An Exegetical
Bibliography
of the
New Testament

JOHN AND 1, 2, 3 JOHN

MERCER UNIVERSITY PRESS • MACON, GEORGIA

An
Exegetical
Bibliography
of the
New Testament

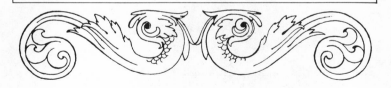

EDITED BY

GÜNTER WAGNER

ΛΛΥ3999

ISBN 0-86554-157-4

Copyright © 1987
Mercer University Press
Macon GA 31207
All rights reserved
Printed in the United States of America

Library of Congress Cataloging-in-Publication Data
Main entry under title.
An Exegetical bibliography of the New Testament
 5 vols. 1983–
  1. Bible, N.T.—Bibliography. I. Wagner, Günter, 1928–
Z7772.L1E93 1987 [BS2361.2] 016.225 83-969
ISBN 0-86554-013-6 [vol. 1, Matthew–Mark]
ISBN 0-86554-140-X [vol. 2, Luke-Acts]
ISBN 0-86554-157-4 [vol. 3, John and 1, 2, 3 John]

Preface

This bibliography is an "unwanted child," but it may well deserve its place. When I started teaching in 1958, I devised a detailed system for the collection of bibliographical information relevant to New Testament studies, ranging from the Old Testament background to the theology of the Early Church. Year after year I used—or misused—all available student help and secretarial assistance to work through our library holdings and current additions to glean references to all sorts of materials and to type each individual reference that was considered useful on a separate card. The card was then filed under its proper heading, so that it would take me—or any student who wished to use the file—no more than a minute to pick up a sizable pile of cards representing a basic bibliography on any topic in the entire New Testament field. The purpose of the whole undertaking was to enable the student as quickly as possible to get down to research without wasting days, even weeks, on the search for literature.

The students who helped me represented more than a dozen nationalities and spoke as many different mother tongues. Knowing or not knowing French, German, Spanish, Danish, Italian, Polish, etc., naturally proved to be both an asset and a liability, in regard to accuracy and consistency; however, as the whole collection was intended to be nothing but a tool for our research, perfectionism in matters of form did not plague us. Postgraduate students who majored in the field of New Testament and later started teaching in various parts of the world got "homesick" for that monstrous steel cabinet in my office and wondered how they could still have access to it. We decided to type up the data of the exegetical section and to photocopy a reduced size of the condensed text, again on separate cards—so that everyone could add further references to his own card file.

Between 1973 and 1979 we made available ''Bibliographical Aids'' on all New Testament writings. Since 1981 I am editing the Second Series, copied by offset printing, again in a postcard size, looseleaf edition; upon request we are adding the place of publication from the Second Series onward and hope that our customers will not mind the inconsistency. We are most grateful to Mercer University Press for publishing at this time Series One and Two together in book form in one text. Updates/supplements for the card editions (Series Three) will continue to be available from Rüschlikon in the future.

The first volume of *An Exegetical Bibliography of the New Testament (Matthew and Mark)* was published in 1983, the second one (Luke and Acts) in 1985. Here we present volume three with a bibliography on The Gospel of John and The Johannine Letters. A fourth volume (on the major Pauline Epistles) is in preparation. I am grateful to all who have assisted in the production of these bibliographies, especially to Dietmar Wowra, and my wife Doris, who have helped with the editing, typing, and proofreading of the manuscript of this volume as well. I want to express my appreciation to the administration of the Baptist Theological Seminary, Rüschlikon, for the support given to this project, and to my friends Margaret and Floyd Patterson (Washington DC), whose encouragement and help have been invaluable throughout the years. Doris and I have waited for this volume on Johannine writings to dedicate it to the dearest of friends.

Günter Wagner
Baptist Theological Seminary Rüschlikon—Zürich
4 July 1987

List of Abbreviations

ABenR American Benedictine Review (Atchison, Kansas)
ACR Australasian Catholic Record (Sydney)
AER American Ecclesiastical Review (Washington)
AfrER African Ecclesiastical Review (Kampala)
AJA American Journal of Archaeology (New York)
AJBA Australian Journal of Biblical Archaeology (Sydney)
ALUOS Annual of Leeds University Oriental Society (Leeds)
AnBib Analecta Biblica (Rome)
ANQ Andover Newton Quarterly (Newton Centre, Massachusetts)
AssS Assemblées du Seigneur (Paris)
ASThI Annual of the Swedish Theological Institute (Jerusalem)
AThR Anglican Theological Review (Evanston, Illinois)
AusBR Australian Biblical Review (Melbourne)
AUSS Andrews University Seminary Studies
(Berrien Springs, Michigan)

BA Biblical Archaeologist (Cambridge, Massachusetts)
BASOR Bulletin of the American Schools of Oriental Research
(Cambridge, Massachusetts)
Biblica Biblica (Rome)
BiblOr Bibliotheca Orientalis (Leiden)
BiblSa Bibliotheca Sacra (Dallas)
BibW Biblical World (Chicago)
BiLe Bibel und Leben (Düsseldorf)
BiOr Bibbia e Oriente (Genoa)

BiRe Bible Revue (Ravenna)
BJRL Bulletin of the John Rylands Library (Manchester)
BLE Bulletin de Littérature Ecclésiastique (Toulouse)
BR Biblical Research (Chicago)
BTh Biblical Theology (Belfast)
BThB Biblical Theology Bulletin (Rome)
BTr Bible Translator (London)
BTS Bible et Terre Sainte (Paris)
BuK Bibel und Kirche (Stuttgart)
BuL Bibel und Liturgie (Klosterneuburg)
BVieC Bible et Vie Chrétienne (Bruges)
BZ Biblische Zietschrift (Paderborn)

CahCER Cahiers du Cercle Ernest-Renan (Paris)
CahJos Cahiers de Joséphologie (Montreal)
CBQ Catholic Biblical Quarterly (Washington)
ChrC Christian Century (Chicago)
ChrTo Christianity Today (Washington)
ChSt Chicago Studies (Mundelein, Illinois)
CiCa Civiltà Cattolica (Rome)
CiDi Ciudad de Dios (Madrid)
ClM Clergy Monthly (Ranchi)
ClR Clergy Review (London)
CoTh Collectanea Theologica (Warsaw)
CrCu Cross Currents (West Nyack, New Jersey)
CrQ Crozer Quarterly (Chester, Pennsylvania)
CSR Christian Scholar's Review (St. Paul, Minnesota)
CThJ Calvin Theological Journal (Grand Rapids, Michigan)
CThM Concordia Theological Monthly (St. Louis, Missouri)
CV Communio Viatorum (Prague)

DBM Deltion Biblikon Meleton (Athens)
DDSR Duke Divinity School Review (Durham, North Carolina)
DiThom Divus Thomas (Poscenza)
DoLi Doctrine and Life (Dublin)
DRev Downside Review (Bath)
DTT Dansk Teologisk Tidsskrift (Copenhagen)
DuRev Dunwoodie Review (New York)

EFr Estudios Fransiscanos (Madrid)
EphC Ephemerides Carmeliticae (Rome)
EphL Ephemerides Liturgicae (Rome)
EphM Ephemerides Mariologicae (Madrid)

EphT Ephemerides Theologicae Lovanienses (Louvain)
EQ Evangelical Quarterly (London)
ER Ecumenical Review (Geneva)
EstBi Estudios Biblicos (Madrid)
EstEc Estudios Eclesiásticos (Madrid)
EsVe Escritos del Vedat (Torrente)
EsVie Espirit et Vie (Langres)
ET Expository Times (Birmingham)
ETh Église et Théologie (Ottawa)
EThR Études Théologiques et Religieuses (Montpelliar)
EuA Erbe und Auftrag (Beuren)
EuD Euntes Docete (Rome)
EvKomm Evangelische Theologie (München)
Exp The Expositor (London)
FrR Frieburger Rundbrief (Frieburg)
FSt Franziskanische Studien (Münster)
FZPhTh Freiburger Zeitschrift für Philosphie und Theologie (Fribourg)

GOThR Greek Orthodox Theological Review (Brookline, Massachusetts)
GPM Göttinger Predigtmeditationen (Göttingen)
GRBS Greek, Roman and Byzantine Studies (Durham, North Carolina)
GThT Gereformeerd Theologisch Tijdschrift (Amsterdam)
GuL Geist und Leben (München)

HerKor Herder Korrespondenz (Freiburg)
Herm Hermathena (Dublin)
HeyJ Heythrop Journal (London)
HPR Homiletic and Pastoral Review (New York)
HR History of Religion (Chicago)
HThR Harvard Theological Review (Cambridge, Massachusetts)
HUCA Hebrew Union College Annual (Cincinnati)

IEJ Israel Exploration Journal (Jerusalem)
IES Indian Ecclesiastical Studies (Bangalore)
IJTh Indian Journal of Theology (Serampore)
IKiZ Internationale Kirchliche Zeitschrift (Bern)
IKZ Internationale Katholische Zeitschrift (Rodenkirchen)
IndTheolStu Indian Theological Studies (Bangalore)
Interp Interpretation (Richmond, Virginia)
IThQ Irish Theological Quarterly (Marynooth)

JAAR Journal of the American Academy of Religion (Atlanta, Georgia)
JAC Jahrbuch für Antike und Christentum (Münster)
JAOS Journal of the American Oriental Society (Baltimore)

JBL Journal of Biblical Literature (Atlanta, Georgia)
JEH Journal of Ecclesiastical History (London)
JES Journal of Ecumenical Studies (Philadelphia)
JEThS Journal of the Evangelical Theological Society (Wheaton)
JHebS Journal of Hebraic Studies (New York)
JHS Journal of Hellenic Studies (London)
JJS Journal of Jewish Studies (London)
JR Journal of Religion (Chicago)
JRomS Journal of Roman Studies (London)
JRTh Journal of Religious Thought (Washington)
JSJ Journal for the Study of Judaism (Leiden)
JSS Journal of Semitic Studies (Manchester)
JThS Journal of Theological Studies (Oxford)

KG Katholische Gedanke (Bonn)
KuD Kerygma und Dogma (Göttingen)

LiBi Linguistica Biblica (Bonn)
LM Lutherische Monatshefte (Hamburg)
LQ Lutheran Quarterly (Gettysburg)
LR Lutherische Rundschau (Geneva)
LSt Louvian Studies (Louvain)
LThPh Laval Théologique et Philosophique (Quebec)
LThQ Lexington Theological Quarterly (Lexington, Kentucky)
LuVie Lumière et Vie (Lyons)
LuVit Lumen Vitae (Brussels)
LW Lutheran World (Geneva)

MCh Modern Churchman (Ludlow)
MisC Miscelánea Comillas (Madrid)
MSR Mélanges de Science Religieuse (Lille)
MTh Melita Theologica (La Valetta)
MThZ Münchener Theologische Zeitschrift (München)

NEAJTh North East Asia Journal of Theology (Tokyo)
NedThT Nederlands Theologisch Tijdschrift (The Hague)
NGTT Nederuits Gereformeerde Teologiese Tydskrif (Stellenbosch)
NKZ Neue kirchliche Zeitschrift (Erlangen)
NovT Novum Testamentum (Leiden)
NRTh Nouvelle Revue Théologique (Louvain)
NTS New Testament Studies (Cambridge)
NTT Norsk Teologisk Tidsskrift (Oslo)
NV Nova et Vetera (Geneva)
NW Neue Weg (Zürich)

OCP Orientalia Christiana Periodica (Rome)
OKS Ostkirchliche Studien (Würzburg)
OLZ Orientalistische Literaturzeitung (Berlin)
PaCl Palestra del Clero (Rovigo)
PEQ Palestine Exploration Quarterly (London)
PSThJ Perkins School of Theology Journal (Dallas)
PThR Princeton Theological Review (Princeton)
RAM Rassegna di Ascetica y Mistica (Florence)
RB Revue Biblique (Jerusalem)
RBen Revue Bénédictine (Maredsous)
RBL Ruch Biblijny i Liturgiczny (Cracow)
RBR Ricerche Bibliche e Religiose (Milan)
RCB Revista de Cultura Biblica (São Paulo)
RCIA Revue de Clerge African (Inkisi, Zaire)
RCT Revista de Cultura Teologica (São Paulo)
REA Revue des Études Augustiniennes (Paris)
REB Revista Eclesiástica Brasileira (Petropolis)
RechSR Recherches de Science Religieuse (Paris)
ReL Religion in Life (Nashville)
REsp Revista de Espiritualidad (Madrid)
RestQ Restoration Quarterly (Abilene, Texas)
RET Revista Española de Teología (Madrid)
RevBi Revista Biblica (Buenos Aires)
RevEx Review and Expositor (Louisville)
RevQ Revue de Qumran (Paris)
RevR Revue Réformée (Saint-German-en-Laye)
RevSR Revue des Science Religieuses (Strasbourg)
RHE Revue d'Histoire Ecclésiastique (Strasbourg)
RHPR Revue d'Histoire et de Philosophie Religieuses (Strasbourg)
RHR Revue de l'Histoire des Religions (Paris)
RHSp Revue d'Histoire de la Spiritualité (Paris)
RivAC Rivista di Archeologia Cristiana (Rome)
RivB Rivista Biblica (Brescia)
RQ Römische Quartalschrift (Freiburg)
RSLR Rivista di Storia e Letteratura Religiosa (Turin)
RSPhTh Revue des Sciences Philosophiques et Théologiques (Paris)
RSt Religious Studies (London)
RT Rassegna di Teologia (Naples)
RThAM Recherches de Théologie Ancienne et Médiévale (Louvain)
RThL Revue Théologique de Louvain (Louvain)

RThom Revue Thomiste (Toulouse)
RThPh Revue de Théologie et de Philosophie (Lausanne)
RThR Reformed Theological Review (Hawthorn, Victoria)
RTK Roczniki Teologiczno-Kanoniczne (Lublin)
RUO Revue de l'Université d'Ottawa (Ottawa)

SaDo Sacra Dottrina (Bologna)
SaDoBB Sacra Dottrina Bolletino Bibliografico (Bologna)
SBFLA Studii Biblici Franciscani Liber Annuus (Jerusalem)
SciE Science et Esprit (Montreal)
ScrB Scripture Bulletin (London)
ScrTh Scripta Theologica (Pamplona)
ScuC Scuola Cattolica (Milan)
SEA Svensk Exegetisk Arsbok (Uppsala)
SEAJTh South East Asia Journal of Theology (Singapore)
SJTh Scottish Journal of Theology (Edinburgh)
SouJTh Southwestern Journal of Theology (Fort Worth)
SThV Studia Theologica Varsaviensia (Warsaw)
StLit Studia Liturgica (Rotterdam)
StPa Studia Patavina (Padua)
StPh Studia Philonica (Chicago)
StR/SciR Studies in Religion/Sciences Religieuses (Toronto)
StTh Studia Theologica (Lund)
StZ Stimmen der Zeit (München)
SVThQ St. Vladimir's Theological Quarterly (Crestwood, New York)
SvTK Svensk Teologisk Kvartalskrift (Lund)

TAik Teologinen Aikakauskirja (Helsinki)
TB Tyndale Bulletin (Cambridge)
Th Theology: A Journal of Historic Christianity (London)
ThG Theologie und Glaube (Paderborn)
ThLZ Theologische Literaturzeitung (Leipzig)
ThPh Theologie und Philosophie (Frankfurt)
ThQ Theologische Quartalschrift (Tübingen)
ThR Theologische Rundschau (Tübingen)
ThRv Theologische Revue (Münster)
ThSK Theologische Studien und Kritiken (Hamburg)
ThSt Theological Studies (New York)
ThT Theology Today (Princeton)
ThZ Theologische Zeitschrift (Basel)
TRE Theologische Realenzyklopädie
(Berlin/New York: Walter de Gruyter)

TsTK Tidsskrift for Teologi og Kirke (Oslo)
TT Theologisch Tidschrift (Amsterdam)
TThZ Trierer Theologische Zeitschrift (Trier)
TvTh Tijdschrift voor Theologie (Nijmegen)

US Una Sancta (Niederaltaich)
USQR Union Seminary Quarterly Review (New York)

VChr Vetera Christianorum (Bari)
VD Verbum Domini (Rome)
VE Vox Evangelica (London)
VF Verkündigung und Forschung (München)
VieS Vie Spirituelle (Paris)
VigChr Vigiliae Christianae (Amsterdam)
VR Vox Reformata (Geelong, Victoria)
VT Vetus Testamentum (Leiden)

WThJ Westminster Theological Journal (Philadelphia)
WuW Wissenschaft und Weisheit (Düsseldorf)

ZAW Zeitschrift für die Alttestamentliche Wissenschaft (Berlin)
ZDMG Zeitschrift der Deutschen Morgenländischen Gesellschaft (Wiesbaden)
ZKG Zeitschrift für Kirchengeschichte (Stuttgart)
ZKTh Zeitschrift für Katholische Theologie (Innsbruck)
ZNW Zeitschrift für die Neutestamentliche Wissenschaft (Berlin)
ZRGG Zeitschrift für Religions und Geistesgeschichte (Erlangen)
ZThK Zeitschrift für Theologie und Kirche (Tübingen)
ZyMy Zycie i Mysl (Warsaw)

Notations

ET English Translation
GT German Translation
n Footnote or note

In case of doubt consult S. Schwertner, IATC: *Internationales Abkürzungsverzeichnis für Theologie und Grenzgebiete* (1974) 3-343. This is identical to TRE: *Theologische Realenzyklopädie: Abkürzungsverzeichnis* (1976) 3-343, with supplements.

For
Jessie and C. Penrose St. Amant

John

ΚΑΤΑ ΙΩΑΝΝΗΝ

1-20 KÜMMEL, W. G., Einleitung in das Neue Testament (1973) 173f., 199-201.

1-17 BLAUERT, H., Die Bedeutung der Zeit in der johanneischen Theologie (1953).

1-15 PAPYRUS BODMER XV (1961) V. Martin/R. Kasser eds.

1-14 LEJOLY, R., Annotations pour une étude du Papyrus 75 Bodmer XV, c'est-à-dire du texte grec de Jean 1-14 (Dison 1976).

1-14:26 KLIJN, A. F. J., "Papyrus Bodmer II (John 1-14) and the Text of Egypt," NTS 3 (1956-1957) 327ff. RHODES, E. F. NTS 14 (1967-1968) 271f.

1-12 VAN DEN BUSSCHE, H. "La structure de Jean I-XII," in: L'Evangile de Jean (1958) Boismard et al., eds., 61-109. BALAGUE, M., Jesucristo, Vida y Luz (1963).

1-12 DE JONGE, M. Jesus: Stranger from Heaven and Son of God (Missoula 1977) 175-77.

1-9 FEE, D. G. "Codex Sinaiticus in the Gospel of John: A Contribution to Methodology in establishing textual Relationships," NTS 15 (1968-1969) 34ff. MEES, M. "Unterschiedliche Lesarten in Bodmer Papyrus XV (P^{75}) und Codex Vaticanus aus Joh. 1-9," Augustinianum 9 (2, 1969) 370-79.

1:1-5:38 GRYGLEWICZ, F. NTS 11 (1964-1965) 259f.

1-4 SEGOVIA, F., "The Love and Hatred of Jesus and Johannine Sectarianism" CBQ 43 (1981) 266-67.

1:1-4:54 SCHWANK, B. Das Johannesevangelium (1966) I.

1-2 BALAGUE, M. "Precedentes del milagro de Cana," CultBib 19 (187, 1962) 365-74. VOSS, G., "Koscmiche Bildwirklichkeit in der neutestamentlichen Verkündigung. Ein Versuch zu Joh 1-2" US 32 (1977) 13-38.

1 GARDNER-SMITH, P. Saint John and the Synoptic Gospels (1938) 1-10. KAESEMANN, E. Exegetische Versuche und Besinnungen (1964) II 155ff. SMITH, D. M. The Composition and Order of the Fourth Gospel (1965) 124n, 176, 219, 228. BRAUN, H. Qumran und NT II (1966) 20, 24. NICKELS, P. Targum and New Testament (1967) 52. RICHTER, H.-F. Auferstehung und Wirklichkeit (1969) 286f. FORTNA, R. T. The Gospel of Signs (1970) 29f., 161-89. BETZ, O. in: Wort und Geschichte (1973) H. Gese/P. H. Rüger eds., 9ff. MACK, B. L. Logos und Sophia (1973) 13. ROSS, J. M. "Two More Titles of Jesus," ET 85 (9, 1974) 281. LANG, B., Frau Weisheit. Deutung einer biblischen Gestalt (Düsseldorf 1975) 59-60.

HOOKER, M. D., "Beyond the Things that are Written? St. Paul's Use of Scripture" NTS 27 (1980-1981) 302.

1:1ff GREEN, H. C. "The Composition of St. John's Prologue," ET 66 (10, 1955) 315-18. MAIWORM, J. "Der Prolog des Jo-Evgls als Epilog," BuK 11 (2, 1956) 51-52. CULLMANN, O. Die Christologie des Neuen Testaments (1957) 255ff., 267ff. KAE-SEMANN, E. "Aufbau und Anliegen des Johanneischen Prologs," in: Libertas Christiana (1957) 75-99. WIKENHAUSER, A. Das Evangelium nach Johannes (1957) 51-56. DE JU-LIOTT, H. "Jésus parmi les siens," BVieC 23 (1958) 13-21. POLLARD, T. E. "The Fourth Gospel: Its Background and Early Interpretation," AusBR (1959) 41-53. BLAIR, E. P. Jesus in the Gospel of Matthew (1960) 98. RUDOLPH, K. Die Mandäer I (1960) 77, 79. SCHWEIZER, E. Erniedrigung und Erhöhung bei Jesus und seinen Nachfolgern (1962) § 8m. MANSON, T. W. "The Johannine Logos Doctrine," in: On Paul and John (1963) 136-59. BRAUN, F.-M. "La lumière du monde," RThom 64 (3, 1964) 341-63. BRINKMANN, B. "Prolog und Johannes-Evangelium. Theologische Grundlinien, innere Einheit," BuK 20 (4, 1965) 106-13. HAENCHEN, E. Problem des johanneischen "Prologs", in: Gott und Mensch (1965) 114-44. JEREMIAS, J. "The Revealing Word," in: The Central Message of the New Testament (1965) 71-90. BULT-MANN, R. "Der religionsgeschichtliche Hintergrund des Prologs zum Johannes-Evangelium," in: Exegetica (1967) E. Dinkler ed., 10-36. PETZKE, G. Die Traditionen über Apollonius von Tyana und das Neue Testament (1970) 189, 214. RICHTER, G. "Ist en ein strukturbildendes Element im Logoshymmus Joh 1,1ff.?" Biblica 41 (4, 1970) 539-44.

1:1-18 VON LOEWENICH, W. Das Johannes-Verständnis im Zweiten Jahrhundert (1932) 76-79, 82-85, 97f., 101, 118-120, 132, 138. LEE, E. K. The Religious Thought of St. John (1950) 56-156. RUCKSTUHL, E. Die literarische Einheit des Johannes-evangeliums (1951) 38, 63-97, 159. HOWARD, W. F. The Gospel According to St. John (1952). BOISMARD, M. E. Le Prologue de saint Jean (1953). ET.: St. John's Prologue (1957). AUSEJO, S. de, "Es un Himno a Cristo el Prologo de San Juan?" EstBi 15 (1956) 223-77, 381-427. SCHLIER, H. Die Zeit der Kirche (1956) 274-87. DODD, C. H. "The Prologue to the Fourth Gospel and Christian Worship," in: Studies in the Fourth Gospel (1957) F. L. Cross ed., 9-22. GRANT, F. C. The Gospels (1957) 167ff. KAESEMANN, E. Aufbau und Anliegen des Johanneischben Prologs, in: Libertas Christiana (1957) 75-99. LACAN, M. F. "Le Prologue de saint Jean. Ses thèmes,

sa structure, son mouvement," LuVie 33 (1957) 91-110.
SCHNACKENBURG, R. "Logos-Hymnus und johanneischer
Prolog," BZ 1 (1, 1957) 69-109. STANLEY, D. M. "God so
loved the world," Worship 32 (1, 1957) 16-23. MOE, O. "Lo-
gosbegrepet i Johannesevangeliets sammenhang," SEA 22-23
(1957-1958) 111-18. GRYGLEWICZ, F. "Prolog Ewangelii i
Pierwszego Listu sw. Jana (De prologo evangelii et primae ep-
istolae sancti Joannis)," RBL 11 (1, 1958) 15-22. WILCK-
ENS, W. The Entstehungsgeschichte des vierten Evangeliums
(1958) 118-22. GUINDON, R. "Le théologie de saint Thomas
d'Aquin dans le rayonnement du 'Prologue' de saint Jean," RUO
29 (1, 1959) 5-23, 121-42. SCHULZ, S., Komposition und
Herkunft der Johanneischen Reden (Stuttgart 1960) 7-57.
GRUNDMANN, W. Zeugnis und Gestalt des Johannes-Evan-
geliums (1961) 22-30. FENASSE, J.-M. "Le Prologue de St.
Jean," BibTerreSainte 51 (1962) 2-4. ROBINSON, J. A. T.
"The Relation of the Prologue to the Gospel of St. John," NTS
9 (1962-1963) 120f. AUCOIN, M. A. "Augustine and John
Chrysostom: Commentators on St. John's Prologue," SciEccl
15 (1, 1963) 123-31. GALOPIN, P.-M. "Le Verbe, témoin du
Pére. Jean I,1-18," BVieC 53 (1963) 16-34. GLASSON, T. F.
Moses in the Fourth Gospel (1963) 65ff., 86ff. HAENCHEN,
E. "Probleme des johanneischen 'Prologs'," ZThK 60 (3, 1963)
305-54. SCHWEIZER, E. Neotestamentica (1963) 113-16.
THOMPSON, P. J., "Psalm 119: a Possible Clue to the Structure of the First Epistle of John" StEv 2 (1964) 487-89.
ELTESTER, W. "Der Logos und sein Prophet. Fragen zur
heutigen Erklärung des johanneischen Prologs," in: Apophor-
eta (1964) 109-34. KELLY, R. "El logos," RevBi 26 (113-14,
1964) 146-51. KUYPER, L. J. "Grace and Truth. An Old Tes-
tament Description of God, and Its Use in the Johannine Gos-
pel," Interpretation 18 (1, 1964) 3-19. LAMARCHE, P. "Le
Prologue de Jean," RechSR 52 (4, 1964) 497-537. LINDIJER,
C. H. De Sacramenten in het Vierde Evangelie (1964) 52. MIS-
KOTTE, K. H. in: Herr, tue meine Lippen auf Bd. 3 (1964) G.
Eichholz ed., 41ff. STANLEY, D. M. "Contemplation of the
Incarnation," TheolDig 12 (4, 1964) 275-86. YATES, K. M.
Preaching from John's Gospel (1964) 6-12. BALAGUE, M. "El
Sentido des los Origenes en el Prologo del cuarto Evangelio,"
RevBi 27 (1965) 94-104, 156-62. BEILNER, W. "Aufbau und
Aussage des Johannes-Prologes (Jo 1,1-18)," BuK 20 (4, 1965)
98-105. BROWN, R. B. "The Prologue of the Gospel of John.
John 1:1-18," RevEx 62 (4, 1965) 429-39. LANGKAMMER,
H. "Zur Herkunft des Logostitels im Johannesprolog," BZ 9
(1, 1965) 91-94. ROBINSON, J. A. T. "The Relation of the

Prologue to the Gospel of St. John," in: The Authorship and Integrity of the New Testament (1965) 61-72. SCHATTEN-MANN, J. "Der Prolog des Johannesevangeliums als Hymnus," in: Studien zum Neutestamentlichen Prosahymnus (1965) 26-32. SMITH, D. M. The Composition and Order of the Fourth Gospel (1965) 5, 61-63. BLANK, J. "Das Johannesevangelium. Der Prolog: Jo 1,1-18," BuL 7 (1966) 28-39, (1966) 112-27. BRAUN, H. Qumran und NT II (1966) 36, 38, 123, 127f., 139, 188, 267, 271, 284. RIDDERBOS, H. "The structure and scope of the prologue to the Gospel of John," NovTest 8 (2-4, 1966) 180-201. DEMKE, C. "Der sogenannte Logos-Hymnus im johanneischen Prolog," ZNW 58 (1967) 45-68. JEREMIAS, J. Der Prolog des Johannesevangeliums (1967). FEUILLET, A. Le Prologue du Quatrième Evangile (1968). GAERTNER, B. E. "The Pauline and Johannine Idea of 'To know God' Against the Hellenistic Background," NTS 14 (1968) 209-31. WINK, W. John the Baptist in the Gospel Tradition (1968) 87-89. DEEKS, D. "The Structure of the Fourth Gospel," NTS 15 (1968-1969) 110ff. BRAUN, H. Jesus (1969) 155. CADMAN, W. H. The Open Heaven (1969) G. B. Caird ed., 15-21. KAESEMANN, E. "The Structure and Purpose of the Prologue to John's Gospel," in: New Testament Questions of Today (1969) 138-67. O'NEILL, J. C. "The Prologue to St. John's Gospel," JThS 20 (1, 1969) 41-52. SCHREINER, J. Gestalt und Anspruch des Neuen Testaments (1969) 236-39. QUERDRAY, G. "Le Prologue du Quatrième Evangile. Etude de Théologie johannique," EsVie 79 (11, 1969) 173-75. WILKENS, W., Zeichen und Werke (Zürich 1969) 129-33. BORGEN, P. "Logos var det sanne lys. Momenter til tolkning av Johannesprologen," SEA 35 (1970) 79-95. BORGEN, P. "Observations on the Targumic Character of the Prologue of John," NTS 16 (3, 1970) 288-95. HOOKER, M. D. NTS 16 (1969-1970) 356f. KYSAR, R. "The Background of the Prologue of the Fourth Gospel. A Critique of Historical Methods," CanJourn Theol 16 (3-4, 1970) 250-55. LANGKAMMER, H. "Wokol wspolczesnej problematyki 'Piesni o Logosie' w Prologu Jana,"RTK 17 (1, 1970) 105-13. LANGKAMMER, P. H. "Literarische und Theologische Einzelstücke in I Kor viii. 6," NTS 17 (1970-1971) 195f. SELBY, D. J., Introduction to the New Testament (New York 1971) 35, 230, 232-34, 446-73. IR-OGOIN, J. "La composition rythmique du prologue de Jean (I,1-18)," RevBi 78 (4, 1971) 501-14. BORGEN, P. "Logos was the True Light. Contributions to the Interpretation of the Prologue of John," NovTest 14 (2, 1972) 115-30. CLARK, G. H. The Johannine Logos (1972). WENGST, K. Christologi-

sche Formeln und Lieder des Urchristentums (1972) 200-208.
BEUTLER, J. " 'Und das Wort ist Fleisch geworden. . . .' Zur
Menschwerdung nach dem Johannesprolog," GuL 46 (1, 1973)
7-16. LOPEZ, E. "Dos siglos de critica literaria en torno al
prologo de San Juan," Studium Ovetense 1 (1973) 135-96.
POTVIN, T. R. The Theology of the Primacy of Christ Ac-
cording to St. Thomas and Its Scriptural Foundations (1973) 3,
38, 44, 84-90, 92-96, 268, 269. van UNNIK, W. C., Sparsa
Collecta. I (Leiden 1973) 35-63. FREED, E. D., "Some Old
Testament Influences on the Prologue of John" in: A Light unto
My Path. FS. J. M. Myers (1974) 146-61. BARRETT, C. K.
"The Father is greater than I (Jo 14,28): Subordinationist
Christology in the New Testament," in: Neues Testament und
Kirche (1974) J. Gnilka ed., 148f. TRUDINGER, L. P. "The
Prologue of John's Gospel: Its Extent, Content and Intent,"
RThR 33 (1, 1974) 11-17. ZIMMERMANN, H. "Christu-
shymnus und johanneischer Prolog," in: Neues Testament und
Kirche (1974) J. Gnilka ed., 249-65. HOOKER, M. D., "The
Johannine Prologue and the Messianic Secret" NTS 21 (1974)
40-58. REIM, G., Studien zum Alttestamentlichen Hinter-
grund des Johannesevangeliums (Cambridge 1974) 276-77.
CONZELMANN, H. und LINDEMANN, A., Arbeitsbuch zum
Neuen Testament (Tübingen 1975) 19, 112ff. EPP, E. J.,
"Wisdom, Torah, Word: The Johannine Prologue and the Pur-
pose of the Fourth Gospel" in: G. F. Hawthorne (ed.) Current
Issues in Biblical and Patristic Interpretation. FS. M. C. Tenney (Grand Rapids 1975) 128-46. KING, J. S., "The Prologue
to the Fourth Gospel: Some Unsolved Problems" ET 86 (1975)
372-75. RISSI, M., "Die Logoslieder im Prolog des vierten
Evangeliums" ThZ 31 (1975) 321-46. TEMPLE, S., The Core
of the Fourth Gospel (London 1975) 65-68. CAHILL, P. J.,
"The Johannine Logos as Center" CBQ 38 (1976) 54-72.
DEEKS, D. G., "The Prologue of St. John's Gospel" BThB 6
(1976) 62-78. GOPPELT, L., Theologie des Neuen Testaments. II (Göttingen 1976) 632-33. HERR, T., Naturrecht aus
der kritischen Sicht des Neuen Testaments (München 1976) 195.
KUBOTH, J., "Literatura formo de la johana prologo" BiRe
12 (1976) 55-64. LANGKAMMER, H., "Pieśń o Logosie oraz
jej tlo religijno-historyczne" in: F. Grvglewicz (ed.) Egzegeza
Ewangelii św. Jana (Lublin 1976) 19-32. RAMAROSON, L.
"La structure du prologue de Jean," SciE 28 (1976) 281-96.
BERGER, K., Exegese des Neuen Testaments (Heidelberg
1977) 27-28. BÜHNER, J.-A., Der Gesandte und sein Weg im
4. Evangelium (Tübingen 1977) 100-101. DAVIS, C. T.,
"Alive to Death - Dead to Life: A Human Dilemma" PRSt 4

(1977) 253-65. GESE, H., "Der Johannesprolog" Beiträge zur
Evangelischen Theologie 78 (München 1977) 152-201. IBUKI,
Y., "Lobhymnus und Fleischwerdung - Studie über den johan-
neischen Prolog" AJBI 3 (1977) 132-56. JANSSENS, Y., "Une
source gnostique du Prologue?" Bibliotheca ephemeridum
theologicarum Lovaniensium 44 (Louvain 1977) 355-58.
LANGBRANDTNER, W., Weltferner Gott oder Gott der Liebe
(Frankfurt a.M./Bern/Las Vegas 1977) 38-44. CHARLIER, C.,
Jean l'évangéliste. Structure dramatique du Quatrième évan-
gile. Méditation liturgique du Prologue (Paris 1978). COL-
LINS, R. F., "The Oldest Commentary on the Fourth Gospel"
BiTod 98 (1978) 1769-75. HAYWARD, C. T. R., "The Holy
Name of the God of Moses and the Prologue of St. John's Gos-
pel" NTS 25 (1978) 16-32. KYSAR, R., "Christology and
Controversy: The Contributions of the Prologue of the Gospel
of John to New Testament Christology and their Historical Set-
ting" CuThM 5 (1978) 348-64. NEWMAN, B. M., Jr., "Some
observations regarding a poetic restructuring of John 1.1-18"
BTr 29 (1978) 206-12. ROBINSON, J. M., "Gnosticism and
the New Testament" in: B. Aland et al. (eds.) Gnosis. FS. H.
Jonas (Göttingen 1978) 128-30. SCHENKE, H. M., "Die Ten-
denz der Weisheit zur Gnosis" in: B. Aland et al. (eds.) Gnosis.
FS. H. Jonas (Göttingen 1978) 360-65. BECKER, J., Das
Evangelium nach Johannes (Gütersloh/Würzburg 1979) 66-67
(lit!). DULING, D. C., Jesus Christ Through History (New York
1979) 49-50. DUNCAN, R. L., "The Logos: from Sophocles
to the Gospel of John" CSR 9 (1979) 121-30. FERRANDO, M.
A., "Notas de Exégesis sobre el prólogo del Cuarto Evangelio
(Jn 1,1-18)" TyV 20 (1979) 55-62. HOFRICHTER, P., "
'Egeneto anthropos.' Text und Zusätze im Johannesprolog"
ZNW 70 (1979) 214-37. IBUKI, Y., "Offene Fragen zur Auf-
nahme des Logoshymnus in das vierte Evangelium" AJBI 5
(1979) 105-32. MILLER, E. L., "The *New International Version* on the Prologue of John" HThR 72 (1979) 307-11.
SCHMITHALS, W., "Der Prolog des Johannesevangeliums"
ZNW 70 (1979) 16-43. BERGMEIER, R., Glaube als Gabe nach
Johannes (Stuttgart 1980) 211. CHOW, P. K., "Analogical ap-
plications of information theory to semantic problems" BTr 31
(1980) 310-18. CULPEPPER, R. A., "The Pivot of John's
Prologue" NTS 27 (1980) 1-31. DUNN, J. D., Christology in
the Making (London 1980) 164, 196, 206, 216, 230, 234, 239-
47, 339n.10, 343n.73, 345n.99. HAENCHEN, E., Das
Johannesevangelium (Tübingen 1980) 112-15 (lit!). LINDE-
MANN, A. "Gemeinde und Welt im Johannesevangelium" in:
D. Lührmann/G. Strecker (eds.) Kirche. FS. G. Bornkamm

(Tübingen 1980) 139-42. SCHILLEBEECKX, E., Christ: the Christian Experience in the Modern World (London 1980) 351-68; GT: Christus und die Christen (Freiburg/Basel/Wien 1977) 338-55. STRECKER, G., " 'Biblische Theologie'? Kritische Bemerkungen zu den Entwürfen von Hartmut Gese und Peter Stuhlmacher" in: D. Lührmann/G. Strecker (eds.) Kirche. FS. G. Bornkamm (Tübingen 1980) 440. THYEN, H., " 'Das Heil kommt von den Juden' " in: D. Lührmann/G. Strecker (eds.) Kirche. FS. G. Bornkamm (Tübingen 1980) 170-74. EVANS, C. A., "On the Prologue of John and the *Trimorphic Protennoia*" NTS 27 (1981) 395-401. MATSUNAGA, K., "The 'Theos' Christology as the Ultimate Confession of the Fourth Gospel" AJBI 7 (1981) 125, 127-28. SIEGWALT, G., "Introduction à une théologie chrétienne de la récapitulation (Remarques sur le contenu dogmatique du prologue de Jean)" RThPh 31 (1981) 259-78.

1:1-17   SCHLIER, H. " 'Im Anfang war das Wort'. Zum Prolog des Johannesevangelium," Wort und Wahrheit IX/3, 169-80.

1:1-16   RYAN, W. F. "John's Hymn to the Word," Worship 37 (5, 1963) 285-92. VAWTER, B. This Man Jesus (1973) 160-63. DUNN, J. D. G., Unity and Diversity in the New Testament (London 1977) 137-138.

1:1-14(18)   HEUE, R./GEHRKE, H. "Zweiter Weihnachtstag. Johannes 1,1-14 (18)," in: Predigtstudien (1972-1973) E. Lange ed., 57-66.

1:1-14   GREGERSEN, V. "Die Struktur des Johannesprologs (dän)," DTT XVII (1954) 34-36. IWAND, H.-J. GPM 9 (1954-1955) 24ff. BARCLAY, W. "Great Themes of the New Testament-II. John i.1-14," ET 70 (3, 1958) 114-17. RIPLEY, F. J. The Last Gospel (1961). IWAND, H.-J. Predigtmeditationen (1964) 425-31. FULLER, R. H. The Foundations of New Testament Christology (1965) 222ff. SCHILLE, G. Frühchristliche Hymnen (1965) 121ff. McNAMARA, M. "Logos of the Fourth Gospel and Memra of the Palestinian Targum (Ex 12:42)," ET 79 (4, 1968) 115-17. THURNEYSEN, E. Das Wort Gottes und die Kirche (1971) 185-211. BARRETT, C. K. "The Prologue of St. John's Gospel," in: New Testament Essays (1972) 27-48. SCHOENHERR, A. GPM 27/1 (1972-1973) 42-50. SIMPFENDOERFER, G. "Erster Weihnachtstag: Johannes 1,1-14," in: Predigtstudien (1972-1973) E. Lange ed., 50-56.

1:1-13   BERGMEIER, R., Glaube als Gabe nach Johannes (Stuttgart 1980) 210-11.

1:1-11 SANDERS, J. T. The New Testament Christological Hymns (1971) 20-25, 29-57. PERRIN, N. A Modern Pilgrimage in New Testament Christology (1974) 126-27.

1:1-9 SUMMERS, R. The Secret Sayings of the Living Jesus (1968) 79.

1:1-8 SCHRAGE, W. GPM 21/2 (1966-1967) 157-64.

1:1-5 VAN DEN BUSSCHE, H. "De tout être la Parole était la vie. Jean 1,1-5," BVieC 58 (69, 1966) 57-65. KAESEMANN, E. New Testament Questions of Today (1969) 145, 166. DU-PONT, J. Essais sur la Christologie de Saint Jean (1951) 12, 35-49. RUCKSTUHL, E. Die literarische Einheit des Johannes-evangeliums (1951) 65, 70f., 82, 89-93, 95f. CHARLES-WORTH, J. H. "Qumran, John and the Odes of Solomon," in: John and Qumran (1972) J. H. Charlesworth ed., 123-24. RIESS, M. und KREYSSIG, P., in P. Krusche et al. (eds.) Predigtstudien für das Kirchenjahr 1978-1979. I/1 (Stuttgart 1978) 72-80. IBUKI, Y., "Offene Fragen zur Aufnahme des Logoshymnus in das Vierte Evangelium" AJBI 5 (1979) 107, 109, 112. MILLER, E. L., "The Logos was God" EQ 53 (1981) 66-67, 76.

1:1-4 CREHAN, J. The Theology of St. John (1965) 48-49, 50-52, 55-56. KAESEMANN, E. New Testament Questions of Today (1969) 140, 151. KUENKEL, K. "Das Leben ist erschienen," in: Weihnachten heute gesagt (1970) H. Nitschke ed., 67-73. SCHOTTROFF, L. Der Glaubende und die feindliche Welt (1970) 231-33. SEISS, J. "Das Wort des Lebens," in: Weihnachten heute gesagt (1970) 138-43. PAGELS, E. H. The Johannine Gospel in Gnostic Exegesis (1973) 20-35. FRICKEL, J., "Naassener oder Valentinianer?" in: M. Krause (ed.) Gnosis and Gnosticism (Leiden 1981) 112-15.

1:1-3 SMITH, M. Tannaitic Parallels to the Gospels (1968) 8 b n 10. BACCHIOCCHI, S., "John 5:17: Negation or Clarification of the Sabbath?" AUSS 19 (1981) 13.

1:1-2.4-5 ROBINSON, J. M. Kerygma und historischer Jesus (1960) 176.

1:1-2 RUCKSTUHL, E. Die literarische Einheit des Johannes-evangeliums (1951) 43f., 69, 93, 97, 230, 245. KAESE-MANN, E. New Testament Questions of Today (1969) 164. HAMERTON-KELLY, R. G. Pre-Existence, Wisdom, and The Son of Man (1973) 8, 131, 187, 200-15, 221, 243, 262. DEL-LING, G. Wort und Werk Jesu im Johannes-Evangelium (1966) 120-22. IBUKI, Y. Die Wahrheit im Johannesevangelium (1972) 178f. PERTIÑEZ, J., "La preexistencia de Cristo" Mayeutica 3 (Marcilla 1977) 329-47. CULPEPPER, R. A., "The Pivot of John's Prologue" NTS 27 (1980-1981) 9-10.

1:1.3 NORDEN, E. Agnostos Theos (1956 = 1912) 348ff.

1:1.14 JEREMIAS, J. "Zum Logos-Problem," ZNW 59 (1-2, 1968) 82-85.

1:1 JANNARIS, A. N. ZNW 2 (1901) 13-25. GRILL, J. Untersuchungen über die Entstehung des vierten Evangeliums II (1923) 40, 94, 330, 337, 381. BAUER, W. Das Johannesevangelium (1925) 5-9. BUECHSEL, F. Das Evangelium nach Johannes (1946) 34-36. HOSKYNS, E. C. The Fourth Gospel (1956) 154-63. KOEHLER L. Eine Handvoll Neues Testament (1954) 71-81. STRATHMANN, H. Das Evangelium nach Johannes (1955) 40-43. ORIGENES, Das Evangelium nach Johannes (1959) R. Gögler ed., 112-22, 125, 140-53. WAINWRIGHT, A. W., The Trinity in the New Testament (1962) 60-63. WENNEMER, K. "Theologie des 'Wortes' im Johannesevangelium. Das innere Verhältnis des verkündigten logos theou zum persönlichen Logos," Scholastik 38 (1, 1963) 1-17. HENNECKE, E./SCHNEEMELCHER, W. Neutestamentliche Apokryphen (1964) I 135. DELLING, G. Wort und Werk Jesu im Johannes-Evangelium (1966) 63, 98, 108f., 124. BORIG, R. Der Wahre Weinstock (1967) 99, 208ff., 213f., 217. COUNTESS, R. H. "The Translation of Theos in the New World Translation," BullEvangTheolSoc 10 (3, 1967) 153-60. GUTHRIE, W. C. K. JThS 20 (2, 1969) 622-625. CRAWFORD, R. G., "Pittenger on the Divinity of Christ," MCh 15 (2, 1972) 121-22. HILLERBRAND, H. J. ed., Luther's Works 52 (1974) 47ff., 53. CONZELMANN, H. und LINDEMANN, A., Arbeitsbuch zum Neuen Testament (Tübingen 1975) 17. FRUECHTEL, E., "ἀρχή und das erste Buch des Johanneskommentars des Origenes" TU 117 (1976) 122-44. BOYLE, O'R., "Sermo: Reopening the Conversation on Translating JN 1,1" VChr 31 (1977) 161-68. METZGER, B. M., The Early Versions of the New Testament (Oxford 1977) 145. SWIDLER, L., Biblical Affirmations of Woman (Philadelphia 1979) 68. BEIERWALTES, W., "Deus est veritas" in: E. Dassmann/K. S. Frank (eds.) Pietas. FS. B. Kötting (Münster 1980) 24. DUNN, J. D., Christology in the Making (London 1980) 58, 164, 230, 232, 241, 245-46, 346n.102, 347n.103 and 106, 348n.111. GEORGI, D., "Weisheit Salomos" in: JüdSchr III/4 (1980) 9n.4a, 9n.9a. MILLER, E. L., " 'The *Logos* was God' " EQ 53 (1981) 65-77. PHILONENKO-SAYAR, B. und PHILONENKO, M., "Die Apokalypse Abrahams" in: JüdSchr V/5 (1982) 444.n.3.

1:1b-2 MASSON, C. "Pour une traduction nouvelle de Jean I:1b et 2," RThPh 98 (6, 1965) 376-81. DEWAILLY, L.-M. " 'La Parole parlait à Dieu'?" RThPh 100 (2, 1967) 123-28.

1:2 IBUKI, Y., "Offene Fragen zur Aufnahme des Logoshymnus in das Vierte Evangelium" AJBI 5 (1979) 118.

1:3-23 FORTNA, R. T. The Gospel of Signs (1970) 161.

1:3-7 ORIGENES, Das Evangelium nach Johannes (1959) R. Gögler ed., 153-68.

1:3-5 BRAUN, H. Qumran und NT II (1966) 110, 123ff., 139ff. IBUKI, Y., "Offene Fragen zur Aufnahme des Logoshymnus in das Vierte Evangelium" AJBI 5 (1979) 108.

1:3-4 MEHLMANN, J. "De mente S. Hieronymi circa divisionem versuum Jo 1,3s," Verbum Domini 33 (1955) 86-94. POTTERIE, I. De La, "De Punctuatie en de Exegese van Joh. 1, 3.4 in de Traditie," Bijdragen 16 (1955) 117-35. POTTERIE, I. De La, "De interpunctione et interpretatione versuum Joh 1,3.4," Verbum Domini 33 (4, 1955) 193-208. BARRETT, C. K. The New Testament Background (1956) 84. Van den BUSSCHE, H. "Quod factum est, in ipso vita erat (Jo. 1,3-4)," ColBG 2 (1956) 85-88. LANGKAMMER, H. "Die Zugehörigkeit des Satzteiles ho gegonen in Joh 1,3.4 bei Hieronymus," BZ 8 (2, 1964) 295-98. ALAND, K. "Ueber die Bedeutung eines Punktes," in: Studies in the History and Text of the New Testament (1967) B. L. Daniels/M. J. Suggs eds., 161-87. ALAND, K. "Eine Untersuchung zu Joh 1:3.4. Ueber die Bedeutung eines Punktes," ZNW 59 (3-4, 1968) 174-209. METZGER, F. M. "Explicit references in the works of Origen to variant readings in New Testament manuscripts," in: Historical and Literary Studies (1968) 96. KYSAR, R. "Rudolf Bultmann's Interpretation of the Concept of Creation in John 1,3-4. A Study of Exegetical Method," CBQ 32 (2, 1970) 77-85. SIMONETTI, M. "Per l'interpretazione di Giovanni 1,3-4," VChr 9 (1, 1972) 101-104. HOCKEY, F., "St. Augustine and John 1,3-4" TU 117 (1976) 443-45. MILLER, E. L., "Codex Bezae on John i.3-4. One Dot or Two?" ThZ 32 (1976) 269-71. BRUCE, F. F., "The Gospel Text of Marius Victorinus" in: E. Best/R. McL. Wilson (eds.) Text and Interpretation. FS. M. Black (Cambridge 1979) 72.

1:3.5 HAHN, F. Das Verständnis der Mission im Neuen Testament (1965²) 137.

1:3 Von LOEWENICH, W. Das Johannes-Verständnis im zweiten Jahrhundert (1932) 120-22. RUCKSTUHL, E. Die literarische Einheit des Johannesevangeliums (1951) 52, 64, 69, 78, 82, 87, 90f., 93, 97. MEHLMAN, J. "A Note on John i.3," ET 67 (1956) 340-41. GLASSON, T. F. "A Trace of Xenophon in John i.3?" NTS 4 (3, 1958) 208-209. POLLARD, T. E. "Cosmology and the Prologue of the Fourth Gospel," VigChr 12 (3, 1958) 147-53. WILES, M. F. The Spiritual Gospel (1960) 102-104, 105. HAACKER, K. "Eine formgeschichtliche Beobachtung zu Joh 1,3 fin.," BZ 12 (1, 1968) 119-21. HUNTER, A. M. According to John (1970²) 57ff. IBUKI, Y. Die Wahrheit im Johannesevangelium (1972) 180, 181 A31, 185. PAGELS, E. H. The Johannine Gospel in Gnostic Exegesis (1973) 20-22, 22-23, 24-30, 30-32, 38-40, 40-48, 48-50. POTVIN, T. R. The Theology of the Primacy of Christ According to St. Thomas and Its Scriptural Foundations (1973) 74, 87, 89, 90, 93, 94, 142, 145₂, 147₁.

1:3 SANDMEL, S., We Jews and Jesus (New York 1977) 41. BERGMEIER, R., Glaube als Gabe nach Johannes (Stuttgart 1980) 181. CULPEPPER, R. A., "The Pivot of John's Prologue" NTS 27 (1980-81) 10. GEORGI, D., "Weisheit Salomos" in: JüdSchr III/4 (1980) 7n.12a, 22a, 8n.6a, 9n.9a. BERGER, K., "Das Buch der Jubiläen" in: JüdSchr II/3 (1981) 544n.7a. LANGKAMMER, H., "Zum Ursprung der kosmologischen Christologie im Neuen Testament" BN 16 (1981) 32-33.

1:3b-4a VAWTER, B. "What Came to be in Him was Life (Jn 1,3b-4a)," CBQ 25 (3, 1963) 401-406. SCHLATTER, F. W. "The Problem of Jn 1:3b-4a," CBQ 34 (1, 1972) 54-58.

1:4-18 MUELLER, T. Das Heilsgeschehen im Johannesevangelium n.d., 13-18.

1:4-5 IBUKI, Y. Die Wahrheit im Johannesevangelium (1972) 181-86. DUNN, J. D., Christology in the Making (London 1980) 241-42. CULPEPPER, R. A., "The Pivot of John's Prologue" NTS 27 (1980-1981) 11-12.

1:4 PALLIS, A., Notes on St. John and the Apocalypse (London 1928) 1. DUPONT, J. Essais sur la Christologie de Saint Jean (1951) 81, 100, 101, 216, 217, 218. RUCKSTUHL, E. Die literarische Einheit des Johannesevangeliums (1951) 64, 72, 78, 81f., 87, 90, 97, 243, 246. PREISKER, H. ThLZ 77 (1952) 673-78. TWOMEY, R. L. "Substantial Life in John 14," AER 134 (1956) 324-27. LACAN, M. F. "L'Oeuvre du Verbe Incarné: le Don de la Vie (Jo. I,4)," RechSR 45 (1, 1957) 61-78. WIKENHAUSER, A. Das Evangelium nach Johannes (1957) 218-22. WILES, M. F. The Spiritual Gospel (1960) 71-73, 75. DELLING, G. Wort und Werk Jesu im Johannes-Evangelium (1966) 45, 120f., 123, 139. BARTINA, S. "La vida como historia, en el prologo al cuarto evangelio," Biblica 49 (1, 1968) 91-96. CADMAN, W. H. The Open Heaven (1969) G. B. Caird ed., 12, 35, 66, 76, 77, 82, 107, 117. PAGELS, E. H. The Johannine Gospel in Gnostic Exegesis (1973) 21, 23, 32-35, 48-49. HILLERBRAND, H. J. ed., Luther's Works 52 (1974) 50f., 74. GEORGI, D., "Weisheit Salomos" in: JüdSchr III/4 (1980) 1n.13a, 2n.23a, 7n.10b.

1:5 RUCKSTUHL, E. Die literarische Einheit des Johannesevangeliums (1951) 52, 64, 66f., 72, 75, 79, 81, 89f. WIKENHAUSER, A. Das Evangelium nach Johannes (1957) 95-97. NAGEL, W. " 'Die Finsternis hat's nicht begriffen' (Joh 1:5)," ZNW 50 (1-2, 1959) 132-37. DYER, J. A. "The Unappreciated Light," JBL 79 (2, 1960) 170-71. WILES, M. F. The Spiritual Gospel (1960) 73, 75, 97, 100. ROSSANO, P. " 'Et tenebrae eam non comprehenderunt' (Giov. I,5)," RivB 9 (2, 1961) 187. NICKELS, P. Targum and New Testament (1967) 52. SCHOTTROFF, L. Der Glaubende und die feindliche Welt (1970) 230-32. IBUKI, Y. Die Wahrheit im Johannesevangelium (1972) 187-90.

1:5 BROWN, R. E., "The Qumran Scrolls and the Johannine Gospel and Epistles" in: K. Stendahl (ed.) The Scrolls and the New Testament (New York 1957) 188-89; [orig. in: CBQ 17 (1955) 403-19, 559-74] ; GT: "Die Schriftrollen von Qumran und das Johannesevangelium und die Johannesbriefe" in: K. H. Rengstorf (ed.), Johannes und sein Evangelium (Darmstadt 1973) 497. ATAL, D., Structure et signification des cinq premiers versets de l'hymne johannique au logos (Louvain 1973). RAYAN, S., The Holy Spirit: Heart of the Gospel and Christian Hope (New York 1978) 6. IBUKI, Y., "Offene Fragen zur Aufnahme des Logoshymnus in das Vierte Evangelium" AJBI 5 (1979) 107, 109. BERGMEIER, R., Glaube als Gabe nach Johannes (Stuttgart 1980) 192n.30, 203. CLARK, K. W., "The Making of the Twentieth Century New Testament" in: The Gentile Bias and Other Essays (Leiden 1980) 152.

1:6ff STRATHMANN, H. Das Evangelium nach Johannes (1955) 49f.

1:6-34 BÖCHER, O., "Johannes der Täufer in der neutestamentlichen Ueberlieferung" in: G. Müller (ed.) Rechtfertigung, Realismus, Universalismus in biblischer Sicht. FS. A. Köberle (Darmstadt 1978) 45-52.

1:6-13 RUCKSTUHL, E. Die literarische Einheit des Johannesevangeliums (1951) 86f., 90, 93-95, 97. IBUKI, Y., "Offene Fragen zur Aufnahme des Logoshymnus in das Vierte Evangelium" AJBI 5 (1979) 109.

1:6-10 BERGMEIER, R., Glaube als Gabe nach Johannes (Stuttgart 1980) 16.

1:6-9 SAHLIN, H. "Zwei Abschnitte aus Joh 1 rekonstruiert," ZNW 51 (1-2, 1960) 64-69.

1:6-8.15.19-34 CULLMANN, O. Urchristentum und Gottesdienst (1950) 60ff., 80. CORELL, A. Consummatum Est (1958) 54-56.

1:6-8 RUCKSTUHL, E. Die literarische Einheit des Johannes-evangeliums (1951) 68ff., 71f., 80-83, 96f., 93f. HAHN, F. Das Verständnis der Mission in Neuen Testament (1965²) 140. SMITH, D. M. The Composition and Order of the Fourth Gospel (1965) 1, 2, 5, 6, 7, 9, 10, 62, 64n, 71. KEHL, M. "Der Mensch in der Geschichte Gottes. Zum Johannesprolog 1:6-8," GuL 40 (6, 1967) 404-409. HOOKER, M. D. NTS 16 (1969-1970) 354-58. BEUTLER, J. Martyria (1972) 26f., 29, 41, 237-47, 284f., 311. SCHNIDER, F. Jesus der Prophet (1973) 48f. TRITES, A. A., The New Testament Concept of Witness (Cambridge 1977) 91-92. RIESS, H. und KREYSSIG, P., in: P. Krusche et al. (eds.) Predigtstudien für das Kirchenjahr 1978-1979. I/1 (Stuttgart 1978) 72-80. IBUKI, Y., "Offene Fragen zur Aufnahme des Logoshymnus in das Vierte Evangelium" AJBI 5 (1979) 105-10. BERGMEIER, R., Glaube als Gabe nach Johannes (Stuttgart 1980) 245n.175. SCHILLEBEECKX, E., Christ: the Christian Experience in the Modern World (London 1980) 359-60; GT: Christus und die Christen (Freiburg/Basel/Wien 1977) 346-47. CULPEPPER, R. A., "The Pivot of John's Prologue" NTS 27 (1980-1981) 12-13.

1:6-7 LIGHTFOOT, R. H. St. John's Gospel (1956) 66-68. FORTNA, R. T. The Gospel of Signs (1970) 161-67, 217f., 222.

1:6 BAUER, W. Das Johannesevangelium (1925) 14-16. PALLIS, A., Notes on St. John and the Apocalypse (London 1928) 1-2. ROBINSON, J. A. T. "The Baptism of John and the Qumran Community," HThR 50 (1957) 175-91. RUDOLPH, K. Die Mandäer I (1960) 77. SCHUETZ, R. Johannes der Täufer (1967). FORTNA, R. T. The Gospel of Signs (1970) 163f., 217. BEUTLER, J. Martyria (1972) 223, 240ff. BÖHLIG, A., Die Gnosis III: Der Manichäismus (Zürich/München 1980) 343n.34.

1:7-8 HAHN, F. Christologische Hoheitstitel (1963) 380. BEUTLER, J. Martyria (1972) 23, 27, 32, 36, 163, 209f., 212, 214, 220, 223, 226ff., 237-50, 258, 279, 336, 339, 353.

1:7 LIGHTFOOT, R. H. St. John's Gospel (1956) 23-26. FORTNA, R. T. The Gospel of Signs (1970) 164f., 170, 180, 207n.

1:7 CRIBBS, F. L., "The Agreements that Exist Between John and Acts" in: C. H. Talbert (ed.) Perspectives on Luke-Acts (Danville 1978) 48. BERGMEIER, R., Glaube als Gabe nach Johannes (Stuttgart 1980) 210.

1:8 IBUKI, Y., "Offene Fragen zur Aufnahme des Logoshymnus in das Vierte Evangelium" AJBI 5 (1979) 106, 111. BERGMEIER, R., Glaube als Gabe nach Johannes (Stuttgart 1980) 13.

1:9-14 RIESS, H. und KREYSSIG, P., in: P. Krusche et al. (eds.) Predigtstudien für das Kirchenjahr 1978-1979, I/1 (Stuttgart 1978) 72-80.

1:9-13 IWAND, H.-J. Predigt-Meditationen (1964) 48-53. RUCKSTUHL, E. Die literarische Einheit des Johannesevangeliums (1951) 63, 64, 65, 70f., 74f., 77f., 82, 91. IBUKI, Y., "Offene Fragen zur Aufnahme des Logoshymnus in das Vierte Evangelium" AJBI 5 (1979) 107, 109.

1:9-11 BÜHNER, J.-A., Der Gesandte und sein Weg im 4. Evangelium (Tübingen 1977) 91-93.

1:9-10 IBUKI, Y. Die Wahrheit im Johannesevangelium (1972) 183f., 186ff., 188f. BONSACK, B., "Syntatktische Ueberlegungen zu Joh. 1:9-10" in: J. K. Elliot (ed.) Studies in New Testament Language and Text. FS. G. D. Kilpatrick (Leiden 1976) 52-79. CULPEPPER, R. A., "The Pivot of John's Prologue" NTS 27 (1980-1981) 13-14.

1:9 BAUER, W. Das Johannesevangelium (1925) 18. DUPONT, J. Essais sur la Christologie de Saint Jean (1951) 62, 81, 100, 101. RUCKSTUHL, E. Die literarische Einheit des Johannesevangeliums (1951) 45, 51, 64-68, 71f., 75-83, 87. MEHLMANN, J. "A Note on John 1,9," ET 65 (3, 1953) 93-94. LIGHTFOOT, R. H. St. John's Gospel (1956) 74-76. WIKENHAUSER, A. Das Evangelium nach Johannes (1957) 174-76. GLASSON, T. F. "John 1:9 and a Rabbinic Tradition," ZNW 49 (3-4, 1958) 288-90. WILES, M. F. The Spiritual Gospel (1960) 69-71, 74, 100-101. ACHTEMEIER, E. R. "Jesus Christ, the Light of the World. The Biblical Understanding of Light and Darkness," Interpretation 17 (4, 1963) 439-49. BRANDES, E. "Nur ein fauler Zauber?" in: Kleine Predigt-Typologie III (1965) L. Schmidt ed., 262-67. HAHN, F. Das Verständnis der Mission im Neuen Testament (1965²) 136. BRAUN, H. Qumran und NT II (1966) 110, 123, 139ff. DELLING, G. Wort und Werk Jesu im Johannes-Evangelium (1966) 57, 60, 68, 115, 120, 122f. NICKELS, P. Targum and New Testament (1967) 52. CERNUDA, A. V. "Enganan la oscuridad y el mundo; la luz era y manifesta lo verdadero. (Esclarecimiento mutuo de Jn 1,9; 1 Cor 7,31; 1 Jn 2,8 y 17)," EstBi

27 (2, 1968) 153-57; (3, 1968) 215-32. BEUTLER, J. Martyria (1972) 223, 232, 240, 321. IBUKI, Y., Die Wahrheit im Johannesevangelium (1972) 183ff. PRETE, B., "La concordanza del participio *erchomenon in Giov. 1,9*" BiOr 17 (1975) 195-208. KLIJN, A. F., "Die Syrische Baruch-Apokalypse" in: JüdSchr V/2 (1976) 134n.2a. BRUCE, F. F., "The Gospel Text of Marius Victorinus" in: E. Best/R. Wilson (eds.) Text and Interpretation. FS. M. Black (Cambridge 1979) 72. IBUKI, Y., "Offene Fragen zur Aufnahme des Logoshymnus in das Vierte Evangelium" AJBI 5 (1979) 107, 111. SWIDLER, L., Biblical Affirmations of Woman (Philadelphia 1979) 68.

1:10-11 DAUER, A. Die Passionsgeschichte im Johannesevangelium (1972) 193, 257.

1:10 RUCKSTUHL, E. Die literarische Einheit des Johannesevangeliums (1951) 51, 63, 65, 66, 67, 68, 69, 72, 75, 80-82, 85, 87, 89, 92-97. DELLING, G. Wort und Werk Jesu im Johannes-Evangelium (1966) 39, 58f., 123. KUHL, J. Die Sendung Jesu und der Kirche nach dem Johannes-Evangelium (1967) 88, 162, 164, 222. NICKELS, P. Targum and New Testament (1967) 52. SCHOTTROFF, L. Der Glaubende und die feindliche Weit (1970) 230-33. GEORGI, D., "Weisheit Salomos" in: JüdSchr III/4 (1980) 7n.22a.

1:11-14 HARNACK, A. von, Studien zur Geschichte des Neuen Testaments und der Alten Kirche (1951) 115ff., 144ff.

1:11-12 BARRETT, C. K. The New Testament Background (1956) 89.

1:11 RUCKSTUHL, E. Die literarische Einheit des Johannesevangeliums (1951) 52, 65f., 69f., 72, 75, 80-82, 92, 95, 175f. JERVELL, J. " 'Er kam in sein Eigentum.' Zu Joh. 1,11," StTh 10 (1, 1956) 14-27. WILLEMSE, J. NTS 11 (1964-1965) 363f. FLORIVAL, E. " 'Les siens ne l'ont pas reçu' (Jn 1,11). Regard évangélique sur la question juive," NRTh 89 (1, 1967) 43-66. SMITH, M. Tannaitic Parallels to the Gospels (1968) 8 b n 5. CHRIST, F. Jesus Sophia (1970) 65, 67, 83, 127. IBUKI, Y., Die Wahrheit im Johannesevangelium (1972) 201ff. DAVIES, W. D. The Gospel and the Land (1974) 319, 320, 320 n.64, 324, 326, 334, 334 n.95. BERGMEIER, R., Glaube als Gabe nach Johannes (Stuttgart 1980) 215, 246n.177. CULPEPPER, R. A., "The Pivot of John's Prologue" NTS 27 (1980-1981) 14-15.

1:12-13 DUPONT, J. Essais sur la Christologie de Saint Jean (1951) 51, 52. DELLING, G. Die Taufe im Neuen Testament (1963) 90f. DAUER, A. Die Passionsgeschichte im Johannesevangelium (1972) 193. VELLANICKAL, M., The Divine Sonship of

Christians in the Johannine Writings (Rome 1977) 105-52.
POTTERIE, I. de la, "Concepcion y nacimiento virginal de Jesus, segun el cuarto evangelio" Sal Terrae 66 (1978) 567-78.
SCHILLEBEECKX, E., Christ: The Christian Experience in the Modern World (London 1980) 360; GT: Christus und die Christen (Freiburg/Basel/Wien 1977) 347.

1:12 RUCKSTUHL, E. Die literarische Einheit des Johannesevangeliums (1951) 63, 65-68, 70, 75, 85, 87, 92, 161. DELLING, G. Die Zueignung des Heils in der Taufe (1961) 60. DELLING, G. Wort und Werk Jesu im Johannes-Evangelium (1966) 42, 62, 64, 67, 128. UNTERGASSMAIR, F. G., Im Namen Jesu: Der Namensbegriff im Johannesevangelium (Stuttgart 1973) 171-75. FORESTELL, J. T., The Word of the Cross: Salvation as Revelation in the Fourth Gospel (Rome 1974) 103, 168, 171, 176, 177, 187, 198. DELLING, G., "Die 'Söhne(Kinder) Gottes' im Neuen Testament" in: R. Schnackenburg (ed.) Die Kirche des Anfangs. FS. H. Schürmann (Freiburg 1978) 623-24. BERGMEIER, R., Glaube als Gabe nach Johannes (Stuttgart 1980) 9, 219, 254n.307f. GEORGI, D., "Weisheit Salomos" in: JüdSchr III/4 (1980) 7n.14a. CULPEPPER, R. A., "The Pivot of John's Prologue" NTS 27 (1980-1981) 15, 17.

1:13-14 HOFRICHTER, P., Nicht aus Blut sondern monogen aus Gott geboren. Textkritische, dogmengeschichtliche und exegetische Untersuchung zu Joh 1,13-14 (Würzburg 1978).

1:13 BLASS, F. Philosophy of the Gospels (1898) 234ff. GRILL, J. Untersuchungen über die Entstehung des vierten Evangeliums II (1923) 90f., 395. PALLIS, A., Notes on St. John and the Apocalypse (London 1928) 2. BRAUN, F. M. "Qui ex Deo natus est," in: Aux Sources de la Tradition Chrétienne (1950) M. M. Goguel ed., 11-31. RUCKSTUHL, E. Die literarische Einheit des Johannesevangeliums (1951) 64, 66, 67, 68, 85-87, 92. CASTELLINI, G. "De Jo 1,13 in quibusdam citationibus patristicis," Verbum Domini 32 (1954) 155-57. CROSSAN, D. M. "Mary's virginity in St. John-An exegetical study," Marianum 19 (1, 1957) 115-26. SCHMID, J. "Joh 1,13," BZ 1 (1, 1957) 118-25. VIARD, A. "Singulier ou pluriel dans S. Jean I,13," AmiCler 68 (33-36, 1958) 516-20. HAHN, F. Christologische Hoheitstitel (1963) 304. DES PLACES, E. "La syngeneia chrétienne," Biblica 44 (3, 1963) 304-32. CROSSAN, D. "Mary and the Church in John 1:13," BibToday 1 (20, 1965) 1318-24. DELLING, G. Wort und Werk Jesu im Johannes-Evangelium (1966) 127f. Galot, J. Etre né de Dieu (1969). SCHWANK, B. "Eine textkritische Fehlentscheidung (Joh

1,13) und ihre Auswirkungen im Holländischen Katechismus," BuK 24 (1, 1969) 16-17. BARROSSE, T. CBQ 32 (1, 1970) 120-21. SABOURIN, L., " 'Who Was Begotten . . . of God' (Jn 1.13)" BThB 6 (1976) 86-90. METZGER, B. M., The Early Versions of the New Testament (Oxford 1977) 458. JEWETT, P. K., Infant Baptism and the Covenant of Grace (Grand Rapids 1978) 236. BERGMEIER, R., Glaube als Gabe nach Johannes (Stuttgart 1980) 213, 216, 219ff., 254n.307f., 255n.320, 324, 259n.413. SALVONI, F., "Nascita verginale di Gesù" RBR 15 (1980) 165-74. CULPEPPER, R. A., "The Pivot of John's Prologue" NTS 27 (1980-1981) 14-15.

1:14-34 "Aloger" in: TRE 2 (1978) 290.

1:14-18 RUCKSTUHL, E. Die literarische Einheit des Johannesevangeliums (1951) 71-73, 83, 88, 92, 93, 94. ACHTEMEIER, E. The Old Testament and the Proclamation of the Gospel (1973) 189ff. THYEN, H., "Aus der Literatur zum Johannesevangelium" ThR 39 (1974) 222-52. HANSON, A. T., "John i. 14-18 and Exodus xxxiv" NTS 23 (1976) 90-101. THYEN, H., ". . . denn wir lieben die Brüder" in: J. Friedrich et al. (eds.) Rechtfertigung. FS. E. Käsemann (Göttingen 1976) 532-33. de la POTTERIE, I., La Vérité dans Saint Jean I/II (Rome 1977) 127-41. IBUKI, Y., "Offene Fragen zur Aufnahme des Logoshymnus in das Vierte Evangelium" AJBI 5 (1979) 107-109. BERGMEIER, R., Glaube als Gabe nach Johannes (Stuttgart 1980) 209ff., 244n.149. HANSON, A. T., The New Testament Interpretation of Scriptures (London 1980) 97-109.

1:14-17 BRAUN, H. Qumran und NT II (1966) 3, 20, 66, 129, 133, 139, 183, 219, 272.

1:14,16-18 ORIGENES, Das Evangelium nach Johannes (1959) H. Gögler ed., 173-82.

1:14 DEISSMANN, A. Licht vom Osten (1925) 99f. GRILL, J. Untersuchungen über die Entstehung des vierten Evangeliums II (1923) 3, 48, 92, 103, 150, 210, 222, 226, 227, 241, 243, 292, 389, 390. BAUER, W. Das Johannesevangelium (1925) 22f. VOLZ, P. Die Eschatologie der jüdischen Gemeinde (1934) 395. RICHARDSON, A. The Miracle-Stories of the Gospels (1948) 14f. FEINE, D. P./BEHM, D. J. Einleitung in das Neue Testament (1950) 261f. DUPONT, J. Essais sur la Christologie de Saint Jean (1951) 11, 39, 47, 49, 50, 51, 52, 53, 54, 55, 56, 57, 235, 278, 279, 283. RUCKSTUHL, E. Die literarische Einheit des Johannesevangeliums (1951) 64-69, 72f., 83-88, 94f., 260f. DONAGHY, H. "God with Us," Worship 31 (5,

1957) 276-84. WIKENHAUSER, A. Das Evangelium nach Johannes (1957) 181f. DE AUSEJO, S. "El concepto de 'carne' aplicado a Cristo en el IV Evangelio," EstBi 17 (4, 1958) 411-27. JERVELL, J. Imago Dei (1960) 180, 191, 195, 216, 220f., 224. ROBINSON, J. M. Kerygma und historischer Jesus (1960) 71, 107. WILES, M. F. The Spiritual Gospel (1960) 9, 69, 84, 96, 97, 105, 131. DILLISTONE, F. W. "The Advent and Theological Language," in: The Communication of the Gospel in New Testament Times (1961) 87-93. RUDOLPH, K. Die Mandäer II (1961) 149, 1. WAINWRIGHT, A. W. The Trinity in the New Testament (1962) 62-63. BARROSSE, T. "The Word Became Flesh," Bible Today 1 (9, 1963) 590-95. DELLLING, G. Die Taufe im Neuen Testament (1963) 91. GLASSON, T. F. Moses in the Fourth Gospel (1963) 34, 106, Ch. IX. HAHN, F. Christologische Hoheitstitel (1963) 316. SMITH, D. M. NTS 10 (1963-1964) 344f. BASELGA, E. " 'Verbum caro factum est'," Manresa 36 (138, 1964) 23-28. GRASSI, J. A. " 'And the Word Became Flesh and Dwelt Among Us'," BibToday 1 (15, 1964) 975-79. HENNECKE, E./SCHNEEMELCHER, W. Neutestamentliche Apokryphen (1964) I 128; II 333. BULTMANN, R. Theologie des Neuen Testaments (1965) 392ff. GAERTNER, B. The Temple and the Community in Qumran and the New Testament (1965) 53, 119. MUSSNER, F. Die Johanneische Sehweise und die Frage nach dem historischen Jesus (1965) 13, 15, 19, 21, 43, 61, 66f., 81. SCHOENHERR, A. "Seine Herrlichkeit," in: Kleine Predigt-Typologie III (1965) L. Schmidt ed., 84-88. SMITH, D. M. The Composition and Order of the Fourth Gospel (1965) 6, 20, 21, 61, 62, 63, 64n., 71, 92. BOUSSET, W. Die Religion des Judentums im Späthellenistischen Zeitalter (1966 = 1926) 346. DELLING, G. Wort und Werk Jesu im Johannes-Evangelium (1966) 15f., 122-25. SCHNACKENBURG, R. NTS 13 (1966-1967) 202ff. FUCHS, E. Programm der Entmythologisierung (1967) 41-50. ISABEL, M. " 'Dioe con nosotros.' 'Y el Verbo se hizo carne y habito entre nosotros'. (Jn 1,14), RevBi 29 (3, 1967) 143-65. KUHL, J. Die Sendung Jesu und der Kirche nach dem Johannes-Evangelium (1967) 74, 76, 86, 176, 217. NICKELS, P. Targum and New Testament (1967) 52. SMITH, M. Tannaitic Parallels to the Gospels (1968) 2 b n 113;4.8;8.4. DU TOIT, A. B. "The incarnate word-a study of John 1:14," Neotestamentica 2 (1968) 9-21. CADMAN, W. H. The Open Heaven (1969) 11, 13, 36, 51, 83, 107, 123, 138, 161, 172, 205, 209. MEAGHER, J. C. "John 1:14 and the New Temple," JBL 88 (1, 1969) 57-68. RICHTER, H.-F. Auferstehung und Wirklichkeit (1969) 233f. RIST, J. M. "St. John and Amelius," JThS 20 (1, 1969) 230-31. SANDVIK, B. Das Kommen des Herrn beim Abendmahl (1970) 124. SCHOTTROFF, L. Der Glaubende und die feindliche Welt (1970) 230, 235-36, 242-44, 262f., 271f., 280, 283, 289, 296. CULLIN, S. The Nature of Truth in "The Gospel of Truth" and in the Writings of Justin Martyr (1970). THUESING, W. Die Erhöhung und Verherrlichung Jesu im Johannesevangelium (1970) 227-29. SMALLEY, S. S. "Diversity and Development in John," NTS 17 (1970-1971) 288f. RICHTER, G. "Die Fleischwerdung des Logos im Johannesevangelium," NovTest 13 (2, 1971) 81-126. BEUTLER, J. Martyria (1972) 239, 248, 250, 269, 350. IBUKI, Y. Die Wahrheit im Johannesevangelium (1972) 188-201. NICOL, W. The Sēmeia in the Fourth Gospel (1972) 120, 122, 130f., 133. RICHTER, G. "Die Fleischwerdung des Logos im Johannesevangelium (Fortsetzung)," NovTest 14 (4, 1972) 257-76. KLIJN, A. F. J./REININK, G. J. Patristic Evidence for Jewish-Christian Sects (1973) 21. KUEMMEL, W. G. Einleitung in das Neue Testament (1973) 194f. PAGELS, E. H. The Johannine Gospel in Gnostic Exegesis (1973) 32, 37-40, 42. POTVIN, T. R. The Theology of the Primacy of Christ According to St. Thomas and Its Scriptural Foundations (1973) 78, 79_1, 85, 90, 93, 96, 109, 238, 266. ROBINSON, J. A. T. "The Use of the Fourth Gospel for Christology Today," in: Christ and the Spirit in the New Testament (1973) B. Lindars/S. S. Smalley eds., 70f., 78. LADD, G. E. A Theology of the New Testament (1974) 222, 224, 234, 238, 242, 247, 263. DAVIES, W. D., The Gospel and the Land (London 1974) 296, 298, 333, 335n.95. FORESTELL, J. T., The Word of the Cross: Salvation as Revelation in the Fourth Gospel (Rome 1974) 110, 168, 191, 192, 202. MÜLLER, U. B., Die Geschichte der Christologie in der johanneischen Gemeinde (Stuttgart 1975) passim. de la POTTERIE, I., "Xápis paulinienne et Xápis johannique" in: E. Ellis/E. Grässer (eds.) Jesus und Paulus, FS. W. G. Kümmel (Göttingen 1975) 256ff., 269ff. COLLINS, R. F., " 'He Came to Dwell Among Us' (Jn 1:14)" MTh 28 (1976) 44-59. "Abendmahl" in: TRE 1 (1977) 67, 113. BÜHNER, J.-A., Der Gesandte und sein Weg im 4. Evangelium (Tübingen 1977) 91-93. DUNN, J. D. G., Unity and Diversity in the New Testament (London 1977) 300-301. ELLIOTT, J. K., "John 1:14 and the New Testament's Use of *plērēs*" BTr 28 (1977) 151-53. de la POTTERIE, I., La Vérité dans Saint Jean I/II (Rome 1977) 76-78, 117-27, 134-41, 169-211. SAITO, T., Die Mosevorstellungen im Neuen Ttestament (Bern 1977) 118-21. HARRISON, E. F., "A Study of John 1:14" in: R. A. Guelich (ed.) Unity and Diversity in New Testament Theology. FS. G.

E. Ladd (Grand Rapids 1978) 23-36. LAMPARTER, H., "Das Christuszeugnis in den Psalmen" in: G. Müller (ed.) Rechtfertigung, Realismus, Universalimus in biblischer Sicht. FS. A. Köberle (Darmstadt 1978) 25. RUDOLPH, K., Die Gnosis (Göttingen 1978) 173. BRUCE, F. F., "The Gospel Text of Marius Victorinus" in: E. Best/R. McWilson (eds.) Text and Interpretation. FS. M. Black (Cambridge 1979) 72. IBUKI, Y., "Offene Fragen zur Aufnahme des Logoshymnus in das vierte Evangelium" ABJI 5 (1979) 108, 113, 116-18, 122, 126. SCHNACKENBURG, R., " 'Und das Wort ist Fleisch geworden' " IKZ 8 (1979) 1-9. BEIERWALTES, W., "Deus est Veritas" in: E. Dassmann/K. S. Frank (eds.) Pietas, FS. B. Kötting (Münster 1980) 24. BERGMEIER, R., Glaube als Gabe nach Johannes (Stuttgart 1980) 209ff., 244n.160.162.163, 245n.165.168, 264n.484, 273n.612. DUNN, J. D. G., Christology in the Making (London 1980) 57-58, 164-65, 213-14, 241-45, et al. SCHILLEBEECKX, E., Christ: the Christian Experience in the Modern World (London 1980) 360-62; GT: Christus und die Christen (Freiburg/Basel/Wien 1977) 347-49. CULPEPPER, R. A., "The Pivot of John's Prologue" NTS 27 (1980-1981) 13-14. CRANFIELD, C. E. B., "John 1:14: 'Became' " ET 93 (1982) 215. "Eckart" in: TRE 9 (1982) 259.

1:14a BERGER, K. "Zu 'Das Wort ward Fleisch' Joh. 1:14a," NovTest 16 (3, 1974) 161-66.

1:15-18 DIEM, H. in: Herr, tue meine Lippen auf Bd. 3 (1964) G. Eichholz ed., 27ff., WEBER, O. Predigtmeditationen (1967) 24-27. NÖRENBERG, K.-D. und HASSELMANN, N., in: P. Krusche et al. (eds.) Predigtstudien für das Kirchenjahr 1980-1981. III/1 (Stuttgart 1980) 83-90. PAHNKE, R., in: GPM 35 (1980) 88-95.

1:15 RUCKSTUHL, E. Die literarische Einheit des Johannesevangeliums (1951) 38, 46, 63f., 68, 71, 77f., 83-88, 92, 94, 152. RUDOLPH, K. Die Mandäer I (1960) 77. HAHN, F. Christologische Hoheitstitel (1963) 380. SMITH, D. M. The Composition and Order of the Fourth Gospel (1965) 1, 2, 5, 6, 7, 9. 10n., 64n., 71, 122. HOOKER, M. D. NTS 16 (1969-1970) 354-58. BEUTLER, J. Martyria (1972) 23, 26f., 41, 220, 223, 234, 237-50, 285, 311, 339, 343, 353. SCHNIDER, F. Jesus der Prophet (1973) 47ff. METZGER, B. M., The Early Versions of the New Testament (Oxford 1977) 245. TRITES, A. A., The New Testament Concept of Witness (Cambridge 1977) 91-92. IBUKI, Y., "Offene Fragen zur Aufnahme des Logoshymnus in das vierte Evangelium" AJBI 5 (1979) 105-14. BERGMEIER, R., Glaube als Gabe nach Johannes (Stuttgart 1980) 16, 209-10, 244n.159.163. SCHILLEBEECKX, E., Christ: the Christian Experience in the Modern World (London 1980) 359-60; GT: Christus und die Christen (Freiburg/Basel/ Wien 1977) 346-47. CULPEPPER, R. A., "The Pivot of John's Prologue," NTS 27 (1980-1981) 12-13.

1:16-18 SWIDLER, L., Biblical Affirmations of Woman (Philadelphia 1979) 72. BERGMEIER, R., Glaube als Gabe nach Johannes (Stuttgart 1980) 244n.149.

1:16-17 JERVELL, J. Imago Dei (1960) 216, 220f., 224.

1:16 BOVER, J. M. Biblica 6 (1925) 454-60. PALLIS, A., Notes on St. John and the Apocalypse (London 1928) 2-3. RUCK-STUHL, E. Die literarische Einheit des Johannesevangeliums (1951) 38, 64, 66, 67, 83-88, 92, 97. SMITH, D. M. The Composition and Order of the Fourth Gospel (1965) 20, 61, 71, 92, 234. NICKELS, P. Targum and New Testament (1967) 52. IBUKI, Y. Die Wahrheit im Johannesevangelium (1972) 201f. van ROON, A., The Authenticity of Ephesians (Leiden 1974) 251. MÜLLER, U. B., Die Geschichte der Christologie in der johanneischen Gemeinde (Stuttgart 1975) passim. de la POTTERIE, I., "Xápis paulinienne et Xápis johannique" in: E. Ellis/E. Grässer (eds.) Jesus und Paulus. FS. W. G. Kümmel (Göttingen 1975) 256f., 261ff., 278ff. de la POTTERIE, I., La Vérité dans Saint Jean I/II (Rome 1977) 142-50. VELLANICKAL, M., The Divine Sonship of Christians in the Johannine Writings (Rome 1977) 152-56. HODGES, Z. C., "Grace after Grace—John 1:16. Part 1 of *Problem Passages in the Gospel of John*" BiblSa 135 (1978) 34-45. IBUKI, Y., "Offene Fragen zur Aufnahme des Logoshymnus in das vierte Evangelium" AJBI 5 (1979) 108, 113. BERGMEIER, R., Glaube als Gabe nach Johannes (Stuttgart 1980) 209ff., 244n.162f. GEORGI, D., "Weisheit Salomos" in: JüdSchr III/4 (1980) 7n.11b, 8n.5a. CULPEPPER, R. A., "The Pivot of John's Prologue" NTS 27 (1980-1981) 11-12.

1:17-48 GLASSON, T. F. Moses in the Fourth Gospel (1963) 24ff., 70, 81, 86. DAUER, A. Die Passionsgeschichte im Johannesevangelium (1972) 301f. IBUKI, Y., Die Wahrheit im Johannesevangelium (1972) 202-207. SAITO, T., Die Mosevorstellungen im Neuen Testament (Bern 1977) 118-21, 137-41, 143, 147. BERGMEIER, R., Glaube als Gabe nach Johannes (Stuttgart 1980) 16. CALLAN, T., "Pauline Midrash: The Exegetical Background of Gal. 3:19b" JBL 99 (1980) 558. SCHILLEBEECKX, E., Christ: the Christian Experience in the Modern World (London 1980) 360-62; GT: Christus und die Christen (Freiburg/Basel/Wien 1977) 347-49.

1:17 BONHOEFFER, A. Epiktet und das Neue Testament (1911)
289, 310. GRILL, J. Untersuchungen über die Entstehung des
vierten Evangeliums II (1923) 92, 236, 356, 375. DUPONT, J.
Essais sur la Christologie de Saint Jean (1951) 38, 39. RUCK-
STUHL, E. Die literarische Einheit des Johannesevangliums
(1951) 38, 63, 66-68, 83-88, 92, 97. WILES, M. F. The Spiritual Gospel (1960) 68-70, 100-102. BORNKAMM-BARTH-
HELD, Ueberlieferung und Auslegung im Matthäus-Evangelium (²1961) 32. HAHN, F. Christologische Hoheitstitel (1963)
391. GRAESSER, E. NTS 11 (1964-1965) 78f. HAHN, F. Das
Verständnis der Mission im Neuen Testament (²1965) 138.
NICKELS, P. Targum and New Testament (1967) 52. OTTO,
G. Denken - um zu glauben (1970) 9-13. HAACKER, K. Die
Stiftung des Heils (1972) 25-36. LADD, G. E. A Theology of
the New Testament (1974) 140, 227, 230. PANIMOLLE, S. A.,
Il dono della Legge e la Grazia della Verità (Gv 1,17) (Rome
1973). PANCARO, S., The Law in the Fourth Gospel (Leiden
1975) 519, 526, 534-46. de la POTTERIE, I., "Xápis pauli-
nienne et Xápis johannique" in: E. Ellis/E. Grässer (eds.) Jesus
und Paulus. FS. S. G. Kümmel (Göttingen 1975) 256ff., 269,
272-73, 279ff. de la POTTERIE, I., La Vérité dans Saint Jean
I/II (Rome 1977) 117-27, 134-41, 156-58, 158-69. HENGEL,
M., Zur Urchristlichen Geschichtsschreibung (Stuttgart 1979)
41; ET: J. Bowden (trans.) Acts and the History of Earliest
Christianity (London 1979) 42. "Barmherzigkeit" in: TRE
(1980) 218. BERGMEIER, R., Glaube als Gabe nach Johannes
(Stuttgart 1980) 13, 209-10, 244n.162, 245n.163-164. CUL-
PEPPER, R. A., "The Pivot of John's Prologue" NTS 27 (1980-
1981) 10.

1:18 RUCKSTUHL, E. Die literarische Einheit des Johannesevangeliums (1951) 66-68, 85-88. WILES, M. F. The Spiritual
Gospel (1960) 91-93, 97, 121. POTTERIE, I. de la, "L'emploi
dynamique de *eís* dans Saint Jean et ses incidences Théologiques," Biblica 43 (1962) 366-87. WAINWRIGHT, A. W.
The Trinity in the New Testament (1962) 60-63. DELLING, G.
Die Taufe im Neuen Testaments (1963) 91. HAHN, F., Christologische Hoheitstitel (1963) 329. SMITH, D. M. The Composition and Order of the Fourth Gospel (1965) 6, 9, 64n., 71,
92. DELLING, G. Wort und Werk Jesu im Johannes-Evangelium (1966) 66f., 108f. LOUW, J. P. "Narrator of the Father-
EXĒGEISTHAI and related terms in Johannine Christology,"
Neotestamentica 2 (1968) 32-40. CADMAN, W. H. The Open
Heaven (1969) 3, 8, 9, 10, 95, 103, 148, 172, 187, 206. JOHN-
STON, G. The Spirit-Paraclete in the Gospel of John (1970) 62,
67, 127, 155, 156, 161. IBUKI, Y. Die Wahrheit im Johannes-

evangelium (1972) 146ff., 154f. PAGELS, E. H. The Johan-
nine Gospel in Gnostic Exegesis (1973) 37, 51-52, 55.
ROBINSON, J. A. T. "The Use of the Fourth Gospel for
Christology Today," in: Christ and the Spirit in the New Tes-
tament (1973) B. Lindars/S. S. Smalley eds., 71, 74f. LADD,
G. E. A Theology of the New Testament (1974) 242, 247, 249,
250, 263, 272, 632. ROSS, J. M. "Two More Titles of Jesus,"
ET 85 (9, 1974) 281. MUELLER, T. Das Heilsgeschehen im
Johannesevangelium n.d., 18-20, 37, 135f. Hahn,
F. "Beobachtungen zu Joh 1:18,34" in: J. K. Elliott (ed.) Stud-
ies in New Testament Language and Text. FS. G. D. Kilpatrick
(Leiden 1976) 239-45. BÜHNER, J.-A., Der Gesandte und sein
Weg im 4. Evangelium (Tübingen 1977) 375-76. de la POT-
TERIE, I., La Vérité dans Saint Jean I/II (Rome 1977) 211-49.
RUDOLPH, K., Die Gnosis (Göttingen 1978) 163, 173, 327.
BRUCE, F. F., "The Gospel Text of Marius Victorinus" in: E.
Best/R. Wilson (eds.) Text and Interpretation. FS. M. Black
(Cambridge 1979) 72. FREED, E. D., "Theological Prelude to
the Prologue of John's Gospel" SJTh 32 (1979) 257-69.
BERGMEIER, R., Glaube als Gabe nach Johannes (Stuttgart
1980) 17, 244n.162, 245n.164. CLARK, K. W., "The Text of
the Gospel of John in Third-Century Egypt" in: The Gentile Bias
and other Essays (Leiden 1980) 159-69. DUNN, J. D., Chris-
tology in the Making (London 1980) 29, 58, 244, 245, 250,
290n.229, 348n.111, 350n.123, 350n.125. HANSON, A. T.,
The New Testament Interpretation of Scripture (London 1980)
162-66. THYEN, H., " 'Das Heil kommt von den Juden' " in:
D. Lührmann/G. Strecker (eds.) Kirche. FS. G. Bornkamm
(Tübingen 1980) 183. CULPEPPER, R. A., "The Pivot of
John's Prologue" NTS 27 (1980-1981) 9-10. MILLER, E. L.,
"The Logos was God" EQ 53 (1981) 65, 75-76.

1:19-5:47 TALBERT, C. H. "Artistry and Theology," CBQ 32 (3, 1970)
341-66.

1:19-4:54 GRUNDMANN, W. "Verkündigung und Geschichte in dem
Bericht vom Eingang der Geschichte Jesu im Johannes-Evan-
gelium," in: Der historische Jesus und der Kerygmatische
Christus (²1961) H. Ristow/K. Matthiae eds., 289-309. DEEKS,
D., "The Structure of the Fourth Gospel," NTS 15 (1968-1969)
112. SELBY, D. J., Introduction to the New Testament (New
York 1971) 234-41. RIEDL, J. Das Heilswerk Jesu nach Jo-
hannes (1973) 63-68.

1:19-4:42 GRUNDMANN, W. Zeugnis und Gestalt des Johannes-Evangeliums (1961) 31-38.

1:19-2:12 MATUS, T. "First and Last Encounter," BibToday 42 (1969) 2893-97. SERRA, A. M. "Le tradizioni della teofania sinaitica nel Targum dello pseudo-Jonathan Es. 19.24 e in Giov. 1,19-2,12," Marianum 33 (1, 1971) 1-39. CAZEAUX, J., " 'C'est Moïse qui vous condamnera . . .,' " LuVie 29 (1980) 75-88.

1:19-2:11 BOISMARD, M. E. De Baptême à Cana (Jean 1.19-2.11) (1956). BARROSSE, T. "The Seven Days of the New Creation in St. John's Gospel," CBQ 21 (4, (1959) 507-16.

1:19ff KNOX, W. L. The Sources of the Synoptic Gospels II (1957) 145. WILKENS, W. Die Entstehungsgeschichte des vierten Evangeliums (1958) 32, 33, 34, 35, 36, 37, 38. KAESEMANN, E. New Testament Questions of Today (1969) 167.

1:19-51 GLASSON, T. F. "John the Baptist in the Fourth Gospel," ET 67 (8, 1956) 245-46. van den BUSSCHE, H., "La Structure de Jean I-XI" in: M. Boismard et al., L'Evangile de Jean: études et problèmes (Bruges 1958) 67-76. YATES, E. M. Preaching from John's Gospel (1963) 13-17. BRAUN, H. Qumran und NT II (1966) 20, 25. WINK, W. John the Baptist in the Gospel Tradition (1968) 89-93. OLSSON, B., Structure and Meaning in the Fourth Gospel (Lund 1974) 23-25, 28-29, 51-52, 101-102, 104-108, 136-38, 254-56, 276-79, et al. de JONGE, M., Jesus: Stranger from Heaven and Son of God (Missoula 1977) 79, 82-85. NICCACCI, A., "La fede nel Gesù storico et la fede nel Cristo risorto (Gv 1,19-51/20,1-20)" Antonianum 53 (1978) 423-42.

1:19-36 VAN IERSEL, B. M. F. "Tradition und Redaktion in Joh. i 19-36," NovTest 6 (4, 1962) 245-67. BOISMARD, M.-E. "Les traditions johanniques concernant le Baptiste," RevBi 70 (1, 1963) 5-42.

1:19-34 RUCKSTUHL, E. Die literarische Einheit des Johannesevangeliums (1951) 33f., 149-59. GILMORE, A. Christian Baptism (1959) 151ff. BROX, N. Zeuge und Märtyrer (1961) 70f. LINDIJER, C. H. De Sacramenten in het Vierde Evangelie (1964) 52f. SMITH, D. M. The Composition and Order of the Fourth Gospel (1965) 119-25, 126, 148, 229. BRAUN, H. Qumran und NT II (1966) 12-14, 19f., 28f., 78-81. BIEDER, W. Die Verheissung der Taufe im Neuen Testament (Zürich 1966) 259-60. FORTNA, R. T. The Gospel of Signs (1970) 167-78, 217n. BEUTLER, J. Martyria (1972) 23, 220, 251, 254, 257, 285f., 311, 352f. PAGELS, E. H. The Johannine Gospel in Gnostic Exegesis: Heracleon's Commentary on John (1973) 51-65. TEMPLE, S., The Core of the Fourth Gospel (London 1975) 68-81. de JONGE, M., Jesus: Stranger from Heaven and Son of God (Missoula 1977) 52-54, 85-90. de la POTTERIE,

I., La Vérité dans Saint Jean I/II (Rome 1977) 95-96, 98.
TRITES, A. A., The New Testament Concept of Witness
(Cambridge 1977) 91-92. BECKER, J., Das Evangelium nach
Johannes (Gütersloh/Würzburg 1979) 88 (lit!). SCHILLE-
BEECKX, E., Christ: the Christian Experience in the Modern
World (London 1980) 368-73; GT: Christus und die Christen
(Freiburg/Basel/Wien 1977) 355-58.

1:19-31 TEMPLE, S., The Core of the Fourth Gospel (London 1975)
69-73. BARTH, M., Die Taufe - ein Sakrament? (Zürich 1951)
385ff. IBUKI, Y., "Offene Fragen zur Aufnahme des Logoshymnus in das Vierte Evangelium" AJBI 5 (1979) 112-13.
HAENCHEN, E., Das Johannesevangelium (Tübingen 1980)
154-55 (lit!). KRAFT, H., Die Entstehung des Christentums
(Darmstadt 1981) 15-16. BARIE, H. und MEIER, C., in: P.
Krusche et al. (eds.) Predigtstudien für das Kirchenjahr 1982/
1983. V/1 (Stuttgart 1982) 34-41.

1:19-28 HARBSMEIER, GPM 4 (1949-1950) 21ff. IWAND, H.-J.
GPM 9 (1954-1955) 16ff. BRUNNER, P. in: Herr, tue meine
Lippen auf Bd. 1 (1957) G. Eichholz ed., 15-20. DOERNE, M.
Er kommt auch noch heute (1961) 17-20. IWAND, H.-J. Predigt-Meditationen (1964) 420-24. UNGEFROREN, H. "Jo-
hannes-der adventische Bote," in: Kleine Predigt-Typologie III
(1965) L. Schmidt ed., 232-38. WILLIAMS, F. E. "Fourth
Gospel and Synoptic Tradition: Two Johannine Passages," JBL
86 (3, 1967) 311-19. HOOKER, M. NTS 16 (1969-1970) 354-
58. JOHNSTON, G. The Spirit-Paraclete in the Gospel of John
(1970) 52-55. KRECK, W. GPM 27 (1, 1972) 27-32. SCHULZ,
H./SPIEGEL, Y. "Vierter Advent: Johannes 1,19-28," in:
Predigtstudien (1972) E. Lange ed., 37-43. SCHNIDER, F. Jesus der Prophet (1973) 47, 206f.

1:19-27 MAURER, C. Ignatius von Antiochien und das Johannesevangelium (1949) 19-22.

1:19-25 SAHLIN, H. "Zwei Abschnitte aus Joh I rekonstruiert," ZNW
51 (1-2, 1960) 64-69.

1:19-23 NICKELS, P. Targum and New Testament (1967) 52.
FORTNA, R. T. The Gospel of Signs (1970) 169-72.

1:19.27 BAILEY, J. A. The Traditions Common to the Gospels of Luke
and John (1963) 9-11.

1:19-21 METZGER, B. M., Manuscripts of the Greek Bible (Oxford
1981) 124.

1:19 BAUER, W. Das Johannesevangelium (1925) 28f. BUECH-
SEL, F. Das Evangelium nach Johannes (1946) 37f. BAR-
RETT, C. K. ThLZ 79 (1954) 762. LIGHTFOOT, R. H. St.

John's Gospel (1956) 64-66. HAHN, F. Christologische Hoheitstitel (1963) 380. FORTNA, R. T. The Gospel of Signs (1970) 166, 170, 179, 180. BEUTLER, J. Martyria (1972) 29, 212, 227, 230, 234, 237, 239, 243, 250-52, 259, 281, 286, 339. IBUKI, Y., "Offene Fragen zur Aufnahme des Logoshymnus in das Vierte Evangelium" AJBI 5 (1979) 111.

1:20-21 HAHN, F. Christologische Hoheitstitel (1963) 359, 370, 374, 380. MARTYN, J. L., The Gospel of John in Christian History (New York 1978) 13-16, 28, 37, 38, 41.

1:20 RUDOLPH, K. Die Mandäer I (1960) 77. FORTNA, R. T. The Gospel of Signs (1970) 170f., 185n. BEUTLER, J. Martyria (1972) 30, 220, 342f., 353. CRIBBS, F. L. in: SBL Seminar Papers 2 (1973) MacRae, G. ed., 3. CRIBBS, F. L., "The Agreements that Exist Between John and Acts" in: C. H. Talbert (ed.) Perspectives on Luke - Acts (Danville 1978) 47-48. FREED, E. D., "*Egō Eimi* in John 1:20 and 4:25" CBQ 41 (1979) 288-91.

1:21-25 SCHNIDER, F. Jesus der Prophet (1973) 47, 191, 215, 223ff. BÜHNER, J.-A. Der Gesandte und sein Weg im 4. Evangelium (Tübingen 1977) 106-107.

1:21 BAUER, W. Das Johannesevangelium (1925) 30f. VOLZ, P. Die Eschatologie der jüdischen Gemeinde (1934) 193. DAVIES, W. D. Torah in the Messianic Age and/or the Age to come (1952) 44. RICHTER, G. " 'Bist du Elias?' (Joh. 1,21)," BZ 6 (1, 1962) 79-92; (2, 1962) 238-56; 7 (1, 1963) 63-80. SMITH, D. M. The Composition and Order of the Fourth Gospel (1965) 12, 120, 121, 122, 123n. BOUSSET, W. Die Religion des Judentums im Späthellenistischen Zeitalter (1966 = 1926) 233. MEEKS, W. A. The Prophet-King, Moses Traditions and the Johannine Christology (1967) 21-26, 33, 89. NÖTSCHER, F., Altorientalischer und alttestamentlicher Auferstehungsglaube (Darmstadt 1970 = 1926) 127. REIM, G., Studien zum Alttestamentlichen Hintergrund des Johannesevangeliums (Cambridge 1974) 119. SAITO, T., Die Mosevorstellungen im Neuen Testament (Bern 1977) 113-15. SCHRAGE, W., "Die Elia-Apokalypse" in: JüdSchr V/3 (1980) 207, 275n.44e. TEMPLE, S., The Core of the Fourth Gospel (London 1975) 73-75. LANGBRANDTNER, W., Weltferner Gott oder Gott der Liebe (Frankfurt a.M./Bern/Las Vegas 1977) 76-79.

1:22-24 SMITH, D. M. The Composition and Order of the Fourth Gospel (1965) 119, 120, 121, 122, 237.

1:23-34 LENTZEN-DEIS, F. Die Taufe Jesu nach den Synoptikern (1970) 78.

1:23-31 ORIGENES, Das Evangelium nach Johannes (1969) R. Gögler ed., 182-208.

1:23 RUDOLPH, K. Die Mandäer I (1960) 77. FREED, E. D. Old Testament Quotations in the Gospel of John (1965) 1-7. BLINZLER, J., Die Brüder und Schwestern Jesu (Stuttgart 1967) 78-79. REIM, G., Studien zum Alttestamentlichen Hintergrund des Johannesevangeliums (Cambridge 1974) 4-10, 89-93. BERGMEIER, R., Glaube als Gabe nach Johannes (Stuttgart 1980) 230. HANSON, A. T., The New Testament Interpretation of Scripture (London 1980) 157.

1:24-28 FORTNA, R. T. The Gospel of Signs (1970) 172-74.

1:25 DAVIES, W. D. Torah in the Messianic Age and/or the Age to come (1952) 44. HAHN, F. Christologische Hoheitstitel (1963) 359. NÖTSCHER, F., Altorientalischer und alttestamentlicher Auferstehungsglaube (Darmstadt 1970 = 1926) 127. SAITO, T., Die Mosevorstellungen im Neuen Testament (Bern 1977) 113-15. MARTYN, J. L., The Gospel of John in Christian History (New York 1978) 13-16.

1:26.29-30 BROWN, R. E. "Three Quotations from John the Baptist in the Gospel of John," CBQ 22 (3, 1960) 292-98.

1:26.31.33 DELLING, G. Die Taufe im Neuen Testament (1963) 46.

1:26-27 LANGBRANDTNER, W., Weltferner Gott oder Gott der Liebe (Frankfurt a.M./Bern/Las Vegas 1977) 76-79.

1:26 BIEDER, W., Die Verheissung der Taufe im Neuen Testament (Zürich 1955) 87-88. PORSCH, F., Pneuma und Wort (Frankfurt 1974) 47-49. METZGER, B. M., The Early Versions of the New Testament (Oxford 1977) 437.

1:27 BEUTLER, J. Martyria (1972) 220, 239, 248, 285, 353. PARKER, P., "The Kinship of John and Acts" in: J. Neusner (ed.) Christianity, Judaism and Other Greco-Roman Cults. I. FS. M. Smith (Leiden 1975) 187-91. SANDMEL, S., We Jews and Jesus (New York 1977) 120. CRIBBS, F. L., "The Agreements that Exist Between John and Acts" in: C. H. Talbert (ed.) Perspectives on Luke-Acts (Danville 1978) 48, 60. PROULX, P. and SCHÖKEL, L. A., "Las Sandalias del Mesías Esposo" Biblica 59 (1978) 1-37. IBUKI, Y., "Offene Fragen zur Aufnahme des Logoshymnus in das Vierte Evangelium" AJBI 5 (1979) 113-14. KIEFFER, R., " 'Mer-än' kristologin hos synoptikerna" SEA 44 (1979) 134-47; FT: "La christologie de supériorité dans les Evangiles Synoptiques" EThR 54 (1979) 579-91.

1:28 PARKER, P. "Bethany beyond Jordan," JBL 74 (4, 1955) 257-
61. Also in: BTr 9 (3, 1958) 137-38. RUDOLPH, K. Die Mandäer I (1960) 231. DALMAN, G. Orte und Wege Jesu (1967)
99f. WIEFEL, W. "Bethabara jenseits des Jordan (Joh.
1,28)," ZDPV 83 (1, 1967) 52-81. METZGER, B. M. "Explicit references in the works of Origen to variant readings in New Testament manuscripts," in: Historical and Literary Studies (1968)
96f. CRIBBS., F. L. in: SBL Seminar Papers 2 (1973) MacRae,
G. ed., 3. DAVIES, W. D. The Gospel and the Land (1974)
318-21 passim. METZGER, B. M., The Early Versions of the
New Testament (Oxford 1977) 172. KRAFT, H., Die Entstehung des Christentums (Darmstadt 1981) 11-12.

1:29 - 3:26 MIZZI, J., "The Old-Latin Element in Jn. I,29 - III,26 of Cod.
Sangallensis 60" Sacris Erudiri 23 (Brugge 1978-1979) 33-62.

1:29-2:12 TRUDINGER, L. P. "The Seven Days of the New Creation in
St. John's Gospel: Some Further Reflections," EQ 55 (3, 1972)
154-58.

1:29-51 DE GOEDT, M. "Un Schème de Révélation dans le Quatrième
Evangile," NTS 8 (2, 1962) 142-50.

1:29-36 BURROWS, E. W. "Did John the Baptist Call Jesus 'The Lamb
of God'?" ET 85 (8, 1974) 245-49. LEROY, H., Zur Vergebung der Sünden (Stuttgart 1974) 82-86.

1:29-34 BAUER, W. Das Johannesevangelium (1925) 35f. GIBLET, J.
"Pour rendre témoignage à la Lumière (John I,29-34),"BVieC
16 (1956-1957) 80-86. BARTH, M., Die Taufe - ein Sakrament? (Zürich 1951) 385-94. HOWTON, D. J. NTS 10 (1963-
1964) 231f.BIEDER, W., Die Verheissung der Taufe im Neuen
Testament (Zürich 1966) 87-88. MARCONCINI, B. "Dal Battista 'storico' al Battista 'giovanneo' : interpretazione storica e
interpretazione esistenziale," RivB 20 (suppl., 1972) 467-80.
FORESTELL, J. T., The Word of the Cross: Salvation as Revelation in the Fourth Gospel (Rome 1974) 20, 21, 25. PORSCH,
F., Pneuma und Wort (Frankfurt 1974) 32-34. ROBERGE, M.,
"Structures littéraires et christologie dans le 4e évangile. Jean
1,29-34" in: M. Gervais et al. (eds.) Le Christ hier, aujour-
d'hui et demain (Laval 1976) 467-77. ALDAY, S. C., "Cristo
Jesús: El que Bautiza en Espíritu Santo. Jn 1,29-34," ISEELA
6 (1976-1977) 167-75. LANGBRANDTNER, W., Weltferner
Gott oder Gott der Liebe (Frankfurt a.M./Bern/Las Vegas 1977)
76-79. IBUKI, Y., "Offene Fragen zur Aufnahme des Logoshymnus in das Vierte Evangelium" AJBI 5 (1979) 113. GAR-
NET, P., "The Baptism of Jesus and the Son of Man Idea"
JSNT 9 (1980) 49-65. HAENCHEN, E., Das Johannesevangelium (Tübingen 1980) 164-65 (lit!). VANDANA, Sr.,

"Waters of Recognition and Awakening. John 1:29-34" BB 6 (1980) 289-301. MATSUNAGA, K., "Is John's Gospel Anti-Sacramental?—A New Solution in the Light of the Evangelist's Milieu" NTS 27 (1981) 521-22. "Epiphaniasfest" in: TRE 9 (1982) 769, 770. MEYER-ROSCHER, W. und HEUE, R., in: P. Krusche et al. (eds.) Predigtstudien für das Kirchenjahr 1982-1983. V/I (Stuttgart 1982) 90-97.

1:29-31 FORTNA, R. T. The Gospel of Signs (1970) 175f.

1:29-30 BROWN, R. E. "Three Quotations from John the Baptist in the Gospel of John," CBQ 22 (3, 1960) 292-98. YATES, J. E. The Spirit and the Kingdom (1963) 213ff.

1:29.36 GILS, F. Jésus Prophète D'Après Les Evangiles Synoptiques (1957) 58-64. STANLEY, D. M. "John the Witness," Worship 32 (7, 1958) 409-16. ZIENER, G. "Johannesevangelium und urchristliche Passafeier," BZ 2 (2, 1958) 263-74. SQUILLACI, D. "La testimonoanza del Battista. Ecce Agnus Dei (Giov. 1,29.36)," PaCl 39 (12, 1960) 642-46. GRYGLEWICZ, F. "Das Lamm Gottes," NTS 13 (2, 1967) 133-146. ROBERTS, J. H. "The Lamb of God," Neotestamentica 2 (1968) 41-56. TOBIN, W. J. "Reflections on the Title and Function of the 'Lamb of God'," BibToday 34 (1968) 2367-76. MIKALSEN, T. The Traditio-Historical Place of the Christology of 1 Peter in Light of 1.18-21 (Rüschlikon 1971) 52ff.

1:29 GRILL, J. Untersuchungen über die Entstehung des vierten Evangeliums II (1923) 23, 83, 87, 94, 141, 147f., 152f., 192, 227, 365. BAUER, W. Das Johannesevangelium (1925) 33f. TAYLOR, V. Jesus and His Sacrifice (1948) 47, 225-28, 230, 237, 258, 264. FEINE, D. P./BEHM, D. J. Einleitung in das Neue Testament (1950) 113f. MUSSNER, F. ZΩH. Die Anschauung vom "Leben" im vierten Evangelium (1952) 101f. NOACK, B. Zur Johanneischen Tradition (1954) 72, 149f. BARRETT, C. K. "The Lamb of God," NTS 1/3 (1955) 210-18. DENNEY, J. The Death of Christ (1956³) 140, 147f. DE LA POTTERIE, I. "Ecco l'Agnello di Dio," BiOr 1 (6, 1959) 161-69. SCHWEIZER, E. Erniedrigung und Erhöhung bei Jesus und seinen Nachfolgern (1962) § 6e. GLASSON, T. F. Moses in the Fourth Gospel (1963) 16, 34, 96ff. HAHN, F. Christologische Hoheitstitel (1963) 55. TAYLOR, E. K. "The Lamb of God," ClR 48 (5, 1963) 285-92. YATES, J. E., The Spirit and the Kingdom (1963) 212-15. HENNECKE, E./SCHNEEMELCHER, W. Neutestamentliche Apokryphen (1964) I 349. BLENKINSOPP, J. "The Lamb of God," ClR 50 (1965) 868-72. HAHN, F. Das Verständnis der Mission im Neuen Testament (1965²) 136. ROSE, A. "Jésus-Christ, Ag-

neua de Dieu," BVieC 62 (1965) 27-32. LAZURE, N., Les
Valeurs Morales de la Théologie Johannique (Paris 1965) 291-
92. McNAMARA, M. The New Testament and the Palestinian
Targum to the Pentateuch (1966) 94 n.62, 167. NICKELS, P.
Targum and New Testament (1967) 52. STROBEL, A. Erkenntnis und Bekenntnis der Sünde in neutestamentlicher Zeit
(1968) 46. WOOD, J. W. "Isaac Typology in the New Testament," NTS 14 (1968) 583-89. WILKENS, W., Zeichen und
Werke (Zürich 1969) 76-77. LYONNET, S. Sin, Redemption,
and Sacrifice (1970) 39-42. BOHREN, R. Predigtlehre (1971)
257f. SCHWEIZER, E. Gott Versöhnt (1971) 57-67. DAUER,
A. Die Passionsgeschichte im Johannesevangelium (1972) 137-
39, 256, 257, 286, 293, 321. BERTRAND, D. A. Le Baptr̂e
de Jésus (1973) 18, 19, 34, 35, 69, 74, 96, 108, 119. LADD,
G. E. A Theology of the New Testament (1974) 43, 226, 249,
280. MUELLER, T. Das Heilsgeschehen im Johannesevangelium n.d., 39-46, 58, 63, 67, 73f., 110, 130, 132-35.
FORESTELL, J., The Word of the Cross: Salvation as Revelation in the Fourth Gospel (Rome 1974) 16, 21, 25, 61, 91, 148,
152. LEROY, H., Zur Vergebung der Sünden (Stuttgart 1974)
84-86. OLSSON, B., Structure and Meaning in the Fourth Gospel (Lund 1974) 51, 61, 106-107, 131-33, 150, 245. PORSCH,
F., Pneuma und Wort (Frankfurt 1974) 39-42. REIM, G., Studien zum Alttestamentlichen Hintergrund des Johannesevangeliums (Cambridge 1974) 176-80. TEMPLE, S., The Core
of the Fourth Gospel (London 1975) 78-79. ASHBY, G., "The
Lamb of God" JThSA 21 (1977) 63-65; 25 (1978) 62-65. BEST,
E., From Text to Sermon (Atlanta 1978) 25. RAYAN, S., The
Holy Spirit: Heart of the Gospel and Christian Hope (New York
1978) 128. SCHILLEBEECKX, E., Christ: the Christian Ex-
perience in the Modern World (London 1980) 407-409 GT:
Christus und die Christen (Freiburg/Basel/Wien 1977) 393-95.
CAREY, G. L., "The Lamb of God and Atonement Theories"
TR 32 (1981) 97-122.

1:30-31 IBUKI, Y. Die Wahrheit im Johannesevangelium (1972) 238ff.
HANSON A., The New Testament Interpretation of Scripture
(London 1980) 166.

1:30 BEUTLER, J. Martyria (1972) 220, 239, 248f., 285, 343, 353.
METZGER, B. M., The Early Versions of the New Testament
(Oxford 1977) 369n.1. IBUKI, Y., "Offene Fragen zur Aufnahme des Logoshymnus in das Vierte Evangelium" AJBI 5
(1979) 113-14.

1:31-34 STRATHMANN, H. Das Evangelium nach Johannes (1955) 49.
DUNN, J. D. G. Baptism in the Holy Spirit (1970) 16, 33.

JOHNSTON, G. The Spirit-Paraclete in the Gospel of John (1970) 17-21.

1:31 McNAMARA, M. The New Testament and the Palestinian Targum to the Pentateuch (1966) 249. PANCARO, S. NTS 16 (1969-1970) 123-25. KLIJN, A. F., "Die Syrische Baruch-Apokalypse" in: JüdSchr V/2 (1976) 141n.3a. METZGER, B. M., The Early Versions of the New Testament (Oxford 1977) 433.

1:32-34 FORTNA, R. T. The Gospel of Signs (1970) 176-78. RICHTER, G. "Zu den Tauferzählungen Mk 1,9-11 und Joh 1,32-34," ZNW 65 (1974) 43-56. PORSCH, F., Pneuma und Wort (Frankfurt 1974) 31-42. FEUILLET, A., "L'historicité des récits évangéliques du baptême de Jésus" NV 52 (1977) 178-87. MARTIN, A. G., "La Saint-Esprit et l'Evangile de Jean dans une perspective trinitaire" RevR 29 (1978) 141-51.

1:32-33 McNAMARA, M. The New Testament and the Palestinian Targum to the Pentateuch (1966) 235 n.129. HEISE, J. Bleiben (1967) 61-63. BEUTLER, J. Martyria (1972) 252-54. PORSCH, F., Pneuma und Wort (Frankfurt 1974) 19-42. DUNN, J. D. G., Christology in the Making (London 1980) 139, 141.

1:32 HAHN, F. Christologische Hoheitstitel (1963) 380. BERGER, K. "Zu den sogenannten Sätzen Heiligen Rechts," NTS 17 (1970-1971) 10-40. KECK, L. E. "The Spirit of the Dove," NTS 17 (1970-1971) 41-67. BEUTLER, J. Martyria (1972) 213, 216f., 253, 277, 282, 285, 311, 326, 340. IBUKI, Y. Die Wahrheit im Johannesevangelium (1972) 239f. QUISPEL, G. "Qumran, John and Jewish Christianity," in: John and Qumran (1972) J. H. Charlesworth ed., 140-41. BERTRAND, D. A. Le Baptême de Jésus (1973) 18, 34, 35, 111, 112, 119. BERGMEIER, R., Glaube als Gabe nach Johannes (Stuttgart 1980) 242n.117.

1:33-34 HARNACK, A. von, Studien zur Geschichte des Neuen Testaments und der Alten Kirche (1931) 127ff., 144ff.

1:33 GRILL, J. Untersuchungen über die Entstehung des vierten Evangeliums II (1923) 23, 220, 223, 238, 290, 339, 357, 373. FLEW, R. N. Jesus and His Church (1956) 173. WIKENHAUSER, A. Das Evangelium nach Johannes (1957) 269-72. YATES, J. E. The Spirit and the Kingdom (1963) 2ff., 217ff. DUNN, J. D. G. Baptism in the Holy Spirit (1970) 19-21. JOHNSTON, G. The Spirit-Paraclete in the Gospel of John (1970) 10, 31, 49, 68, 71. PORSCH, F., Pneuma und Wort (Frankfurt 1974) 42-51. RAYAN, S., The Holy Spirit: Heart of the Gospel and Christian Hope (New York 1978) 2. SWID-

LER, L., Biblical Affirmations of Woman (Philadelphia 1979)
60. RUSSELL, E. A., "The Holy Spirit in the Fourth Gospel.
Some observations" IBS 2 (1980) 84-94. LÉON-DUFOUR, X.,
"Toward a Symbolic Reading of the Fourth Gospel" NTS 27
(1981) 450.

1:34 BAUER, W. Das Johannesevangelium (1925) 34f. GILS, F.
Jésus Prophète D'Après Les Evangiles Synoptiques (1957) 58-
61. SCHILDENBERGER, J. "Parallelstellen als Ursache von
Textveränderungen," Biblica 40 (1959) 189-90. HAHN, F.
Christologische Hoheitstitel (1963) 330, 380. KAESEMANN,
E. Exegetische Versuche und Besinnungen (1964) I 249.
MARSHALL, I. H. "The Son of Man or Servant of Yahweh?
- A Reconsideration of Mark 1:11," NTS 15 (1968-1969) 327ff.
FORTNA, R. T. The Gospel of Signs (1970) 177f., 179, 182.
JEREMIAS, J. Neutestamentliche Theologie I (1971) 60f.
BEUTLER, J. Martyria (1972) 163, 214, 254, 260, 286, 311,
326, 340. LADD, G. E. A Theology of the New Testament
(1974) 44, 247, 275. ROSS, J. M. "Two More Titles of Je-
sus," ET 85 (9, 1974) 281. PORSCH, F. Pneuma und Wort
(Frankfurt 1974) 37-38. HAHN, F., "Beobachtungen zu Joh
1:18,34" in: J. K. Elliot (ed.) Studies in New Testament Language and Text. FS. G. D. Kilpatrick (Leiden 1976) 239-45.
METZGER, B. M., The Early Versions of the New Testament
(Oxford 1977) 40. CRIBBS, F. L., "The Agreements that Exist Between John and Acts" in: C. H. Talbert (ed.) Perspectives
on Luke-Acts (Danville 1978) 60. CLARK, K. W., "The Text
of the Gospel of John in Third-Century Eygpt" in: The Gentile
Bias and other Essays (Leiden 1980) 160.

1:35ff SCHWEIZER, E. Erniedrigung und Erhöhung bei Jesus und
seinen Nachfolgern (1962) § 11f. HAHN, F. Christologische
Hoheitstitel (1963) 75. HAHN, F. Das Verständnis der Mission
im Neuen Testament (1965²) 138.

1:35-2:22 WAHLDE, U. C. von, "The Witness to Jesus in John 5:31-40
and Belief in the Fourth Gospel" CBQ 43 (1981) 399-404.

1:35-51 BAUER, W. Das Johannesevangelium (1925) 40f. RUCK-
STUHL, E. Die literarische Einheit des Johannesevangeliums
(1951) 65, 102, 110-13, 137, 148, 217. WIKENHAUSER, A.
Das Evangelium nach Johannes (1957) 71f. SCHULZ, A.
Nachfolge und Nachahmen (1962) 110-16, 141f. HAHN, F.
Christologische Hoheitstitel (1963) 224, 235. BRAUN, H.
Qumran und NT II (1966) 20, 25, 110, 133, 139, 183, 328. IT-
TEL, G. W. Jesus und die Jünger (1970) 25-27. OTOMO, Y.
Nachfolge Jesu und Anfänge der Kirche im Neuen Testament
(1970) 34-37, 129. NICOL, W. The Sēmeia in the Fourth Gos-

pel (1972) 39, 61, 74f. HAHN, F. "Die Jüngerberufung Joh 1,35-51," in: Neues Testament und Kirche (1974) J. Gnilka ed., 172-90. CULLMANN, O., Der johanneische Kreis (Tübingen 1975) 64, 74, 76, 82, 93. TEMPLE, S., The Core of the Fourth Gospel (London 1975) 81-90. TRITES, A. A., The New Testament Concept of Witness (Cambridge 1977) 92-93. BECKER, J., Das Evangelium nach Johannes (Gütersloh/Würzburg 1979) 99 (lit!). EGGER, W., Nachfolge als Weg zum Leben (Klosterneuburg 1979) 161-64. KUHN, H.-W., "Nachfolge nach Ostern" in: D. Lührmann/G. Strecker (eds.) Kirche. FS. Günther Bornkamm (Tübingen 1980) 107-10.

1:35-50 FORTNA, R. T. The Gospel of Signs (1970) 155, 161, 180-87.

1:35-42 DIEM, H. in: Herr, tue meine Lippen auf Bd. 3 (1964) G. Eichholz ed., 76ff. LORENZEN, T. Die Bedeutung des Lieblingsjüngers für die Johanneische Theologie (Rüschlikon 1969) 33-43. LORENZEN, T. Der Lieblingsjünger im Johannesevangelium (1971) 37ff. VELLANICKAL, M., " 'Discipleship' according to the Gospel of John" Jeevadhara 10 (Kottayam, India 1980) 131-47. GABATHULER, H. J., und GUGGISBERG, K., in: P. Krusche et al. (eds.) Predigtstudien für das Kirchenjahr 1980-1981. III/2 (Stuttgart 1981) 131-38. LEIDIG, E., Jesu Gespräch mit der Samaritanerin (Basel 1981) 175-79. STOEVESANDT, H., in: GPM 35 (1981) 352-61.

1:35-40 HANHART, K., " 'About the tenth hour' . . . on Nisan 15 (Jn 1:35-40)" Bibliotheca ephemeridum theologicarum Lovaniensium 44 (Louvain 1977) 335-46.

1:35-39 SURKAU, H.-W., GPM 25 (4, 1970) 58-66. DAUER, A. Die Passionsgeschichte im Johannesevangelium (1972) 35f. TEMPLE, S., The Core of the Fourth Gospel (London 1975) 82-89. HAENCHEN, E., Das Johannesevangelium (Tübingen 1980) 172 (lit!)

1:35 METZGER, B. M., The Early Versions of the New Testament (Oxford 1977) 42.

1:36 GRILL, J. Untersuchungen über die Entstehung des vierten Evangeliums II (1923) 23, 94, 141, 192, 227, 237. NOACK, B. Zur Johanneischen Tradition (1954) 72, 149f. DE LA POTTERIE, I. "Ecco l'Agnello di Die," BiOr 1 (6, 1959) 161-69. VIRGULIN, S. "Recent Discussion of the Title 'Lamb of God'," in: Scripture 13 (23, 1961) 74-80. HAHN, F. Christologische Hoheitstitel (1963) 55. WILKENS, W., Zeichen und Werke (Zürich 1969) 76-77. REIM, G., Studien zum Alttestamentlichen Hintergrund des Johannesevangeliums (Cambridge 1974) 178-79. METZGER, B. M., The Early Ver-

sions of the New Testament (Oxford 1977) 42. SCHILLE-
BEECKX, E., Christ: the Christian Experience in the Modern
World (London 1980) 407-409; GT: Christus und die Christen
(Freiburg/Basel/Wien 1977) 393-95.

1:38-49 FLEW, R. N. Jesus and His Church (1956) 177.

1:38-39 HEISE, J., Bleiben. μένειν in den Johanneischen Schriften
(Tübingen 1967) 47-50. SMITH, M. Tannaitic Parallels to the
Gospel (1968) 2.68. "Amt" in: TRE 2 (1978) 511.

1:38 KNOX, W. L., The Sources of the Synoptic Gospels (1957) II
87. WULF, F. " 'Meister, wo wohnst du?' (Joh 1,38)," GuL
31 (4, 1958) 241-44. HAHN, F. Christologische Hoheitstitel
(1963) 75. OLSSON, B., Structure and Meaning in the Fourth
Gospel (Lund 1974) 31, 131, 157, 219-21, 262-63. METZ-
GER, B. M., The Early Versions of the New Testament (Oxford 1977) 252. COLLINS, R. F., "The Search for Jesus.
Reflections on the Fourth Gospel" LThPh 34 (1978) 27-48.

1:39 McNAMARA, M. The New Testament and the Palestinian
Targum to the Pentateuch (1966) 167 n.48.

1:40-51 HAENCHEN, E., Das Johannesevangelium (Tübingen 1980)
177-78 (lit!).

1:40-49 ENCISO VIANA, J. "La vocacion de Natanael y el Salmo 24,"
EstBi 19 (3, 1960) 229-36.

1:40-42 MORGAN, G. C. The Parables and Metaphors of Our Lord
(1943) 249ff. BROWN, R. E. et al. (eds.) Peter in the New
Testament (Minneapolis 1973) 131-32. MARTYN, J. L., The
Gospel of John in Christian History (New York 1978) 35, 36,
38-40.

1:40-41 KUEMMEL, W. G. Einleitung in das Neue Testament (1973)
202f. TEMPLE, S., The Core of the Fourth Gospel (London
1975) 84-88.

1:40 TURNER, N. Grammatical Insights into the New Testament
(1965) 135ff.

1:41 HAHN, F. Christologische Hoheitstitel (1963) 208f. MEHL-
MANN, J. "A vocaçâo de Sao Tiago Maior em Jo 1,41," RCB
1 (2-3, 1964) 209-21; 4 (8-9, 1967) 127-46. LADD, G. E. A
Theology of the New Testament (1974) 139, 140, 243. "Aramäisch" in: TRE 3 (1978) 608.

1:42 STRECKER, G. Der Weg der Gerechtigkeit (1962) 206n.4.
FITZMYER, J. A. Essays on the Semitic Background of the
New Testament (1971) 105-12. VOEGTLE, A. "Zum Problem
der Herkunft von Mt 16,17-19," in: Orientierung an Jesus (1973)
P. Hoffmann ed., 380-82, 390f. "Aramäisch" in: TRE 3 (1978)

606. FITZMYER, J. A., " 'Aramaic Kepha' and Peter's Name in the New Testament" in: F. Best/R. McWilson (eds.) Text and Interpretation. FS. M. Black (Cambridge 1979) 124-30.

1:43-51 BUECHSEL, F. Das Evangelium nach Johannes (1946) 43. DIEM, H. in: Herr,tue meine Lippen auf Bd. 3 (1964) G. Eichholz ed., 81ff. KIIVIT, J. GPM 19 (4, 1964) 68-74. SAUTER, G. in: Hören und Fragen Bd. 5, 3 (1967) G. Eichholz/M. Falkenroth eds., 115ff. LANGE, E. ed., Predigtstudien für das Kirchenjahr 1970-1971 (1970) 102-106. WINTER, F. GPM 25 (4, 1970) 89-95. HENKE, D. und NEHB, H., in: P. Krusche et al. (eds.) Predigtstudien für das Kirchenjahr 1976-1977. V/1 (Stuttgart 1976) 83-89. HANSON, A. T., The New Testament Interpretation of Scripture (London 1980) 166. POKORNÝ, P., in: GPM 35 (1980) 84-87.

1:43-45 TEMPLE, S., The Core of the Fourth Gospel (London 1975) 84-88.

1:43 WILLIAMS, J., "Proposed Renderings for Some Johannine Passages" BTr 25 (1974) 351-53. LANGBRANDTNER, W., Weltferner Gott oder Gott der Liebe (Frankfurt a.m./Bern/Las Vegas 1977) 69-71. MARTYN, J. L., The Gospel of John in Christian History (New York 1978) 33-38, 40-41, 43-44, 46-49, 51, 93-94, 95.

1:44-51 LO GIUDICE, C. "La fede degli apostoli nel IV Vangelo," Biblica 28 (1947) 62-65.

1:44 DALMAN, G. Orte und Wege Jesu (1967) 176f. "Aramäisch" in TRE 3 (1978) 604.

1:45-51 PAINTER, J., "Christ and the Church in John 1,45-51" Bibliotheca ephemeridum theologicarum Lovaniensium 44 (Louvain 1977) 359-62. LEIDIG, E., Jesu Gespräch mit der Samaritanerin (Basel 1981) 179-84.

1:45-49 PANCARO, S., The Law in the Fourth Gospel (Leiden 1975) 288-304, 331.

1:45-47 SMITH, M. Tannaitic Parallels to the Gospels (1968) 2, 65, 67, 68. MARTYN, J. L., The Gospel of John in Christian History (New York 1978) 34-38, 40, 43, 68, 108.

1:45-46 KRAFT, H., Die Entstehung des Christentums (Darmstadt 1981) 79, 83.

1:45 BERGER, K. Die Gesetzesauslegung Jesu (1972) 209-27. RUCKSTUHL, E. Die literarische Einheit des Johannesevangeliums (1951) 135f. KAESMANN, E. Exegetische Versuche und Besinnungen (1964) I 254. BOUSSET, W. Die Religion des Judentums im Späthellenistischen Zietalter

(1966 = 1926) 144. LADD, G. E., A Theology of the New Testament (1974) 243, 266, 279.. SAITO, T., Die Mosevorstellungen im Neuen Testament (Bern 1977) 141-47.

1:46ff DALMAN, G. Orte und Wege Jesu (1967) 113f.

1:47-51 MORGAN, G. C. The Parables and Metaphors of Our Lord (1943) 254ff. DE GOEDT, M. "Un Schême Révélation dans le Quatrième Evangile" NTS 8 (1961-1962) 144f.

1:47 HAHN, F. Das Verständnis der Mission im Neuen Testament (1965²) 138. KUHLI, H., "Nathanael - 'wahrer Israelit'? Zum angeblich attributiven Gebrauch von ἀληθῶς in Joh 1:47" BN 9 (1979) 11-19. SCHWARZ, G., "αληθως Ισραηλιτης" BN 10 (1979) 41-42.

1:48-50 TELFORD, W. R., The Barren Temple and the Withered Tree (Sheffield 1980) 218-23.

1:48 MICHAELS, J. R. "Nathanael Under the Fig Tree," ET 78 (6, 1967) 182-83.

1:49 HAHN, F. Christologische Hoheitstitel (1963) 330. LINDARS, B. "The Son of Man in the Johannine Christology," in: Christ and the Spirit in the New Testament (1973) B. Lindars/ S. S. Smalley eds., 45f. PANCARO, S., The Law in the Fourth Gospel (Leiden 1975) 74, 79, 85, 149, 244, 290-302. DE JONGE, M., Jesus: Stranger from Heaven and Son of God (Missoula 1977) 58-59.

1:50-51 GLASSON, T. F. Moses in the Fourth Gospel (1963) 34f.

1:50 HAHN, F. Christologische Hoheitstitel (1963) 39f., 75, 76.

1:51 GRILL, J. Untersuchung über die Entstehung des vierten Evangeliums II (1923) 3, 69, 242f., 301, 367. QUISPEL, G. "Nathanael und der Menschensohn (Joh 1, 51)," ZNW 57 (1956) 281-83. SCHULZ, S., Untersuchungen zur Menschensohn-Christologie im Johannesevangelium (Göttingen 1957) 97-103. FRITSCH, I. " '. . . videbitis . . . angelos Dei ascendentes et descendentes super Filium hominis' (Io. 1,51)," VerbDom 37 (1, 1959) 3-11. GIBLET, J. "Tu verras le ciel ouvert (Jean 1,51)," BVieC 36 (1960) 26-30. MICHAELIS, W. "Joh. 1,51, Gen 28,12 und das Menschensohn-Problem," ThLZ 85 (8, 1960) 561-78. WILES, M. F. The Spiritual Gospel (1960) 38-39. SCHWEIZER, E. Erniedrigung und Erhöhung bei Jesus und seinen Nachfolgern (1962) § 5efh, 6g. HAHN, F. Christologische Hoheitstitel (1963) 39(f.)₆. GAERTNER, B. The Temple and the Community in Qumran and the New Testament (1965) 118. BOUSSET, W. Die Religion des Judentums im Späthellenistischen Zeitalter (1966 = 1926) 268. DELLING, G. Wort

und Werk Jesu im Johannes-Evangelium (1966) 37, 67, 96, 110.
ODEBERG, H. The Fourth Gospel (1968) 33-42. SMALLEY,
S. S. "The Johannine Son of Man Sayings," NTS 15 (1968-
1969) 298ff. CADMAN, W. H. The Open Heaven (1969) G.
B. Caird ed., 26, 27, 28, 43, 60, 61. LENTZEN-DEIS, F. Die
Taufe Jesu nach den Synoptikern (1970) 115ff. JEREMIAS, J.
Neutestamentliche Theologie I (1971) 44, 248, 251, 259.
DAUER, A. Die Passionsgeschichte im Johannesevagnelium
(1972) 141, 301, 304. MEEKS, W. A. "The Man From Heaven
in Johannine Sectarianism," in: proceedings 1 (1972) L. C.
McGaughy ed., 285-313. HAMERTON-KELLY, R. G. Pre-
Existence, Wisdom, and the Son of Man (1973) 198, 225-30,
232, 236. LINDARS, B. "The Son of Man in the Johannine
Christology," in: Christ and the Spirit in the New Testament
(1973) B. Lindars/S. S. Smalley eds., 46ff., 57. MICHON, E.,
"Znaczenie i teologiczna interpretacja logionu J 1,51" Studia
Warminskie 10 (1973) 133-91; 11 (1974) 249-307. OLSSON,
B., Structure and Meaning in the Fourth Gospel (Lund 1974)
19, 32, 46, 74-76. PERRIN, N., A Modern Pilgrimage in New
Testament Christology (Philadelphia 1974) 127-28. REIM, G.,
Studien zum Alttestamentlichen Hintergrund des Johannes-
evangeliums (Cambridge 1974) 100-104. DAVIES, W. D. The
Gospel and the Land (1974) 296-99 passim, 316, 317. SMAL-
LEY, S. S., "Johannes 1,51 und die Einleitung zum vierten
Evangelium" in: R. Pesch/R. Schnackenburg (eds.) Jesus und
der Menschensohn (Freiburg 1975) 300-13. BÜHNER, J.-A.
Der Gesandte und sein Weg im 4. Evangelium (Tübingen 1977)
391-92, 398-99. DUNN, J. D., Christology in the Making
(London 1980) 89-90, 154. HANSON, A. T., The New Testament Interpretation of Scripture (London 1980) 110-14, 158,
162-66. SCHÜRMANN, H., "Christliche Weltverantwortung
im Lichte des Neuen Testaments" Catholica 34 (1980) 111.

2-12 SMITH, T. C. "The Book of Signs. Joh 2-12," RevEx 62 (4,
1965) 441-57.

2-4 GARDNER-SMITH, P. Saint John and the Synoptic Gospels
(1938) 11-24. BRAUN, F.-M. "Le Don de Dieu et l'Initiation
Chrétienne (Jn. 2-3)," NRTh 86 (10, 1964) 1025-48. HANI-
MANN, J. "L'heure de Jésus et le noces de Cana. Le sens de

la résponse de Jésus: 'Mon heure n'est pas encore venue',''
RThom 64 (1963) 569-83. GALBIATI, E. ''Nota sulla struttura del 'libro dei segni' (Gv. 2-4),'' EuD 25 (1, 1972) 139-44.

2 CULLMANN, O. Urchristentum und Gottesdienst (1950) 98,
103f. HENNECKE, E./SCHNEEMELCHER, W. Neutestamentliche Apokryphen (1964) I 128. KAESEMANN, E. Exegetische Versuche und Besinnungen (1964) I 216.

2:1ff WILKENS, W. Die Entstehungsgeschichte des vierten Evan-
geliums (1958) 38, 39, 40, 41. GLASSON, T. F. Moses in the
Fourth Gospel (1963) 26, 57f., 71, 88, 103. SCHILLE, G.
Frühchristliche Hymnen (1965) 145f. HOFBECK, S. Semeion
(1966) 91-105. PETZKE, G. Die Traditionen über Apollonius
von Tyana und das Neue Testament (1970) 165, 178, 225.
MÜLLER, U. B. ''Die griechische Esra-Apokalypse'' in:
JüdSchr V/2 (1976) 96n.276.

2:1-22 YATES, K. M. Preaching from John's Gospel (1964) 18-21.
LAURENTIN, R. Jésus au Temple (1966) 125-218.

2:1-12:50 PERRIN, N., The New Testament: An Introduction (New York
1974) 233-42.

2:1-4:54 van den BUSSCHE, H., ''La Structure de Jean I-XII'' in: M.
Boismard et al., L'Evangile de Jean: études et problèmes (Bruges
1958) 76-88. MOLONEY, F. J., ''From Cana to Cana (Jn. 2:1-
4:54) and the fourth Evangelist's concept of correct (and incorrect) faith'' Salesianum 40 (Rome 1978) 817-43, also in: E. A.
Livingstone (ed.) Studia Biblica 1978/II (Sheffield 1980) 185-
213.

2:1-12 LO GIUDICE, C. ''La fede degli apostoli nel IV Vangelo,''
Biblica 28 (1947) 66-68. RUCKSTUHL, E. Die literarische
Einheit des Johannesevangeliums (1951) 99, 140, 217. AN-
ZALONE, V. ''Gesù e Maria alle nozze di Cana (Giov. 2,1-
12),'' DiThom 65 (1, 1962) 65-80. BAKKER, J. T. '' 'De
moeder van Jezuz was daar': Een reactie'' HomBib 21 (3, 1962)
51-54. VAN HALSEMA, J. H. ''De moeder van Jezus was
daar'' HomBib 21 (2, 1962) 25-28. DEEKS, D. ''The Structure
of the Fourth Gospel,'' NTS 15 (1968-1969) 124ff. GEOL-
TRAIN, P., ''Les noces à Cana. Jean 2,1-12. Analyse des
structures narratives'' FV 73 (1974) 83-90. LOHSE, E., ''Miracles in the Fourth Gospel'' in: M. Hooker/C. Hickling (eds.)
What About the New Testament? FS. C. Evans (London (1975)
68-69. BREUSS, J., Das Kanawunder. Hermeneutische und
pastorale Ueberlegungen aufgrund einer phänomenologischen
Analyse von Joh 2,1-12 (Fribourg 1976) passim. LANG-
BRANDTNER, W., Weltferner Gott oder Gott der Liebe

(Frankfurt a.M./Bern/Las Vegas 1977) 71-76. WULF, F., "Das marianische Geheimnis der Kirche im Licht des Johannesevangeliums" GuL 50 (1977) 326-34. RUEGG, U., "Jesus an der Hochzeit zu Kana (Johannes 2,1-12)" in: A. Steiner/V. Weymann (eds.) Wunder Jesu (Basel/Zürich 1978) 147-66. ALFARO, J. I., "La mariología del Cuarto Evangelio. Ensayo de teología bíblica" RevBi 41 (1979) 193-209. BECKER, J., Das Evangelium nach Johannes (Gütersloh/Würzburg 1979) 105-106 (lit!). SWIDLER, L., Biblical Affirmations of Woman (Philadelphia 1979) 177, 220, 223. ZECHNER, A., Wer hat bei der Hochzeit von Kana geheiratet? Studientext zum literarisch-theologischen Zusammenhang und seinen historischen Implikationen (Linz 1979). COLLINS, R. F., "Cana (Jn. 2:1-12)— The first of his signs or the key to his signs?" IThQ 47 (1980) 79-95. HAENCHEN, E., Das Johannesevangelium (Tübingen 1980) 186-87 (lit!). LEIDIG, E., Jesu Gespräch mit der Samaritanerin (Basel 1981) 248-55.

2:1-11 BAUER, W. Das Johannesevangelium (1925) 43f. LORTZING, J., "Die inneren Beziehungen zwischen Jo 2:1-11 und Offb 12. Eine Auseinandersetzung mit der religionsgeschichtliche Schule" ThG 29 (1937) 498-529. HOSKYNS, E. C. The Fourth Gospel (1947) 190-92. CULLMANN, O. Urchristentum und Gottesdienst (1950) 67ff. SCHNACKENBURG, R. Das erste Wunder Jesu (1951). ADRIEN, B. "Les noces de Cana," EThR VIII (1952) 9-22. ILLINGWORTH, P. A. "The Miracle of Cana," ET 65 (9, 1954) 287. MAESO, D. C. "Sprachliche Erklärung der Geschichte von der Hochzeit zu Kana" (span), Cultura Biblica A 11, no. 122-127 (1954) 352-64. MICHL, J. "Die Hochzeit zu Kana. Kritik einer Auslegung," ThG 45 (5, 1955) 334-48. STEPHENSON, A. M. G. "The Miracle at Cana," ET 66 (6, 1955) 177. SCHULZE-KADELBACH, G. "Zur Pneumatologie des Johannesevangeliums," ThL 81 (1956) 351-54. BROWNLEE, W. H. "Messianic Motifs of Qumran and the New Testament, II," NTS 3 (1956-1957) 206. OBENDIET, H. in: Herr, tue meine Lippen auf Bd. 1 (1957) G. Eichholz ed., 53-58. ZIENER, G. "Weisheitsbuch und Johannesevangelium," Biblica 38 (1957) 413-14. CORELL, A. Consummatum Est (1958) 56-58. STANLEY, D. M. "Cana as Epiphany," Worship 32 (2, 1958) 83-89. van den BUSSCHE, H., "La Structure de Jean I-XII" in: M. Boismard et al., L'Evangile de Jean: études et problèmes (Bruges 1958) 79-83. HAIBLE, E. "Das Gottesbild der Hochzeit von Kana. Zur biblischen Grundlegung der Eingottlehre," MThZ 10 (3, 1959) 189-99. FEUILLETT, A. "L'heure de Jésus et le signe de Cana. Contribution à l'étude de la structure du quatrième évangile,"

EphT 36 (1, 1960) 5-22. HARTDEGEN, S. "The Marian Significance of Cana (John 2:1-11)," MarStud 11 (1960) 85-103. NOETZEL, H. Christus und Dionysos (1960). WILES, M. F. The Spiritual Gospel (1960) 34, 42-44, 45. ARMERDING, C. "The Marriage in Cana," BiblSa 118 (472, 1961) 320-26. DOERNE, M. Er kommt auch noch heute (1961) 35-38. TAYLOR, E. K. "The Woman of Cana," Furrow 12 (5, 1961) 304-10. DILLON, R. J. "Wisdom Tradition and Sacramental Retrospect in the Cana Account (Jn 2,1-11)," CBQ 24 (3, 1962) 268-96. MICHAUD, J.-P. "Le signe de Cana dans son contexte johannique," LThPh 18 (2, 1962) 239-85. TEMPLE, S. "The Two Signs in the Fourth Gospel," JBL 81 (2, 1962) 169-74. DERRETT, J. D. M. "Water into Wine," BZ 7 (1, 1963) 80-97. LEROY, H. "Das Weinwunder zu Kana. Eine exegetische Studie zu Jo 2,1-11," BuL 4 (3, 1963) 168-73. MICHAUD, J.-P. "Le signe de Cana dans son contexte johannique," LThPh 19 (2, 1963) 257-83. HANIMANN, J. "L'heure de Jésus et les noces de Cana. Le sens de la réponse de Jésus: 'Mon heure n'est pas encore venue'," RThom 64 (1964) 569-83. LINDIJER, C. H. De Sacramenten in het Vierde Evangelie (1964) 54ff. FEUILLET, A. "La signification fondamentale du premier miracle de Cana (Jo. II,1-11) et le symbolisme johannique," RThom 65 (4, 1965) 517-35. HINNEBUSCH, P. "Cana and the Paschal Mystery," Bib-Today 1 (29, 1965) 1325-33. BIEDER, W., Die Verheissung der Taufe im Neuen Testament (Zürich 1966) 260-61. BRAUN, F.-M. Jean le Théologien (1966) 79-81. BRAUN, H. Qumran und NT II (1966) 76, 133, 318. RIEDL, J. "El 'principio' de los milagros de Jesus en Cana de Galilea," RevBi 28 (3, 1966) 131-47. SMITMANS, A. Das Weinwunder von Kana (1966). DEQUEKER, L. "De bruiloft te Kana (Jo. II,1-11)," Coll-Mech 52 (3, 1967) 177-93. NICKELS, P. Targum and New Testament (1967) 53. RISSI, M. "Die Hochzeit in Kana (Joh 2,1-11)," in: Oikonomia (1967) F. Christ ed., 76-92. WILLIAMS, F. E. "Fourth Gospel and Synoptic Tradition: Two Johannine Passages," JBL 86 (3, 1967) 311-19. WINK, W. John the Baptist in the Gospel Tradition (1968) 92-93. WORDEN, T. "The Marriage Feast at Cana (John 2.1-11)," Scripture 29 (52, 1968) 97-106. CADMAN, W. H. The Open Heaven (1969) G. B. Caird ed., 60, 61, 62. SEGALLA, G. StPa 16 (2, 1969) 324-33. WILKENS, W., Zeichen und Werke (Zürich 1969) 30-33. DERRETT, J. D. M. Law in the New Testament (1970) 228-46, FORTNA, R. T. The Gospel of Signs (1970) 29-38. LE FORT, P. Les Structures de L'Eglise militante selon saint Jean (1970) 153-55. SCHUERMANN, H. Ursprung und Gestalt

(1970) 20-22. BATEY, R. A. New Testament Nuptial Imagery (1971) 51-52. JEREMIAS, J. Neutestamentliche Theologie I (1971) 92f., 109. GRASSI, J. A. "The Wedding at Cana (John II 1-11): A Pentecostal Meditation?" NovTest 14 (2, 1972) 131-36. HARSCH, H. "Tiefenpsychologische Interpretation von Joh 2,1-11," in: Versuche mehrdimensionaler Schriftauslegung (1972) G. Voss/H. Harsch eds., 89ff. LEROY, H. "Diskussionsbeiträge zur Exegese von Joh 2,1-11," in: Versuche mehrdimensionaler Schriftauslegung (1972) G. Voss/ H. Harsch eds., 86ff. NICOL, W. The Sēmeia in the Fourth Gospel (1972) 30f., 53f., 106f., 110f. SCHADE, H. "Zu den frühen Darstellungen der Hochzeit von Kana," in: Versuche mehrdimensionaler Schriftauslegung (1972) G. Voss/H. Harsch eds., 104ff. SMITMANS, A. "Exegese von Joh 2,1-11 im Zusammenhang des Johannesevangeliums," in: Versuche mehrdimensionaler Schriftauslegung (1972) G. Voss/H. Harsch eds.,72ff. SMITMANS, A. "Die Botschaft von John 2,1-11 nach der Auslegung der Väter," in: Versuche mehrdimensionaler Schriftauslegung (1972) G. Voss/H. Harsch eds., 124ff. WALTER, N. GPM 27/1 (1972-1973) 75-81. KARZEL, H./FAK, E. "Zweiter Sonntag nach Epiphanias: Johannes 2,1-11," in: Predigtstudien (1972-1973) E. Lange ed., 85-89. CRIBBS, F. L. in: SBL Seminar Papers 2 (1973) MacRae, G. ed., 3. OLSSON, B. Structure and Meaning in the Fourth Gospel (1974). SPICQ, C. "Il primo miracolo di Gesù dovuto a sua Madre (Giov. 2,1-11)," SaDo 18 (69-70, 1973) 125-44. KYSAR, R., The Fourth Evangelist and His Gospel (Minneapolis 1974) 249. LINNEMANN, E., "Die Hochzeit zu Kana und Dionysos oder das Unzureichende der Kategorien. Uebertragung und Identifikation zur Erfassung der religionsgeschichtlichen Beziehungen" NTS 20 (1974) 408-18. MURTONEN, A., " 'Wedding at Cana.' On Comparative Socio-Linguistic Background" Milla Wa-Milla 14 (Melbourne 1974) 32-46. BARTLETT, D., Fact and Faith (Valley Forge 1975) 60-61. van BELLE, G., De Semeia-Bron in het Vierde Evangelie (Leuven 1975) 59-65. TEMPLE, S., The Core of the Fourth Gospel (London 1975) 90-91. AGOURIDIS, S., "Iōan. 2,1-11 (Biblikē meletē)" DBM 4 (1976) 86-96. CZAJKOWSKI, M., "Maria u progu i kresu dziela Mesjaszai; J 2,1-11; 19,25-27 (Maria am Anfang und am Ende des Wirkens des Messias; Joh 2,1-11; 19,25-27)" in: F. Gryglewicz (ed.) Egzegeza Ewangelii św. Jana (Lublin 1976) 101-12. OLSSON, B., "Att umgås med texter" SvTK 52 (1976) 49-58. de JONGE, M., Jesus: Stranger from Heaven and Son of God (Missoula 1977) 122-24. SHEA, M. C., "Cana. A Scriptural Basis for the Immaculate Conception?" DRev 95

(1977) 124-32. TOUSSAINT, S. D., "The Significance of the
First Sign in John's Gospel" BiblSa 134 (1977) 45-57. TRITES,
A. A., The New Testament Concept of Witness (Cambridge
1977) 93-94. RAMOS, F. F., "El Espiritu Santo y Maria en los
escritos joanicos" EphM 28 (1978) 169-90. COOPER, K. T.,
"The Best Wine: John 2:1-11" WThJ 41 (1979) 364-80. MAC-
KÓWSKI, R. M., " 'Scholars' Qanah.' A Re-examination of
the Evidence in Favor of Khirbet-Qanah" BZ 23 (1979) 278-
84. de la POTTERIE, I., "La madre de Gesù e il mistero di
Cana" CiCa 130 (1979) 425-40. RUETHER, R. R., Mary - The
Feminine Face of the Church (London 1979) 31-35. BUSSE,
U. und MAY, A., "Das Weinwunder von Kana (Joh 2,1-11).
Erneute Analyse eines 'erratischen Blocks' " BN 12 (1980) 35-
61. FEUILLET, A., "La doctrine mariale du Nouveau Testa-
ment et la Médaille Miraculeuse. Une révélation privée au ser-
vice de la Grande Révélation" EsVie 90 (1980) 657-75.
GIBLIN, C. H., "Suggestion, Negative Response, and Posi-
tive Action in St John's Portrayal of Jesus (John 2.1-11; 4.46-
54; 7.2-14, 11.1-44)" NTS 26 (1980) 197-211. GILL, J. H.,
"Jesus, Irony, and the 'New Quest' " Encounter 15 (Indianap-
olis 1980) 139-51. MENOUD, P.-H., "Die Bedeutung des
Wunders nach dem Neuen Testament" in: A. Suhl (ed.) Der
Wunderbegriff im Neuen Testament (Darmstadt 1980) 289-90.
MOLONEY, F. J., "From Cana to Cana (John 2:1-4:54) and
the Fourth Evangelist's Concept of Correct (and Incorrect)
Faith" in: E. A. Livingstone (ed.) Studia Biblica 1978/II (Sheffield 1980) 189-93. TOUS, L., "Maria y la Iglesia. La madre
de Jesús en el IV evangelio" Biblia y Fe 6 (Madrid 1980) 226-
34. TRAUB, G., "Die Wunder im Neuen Testament" in: A.
Suhl (ed.) Der Wunderbegriff im Neuen Testament (Darmstadt
1980) 172-74. BOVON, F., "La vie des apôtres: traditions bibliques et narrations apocryphes" in: F. Bovon et al. (eds.) Les
Actes Apocryphes des Apôtres (Geneva 1981) 155.

2:1-10 SUMMERS, R. The Secret Sayings of the Living Jesus (1968)
40. "Abendmahl" in: TRE 1 (1977) 57.

2:1-2 BLINZLER, J., Die Brüder und Schwestern Jesu (Stuttgart
1967) 27-28. BRAUN, F. M., "La Réduction du Pluriel au
Singulier dans l'Evangile et la Première Lettre de Jean" NTS
24 (1977) 55. "Ehe" in: TRE 9 (1982) 318.

2:1 MANNS, F., "Le troisième jour il y eut des noces à Cana"
Marianum 40 (1978) 160-63. SCHWARZ, G., "τη ημερα τη
τριτη (Johannes 2,1)," BN 13 (1980) 56. PARKIN, V., " 'On
the third day there was a marriage in Cana of Galilee' (John 2.1)"
IBS 3 (1981) 134-44. BRAUN, F. M., "La Réduction du Plu-

riel au Singulier dans L'Evangile et la Première Lettre de Jean''
NTS 24 (1977) 52, 55.

2:2 LIGHTFOOT, R. H. St. John's Gospel (1956) 68-73.

2:3ff TEMPLE, G. "Conversation Piece at Cana," Dominican Studies VII (1954) 104-13.

2:3-5 KILMARTIN, E. J. "The Mother of Jesus was there. (The Significance of Mary in Jn 2,3-5 and Jn 19,25-27)," SciEccl 15 (1, 1963) 213-26.

2:3-4 PEINADOR, M. "La respuesta de Jesus a su Madre en las bodas de Cana. 'Quid mihi et tibi est, mulier? Nondum venit hora mea' Jo. II,2-4," EphM 8 (1, 1958) 61-104. PEINADOR, M. "Breves observaciones adicionales a 'La respuesta de Jesus a su Madre en las bodas de Cana,' " EphM 9 (1, 1959) 113-16. REUSS, J. "Joh 2,3f in Johanneskommentaren der griechischen Kirche," in: Neutestamentliche Aufsätze (1963) J. Blinzler/O. Kuss/F. Mussner eds., 207-13. ZEHRER, F. "Das Gespräch Jesu mit seiner Mutter auf der Hochzeit zu Kana (Joh 2,3f.) im Licht der traditions- und redaktionsgeschichtlichen Forschung," BuLit 43 (3, 1970) 14-27.PAX, E. "Bemerkungen zum patriarchalischen Stil," SBFLA 22 (1972) 315-34. BRAUN, F. M., "La Réduction du Pluriel au Singulier dans l'Evangile et la Première Lettre de Jean" NTS 24 (1977) 48, 49, 51.

2:3 PALLIS, A., Notes on St. John and the Apocalypse (London 1928) 50-51.

2:4-11 MARTYN, J. L., The Gospel of John in Christian History (New York 1978) 22.

2:4 GRILL, J. Untersuchungen über die Entstehung des vierten Evangeliums II (1923) 3, 5, 82, 112, 113, 116, 162, 195. KURFESS, A. ZNW 44 (1952-1953) 257. SPADAFORA, F. "Maria alle nozze di Cana," RivB II (3, 1954) 220-47. TESTA, E. "La mediazione di Maria a Cana," SBFLA V (1954-1955) 139-90. MICHL, J. "Bemerkungen zu Joh. 2,4," Biblica 46 (4, 1955) 492-509. CORTES, J. "Las Bodas de Cana. La respuesta de Cristo a su Madre," Marianum 20 (2, 1958) 155-89. SQUILLACI, D. "La Madonna alle nozze di Cana. 'Quid mihi et tibi, Mulier? Nondum venit hora mea' (Giov. 2,4)," PaCl 37 (4, 1958) 183-86. CEROKE, C. P. "The Problem of Ambiguity in John 2,4," CBQ 21 (3, 1959) 316-40. GRILL, S. "Syrisches einfaches 'non' in der Bedeutung von 'nonne'," ThZ 16 (2, 1960) 134-35. SQUILLACI, D. "La Donna nel Protovangelo, nel Vangelo e nell Apocalisse," PaCl 39 (13, 1960) 700-708. HENZ, C. M. " 'Quid mihi et tibi, mulier? Nondum

venit hora mea' (Io. 2,4)," Marianum 23 (4, 1961) 471-79.
BRESOLIN, A. "L'esegesi di Giov. 2,4 nei Padri Patini," REA
8 (3, 1962) 243-73. LANGHAMMER, T. "J 2,4 w swietle
najnowszej egzegezy (De recentis exegesi J 2,4)," RBL 15 (2,
1962) 82-91. STRECKER, G. Der Weg der Gerechtigkeit
(1962) 87$_6$. SALVONI, F. "Nevertheless, My Hour Has Not
Yet Come (John 2:4)," RestQ 7 (4, 1963) 236-41. EYQUEM,
M.-B. "La foi de Marie et les noces de Cana," VieS 117 (541,
1967) 169-81. DERRETT, J. D. M. Law in the New Testament
(1970) 238-43. FORTNA, R. T. The Gospel of Signs (1970)
31f. THUESING, W. Die Erhöhung und Verherrlichung Jesu
im Johannesevangelium (1970) 92-96. NICOL, W. The Sēmeia
in the Fourth Gospel (1972) 30, 52, 128f. FORESTELL, J. T.,
The Word of the Cross: Salvation as Revelation in the Fourth
Gospel (Rome 1974) 71, 72, 73. VANHOYE, A. "Interriga-
tion johannique et exégèse de Can (Jn 2,4)," Biblica 55 (2, 1974)
157-67. CARLE, P.-L., "La Vierge et la prière d'intercession.
Cana - 'Qu'y a-t-il entre toi et moi?' " NV 50 (1975) 191-201.
BÄCHLI, O., " 'Was habe ich mit Dir zu schaffen?' Eine for-
melhafte Frage im AT und NT" ThZ 33 (1977) 69-80. METZ-
GER, B. M., The Early Versions of the New Testament (Oxford
1977) 173, 243.

2:5 BRUNNER, A. " 'Was er euch sagen wird, das tut' (Joh 2,5),"
GuL 34 (2, 1961) 81-84. NICKELS, P. Targum and New Testament (1967) 53.

2:6 DELLING, G. Die Taufe im Neuen Testament (1963) 40.
OLSSON, B., Structure and Meaning in the Fourth Gospel
(Lund 1974) 154, 156, 260-62. VILLESCAS, J., "John 2.6:
The capacity of the six jars" BTr 28 (1977) 447.

2:7-8 GRILL, J. Untersuchungen über die Entstehung des vierten
Evangeliums II (1923) 3-5.

2:9 PALLIS, A., Notes on St. John and the Apocalypse (London
1928) 3. DACQUINO, P. "Aqua vinum facta (Io 2,9),"
VerbDom 39 (2, 1961) 92-96. OLSSON, B., Structure and
Meaning in the Fourth Gospel (Lund 1974) 161-63.

2:10 MEYER, P. W. "John 2:10," JBL 86 (2, 1967) 191-97.
FORTNA, R. T. The Gospel of Signs (1970) 33f., 215. LIN-
DARS, B. "Two Parables in John," NTS 16 (4, 1970) 318-29.

2:11 GRILL, J. Untersuchungen über die Entstehung des vierten
Evangeliums II (1923) 2, 3, 4, 5, 39, 48, 50, 68f., 76, 82, 104,
111f., 366, 372. RUCKSTUHL, E. Die literarische Einheit des
Johannesevangeliums (1951) 107, 109f., 136, 223, 260.
LIGHTFOOT, H. H. St. John's Gospel (1956) 21-23. KNOX,

W. L. The Sources of the Synoptic Gospels II (1957) 8. DEL-LING, G. Wort und Werk Jesu im Johannes-Evangelium (1966) 16, 23, 31, 37, 43, 75. CADMAN, W. H. The Open Heaven (1969) G. B. Caird ed., 11, 23, 24, 36, 37, 63, 65, 81, 107, 123, 129, 132, 138, 144, 161, 172, 205. FORTNA, R. T. The Gospel of Signs (1970) 34-37. SCHOTTROFF, L. Der Glaubende und die feindliche Welt (1970) 245-47, 252-55. SMALLEY, S. S. "Diversity and Development in John," NTS 17 (1970-1971) 288f. NICOL, W. The Sēmeia in the Fourth Gospel (1972) 114, 121f., 128. LADD, G. E. A Theology of the New Testament (Grand Rapids 1974) 231, 273, 276. BERG-MEIER, R., Glaube als Gabe nach Johannes (Stuttgart 1980) 273n.612.

2:12ff HOWARD, W. F. "The Position of the Temple Cleansing in the Fourth Gospel," ET 44 (1933) 84-85. LEWIS, G. P. "Dislocations in the Fourth Gospel: The Temple Cleansing and the Visit of Nicodemus," ET 44 (1933) 228-30. LEWIS, F. W. "Disarrangement in the Fourth Gospel," ET 44 (1933) 382. LIGHTFOOT, R. H. "Unresolved New Testament Problems - The Cleansing of the Temple in St. John's Gospel," ET 60 (1948-1949) 64-68.

2:12-25 FEE, G. D. "The Lemma of Origen's Commentary on John, Book X - An Independent Witness to the Egyptian Textual Tradition?" NTS 20 (1, 1973) 78-81. TEMPLE, S., The Core of the Fourth Gospel (London 1975) 91-98. TRITES, A. A., The New Testament Concept of Witness (Cambridge 1977) 94-95.

2:12-22 CULLMANN, O. Urchristentum und Gottesdienst (1950) 72-76. BIEDER, W., Die Verheissung der Taufe im Neuen Testament (Zürich 1968) 261-62.

2:12-19 ORIGENES, Das Evangelium nach Johannes (1959) R. Gögler ed., 209-34.

2:12 BLINZLER, J., Die Brüder und Schwestern Jesu (Stuttgart 1967) 27-28. HEISE, J., Bleiben. μένειν in den Johanneischen Schriften (Tübingen 1967) 47-50. BRAUN, F. M., "La Réduction du Pluriel au Singulier dans l'Evangile et la Première Lettre de Jean" NTS 24 (1977) 55. ROBINSON, B. P., "The Meaning and Significance of 'The Seventh Hour' in John 4:52" in: E. A. Livingstone (ed.) Studia Biblica 1978/II (Sheffield 1980) 260-61.

2:13ff MENDNER, S. "Die Tempelreinigung," ZNW 47 (1956) 93-112. HAHN, F. Christologische Hoheitstitel (1963) 171. GAERTNER, B. The Temple and the Community in Qumran and the New Testament (1965) 120.

2:13-25 LINDIJER, C. H. De Sacramenten in het Vierde Evangelie (1964) 59f. YATES, K. M. Preaching from John's Gospel (1964) 22-27. OLSSON, B., Structure and Meaning in the Fourth Gospel (Lund 1974) 44, 61, 101, 245, 247, 264-66, 280. LANGBRANDTNER, W., Weltferner Gott oder Gott der Liebe (Frankfurt a.M./Bern/Las Vegas 1977) 14-18.

2:13-22 MORGAN, G. C. The Parables and Metaphors of Our Lord (1943) 260ff. KAESEMANN, E. GPM 9 (1954-1955) 250ff. SABBE, M. "Tempelreiniging en Tempellogion," ColBG 2 (1956) 289-99; 466-80. WIKENHAUSER, A. Das Evangelium nach Johannes (1957) 82f. VAN DEN BUSSCHE, H. "Le signe du Temple (Jean 2, 13-22)," BVieC 20 (1957-1958) 92-100. BUSE, I. "The Cleansing of the Temple in the Synoptics and in John," ET 70 (1, 1958) 22-24. WILKENS, W. Die Entstehungsgeschichte des vierten Evangeliums (1958) 15, 16, 17, 18, 26, 27, 28. WILES, M. F. The Spiritual Gospel (1960) 44-45. BALAGUE, M. "La senal del templo. Sustitucion de la religion material (de las tinieblas) por la espiritual (de la luz). Jn 2,13-22," CultBib 19 (186, 1962) 259-81. MUSSNER, F. Die Johanneische Sehweise und die Frage nach dem historischen Jesus (1965) 38ff. HAHN, F. Das Verständnis der Mission im Neuen Testament (1965²) 30. BRAUN, F.-M. Jean le Theologien (1966) 81-85. BRAUN, H. Qumran und NT II (1966) 133, 183, 271, 327. MUSSNER, F. " 'Kultische' Aspekte im johanneischen Christusbild," in: Praesentia Salutis (1967) 133. GASTON, L. No Stone on Another (1970) 83, 86, 102, 206-209. ROLOFF, J. Das Kerygma und der irdische Jesus (1970) 102-10. HAACKER, K. Die Stiftung des Heils (1972) 39-42. APPOLD, M. L., The Oneness Motif in the Fourth Gospel (Tübingen 1976) 105, 114-21. DALY, R. J., Christian Sacrifice (Washington D.C. 1978) 213-14. BECKER, J., Das Evangelium nach Johannes (Gütersloh/Würzburg 1979) 121 (lit!). HAENCHEN, E., Das Johannesevangelium (Tübingen 1980) 197-98. MOLONEY, F. J., "From Cana to Cana (John 2:1-4:54) and the Fourth Evangelist's Concept of Correct (and Incorrect) Faith" in: E. A. Livingstone (ed.) Studia Biblica 1978/II (Sheffield 1980) 193. DEMKE, C., in: GPM 35 (1981) 380-84. HASSELMANN, N. und STECK, W., in: P. Krusche et al. (eds.) Predigtstudien für das Kirchenjahr 1980-1981. III/2 (Stuttgart 1981) 169-77.

2:13-21 BAUER, W. Das Johannesevangelium (1925) 46f.

2:13-19 RUCKSTUHL, E. Die literarische Einheit des Johannesevangeliums (1951) 217f.

2:13-17 LIGHTFOOT, R. H. The Gospel Message of St. Mark (1950) 70-79. DEHN, G. in: Herr, tue meine Lippen auf Bd. 3 (1964) G. Eichholz ed., 480ff. PATSCH, H. Abendmahl und historischer Jesus (1972) 43f. MEYER, B. F., The Aims of Jesus (London 1979) 197-202. DERRETT, J. D. M., "Fresh Light on the Lost Sheep and the Lost Coin" NTS 26 (1980) 36-60. KRAFT, H., Die Entstehung des Christentums (Darmstadt 1981) 187-91. MOHR, T. A., Markus - und Johannespassion (Zürich 1982) 86-99.

2:13 ROBINSON, J. M. Kerygma und historischer Jesus (1960) 146. BOUSSET, W. Die Religion des Judentums im Späthellenistischen Zeitalter (1966 = 1926) 111.

2:14-22 SCHNIDER, F./STENGER, W. Johannes and die Synoptiker (1971) 26-53.

2:14-19 FORTNA, R. T. The Gospel of Signs (1970) 144-49.

2:14-16 TEMPLE, S., The Core of the Fourth Gospel (London 1975) 93-96.

2:14 KLAWEK, A. "Hymn anielski Lk 2,14," RBL 23 (2-3, 1970) 65-72.

2:15 MOULTON, H. K. "Pantas in John 2:15," BTr 18 (3, 1967) 126-27.

2:16-22 LEUNG TSUNG-YAT, T., " 'Memory' in John's Gospel" Theology Annual 2 (Hong Kong 1978) 3-17.

2:16 NOACK, B. Zur Johanneischen Tradition (1954) 102f. BRUCE, F. F. "The Book of Zechariah and the Passion Narrative," BJRL 43 (1960-1961) 351. HAHN, F. Christologische Hoheitstitel (1963) 172.

2:17-22 HANSON, A. T., The New Testament Interpretation of Scripture (London 1980) 114-17.

2:17 LINDARS, B. New Testament Apologetic (1961) 104ff., 266f. EDGAR, S. L. "Respect for Context in Quotations from the Old Testament," NTS 9 (1962) 58. FREED, E. D. Old Testament Quotations in the Gospel of John (1965) 8-10. ROTHFUCHS, W. Die Erfüllungszitate des Matthäus-Evangeliums (1969) 163f. DAUER, A. Die Passionsgeschichte im Johannesevangelium (1972) 184, 301, 304, 305. DORMEYER, D., Die Passion Jesu als Verhaltensmodell (Münster 1974) 250n.47. OLSSON, B., Structure and Meaning in the Fourth Gospel (Lund 1975) 51, 72, 79, 262, 264-66, 271, 280. REIM, G., Studien zum Alttestamentlichen Hintergrund des Johannesevangeliums (Cambridge 1974) 10-12, 89-91, 93-95. HANSON, A. T., The New Testament Interpretation of Scripture (London 1980) 158.

2:18ff GRILL, J. Untersuchungen über die Entstehung des vierten Evangeliums II (1923) 68, 70, 71, 79, 242. GAERTNER, B. The Temple and the Community in Qumran and the New Testament (1965) 107.

2:18-22 WILKENS, W., Zeichen und Werke (Zürich 1969) 62-65. MOHR, T. A., Markus- und Johannespassion (Zürich 1982) 100-108.

2:19ff GREER, R. A. The Captain of Our Salvation (1973) 160-61.

2:19-22 VOGELS, H. "Die Tempelreinigung und Golgatha (Joh 2:19-22)," BZ 6 (1, 1962) 102-107. LEROY, H. Rätsel und Missverständnis (1968) 137-47. THUESING, W. Die Erhöhung und Verherrlichung Jesu im Johannesevangelium (1970) 279-83.

2:19-21 DALY, R. J., Christian Sacrifice (Washington D.C. 1978) 214-15, 229.

2:19-20 HAHN, F. Christologische Hoheitstitel (1963) 176.

2:19 GRILL, J. Untersuchungen über die Entstehung des vierten Evangeliums II (1923) 6, 8, 79, 83, 161, 192f., 210, 357. DODD, C. H. The Interpretation of the Fourth Gospel (1953) 301. DENNEY, J. The Death of Christ (1956³) 141. FLEW, R. N. Jesus and His Church (1956) 40-42. MENDNER, S. "Die Tempelreinigung," ZNW 47 (1956) 98ff. STANLEY, D. M. "The Christian Mystery and the New Temple," Worship 32 (4, 1958) 233-39. GAERTNER, B. The Temple and the Community in Qumran and the New Testament (1965) 113, 120. HAHN, F. Das Verständnis der Mission im Neuen Testament (1965²) 29f., 100. SANDVIK, B. Das Kommen des Herrn beim Abendmahl (1970) 56, 81, 139. DORMEYER, R. D., Die Passion Jesu als Verhaltensmodell (Münster 1974) 159-62. WILLIAMS, J. A., A Conceptual History of Deuteronomism in the Old Testament, Judaism, and the New Testament (Ph.D. Diss., Louisville 1976) 294-97. DUNN, J. D. G., Unity and Diversity in the New Testament (London 1977) 303. NEREPARAMPIL, L., Destroy This Temple. An Exegetico-Theological Study on the Meaning of Jesus' Temple-Logion in Jn 2:19 (Bangalore 1978). MEYER, B. F., The Aims of Jesus (London 1979) 181-85. VIELHAUER, P., "Das Bild vom Bau in der Christlichen Literatur vom Neuen Testament bis Clemens Alexandrinus" in: G. Klein (ed.) Oikodome. FS. P. Vielhauer (München 1979).

2:20 GAERTNER, B. The Temple and the Community in Qumran and the New Testament (1965) 111. HAHN, F. Das Verständnis der Mission im Neuen Testament (1965²) 76.

2:21-22 ORIGENES, Das Evangelium nach Johannes (1959) R. Gögler ed., 234-40. OLSSON, B., Structure and Meaning in the Fourth Gospel (Lund 1974) 79, 262-64, 266, 271, 280.

2:21 GAERTNER, B. The Temple and the Community in Qumran and the New Testament (1965) 120, 140. SANDVIK, B. Das Kommen des Herrn beim Abendmahl (1970) 124, 125. DAVIES, W. D. The Gospel and the Land (1974) 290, 296, 335 n.98. MEYER, B. F., The Aims of Jesus (London 1979) 181-85.

2:22 PALLIS, A., Notes on St. John and the Apocalypse (London 1928) 51. DELLING, G. Die Taufe im Neuen Testament (1963) 93. HAHN, F. Christologische Hoheitstitel (1963) 204. GAERTNER, B. The Temple and the Community in Qumran and the New Testament (1965) 120. DELLING, G. Wort und Werk Jesu im Johannes-Evangelium (1966) 45f. DAUER, A. Die Passionsgeschichte im Johannesevangelium (1972) 33, 198, 205, 238. BRAUN, F. M., "La Réduction du Pluriel au Singulier dans l'Evangile et la Première de Lettre Jean" NTS 24 (1977) 58, 59. METZGER, B. M., The Early Versions of the New Testament (Oxford 1977) 254.

2:23-3:36 RUCKSTUHL, E., "Abstieg und Erhöhung des johanneischen Menschensohns" in: R. Pesch/R. Schnackenburg (eds.) Jesus und der Menschensohn (Freiburg 1975) 315-17.

2:23-3:21 STANLEY, D. M. "Israel's Wisdom meets the Wisdom of God," Worship 32 (5, 1958) 280-87. DE LA POTTERIE, I. "Ad dialogum Jesu cum Nicodemo (2,23-3,21). Analysis litteraria," VerbDom 47 (3, 1969) 141-50. TOPEL, L. J. "A Note on the Methodology of Structural Analysis in Jn 2:23-3:21," CBQ 33 (2, 1971) 211-20. GAETA, G., Il dialogo con Nicodemo. Per l'interpretazione del capitolo terzo dell' evangelo di Giovanni (Brescia 1974). OSCULATI, R., Fare la verità. Analisi fenomenologica di un linguaggio religioso (Giovanni: 2,23 - 3,21) (Milan 1974). TSUCHIDO, K., "The Composition of the Nicodemus-Episode, John ii 23 - iii 21" AJBI 1 (1975) 91-103. BECKER, J., Das Evangelium nach Johannes (Gütersloh/ Würzburg 1979) 128-29 (lit!). de BURGOS NÚÑEZ, M., Catequesis sobre el amor de Dios, la fe en el Hijo y la salvación del mundo en Jn 2,23 - 3,21. El diálogo con Nicodemo" Communio 12 (1979) 3-51.

2:23-3:19 BLIGH, J. "Four Studies in St. John, II: Nicodemus," HeyJ 8 (1, 1967) 40-51.

2:23ff KAESEMANN, E. Exegetische Versuche und Besinnungen (1964) I 226. BEUTLER, J. Martyria (1972) 162, 176, 307ff., 357.

2:23-25 WILKENS, W. Die Entstehungsgeschichte des vierten Evangeliums (1958) 133, 134, 135. LANGBRANDTNER, W., Weltferner Gott oder Gott der Liebe (Frankfurt 1977) 16-17.

HODGES, Z. C., "Problem Passages in the Gospel of John. Part 2: Untrustworthy Believers — John 2:23-25" BiblSa 135 (1978) 139-52. HAENCHEN, E., Das Johannesevangelium (Tübingen 1980) 211 (lit!).

2:23-24 WILES, M. F. The Spiritual Gospel (1960) 87-88, 90.

2:23 GRILL, J. Untersuchungen über die Entstehung des vierten Evangeliums II (1923) 4, 6, 361. PALLIS, A., Notes on St. John and the Apocalypse (London 1928) 4. CULLMANN, O. Urchristentum und Gottesdienst (1950) 44f. DELLING, G. Die Zueignung des Heils in der Taufe (1961) 60. DELLING, G. Wort und Werk Jesu im Johannesevangelium (1966) 16, 42f. SCHOTTROFF, L. Der Glaubende und die feindliche Welt (1970) 245, 246, 250-52. UNTERGASSMAIR, F. G., Im Namen Jesu: der Namenbegriff im Johannesevangelium (Stuttgart 1973) 171-75. LADD, G. E. A Theology of the New Testament (1974) 231, 273, 276.

2:24 BRAUN, F. M., "La Réduction du Pluriel au Singulier dans l'Evangile et la Première Lettre de Jean" NTS 24 (1977) 50, 58.

2:28 BRAUN, F. M., "La Réduction du Pluriel au Singulier dans l'Evangile et la Première Letter de Jean" NTS 24 (1977) 54.

3-4 DE JULLIOT, H. "L'eau et l'Esprit," BVieC 27 (1959) 35-42. POTTERIE, I. "Structura primae partie Evangelii Johannis," VD 47 (3, 1969) 130-40.

3 CULLMANN, O. Urchristentum und Gottesdienst (1950) 51f., 83. NOACK, B. Zur Johanneischen Tradition (1954) 13, 19-20. BECKER, H., Die Reden des Johannesevangeliums und der Stil der gnostischen Offenbarungsrede (Göttingen 1956) 94-96, 116-17.. WIKENHAUSER, A. Das Evangelium nach Johannes (1957) 102. SCHNACKENBURG, R. "Die 'situationsgelösten' Redestücke in Joh 3," ZNW 49 (1-2, 1958) 88-99. SMTIH, D. M. The Composition and Order of the Fourth Gospel (1965) 124n., 125-127, 135. BRAUN, H. Qumran und NT II (1966) 133. BORNKAMM,G. Geschichte und Glaube (1968) 65f. LOHSE, E. et al., eds., Der Ruf Jesu und die Antwort der Gemeinde (1970) 119-21. SMITH, M. Clement of Alexandria and a secret Gospel of Mark (1973) 115, 175, 183, 200, 210,

244, 246f. RIEDL, J. Das Heilswerk Jesu nach Johannes (1973) 379-406. MUELLER, T. Das Heilsgeschehen im Johannesevangelium n.d., 46-54. ZIMMERMANN, H. "Die Christliche Taufe nach Joh. 3. Ein Beitrag zur Logoschristologie des vierten Evangeliums" Catholica 30 (1976) 81-93. LANG-BRANDTNER, W., Weltferner Gott oder Gott der Liebe (Frankfurt a.M./Bern/Las Vegas 1977) 18-25. BERGMEIER, R., Glaube als Gabe nach Johannes (Stuttgart 1980) 216, 221. NEYREY, J. H., "John III — A Debate over Johannine Epistemology and Christology" NovT 23 (1981) 115-27.

3:1ff BAUER, W. Das Johannesevangelium (1925) 58f.

3:1-36 YATES, K. M. Preaching from John's Gospel (1964) 28-37.

3:1-21.31-36 WILKENS, W. Die Entstehungsgeschichte des vierten Evangeliums (1958) 133, 134, 135.

3:1-21 WUHRMANN, I. U. Vom Alten zum Neuen (1912). BUECH-SEL, F. Das Evangelium nach Johannes (1946) 56f. CULL-MANN, O. Urchristentum und Gottesdienst (1950) 76ff. BRAUN, F. M. "La vie d'en haut," RSPT 40 (1956) 3-24. CORELL, A. Consummatum Est (1958) 58-60. MENDNER, S. "Nikodemus." JBL 77 (4, 1958) 293-323. van den BUSSCHE, H., "La Structure de Jean I-XII" in: M. Boismard et al., L'Evangile de Jean: études et problèmes (Bruges 1958) 83-84. BALAGUE, M., "Dialogo con Nicodemo," CultBib 16 (167, 1959) 193-206. COUREL, F. "Jesus et Nicodème," Christus 8 (30, 1961) 207-12. LINDIJER, C. H. De Sacramenten in het Vierde Evangelie (1964) 60ff. CADMAN, W. H., The Open Heaven (1969) G. B. Caird ed., 63-71. DE JONGE, M. "Nicodemus and Jesus: Some Observations on Misunderstanding and Understanding in the Fourth Gospel," BJRL 55 (2, 1971) 337-59. BEUTLER, J. Martyria (1972) 307, 314, 356f. MEEKS, W. A. "The Man from Heaven in Johannine Sectarianism," in: Proceedings 1 (1972) L. C. McGaughy ed., 293-98. BECKER, J. "J 3,1-21 als Reflex johannischer Schuldiskussion," in: Das Wort und die Wörter (1973) H. Balz/S. Schulz eds., 85-95. STACHOWIAK, L. "Spotkanie Jezusa z Nikodemen (J 3,1-21)," RTK 20 (1, 1973) 69-81. BIEDER, W., Die Verheissung der Taufe im Neuen Testament (Zürich 1966) 262-69. PORSCH, F., Pneuma und Werk (Frankfurt 1974) 84-85. RUCKSTUHL, E., "Abstieg und Erhöhung des Johanneischen Menschensohns" in: R. Pesch/R. Schnackenburg (eds) Jesus und der Menschensohn (Freiburg 1975) 317-40. TEMPLE, S., The Core of the Fourth Gospel (London 1975) 99-107. de JONGE, M., Jesus: Stranger from Heaven and Son of God (Missoula 1977) 37-42. TRITES, A. A., The New Tes-

tament Concept of Witness (Cambridge 1977) 95-97. WAL-
TER, L., "Lecture d'Evangile. Jean III, 1-21: selon la foi et
l'incredulité" EsVie 87 (1977) 369-78, 385-90. BOJORGE, H.,
"La entrada en la tierra prometida y la entrada en el Reino. El
trasfondo teológico del diá-Logo de Jesús con Nicodemo (Jn 3)"
RevBi 41 (1979) 171-86. HAENCHEN, E., Das Johannesevangelium (Tübingen 1980) 214-15 (lit!). MOLONEY, F. J.,
"From Cana to Cana (John 2:1-4:54) and the Fourth Evangelist's Concept of Correct (and Incorrect) Faith," in: E. A. Livingstone (ed.) Studia Biblica 1978/II (Sheffield 1980) 194.
LEIDIG, E., Jesu Gespräch mit der Samaritanerin (Basel 1981)
184-90. LINDARS, B., "Discourse and Tradition: The Use of
the Sayings of Jesus in the Discourses of the Fourth Gospel"
JSNT 13 (1981) 85-87. MILLER, D. G., "John 3.1-21" Interp
35 (1981) 174-79.

3:1-15 IWAND, H.-J. GPM 4 (1949-1950) 173ff. BORNKAMM, G.
GPM 9 (1954-1955) 156ff. GOLLWITZER, H., GPM 15 (1960-
1961) 179ff. DOERNE, M. Er kommt auch noch heute (1961)
99-101. EICHHOLZ, G. in: Herr, tue meine Lippen auf Bd. 1
(1957) G. Eicholz ed., 194-203. IWAND, H.-J. Predigt-Meditationen (1964) 222-29. VOOBUS, A. The Gospels in Study
and Preaching (1966) 1-30. COLLINS, R. F., "Jesus' Conversation with Nicodemus" BiTod 93 (1977) 1409-19. STO-
EVESANDT, H., in: GPM 33 (1979) 261-72. CANTWELL,
L., "The Quest for the Historical Nicodemus" RSt 16 (1980)
481-86.

3:1-13 LOCKYER, H. All the Parables of the Bible (1963) 314ff. GO-
LEBIOWSKI, F., "Powiazania literackie i znaczenie teologiczne trzech perykop w Ewangelii Janowej" RBL 28 (1975)
182-99.

3:1-12 BLANK, J. Krisis (1964) 56. BRAUN, F.-M. Jean le Théolo-
gien(1966) 85-90. PESCH, H. " 'Ihr müsst von oben geboren
werden,' Eine Auslegung von Jo 3,1-12," BuL 7 (3, 1966) 208-
19. KUHL, J. Die Sendung Jesu und der Kirche nach dem Jo-
hannes-Evangelium (1967) 189-91. LANGBRANDTNER, W.,
Weltferner Gott oder Gott der Liebe (Frankfurt 1977) 19-22.
VOUGA, F., Le cadre historique et l'intention théologique de
Jean (Paris 1977) 16-23. HORST, U., "Heilsverlangen und
Wiedergeburt. Zu Joh. 3.1-12" Anzeiger für die katholische
Geistlichkeit 88 (1979) 408.

3:1-10 DE LA POTTERIE, I. "Jesus et Nicodemus: de necessitate ge-
nerationis ex Spiritu (Jo 3,1-10)," VerbDom 47 (4, 1969) 193-
214. RUCKSTUHL, E., "Abstieg und Erhöhung des johanneischen Menschensohns" in: R. Pesch/R. Schnackenburg

(eds.) Jesus und der Menschensohn (Freiburg 1975) 317-40. NEYREY, J. H., "John III — A Debate over Johannine Epistomology and Christology," NovT 23 (1981) 118-21.

3:1-8 BERGMEIER, R., Glaube als Gabe nach Johannes (Stuttgart 1980) 219.

3:1-5 HERMISSON, H.-J., GPM 29 (1975) 266ff.

3:1-3 TEMPLE, S., The Core of the Fourth Gospel (London 1975) 100-102.

3:1-2 TEMPLE, S., The Core of the Fourth Gospel (London 1975) 288-89. VOUGA, F., Le cadre historique et l'intention théologique de Jean (Paris 1977) 17-18.

3:1 FORTNA, R. T. The Gospel of Signs (1970) 128-34, 210, 216, 217. BEUTLER, J. Martyria (1972) 241f., 307f.

3:2 HAHN, F. Christologische Hoheitstitel (1963) 75f., 77, 80f., 397. HENNECKE, E./SCHNEEMELCHER, W. Neutestamentliche Apokryphen (1964) I 60. SMITH, M. Tannaitic Parallels to the Gospels (1968) 2.70*. BEUTLER, J. Martyria (1972) 243, 308ff., 317, 357. REIM, G., Studien zum Alttestamentlichen Hintergrund des Johannesevangeliums (Cambridge 1974) 119-20. METZGER, B. M., The Early Versions of the New Testament (Oxford 1977) 253. CRIBBS, F. L., "The Agreements that Exist Between John and Acts" in: C. H. Talbert (ed.) Perspectives on Luke-Acts (Danville 1978) 60. BERGMEIER, R., Glaube als Gabe nach Johannes (Stuttgart 1980) 219.

3:3ff MUSSNER, F. ZΩH. Die Anschauung vom "Leben" im vierten Evangelium (1952) 119f. BEASLEY-MURRAY, G. R. Baptism in the New Testament (1962) 226ff. SMITH, M. Clement of Alexandria and a secret Gospel of Mark (1973) 120, 153f., 169, 183f., 236, 247. BERGMEIER, R. Glaube als Gabe nach Johannes (Stuttgart 1980) 250n.234.

3:3-21 PORSCH, F., Pneuma und Wort (Frankfurt 1974) 96-110.

3:3-10 VELLANICKAL, M., "Christian: Born of the Spirit" BB 2 (1976) 153-74. VELLANICKAL, M., The Divine Sonship of Christians in the Johannine Writings (Rome 1977) 163-213.

3:3-8 BRAUN, H. Qumran und NT II (1966) 28, 123, 130f., 133, 222, 251, 254, 299f. PORSCH, F., Pneuma und Wort (Frankfurt 1974) 83-135. DELLING, G., "Die 'Söhne (Kinder) Gottes' im Neuen Testament" in: R. Schnackenburg et al. (eds.), Die Kirche des Anfangs. FS. H. Schürmann (Freiburg 1978) 624-26. SCHWEIZER, E., Heiliger Geist (Berlin 1978) 98-99. BERGMEIER, R., Glaube als Gabe nach Johannes (Stuttgart 1980) 213, 220.

3:3-5 DUPONT, J. Essais sur la Christologie de Saint Jean (1951) 166, 167. LE FROIS, J. "Die geistige Mutterschaft Mariens nach Jo 3,3-5 (span)," RevBi 75 (17, 1955) 1-4. DELLING, G. Die Taufe im Neuen Testament (1963) 89-92. LEROY, H. Rätsel und Missverständnis (1968) 124-37. BERGMEIER, R., Glaube als Gabe nach Johannes (Stuttgart 1980) 216-27, 219. MOUNCE, W. D., The Origin of the New Testament Metaphor of Rebirth (Ph.D.Diss., Aberdeen 1981) 125-62.

3:3-4 BEUTLER, J. Martyria (1972) 308f., 316, 357. PORSCH, F., Pneuma und Wort (Frankfurt 1974) 96-98.

3:3 GRILL, J. Untersuchungen über die Entstehung des vierten Evangeliums II (1923) 5, 8, 87f., 290, 362, 395. BAUER, W. Das Johannesevangelium (1925) 48ff. CULLMANN, O. Urchristentum und Gottesdienst (1950) 61. STRATHMANN, H. Das Evangelium nach Johannes (1955) 75f. WIKENHAUSER, A. Das Evangelium nach Johannes (1957) 91-94. ROBINSON, J. M. Kerygma und historischer Jesus (1960) 162, 168, 170. DELLING, G. Die Taufe im Neuen Testament (1963) 135. DELLING, G. Wort und Werk Jesu im Johannes-Evangelium (1966) 11, 17, 67, 127f., 142. JUENGEL, E. Paulus und Jesus (1966) 162. SHIMADA, K., The Formulary Material in First Peter (Th.D.Diss., Ann Arbor 1966) 186-91, 196-98. SANFORD, J. A., The Kingdom Within (New York 1970) 46-47, 53. JEREMIAS, J. Neutestamentliche Theologie I (1971) 21, 40, 43f. LADD, G. E. A Theology of the New Testament (1974) 160, 216, 268, 298, 303, 591, 615. VOUGA, F., Le cadre historique et l'intention théologique de Jean (Paris 1977) 18. JEWETT, P. K., Infant Baptism and the Coveneant of Grace (Grand Rapids 1978) 67, 223. BARTH, G., Die Taufe in frühchristlicher Zeit (Neukirchen-Vluyn 1981) 12, 60, 70, 72, 74, 106, 108-109, 143. LINDARS, B., "Discourse and Tradition: The Use of the Sayings of Jesus in the Discourses of the Fourth Gospel" JSNT 13 (1981) 85-86, 91, 96. LINDARS, B., "John and the Synoptic Gospels: A Test Case" NTS 27 (1981) 287-94.

3:4-6 TEMPLE, S., The Core of the Fourth Gospel (London 1975) 102-105.

3:4 PALLIS, A., Notes on St. John and the Apocalypse (London 1928) 5. LINDARS, B., "John and the Synoptic Gospels: A Test Case" NTS 27 (1980-1981) 291.

3:5ff BETZ, O. "Die Geburt der Gemeinde durch den Lehrer," NTS 3 (1956-1957) 323ff. ODEBERG, H. The Fourth Gospel (1968) 48-71.

3:5.6.8 FLEW, R. N. Jesus and His Church (1956) 173.

3:5-6 JOHNSTON, G. The Spirit-Paraclete in the Gospel of John (1970) 40-43, 84.

3:5 GRILL, J. Untersuchungen über die Entstehung des vierten Evangeliums II (1923) 8, 87f., 91, 238, 290, 291, 339, 395. PALLIS, A., Notes on St. John and the Apocalypse (London 1928) 5. MASSAUX, E. Influence de l'Evangile de saint Matthieu sur la litterature chrétienne avant saint Irénée (1950) 293-300. RUCKSTUHL, E. Die literarische Einheit des Johannesevangeliums (1951) 17, 34, 46, 171f., 174. BARTH, M., Die Taufe - ein Sakrament? (Zürich 1951) 434ff. NIEWALDA, P. Sakramentssymbolik im Johanesevangelium? (1958) 2-3. ROBINSON, J. M. Kerygma und historischer Jesus (1960) 162, 168, 170. RUDOLPH, K. Die Mandäer I (1960) 77, 240. DE LA POTTERI, I. " 'Naître de l'eau et naître de l'Esprit.' Le texte baptismal de Jn 3,5," SciEccl 14 (3, 1962) 417-43. DELLING, G. Die Taufe im Neuen Testament (1963) 13, 67, 95, 96. HENNECKE, E./SCHNEEMELCHER, W. Neutestamentliche Apokryphen (1964) II 77. HAMMER, P. L. "Baptism with Water and the Spirit," TheolLife 8 (1, 1965) 35-43. DELLING, G. Wort und Werk Jesu im Johannes-Evangelium (1966) 17, 67f., 127f., 136. ROBINSON, D. W. B. "Born of Water and Spirit: Does John 3:5 Refer to Baptism?" RThR 25 (1966) 15-23. SHIMADA, K., The Formulary Material in First Peter (PhD. Diss., Ann Arbor 1966) 186-91, 196-98. KUHL, J. Die Sendung Jesu und der Kirche nach dem Johannes-Evangelium (1967) 135, 189-91. NICKELS, P. Targum and New Testament (1967) 53. RICHTER, G. Die Fusswaschung im Johannesevangelium (1967) 9, 20, 55, 59, 62, 66, 116, 186, 277, 297. SCHWEIZER, E. NTS 14 (1967-1968) 4f. DUNN, J. D. G. Baptism in the Holy Spirit (1970) 168, 175, 183, 186, 188ff., 204, 226. KASPER, W. ed., Christsein ohne Entscheidung oder soll die Kirche Kinder taufen? (1970) 66-68. FOWLER, R. "Born of water and the Spirit (Jn 3:5)," ET 82 (5, 1971) 159. JEREMIAS, J. Neutestamentliche Theologie I (1971) 40f., 43f., 153. KUEMMEL, W. G. Einleitung in das Neue Testament (1973) 175f. KYSAR, R., The Fourth Evangelist and His Gospel (Minneapolis 1974) 250-51. LADD, G. E. A Theology of the New Testament (1974) 96, 216, 284, 298, 303. RICHTER, G., "Zum sogenannten Tauftext (Joh 3,5" MThZ 26 (1975) 101-25. SPRIGGS, D. G. "Meaning of 'Water' in John 3:5," ET 85 (5, 1974) 149-50. PORSCH, F., Pneuma und Wort (Frankfurt 1974) 91-92, 98-101, 125-30. BECKER, J., Auferstehung der Toten im Urchristentum (Stuttgart 1976) 135, 136, 137, 138, 139, 140. DUNN, J. D. G., Unity and Diversity in the New Testament (London 1977) 169-

70. HODGES, Z. C., "Problem Passages in the Gospel of John. Part 3: Water and Spirit — John 3:5" BiblSa 135 (1978) 206-20. JEWETT, P. K., Infant Baptism and the Covenant of Grace (Grand Rapids 1978) 42, 58, 76. BELLEVILLE, L., " 'Born of Water and Spirit': John 3:5" TJ 1 (1980) 125-41. BARTH, G., Die Taufe in frühchristlicher Zeit (Neukirchen-Vluyn 1981) 12, 60, 70, 72, 74, 106, 108-109, 143. LEON-DUFOUR, X., "Towards a Symbolic Reading of the Fourth Gospel" NTS 27 (1980-1981) 449. LINDARS, B., "Discourse and Tradition: The Use of the Sayings of Jesus in the Discourses of the Fourth Gospel" JSNT 13 (1981) 85-86, 91, 96. LINDARS, B., "John and the Synoptic Gospels: A Test Case" NTS 17 (1980-1981) 287, 290-92.

3:6 REUSS, J. "Presbyter Ammonius Kommentar zum Jo-Evangelium," Biblica 44 (1963) 162. KAESEMANN, E. Exegetische Versuche und Besinnungen (1964) II 172. KAESEMANN, E. New Testament Questions of Today (1969) 157. METZGER, B. M., The Early Versions of the New Testament (Oxford 1977) 40. JEWETT, P. K., Infant Baptism and the Covenant of Grace (Grand Rapids 1978) 223. BERGMEIER, R., Glaube als Gabe nach Johannes (Stuttgart 1980) 213, 220-21, 254n.310.311.

3:7 SMITH, M. Tannaitic Parallels to the Gospels (1968) 2.80*. METZGER, B. M., The Early Versions of the New Testament (Oxford 1977) 252. BERGMEIER, R., Glaube als Gabe nach Johannes (Stuttgart 1980) 219, 254n.312.

3:8 MORGAN, G. C. The Parables and Metaphors of Our Lord (1943) 266ff. MAURER, C., Ignatius von Antiochien und das Johannesevangelium (Zürich 1949) 25-30, 45-58. RUCKSTUHL, E. Die literarische Einheit des Johannesevangeliums (1951) 52, 171f. DONN, T. M. "The Voice of the Spirit (Jo 3,8)," ET 66 (1, 1954) 32. ORIGENES, Das Evangelium nach Johannes (1959) R. Gögler ed., 240-41. DELLING, G., Die Taufe im Neuen Testament (1963) 89. HUNTER, A. M. According to John (1970) 79. SMITH, C. H. "houtōs estin pas ho gegennēmenos ek tou pneumatos (Jn 3:8)," ET 81 (6, 1970) 181. DAVIES, W. D. The Gospel and the Land (1974) 220, 302, 317. METZGER, B. M., The Early Versions of the New Testament (Oxford 1977) 49. JEWETT, P. K., Infant Baptism and the Covenant of Grace (Grand Rapids 1978) 223. BERGMEIER, R., Glaube als Gabe nach Johannes (Stuttgart 1980) 216, 219, 253n.300. BUETUBELA, B., "Jn 3,8: l'Esprit-Saint ou le Vent naturel?" RATh 4 (1980) 55-64.

3:9ff NORDEN, E. Agnostos Theos (1956 = 1912) 299f.

3:9-13 ROBINSON, J. A. T. "The One Baptism," in: Twelve New Testament Studies (1962) 158-75.

3:9-12 VOUGA, F., La cadre historique et l'intention théologique de Jean (Paris 1977) 20-21.

3:9-10 BEUTLER, J. Martyria (1972) 308ff.

3:9 BERGMEIER, R., Glaube als Gabe nach Johannes (Stuttgart 1980) 219, 254n.310.

3:10 BISHOP, E. F. F. "The authorised teacher of the Israel of God (John 3,10)," BTr 7 (2, 1956) 81-83. STROBEL, A. Erkenntnis and Bekenntnis der Sünde in neutestamentlicher Zeit (1968) 46. PANCARNO, B. NTS 16 (1969-1970) 123-25. LÉON-DUFOUR, X., "Towards a Symbolic Reading of the Fourth Gospel" NTS 27 (1980-1981) 451.

3:11-13:31 GEORGI, D., "Weisheit Salomos" in: JüdSchr III/4 (1980) 9n.16a.

3:11-21 VAN DEN BUSSCHE, H. "L'élévation du Fils de l'homme (Jean 3,11-21)," BVieC 35 (1960) 16-25. DE LA POTTERIE, I. "Jesus et Nicodemus: de revelatione Jesu et vera fide in eum (Jo 3,11-21)," VerbDom 47 (4, 1969) 257-83. BEUTLER, J. Martyria (1972) 217, 307, 309, 313f. VELLANICKAL, M., The Divine Sonship of Christians in the Johannine Writings (Rome 1977) 208-13.

3:11-17 NEYREY, J. H., "John III — A Debate over Johannine Epistomology and Christology" NovT 23 (1981) 121-22.

3:11-13 HAACKER, K. Die Stiftung des Heils (1972) 108-11. BÜHNER, J.-A., Der Gesandte und sein Weg im 4. Evangelium (Tübingen 1977) 378.

3:11-12 HAHN, F. Das Verständnis der Mission im Neuen Testament (1965²) 140. BERGER, K. Die Amen-Worte Jesu (1970) 107-109. BEUTLER, J. Martyria (1972) 23f., 26ff., 210f., 217ff., 227ff., 307-13, 315-18, 326f., 365f. PORSCH, F., Pneuma und Wort (Frankfurt 1974) 101-105. RUCKSTUHL, E., "Abstieg und Erhöhung des johanneischen Menschensohns" in: R. Pesch/ R. Schnackenburg (eds.) Jesus und der Menschensohn (Freiburg 1975) 320-23. MATSUNAGA, K., "Is John's Gospel Anti-Sacramental? — A New Solution in the Light of the Evangelist's Milieu" NTS 27 (1980-1981) 518.

3:11 BÜHNER, J.-A., Der Gesandte und sein Weg im 4. Evangelium (Tübingen 1977) 109-10, 378-80. BERGMEIER, R., Glaube als Gabe nach Johannes (Stuttgart 1980) 255n.339.

3:12ff THUESING, W. Die Erhöhung und Verherrlichung Jesu im Johannesevangelium (1970) 254-61.

3:12-13 GEORGI, D., "Weisheit Salomos" in: JüdSchr III/4 (1980) 9n.10a.

3:12 LADD, G. E. A Theology of the New Testament (1974) 216, 224, 245. COURTHIAL, P., "Note sur Jean 3/12" RevR 31 (1980) 265-69.

3:13-21 BLANK, J. Krisis (1964) 96. PORSCH, F., Pneuma und Wort (Frankfurt 1974) 106-10. SCHILLEBEECKX, E., Christ: the Christian Experience in the Modern World (London 1980) 324-28, GT: Christus und die Christen (Freiburg/Basel/Wien 1977) 311-15.

3:13-15 SCHULZ, S., Untersuchungen zur Menschensohn-Christologie im Johannesevangelium (Göttingen 1957) 104-106.

3:13-14 BORGEN, P., "Some Jewish Exegetical Traditions as Background for Son of Man Sayings in John's Gospel (Jn 3,13-14 and context)" Bibliotheca ephemeridum theologicarum Lovaniensium 44 (Louvain 1977) 243-58. BERGMEIER, R., Glaube als Gabe nach Johannes (Stuttgart 1980) 242n.117, 246-47n.191.

3:13 SCHULZ, S., Untersuchungen zur Menschensohn-Christologie im Johannesevangelium (Göttingen 1957) 105-106. SIDEBOTTOM, E. M. "The Ascent and Descent of the Son of Man in the Gospel of St. John," AThR 2 (2, 1957) 115-22. WILES, M. F. The Spiritual Gospel (1960) 97, 114, 132, 134, 136. SCHNACKENBURG, R. NTS 11 (1964-1965) 125f. BOUSSET, W. Die Religion des Judentums im Späthellenistischen Zeitalter (1966 = 1926) 268. DELLING, G. Wort und Werk Jesu im Johannes-Evangelium (1966) 61, 88, 96, 110, 123. McNAMARA, M. The New Testament and the Palestinian Targum to the Pentateuch (1966) 73, 74n.15. NICKELS, P., Targum and New Testament (1967) 53. ODEBERG, H. The Fourth Gospel (1968) 72-99. CADMAN, W. H. The Open Heaven (1969) G. B. Caird ed., 28-31, 34, 103, 148. THUESING, W. Die Erhöhung und Verherrlichung Jesu im Johannesevangelium (1970) 255-61. IBUKI, I. Die Wahrheit im Johannesevangelium (1972) 155f. HAMERTON-KELLY, R. G. Pre-Existence, Wisdom, and the Son of Man (1973) 225, 230-31, 238. LINDARS, B. "The Son of Man in the Johannine Christology," in: Christ and the Spirit in the New Testament (1973) B. Lindars/S. S. Smalley eds., 44, 47f. RUCKSTUHL, E., "Abstieg und Erhöhung des johanneischen Menschensohns" in: R. Pesch/R. Schnackenburg (eds.) Jesus und der Menschensohn (Freiburg 1975) 324-29. BÜHNER, J.-A., Der

Gesandte und sein Weg im 4. Evangelium (Tübingen 1977) 65-
66, 112, 306f., 378, 380-85, 391-95, 398-99. METZGER, B.
M., The Early Versions of the New Testament (Oxford 1977)
41. MARTYN, J. L., The Gospel of John in Christian History
(New York 1978) 20-21, 28. SCHMITHALS, W., "Zur Herkunft der gnostischen Elemente in der Sprache des Paulus" in:
B. Aland et al. (eds.) Gnosis. FS. H. Jonas (Göttingen 1978)
403. DUNN, J. D., Christology in the Making (London 1980)
29, 56, 89-90, 186, 302n.127, 319n.67.

3:14-19 DUPONT, J. Essais sur la Christologie de Saint Jean (1951) 174-
75, 259, 260. LANGBRANDTNER, W., Weltferner Gott oder
Gott der Liebe (Frankfurt 1977) 23-24.

3:14-16 SCHELKLE, K. H. Die Passion Jesu in der Verkündigung des
Neuen Testaments (1949) 124f., 130f. KUHL, J. Die Sendung
Jesu und der Kirche nach dem Johannes-Evangelium (1967) 117-
19, 204.

3:14-15 TAYLOR, V. Jesus and His Sacrifice (1948) 221-24, 237.
MUSSNER, F. ΖΩΗ. Die Anschauung vom "Leben" im vier-
ten Evangelium (1952) 105f. HAHN, F. Das Verständnis der
Mission im Neuen Testament (1965²) 138. HIGGINS, A. J. B.
Menschensohn-Studien (1965) 28-32. BRAUN, F.-M. Jean le
Théologien (1966) 173f. NICKELS, P. Targum and New Tes-
tament (1967) 53. ODEBERG, H. The Fourth Gospel (1968)
99-113. THUESING, W. Die Erhöhung und Verherrlichung
Jesu im Johannesevangelium (1970) 258-61.

3:14 MORGAN, G. C. The Parables and Metaphors of Our Lord
(1943) 272ff. CULLMANN, O. Urchristentum und Gottesdienst (1950) 51f. RUCKSTUHL, E. Die literarische Einheit des
Johannesevangeliums (1951) 178f., 256. COLWELL, E. C./
TITUS, E. L. The Gospel and the Spirit (1953) 59, 68, 81, 97
n.61, 101. DENNEY, J. The Death of Christ (1956³) 141.
SCHULZ, S., Untersuchungen zur Menschensohn-Chri-
stologie im Johannesevangelium (Göttingen 1957) 106-109.
ROBINSON, J. M. Kerygma und historischer Jesus (1960) 71.
GLASSON, T. F. Moses in the Fourth Gospel (1963) Ch. IV,
43. HAHN, F. Christologische Hoheitstitel (1963) 53, 130.
CULLMANN, O. NTS 11 (1964-1965) 116f. DELLING, G.
Wort und Werk Jesu im Johannes-Evangelium (1966) 62, 80,
84, 95. McNAMARA, M. The New Testament and the Palestinian Targum to the Pentateuch (1966) 146. SMALLEY, S. S.
"The Johannine Son of Man Sayings," NTS 15 (1968-1969)
291ff. DAUER, A. Die Passionsgeschichte im Johannesevangelium (1972) 141, 264, 266, 278f., 301, 304, 324. HAM-
ERTON-KELLY, R. G. Pre-Existence, Wisdom, and the Son

of Man (1973) 225, 231-34, 236, 238. LINDARS, B. "The Son
of Man in the Johannine Christology," in: Christ and the Spirit
in the New Testament (1973) B. Lindars/S. S. Smalley eds., 44,
48, 53, 56f. CAVALLIN, H. C. C. Life After Death (1974) 7,
2 n.18. FORESTELL, J. T., The Word of the Cross: Salvation
as Revelation in the Fourth Gospel (Rome 1974) 43, 60, 61, 63,
89. PANCARO, S., The Law in the Fourth Gospel (Leiden
1975) 320, 332-36, 337, 351, 352. RUCKSTUHL, E., "Abstieg und Erhöhung des johanneischen Menschensohns" in: R.
Pesch/R. Schnackenburg (eds.) Jesus und der Menschensohn
(Freiburg 1975) 330-35. SAITO, T., Die Mosevorstellungen im
Neuen Testament (Bern 1977) 115-16, 143. KJESETH, P.,
"Nehushtan and Ernst Bloch — Raymond Brown and Biblical
Studies" Dialog 17 (1978) 280-86. SCHWEIZER, E., Heiliger
Geist (Berlin 1978) 132-33. ROLOFF, J., Neues Testament
(Neukirchen-Vluyn 1979) 193f.

3:15-21 BRAUN, H. Qumran und NT II (1966) 91, 105, 120, 122f., 125,
127f., 138, 171, 245, 249, 271, 284.

3:15-16 TAYLOR, V. Jesus and His Sacrifice (1948) 221-24, 230, 237.

3:15 DELLING, G. Die Zueignung des Heils in der Taufe (1961) 60.
IBUKI, Y. Die Wahrheit im Johannesevangelium (1972) 337-
40. METZGER, B. M., The Early Versions of the New Testament (Oxford 1977) 42, 369n.1. BERGMEIER, R., Glaube
als Gabe nach Johannes (Stuttgart 1980) 192n.34. GEORGI, D.,
"Weisheit Salomos" in: JüdSchr III/4 (1980) 9n.10a.

3:16ff BERGMEIER, R., Glaube als Gabe nach Johannes (Stuttgart
1980) 232.

3:16-21 TRILLHAAS, GPM 4 (1949-1950) 170ff. KRAUS, GPM 9
(1954-1955) 150ff. BONHOEFFER, D. in: Herr, tue meine
Lippen auf Bd. 1 (1957) G. Eichholz ed., 189-94. MERKEL/
GEORGI/BALTZER, GPM 15 (1960-1961) 172ff. DOERNE,
M. Er kommt auch noch beute (1961) 96-99. ODEBERG, H.
The Fourth Gospel (1968) 113-49. LINDARS, B. "Δικαιο
σύνη in Jn 16.8 and 10," in: Mélanges Bibliques en hommage
au R. P. Béda Rigaux (1970) A. Descamps/A. de Halleux eds.,
282-83. MARQUARDT, F.-W. GPM 27 (2, 1973) 285-91.
RUCKSTUHL, E., "Abstieg und Erhöhung des johanneischen
Menschensohns" in: R. Pesch/R. Schnackenburg (eds.) Jesus
und der Menschensohn (Freiburg 1975) 335-37. RHEIN, C. und
LÜTCKE, K.-H., in: P. Krusche et al. (eds.) Predigtstudien für
das Kirchenjahr 1980-1981. III/I (Stuttgart 1980) 38-45.

3:16-19 KUHL, J. Die Sendung Jesu und der Kirche nach dem Johannes-Evangelium (1967) 76, 210f.

3:16-18   HAHN, F. Christologische Hoheitstitel (1963) 330. BÜHNER,
J.-A., Der Gesandte und sein Weg im 4. Evangelium (Tübingen 1977) 171-72, 411-12. LINDEMANN, A., "Gemeinde
und Welt im Johannesevangelium" in: D. Lührmann/G.
Strecker (eds.) Kirche. FS. G. Bornkamm (Tübingen 1980) 143-45.

3:16-17   HAHN, F. Christologische Hoheitstitel (1963) 329. DEL-
LING, G. Wort und Werk Jesu im Johannes-Evangelium (1966)
58, 83, 133, 138. SCHOTTROFF, L. Der Glaubende und die
feindliche Welt (1970) 235-36, 243-44, 283-89. SCHWEIZER,
E. Beiträge zur Theologie des Neuen Testaments (1970) 83-95.
SANDERS, J. T., Ethics in the New Testament (Philadelphia
1975) 94. BÜHNER, J.-A. Der Gesandte und sein Weg im 4.
Evangelium (Tübingen 1977) 94-95, 263-65, 412-13.
SCHMITHALS, W., "Zur Herkunft der gnostischen Elemente
in der Sprache des Paulus" in: B. Aland et al. (eds.) Gnosis.
FS. H. Jonas (Göttingen 1978) 403. BERGMEIER, R., Glaube
als Gabe nach Johannes (Stuttgart 1980) 215, 233.

3:16   GRILL, J. Untersuchungen über die Entstehung des vierten
Evangeliums II (1923) 143f., 152f., 218. CULLMANN, O.
Urchristentum und Gottesdienst (1950) 52. SCHULZ, S., Un-
tersuchungen zur Menschensohn-Christologie im Johannes-
evangelium (Göttingen 1957) 140-42. MOODY, D., "God's
Only Son: The Translation of John 3:16 in the Revised Standard
Version," BTr 10 (1959) 145-47. KRAMER, W. Christos
Kyrios Gottessohn (1963) § 26a. HAHN,F. Das Verständnis der
Mission im Neuen Testament (1965²) 136, 138. DELLLING,
G. Wort und Werk Jesu im Johannes-Evangelium (1966) 41f.,
61, 64, 68, 78, 80, 104, 107, 143, 146. LUTHER, M. Predig-
ten über die Christus-Botschaft (1966) 239-46. McNAMARA,
M. The New Testament and the Palestinian Targum to the Pen-
tateuch (1966) 164. KUHL, J. Die Sendung Jesu und der Kirche
nach dem Johannes-Evangelium (1967) 104-106, 118f., 137,
213. NICKELS, P. Targum and New Testament (1967) 53.
POPKES, W. Christus Traditus (1967) 56f., 120, 190, 198,
202f., 211ff., 215, 245f., 250f., 255, 261, 282. SMITH, M.
Tannaitic Parallels to the Gospels (1968) 8 b n 10*. CADMAN,
W. H. The Open Heaven (1969) G. B. Caird ed., 10, 12, 17,
54, 67, 73, 107, 130, 182, 207. BEUTLER, J. Martyria (1972)
217, 281, 284, 308, 312. DAUER, A. Die Passionsgeschichte
im Johannesevangelium (1972) 255, 260, 286, 289, 294.
IBUKI, Y. Die Wahrheit im Johannesevangelium (1972) 156-
60, 263f., 337-40. ROBERTS, R. L. "The Rendering 'Only
Begotten' In John 3:16," RestQ 16 (1, 1973) 2-22. KUEM-
MEL, W. G. Römer 7 und das Bild des Menschen im Neuen

Testament (1974) 200, 202f. LADD, G. E. A Theology of the
New Testament (1974) 226, 227, 229, 280, 294. LOHSE, E.
Grundriss der neutestamentlichen Theologie (1974) 14, 130f.,
133. THYEN, H., "... denn wir lieben die Brüder" in: J.
Friedrich et al. (eds.) Rechtfertigung. FS. E. Käsemann (Tü-
bingen/Göttingen 1976) 536, 538-39. BERGER, K., Exegese
des Neuen Testaments (Heidelberg 1977) 182-83. METZGER,
B. M., The Early Versions of the New Testament (Oxford 1977)
255. "Agende" in: TRE 2 (1978) 3. BERGMEIER, R., Glaube
als Gabe nach Johannes (Stuttgart 1980) 21, 268n.524. "Dordrechter Synode" in: TRE 9 (1982) 141.

3:17ff HAHN, F. Das Verständnis der Mission im Neuen Testament
(1965²) 137. BEUTLER, J. Martyria (1972) 242, 269, 312.

3:17-18 BERGMEIER, R., Glaube als Gabe nach Johannes (Stuttgart
1980) 215.

3:17 GRILL, J. Untersuchungen über die Entstehung des vierten
Evangeliums II (1923) 67, 143, 296, 335, 359. BAUER, W.
Das Johannesevangelium (1925) 55. DELLING, G. Wort und
Werk Jesu im Johannes-Evangelium (1966) 58, 61, 65, 99f.,
114, 141. SCHRAGE, W., "Die Elia-Apokalypse" in: Jüd-
Schr V/3 (1980) 232n.20d.

3:18-21 BENOIT, P. "Paulinisme et Johannisme," NTS 9 (1962-1963)
201f. NEYREY, J. H., "John III — A Debate over Johannine
Epistomology and Christology" NovT 23 (1981) 122-23.

3:18 WILES, M. F. The Spiritual Gospel (1960) 80-81, 88. DEL-
LING, G. Die Zueignung des Heils in der Taufe (1961) 60.
HAHN, F. Christologische Hoheitstitel (1963) 330. DEL-
LING, G. Wort und Werk Jesu im Johannes-Evangelium (1966)
41f., 44, 67, 100, 104, 108. CADMAN, W. H. The Open
Heaven (1969) G. B. Caird ed., 10, 17, 44, 130. RICHTER,
H.-F. Auferstehung und Wirklichkeit (1969) 233, 275, 288.
IBUKI, Y. Die Wahrheit im Johannesevangelium (1972) 338ff.
UNTERGASSMAIR, F. G., Im Namen Jesu: Der Namensbe-
griff im Johannesevangelium (Stuttgart 1973) 171-75. LADD,
G. E. A Theology of the New Testament (1974) 307. BERG-
MEIER, R., Glaube als Gabe nach Johannes (Stuttgart 1980)
192n.34, 204, 211, 233. BERGER, K., "Das Buch der Jubi-
läen" in: JüdSchr II/3 (1981) 509n.17h.

3:19ff IBUKI,Y. Die Wahrheit im Johannesevangelium (1972) 338-
43, 344ff., 348-54.

3:19-21 de la POTTERIE, I., La Vérité dans Saint Jean I/II (Rome 1977)
496-502. BERGMEIER, R., Glaube als Gabe nach Johannes

(Stuttgart 1980) 15-16, 19, 27, 35n.123, 85, 204, 232-33, 244n.159, 256n.346.347, 270n.559.

3:19-20 BROWN, R. E., "The Qumran Scrolls and the Johannine Gospel and Epistles" in: K. Stendahl (ed.) The Scrolls and the New Testament (New York 1957) 191-92; [orig. in CBQ 17 (1955) 403-19, 559-74]; GT: "Die Schriftrollen von Qumran und das Johannesevangelium und die Johannesbriefe" in: K. H. Rengstorf (ed.) Johannes und sein Evangelium (Darmstadt 1973) 501-502. BEUTLER, J. Martyria (1972) 224, 267, 312f., 321.

3:19 PALLIS, A., Notes on St. John and the Apocalypse (London 1928) 52. MUSSNER, F. ZΩH. Die Anschauung vom "Leben" im vierten Evangelium (1952) 166f. KUHL, J. Die Sendung Jesu und der Kirche nach dem Johannes-Evangelium (1967) 71, 82, 161, 165, 209, 214. NICKELS, P. Targum and New Testament (1967) 53. LATTKE, M., Einheit im Wort. Die spezifische Bedeutung von "agape," "agapan" und "filein" im Johannes-Evangelium (München 1975) 12, 80-81, 83-84. KLIJN, A. F., "Die syrische Baruch-Apokalypse" in: JüdSchr V/2 (1976) 134n.2a.

3:20-21 BROWN, R. E., "The Qumran Scrolls and the Johannine Gospel and Epistles" in: K. Stendahl (ed.) The Scrolls and the New Testament (New York 1957) 197; [orig. in CBQ 17 (1955) 403-19, 559-74]; GT: "Die Schriftrollen von Qumran und das Johannesevangelium und die Johannesbriefe" in: K. H. Rengstorf (ed.) Johannes und sein Evangelium (Darmstadt 1973) 511. HODGES, Z. C., "Problem Passages in the Gospel of John. Part 4: Coming to the Light — John 3:20-21" BiblSa 135 (1978) 314-22.

3:20 GEORGI, D., "Weisheit Salomos" in: JüdSchr III/4 (1980) 2n.14a. PAINTER, J., "The Farewell Discourses and the History of Johannine Christianity" NTS 27 (1980-1981) 538.

3:21 VOLZ, P. Die Eschatologie der jüdischen Gemeinde (1934) 366. BARRETT, C. K. The New Testament Background (1956) 222. LAZURE, N., Les Valeurs Morales de la Théologie Johannique (Paris 1965) 80-81. de la POTTERIE, I., La Vérité dans Saint Jean I/II (Rome 1977) 486-520, 530-35.

3:22-4:42 FARRER, A. St Matthew and St Mark (1954) 54.

3:22-4:3 LINDIJER, C. H. De Sacramenten in het Vierde Evangelie (1964) 63f. WINK, W. John the Baptist in the Gospel Tradition (1968) 93-95, 98-99. JEREMIAS, J. Neutestamentliche Theologie I (1971) 52f. JEWETT, P. K., Infant Baptism and the Covenant of Grace (Grand Rapids 1978) 66.

3:22-4:1 GOULDER, M. D., "The Apocalypse as an Annual Cycle of Prophecies" NTS 27 (1980-1981) 372.

3:22ff. KNOX, W. L. The Sources of the Synoptic Gospels II (1957) 145. RUDOLPH, K. Die Mandäer I (1960) 77, 232. BEASLEY-MURRAY, G. R. Baptism in the New Testament (1962) 67ff. LENTZEN-DEIS, F. Die Taufe Jesu nach den Synoptikern (1970) 78.

3:22-36 GRILL, J. Untersuchungen über die Entstehung des vierten Evangeliums II (1923) 63f., 360, 367, 383. CULLMANN, O. Urchristentum und Gottesdienst (1950) 60, 80f. ROBINSON, J. A. T. "The One Baptism," in: Twelve New Testament Studies (1962) 158-75. VAN DEN BUSSCHE, H. "Les paroles de Dieu. Jean 3,22-36," BVieC 55 (1964) 23-28. BIEDER, W., Die Verheissung der Taufe im Neuen Testament (Zürich 1966) 269-70. OLSSON, B., Structure and Meaning in the Fourth Gospel (Lund 1974) 27-29. 54, 125, 128, 133-36, 138, 159, 161-62, 172, 209, 233, 239, 251, 255, 277. TEMPLE, S., The Core of the Fourth Gospel (London 1975) 104-11. HAENCHEN, E., Das Johannesevangelium (Tübingen 1980) 230 (lit!.). WILSON, J., "The Integrity of John 3:22-36" JSNT 10 (1981) 34-41.

3:22-30 WILKENS, W. Die Entstehungsgeschichte des vierten Evangeliums (1958) 127-29. van den BUSSCHE, H., "La Structure de Jean I-XII" in: M. Boismard et al., L'Evangile de Jean: études et problèmes (Bruges 1958) 84-85. GILMORE, A. Christian Baptism (1959) 151f. BOISMARD, M. E. "Les traditions johanniques concernant le Baptiste," RB 70 (1963) 5, 42. DEEKS, D. "The Structure of the Fourth Gospel," NTS 15 (1968-1969) 114ff. BATEY, R. A. New Testament Nuptial Imagery (1971) 47-50. BEUTLER, J. Martyria (1972) 217, 286, 313f., 352. SCHNIDER, F. Jesus der Prophet (1974) 39, 48f. PORSCH, F., Pneuma und Wort (Frankfurt 1973) 87-89. LANGBRANDTNER, W., Weltferner Gott oder Gott der Liebe (Frankfurt a.M./Bern/Las Vegas 1977) 76-79. TRITES, A. A., The New Testament Concept of Witness (Cambridge 1977) 97-98. BECKER, J., Das Evangelium nach Johannes (Gütersloh/Würzburg 1979) 152 (lit!.).

3:22-26 LEGASSE, S., "Le Baptême administré par Jesus (Jn 3,22-26; 4,1-3) et l'origine du baptême chrétien" BLE 78 (1977) 3-30.

3:22 GRILL, J. Untersuchungen über die Entstehung des vierten Evangeliums II (1923) 63f., 360, 367, 383. RUCKSTUHL, E. Die literarische Einheit des Johannesevangeliums (1951) 173, 174, 175. FLEW, R. N. Jesus and His Church (1956) 119. DELLING, G. Die Taufe im Neuen Testament (1963) 57.

STROBEL, A. Erkenntnis und Bekenntnis der Sünde in neutestamentlicher Zeit (1968) 57. DAVIES, W. D. The Gospel and the Land (1974) 323, 325, 329, 329 n.83. OLSSON, B., Structure and Meaning in the Fourth Gospel (Lund 1974) 23, 26, 53, 125-26, 134-35, 149, 156. JEWETT, P. K., Infant Baptism and the Covenant of Grace (Grand Rapids 1978) 233.

3:23-24 FORTNA, R. T. The Gospel of Signs (1970) 161-89.

3:23 DELLING, G. Die Taufe im Neuen Testament (1963) 48, 57. BRAUN, H. Qumran und NT II (1966) 16. BOISMARD, M.-E. "Aenon, près de Salem (Jean, III,23)," RevBi 80 (2, 1973) 218-29. CRIBBS, F. L. in: SBL Seminar Papers 2 (1973) G. MacRae ed., 3. OLSSON, B., Structure and Meaning in the Fourth Gospel (Lund 1974) 30, 53-54, 135-37, 154, 197, 261-62.

3:24 FEINE, D. P./BEHM, D. J. Einleitung in das Neue Testament (1950) 113ff.

3:25-36 CADMAN, W. H. The Open Heaven (1969) G. B. Caird ed., 71-73.

3:25-26 MOLONEY, F. J., "From Cana to Cana (John 2:1-4:54) and the Fourth Evangelist's Concept of Correct (and Incorrect) Faith" in: E. A. Livingstone (ed.) Studia Biblica 1978/II (Sheffield 1980) 194-95.

3:25 PALLIS,, A., Notes on St. John and the Apocalypse (London 1928) 5-7. OLSSON, B., Structure and Meaning in the Fourth Gospel (Lund 1974) 25, 51, 125, 135-37, 157. WAHLDE, U. C., "The Johannine 'Jews': A Critical Survey" NTS 28 (1982) 49-50.

3:26 HAHN, F. Christologische Hoheitstitel (1963) 75, 380. BEUTLER, J. Martyria (1972) 23, 220f., 252, 281, 285f., 311. OLSSON, B., Structure and Meaning in the Fourth Gospel (Lund 1974) 28-29, 53, 126, 135-37, 220, 239. BERGMEIER, R., Glaube als Gabe nach Johannes (Stuttgart 1980) 238n.39.

3:27-36 BLACK, M. An Aramaic Approach to the Gospels and Acts (1967) 146f.

3:27-30 TEMPLE, S., The Core of the Fourth Gospel (London 1975) 109-11.

3:27 KNOX, W. L. The Sources of the Synoptic Gospels II (1957) 91. NICKELS, P. Targum and New Testament (1967) 53. BERGMEIER, R., Glaube als Gabe nach Johannes (Stuttgart 1980) 215, 242n.117.

3:28.32 HAHN, F. Das Verständnis der Mission im Neuen Testament (1965²) 140.

3:28 RUDOLPH, K. Die Mandäer I (1960) 77. HAHN, F. Christologische Hoheitstitel (1963) 380. BEUTLER, J. Martyria (1972) 216f., 242. CRIBBS, F. L., "The Agreements that Exist Between John and Acts" in: C. H. Talbert (ed.) Perspectives on Luke-Acts (Danville 1978) 47-48.

3:29 GRILL, J. Untersuchungen über die Entstehung des vierten Evangeliums II (1923) 64, 74, 81f., 110. BROWNLEE, W. H. "Messianic Motifs of Qumran and the New Testament," NTS 3 (1956-1957) 206. WILES, M. F. The Spiritual Gospel (1960) 38-39. WAINWRIGHT, A. W. The Trinity in the New Testament (1962) 91-92. KAESEMANN, E. Exegetische Versuche und Besinnungen (1964) I 249. BRAUN, H. Qumran und NT II (1966) 318. NICKELS, P. Targum and New Testament (1967) 53. HUNTER, A. M. According to John (1970²) 78f.

3:30 MEHLMANN, J. "E Preciso Que Aquêle Cresça E Eu Diminua (Jo 3,30)," RCT 3 (2, 1963) 85-105.

3:31-36 BLANK, J. Krisis (1964) 63. KUHL, J. Die Sendung Jesu und der Kirche nach dem Johannes-Evangelium (1967) 66-69, 81. QUERVAIN, A. de, in: Hören und Fragen Bd. 5,3 (1967) G. Eichholz/A. Falkenroth eds., 51ff. WEBER, O. Predigtmeditationen (1967) 175-78. DUNN, J. D. G. Baptism in the Holy Spirit (1970) 19f. LANGE, E. ed., Predigtstudien (1970) 56-66. LOEWE, H. GPM 25 (4, 1970) 45-50. BEUTLER, J. Martyria (1972) 36, 217ff., 227f., 281, 307, 308, 310, 313ff., 324, 326f., 336, 356, 366. PORSCH, F., Pneuma und Wort (Frankfurt 1974) 85-89, 101-105. ADOLPHSEN, H. und KNUTH, H.-S., in: P. Krusche et al. (eds.) Predigtstudien für das Kirchenjahr 1976-1977. V/1 (Stuttgart 1976) 47-53. SCHMITHALS, W., in: GPM 31 (1976) 37-42. de JONGE, M., Jesus: Stranger from Heaven and Son of God (Missoula 1977) 37-42. LANGBRANDTNER, W., Weltferner Gott oder Gott der Liebe (Frankfurt 1977) 21-23, 24. BECKER, J., Das Evangelium nach Johannes (Gütersloh/Würzburg 1979) 156 (lit!). BERGMEIER, R., Glaube als Gabe nach Johannes (Stuttgart 1980) 212, 220-21, 246-47n.191. SCHILLEBEECKX, E., Christ: the Christian Experience in the Modern World (London 1980) 323-24, 325-28; GT: Christus und die Christen (Freiburg/Basel/Wien 1977) 310-11, 312-15. NEYREY, J. H., "John III — A Debate over Johannine Epistemology and Christology" NovT 23 (1981) 123-24. CASPARY, H.-N. und KUHLI, H., in: P. Krusche et al. (eds.) Predigtstudien für das Kirchenjahr 1982-1983. V/1 (Stuttgart 1982) 50-61.

3:31-35 IBUKI,Y. Die Wahrheit im Johannesevangelium (1972) 144-155, 263f.

3:31-32 ALAND, K. NTS 12 (1965-1966) 19ff. KUHL, J. Die Sendung Jesu und der Kirche nach dem Johannes-Evangelium (1967) 60, 71, 75, 79, 89, 92, 177, 190.

3:31.33.35 DELLING, Die Taufe im Neuent Testament (1963) 90, 94, 105.

3:31.34 ORIGENES, Das Evangelium nach Johannes (1959) R. Gögler ed., 241-42.

3:31 RUCKSTUHL, E. Die literarische Einheit des Johannesevangeliums (1951) 17, 44, 46, 69, 77, 146. KNOX, W. L. The Sources of the Synoptic Gospels II (1957) 91. WILES, M. F. The Spiritual Gospel (1960) 76-78. KUEMMEL, W. G., Römer 7 und das Bild des Menschen im Neuen Testament (1974) 203. SCHMITHALS, W., "Zur Herkunft der gnostischen Elemente in der Sprache des Paulus" in: B. Aland (ed.) Gnosis FS. H. Jonas (Göttingen 1978) 403. BERGMEIER, R., Glaube als Gabe nach Johannes (Stuttgart 1980) 176n.526, 220ff., 242n.117, 248n.212.

3:32-35 BÜHNER, J.-A., Der Gesandte und sein Weg im 4. Evangelium (Tübingen 1977) 402-403.

3:32-34 RAYAN, S., The Holy Spirit: Heart of the Gospel and Christian Hope (New York 1978) 84.

3:32 DELLING, G. Wort und Werk Jesu im Johannes-Evangelium (1966) 35, 37, 47-49. BERGMEIER, R., Glaube als Gabe nach Johannes (Stuttgart 1980) 255n.339.

3:33 PALLIS, A., Notes on St. John and the Apocalypse (London 1928) 7.

3:34-35 THUESING, W. Die Erhöhung und Verherrlichung Jesu im Johannesevangelium (1970) 153-56. BEIERWALTES, W., "Deus est veritas" in: E. Dassmann/K. S. Frank (eds.) Pietas. FS. B. Kötting (Münster 1980) 23-24.

3:34 FLEW, R. N. Jesus and His Church (1956) 173. GOLUB, J. " . . . non enim ad mensuram dat Spiritum (Jo 3,34b)," VerbDom 43 (2, 1965) 62-70. METZGER, B. M. "Explicit references in the works of Origen to variant readings in New Testament manuscripts," in: Historical and Literary Studies (1968) 97. CADMAN, W. H. The Open Heaven (1969) 6, 8, 65, 105, 115. DUNN, J. D. G. Baptism in the Holy Spirit (1970) 20, 29n, 32, 33, 198. JOHNSTON, G. The Spirit-Paraclete in the gospel of John (1970) 13-15. DAUER, A. Die Passionsgeschichte im Johannesevangelium (1972) 248, 259, 288. PORSCH, F., Pneuma und Wort (Frankfurt 1974) 103-105. BÜHNER, J.-A., Der Gesandte und sein Weg im 4. Evangelium (Tübingen 1977) 109-10. CLARK, K. W., "The Text of the Gospel of John in Third-Century Egypt'' in: The Gentile Bias and other Essays (Leiden 1980) 161-62. DUNN, J. D., Christology in the Making (London 1980) 141.

3:35-36 SCHULZ, S., Untersuchungen zur Menschensohn-Christologie im Johannesevangelium (Göttingen 1957) 125-27. DELLING, G. Wort und Werk Jesu im Johannes-Evangelium (1966) 101-104. BECKER, J., Auferstehung der Toten im Urchristentum (Stuttgart 1976) 120-28. ''Agende'' in: TRE 2, 1978) 3.

3:35 DUPONT, J. Esais sur la Christologie de Saint Jean (1951) 176, 200, 288, 289. STRECKER, G. Der Weg der Gerechtigkeit (1962) 209n2. HAHN, F. Christologische Hoheitstitel (1963) 329. GRUNDMANN, W. NTS 12 (1965-1966) 43f. CADMAN, W. H. The Open Heaven (1969) G. B. Caird ed., 16, 98, 119, 180. CHRIST, F. Jesus Sophia (1970) 86, 87, 88. LADD, G. E. A Theology of the New Testament (1974) 248, 259, 288. LATTKE, M., Einheit im Wort. Die spezifische Bedeutung von ''Agape,'' ''agapan'' und ''filein'' im Johannes-Evangelium (München 1975) 13, 19, 86-95. BÜHNER, J.-A., Der Gesandte und sein Weg im 4. Evangelium (Tübingen 1977) 198-99. GEORGI, D., ''Weisheit Salomos'' in: JüdSchr III/4 (1980) 8n.3b.

3:36 MORRIS, L. The Apostolic Preaching of the Cross (1955) 163f. HAHN, F. Christologische Hoheitstitel (1963) 329f. BRAUN, H. Qumran und NT II (1966) 135, 270, 283. HEISE, J. Bleiben (1967) 57-60. DAUER, A. Die Passionsgeschichte im Johannesevangelium (1972) 257, 260, 289. LADD, G. E. A Theology of the New Testament (1974) 216, 229, 232, 256, 279. LOHSE, E. Grundriss der neutestamentlichen Theologie (1974) 136f. BERGMEIER, R., Glaube als Gabe nach Johannes (Stuttgart 1980) 40n.218, 211, 233. LINDARS, B., ''John and the Synoptic Gospels: A Test Case'' NTS 27 (1980-1981) 292. ''Dordrechter Synode'' in: TRE 9 (1982) 141.

_____

4-5.9 HOSKINS, E. C. The Fourth Gospel (1947) 363-65.

4 VON LOEWENICH, W. Das Johannes-Verständnis im zweiten Jahrhundert (1932) 68, 85-92, 93, 94, 136. SCHWEIZER, E., Ego Eimi (Göttingen 1939) 161-66. GRAF, E. ''Theology

at Jacob's Well. Chapters from the Gospel of St. John,'' HPR 59 (12, 1959) 1099-1104. BALAGUE, M. ''Hacia la religion del espiritu,'' CultBib 18 (178, 1961) 151-66. DELLING, G. Die Taufe im Neuen Testament (1963) 92. GLASSON, T. F. Moses in the Fourth Gospel (1963) 53ff., 89, 91, BRAUN, H. Qumran und NT II (1966) 116. FEE, D. G. ''Codex Sinaiticus in the Gospel of John: A Contribution to Methodology in establishing textual Relationships,'' NTS 15 (1968-1969) 29ff. LOHSE, E. et al., eds., Der Ruf Jesu und die Antwort der Gemeinde (1970) 121-23. KIPPENBERG, H. G. Garizim und Synagoge (1971) 115f., passim. BONNEUA, N. R. ''The Woman at the Well. John 4 and Genesis 24,'' BibToday 67 (1973) 1252-59. DAVIES, W. D. The Gospel and the Land (1974) 296-99 passim, 305-12, 324, 327, 342. KING, J. S., ''Sychar and Calvary. A Neglected Theory in the Interpretation of the Fourth Gospel'' Th 77 (1974) 417-22. OLSSON, B., Structure and Meaning in the Fourth Gospel (Lund 1974) 34, 54, 60, 67, 80, 93, 112, 115-257, 259-61, 277-80, 284, 287-88. CULLMANN, O., Der johanneische Kreis (Tübingen 1975) 16, 47, 51, 52, 55, 58, 93.

4:1ff HAHN, F. Das Verständnis der Mission im Neuen Testament (1965²) 23, 50, 64f. THYEN, H. Studien zur Sündenvergebung (1970) 142f., 146.

4:1-47 BRAUN, F.-M. Jean le Théologien (1966) 103-107.

4:1-45 DEEKS, D. ''The Structure of the Fourth Gospel,'' NTS 15 (1968-1969) 125ff. MARSHALL, I. H., ''The Problem of New Testament Exegesis'' JEThS 17 (1974) 67-73. TEMPLE, S. The Core of the Fourth Gospel (London 1975) 111-19. HUDRY-CLERGEON, L., ''De Judée en Galilée. Étude de Jean 4, 1-45'' NRTh 103 (1981) 818-30.

4:1-42 TAYLOR, V. The Formation of the Gospel Tradition (1949) 163f. RUCKSTUHL, E. Die literarische Einheit des Johannesevangeliums (1951) 110, 113-17. DEHN, G. Jesus und die Samarither (1956). ROUSTANG, F. ''Les moments de l'Acte de Foi et ses conditions de possibilité. Essai d'interprétation du dialogue avec la Samaritaine,'' RechSR 46 (3, 1958) 344-78. van den BUSSCHE, H., ''La Structure de Jean I-XII'' in: M. Boismard et al., L'Evangile de Jean: études et problèmes (Bruges 1958) 85-87. GRUNDMANN, W. ''Verständnis und Bewegung des Glaubens im Johannes-Evangelium,'' KuD 6 (1960) 146ff. STANLEY, D. M. ''Interlude samaritain,'' BibTerre-Sainte 28 (1960) 2-3. WILES, M. F. The Spiritual Gospel (1960) 45-49, 60. BLIGH, J. ''Jesus in Samaria,'' HeyJ 3 (4, 1962) 329-46. PRETE, B. ''La Samaritana (Giov. 4,1-42),'' SaDo 9

(34, 1964) 252-68. YATES, K. M. Preaching from John's Gospel (1964) 38-46, SMITH, D. M. The Composition and Order of the Fourth Gospel (1965) 34, 35, 36, 51, 66, 111n., 215n., 227. BIEDER, W., Die Verheissung der Taufe im Neuen Testament (Zürich 1966) 270-71. NICOL, W. The Semeia in the Fourth Gospel (1972) 40, 61, 78f., 92, 102. SCHNIDER, F. Jesus der Prophet (1973) 173, 191, 203, 238. MUELLER, T. Das Heilsgeschehen im Johannesevangelium n.d., 29-31. HOGAN, M. P., "The Woman at the Well (John 4:1-42)" BiTod 82 (1976) 663-69. TRITES, A. A., The New Testament Concept of Witness (Cambridge 1977) 98-99. de VRIES, E., "Johannes 4:1-42. In geest en hoofdzaak" GThT 78 (1978) 93-114. BECKER, J., Das Evangelium nach Johannes (Gütersloh/ Würzburg 1979) 165 (lit!). BROWN, R. E., The Community of the Beloved Disciple (London 1979) 187-89. SWIDLER, L., Biblical Affirmations of Woman (Philadelphia 1979) 192. CARMICHAEL, C. M., "Marriage and the Samaritan Woman" NTS 26 (1980) 332-46, HAENCHEN, E., Das Johannesevangelium (Tübingen 1980) 236-37 (lit!). LEIDIG, E., Jesu Gespräch mit der Samaritanerin (Basel 1981) 1-160, 190-207. CAHILL, P. J., "Narrative Art in John IV" Religious Studies Bulletin 2 (1982) 41-48. CHAPPUIS, J.-M., "Jesus and the Samaritan Woman. The Variable Geometry of Communication" EcumRev 34 (1982) 8-34.

4:1-40 REIM, G., Studien zum Alttestamentlichen Hintergrund des Johannesevangeliums (Cambridge 1974) 106-107. MEIS, A., "Problematica de la Carismatica Neotestamentaria" TyV 17 (1976) 193-208. LÉGASSE, S., "Le Baptême administré par Jésus (Jn 3,22-26; 4:1-3) et l'origine du Baptême chrétien" BLE 78 (1977) 3-30. METZGER, B. M., The Early Versions of the New Testament (Oxford 1977) 248. de JONGE, M., Jesus: Stranger from Heaven and Son of God (Missoula 1977) 63-66, 102-106. van UNNIK, W. C., "A Greek Characteristic of Prophecy in the Fourth Gospel"1 in: E. Best/R. McL. Wilson (eds.) Text and Interpretation. FS. M. Black (Cambridge 1979) 211-29.

4:1-30 CULLMANN, O. Urchristentum und Gottesdienst (1950) 82ff.

4:1-14 MORGAN, G. C. The Parables and Metaphors of Our Lord (1943) 278ff. CORELL, A. Consummatum Est (1956) 60-62.

4:1-3 GILMORE, A. Christian Baptism (1959) 151ff. QUISPEL, G. "Qumran, John and Jewish Christianity," in: John and Qumran (1972) J. H. Charlesworth ed., 141-42.

4:1.3.44-45 WILKENS, W. Die Entstehungsgeschichte des vierten Evangeliums (1958) 127, 128, 129, 130.

4:1-2 FLEW, R. N. Jesus and His Church (1956) 119. DELLING, G. Die Taufe im Neuen Testament (1963) 57.

4:1 RUCKSTUHL, E. Die literarische Einheit des Johannesevangeliums (1951) 173f., 177. HAHN, F. Christologische Hoheitstitel (1963) 94. STROBEL, A. Erkenntnis und Bekenntnis der Sünde in neutestamenticher Zeit (1968) 67.

4:2 RUDOLPH, K. Die Mandäer I (1960) 77.

4:3 HEUSS, J. '' 'Presbyter Ammonius' Kommentar zum Jo-Evangelium,'' Biblica 44 (1963) 162-63.

4:4-42 LINDIJER, C. H. De Sacramenten in het Vierde Evangelie (1964) 65f. FRIEDRICH, G. Wer ist Jesus? (1967). FORTNA, R. T. The Gospel of Signs (1970) 189-93.

4:4-26 ODEBERG, H. The Fourth Gospel (1968) 173ff. VOUGA, F., Le cadre historique et l'intention théologique de Jean (Paris 1977) 24-32. VELLANICAL, M., "Drink from the Source of the Living Water," BB 5 (1979) 309-18.

4:4-6 TEMPLE, S., The Core of the Fourth Gospel (London 1975) 113-15. VOUGA, F., Le cadre historique et l'intention théologique de Jean (Paris 1977) 26-27.

4:5-42 SWIDLER, L., Biblical Affirmations of Woman (Philadelphia 1979) 220, 223.

4:5-26 BAUER, W. Das Johannesevangelium (1925) 72f.

4:5-15 IWAND, H.-J. Predigt-Meditationen (1964) 290-93. SCHOTTROFF, L. "Johannes 4:5-15 und die Konsequenzen des johanneischen Dualismus," ZNW 60 (3-4, 1969) 199-214.

4:5-14 DIEM, H. in: Herr, tue meine Lippen auf Bd. 3 (1964) G. Eichholz ed., 87ff. STECK, K. G. GPM 23 (1, 1968) 82-90.

4:5-6 SCHENKE, H.-M. "Jacobsbrunnen-Josephsgrab-Sychar. Topographische Untersuchungen und Erwägungen in der Perspektive von Joh. 4,5.6." ZDPV 84 (2, 1968) 159-84.

4:5 METZGER, B. M. The Early Versions of the New Testament (Oxford 1977) 172. BERGER, K., "Das Buch der Jubiläen" in: JüdSchr II/3 (1981) 492n4h.

4:6ff STURCH, R. L., "The Alleged Eyewitness Material in the Fourth Gospel" in: E. A. Livingstone (ed.) Studia Biblica 1978/II (Sheffield 1980) 317-18.

4:6-15 BRAUN, F.-M. Jean le Théologien (1966) 90-92.

4:6 PALLIS, A., Notes on St. John and the Apocalypse (London 1928) 8.BRUNS, J. E. NTS 13 (1966-1967) 386ff. BISHOP, F. F. E. "Constantly on the Road," EQ 41 (1, 1969) 14-18.

4:7ff STROBEL, A. Erkenntnis und Bekenntnis der Sünde in neutestamentlicher Zeit (1968) 60.

4:7-42 PAGELS, E. H. The Johannine Gospel in Gnostic Exegesis (1973) 83-86. FARICY, R., Praying for Inner Healing (London 1979) 15-16.

4:7-26 PORSCH, F., Pneuma und Wort (Frankfurt 1974) 137-39. VELLANICKAL, M., "Drink from the Source of the Living Water" BB 5 (1979) 309-18.

4:7-15 ODEBERG, H. The Fourth Gospel (1968) 149-69. MOLO-NEY, F. J., "From Cana to Cana (John 2:1-4:54) and the Fourth Evangelist's Concept of Correct (and Incorrect) Faith" in: E. A. Livingstone (ed.) Studia Biblica 1978/II (Sheffield 1980) 196-97.

4:7-10 VOUGA, F., Le cadre historique et l'intention théologique de Jean (Paris 1977) 27-28.

4:8-15 WEAD, D. W. The Literary Devices in John's Gospel (1970) 86-87.

4:9 BUECHSEL, F. Das Evangelium nach Johannes (1946) 61f. RUCKSTUHL, E. Die literarische Einheit des Johannes-evangeliums (1951) 84, 175f. HENNECKE, E./SCHNEE-MELCHER, W. Neutestamentliche Apokryphen (1964) II 14. ALAND, K. NTS 12 (1965-1966) 199f. BOUSSET, W. Die Religion des Judentums im Späthellenistischen Zeitalter (1966 = 1926) 87. KILPATRICK, G. D. "John 4:9," JBL 87 (3, 1968) 327-28. HALL, D. R. "The Meaning of sygchraomai in John 4:9," ET 83 (2, 1971) 56-57. METZGER, B. M., The Early Versions of the New Testament (Oxford 1977) 41. RAYAN, S., The Holy Spirit: Heart of the Gospel and Christian Hope (New York 1978) 54-55.

4:10ff IBUKI, Y. Die Wahrheit im Johannesevangelium (1972) 317ff.

4:10-26 NEYREY, J. A. "Jacob Traditions and the Interpretation of John 4:10-26" CBQ 41 (1979) 419-37.

4:10-15 LEROY, H. Rätsel und Missverständnis (1968) 88-99. PORSCH, F., Pneuma und Wort (Frankfurt 1974) 139-45. PANCARO, S., The Law in the Fourth Gospel (Leiden 1975) 359, 453, 473-85. BERGMEIER, R., Glaube als Gabe nach Johannes (Stuttgart 1980) 270n.556.

4:10-14 BRAUN, H. Qumran und NT II (1966) 129, 133, 191, 253. SMITH, M. Tannaitic Parallels to the Gospels (1968) 8 b n 10. BRAUN, F.-M. "Avoir soif et boire (Jn 4,10-14; 7,37-39)," in: Mélanges Bibliques en hommage au R. P. Béda Rigaux (1970) A. Descamps/A. de Halleux eds., 247-58. DUNN, J. D.

G. Baptism in the Holy Spirit (1970) 180, 187. HAHN, F. "Die Worte vom lebendigen Wasser im Johannesevangelium. Eigenart und Vorgeschichte von Joh 4:10,13-14,6:35,7:37-39" in: J. Jerwell/W. A. Meeks (eds.) God's Christ and His People. FS. N. A. Dahl (New York 1977) 51-70. RAYAN, S., The Holy Spirit: Heart of the Gospel and Christian Hope (New York 1978) 115-16.

4:10-11   RUDOLPH, K. Die Mandäer I (1960) 232. NÖTSCHER, F., Altorientalischer und alttestamentlicher Auferstehungsglaube (Darmstadt 1970 = 1926) 322-23. BERGMEIER, R., Glaube als Gabe nach Johannes (Stuttgart 1980) 207.

4:10   BARRETT, C. K. The New Testament Background (1956) 89. RUDOLPH, K. Die Mandäer II (1961) 387. MacGREGOR, G. H. C. "The Eucharist in the 4th Gospel," NTS 9 (1962-1963) 111f. GAERTNER, B. The Temple and the Community in Qumran and the New Testament (1965) 75. METZGER, B. M., The Early Versions of the New Testament (Oxford 1977) 255. FRICKEL, J., "Naassener oder Valentinianer?" in: M. Krause (ed.) Gnosis and Gnosticism (Leiden 1981) 115-16.

4:11-15   VOUGA, F., Le cadre historique et l'intention théologique de Jean (Paris 1977) 28-29.

4:11-12   BAGATTI, B. "Nuovi apporti archeologici sul pozzo di Giacobbe in Samaria," SBFLA 16 (1965-1966) 127-64.

4:11   HAHN, F. Christologische Hoheitstitel (1963) 94.

4:12.20ff   KAESEMANN, E. Exegetische Versuche und Besinnungen (1964) I 181.

4:12   NICKELS, P. Targum and New Testament (1967) 54. BERGMEIER, R., Glaube als Gabe nach Johannes (Stuttgart 1980) 215, 242n.118.

4:13-16.19-20   ORIGENES, Das Evangelium nach Johannes (1959) R. Gögler ed., 243-55.

4:13-14   BERGMEIER, R., Glaube als Gabe nach Johannes (Stuttgart 1980) 207.

4:14   BAUER, W. Das Johannesevangelium (1925) 65. DUPONT, J. Essais sur la Christologie de Saint Jean (1951) 193, 203, 204. BROWN, R. E., "The Qumran Scrolls and the Johannine Gospel and Epistles" in: K. Stendahl (ed.) The Scrolls and the New Testament (New York 1957) 200, [orig. in: CBQ 17 (1955) 403-19, 559-74]; GT: Die Schriftrollen von Qumran und das Johannesevangelium und die Johannesbriefe" in: K. H. Rengstorf (ed.) Johannes und sein Evangelium (Darmstadt 1973) 511. RUDOLPH, K. Die Mandäer I (1960) 232; II (1961) 127. DEL-

LING, G. Die Taufe im Neuen Testament (1963) 92. GAERT-NER, B. The Temple and the Community in Qumran and the New Testament (1965) 119. DELLING, G. Wort und Werk Jesu im Johannes-Evangelium (1966) 119, 143f. McNAMARA, M. The New Testament and the Palestinian Targum to the Pentateuch (1966) 149. LADD, G. E., A Theology of the New Testament (1974) 252, 257, 284, 289. BRUCE, F. F., The Time is Fulfilled (Exeter 1978) 44-46. BÖHLIG, A., Die Gnosis III: Der Manichäismus (Zürich/München 1980) 343n.28. FRICKEL, J., "Naassener oder Valentinianer?" in: M. Krause (ed.) Gnosis and Gnosticism (Leiden 1981) 115-16.

4:15 HAHN, F. Christologische Hoheitstitel (1963) 94. NICKELS, P. Targum and New Testament (1967) 54.

4:16-26 DAVIES, W. D. The Gospel and the Land (1974) 300-301. MOLONEY, F. J., "From Cana to Cana (John 2:1-4:54) and the Fourth Evangelist's Concept of Correct (and Incorrect) Faith" in: E. A. Livingstone (ed.) Studia Biblica 1978/II (Sheffield 1980) 197-98.

4:16-19 FORTNA, R. T. The Gospel of Signs (1970) 190f. BERGMEIER, R., Glaube als Gabe nach Johannes (Stuttgart 1980) 270n.556.

4:16-18 VOUGA, F., Le cadre historique et l'intention théologique de Jean (Paris 1977) 29-30.

4:17-18 STROBEL, A. Erkenntnis und Bekenntnis der Sünde in neutestamentlicher Zeit (1968) 46.

4:19ff HAHN, F. Das Verständnis der Mission im Neuen Testament (1965²) 64. SCHNACKENBURG, R. Christliche Existenz nach dem Neuen Testament (1968) 75-96.

4:19-30.39-42 SOUCEK, J. B. GPM 17 (1, 1963) 224-27. HAAR, J. GPM 23 (2, 1968) 222-28. HARDER, G. GPM 29 (2, 1975) 272ff. RUDDAT, G./SCHROER, H. "Johannes 4,19-30.39-42: Offenbarung durch Erfahrung," in: Predigtstudien (1975) P. Krusche/E. Lange/D. Rössler/R. Roessler eds., 83-92.

4:19-30 HARDER, G., in: GPM 29 (1975) 272-80.

4:19-26 VOUGA, F., Le cadre historique et l'intention théologique de Jean (Paris 1977) 30-31.

4:19 HAHN, F. Christologische Hoheitstitel (1963) 94, 397. ODEBERG, H. The Fourth Gospel (1968) 169-73. IBUKI, Y. Die Wahrheit im Johannesevangelium (1972) 319f. SCHNIDER, F. Jesus der Prophet (1973) 121, 205, 223ff. REIM, G., Studien zum Alttestamentlichen Hintergrund des Johannesevangeliums (Cambridge 1974) 120-21.

4:20-26　HAACKER, K. Die Stiftung des Heils (1972) 42-48. PORSCH, F. Pneuma und Wort (Frankfurt 1974) 145-60. BERGMEIER, R., Glaube als Gabe nach Johannes (Stuttgart 1980) 270n.556.

4:20-24　GRILL, J. Untersuchungen über die Entstehung des vierten Evangeliums II (1923) 77f., 244, 392.

4:20　BULL, R. J., "An Archaeological Context for Understanding John 4:20" BA 38 (1975) 54-59. BULL, R. J., An Archaeological Footnote to 'Our Fathers worshipped on this Mountain', John iv. 20" NTS 23 (1977) 460-62. BERGMEIER, R., Glaube als Gabe nach Johannes (Stuttgart 1980) 242n.118.

4:21ff　SEIDENSTICKER, P. Lebendiges Opfer (1954) 125ff. GAERTNER, B. The Temple and the Community in Qumran and the New Testament (1965) 108.

4:21-30　MOULE, C. F. D., The Holy Spirit (London 1978) 38.

4:21-26　WESTEMEYER, D., " 'Weder auf diesem Berge noch in Jerusalem'. Zu Joh 4,21-26" Dienender Glaube 51 (1975) 184-90.

4:22　RUCKSTUHL, E. Die literarische Einheit des Johannesevangeliums (1951) 175f. BESNARD, P. " 'Vous adorez ce que vous ne connaissez pas'," BibTerreSainte 28 (1960) 3. HAHN, F. Das Verständnis der Mission im Neuen Testament (1965²) 65, 138. SMITH, D. M. The Composition and Order of the Fourth Gospel (1965) 224, 233f., 234. HAACKER, K., "Gottesdienst ohne Gotteserkenntnis. Joh 4,22 vor dem Hintergrund der jüdisch-samaritanischen Auseinandersetzung" in: B. Benzing et al. (eds.) Wort und Wirklichkeit. FS. E. Rapp (Meisenheim am Glan 1976) 110-26. HAHN, F., " 'Das Heil kommt von den Juden'. Erwägungen zu Joh 4,22b" in: B. Benzing et al. (eds.) Wort und Wirklichkeit. FS. E. Rapp (Meisenheim am Glan 1976) 66-84. MUSSNER, F., "Eine christliche Theologie des Judentums. Ein Angebot zur Verständigung" in: P. Lapide et al., Was Juden und Christen voneinander denken (Basel/Freiburg/Wien 1978) 55-57. THYEN, H., " 'Das Heil kommt von den Juden' " in: D. Lührmann/G. Strecker (eds.) Kirche. FS. G. Bornkamm (Tübingen 1980) 163-84.

4:23-24　BUECHSEL, D. F. Der Geist Gottes im Neuen Testament (1926) 501-502, 504-505. MYERS, J. M./REIMHERR, O./ BREAM, H. N. Search the Scriptures (1969) 33-48. JOHNSTON, G. The Spirit-Paraclete in the gospel of John (1970) 43-47, 70. IBUKI, Y. Die Wahrheit im Johannesevangelium (1972) 311-15. PORSCH, F., Pneuma und Wort (Frankfurt 1974) 137-60. LEON, D. M., "Adoracion en espiritu y verdad. Aportacion targumica a la inteligencia de Jn 4,23.24" in: Homenaje a

Juan Prado (Madrid 1975) 387-403. DUNN, J. D. G., Unity and Diversity in the New Testament (London 1977) 131, 353-54. de la POTTERIE, I., La Vérité dans Saint Jean I/II (Rome 1977) 673-706. DAY, R. J., Christian Sacrifice (Washington D.C. 1978) 287-90. "Benediktionen" in: TRE 5 (1980) 569.

4:23.25 BRAUN, H. Qumran und NT II (1966) 79, 133, 183, 263f.

4:23 GRONKOWSKI, W. "In spiritu et veritate (Joh 4,23)," RBL 7 (1954) 194-204. SCHNACKENBURG, R. "Die 'Anbetung in Geist und Wahrheit' (Joh 4:23) im Lichte von Qumran-Texten," BZ 3 (1, 1959) 88-94. LAZURE, N., Les Valeurs Morales de la Théologie Joahnnique (Paris 1965) 78-80. "Antisemitismus" in: TRE 3 (1978) 126. KUHL, J. Die Sendung Jesu und der Kirche nach dem Johannes-Evangelium (1967) 112, 135, 152, 176, 188, 224. BERGMEIER, R., Glaube als Gabe nach Johannes (Stuttgart 1980) 13. FRICKEL, J., "Naassener oder Valentinianer?" in: M. Krause (ed.) Gnosis and Gnosticism, (Leiden 1981) 117-19.

4:24-26.28.31 ORIGENES, Das Evangelium nach Johannes (1959) R. Gögler ed., 255-78.

4:24 GRILL, J. Untersuchungen über die Entstehung des vierten Evangeliums (1923) II 394f. WILES, M. F. The Spiritual Gospel (1960) 67-70, 72. LAZURE, N., Les Valeurs Morales de la Théologie Johannique (Paris 1965) 94. CLARK, K. W., "The Text of the Gospel of John in Third Century Egypt" in: The Gentile Bias and Other Essays (Leiden 1980) 160.

4:25-30 BOUSSET, W. Die Religion des Judentums im Späthellenistischen Zeitalter (1966 = 1926) 225. FORTNA, R. T. The Gospel of Signs (1970) 191f.

4:25-26 WIKENHAUSER, A. Das Evangelium nach Johannes (1957) 113-15. SMALLEY, S. S. "Diversity and Development in John," NTS 17 (1970-1971) 288f. BERGMEIER, R., Glaube als Gabe nach Johannes (Stuttgart 1980) 208.

4:25 VOLZ, P. Die Eschatologie der jüdischen Gemeinde (1934) 200. BOISMARD, M. E., "Importance de la critique textuelle pour établir l'origine araméenne du quatrième évangele" in: M. Boismard et al., L'Evangile de Jean: études et problèmes (Bruges 1958) 46-47. HAHN, F.Christologische Hoheitstitel (1963) 208f., 362, 397. REIM, G., Studien zum alttestamentlichen Hintergrund des Johannesevangeliums (Cambridge 1974) 120-21, 249-51. METZGER, B. M., The Early Versions of the New Testament (Oxford 1977) 254. "Aramäisch" in: TRE 3 (1978) 608. FREED, E. D., "Ego Eimi in John 1:20 and 4:25," CBQ 41 (1979) 288-91. VAN UNNIK, W. C., "A Greek Characteristic of Prophecy in the Fourth Gospel" in: E. Best/R. McL. Wilson (eds.) Text and Interpretation. FS. M. Black (Cambridge 1979) 211-29.

4:26 HARNER, P. B. The "I am" of the Fourth Gospel (1970) 45-47. IBUKI, Y. Die Wahrheit im Johannesevangelium (1972) 49, 319f., 322, 335. HOWARD, V. P., Das Ego Jesu in den Synoptischen Evangelien (Marburg 1975) 253. SWIDLER, L., Biblical Affirmations of Woman (Philadelphia 1979) 223.

4:27-42 WEBER, O. Predigtmeditationen (1967) 256-59. HEER, J. "Johanneische Botschaft: Die Mission in Samaria," Sein und Sendung 33 (3, 1968) 99-112.

4:27-30 MOLONEY, F. J., "From Cana to Cana (John 2:1-4:54) and the Fourth Evangelist's Concept of Correct (and Incorrect) Faith" in: E. A. Livingstone (ed.) Studia Biblica 1978/II (Sheffield 1980) 198-99.

4:27 MOORE, G. F. Judaism II (1946) 270.

4:28ff HAHN, F. Das Verständnis der Mission im Neuen Testament (1965²) 141.

4:29 IBUKI, Y. Die Wahrheit im Johannesevangelium (1972) 319f., 330, 333. REIM, G., Studien zum Alttestamentlichen Hintergrund des Johannesevangeliums (Cambridge 1974) 121. BERGMEIER, Glaube als Gabe nach Johannes (Stuttgart 1980) 208, 270n.556.

4:31-42 DIEM, H. in: Herr, tue meine Lippen auf Bd. 3 (1964) G. Eichholz ed., 91ff.

4:31-38 LOEWE, R. in: Hören und Fragen Bd. 5, 3 (1967) G. Eichholz/ A. Falkenroth eds., 569ff. KRUSE, M. GPM 25 (2, 1971) 396-402.

4:31-34 LEROY, H. Rätsel und Missverständnis (1968) 147-55. IBUKI, Y. Die Wahrheit im Johannesevangelium (1972) 325-28.

4:31 HAHN, F. Christologische Hoheitstitel (1963) 75.

4:32.34 ODEBERG, H. The Fourth Gospel (1968) 187ff. RIEDL, J. Das Heilswerk Jesu nach Johannes (1973) 43-68, 183-86.

4:34 KUHL, J. Die Sendung Jesu und der Kirche nach dem Johannes-Evangelium (1967) 94f., 112-15, 177, 196, 211. THUESING, W. Die Erhöhung und Verherrlichung Jesu im Johannesevangelium (1970) 51-53. DAUER, A. Die Passionsgeschichte im Johannesevangelium (1972) 47, 210, 214, 249, 258, 282, 287f., 290, 291, 294. PANCARO, S., The Law in the Fourth Gospel (Leiden 1975) 372, 374, 375-76, 384-89. BÜHNER, J.-A., Der Gesandte und sein Weg im 4. Evan-

gelium (Tübingen 1977) 135-36, 203, 208-209. BACCHIOC-
CHI, S., "John 5:17: Negation or Clarification of the Sabbath?"
AUSS 19 (1981) 14. "Consilia Evangelica" in: TRE 8 (1981)
195. "Demut" in: TRE 8 (1981) 464.

4:35-39 HAHN, F. Das Verständnis der Mission im Neuen Testament
(1965²) 32, 142.

4:35ff KAESEMANN, E. New Testament Questions of Today (1969)
163.

4:35-38 KUHL, J. Die Sendung Jesu und der Kirche nach dem Johannes-Evangelium (1967) 95, 140-42, 224f. HUNTER, A. M.
According to John (1970²) 79f. THUESING, W. Die Erhöhung
und Verherrlichung Jesu im Johannesevangelium (1970) 53-58.
IBUKI, Y. Die Wahrheit im Johannesevangelium (1972) 328ff.

4:35-36 SMITH, M. Tannaitic Parallels to the Gospels (1968) appendix
A.

4:35 WILES, M. F. The Spiritual Gospel (1960) 24, 39-40. BORN-
KAMM-BARTH-HELD, Überlieferung und Auslegung im
Matthäus-Evangelium (1961²) 16. BRAUN, H. Qumran und NT
II (1966) 134. ARGYLE, A. W. "A Note on John 4:35. (eti)
tetramēnos estin chō therimos erchetai," ET 82 (8, 1971) 247-
48. METZGER, B. M., The Early Versions of the New Testament (Oxford 1977) 179.

4:36-38 NICCACCI, A., "Siracide 6,19 e Giovanni 4,36-38," BibOr
23 (1981) 149-53.

4:36 BRAUN, F.-M. Jean le Théologien (1966) 93-95. RUDOLPH,
K., Die Gnosis (Göttingen 1978) 213.

4:37-38 MAURER, C. Ignatius von Antiochien und das Johannesevangelium (1949) 49.

4:37 WATSON, W. G. E. "Antecedents of a New Testament prov-
erb," VT 20 (3, 1970) 368-70. CLARK, K. W., "The Text of
the Gospel of John in Third-Century Egypt" in: The Gentile Bias
and other Essays (Leiden 1980) 162.

4:38-39 HENGEL, M., Zur urchristlichen Geschichtsschreibung (Stuttgart 1979) 69; ET: J. Bowden (trans.) Acts and the History of
Earliest Christianity (London 1979) 79.

4:38 MANEK, J. "The Biblical Concept of Time and our Gospels,"
NTS 6 (1959-1960) 45f. ROBINSON, J. A. T. "The 'Others'
of John 4,38," in: Twelve New Testament Studies (1962) 61-
66. BRAUN, H. Qumran und NT II (1966) 133, 140, 183.
BLACK, M. An Aramaic Approach to the Gospels and Acts
(1967) 283f.

4:39-42 WALKER, R. "Jüngerwort und Herrenwort. Zur Auslegung von Joh 4:39-42," ZNW 57 (1-2, 1966) 49-54. HAAR, J. GPM 23 (2, 1968) 222-28. IBUKI, Y. Die Wahrheit im Johannes-evangelium (1972) 330-34. HARDER, G., in: GPM 29 (1975) 272-80. MOLONEY, F. J., "From Cana to Cana (John 2:1-4:54) and the Fourth Evangelist's Concept of Correct (and Incorrect) Faith" in: E. A. Livingstone (ed.) Studia Biblica 1978/ II (Sheffield 1980) 198-99.

4:39-40 BROX, N. Zeuge und Märtyrer (1961) 84f.

4:39 BEUTLER, J. Martyria (1972) 215ff., 282, 326.. REIM, G., Studien zum Alttestamentlichen Hintergrund des Johannes-evangeliums (Cambridge 1974) 121. CRIBBS, F. L., "The Agreements that Exist Between John and Acts" in: C. H. Talbert (ed.) Perspectives on Luke-Acts (Danville 1978) 58. GERSTENBERGER, E. S. und SCHRAGE, W., Frau und Mann (Stuttgart 1980) 140.

4:40 HEISE, J., Bleiben. μένειν in den Johanneischen Schriften (Tübingen 1967) 47-50.

4:41-42 DELLING, Wort und Werk Jesu im Johannesevangelium (1966) 40, 44f. REIM, G., Studien zum Alttestamentlichen Hintergrund des Johannesevangeliums (Cambridge 1974) 121.

4:41 KILPATRICK, G. D., "John iv 41 *PLEION* or *PLEIOUS*" NovT 18 (1976) 131-32.

4:42 GRILL, J. Untersuchungen über die Entstehung des vierten Evangeliums II (1923) 8, 52, 67, 142, 143, 144, 153, 370. HAHN, F. Das Verständnis der Mission im Neuen Testament (1965²) 136. BECKER, J. NTS 16 (1969-1970) 139f. BARRETT, C. K. "Conversion and Conformity: the Freedom of the Spirit in the Institutional Church," in: Christ and the Spirit in the New Testament (1973) B. Lindars/S. S. Smalley eds., 373f. BERGMEIER, R., Glaube als Gabe nach Johannes (Stuttgart 1980) 260n.428.

4:43-54 BUECHSEL, F. Das Evangelium nach Johannes (1946) 69. STRATHMANN, H. Das Evangelium nach Johannes (1955) 95. ZIENER, G. "Weisheitsbuch und Johannesevangelium," Biblica 38 (1957) 409-11. GRUNDMANN, W. Zeugnis und Gestalt des Johannes-Evangeliums (1961) 39-43. YATES, K. M. Preaching from John's Gospel (1964) 47-53. BRAUN, F.-M. Jean le Théologien (1966) 95-98. MEEKS, W. A. The Prophet-King, Moses Traditions and the Johannine Christology (1967) 39-41. HEER, J. "Der Glaube des 'Königlichen'," Sein und Sendung 33 (4, 1968) 147-64. MATSUNAGA, K., "The Galileans in the Fourth Gospel" AJBI 2 (1976) 139-58. BECKER, J., Das Evangelium nach Johannes (Gütersloh/Würzburg 1979)

185. (lit!). HAENCHEN, E., Das Johannesevangelium (Tübingen 1980) 257 (lit!).

4:43 DAVIES, W. D. The Gospel and the Land (1974) 238, 321, 323, 324, 325.

4:44.46-53.54 ORIGENES, Das Evangelium nach Johannes (1959) R. Gögler ed., 278-84.

4:44 PALLIS, A., Notes on St. John and the Apocalypse (London 1928) 9. WILLEMSE,J. "La Patrie de Jésus selon Saint Jean iv, 44," NTS 11 (4, 1965) 349-64. SUMMERS, R. The Secret Sayings of the Living Jesus (1966) 36. BEUTLER, J. Martyria (1972) 215, 217, 325f. KUEMMEL, W. G. Einleitung in das Neue Testament (1973) 167f. OLSSON, B., Structure and Meaning in the Fourth Gospel (Lund 1974) 26-28, 127, 131, 134, 144-45, 262. REIM, G., "John iv 44 — Crux or Clue?" NTS 22 (1976) 476-80. STURCH, R. L., "The 'PATRIS' of Jesus" JThS 28 (1977) 94-96. THYEN, H., " 'Das Heil kommt von den Juden' " in: D. Lührmann/G. Strecker (eds.) Kirche. FS. G. Bornkamm (Tübingen 1980) 178-79.

4:45ff SMITH, M. Clement of Alexandria and a secret Gospel of Mark (1973) 147, 153f.

4:45-54 LEIDIG, E., Jesu Gespräch mit der Samaritanerin (Basel 1981) 253-57.

4:45 NICOL, W. The Sēmeia in the Fourth Gospel (1972) 99f. DAVIES, W. D. The Gospel and the Land (1974) 322-26 passim, 412. METZGER, B. M., The Early Versions of the New Testament (Oxford 1977) 248.

4:46ff SCHWEIZER, E. "Die Heilung des Königlichen: Joh 4, 46ff.," EvTh 11 (1951-1952) 64-71. KNOX, W. L. The Sources of the Synoptic Gospels II (1957) 8.

4:46-54 SCHNIEWIND, J., Die Parallelperikopen bei Lukas und Johannes (Darmstadt 1958 = 1914) 16-21. FEUILLET, A. "La signification théologique du second miracle de Cana (Jo IV,46-54)," RechSR 48 (1-2, 1960) 62-74. GRUNDMANN, W. "Verständnis und Bewegung des Glaubens im Johannes-Evangelium," KuD 6 (1960) 137-39. WILES, M. F., The Spiritual Gospel (1060) 49-50. BOISMARD, M.-E., "Saint Luc et la rédaction du quatrième évangile (Jn, iv, 46-54)," RevBi 69 (2, 1962) 185-211. SCHWEIZER, E. Neotestamentica (1963) 407-15. SCHNACKENBURG, R. "Zur Traditionsgeschichte von Joh 4,46-54," BZ 8 (1, 1964) 56-58. HOFBECK, S. Semeion (1966) 105-109. ERDOZAIN, L. La funcion del signo en la fe segun el cuarto evangelio (1968). SIEGMAN, E. F. "St. John's Use of the Synoptic Material," CBQ 30 (2, 1968) 182-98.

BLANK, J. Schriftauslegung in Theorie und Praxis (1969) 107, 112ff., WEISER, A. Glaube und Wunder (1969). WILKENS, W., Zeichen und Werke (Zürich 1969) 33-35. FORTNA, R. T. The Gospel of Signs (1970) 38-48. SCHNIDER, F./STENGER, W. Johannes und die Synoptiker (1971) 54-88. SELBY, D. J., Introduction to the New Testament (New York 1971) 198, 209, 220, 249-50. NICOL, W. The Sēmeia in the Fourth Gospel (1972) 31, 41f., 55f., 73f., 107. PAGELS, E. H. The Johannine Gospel in Gnostic Exegesis (1973) 83-85. TALBERT, C. H. Literary Patterns, Theological Themes, and the Genre of Luke-Acts (1974) 19. REIM, G., Studien zum Alttestamentlichen Hintergrund des Johannesevangeliums (Cambridge 1974) 235-39. van BELLE. G., De Semeia-Bron in het Vierde Evangelie (Leuven 1975) 59-65. LOHSE, E., "Miracles in the Fourth Gospel" in: M. Hooker/C. Hickling (eds.) What About the New Testament? FS. C. Evans (London 1975) 65-66. TEMPLE, S., The Core of the Fourth Gospel (London 1975) 119-21. de JONGE, M., Jesus: Stranger from Heaven and Son of God (Missoula 1977) 122-24. LANGBRANDTNER, W., Weltferner Gott oder Gott der Liebe (Frankfurt a.M./Bern/Las Vegas 1977) 71-76. TRITES, A. A., The New Testament Concept of Witness (Cambridge 1977) 99-100. DAHINTEN, G., in: GPM 35 (1980) 104-107. GIBLIN, C. H., "Suggestion, Negative Response, and Positive Action in St. John's Portrayal of Jesus (John 2.1-11.; 4.46-54.; 7.2-14.; 11.1-44.)" NTS 26 (1980) 197-211. HENGEL, M. und HENGEL, R., "Die Heilungen Jesu und medizinisches Denken" in: A. Suhl (ed.) Der Wunderbegriff im Neuen Testament (Darmstadt 1980) 351-52. MOLONEY, F. J., "From Cana to Cana (John 2:1-4:54) and the Fourth Evangelist's Concept of Correct (and Incorrect) Faith" in: E. A. Livingstone (ed.) Studia Biblica 1978/II (Sheffield 1980) 189-93.

4:46-53 MOORE, G. F. Judaism (1946) I 377n., II 263n. HAHN, F. Das Verständnis der Mission im Neuen Testament (1965²) 24f.

4:46-52 MARTYN, J. L., The Gospel of John in Christian History (New York 1978) 21, 23.

4:46 RUCKSTUHL, E. Die literarische Einheit des Johannesevangeliums (1951) 109f., 136. FORTNA, R. T. The Gospel of Signs (1970) 39, 75, 89, 99n., 104, 216. OLSSON, B., Structure and Meaning in the Fourth Gospel (Lund 1974) 26-28, 53, 56, 65, 143-44, 279.

4:47-54 KRECK, GPM 4 (1949-1950) 274ff. FRIEDRICH, GPM 9 (1954-1955) 246ff. DEHN, G. in: Herr, tue meine Lippen auf Bd. 1 (1957) G. Eichholz ed., 305-10. STECK, GPM 15 (1960-

1961) 294ff. DOERNE, M. Er kommt auch noch heute (1961) 147-49.

4:47-5:6 METZGER, B. M., Manuscripts of the Greek Bible (Oxford 1981) 98.

4:47-53 HAHN, F. "Predigt über Johannes 4,47-52," in: Predigtstudien (1972-1973) E. Lange ed., 94-98.

4:47 FORTNA, R. T. The Gospel of Signs (1970) 39-41.

4:48.50.53-54 SCHOTTROFF, L. Der Glaubende und die feindliche Welt (1970) 248-52, 263-67.

4:48 KNOX, W. L. The Sources of the Synoptic Gospels II (1957) 8. KAESEMANN, E. Exegetische Versuche und Besinnungen (1964) I 216. THEYSSEN, G. W. "Unbelief" in the New Testament (Rüschlikon, 1965) 49ff. BEUTLER, J. Martyria (1972) 294f. NICOL, W. The Sēmeia in the Fourth Gospel (1972) 10f., 28f., 104f., 113. DUNN, J. D. G., Unity and Diversity in the New Testament (London 1977) 302-303. METZGER, B. M., The Early Versions of the New Testament (Oxford 1977) 255.

4:49 HAHN, F. Christologische Hoheitstitel (1963) 94.

4:50-51 FORTNA, R. T. The Gospel of Signs (1970) 41ff.

4:50 BERGMEIER, R., Glaube als Gabe nach Johannes (Stuttgart 1980) 180.

4:51 KILPATRICK, G. D. "John IV. 51 PAIS or YIOS?" JThS 14 (2, 1963) 393. FREED, E. D. "John IV.51 PAIS or HUIOS?" JThS 16 (2, 1965) 448-49.

4:52 METZGER, B. M., The Early Versions of the New Testament (Oxford 1977) 42. ROBINSON, B. P., "The Meaning and Significance of 'The Seventh Hour' in John 4:52" in: E. A. Livingstone (ed.) Studia Biblica 1978/II (Sheffield 1980) 255-63.

4:53 JEWETT, P. K., Infant Baptism and the Covenant of Grace (Grand Rapids 1978) 51.

4:54 OLSSON, B., Structure and Meaning in the Fourth Gospel (Lund 1974) 28, 64-68, 143-44, 262, 279.

5-12 SELBY, D. J., Introduction to the New Testament (New York 1971) 241-52. GNILKA, J., ThR 69 (1, 1973) 1-7. SEGOVIA,

F., "The Love and Hatred of Jesus and Johannine Sectarianism" CBQ 43 (1981) 267-68, 271.

5.6.7-12 GUILDING, A. The Fourth Gospel and Jewish Worship (1960) 51-52.

5-10 GARDNER-SMITH, P. Saint John and the Synoptic Gospels (1938) 25-41.

5-8 van den BUSSCHE, H., "La Structure de Jean: I-XII" in: M. Boismard et al., L'Evangile de Jean. études et problèmes (Bruges 1958) 88-103.

5:31-7:24 VOUGA, F., Le cadre historique et l'intention théologique de Jean (Paris 1977) 38-50.

5-6 WIKENHAUSER, A. Das Evangelium nach Johannes (1957) 118-21. KUZENZAMA, K. P. M., "Jn 5-6 ou Jn 6-5? Une question embarrassante de critique littéraire" RATh 3 (1979) 61-69.

5 FEINE, P./BEHM, J. Einleitung in das Neue Testament (1950) 120f. BECKER, H., Die Reden des Johannesevangeliums und der stil der gnostischen Offenbarungsrede (Göttingen 1956) 70-75, 118-19. van den BUSSCHE, A., "La Structure de Jean I-XII" in: H. Boismard et al., L'Evangile de Jean: études et problèmes (Bruges 1958) 89-94. GRUNDMANN, W. "Verständnis und Bewegung des Glaubens im Johannes-Evangelium," KuD 6 (1960) 139f. BLIGH, J. "Jesus in Jerusalem," HeyJ 4 (12, 1963) 115-34. DELLING, G. Die Taufe im Neuen Testament (1963) 92. SMITH, D. M. The Composition and Order of the Fourth Gospel (1965) 117, 139, 140f., 156, 158, 160, 175, 216, 230, 231. DELLING, G. Wort und Werk Jesu im Johannes-Evangelium (1966) 21f., 26. MEEKS, W. A. The Prophet-King, Moses Traditions and theJohannine Christology (1967) 59, 293-95, 315n., 317. JEREMIAS, J. Biblica 54 (1, 1973) 152-55. DAVIES, W. D. The Gospel and the Land (1974) 296, 304, 312, 313, 315. KLINGER, J. (Betezda a uniwersalizm Logosu" Rozniki Teologiczne Chrescijanskiej Akademii Teologicznej 16 (1974) 275-95. LOHSE, E., "Miracles in the Fourth Gospel" in: M. Hooker/C. Hickling (eds.) What About the New Testament? FS. C. Evans (London 1975) 69. TEMPLE, S., The Core of the Fourth Gospel (London 1975) 121-31. TRITES, A. A., The New Testament Concept of Witness (Cambridge 1977) 100-103. SCHILLEBEECKX, E., Christ, the Christian Experience in the Modern World (London 1980) 386-87; GT: Christus und die Christen (Freiburg/Basel/Wien 1977) 372-73.

5:1ff DAVIES, W. D. The Gospel and the Land (1974) 306-13 passim.

5:1-47 NOACK, B. Zur Johanneischen Tradition (1954) 114f., 126. YATES, K. M. Preaching from John's Gospel (1964) 54-62. SMITH, D. M. The Composition and Order of the Fourth Gospel (1965) 130-34, 149. SCHREINER, J. Gestalt and Anspruch des Neuen Testaments (1969) 239-42.

5:1-31 HOFBECK, S. Semeion (1966) 109-13.

5:1-30 HEER, J. "An Jesus entscheidet sich das Heil," Sein und Sendung 33 (6, 1968) 243-61. BERNARD, J., La guérison de Béthesda. Harmoniques judéo-hellenistiques d'un récit de miracle un jour de sabbat" MSR 33 (1976) 3-34; 34 (1977) 13-44. HAENCHEN, E., Das Johannesevangelium (Tübingen 1980) 265-66 (lit!).

5:1-29 CORELL, A. Consummatum Est (1958) 62-63.

5:1-21 HERMAN, J., "Mi törté a Bethesda tavánál?" Reformatus Szemle 71 (1978) 122-28.

5:1-19 CULLMANN, O. Urchristentum und Gottesdienst (1950) 86ff. BIEDER, W. Die Verheissung der Taufe im Neuen Testament (Zürich 1965) 271-72. BARTLETT, D. L., Fact and Faith (Valley Forge 1975) 61-62.

5:1-18 BALAGUE, M. "El Bautismo como resurreccion del pecado," CultBib 18 (177, 1961) 103-10. LINDIJER, C. H. De Sacramenten in het Vierde Evangelie (1964) 66ff. VAN DEN BUSSCHE, H. "Guérison d'un paralytique à Jerusalem le jour du sabbat. Jean 5,1-18," BVieC 61 (1965) 18-28. OTTO, G. Denken - um zu glauben (1970) 97-101. PANCARO, S., The Law in the Fourth Gospel (Leiden 1975) 7, 9-16, 159, 161, 169, 173. CRIBBS, F. L., "The Agreements that Exist between John and Acts" in: C. H. Talbert (ed.) Perspectives on Luke-Acts (Danville 1978) 45. BECKER, J., Das Evangelium nach Johannes (Gütersloh/Würzburg 1979) 229 (lit!).

5:1-16 WILES, M. F. The Spiritual Gospel (1960) 51-52. WILKENS, W. Zeichen und Werke (Zürich 1969) 39-41. BOYENS, A. und BALTENSWEILER, H., in: P. Krusche et al. (eds.) Predigtstudien für das Kirchenjahr 1976-1977 V/2 (Stuttgart 1977) 215-21. LEIDIG, E., Jesu Gespräch mit der Samaritanerin (Basel 1981) 207-12.

5:1-14 GOLLWITZER, H. GPM 11 (4, 1957) 246-51. KLAAS, W. in: Herr, tue meine Lippen auf Bd. 3 (1964) G. Eichholz ed., 393ff. NAUCK, W. in: Hören und Fragen Bd. 5,3 (1967) G. Eichholz/A. Falkenroth eds., 499ff. LANGE, E. ed., Predigtstudien (1971) 222-28. TROEGER, K.-W. GPM 25 (4, 1971) 413-21.

5:1-9 ZIENER, G. "Weisheitsbuch und Johannesevangelium," Biblica 38 (1957) 409-11. BAGATTI, B. "Il lento disseppellimento della piscina probatica a Gerusalemme," BiOr 1 (1, 1959) 12-14. DELLING, G. Wort und Werk Jesu im Johannes-Evangelium (1966) 23, 75, 113, 137. DUPREZ, A. Jésus et les dieux guérisseurs (1970). FORTNA, R. T. The Gospel of Signs (1970) 48-54, 55, 103, 107, 108, 196. NICOL, W. The Sēmeia in the Fourth Gospel (1972) 15f., 31f. 44, 56, 107. LOHSE, E. Die Einheit des Neuen Testaments (1973) 62f. DAVIES, W. D. The Gospel and the Land (1974) 302-303, 304-307 passim. PANCARO, S., The Law in the Fourth Gospel (Leiden 1975) 10-12, 18. DEL VERME, M., "La piscina probatica. Gv. 5,1-9. Un problema di critica testuale e di esegesi di fronte ai risultati degli ultimi scavi" BiOR 18 (1976) 109-19. BECKER, J., "Wunder und Christologie. Zum literar-kritischen und christologischen Problem der Wunder im Johannesevangelium" in: A. Suhl (ed.) Der Wunderbegriff im Neuen Testament (Darmstadt 1980) 446-48.

5:1-6 STEIGER, L. "Stehe auf, nimm dein Bett und gehe hin," in: Parrhesia (1966) 3-10.

5:1 MOORE, G. F. Judaism II (1946) 52n. ROBINSON, J. M. Kerygma und historischer Jesus (1960) 146. DELLING, G. Die Taufe im Neuen Testament (1963) 29. GRAESSER, E. NTD 11 (1964-1965) 76f. BOWMAN, J. "The Identity and Date of the Unnamed Feast of John 5:1," in: Near Eastern Studies in Honor of William Foxwell Albright (1973) H. Goedicke ed., 43-56. BOWMAN, J., The Fourth Gospel and the Jews (Pittsburgh 1975) 111-32. KLIJN, A. F., "Die Syrische Baruch-Apokalypse" in: JüdSchr V/2 (1976) 146n.7b.

5:2-47 GRUNDMANN, W. Zeugnis und Gestalt des Johannes-Evangeliums (1961) 44-50.

5:2-9 ORIGENES, Das Evangelium nach Johannes (1959) R. Gögler ed., 284-85. VARDAMAN, E. J. "The Pool of Bethesda," BTr 14 (1, 1963) 27-29. DUNN, J. D. G. Baptism in the Holy Spirit (1970) 186f.

5:2 BLASS, F. Philosophy of the Gospels (1898) 241ff. PALLIS, A., Notes on St. John and the Apocalypse (London 1928) 9. REUSS, J. "Presbyter Ammonius' Kommentar zum Jo-Evangelium," Biblica 44 (1963) 163-64. WIEAND, D. J. "John v. 2 and the Pool of Bethesda," NTS 12 (4, 1966) 392-404. NICOL, W. The Sēmeia in the Fourth Gospel (1972) 44f. DAVIES, W. D., The Gospel and the Land (London 1974) 307n.35, 308, 311. METZGER, B. M., The Early Versions of the New Testament (Oxford 1977) 172.

5:3-4 ALAND, K., Der Text des Neuen Testaments (Stuttgart 1982) 305.

5:3 PALLIS, A., Notes on St. John and the Apocalypse (London 1928) 9-10. HODGES, Z. C., "Problem Passages in the Gospel of John. Part 5: The Angel at Bethesda — John 5:4" BiblSa 136 (1979) 25-39.

5:6-8 BROER, I. Die Urgemeinde und das Grab Jesu (1972) 212f.

5:6 STAEHLIN, W. "Willst du gesund Werden?" in: Forschung und Erfahrung im Dienst der Seelsorge (1961) 97-100.

5:7 HAHN, F. Christologische Hoheitstitel (1963) 94. BLACK, M. An Aramaic Approach to the Gospels and Acts (1967) 77f. NICKELS, P. Targum and New Testament (1967) 54. METZGER, B. M., The Early Versions of the New Testament (Oxford 1977) 162.

5:8 BUSE, I. "John V.8 and Johannine-Marcab Relationships," NTS 1 (2, 1954) 134-36. BETZ, H. D. Lukian von Samosata und das Neue Testament (1961) 155, 158. JOHNSON, D. B. "A Neglected Variant in Gregory 33 (John v.8)," BTS 18 (2, 1972) 231-32.

5:9-16 MEYER, B. F., The Aims of Jesus (London 1979) 162-68.

5:9 FORTNA, H. T. The Gospel of Signs (1970) 52f.

5:10ff BOUSSET, W. Die Religion des Judentums im Späthellenistischen Zeitalter (1966 = 1926) 126.

5:10-10:39 PERRIN, N., The New Testament (New York 1974) 235-40.

5:10 SWIDLER, L., Biblical Affirmations of Woman (Philadelphia 1979) 181. BACCHIOCCHI, S., "John 5:17: Negation or Clarification of the Sabbath?" AUSS 19 (1981) 18. BERGER, K., "Das Buch der Jubiläen" in: JüdSchr II/3 (1981) 553n.8k.

5:11 RAYAN, S., The Holy Spirit: Heart of the Gospel and Christian Hope (New York 1978) 82.

5:13 LIGHTFOOT, R. H. St. John's Gospel (1956) 63f.

5:14 KAESEMANN, E. Exegetische Versuche und Besinnungen (1964) I 246. LAZURE, N., Les Valeurs Morales de la Théologie Johannique (Paris 1965) 292-95. PANCARO, S., The Law in the Fourth Gospel (Leiden 1975) 10-12, 13, 18.

5:15 "Amt" TRE 2 (1978) 517.

5:16-47 CADMAN, W. H. The Open Heaven (1969) G. B. Caird ed., 74-80.

5:17ff BEUTLER, J. Martyria (1972) 254, 256, 273, 356. NICOL, W. The Sēmeia in the Fourth Gospel (1972) 117f.

.

5:17-47 STANLEY, D. M. "The Mission of the Son," Worship 33 (1, 1958) 27-34.

5:17-30 SUNDBERG, A. C. "Isos To Theo Christology in John 5:17-30," BR 15 (1970) 19-31. THUESING, W. Die Erhöhung und Verherrlichung Jesu im Johannesevangelium (1970) 59-61. de JONGE, M., Jesus: Stranger from Heaven and Son of God (Missoula 1977) 148-49.

5:17-18 PANCARO, S., The Law in the Fourth Gospel (Leiden 1975) 7, 16, 53, 54-56, 498.

5:17.20.36 RIEDL, J. Das Heilswerk Jesu nach Johannes (1973) 187-282.

5:17 BARRETT, C. K. The New Testament Background (1956) 175. MAURER, C. "Steckt hinter Joh. 5,17 ein Übersetzungsfehler?" in: Wort und Dienst Bd. 5 (1957) A. Adam ed., 130-40. GIBLET, J., "Jésus et le 'Pere' dans le IVe évangile" in: M. Boismard et al., L'Evangile de Jean: études et problèmes (Bruges 1958) 114-20. CULLMANN, O. "Sabbat und Sonntag nach dem Johannesevangelium," in: Vorträge und Aufsätze (1966) K. Fröhlich ed., 187-91. CADMAN, W. H. The Open Heaven (1969) G. B. Caird ed., 81, 115, 156, 205. FERRARO, G. "Il senso di 'heos arti' nel testo in Giovanni 5,17." RivB 20 (suppl., 1972) 529-45. BACCHIOCCHI,S., "John 5:17: Negation or Clarification of the Sabbath?" AUSS 19 (1981) 3-19. "Chiliasmus" in: TRE 7 (1981) 728.

5:18 DAUER, A. Die Passionsgeschichte im Johannesevangelium (1972) 88, 180, 247, 251, 265. BEYSCHLAG, K. Simon Magus und die Christliche Gnosis (1974) 103(10), 103(12), 110(27). GEORGI, D., "Weisheit Salomos" in: JüdSchr III/4 (1980) 2n.16b. BACCHIOCCHI, S., "John 5:17: Negation or Clarification of the Sabbath?" AUSS 19 (1981) 17. DAVIES, S. L., "Who is Called Bar Abbas?" NTS 27 (1980-1981) 262. MATSUNAGA, K., "The 'Theos' Christology as the Ultimate Confession of the Fourth Gospel" AJBI 7 (1981) 129-30, 135.

5:19ff BERGMEIER, R., Glaube als Gabe nach Johannes (Stuttgart 1980) 243n.120, 123.

5:19-47 MEEKS, W. A. The Prophet-King, Moses Traditions and the Johannine Christology (1967) 303-305. BEAUVERY, R. " 'Mon Père et votre Père'," LuVie 20 (104, 1971) 75-87. WALTER, L., L'incroyance des croyants selon saint Jean (Paris 1979) 59-63.

5:19-30 RUCKSTUHL, E. Die literarische Einheit des Johannesevangeliums (1951) 159, 162, 167-70, 247, 252f, 255f. SCHULZ, S., Untersuchungen zur Menschensohn-Christologie im Johannesevangelium (Göttingen 1957) 135-42.

LEON-DUFOUR, X. NTS 7 (1960-1961) 253f. GAECHTER, P. "Zur Form von Joh 5,19-30," in: Neutestamentliche Aufsätze (1963) J. Blinzler/O. Kuss/F. Mussner eds., 65-68. BLANK, J. Krisis (1964) 109. DODD, C. R. "A Hidden Parable in the Fourth Gospel," in: More New Testament Studies (1968) 30-40. VANHOYE, A. "La composition de Jn 5,19-30," in: Mélanges Bibliques en hommage au R. P. Béda Rigaux (1970) A. Descamps./A. de Halleux eds., 259-74. BEUTLER, J. Martyria (1972) 28, 254ff, 265, 269, 352, 346. BECKER, J., Auferstehung der Toten im Urchristentum (Stuttgart 1976) 125-28. LANGBRANDTNER, W., Weltferner Gott oder Gott der Liebe (Frankfurt a.M./Bern/Las Vegas 1977) 11-14. BECKER, J., Das Evangelium nach Johannes (Gütersloh/Würzburg 1979) 234-35 (lit!).

5:19-29 WEBER, O. Predigtmeditationen (1967) 188-90. ODEBERG, H. The Fourth Gospel (1968) 190ff.

5:19-23 SCHULZ, S., Untersuchungen zur Menschensohn-Christologie im Johannesevangelium (Göttingen 1957) 128-35. HAHN, F. Christologische Hoheitstitel (1963) 329. DELLING, G. Wort und Werk Jesu im Johannes-Evangelium (1966) 100f.

5:19-21 GRUNDMANN, W. NTS 12 (1965-1966) 44f.

5:19-20 WILKENS, W. Die Entstehung des vierten Evangeliums (1958) 98-108. DODD, C. H. "Une parabole cachée dans le quatrième Evangile," RHPhR 42 (1962) 107-15. HAHN, F. Christologische Hoheitstitel (1963) 40f., 330. NIESEL, W. in: Herr, tue meine Lippen auf Bd. 3 (1964) G. Eichholz ed., 458ff. HUNTER, A. M. According to John (1970²) 80f. JEREMIAS, J. Neutestamentliche Theologie I (1971) 44, 64, 66f. IBUKI, Y. Die Wahrheit im Johannesevangelium (1972) 46f., 58f., 167ff. GOPPELT, L. Theologie des Neuen Testaments I (1975) J. Roloff ed., 251f.

5:19.24.25 BERGER, K. Die Amen-Worte Jesu (1970) 109-10.

5:19 PALLIS, A., Notes on St. John and the Apocalypse (London 1928) 10. WILES, M. F. The Spiritual Gospel (1960) 120, 121, 124, 133, 139. DELLING, G. Wort und Werk Jesu im Johannes-Evangelium (1966) 60, 66, 73, 105, 112f. BÜHNER, J.-A., Der Gesandte und sein Weg im 4. Evangelium (Tübingen 1977) 241-42. "Autorität" in: TRE 5 (1980) 47. CLARK, S. B., Man and Woman in Christ (Ann Arbor, Mich. 1980) 64. BACCHIOCCHI, S., "John 5:17: Negation or Clarification of the Sabbath?" AUSS 19 (1981) 17.

5:20 BARRETT, C. K. The New Testament Background (1956) 90. DELLING, G. Die Taufe im Neuen Testament (1963) 94. KASEMANN, E. Exegetische Versuche und Besinnungen (1964) II 101. CADMAN, W. H. The Open Heaven (1969) G. B. Caird ed., 5, 16, 98, 119, 146. KAESEMANN, E. New Testament Questions of Today (1969) 103. THUESING, W. Die Erhöhung und Verherrlichung Jesu im Johannesevangelium (1970) 59-61. LATTKE, M., Einheit im Wort (München 1975) 13, 19, 96-101. GEORGI, D., "Weisheit Salomos" in: JüdSchr III/4 (1980) 8n. 3n, 9n. 9a.

5:21ff HAHN, F. Das Verständnis der Mission im Neuen Testament (1965²) 137.

5:21-30 DUPONT, J. Essais zur la Christologie de Saint Jean (1951) 171-74, 175, 195. ALONSO DÍAZ, J., "El Mesías y la realizacíon de la justicia escatológica" Salmanticensis 23 (1976) 61-84. BÜHNER, J.-A., Der Gesandte und sein Weg im 4. Evangelium (Tübingen 1977) 245-46.

5:21-29 HAHN, F. Christologische Hoheitstitel (1963) 40f., 330.

5:21-27 LANGBRANDTNER, W., Weltferner Gott oder Gott der Liebe (Frankfurt 1977) 308-309.

5:21-22 FORESTELL, J. T., The Word of the Cross: Salvation as Revelation in the Fourth Gospel (Rome 1974) 51, 52, 53, 54.

5:21 RUCKSTUHL, E., Die literarische Einheit des Johannesevangeliums (1951) 52, 179, 194, 249, 250. GRUNDMANN,W. NTS 12 (1965-1966) 45f. NÖTSCHER, F., Altorientalischer und alttestamentlicher Auferstehungsglaube (Darmstadt 1970 = 1926) 305. FORESTELL, J. T., The Word of the Cross: Salvation as Revelation in the Fourth Gospel (Rome 1974) 51, 52, 53, 54. "Auferstehung" in: TRE 4 (1979) 459. BERGMEIER, R., Glaube als Gabe nach Johannes (Stuttgart 1980) 218. BACCHIOCCHI, S., "John 5:17: Negation or Clarification of the Sabbath?" AUSS 19 (1981) 17.

5:22ff WILCKENS, W. Die Entstehungsgeschichte des vierten Evangeliums (1958) 50, 51.

5:22-23 BACCHIOCCHI, S., "John 5:17: Negation or Clarification of the Sabbath?" AUSS 19 (1981) 17.

5:22 BARRETT, C. K. The New Testament Background (1956) 255. WILES, M. F. The Spiritual Gospel (1960) 80, 115, 121, 137. KUHL, J. Die Sendung Jesu und der Kirche nach dem Johannesevangelium (1967) 209-12. BERGMEIER, R., Glaube als Gabe nach Johannes (Stuttgart 1980) 40n.218, 211.

5:23-24 HAHN, F. Das Verständnis der Mission im Neuen Testament (1965²) 141.

5:23 KUHL, J. Die Sendung Jesu und der Kirche nach dem Johannesevangelium (1967) 76, 128, 143, 217. MEEKS, W. A. The Prophet-King, Moses Traditions and the Johannine Christology (1967) 301-302.

5:24-30 BRAUN, F.-M. Jean le Théologien (1966) 122-26.

5:24-29 BOROWICZ, C. "Resurrectio prima-resurrectio secunda," RBL 16 (5-6, 1963) 235-51. MARSCH, W. D. in: Hören und Fragen Bd. 5, 3 (1967) G. Eicholz/A. Falkenroth eds., 541ff.

5:24-27 BERGMEIER, R. Glaube als Gabe nach Johannes (Stuttgart 1980) 243n.120.

5:24-26 BORNKAMM, G. Geschichte und Glaube II (1971) 63f. "Auferstehung" in: TRE 4 (1979) 459.

5:24-25 RUDOLPH, K., Die Gnosis (Göttingen 1978) 324. BERG-MEIER, R., Glaube als Gabe nach Johannes (Stuttgart 1980) 13, 204-205, 207, 220, 232, 268n.524, 269n.544.

5:24.38 FLEW, R. N. Jesus and His Church (1956) 117n.

5:24 DUPONT, J. Essais sur la Christologie de Saint Jean (1951) 21, 164, 182, 183, 184. MUSSNER, F. ΖΩΗ. Die Anschauung vom "Leben" im vierten Evangelium (1962) 96f., HAHN, F. Christologische Hoheitstitel (1963) 40f. HENNECKE, E./ SCHNEEMELCHER, W. Neutestamentliche Apokryphen (1964) I 138. DELLING, G. Wort und Werk Jesu im Johannes-Evangelium (1966) 41, 45, 54, 113f., 141, 143f. MEEKS, W. A. The Prophet-King, Moses Traditions and the Johannine Christology (1967) 301-302. IBUKI, Y., Die Wahrheit im Johannesevangelium (1972) 31f., 169. LADD, G. E., A Theology of the New Testament (1974) 229, 271, 307. FORES-TELL, J. T. The Word of the Cross: Salvation as Revelation in the Fourth Gospel (Rome 1974) 51, 53, 54, 55, 115, 119, 126. LATTKE, M., Einheit im Wort (München 1975) 101-107. SANDERS, J. T., Ethics in the New Testament (Philadelphia 1975) 96, 98-99., BÜHNER, J.-A., Der Gesandte und sein Weg im 4. Evangelium (Tübingen 1977) 167-169. LANG-BRANDTNER, W., "Weltlerner Gott oder Gott der Liebe (Frankfurt a.m. Bern/Las Vegas 1977) 390-91. SCHMIT-HALS, W., "Zur Herkunft der gnostischen Elemente in der Sprache des Paulus" in: B. Aland et al. (eds.) Gnosis. FS. H. Jonas (Göttingen 1978) 403. GEORGI, D., "Weisheit Sa-lomos" in: JüdSchr III/4 (1980) 2n.23a. LÉON-DUFOUR, X. "Towards a Symbolic Reading of the Fourth Gospel" NTS 27 (1980-1981) 450.

5:25ff "Apokalyptik" in: TRE 3 (1978) 254.

5:25-29 ESSAME, W. G. "Matthew xxviii. 51-54 and John v. 25-29," ET 76 (2, 1964) 103. DAVIES, W. D., The Gospel and the Land (London 1974) 331.

5:25-26 SCHULZ, S., Untersuchungen zur Menschensohn-Christologie im Johannesevangelium (Göttingen 1957) 128-35.

5:25 RUCKSTUHL, E. The Literarische Einheit des Johannesevangeliums (1951) 17, 162f. HAHN, F. Christologische Hoheitstitel (1963) 330. CAVALIER, H. C. C. Life After Death (1974) 4, 1n.30. LADD, G. E. A Theology of the New Testament (1974) 231, 246, 258. FORESTELL, J. T. The Word of the Cross: Salvation as Revelation in the Fourth Gospel (Rome 1974) 51, 53, 54, 55, 84, 100, 115. "Auferstehung" in: TRE 4 (1979) 484. CLARK, K. W., "The Text of the Gospel of John in Third-Century Egypt" in: The Gentile Bias and Other Essays (Leiden 1980) 161.

5:26 GRILL, J. Untersuchungen über die Entstehung des vierten Evangeliums II (1923) 40, 209f., 220. DUPONT, J. Essais sur la Christologie de Saint Jean (1951) 195, 196, 198. RUCK-STUHL, E., Die literarische Einheit des Johannesevangeliums (1951) 51, 246, 249, 250. WILES, M. F. The Spiritual Gospel (1960) 121-22, 140. HAHN, F. Christologische Hoheitstitel (1963) 49, 329f. CADMAN, W. H. The Open Heaven (1969) G. B. Caird ed., 7, 12, 13, 17, 18, 19, 34, 50, 59, 82, 107, 150, 175, 204. IBUKI, Y., Die Wahrheit im Johannesevangelium (1972) 59. LADD, G. E., A Theology of the New Testament (1974) 248, 257, 258. BERGMEIER, R., Glaube als Gabe nach Johannes (Stuttgart 1980) 13, 16. GEORGI, D., "Weisheit Salomos" in: JüdSchr III/4 (1980) 2n.23a.

5:27-29 SCHULZ, S., Untersuchungen zur Menschensohn-Christologien im Johannesevangelium (Göttingen 1957) 109-14. RUCKSTUHL, E. Die literarische Einheit des Johannesevangeliums (1951) 159-69. HAHN, F. Christologische Hoheitstitel (1963) 39 (ff.)6. REIM, G., Studien zum Alttestamentlichen Hintergrund des Johannesevangeliums (Cambridge 1974) 253-54.

5:27-28 REUSS, J. "Presbyter Ammonius' Kommentar zum Jo-Evangelium,"Biblica 44 (1963) 164-65.

5:27 BARRETT, C. K. The New Testament Background (1956) 90, 255. SCHULZ, S., Untersuchungen zur Menschensohn-Christologie im Johannesevangelium (Göttingen 1957) 111-13. WILES, M. F., The Spiritual Gospel (1960) 114-15, 140. SCHNACKENBURG, R. NTS 11 (1964-1965) 125f. HIGGINS, A. J. B. Menschensohn-Studien (1965) 32-35. BOUS-

SET, W. Die Religion des Judentums im Späthellenistischen Zeitalter (1966 = 1926) 268. KUHL, J. Die Sendung Jesu und der Kirche nach dem Johannes-Evangelium (1967) 209-12. LEIVESTAD, R., "Der Apokalyptische Menschensohn ein theologisches Phantom," in: ASThI VI (1967-1968) H. Kosmala ed., 49-105. BÖHLIG, A., "Griechische und Orientalische Einflüsse im Urchristentum" in: Mysterion und Wahrheit (Leiden 1968) 55-56. LINDARS, B. "The Son of Man in the Johannine Christology," in: Christ and the Spirit in the New Testament (1973) B. Lindars/S. S. Smalley, eds., 43f., 46, 51, 53, 56f. BÜHNER, J.-A., Der Gesandte und sein Weg im 4. Evangelium (Tübingen 1977) 391, 398, 406-407. BERGMEIER, R., Glaube als Gabe nach Johannes (Stuttgart 1980) 40n.218, 211, 243n.123, 270n.552.

5:28-29   VOLZ, P. Die Eschatologie der jüdischen Gemeinde (1934) 270. SCHULZ., S. Untersuchungen zur Menschensohn-Christologie im Johannesevangelium (Göttingen 1957) 113-14. SMITH, D. M. The Composition and Order of the Fourth Gospel (1965) 218, 219, 229, 230, 231, 235, 237, 238. NÖTSCHER, F., Altorientalischer und altestamentlicher Auferstehungsglaube (Darmstadt 1970 = 1926) 305, 307-308. BORNKAMM, G. Geschichte und Glaube II (1971) 63f. CAVALLIN, H. C. C. Life After Death (1974) 2, 2n.10, 4, 1 n 30. LADD, G. E. A Theology of the New Testament (1974) 246, 258, 299, 300, 306, 307. BECKER, J., Auferstehung der Toten im Urchristentum (Stuttgart 1976) 143-45. DUNN, J. D. G., Jesus and the Spirit (London 1975) 118-19. RUDOLPH, K. Die Gnosis (Göttingen 1978) 207. "Auferstehung" in: TRE 4 (1979) 459. HODGES., Z. C., "Problem Passages in the Gospel of John. Part 6: Those Who Have Done Good—John 5:28-29" BiblSa 136 (1979) 158-66. BERGMEIER, R., Glaube als Gabe nach Johannes (Stuttgart 1980) 205, 208, 243n.120, 123, 270n.553. "Chiliasmus" in: TRE 7 (1981) 725.

5:28   DELLING, G. Wort und Werk Jesu im Johannes-Evangelium (1966) 140f. NICKELS, P. Targum and New Testament (1967) 54. SMITH, M. Tannaitic Parallels to the Gospels (1968) 2, 80. CADMAN, W. H. The Open Heaven (1969) G. B. Caird ed., 44, 45, 147, 151, 152, 170, 186. THUESING, W. Die Erhöhung und Verherrlichung Jesu im Johannesevangelium (1970) 283-85.

5:29   CAVALLIN, H. C. C. Life After Death (1974) 3 n.14. FORESTELL, J. T., The Word of the Cross: Salvation as Revelation in the Fourth Gospel (Rome 1974) 33, 51, 119, 128, 129, 130.

5:30-47 ODEBERG, H. The Fourth Gospel (1968) 217ff. BEUTLER, J. Martyria (1972) 26, 266, 331, 355. BERGMEIER, R., Glaube als Gabe nach Johannes (Stuttgart 1980) 211.

5:30-38 WEBER, O. Predigtmeditationen (1967) 246-49.

5:30-37 TRAUB, H. in: Hören und Fragen Bd. 5,3 (1967) G. Eichholz/ A. Falkenroth eds., 67ff.

5:30 PALLIS, A., Notes on St. John and the Apocalypse (London 1928) 11. WILES, M. F. The Spiritual Gospel (1960) 124, 126, 127, 133, 134. HAHN, F. Christologische Hoheitstitel (1963) 40f. REUSS, J. "Presbyter Ammonius' Kommentar zum Jo-Evangelium," Biblica 44 (1963) 165-66. DELLING, G. Wort und Werk Jesu im Johannes-Evangelium (1966) 35, 60, 63, 103, 112f., 142. KUHL, J. Die Sendung Jesu und der Kirche nach dem Johannes-Evangelium (1967) 95f., 143. NICKELS, P. Targum and New Testament (1967) 54. BEUTLER, J. Martyria (1972) 254, 256, 260, 269. BERGMEIER, R., Glaube als Gabe nach Johannes (Stuttgart 1980) 243n.123, 270n.552, 554.

5:31ff RUDOLPH, K. Die Mandäer I (1960) 77. HAHN, F. Das Verständnis der Mission im Neuen Testament (1965²) 140. BEUT-LER, J. Martyria (1972) 27f., 211f., 218f., 223ff., 227f., 229f., 254-65, 270f., 277ff., 285f., 292f. IBUKI, Y. Die Wahrheit im Johannesevangelium (1972) 231-35, 260f.

5:31-47 GIBLET, J. "Le Témoignage Du Père (Jn. 5,31-47)," BVieC 12 (1955) 49-59. KUHL, J. Die Sendung Jesu und der Kirche nach dem Johannes-Evangelium (1967) 64f., 173. WINK, W. John the Baptist in the Gospel Tradition (1968) 96-97. DEEKS, D. "The Structure of the Fourth Gospel," NTS 15(1968-1969) 122ff. BERNARD, J., "Témoignage pour Jésus-Christ: Jean 5:31-47" MSR 36 (1979) 3-55. BECKER, J., Das Evangelium nach Johannes (Gütersloh/Würzburg 1979) 248-49 (lit!), HAENCHEN, E., Das Johannesevangelium (Tübingen 1980) 292 (lit!).

5:31-40 von WAHLDE, U. C., "The Witnesses to Jesus in John 5:31-40 and Belief in the Fourth Gospel" CBQ 43 (1981) 385-404.

5:31-35 VOUGA, F., Le cadre historique et l'intention théologique de Jean (Paris 1977) 40-42.

5:31-32 CREHAN, J. The Theology of St. John (1965) 26-27, 30.

5:32 DELLING, G. Wort und Werk Jesu im Johannes-Evangelium (1966) 47. RUCKSTUHL, E. Die literarische Einheit des Johannesevangeliums (1951) 226f. von WAHLDE, U. C., "The Witnesses to Jesus in John 5:31-40 and Belief in the Fourth Gospel" CBQ 43 (1981) 386, 388.

5:33-35 SEIDENSTICKER, P. Die Auferstehung Jesu in der Botschaft der Evangelisten (1968) 116f.

5:33 HAHN, F. Christologische Hoheitstitel (1963) 380. BRAUN, H. Qumran und NT II (1966) 122. de la POTTERIE, I., La Vérité dans Saint Jean I/II (Rome 1977) 91-100. BERGMEIER, R., Glaube als Gabe nach Johannes (Stuttgart 1980) 19, 203.

5:35 MORGAN, G. C. The Parables and Metaphors of Our Lord (1943) 284ff. BOISMARD, M. E., "Importance de la critique textuelle pour établir l'origine araméenne du quatrième évangile" in: M. Boismard et al. L'Evangile de Jean: études et problèmes (Bruges 1958) 56-57. RUDOLPH, K. Die Mandäer I (1960) 77. NEUGEBAUER, F. "Miszelle zu Joh 5:35," ZNW 52 (1-2, 1986) 130. HAHN, F. Christologische Hoheitstitel (1963) 330. REUSS, J. "Presbyter Ammonius' Kommentar zum Jo-Evangelium," Biblica 44 (1963) 166. KLIJN, A. F., "Die Syrische Baruch-Apokalypse" in: JüdSchr V/2 (1976) 134n2a. HANSON, A. T., The New Testament Interpretation of Scripture (London 1980) 162-66.

5:36-38 VOUGA, F., Le cadre historique et l'intention théologique de Jean (Paris 1977) 42-43.

5:36-37 CREHAN, J. The Theology of St. John (1965) 26, 41-44, 104.

5:36 VANHOYE, A. "Opera Jesu donum Patris," VerbDom 36 (2, 1958) 83-92. VANHOYE, H. "L'oeuvre du Christ, don du Père (Jn. V, 36 et XVII, 4)," RechSR 48 (3, 1960) 377-419. DELLING, G. Wort und Werk Jesu im Johannes-Evangelium (1966) 34, 48f., 60, 65, 67, 73f., 105. KUHL, J. Die Sendung Jesu und der Kirche nach dem Johannes-Evangelium (1967) 92-94, 112-14, 174, 183. DAUER, A. Die Passionsgeschichte im Johannesevangelium (1972) 210, 213, 290, 291. LADD, G. E. A Theology of the New Testament (1974) 267. METZGER, B. M., The Early Versions of the New Testament (Oxford 1977) 84. von WAHLDE, U. C., "The Witnesses to Jesus in John 5:31-40 and Belief in the Fourth Gospel" CBQ 43 (1981) 386, 388.

5:37-38 PANCARO, S., The Law in the Fourth Gospel (Leiden 1975) 180, 183, 209, 210, 216-26.

5:37 BROX, N. Zeuge und Märtyrer (1961) 74f. BAUMERT, N., Täglich Sterben und Auferstehen. Der Literalsinn von 2 Kor 4,12-5,10 (München 1973) 228. BERGMEIER, R., Glaube als Gabe nach Johannes (Stuttgart 1980) 17. von WAHLDE, U. C., "The Witnesses to Jesus in John 5:31-40 and Belief in the Fourth Gospel" CBQ 43 (1981) 386, 388-91, 393-95.

5:38-21:25 GRYGLEWICZ, F. NTS 11 (1964-1965) 259f.

5:38 FLEW, R. N. Jesus and His Church (1956) 177n. BORIG, R. Der Wahre Weinstock (1967) 43, 53f., 62, 225. HEISE, J. Bleiben (1967) 69-70. von WAHLDE, U. C., "The Witnesses to Jesus in John 5:31-40 and Belief in the Fourth Gospel" CBQ 43 (1981) 386-96.

5:39-47 GLASSON, T. F. Moses in the Fourth Gospel (1963) 89f. KLAAS, W. in: Herr, tue meine Lippen auf Bd. 3 (1964) G. Eichholz ed., 106ff. FORCK, G., in: GPM 35 (1981) 308-13. RIESS, R., in: P. Krusche et al. (eds.) Predigtstudien für das Kirchenjahr 1980-1981. III/2 (Stuttgart 1981) 99-108.

5:39.45f. HAHN, F. Das Verständnis der Mission im Neuen Testament (1965²) 138.

5:39-40 DUPONT, J. Essais sur la Christologie de Saint Jean (1951) 27, 164, 206, 207, 208, 215. REIM, G., Studien zum Alttestamentlichen Hintergrund des Johannesevangeliums (Cambridge 1974) 144, 270, 278-79. VOUGA, F., Le cadre historique et l'intention théologique de Jean (Paris 1977) 43-44.

5:39 BOISMARD, M. E., "Importance de la critique textuelle pour établir l'origine ataméenne du quatrième l'évangile" in: M. Boismard et al., L'Evangile de Jean: études et problèmes (Bruges 1958) 51-52. HENNECKE, E./SCHNEEMELCHER, W. Neu-testamentliche Apokryphen (1964) I 59. SUMMERS, R. The Secret Sayings of the Living Jesus (1968) 67. LADD, G. E. A Theology of the New Testament (1974) 232, 256, 266, 275, 279. REIM, G., Studien zum Alttestamentlichen Hintergrund des Johannesevangeliums (Cambridge 1974) 143-45. BRUCE, F. F., The Time is Fulfilled (Exeter 1978) 35-53. BERGMEIER, R., Glaube als Gabe nach Johannes (Stuttgart 1980) 249n.227, 263n.472. "Bibel" in: TRE 6 (1980) 71-72. "Biblizismus" in: TRE 6 (1980) 479. MAGASS, W., "11 Thesen zum Bibellesen - und zum 'Suchen' in der Schrift (Joh 5,39)" LiBi 47 (1980) 5-20. von WAHLDE, U. C., "The Witnesses to Jesus in John 5:31-40 and Belief in the Fourth Gospel" CBQ 43 (1981) 386-88.

5:41-47 WALTER, L., L'incroyance des croyants selon saint Jean (Paris 1976) 59-68.

5:41-44 PANCARO, S., The Law in the Fourth Gospel (Leiden 1975) 233-53, 266, 289, 511, 533. VOUGA, F., Le cadre historique et l'intention théologique de Jean (Paris 1977) 44-45.

5:41 "Ehre" in: TRE 9 (1982) 364.

5:42 WIKENHAUSER, A. Das Evangelium nach Johannes (1957) 287-89.

5:43 DELLING, G. Die Zueignung des Heils in der Taufe (1961) 43, 45. BOUSSET, W. Die Religion des Judentums im Späthellenistischen Zeitalter (1966 = 1926) 255. UNTERGASSMAIR, F. G., Im Namen Jesu: Der Namensbegriff im Johannesevangelium (Stuttgart 1974) 47-56. BÜHNER, J.-A., Der Gesandte und sein Weg im 4. Evangelium (Tübingen 1977) 148-49. "Antichrist" in: TRE 3 (1978) 22, 45.

5:44 THEISSEN, G. W. "Unbelief" in the New Testament (1965) 44f. PANCARO, S., The Law in the Fourth Gospel (Leiden 1975) 239, 241-53. "Ehre" in: TRE 9 (1982) 365.

5:45-47 REIM, G. Studien zum Alttestamentlichen Hintergrund des Johannesevangeliums (Cambridge 1974) 128-29. PANCARO, S., The Law in the Fourth Gospel (Leiden 1975) 231, 232, 233, 254-63. SAITO, T., Die Mosevorstellungen im Neuen Testament (Bern 1977) 116-17, 141-42. VOUGA, F., Le cadre historique et l'intention théologique de Jean (Paris 1977) 45-46.

5:45-46 BERGMEIER, R., Glaube als Gabe nach Johannes (Stuttgart 1980) 16, 249n.227.

5:45 VOLZ, P. Die Eschatologie der jüdischen Gemeinde (1934) 195. KNOX, W. L. The Sources of the Synoptic Gospels II (1957) 153. HENNECKE, E./SCHNEEMELCHER, W. Neutestamentliche Apoktyphen (1964) I 59. GRUNDMANN, W. NTS 12 (1965-1966) 47f.

5:46-47 PANCARO, S., The Law in the Fourth Gospel (Leiden 1975) 255, 258-63.

5:46 SMITH, M. Tannaitic Parallels to the Gospels (1968) 8 b n 5.

5:47 PANCARO, S., The Law in the Fourth Gospel (Leiden 1975) 88, 130, 146, 169, 170-72.

6-12 GUILDING, A. The Fourth Gospel and Jewish Worthip (1960) 213-16.

6-8 LANGBRANDTNER, W., Weltferner Gott oder Gott der Liebe (Frankfurt a. M./Bern/Las Vegas 1977) 79-83.

6-7 GLASSON, T. F. Moses in the Fourth Gospel (1963) 102ff.

6 BAUER, W. Das Johannesevangelium (1925) 97-99. SCHWEIZER, E., Ego Eimi (Göttingen 1939) 151-57.

BUECHSEL, F. Das Evangelium nach Johannes (1946) 93. HOSKYNS, E. C. The Fourth Gospel (1947) 304-307. CULL-MANN, O. Urchristentum und Gottesdienst (1950) 8, 45, 69f., 103f., 109. FEINE, D. P./BEHM, D. J. Einleitung in das Neue Testament (1950) 120f. DENNEY, J. The Death of Christ (1956³) 142. BECKER, H., Die Reden des Johannes-evangeliums und der Stil der gnostischen Offenbarungsrede (Göttingen 1956) 67-70, 117. MOLLAT, D. "Le Chapitre VIᵉ de Saint Jean," LuVie 31 (1957) 107-19. RACETTE, J. "L'unité du discours sur le pain de vie (Jean, VI)," ScienceEccl 9 (1, 1957) 82-85. LEON-DUFOUR, K. "Le mystère du Pain de Vie (Jean VI)," RechSR 46 (4, 1958) 481-523. STANLEY, D. M. "The Bread of Life," Worship 32 (8, 1958) 477-88. van den BUSSCHE, H., "La Structure de Jean I-XI" in: M. Bois-mard et al., L'Evangile de Jean: études et problèmes (Bruges 1958) 94-96. BORGEN, P. "The Unity of the Discourse in John 6," ZNW 50 (3-4, 1959) 277-78. GAERTNER, B. John 6 and the Jewish Passover (1959). LEENHARDT, F.-J. "La struc-ture du chapítre 6 de l'évangile de Jean," RHPhR 59 (1, 1959) 1-13. BORGEN, "'Brød fra himmel og fra jord. Om haggada i palestinsk midrasj, hos Philo og i Johannesevangelie" NTT 61 (4, 1960) 218-40. FEUILLE, A. "Les thèmes bibliques ma-jeurs du discours sur le pain de vie (Jn 6). Contribution a l'étude des sources de la pensée johannique," NRTh 82 (8, 1960) 803-22; (9, 1960) 918-39; (10, 1960) 1040-62. KILMARTIN, E. J. "Liturgical Influence on John 6," CBQ 22 (2, 1960) 183-91. KILMARTIN, E. J. "The Formation of the Bread of Life Dis-course John 6/," Scripture 12 (19, 1960) 75-78. KILMARTIN, E. J., "A First Century Chalice Dispute," SciEccl 12 (3, 1960) 403-408. STOEGER, A. "Die Eucharistie bei Johannes," BuK 13 (2, 1960) 41-43. SCHULZ, S., Komposition und Herkunft der Johanneischen Reden (Stuttgart 1960) 72-74, 94-98. BRENNAN, J. "The Living Bread," Furrow 12 (11, 1961) 647-61. MacGREGOR, G. H. C. "The Eucharist in the Fourth Gos-pel," NTS 9 (1962-1963) 114f. PARKER, D. "Luke and the Fourth Evangelist," NTS 9 (1962-1963) 331f. AMBRO-SANIO, A. "La dottrina eucaristica in S. Giovanni secondo in recenti discussioni tra i protestanti," RivB 11 (2, 1963) 145-65. BORGEN, P. "Observations on the Midrashic character of John 6," ZNW 54 (1963) 232-39. BROOKS, O. S. "The Johannine Eucharist. Another Interpretation," JBL 82 (3, 1963) 293-300. DUNKERLEY, R. "The Sign of the Meal," LondQuart-HolRev 32 (1, 1963) 61-66. GLASSON, T. F., Moses in the Fourth Gospel (1963) ch. VI, 90f., 107. WORDEN, T. "The Holy Eucharist in St. John-I," Scripture 15 (32, 1963) 97-103.

BLIGH, J. "Jesus in Galilee," HeyJ 5 (1, 1964) 3-26. LIN-DIGER, C. H. De Sacramenten in het Vierde Evangelie (1964) 68ff. MOLLAT, D. "The Sixth Chapter of St. John," in: The Eucharist in the New Testament (1964) 143-56. RULAND, V., "Sign and Sacrament. John's Bread of Life Discourse (Chapter 6)," Interpretation 18 (4, 1964) 450-62. BORGEN, P. Bread From Heaven (1965) 22, 26, 27, 35, 42, 44, 45, 55, 67, 68, 74, 85, 97, 99, 114, 152, 153, 154, 156, 158, 178, 180, 185, 188, 189, 190. SCHATTENMANN, J. "Der Hymnus in Johannes 6," in: Studien Zum Neutestamentlichen Prosahymnus (1965) 33-39. SMITH, D. M. The Composition and Order of the Fourth Gospel (1965) 141-52. BRAUN, F.-M. Jean le Théologien (1966) 107-12. BRAUN, H. Qumran und NT II (1966) 42. DELLING, G. Wort und Werk Jesu im Johannes-Evangelium (1966) 16, 22, 61, 76, 118. MOORE, F. J. "Eating the Flesh and Drinking the Blood: A Reconsideration," AThR 48 (1, 1966) 70-75. DEKKER, C. NTS 13 (1966-1967) 77ff. NICK-ELS, P. Targum and New Testament (1967) 54. BER-ROUARD, M.-F. "La multiplication des pains et le discours du pain de vie (Jean, 6)," LuVie 18 (94, 1969) 63-75. GI-BLET, J. "The Eucharist in St. John's Gospel (John 6)," Concilium 40 (1969) 60-69. MEES, M. "Sinn und Bedeutung westlicher Textvarianten in John 6," BZ 13 (2, 1969) 244-51. LE DEAUT, R. "Une aggadah targumique et les 'murmures' de Jean 6," Biblica 51 (1, 1970) 80-83. DUNN, J. D. G. Baptism in the Holy Spirit (1970) 175, 183ff., 189. DUNN, J. D. G. "John VI = A Eucharistic Discourse?" NTS 17 (1970-1971) 328-38. BORNKAMM, G. Geschichte und Glaube II (1971) 51-54. PREISS, T. "Etude sur le chapitre 6 de l'Evangile de Jean," EThR 46 (2, 1971) 143-67. SCHLIER, H. Das Ende der Zeit (1971) 102-23. KUEMMEL, W. G. Einleitung in das Neue Testament (1973) 171f. KYSAR, R. "The Source Analysis of the Fourth Gospel-A Growing Consensus?" NovTest 15 (2, 1973) 134-52. LINDARS, B. "The Son of Man in the Johannine Christology," in: Christ and the Spirit in the New Testament (1973) B. Lindars/S. S. Smalley eds., 45, 48, 62, 58. RIEDL, J. Das Heilswerk Jesu nach Johannes (1973) 283-343. SHORTER, M. "The Position of Chapter VI in the Fourth Gospel," ET 84 (6, 1973) 181-83. DAVIES, W. D. The Gospel and the Land (1974) 296, 304, 322, 325, 349. BARTLETT, L., Fact and Faith (Valley Forge 1975) 62. CROATTO, J. S. "Riletture dell'Esodo nel cap. 6 di San Giovanni" BiblOr 17 (1975) 11-20. HEIN, K., Eucharist and Excommunicaton (Frankfurt 1975) 24-34. LOHSE, E., "Miracles in the Fourth Gospel" in: M. Hooker/C. Hickling (eds.) What About the New Testament? FS.

C. Evans (London 1975) 66-67. TEMPLE, S., The Core of the Fourth Gospel (London 1975) 131-49. WALTER, L., L'incroyance des croyants selon saint Jean (Paris 1976) 69-87. "Abendmahl" in: TRE 1 (1977) 62, 114. de JONGE, M., Jesus: Stranger from Heaven and Son of God (Missoula 1977) 129-30. LANGBRANDTNER, W., Weltferner Gott oder Gott der Liebe (Frankfurt a.m./Bern/Las Vegas 1977) 1-11. TRITES, A. A., The New Testament Concept of Witness (Cambridge 1977) 103-104. "Agende" in: TRE 2 (1978) 27. BRUCE, F. F., The Time is Fulfilled (Exeter 1978) 42-44. RUSCH, F. A., "The Signs and the Discourse—The Rich Theology of John 6" CuThM 5 (1978) 386-90. THYEN, H., "Aus der Literatur zum Johannesevangelium (P. ForTsetzung)" ThR 43 (1978) 328-59. VELLANICKAL, M., "Jesus: the Bread of Life" BB 4 (1978) 30-48. RIGOPOULOS, G. C. *Jesous Christos "Ho Artos ho zōn"* (Athens: privately published, 1979). RUAGER, S., Johannes: 6 og nadveren" TTK 50 (1979) 81-92. GIBLET, J., "La chair du Fils de l'homme" LuVie 29 (1980) 89-103. SCHILLEBEECKX, E., Christ: the Christian Experience in the Modern World (London 1980) 387-88; GT: Christus und die Christen (Freiburg/Basel/Wien 1977) 373-74. LEIDIG, E., Jesu Gespräch mit der Samaritanerin (Basel 1981) 212-18.

6:1ff LIGHTFOOT, R. H. History and Interpretation in the Gospels (1934) 115f. WILKENS, W. Die Entstehungsgeschichte des vierten Evangeliums (1958) 43, 44, 45. GRUNDMANN, W. Zeugnis und Gestalt des Johannes-Evangeliums (1961) 39-43. HAHN, F. Christologische Hoheitstitel (1963) 397. SMITH, D. M. The Composition and Order of the Fourth Gospel (1965) 128ff. 226.

6:1-71 CORELL, A. Consummatum Est (1958) 63-67. DE JULLIOT, H. "Le Pain de Vie (Jean 6,1-71)," BVieC 26 (1959) 38-43. YATES, K. M. Preaching from John's Gospel (1964) 63-70. DEEKS, D. "The Structure of the Fourth Gospel," NTS 15 (1968-1969) 125ff. SCHNIDER, F./STENGER, W. Johannes und die Synoptiker (1971) 89-178.

6:1-59 WORDEN, T. "The Holy Eucharist in St John-II," Scripture 16 (33, 1964) 5-16.

6:1-51 MUELLER, T. Das Heilsgeschehen im Johannesevangelium n.d., 104-108.

6:1-35 HEER, J. "Jesus das Brot des Lebens," Sein und Sendung 33 (7, 1968) 291-308.

6:1-30 MENDER, S. "Zum Problem 'Johannes und die Synoptiker,'" NTS 4 (1958) 285ff.

6:1-26 RUCKSTUHL, E. Die literarische Einheit des Johannesevangeliums (1951) 110, 117-22.

6:1-25 HEIL, J. P., Jesus Walking on the Sea (Rome 1981) 145-52.

6:1-21 BLANK, J. "Die johanneische Brotrede. Einführung: Brotvermehrung und Seewandel Jesu: Jo 6,1-21," BuL 7 (3, 1966) 193-
207. KONINGS, J., "The Pre-Markan Sequence in Jn VI: A
Critical Re-examination" Bibliotheca ephemeridum theologicarum Lovaniensium 34 (Louvain 1974) 147-77. EGGER, W.,
Frohbotschaft und Lehre (Frankfurt a.M. 1976) 123. BECKER,
J., Das Evangelium nach Johannes (Gütersloh/Würzburg 1979)
189 (lit!).

6:1-15 BARTH, GPM 4 (1949-1950) 102ff. FRICK, GPM 9 (1954-
1955) 88ff. IWAND, H.-J., in: Herr, tue meine Lippen auf Bd.
1 (1957) G. Eichholz ed., 106-10. FRIEDRICH, GPM 15 (1960-
1961) 99ff. HAHN, F. Christologische Hoheitstifel (1963) 391.
KNACKSTEDT, J. NTS 10 (1963-1964) 317f. KAMPHAUS,
F. Von der Exegese zur Predigt (1968²) 145-49, 204-206. WIL-
KENS, W., Zeichen und Werke (Zürich 1969) 35-37. NICOL,
W. The Semeia in the Fourth Gospel (1972) 31ff., 43, 57, 74,
79, 111f. PFITZNER, K. "Laetare. Johannes 6,1-15," in:
Predigtstudien (1972-1973) E. Lange ed., 164-70. TREVI-
JANO, E. R., "Crisis mesiánica en la multiplicación de los
panes (Mc 6:30-46 y Jn 6,1-15)" Burgense 16 (1975) 413-39.
WIEBERING, J., in: GPM 33 (1979) 318-22. HAENCHEN,
E., Das Johannesevangelium (Tübingen 1980) 299 (lit!).
TRAUB, G., "Die Wunder im Neuen Testament" in: A. Suhl
(ed.) Der Wunderbegriff im Neuen Testament (Darmstadt 1980)
171-72.

6:1-14 HEISING, A. Die Botschaft der Brotvermehrung (1967).
RUDDICK, C. T. "Feeding and Sacrifice-The Old Testament
Background of the Fourth Gospel," ET 79 (11, 1968) 340-41.
FORTNA, R. T. The Gospel of Signs (1970) 38, 55-64, 86, 95,
105. CRIBBS, F. L. in: SBL Seminar Papers 2 (1973) MacRae,
G., ed., 3. MARTYN, J. L., The Gospel of John in Christian
History (New York 1978) 23-24, 28, 68.

6:1-13.26-65 CULLMANN, O. Urchristentum und Gottesdienst (1950) 89ff.

6:1-13 LEE, E. K. "St. Mark and the Fourth Gospel," NTS 3 (1956-
1957) 51ff. ZIENER, G. "Weisheitsbuch und Johannesevangelium", Biblica 38 (1957) 407-409. JOHNSTON, E. D.
"The Johannine Version of the Feeding of the Five Thousand-
an Independent Tradition?" NTS 8 (2, 1962) 151-54. BECKER,
U./WIBBING, S. Wundergeschichten (1965) 55ff. MEEKS, W.
A. The Prophet-King, Moses Traditions and the Johannine

Christology (1967) 91-98. QUIEVREUX, F. "Le récit de la Multiplication des pains dans le quatrième évangile," RevSR 41 (2, 1967) 97-108. VOEOEBUS, A. Liturgical Tradition in the Didache (1968) 137-57. SCHRAMM, T. Der Markus-Stoff bei Lukas (1971) 129f. KYSAR, R., The Fourth Evangelist and his Gospel (Minneapolis 1974) 252-54. LANGBRANDTNER, W., Weltferner Gott oder Gott der Liebe (Frankfurt 1977) 1-2. SWIDLER, L., Biblical Affirmations of Woman (Philadelphia 1979) 249, 279. BAGATTI, B., "Dove avvenne la moltiplicazione dei pani?" Salmanticensis 28 (1981) 293-98.

6:1 CREHAN, J. The Theology of St. John (1965) 150-51. FORTNA, R. T. The Gospel of Signs (1970) 55f.

6:2 CRIBBS, F. L., "The Agreements that Exist Between John and Acts" in: C. H. Talbert (ed.) Perspectives on Luke-Acts (Danville 1978) 60.

6:4ff STONEHOUSE, N. B. The Witness of Matthew and Mark to Christ (1944) 32.

6:4 GRILL, J. Untersuchungen über die Entstehung des vierten Evangeliums II (1923) 125, 160f. FEINE, D. P.,/BEHM, D. J. Einleitung in das Neue Testament (1950) 113f. SMITH, D. M. The Composition and Order of the Fourth Gospel (1965) 97, 104, 128, 216.

6:5-9 COLSON, J. L'Enigme du disciple que Jésus aimait (1969) 18-40. FORTNA, R. T. The Gospel of Signs (1970) 57ff. STURCH, R. L., " The Alleged Eyewitness Material in the Fourth Gospel" in: E. A. Livingstone (ed.) Studia Biblica 1978/ II (Sheffield 1980) 318-20.

6:7 PARKER, T. H. L. Calvin's New Testament Commentaries (1971).

6:8 KAESEMANN, E. Exegetische Versuche und Besinnungen (1964) I 254.

6:9ff HENNECKE, E./SCHNEEMELCHER, W. Neutestamentliche Apokryphen (1964) I 129.

6:11 GRILL, J. Untersuchungen über die Entstehung des vierten Evangeliums II (1923) 118f. JEREMIAS, J. Die Abendmahlsworte Jesu (1960) 166-68. WANKE, J., Die Emmauserzählung (Leipzig 1973) 104. CLARK, K. W., "The Text of the Gospel of John in Third-Century Egypt" in: The Gentile Bias and Other Essays (Leiden 1980) 160-61.

6:12-15 DUNN, J. D. G., Unity and Diversity in the New Testament (London 1977) 78.

6:12-13 BRAUN, F.-M. ''Quatre 'Signes' Johanniques de L'unité Chrétienne,'' NTS 9 (1962-1963) 147f. FORTNA, H. T. The Gospel of Signs (1970) 59f.

6:14-21 YATES, K. M. Preaching from John's Gospel (1964) 71-74.

6:14-15 VOLZ, P. Die Eschatologie der jüdischen Gemeinde (1934) 194. GLASSON, T. F. Moses in the Fourth Gospel (1963) 27ff. HAHN, F. Christologische Hoheitstitel (1963) 174, 370, 392, 397. KAESEMANN, E. Exegetische Versuche und Besinnungen (1943) I 226. MEEKS, W. A. The Prophet-King, Moses Traditions and the Johannine Christology (1967) 87-91. FORTNA, R. T. The Gospel of Signs (1970) 60-62. KIPPENBERG, H. G. Garizim und Synagoge (1971) 324, passim. NICOL, W. The Sēmeia in the Fourth Gospel (1972) 87f. de JONGE, M., Jesus: Stranger from Heaven and Son of God (Missoula 1977) 57-58.

6:14 DAVIES, W. D. Torah in the Messianic Age and/or the Age to Come (1952) 44/. BOUSSET, W. Die Religion des Judentums im Späthellenistischen Zeitalter (1966 = 1926) 233. VÖÖBUS, A. The Gospels in Studying and Preaching (1966) 217f. MEEKS, W. A. The Prophet-King, Moses Traditions and the Johannine Christology (1967) 22-26. LADD, G. E. A Theology of the New Testament (1974) 225, 273, 274. SCHELKLE, K. H. ''Jesus-Lehrer und Prophet,'' in: Orientierung an Jesus (1973) P. Hoffmann ed., 305f. REIM, G. Studien zum Alttestamentlichen Hintergrund des Johannesevangeliums (Cambridge 1974) 122-23, 133-34, 225-26. METZGER, B. M., The Early Versions of the New Testament (Oxford 1977) 177.

6:15-25 FORTNA, R. T. The Gospel of Signs (1970) 64-70. HEIL, J. P., Jesus Walking on the Sea (Rome 1981) passim.

6:15 BLAIR, E. P. Jesus in the Gospel of Matthew (1960) 52. HAHN, F. Christologische Hoheitstitel (1963) 187. NICKELS, P. Targum and New Testament (1967) 54. JEREMIAS, J. Neutestamentliche Theologie (1971) I 76f. DAUER, A. Die Passionsgeschichte in Johannesevangelium (1972) 107, 123, 253. LADD, G. E. A Theology of the New Testament (1974) 139, 243, 275, 411. HEIL, J. P., Jesus Walking on the Sea (Rome 1981) 75-76.

6:16ff LIGHTFOOT, R. H. History and Interpretation in the Gospels (1934) 189f. WILKENS, W. Die Entstehungsgeschichte des vierten Evangeliums (1958) 43-47.

6:16-27 WILKENS, W., Zeichen und Werke (Zürich 1969) 37-39.

6:16-25 NICOL, W. The Sēmeia in the Fourth Gospel (1972) 34f., 58f., 74, 92. HAENCHEN, E., Das Johannesevangelium (Tübingen 1980) 310 (lit!).

6:16-21 KNACKSTEDT, J. NTS 10 (1963-1964) 310f. MUSSNER, F. Die Wunder Jesu (1967) 61-68. ZARRELLA, P. "Gesù cammina sulle acque. Significato teologico di Giov. 6,16-21," SouC 95 (2, 1967) 146-60. ITTEL, G. W. Jesus und die Jünger (1970) 67-69. HARNER, P. B. The "I Am" of the Fourth Gospel (1970) 47-48. BETH, K., "Di Wunder Jesu" in: A. Suhl (ed.) Der Wunderbegriff im Neuen Testament (Darmstadt 1980) 115-16. TRAUB, G., "Die Wunder im Neuen Testament" in: A. Suhl (ed.) Der Wunderbegriff im Neuen Testament (Darmstadt 1980) 165-71.

6:16-17 HEIL, J. P., Jesus Walking on the Sea (Rome 1981) 76-77.

6:17-18 HEIL, J. P., Jesus Walking on the Sea (Rome 1981) 77.

6:19 HEIL, J. P., Jesus Walking on the Sea (Rome 1981) 77-79.

6:20 HOWARD, V. P., Das Ego in den Synoptischen Evangelien (Marburg 1975) 253. METZGER, B. M., The Early Versions of the New Testament (Oxford 1977) 246. HEIL, J. P., Jesus Walking on the Sea (Rome 1981)79-80.

6:21 RENIE, J. "Une Antilogie Evangélique. Mc 6,51-52; Mt 14,32-33," Biblica 36 (1955) 223-26. METZGER, B. M., The Early Versions of the New Testament (Oxford 1977) 392. HEIL, J. P., Jesus Walking on the Sea (Rome 1981) 80-82.

6:22-71 LEAL, J. "La fe como ascética y mistica en el discurso del lan de la vida (Jn 6,22-71)," Manresa 43 (168, 1971) 195-202. BECKER, J., Das Evangelium nach Johannes (Gütersloh/ Würzburg 1979) 198-99 (lit!).

6:22-59 STACHOWIAK, L. "Literackie i egzetyczne problemy perikopy o chlebie z nieba (Jn 6,22-59)," SThV 11 (2, 1973) 57-74. THOMAS, J., "Le discours dans la synagogue de Capharnaüm. Note sur Jean 6, 22-59" Christus 29 (1982) 218-22.

6:22-66 LINDARS, B., "Discourse and Tradition: The Use of the Sayings of Jesus in the Discourses of the Fourth Gospel" JSNT 13 (1981) 88-89.

6:22-59 "Auferstehung" in: TRe 4 (1979) 460.

6:22-51 WIKENHAUSER, A. Das Evangelium nach Johannes (1957) 134-36.

6:22-50 BLANK, J. " 'Ich bin das Lebensbrot' Jo 6,22-50," BuL 7 (4, 1966) 255-70.

6:22-31 PORSCH, F., Pneuma und Wort (Frankfurt 1974) 171-74.

6:22-29 SCHMAUCH, W. GPM 17 (1, 1963) 142-46. KLEIN, G. GPM 23 (2, 1968) 132-38. SCHMIDT, H. GPM 29 (2, 1975) 169ff. SOLLE, S. und RAISS, H., in: P. Krusche et al. (eds.) Predigtstudien für das Kirchenjahr 1974-1975 III/1 (Stuttgart 1974) 155-64. SCHMIDT, H., in: GPM 29 (1975) 169-75.

6:22-28 HAACKER, K. Die Stiftung des Heils (1972) 106-108.

6:22-24 ROBERGE, M., "Jean VI,22-24. Un problème de critique textuelle?" LThPh 34 (1978) 275-89; 35 (1979) 139-51.

6:22 PALLIS, A., Notes on St. John and the Apocalypse (London 1928) 12.

6:23 HAHN, F. Christologische Hoheitstitel (1963) 94. METZGER, B. M., The Early Versions of the New Testament (Oxford 1977) 422-23.

6:24-71 TEMPLE, S. "A Key to the Composition of the Fourth Gospel," JBL 80 (3, 1961) 220-32.

6:24-29 JENSEM. H. W. in: Herr, tue meine Lippen auf Bd. 3 (1964) G. Eichholz ed., 475ff.

6:24 VOLZ, P. Die Eschatologie der jüdischen Gemeinde (1934) 193.

6:25ff BLAIR, E. P. Jesus in the Gospel of Matthew (1960) 146.

6:25-66 SCHLATTER, D. A. Die Theologie des Neuen Testaments I (1909) 499-502.

6:25-59 ALETTI, J.-N., "Le discours sur le pain de vie (Jean 6). Problèmes de composition et fonction des citations de l'Ancien Testament" RechSR 62 (1974) 169-97. MUÑOZ LEÓN, D., "El sustrato targúmico del Discurso del Pan de Vida. Nuevas aportaciones: La equivalencia 'venir' = 'aprender/creer' (Jn 6,35.37.45) y la conexión 'vida eterna' y 'resurrección' (Jn 6,40.54)" EstBi 36 (1977) 217-26.

6:25-58 GALBIATI, E. "Il pane della vita (Giov. 6,25-58)," BiOr 5 (3, 1963) 101-10.

6:25-51(59) RUCKSTUHL, E. Die literarische Einheit des Johannesevangeliums (1961) 120-22, 159, 170, 247, 251-62.

6:25-51 GAMBINO, G., "Struttura, Composizione e Analisi letterario-teologica di GV 6,25-51" RivB 24 (1976) 337-38. MUELLER, T. Das Heilsgeschehen im Johannesevangelium n.d., 31-33.

6:25-29 COUSINS, P. E. "The Feeding of the Five Thousand," EQ 39 (3, 1967) 152-54.

6:25 HAHN, F. Christologische Hoheitstitel (1963) 75.

6:26-71 ODEBERG, H. The Fourth Gospel (1968) 235ff. CADMAN, W. H. The Open Heaven (1969) G. B. Caird ed., 81-96. SCHNIDER, F./STENGER, W. Johannes und die Synoptiker (1971) 154-70.

6:26-59 MAURER, C. Ignatius von Antiochien und das Johannesevangelium (1949) 34ff., 77ff. HAENCHEN, E., Das
Johannesevangelium (Tübingen 1980) 317-19 (lit!).

6:26-58 PORSCH, F., Pneuma und Wort (Frankfurt 1974) 162-65.
MOLONEY, F. J., "John 6 and the Celebration of the Eucharist" DRev 93 (1975) 243-51. SCHENKE, L., "Die formale
und gedankliche Struktur von Joh 6,26-58" BZ 24 (1980) 21-
41. HEIL, J. P., Jesus Walking on the Sea (Rome 1981) 152-
65.

6:26-51 RICHTER, G. "Die alttestamentlichen Zitate in der Rede vom
Himmelbrot Joh 6,26-51a," in: Schriftauslegung (1972) J.
Ernst, ed., 193-279. GAMBINO, G. "Struttura, composizione
e analis: letterario-teologica di Gv. 6,26-51b" RivB 24 (1976)
337-58.

6:26-40 HEIL, P., Jesus Walking on the Sea (Rome 1981) 153-57.

6:26-35 TEMPLE, S., The Core of the Fourth Gospel (London 1975)
141-44. LANGBRANDTNER, W., Weltferner Gott oder Gott
der Liebe (Frankfurt 1977) 3-4.

6:26-34 PANCARO, S. The Law in the Fourth Gospel (Leiden 1975)
453, 454-72, 473.

6:26-31 WALTER, L., L'incroyance des croyants selon saint Jean (Paris
1976) 70-76.

6:26 KAESEMANN, E. Exegetische Versuche und Besinnungen
(1964) I 216, 226. SCHOTTROFF, L. Der Glaubende und die
feindliche Welt (1970) 250-52, 254f., 257, 263. GROB, F., "
'Vous me cherchez, non parce que vouz avez vu des signes. . .
.' Essai d'explication coheŕente de Jean 6/26" RHPR 60 (1980)
429-39.

6:27-58 WEAD, D. W. The Literary Devices in John's Gospel (1970)
83-86.

6:27-51 SMITH, D. M. The Composition and Order of the Fourth Gospel (1965) 148ff, 150, 151. KUHL, J. The Sendung Jesu und
der Kirche nach dem Johannes-Evangelium (1967) 191f.

6:27 DUPONT, J. Essais sur la Christologie de Saint Jean (1951) 164,
193, 201. RUCKSTUHL, E. Die literarische Einheit des
Johannesevangeliums (1951) 34, 164, 169, 176, 242, 251, 253,
254, 255, 257, 260, 268. SCHULZ, S., Untersuchungen zur
Menschensohn-Christologie im Johannesevangelium (Göttingen 1957) 115-17. DELLING, G. Die Taufe im Neuen Testament (1963) 105. SCHNACKENBURG, R. NTS 11 (1964-65)
124f. SMITH, D. M. The Composition and Order of the Fourth
Gospel (1965) 142f. DELLING, G. Wort und Werk Jesu im Jo-

hannes-Evangelium (1966) 66f., 122, 145f. HEISE, J. Bleiben
(1967) 66-69. KUHL, J. Die Sendung Jesu und der Kirche nach
dem Johannes-Evangelium (1967) 93f. SMALLEY, S. S., "The
Johannine Son of Man Sayings," NTS 15 (1968-69) 293ff.
DUNN, J. D. G. Baptism in the Holy Spirit (1970) 29n, 33, 184.
IBUKI, Y. Die Wahrheit im Johannesevangelium (1972) 350f.
LINDARS, B. "The Son of Man in the Johannine Christol-
ogy," in: Christ and the Spirit in the New Testament (1973) B.
Lindars/S. S. Smalley eds., 44, 58f. LADD, G. E. A Theology
of the New Testament (1974) 245, 257, 274. BERGMEIER, R.,
Glaube als Gabe nach Johannes (Stuttgart 1980) 207, 227,
242n.113.

6:28-35,37- WILKENS, W. Die Entstehungsgeschichte des vierten Evan-
51, 59   geliums (1958) 94, 95, 96, 97, 98.

6:28-29 SMITH, D. M. The Composition and Order of the Fourth Gos-
pel (1965) 135, 136f., 137, 143, 149, 158, 159, 162. BERG-
MEIER, R. "Glaube als Werk? Die 'Werke Gottes' in
Damaskusschrift II,14-15 und Johannes 6,28-29," RevQ 6 (2,
1967) 253-60. IBUKI, Y., Die Wahrheit im Johannes-
evangelium (1972) 350f. PANCARO, S., The Law in the Fourth
Gospel (Leiden 1975) 384, 389-97. de la POTTERIE, I., La
Vérité dans Saint Jean I/II (Rome 1977) 510-12. BERG-
MEIER, R., Glaube als Gabe nach Johannes (Stuttgart 1980)
203, 223-24, 259n.396. von WAHLDE, U. C. "Faith and
Works in Jn vi 28-29. Exegesis or Eisegesis? NovT 22 (1980)
304-15.

6:28 BRAUN, H. Qumran und NT II (1966) 134.

6:29 BACCHIOCCHI, S., "John 5:17: Negation or Clarification of
the Sabbath?" AUSS 19 (1981) 14.

6:30-50 SAITO, T., Die Mosevorstellungen im Neuen Testament (Bern
1977) 109-13, 137-41, 143.

6:30-44 WEBER, O. Predigtmeditationen (1967) 53-57.

6:30-35 HEINRICH, G./ROSENBOOM, E. "Johannes 6,30-35: Wo-
von man leben kann," in: Predigtstudien (1975) P. Krusche/E.
Lange/D. Rössler/R. Rössler eds., 234-40. BERBERS, C. A.
P. und WIEDMANN, H.-G., in: P. Krusche et al (eds.)
Predigtstudien für das Kirchenjahr 1980-81. III/2 (Stuttgart
1981) 146-53.

6:30-33 HAMERTON-KELLY, R. G. Pre-Existence, Wisdom, and The
Son of Man (1973) 237-39.

6:30-31 GRILL, J. Untersuchungen über die Entstehung des vierten Evangeliums II (1923) 75f. HAHN, F. Christologische Hoheitstitel (1963) 391.

6:30 BLACK, M., An Aramaic Approach to the Gospels and Acts (1967) 77f.

6:31ff ELLIS, E. E. Paul's Use of the Old Testament (1957) 89, 131f. BORGEN, P. "Observations on the Midrashic Character of John 6," ZNW 54 (3-4, 1963) 232-40. MALINA, B. J. The Palestinian Manna Tradition (1968) 102-106.

6:31-58 BORGEN, P. Bread from Heaven (1965). RICHTER, G. "Zur Formgeschichte und literarischen Einheit vom Joh. 6:31-58," ZNW 60 (1-2, 1969) 21-55. JOHNSTON, G. The Spirit-Paraclete in the Gospel of John (1970) 131-34. MCDONALD, J. I. H., Kerygma and Didache (Cambridge 1980) 48-50.

6:31-51 PORSCH, F., Pneuma und Wort (Frankfurt 1974) 167-70.

6:31-33.49f.58 RICHARDSON, A. The Miracle-Stories of the Gospels (1948) 95f.

6:31 FREED, E. D. Old Testament Quotations in the Gospel of John (1965) 11-16. NICKELS, P. Targum and New Testament (1967) 54. REIM, G., Studien zum Alttestamentlichen Hintergrund des Johannesevangeliums (Cambridge 1974) 12-15, 89-91, 93-96. BERGMEIER, R., Glaube als Gabe nach Johannes (Stuttgart 1980) 207, 242n.104, 117-18. HANSON, A. T., The New Testament Interpretation of Scripture (London 1980) 159-62. LINDARS, B., "Discourse and Tradition. The Use of the Sayings of Jesus in the Discourses of the Fourth Gospel" JSNT 13 (1981) 88.

6:32ff BORNKAMM-BARTH-HELD, Ueberlieferung und Auslegung im Matthäus-Evangelium (^{2}1961) 32. SMITH, M. Tannaitic Parallels to the Gospels (1968) 2 b n 116, 8 end. BERGMEIER, R., Glaube als Gabe nach Johannes (Stuttgart 1980) 13, 207, 215-16, 242n.117.

6:32-59 BÜHNER, J.-A., Der Gesandte und sein Weg im 4. Evangelium (Tübingen 1977) 175-80.

6:32-58 BAUER, W. Das Johannesevangelium (1925) 95-97.

6:32-35 LEROY, H. Rätsel und Missverständnis (1968) 100-109. HORST, U., "Brot und Leben" Anzeiger für die katholische Geistlichkeit 88 (1979) 246-48.

6:32-34 HAHN, F. Christologische Hoheitstitel (1963) 391. PORSCH, F., Pneuma und Wort (Frankfurt 1974) 174-75.

6:32-33 RUCKSTUHL, E. Die literarische Einheit des Johannes-evangeliums (1951) 169, 238, 242, 244, 250, 254, 257. LADD, G. E. A Theology of the New Testament (1974) 216, 224, 226, 231, 257, 264, 267.

   6:32 PALLIS, A., Notes on St. John and the Apocalypse (London 1928) 12-13.

6:33-35 SMITH, D. M. The Composition and Order of the Fourth Gospel (1965) 135, 136, 137, 139, 140, 148, 149.

   6:33 DELLING, G. Wort und Werk Jesu im Johannes-Evangelium (1966) 58, 67, 118f., 121f. CADMAN, W. H. The Open Heaven (1969) G. B. Caird, ed., 34, 130, 182, 198. JEWETT, P. K., Infant Baptism and the Covenant of Grace (Grand Rapids 1978) 233.

6:35-58 MORGAN, G. C. The Parables and Metaphors of the Lord (1943) 289ff. BROWN, R. E. "The Eucharist and Baptism in St. John," Proceedings of the Society of Catholic Teachers of Sacred Doctrine 8 (1962) 14-37.

6:35-51 LÉON-DUFOUR, X., "Towards a Symbolic Reading of the Fourth Gospel" NTS 27 (1980-1981) 451-54.

6:35-38 LOCKYER, H. All the Parables of the Bible (1963) 318ff.

6:35-38 SCHNACKENBURG, R. "Das Brot des Lebens," in: Tradition und Glaube (1971) G. Jeremias ed., 328-43.

   6:35 BUECHSEL, F. Das Evangelium nach Johannes (1946) 85f. RUCKSTUHL, E. Die literarische Einheit des Johannes-evangeliums (1951) 50, 169, 242, 246, 250, 253f, 257, 268f. BORIG, R. Der Wahre Weinstock (1967) 25, 29ff., 99, 225. IBUKI, Y., Die Wahrheit im Johannesevangelium (1972) 343f. SCHNACKENBURG, R., Aufsätze und Studien zum Neuen Testament (Leipzig 1973) 349-63. REIM, G., Studien zum Alttestamentlichen Hintergrund des Johannesevangeliums (Cambridge 1974) 150-51. HAHN, F., "Die Worte vom lebendigen Wasser im Johannesevangelium. Eigenart und Wortgeschichte von Joh 4:10,13f., 6:35, 7:37-39" in: J. Jervell/W. A. Meeks (eds.) God's Christ and His People. FS. N.A. Dahl (New York 1977) 51-70. FISCHER, U., Eschatologie und Jenseitserwartung im hellenistischen Diasporajudentum (Berlin 1978) 68. RAYAN, S., The Holy Spirit: Heart of the Gospel and Christian Hope (New York 1978) 116-17. SWIDLER, L., Biblical Affirmations of Woman (Philadelphia 1979) 63, 289. KUZENZAMA, K. P. M., "La préhistoire de l'expression 'pain de vie' (Jn 6,36b, 48). Continuité ou émergence?" RATh 4 (1980) 65-83. KUZENZAMA, K. P. M., "L'expression Le Pain de vie' (Jn 6,35b) et les données néotestamentaires. Originalité johannque?" RATh 5 (1981) 45-55. MAIER, G., "Johannes

und Matthaeus - Zwiespalt oder Viergestalt des Evangeliums?''
in: A. T. France/D. Wenham (eds.) Gospel Perspectives II
(Sheffield 1981) 284-85.

6:36ff BERGMEIER, R., Glaube als Gabe nach Johannes (Stuttgart
1980) 259n.395.

6:36-40 PORSCH, F., Pneuma und Wort (Frankfurt 1974) 175-76.
LANGBRANDTNER, W., Weltferner Gott oder Gott der Liebe
(Frankfurt 1977) 268-71.

6:36 THEYSSEN, G. W. ''Unbelief'' in the New Testament
(Rüschlikon 1965) 49ff.

6:37-44 REBLIN, K. und ONNASCH, K., in: P. Krusche et al. (eds.)
Predigtstudien für das Kirchenjahr 1976-1977. V/2 (Stuttgart
1977) 222-29.

6:37-40.(41- HEINTZE, G. in: Hören und Fragen Bd. 5,3 (1967) G. Eicholz/
43).44 A. Falkenroth eds., 516ff.

6:37-40 SCHOENHERR, A. GPM 29 (1, 1974) 73-80. HERBERT, K.
GPM 23/I (1968-1969) 60-67. BÖTTCHER, W., in: P. Krusche
et al. (eds.) Predigtstudien für das Kirchenjahr 1974-1975. III/
1 (Stuttgart 1974) 79-85. PANCARO, S., The Law in the Fourth
Gospel (Leiden 1975) 372-74.

6:37 RUCKSTUHL, E. Die literarische Einheit des Johannes-
evangeliums (1951) 69, 199, 253f. HAHN, F. Das Verständnis
der Mission im Neuen Testament (²1965) 138. HOFIUS, O.,
''Erwählung und Bewährung. Zur Auslegung von Joh. 6,37''
ThB 8 (1977) 24-29. RAYAN, S., The Holy Spirit: Heart of the
Gospel and Christian Hope (New York 1978) 82. BERG-
MEIER, R., Glaube als Gabe nach Johannes (Stuttgart 1980)
27, 160n.255, 189, 236, 249n.225, 269n.530.

6:38 RUCKSTUHL, E. Die literarische Einheit des Johannes-
evangeliums (1951) 46, 253, 257, 266. WILES, M. F. The
Spiritual Gospel (1960) 121, 124, 126, 132. HAHN, F. Das
Verständnis der Mission im Neuen Testament (²1965) 140.
KUHL, J. Die Sendung Jesu und der Kirche nach dem Johan-
nes-Evangelium (1967) 95f.

6:39ff VOLZ, P. Die Eschatologie der jüdischen Gemeinde (1934) 270.

6:39-40 RUCKSTUHL, E. Die literarische Einheit des Johannesevangeliums (1951) 34, 159-70, 244, 253-55.. SMITH, D. M.
The Composition and Order of the Fourth Gospel (1965) 135,
138, 218, 226, 231, 232, 235, 237. LADD, G. E. A Theology
of the New Testament (1974) 248, 258, 263, 272, 299, 300, 305.
''Apokalyptik'' in: TRE 3 (1978) 234. BERGMEIER, R.

Glaube als Gabe nach Johannes (Stuttgart 1980) 27, 205, 208, 236, 249n.225, 269n.530.

6:40 DELLING, G. Die Zueignung des Heils in der Taufe (1961) 60. GLASSON, T. F. Moses in the Fourth Gospel (1963) 34f. HAHN, F. Christologische Hoheitstitel (1963) 329f. DELLING, G. Wort und Werk Jesu im Johannes-Evangelium (1966) 143f. CADMAN, W. H. The Open Heaven (1969) G. B. Caird ed., 12, 101, 147, 175. NÖTSCHER, F., Altorientalischer und alttestamentlicher Auferstehungsglaube(Darmstadt 1970 = 1926) 308. METZGER, B. M., The Early Versions of the New Testament (Oxford 1977) 91, 390.

6:41-52 BEAUVERY, R. "Le fils de Joseph! Manne descendue du ciel? Jn 6.41-52," AssS 50 (1974) 43-49.

6:41-47 LANGBRANDTNER, W. Weltferner Gott oder Gott der Liebe (Frankfurt 1977) 5-6. HEIL, P., Jesus Walking on the Sea (Rome 1981) 157-60.

6:41-43. LeDEAUT, R. "Une aggadah targumique et les 'murmures' de 58-61 Jean 6," Biblica 51 (I, 1970) 80-83.

6:41-42 LEROY, H. Rätsel und Missverständis (1968) 100-109. BERGMEIER, Glaube als Gabe nach Johannes (Stuttgart 1980) 215, 216, 242n.117.

6:41 LEIPOLDT, J. "Johannesevangelium und Gnosis," in: Neutestamentliche Studien (1914) A. Deissmann/H. Windisch eds., 147-49. GRILL, J. Untersuchungen über die Entstehung des vierten Evangeliums II (1923) 25, 224f., 360. RUCKSTUHL, E. Die literarische Einheit des Johannesevangeliums (1951) 253f. von WAHLDE, U. C., "The Johannine 'Jews': A Critical Survey" NTS 28 (1982) 38, 41-44, 45-46, 49, 54.

6:42-47 DERRETT, J. D. M., "Matthew 23:8-10 a Midrash on Isaiah 54:13 and Jeremiah 31:33-34." Biblica 62 (1981) 382.

6:42 PETZKE, G. Die Traditionen über Apollonius von Tyana und das Neue Testament (1970) 163, 165.

6:43-47 PORSCH, F., Pneuma und Wort (Frankfurt 1974) 177-83.

6:44-46 THUESING, W. Die Erhöhung und Verherrlichung Jesu im Johannesevangelium (1970) 26-28.

6:44 RUCKSTUHL, E. Die literarische Einheit des Johannesevangeliums (1951) 159-70. FEUILLET, A. "Note sur la traduction de Jér. xxxi 3c," VT 12 (1, 1962) 122-24. HAHN, F. Das Verständnis der Mission im Neuen Testament (²1965) 138. DELLING, G. Wort und Werk Jesu im Johannesevangelium (1966) 64f. IBUKI, Y. Die Wahrheit im Johannesevangelium

(1972) 343f. LADD, G. E. A Theology of the New Testament (1974) 248, 277, 299, 300, 305. PORSCH, F., Pneuma und Wort (Frankfurt 1974) 113-14. "Apokalyptik" in: TRE 3 (1978) 254. BERGMEIER, R., Glaube als Gabe nach Johannes (Stuttgart 1980) 45n.320, 189, 205, 208, 216, 236, 269n.530. FRICKEL, J., "Naassener oder Valentinianer?" in: M. Krause (ed.) Gnosis and Gnosticism (Leiden 1981) 100, 104.

6:45 DENNEY, J. The Death of Christ (³1956) 165. FREED, E. D. Old Testament Quotations in the Gospel of John (1965) 17-20. DUNN, J. D. G. Baptism in the Holy Spirit (1970) 184f. RICHTER, G. "Die alttestamentlichen Zitate in der Rede vom Himmelsbrot Joh 6,26-51a," in: Schriftauslegung (1972) J. Ernst ed., 251-76. FORESTELL, J. T., The Word of the Cross: Salvation as Revelation in the Fourth Gospel (Rome 1974) 95, 111-12. REIM, G., Studien zum Alttestamentlichen Hintergrund des Johannesevangeliums (Cambridge 1974) 16-18, 89-95, 279. PANCARO, S., The Law in the Fourth Gospel (Leiden 1975) 453, 454-72, 538. METZGER, B. M., The Early Versions of the New Testament (Oxford 1977) 390. de la POTTERIE, I., La Vérité dans Saint Jean I/II (Rome 1977) 502-509. BERGMEIER, R., Glaube als Gabe nach Johannes (Stuttgart 1980) 27, 216, 224, 228, 249n.233, 270n.546. HANSON, A. T., The New Testament Interpretation of Scripture (London 1980) 159-62. LÉON-DUFOUR, X., "Towards a Symbolic Reading of the Fourth Gospel" NTS 27 (1980-1981) 450. LINDARS, B., "Discourse and Tradition: The Use of the Sayings of Jesus in the Discourses of the Fourth Gospel" JSNT 13 (1981) 88.

6:46 NICKELS, P. Targum and New Testament (1967) 54. IBUKI, Y. Die Wahrheit im Johannesevangelium (1972) 50f. BÜHNER, J.-A., Der Gesandte und sein Weg im 4. Evangelium (Tübingen 1977) 375-76. BERGMEIER, R., Glaube als Gabe nach Joahnnes (Stuttgart 1980) 17, 244n.162, 248n.213.

6:47-63 IWAND, H.-J. Predigt-Meditationen (1964) 62-67. "Agende" in: TRE 2 (1978) 30.

6:47-57 BORNKAMM, G. in: Herr, tue meine Lippen auf Bd. 3 (1964) G. Eichholz ed., 154ff. HAAR, J. GPM 19 (1, 1965) 129-34. FUERST, W. in: Hören und Fragen Bd. 5,3 (1967) G. Eichholz/A. Falkenroth eds., 208ff. LANGE, E. ed., Predigtstudien für das Kirchenjahr 1970-1971 (1970) 159-65. TRAUB, H. GPM 25 (1, 1971) 150-57. RUCK, H. und HARTMANN, G., in: P. Krusche et al. (eds.) Predigtstudien für das Kirchenjahr 1976-1977. V/1 (Stuttgart 1976) 155-62. SCHRÖER, A., in: GPM 31 (1977) 146-51.

6:47-51 BERGMEIER, R., Glaube als Gabe nach Johannes (Stuttgart 1980) 207, 242n.102. CHRISTIANSEN, R. und WREGE, H.-T., in: P. Krusche et al. (eds.) Predigtstudien für das Kirchenjahr 1982-1983 V/1 (Stuttgart 1982) 159-66.

6:47 RUCKSTUHL, E. Die literarische Einheit des Johannesevangeliums (1951) 254f., 267f. BORNKAMM, G. Geschichte und Glaube II (1971) 59-61.

6:48-63 CLEMEN, C. Primitive Christianity and Its Non-Jewish Sources (1912) 253f.

6:48-59 KRAFT, M., Die Entstehung des Christentums (Darmstadt 1981) 174-80.

6:48-58 LANGBRANDTNER, W., Weltferner Gott oder Gott der Liebe (Frankfurt 1977) 6-9, 10, 286.

6:48-51 SCHUERMANN, H. Ursprung und Gestalt (1970) 158, 159, 160, 162. HEIL, P., Jesus Walking on the Sea (Rome 1981) 160-61.

6:48 RUCKSTUHL, E. Die literarische Einheit des Johannesevangeliums (1951) 268f. SCHNACKENBURG, R., Aufsätze und Studien zum Neuen Testament (Leipzig 1973) 349-63. BERGMEIER, R., Glaube als Gabe nach Johannes (Stuttgart 1980) 216. KUZEMZAMA, K. P. M., "La préhistoire de l'expression 'pain de vie' (Jn. 6:35b,48). Continuité ou émergence?" RATh 4 (1980) 65-83.

6:49-58 BORGEN, P. Bread from Heaven (1965) 86-98.

6:49-50 WREGE, H.-T. Die Ueberlieferungsgeschichte der Bergpredigt (1968) 93f. PANCARO, S., The Law in the Fourth Gospel (Leiden 1975) 453, 454-72.

6:49 NICKELS, P. Targum and New Testament (1967) 55. METZGER, B. M. The Early Versions of the New Testament (Oxford 1977) 42. BERGMEIER, R., Glaube als Gabe nach Johannes (Stuttgart 1980) 242n.118.

6:50ff NÖTSCHER, F., Altorientalischer and alttestamentlicher Auferstehungsglaube (Darmstadt 1970 = 1926) 313, 324.

6:50-51 BERGMEIER, R., Glaube als Gabe nach Johannes (Stuttgart 1980) 215, 216, 242n.177.

6:51ff FEINE, P. The Apostel Paulus (1927) 371f. MAURER, C. Ignatius von Antiochien und das Johannesevangelium (1949) 38ff. BORNKAMM, G. "Di eucharistische Rede im Johannesevangelium," ZNW 47 (1956) 161-69.

6:51bff ANDERSEN, A., "Zu Jn 6:51bff," ZNW 9 (1908) 163. CULLMANN, O. Urchristentum und Gottesdienst (1950) 6, 59(19), 111(131).

6:51-63 DELLING, G. Die Taufe im Neuen Testament (1963) 91.

6:51-59 GAUGLER, E. Das Abendmahl im Neuen Testament (1943) 58. MENOUD, P. H. L'évangile de Jean d'après des recherches récentes (²1950) 53f. SCHNEIDER, J. "Zur Frage der Komposition von Joh 6,27-58(59)," in: In Memoriam Ernst Lohmeyer (1951) 132ff. DELLING, G. Wort und Werk Jesu im Johannes-Evangelium (1966) 134f. HEER, J. "Jesus - das eucharistische Lebensbrot," Sein und Sendung 33 (9, 1968) 387-404. KYSAR, R. The Fourth Evangelist and His Gospel (Minneapolis 1974) 252-54.

6:51-58 GRILL, J. Untersuchungen über die Entstehung des vierten Evangeliums II (1923) 118, 224, 349, 355, 373, 384, 390. RUCKSTUHL, E. Die literarische Einheit des Johannes-evangeliums (1951) 16f., 121f., 169-72, 220-71. SCHWEIZER, E. "Das johanneische Zeugnis vom Herrenmahl," EvTh 12 (1952-1953) 341-63. BORNKAMM, G. "Die eucharistische Rede im Johannes-Evangelium," ZNW 47 (1956) 161-69. BORGEN, P. "The Unity of the Discourse in John 6," ZNW 50 (1959) 277-78. BEHLER, G. M. "Le pain de vie (Jean 6,51-58)," BVieC 32 (1960) 15-26. DELLING, G. Die Taufe im Neuen Testament (1963) 90, 96. SCHWEIZER, E. Neotestamentica (1963) 384-96. SMITH, D. M. The Composition and Order of the Fourth Gospel (1965) 134-52. KAESEMANN, E. New Testament Questions of Today (1969) 157. DUNN, J. D. G. Baptism in the Holy Spirit (1970) 183ff., 226. BORN-KAMM, G. Geschichte und Glaube II (1971) 51-64. KUEM-MEL, W. G. Einleitung in das Neue Testament (1973) 175f. LOHSE, E. Die Einheit des Neuen Testaments (1973) 193, 199-203, 205-208. WANKE, J., Die Emmauserzählung (Leipzig 1973) 104. PORSCH, F., Pneuma und Wort (Frankfurt 1974) 162-64, 165-67. BECKER, J., Auferstehung der Toten im Urchristentum (Stuttgart 1976) 138-40. GOPPELT, L., Theologie des Neuen Testaments II (Göttingen 1976) 638-39. "Abend-mahl" in: TRE 1 (1977) 57. DUNN, J. D. G., Unity and Diversity in the New Testament (London 1977) 170-71, 302. BERGMEIER, R., Glaube als Gabe nach Johannes (Stuttgart 1980) 207-208, 212, 242n.102, 104. HAHN, F., "Thesen zur Frage einheitsstiftender Elemente in Lehre und Praxis des urchristlichen Herrenmahls" in: D. Lührmann/G. Strecker (eds.) Kirche. FS. G. Bornkamm (Tübingen 1980) 419. HEIL, J. P., Jesus Walking on the Sea (Rome 1981) 161-65.

6:51b-58 NIEWALDA, P. Sakramentsymbolik im Johannesevangelium (1958) 4-6.

6:51c-58 MUSSNER, F. ZWH. Die Anschauung vom "Leben" im vierten Evangelium (1952) 130f. JEREMIAS, J. "Joh 6,51c-58 - redaktionell?" ZNW 44 (1952-1953) 256f. WILKENS, W. Die Entstehungsgeschichte des vierten Evangeliums (1958) 20-24. McPOLIN, J. "Bultmanni theoria litteraria et Jo 6,51c-58c," VerbDom 44 (5-6, 1966) 243-58. BORNKAMM, G. "Die Eucharistische Rede im Johannes-Evagelium," Geschichte und Glaube I (1968) 60-67. WILCKENS, U. "Der eucharistische Abschnitt der johanneischen Rede vom Lebensbrot (Joh 6:51c-58)." in: Neues Testament und Kirche (1974) J. Gnilka ed., 220-48. MUELLER, T. Das Heilsgeschehen im Johannesevangelium n.d., 104-108.

6:51-57 "Blut" in: TRE 6 (1980) 734. CARSON, D. A., "Historical Tradition in the Fourth Gospel: After Dodd, What?" in: R. T. France/D. Wenham (eds.) Gospel Perspectives. II (Sheffield 1981) 125-26.

6:51-56 GRILL, J. Untersuchungen über die Entstehung des vierten Evangeliums II (1923) 225f. ROBINSON, J. M. Kerygma und historischer Jesus (1960) 107. NICKELS, P. Targum and New Testament (1967) 55. SKRINJAR, A. "De terminologia sacrificali in J 6,51-56," DiThom 74 (2, 1971) 189-97.

6:51-53 LEROY, H. Rätsel und Missverständnis (1968) 109-24.

6:51 MAURER, C. Ignatius von Antiochien und das Johannesevangelium (1949) 78ff., 81ff. RUCKSTUHL, E. Die literarische Einheit des Johannesevangeliums (1951) 256-58, 268f. FLEW, R. N. Jesus and His Church (1956) 178n.HAHN, F. Christologische Hoheitstitel (1963) 57, 60. GAERTNER, B. The Temple and the Community in Qumran and the New Testament (1965) 75. SMITH, D. M. The Composition and Order of the Fourth Gospel (1965) 136, 139, 145, 146, 147, 149, 151. DELLING, G. Wort und Werk Jesu im Johannes-Evangelium (1966) 57f., 135f. KUHL, J. Die Sendung Jesu und der Kirche nach dem Johannes-Evangelium (1967) 107-109, 192f. DAUER, A. Die Passionsgeschichte im Johannesevangelium (1972) 142, 256, 257. DELLING, G. Der Kreuzestod Jesu in der urchristlichen Verkündigung (1972) 33f., 98f. LADD, G. E. A Theology of the New Testament (1974) 224, 245, 246, 258, 275, 291. BÜHNER, J.-A., Der Gesandte und sein Weg im 4. Evangelium (Tübingen 1977) 175-76. METZGER, B. M., The Early Versions of the New Testament (Oxford 1977) 255. BÖHLIG, A., Die Gnosis III: Der Manichäismus (Zürich/München 1980) 343n.27.

6:51c SCHUERMANN, H. "Joh. 6,51c-ein Schlüssel zur johanneischen Brotrede," BZ 2 (1, 1958) 244-62. SCHUERMANN, H. Ursprung und Gestalt (1970) 151-66.

6:52-71 KIEFFER, R. Au delà des recensions? (1968). BROWN, R. E.
CBQ 31 (2, 1969) 262-64. BIRDSALL, J. N. JThS 20 (2, 1969)
610-14.

6:52-59 BUECHSEL, F. Das Evangelium nach Johannes (1946) 88f.

6:52-58 WILLIAMS, J. A. A Conceptual History of Deuteronomism in
the Old Tesament, Judaism, and the New Testament (Ph.D.
Diss. Louisville 1976) 314.

6:52-60 FLEW, R. N. Jesus and His Church (1956) 178.

6:52-62 MUSSNER, F. ZWH. Die Anschauung vom "Leben" im vierten Evangelium (1952) 132f.

6:52 SCHNACKENBURG, R. "Zur Rede vom Brot aus dem Him-
mel: eine Beobachtung zu Joh 6,52," BZ 12 (2, 1968) 248-52.
METZGER, B. M., The Early Versions of the New Testament
(Oxford 1977) 324. CLARK, K. W., "The Text of the Gospel
of John in Third-Century Egypt" in: The Gentile Bias and Other
Essays (Leiden 1980) 161. LÉON-DUFOUR, X., "Towards a
Symbolic Reading of the Fourth Gospel" NTS 27 (1980-1981)
452. von WAHLDE, U. C., "The Johannine 'Jews': A Critical
Survey" NTS 28 (1982) 38, 41-44, 46, 49, 54.

6:53ff HOWARD, W. F. Christianity According to St. John (1943)
204. LEE, E. K. The Religious Thought of St. John (1950) 184-
88.

6:53-58 MORGAN, G. C. The Parables and Metaphors of Our Lord
(1943) 294ff. SCHUERMANN, H. "Die Eucharistie als Re-
präsentation und Applikation des Heilsgeschehens nach Joh
6,53-58," TThZ 68 (2, 1959) 30-45; (2, 1959) 108-18. KUHL,
J. Die Sendung Jesu und der Kirche nach dem Johannes-Evangelium (1967) 191-94. SCHUERMANN, H. Ursprung und
Gestalt (1970) 151-66, 167-87. LÉON-DUFOUR, X., "Towards a Symbolic Reading of the Fourth Gospel" NTS 27 (1980-
1981) 451-54.

6:53-57 BÜHNER, J.-A., Der Gesandte und sein Weg im 4. Evangelium (Tübingen 1977) 408.

6:53-56 RUCKSTUHL, E. Die literarische Einheit des Johannesevangeliums (1951) 243f., 245-57, 265-71.

6:53-54 SMITH, D. M. The Composition and Order of the Fourth Gospel (1965) 90, 135, 138, 140, 218, 231, 232, 235, 237.
"Abendmahl" in: TRE 1 (1977) 124. "Auferstehung" in: TRE
4 (1979) 516.

6:53 SCHULZ, S., Untersuchungen zur Menschensohn-Christologie im Johannesevangelium (Göttingen 1957) 115-17.
HIGGINS, A. J. B. Menschensohn-Studien (1965) 40-43, 48.

SMALLEY, S. S. "The Johannine Son of Man Sayings," NTS 15 (1968-1969) 293ff. BARRETT, C. K., "Das Fleisch des Menschensohnes" (Joh 6.53)" in: R. Pesch/R. Schnackenburg (eds.), Jesus und der Menschensohn (Freiburg 1975) 342-54. "Abendmahl" in: TRE 1 (1977) 67, 68. JEWETT, P. K., Infant Baptism and the Covenant of Grace (Grand Rapids 1978) 42, 147. RUDOLPH, K., Die Gnosis (Göttingen 1978) 210.

6:54-55 SIEDLECKI, E. J. A Patristic Synthesis of John VI, 54-55 (1956).

6:54.56.57 DELLING, G. Wort und Werk Jesu im Johannes-Evangelium (1966) 65f., 129f., 143f.

6:54 WAINWRIGHT, A. W. The Trinity in the New Testament (1962) 168-69. BERGMEIER, R., Glaube als Gabe nach Johannes (Stuttgart 1980) 205.

6:55-65 ROEPKE, C.-J. und BOGDAHN, M., in: P. Krusche et al. (eds.) Predigtstudien für das Kirchenjahr 1980-1981. III/1 (Stuttgart 1980) 157-64. HINZ, C., in: GPM 35 (1981) 170-73.

6:55 MAURER, C. Ignatius von Antiochien und das Johannesevangelium (1949) 86ff.

6:56 BORIG, R. Der Wahre Weinstock (1967) 215f. HEISE, J. Bleiben (1967) 92-93.

6:57-58 MATSUNAGA, K., "Is John's Gospel Anti-Sacramental? — A New Solution to the Light of the Evangelist's Milieu" NTS 27 (1980-1981) 518.

6:57 DUPONT, J. Essais sur la Christologie de Saint Jean (1951) 197, 198, 200. CROCETTI, G. "Le linee fondamentali del concetto di vita in Jo. 6,57," RivB 19 (4, 1971) 375-94.

6:58.59 SMITH, D. M. The Composition and Order of the Fourth Gos-
60-91 pel (1965) 131, 137, 139-41, 149, 150-52, 166-68.

6:58 METZGER, B. M., The Early Versions of the New Testament (Oxford 1977) 390. BERGMEIER, R., Glaube als Gabe nach Johannes (Stuttgart 1980) 242n.117f.

6:59-71 HEIL, P., Jesus Walking on the Sea (Rome 1981) 165-70.

6:60ff CULLMANN, O. Urchristentum und Gottesdienst (1950) 108f.

6:60-71 WILKENS, W. Die Entstehungsgeschichte des vierten Evangeliums (1958) 138-41. SCHUERMANN, H. Ursprung und Gestalt (1970) 175-79. FERRARO, G., "Giovanni 6,60-71. Osservazioni sulla struttura letteraria e il valore della pericope nel quarto vangelo" RivBi 26 (1978) 33-69. HAENCHEN, E., Das Johannesevangelium (Tübingen 1980) 337 (lit!).

6:60-69 STECK, K. G. in: Herr, tue meine Lippen auf Bd. 3 (1964) G. Eichholz ed., 233ff. FRICK, R. GPM 23/2 (1968-1969) 193-99. BEAUVERY, R. " 'Voulez-vous partir, vous aussi?' Jn. 6,60-69," AssS 52 (1974) 44-51.

6:60-66 BRAUN, F.-M. Jean le Théologien (1966) 126f. WALTER, L., L'incroyance des croyants selon saint Jean (Paris 1976) 77-87.

6:60-65 BORNKAMM, G. Geschichte und Glaube I (1968) 63f.; II (1971) 57-59. PORSCH, F., Pneuma und Wort (Frankfurt 1974) 162-70, 185-86. MATSUNAGA, K., "Is John's Gospel Anti-Sacramental?—A New Solution in the Light of the Evangelist's Milieu" NTS 27 (1980-1981) 517-18, 521.

6:60 BERGER, K., "Das Buch der Jubiläen" in: JüdSchr II/3 (1981) 504n.23e.

6:61 PALLIS, A., Notes on St. John and the Apokalypse (London 1928) 14.

6:62-63 SCHWEIZER, E., Neotestamentica (1963) 388-90. DUNN, J. D. G. Baptism in the Holy Spirit (1970) 175, 184ff. JOHNSTON, G. The Spirit-Paraclete in the Gospel of John (1970) 22-28. SCHUERMANN, H. Ursprung und Gestalt (1970) 160, 163, 170, 171, 180. PORSCH, F., Pneuma und Wort (Frankfurt 1974) 204-10.

6:62 WILES, M. F. The Spiritual Gospel (1960) 132-34, 136. SCHNACKENBURG, R. NTS 11 (1964-1965) 125f. BOUSSET, W. Die Religion des Judentums im Späthellenistischen Zeitalter (1966 = 1926) 268. DELLING, G. Wort und Werk Jesu im Johannes-Evangelium (1966) 61, 85f., 96, 136. KUHL, J. Die Sendung Jesu und der Kirche nach dem Johannes-Evangelium (1967) 75f., 123, 194. THUESING, W. Die Erhöhung und Verherrlichung Jesu im Johannesevangelium (1970) 261-63, 269-75. LADD, G. E. A Theology of the New Testament (1974) 216, 224, 241. SCHULZ, S. Untersuchungen zur Menschensohn-Christologie im Johannesevangelium (Göttingen 1957) 117-18. BÜHNER, J.-A., Der Gesandte und sein Weg im 4. Evangelium (Tübingen 1977) 408. DUNN, J. D. G., Christology in the Making (London 1980) 29, 56, 89-90, 302n.127.

6:63 DUPONT, J. Essais sur la Christologie de Saint Jean (1951) 20, 26, 164, 199. FLEW, R. N. Jesus and His Church (1956) 174. DELLING, G. Die Taufe im Neuen Testament (1963) 91, 95. KAESEMANN, E. Exegetische Versuche und Besinnungen (1964) II 172. DELLING, G. Wort und Werk Jesu im Johannes-Evangelium (1966) 45, 57, 72, 121. WREGE, H.-T. Die Ueberlieferungsgeschichte der Bergpredigt (1968) 170f. KAESEMANN, E. New Testament Questions of Today (1969) 157.

THUESING, W. Die Erhöhung und Verherrlichung Jesu im Johannesevangelium (1970) 154f. DI MARINO, A. "Fondamenti biblici della teologia morale. Riflessioni di un moralista," RT 14 (1, 1973) 10-14. CAVALLIN, H. C. C. Life After Death (1974) 4, In31. LADD, G. E. A Theology of the New Testament (1974) 224, 257, 291, 292. PORSCH, E., Pneuma und Wort (Frankfurt 1974) 161-212. STENGER, W., " 'Der Geist ist es, der lebendig macht, das Fleisch nützt nichts' (Joh 6,63)" TThZ 85 (1976) 116-22. METZGER, B. M., The Early Versions of the New Testament (Oxford 1977) 139. SCHWEIZER, E., Heiliger Geist (Berlin 1978) 99-100. BERGMEIER, R., Glaube als Gabe nach Johannes (Stuttgart 1980) 218, 254n.310f. GEORGI, D., "Weisheit Salomos" in: JüdSchr III/4 (1980) 16n.12a.26c. MUELLER, T. Das Heilsgeschehen im Johannesevangelium n.d., 104-108.

6:64-71 BAUER, W. Das Johannesevangelium (1925) 192.

6:64-69 STECK, K. G. GPM 17 (1, 1963) 195-200. LOHSE, E. Das Aergernis des Kreuzes (1969) 30-35. HAAR, J. GPM 29 (2, 1975) 232-38. RAISS, H./KIRCHGAESSNER, A. "Johannes 6,646-69: Die Zumutung der Nachfolge," in: Predigtstudien für das Kirchenjahr 1975 (1975) P. Krusche/E. Lange/D. Rössler/ R. Roessler eds., 45-50.

6:65 BERGMEIER, R., Glaube als Gabe nach Johannes (Stuttgart 1980) 215, 236, 269n.530.

6:66ff STRECKER, G. Der Weg der Gerechtigkeit (1962) 202n.4.

6:66-71 STRATHMANN, H. Das Evangelium nach Johannes (1955) 130. HAHN, F. Christologische Hoheitstitel (1963) 228(f.)₄. HAENCHEN, E. "Die Komposition von Mk vii 27 - ix l und Par." in: ΧΑΡΙΣ ΚΑΙ ΣΘΦΙΑ (1964) 81-109. HAENCHEN, E. "Leidensnachfolge," Die Bibel und Wir (1968) 102-34. ITTEL, G. W. Jesus undd die Jünger (1970) 76-78. MATSUNAGA, K., "Is John's Gospel Anti-Sacramental? — A New Solution in the Light of the Evangelist's Milieu" NTS 27 (1980-1981) 517-20.

6:66 CONZELMANN, H. und LINDEMANN, A., Arbeitsbuch zum Neuen Testament (Tübingen 1975) 345.

6:67ff SATAKE, A., Die Gemeindeordnung in der Johannesapokalypse (Neukirchen-Vluyn 1966) 15.

6:67-71 FORTNA, R. T. The Gospel of Signs (1970) 195-97.

6:67-69 BROWN, R. E. et al. (eds.) Peter in the New Testament (Minneapolis 1973) 131-32.

6:67-68 MATSUNAGA, K., "Is John's Gospel Anti-Sacramental? — A New Solution in the Light of the Evangelist's Milieu" NTS 27 (1980-1981) 517.

6:67 SWIDLER, L., Biblical Affirmations of Woman (Philadelphia 1979) 289.

6:68-70 BUECHSEL, F. Das Evangelium nach Johannes (1946) 92f.

6:68 LO GIUDICE, C. "Le fede degli apostoli nel IV Vangelo." Biblica 28 (1947) 68-70. BÜHNER, J.-A., Der Gesandte und sein Weg im 4. Evangelium (Tübingen 1977) 169-70. "Amt" in: TRE 2 (1978) 517. GEORGI, D., "Weisheit Salomos" in: JüdSchr III/4 (1980) 16n.26c.

6:69 GRILL, J. Untersuchungen über die Entstehung des vierten Evangeliums II (1923) 40, 45, 73, 92, 205, 372f. BAUER, W. Das Johannesevangelium (1925) 99-101. BUECHSEL, F. Das Evangelium nach Johannes (1946) 92. FLEW, R. N., Jesus and His Church (1956) 177. JOUBERT, H. L. N. " 'The Holy One of God' (John 6:69)," Neotestamentica 2 (1968) 57-69. METZGER, B. M., The Early Versions of the New Testament (Oxford 1977) 41. CRIBBS, F. L., "The Agreements that Exist Between John and Acts" in: C. H. Talbert (ed.) Perspectives on Luke-Acts (Danville 1978) 55. FRIEDRICH, G., "Beobachtungen zur Messianischen Hohepriestererwartung in den Synoptikern" in: Auf das Wort kommt es an. Gesammelte Aufsätze (Göttingen 1978) 66-69. BÖHLIG, A., Die Gnosis III: Der Manichäismus (Zürich/München 1980) 343n.23. GEORGI, D., "Weisheit Salomos" in: JüdSchr III/4 (1980) 15n.3a.

6:70 GRILL, J. Untersuchungen über die Entstehung des vierten Evangeliums II (1923) 34f. DELLING, G. Die Taufe im Neuen Testament (1963) 95. CADMAN, W. H. The Open Heaven (1969) G. B. Caird ed., 97, 136, 137, 173, 184. METZGER, B. M., The Early Versions of the New Testament (Oxford 1977) 88. "Antichrist" in: TRE 3 (1978) 22.

6:71 DORMEYER, D., Die Passion Jesu als Verhaltensmodell (Münster 1974) 83, 136.

_____

7-11 HUNTER, A. M. According to John (1970²) 60ff.

7-10 de la POTTERIE, I., La Vérité dans Saint Jean I/II (Rome 1977) 816-19.

7-8 GUILDING, A. The Fourth Gospel and Jewish Worship (1960) 122-23. LAURENTIN, R. Jésus au Temple (1966) 128-32. LOHSE, E. et al., eds., Der Ruf Jesu und die Antwort der Gemeinde (1970) 123-26, 129. TRITES, A. A., The New Testament Concept of Witness (Cambridge 1977) 104-107. SCHILLEBEECKX, E., Christ: The Christian Experience in the Modern World (London 1980) 388-91; GT: Christus und die Christen (Freiburg/Basel/Wien 1977) 374-77. DAHMS, J. V., "Isaiah 55:11 and the Gospel of John" EQ 53 (1981) 79-82, 84.

7 SCHNEIDER, J. "Zur Komposition von Joh 7," ZNW 45 (1954) 108-19. BECKER, H., Die Reden des Johannesevangeliums und der Stil der gnostischen Offenbarungsrede (Göttingen 1956) 75-77. WIKENHAUSER, A. Das Evangelium nach Johannes (1957) 155. van den BUSSCHE, M., "La Structure de Jean I-XII" in: M. Boismard et al., L'Evangile de Jean: études et problèmes (Bruges 1958) 96-100. GRUNDMANN, W. "Verständnis und Bewegung des Glaubens im Johannes-Evangelium," KuD 6 (1960) 140f. SMITH, D. M. The Composition and Order of the Fourth Gospel (1965) 152-55. MEEKS, W. A. The Prophet-King, Moses Traditions and the Johannine Christology (1967) 42-57, 57-61. RIEDL, J. Das Heilswerk Jesu nach Johannes (1973) 344-78. DAVIES, W. D. The Gospel and the Land (1974) 290, 315, 327, 330. de JONGE, M., Jesus: Stranger from Heaven and Son of God (Missoula 1977) 130-31, 142-44. BRUCE, F. F., The Time is Fulfilled (Exeter 1978) 41-42.

7:1-52 GUILDING, A. The Fourth Gospel and Jewish Worship (1960) 98-106. YATES, K. M. Preaching from John's Gospel (1964) 75-79.

7:1-39 CADMAN, W. H. The Open Heaven (1969) G. B. Caird ed., 97-106.

7:1-36 TEMPLE, S., The Core of the Fourth Gospel (London 1975) 150-55. ATTRIDGE, H. W.,"Thematic Development and Source Elaboration in John 7:1-36" CBQ (1980) 160-70.

7:1-13 NICOL, W. The Sēmeia in the Fourth Gospel (1972) 128f. BECKER, J., "Wunder und Christologie. Zum literar-kritischen und christologischen Problem der Wunder im Johannesevangelium" in: A. Suhl (ed.) Der Wunderbegriff im Neuen Testament (Darmstadt 1980) 441-42. HAENCHEN, E., Das Johannesevangelium (Tübingen 1980) 344 (lit!). LEIDIG, E., Jesu Gespräch mit der Samaritanerin (Basel 1981) 257-60.

7:1-10 CULLMANN, O. Urchristentum und Gottesdienst (1950) 67ff. ESTALAYO ALONSO, V., "Análisis Literario de Jn 7,1-10" Estudios Teologicos 4 (Guatemala City 1977) 3-106.

7:1-9 SEGOVIA, F., "The Love and Hatred of Jesus and Johannine Sectarianism" CBQ 43 (1981) 267, 270, 272.

7:1-2 STRECKER, G. Der Weg der Gerechtigkeit (1962) 87.

7:1 BUESCHEL, F. Das Evangelium nach Johannes (1946) 95. LEE, E. K. "St. Mark and the Fourth Gospel," NTS 3 (1956-1957) 53ff.

7:2ff WILKENS, W. Die Entstehungsgeschichte des vierten Evangeliums (1958) 48, 49.

7:2-14 GIBLIN, C. H., "Suggestion, Negative Response, and Positive Action in St. John's Portrayal of Jesus (John 2:1-11; 4:46-54; 7:2-14; 11.1-44)" NTS 26 (1980) 197-211.

7:2-13 BECKER, J. Das Evangelium nach Johannes (Gütersloh/Würzburg 1979) 261 (lit!).

7:2 GRILL, J. Untersuchungen über die Entstehung des vierten Evangeliums II (1923) 22, 125, 160f. DANIELOU, J. "Les Quatre-Temps de septembre et la fête des Tabernacles," la Maison-Dieu 46 (1956) 114-36. BERGMEIER, R., Glaube als Gabe nach Johannes (Stuttgart 1980) 227.

7:3ff FORTNA, R. T. The Gospel of Signs (1970) 103, 196f.

7:3-8 ODEBERG, H. The Fourth Gospel (1958) 270ff.

7:3-5 GRILL, J. Untersuchungen über die Entstehung des vierten Evangeliums II (1923) 25f. HENNECKE, E./SCHNEE-MELCHER, W. Neutestamentliche Apokryphen (1964) I 312.

7:3 PALLIS, A., Notes on St. John and the Apokalypse (London 1928) 14-15.

7:4 McNAMARA, M. The New Testament and the Palestinian Targum to the Pentateuch (1966) 249. LINDEMANN, A., "Gemeinde und Welt im Johannesevangelium" in: R. Lührmann/G. Strecker (ed.) Kirche. FS. G. Bornkamm (Tübingen 1980) 145.

7:5 BLINZLER, J., Die Brüder und Schwestern Jesu (Stuttgart 1967) 122-23.

7:6.8 THUESING, W. Die Erhöhung und Verherrlichung Jesu im Johannesevangelium (1970) 90-92.

7:7 OLBRICHT, T. H. "Its Works Are Evil (John 7:7)," RestQ 7 (4, 1963) 242-44. BEUTLER, J. Martyria (1972) 26, 210, 216, 224, 260. DAUER, A. Die Passionsgeschichte im Johannesevangelium (1972) 247, 249, 256, 257, 260. BERGMEIER, R., Glaube als Gabe nach Johannes (Stuttgart 1980) 221, 233,

256n.346f., 259n.397. GEORGI, D., "Weisheit Salomos" in: JüdSchr III/4 (1980) 2n.14a. LINDEMANN, A., "Gemeinde und Welt im Johannesevangelium" in: D. Lührmann/G. Strecker (eds.) Kirche. FS. G. Bornkamm (Tübingen 1980) 145.

7:8 ROBINSON, J. M. Kerygma und historischer Jesus (1960) 146. STRECKER, G. Der Weg der Gerechtigkeit (1962) 87. NEI-RYNCK, F. "Les Femmes au Tombeau: Etude de la Rédaction Matthénne (Matt. XXVIII 1-10)," NTS 15 (1968-1969) 187ff.

7:9 HEISE, J., Bleiben. μένειν in den Johanneischen Schriften (Tübingen 1967) 47-50.

7:10-52 de JONGE, M., Jesus: Stranger from Heaven and Son of God (Missoula 1977) 80-82.

7:10-18 IWAND, H.-J. Predigt-Meditationen (1964) 294-98. KRECK, W. GPM 19 (4, 1964) 95-99. HELD, H. J. in: Hören und Fragen Bd 5,3 (1967) G. Eichholz/A. Falkenroth eds., 157ff. BORNKAMM, G. GPM 25 (4, 1970) 108-13. BIRKHOLZER, H. und WIEDEMANN, H.-G.,in: P. Krusche et al. (eds.) Predigtstudien für das Kirchenjahr 1976-1977. V/1 (Stuttgart 1976) 105-11. CASALIS, G., GPM 31 (1976) 89-96.

7:10-13 GRUNDMANN, W. Zeugnis und Gestalt des Johannes-Evangeliums (1961) 44-50.

7:10 STRECKER, G. Der Weg der Gerechtigkeit (1962) 87n.6.

7:11ff IBUKI, Y. Die Wahrheit im Johannesevangelium (1972) 66f.

7:13 CLARK, K. W., "The Text of the Gospel of John in Third-Century Egypt" in: The Gentile Bias and Other Essays (Leiden 1980) 162.

7:14-53 O'ROURKE, J. "Jn 7,14-53: Another combined narrative?" StudMontReg 9 (1, 1966) 143-46.

7:14-52 SCHNIDER, F. Jesus der Prophet (1973) 214ff., 239.

7:14-39 ODEBERG, H. The Fourth Gospel (1968) 281ff.

7:14-36 VAN DEN BUSSCHE, H. "Leurs écritures et Son enseignement. Jean 7,14-36," BVieC 58 (72, 1966) 21-30.

7:14, 25-30, WILKENS, W. Die Entstehungsgeschichte des vierten Evan-37-44 geliums (1958) 131.

7:14–10:21 PERRIN, N., The New Testament: An Introduction (New York 1974) 237-40. de la POTTERIE, I., La Vérité dans Saint Jean I/II (Rome 1977) 819-22.

7:14-8:59 BERGMEIER, R., Glaube als Gabe nach Johannes (Stuttgart 1980) 224.

7:14-52 HAENCHEN, E., Das Johannesevangelium (Tübingen 1980) 350-51 (lit!).

7:14-24 DAVIES, W. D., The Sermon on the Mount (Cambridge 1966) 120-21. PANCARO, S., The Law in the Fourth Gospel (Leiden 1975) 169-74.

7:14-18 PANCARO, S., The Law in the Fourth Gospel (Leiden 1975) 106, 130, 131, 132, 134-36. KÖHLER, C. und HANUSCH, R., in: P. Krusche et al. (ed.) Predigtstudien für das Kirchenjahr 1982-1983. V/1 (Stuttgart 1982) 82-90.

7:14 SMITH, D. M. The Composition and Order of the Fourth Gospel (1965) 131, 133, 152, 155. DAVIES, W. D. The Gospel and the Land (1974) 290, 291-92.

7:15-8:49 GRUNDMANN, W. Zeugnis und Gestalt des Johannes-Evangeliums (1961) 44-50.

7:15-24 SMITH, D. M. The Composition and Order of the Fourth Gospel (1965) 130-34, 140, 154, 160. BEUTLER, J. Martyria (1972) 264ff., 355. BECKER, J., Das Evangelium nach Johannes (Gütersloh/Würzburg 1979) 248-49 (lit!).

7:15-18.21-24 WILKENS, W. Die Entstehungsgeschichte des vierten Evangeliums (1958) 98-108.

7:15 PANCARO, S., The Law in the Fourth Gospel (Leiden 1975) 170-72, 455. BERGER, K., "Das Buch der Jubiläen" in: JüdSchr II/3 (1981) 423n.14b. von WAHLDE, U. C., "The Johannine 'Jews': A Critical Survey" NTS 28 (1982) 44-45.

7:16-17 VOUGA, F., Le cadre historique et l'intention théologique de Jean (Paris 1977) 46-47.

7:17 FLEW, R. N. Jesus and His Church (1956) 179n. PANCARO, S., The Law in the Fourth Gospel (Leiden 1975) 372, 373, 375, 377-80, 395. BERGMEIER, R., Glaube als Gabe nach Johannes (Stuttgart 1980) 214, 220, 259n.403.

7:18 RUCKSTUHl, E. Die literarische Einheit des Johannesevangeliums (1951) 44, 69, 70, 237, 239, 249. HAHN, F. Das Verständnis der Mission im Neuen Testament (²1965) 141. BRAUN, H. Qumran und NT (1966) 130, 255. KUHL, J. Die Sendung Jesu und der Kirche nach dem Johannes-Evangelium (1967) 90, 216-18. BÜHNER, J.-A., Der Gesandtle und sein Weg im 4. Evangelium (Tübingen 1977) 237-40, 249-59. de la POTTERIE, I., La Vérité dans Saint Jean I/II (Rome 1977) 986-88. VOUGA, F., Le cadre historique et l'intention théologique de Jean (Paris 1977) 47.

7:19-24 SAITO, T., Die Mosevorstellungen im Neuen Testament (Bern 1977) 147.

7:19-22 GLASSON, T. F. Moses in the Fourth Gospel (1963) 90-92.

7:19-20 PANCARO, S., The Law in the Fourth Gospel (Leiden 1975) 130, 131, 134-36, 158.

7:19 GRILL, J. Untersuchungen über die Entstehung des vierten Evangeliums II (1923) 13f., 356. PALLIS, A., Notes on St. John and the Apocalypse (London 1928) 15. LJUNGMAN, H. Das Gesetz Erfüllen (1954) 70-73. KUEMMEL, W. G. Römer 7 und das Bild des Menschen im Neuen Testament (1974) 203. VOUGA, F., Le cadre historique et l'intention théologique de Jean (Paris 1977) 47-48.

7:21-24 VOUGA, F., Le cadre historique et l'intention théologique de Jean (Paris 1977) 47-48. "Beschneidung" in: TRE 5 (1980) 722.

7:21-23 PANCARO, S., The Law in the Fourth Gospel (Leiden 1975) 147, 156, 157, 158-66.

7:21 GRILL, J. Untersuchungen über die Entstehung des vierten Evangeliums II (1923) 361f. IBUKI, Y. Die Wahrheit im Johannesevangelium (1972) 64f. PALLIS, A., Notes on St. John and the Apocalypse (London 1928) 15.

7:22-24 BACCHIOCCHI, S., "John 5:17: Negation or Clarification of the Sabbath?" AUSS 19 (1981) 17-18.

7:22-23 SUMMERS, R. The Secret Sayings of the Living Jesus (1968) 67. REIM, G., Studien zum Alttestamentlichen Hintergrund des Johannesevangeliums (Cambridge 1974) 141-42.

7:22 BERGMEIER, R., Glaube als Gabe nach Johannes (Stuttgart 1980) 242n.118.

7:23 LJUNGMAN, H. Das Gesetz Erfüllen (1954) 71-73. BOUSSET, W. Die Religion des Judentums im Späthellenistischen Zeitalter (1966 = 1926) 126. SMITH, M. Tannaitic Parallels to the Gospels (1968) 6 b n 5.

7:24 PALLIS, A. Notes on St. John and the Apocalypse (London 1928) 15-16. BLANK, J. Krisis (1963) 48. PANCARO, S., The Law in the Fourth Gospel (Leiden 1975) 166-68, 169, 170, 173. BERGMEIER, R., Glaube als Gabe nach Johannes (Stuttgart 1980) 215.

7:25-52 SMITH, D. M. The Composition and Order of the Fourth Gospel (1965) 133, 152-55.

7:25-36 BECKER, J., Das Evangelium nach Johannes (Gütersloh/ Würzburg 1979) 266 (lit!).

7:25-29 KUHL, J. Die Sendung Jesu und der Kirche nach dem Johannes-Evangelium (1967) 58-60.

7:25-26 IBUKI, Y., Die Wahrheit im Johannesevangelium (1972) 48.

7:26   SMITH, M. Tannaitic Parallels to the Gospels (1968) 8 b n 7.

7:27ff de JONGE, M., Jesus: Stranger from Heaven and Son of God (Missoula 1977) 90-91.

7:27   VOLZ, P. Die Eschatologie der jüdischen Gemeinde (1934) 208. HAHN, F. Christologische Hoheitstitel (1963) 224. SQUIL-LACI, D. "Il Cuore di Gesù fonte della grazia," PaCl 43 (June 1, 1964) 593-95. BOUSSET, W. Die Religion des Judentums im Späthellenistischen Zeitalter (1966 = 1926) 230. DEL-LING, G. Wort und Werk Jesu im Johannes-Evangelium (1966) 91f. McNAMARA, M. The New Testament and the Palestinian Targum of the Pentateuch (1966) 250. NICKELS, P. Targum and New Testament (1967) 55. METZGER, B. M., The Early Versions of the New Testament (Oxford 1977) 390.

7:28-30 HAHN, F. Das Verständnis der Mission im Neuen Testament (²1965) 140.

7:28-29 KUHL, J. Die Sendung Jesu und der Kirche nach dem Johan-nes-Evangelium (1967) 58-65. DAHMS, J. V., "Isaiah 55:11 and the Gospel of John" EQ 53 (1981) 78-88.

7:28   PALLIS, A., Notes on St. John and the Apocalypse (London 1928) 16. RUCKSTUHL, E. Die literarische Einheit des Johannesevangeliums (1951) 247f.

7:29   PALLIS, A., Notes on St. John and the Apocalypse (London 1928) 16-17. BERGMEIER, R., Glaube als Gabe nach Johan-nes (Stuttgart 1980) 248n.213.

7:30   HENNECKE, E./SCHNEEMELCHER, W. Neutestament-liche Apokryphen (1964) I 60. SMITH, D. M. The Composi-tion and Order of the Fourth Gospel (1965) 153, 154, 155, 157, 241. CADMAN, W. H. The Open Heaven (1969) G. B. Caird ed., 36, 62, 98, 99. PETZKE, G. Die Traditionen über Apol-lonius von Tyana und das Neue Testament (1970) 177, 181. DAUER, A. Die Passionsgeschichte im Johannesevangelium (1972) 237, 247, 278.

7:31-36 SMITH, D. M. The Composition and Order of the Fourth Gos-pel (1965) 152, 153, 154, 155.

7:31   HAHN, F. Christologische Hoheitstitel (1963) 224. de JONGE, M., Jesus: Stranger from Heaven and Son of God (Missoula 1977) 91-92. CRIBBS, F. L., "The Agreements that Exist Be-tween John and Acts" in: C. H. Talbert (ed.) Perspectives on Luke-Acts (Danville 1978) 58. MARTIN, A. G., "La Saint-Esprit et l'Evangile de Jean dans une perspective trinitaire" RevR 29 (1978) 141-51.

7:32-36 KUHL, U. Die Sendung Jesu und der Kirche nach dem Johannes-Evangelium (1967) 124f. COLLINS, R. F., "The Search for Jesus. Reflections on the Fourth Gospel" LThPh 34 (1978) 27-48.

7:32 GRILL, J. Untersuchungen über die Entstehung des vierten Evangeliums II (1923) 13f., 17f., 125. STRECKER, G. Der Weg der Gerechtigkeit (1962) 113. DAUER, A. Die Passionsgeschichte im Johannesevangelium (1972) 28, 88, 247.

7:33-39 STECK, K. G. in: Her, tue meine Lippen auf Bd. 3 (1964) G. Eichholz ed., 256ff.

7:33-36 LEROY, H. "Das johanneische Missverständnis als literarische Form," BuL 9 (3, 1968) 196-207. LEROY, H. Rätsel und Missverständnis (1968) 51-67.

7:33 KAESEMANN, E. Exegetische Versuche und Besinnungen (1964) I 181. DAHM, J. V., "Isaiah 55:11 and the Gospel of John" EQ 53 (1981) 78-88.

7:34 BERGMEIER, R., Glaube als Gabe nach Johannes (Stuttgart 1980) 255n.326.

7:35-36 HAHN, F. Das Verständnis Mission im Neuen Testament (²1965) 138.

7:35 BAMMEL, E. "Joh. 7:35 in Manis Lebensbeschreibung," NovTest 15 (5, 1973) 191-92. METZGER, B. M., The Early Versions of the New Testament (Oxford 1977) 390. HANSON, A. T., The New Testament Interpretation of Scripture (London 1980) 159-62. SAUER, G., "Das 'Prophetische Amt Christ' und das 'Amt' des Propheten" EvTh 41 (1981) 290, 292. von WAHLDE, U. C. "The Johannine 'Jews': A Critical Survey" NTS 28 (1982) 44-45.

7:37ff CULLMANN, O. Urchristentum und Gottesdienst (1950) 77, 83f. GLASSON, T. F. Moses in the Fourth Gospel (1963) Ch. VII,72, 106f. IBUKI, Y. Die Wahrheit im Johannesevangelium (1972) 47, 72, 316f.

7:37-52 MEEKS, W. A. The Prophet-King, Moses Traditions and the Johannine Christology (1967) 32-41. TEMPLE, S., The Core of the Fourth Gospel (London 1975) 155-58. BECKER, J., Das Evangelium nach Johannes (Gütersloh/Würzburg 1979) 271 (lit!).

7:37-44 SAITO, T., Die Mosevorstellungen im Neuen Testament (Bern 1977) 113-15, 137-41.

7:37-39 MORGAN, G. C. The Parables and Metaphors of Our Lord (1943) 298ff. MUSZNER, F. ZΩH. Die Anschauung vom "Leben" im vierten Evangelium (1952) 116f. CORELL, A. Consummatum Est (1958) 60-62. BLENKINSOPP, J. "John

vii. 37-39: Another Note on a Notorious Crux," NTS 6 (1, 1959) 95-98. BLENKINSOPP, J., "The Quenching of Thirst: Reflections on the Utterance in the Temple, John 7:37-9," Scripture 12 (18, 1960) 39-48. KOHLER, M. "Des fleuves d'eau vive. Exégèse de Jean 7:37-39," RThP 10 (3, 1960) 188-201. POWER, F. "Living Water," Review for Religious 19 (1, 1960) 5-11. WILES, M. F. The Spiritual Gospel (1960) 48-49, 60. ROBINSON, J. A. T. "The One Baptism," in: Twelve New Testament Studies (1962) 158-75. DELLING, G. Die Taufe im Neuen Testament (1963) 92. HOOKE, S. H. "The Spirit was not yet," NTS 9 (4, 1963) 372-80. LOCKYER, H. All the Parables of the Bible (1963) 320ff. SCHWEIZER, E. GPM 17 (1963) 210-16. LINDIJER, C. H. De Sacramenten in het Vierde Evangelie (1964) 82f. SORG, R. Ecumenic Psalm 87 (1966). KUHL, J. Die Sendung Jesu und der Kirche nach dem Johannes-Evangelium (1967) 178-80. HEER, J. "Wenn Jemand dürstet," Sein und Sendung 33 (10, 1968) 435-48. KRECK, W. GPM 23 (2, 1968)211-17. SCHWEIZER, E. Neues Testament und heutige Verkündigung (1969) 66-73. BRAUN, F.-M. "Avoir soif et boire (Jn 4,10-14; 7:37-39)," in: Mélanges Bibliques en hommage au R. P. Béda Rigaux (1970) A.Descamps/ A. deHalleux, eds., 247-58. JOHNSTON, G. The Spirit-Paraclete in the Gospel of John (1970) 41, 47-49. THUESING, W. Die Erhöhung und Verherrlichung Jesu im Johannesevangelium (1970) 159-65. BEUTLER, J. Martyria (1972) 253, 259, 266, 301. DAUER, A. Die Passionsgeschichte im Johannesevangelium (1972) 215f. HAACKER, K. Die Stiftung des Heils (1972) 48-52. MIGUENS, M. "El Agua y el Espiritu en Jn 7,37-39," EstBi 31 (4, 1972) 369-98. LOEWE, H./ZIPPERT, C. "Johannes 7,37-39: Jenseits von Gier und Ueberdruss," in: Predigtstudien für das Kirchenjahr 1975 (1975) P. Krusche/E. Lange/D. Rössler/R. Roessler eds., 68-76. STOEVESANDT, H. GPM 29 (2, 1975) 257ff. PANCARO, S., The Law in the Fourth Gospel (Leiden 1975) 359, 479-81, 484. HAHN, F., "Die Worte vom lebendigen Wasser im Johannesevangelium. Eigenart und Vorgeschichte von Joh 4:10,13f., 6:35, 7:37-39" in: P. Jervell/W. A. Meeks (eds.) God's Christ and His People. FS. N. A. Dahl (New York 1977) 51-70. de la POTTERIE, I., La Vérité dans Saint Jean I/II (Rome 1977) 692-96. FEE, G. D., "Once More — John 7:37-39" ET 89 (1978) 116-18. RAMOS, F. F., "El Espiritu Santo y Maria en los escritos joanicos" EphM 28 (1978) 169-90. HODGES, Z. C., "Problem Passages in the Gospel of John: Part 7: Rivers of Living Water — John 7:37-39" BiblSa 136 (1979) 239-48. SWIDLER, L., Biblical Affirmations of Woman (Philadelphia 1979)

173, 220, 224. BALTENSWEILER, H. und OTT, H., in: P. Krusche et al. (eds.) Predigtstudien für das Kirchenjahr 1980-1981. III/2 (Stuttgart 1981) 62-69. HÜBNER, E., in: GPM 35 (1981) 272-80.

7:37-38 LATTEY, C. "A Note on John VII, 37-38" Scripture VI (5, 1954) 151-53. BARRETT, C. K. The New Testament Background (1956) 159. QUIRANT, J. C. " 'Torrentes de agua viva.' Una neuva interpretacion de Juan 7,37-38?" EstBi 16 (3-4, 1957) 297-306. KUHN, K. H. "St. John vii. 37-38," NTS 4 (1, 1957) 63-65. BOISMARD, M.-E., "De son ventre couleront des fleuves d'eau (Jo., VII, 37-38)," RevBi 65 (4, 1958) 523-46. BESNARD, A.-M., "La foi accomplit l'attente humaine," VieS 103 (466, 1960) 353-70. KILPATRICK, G. D. "The Punctuation of John vii. 37-38," JThS 11 (2, 1960) 340-43. RUDOLPH, K. Die Mandäer II (1961) 127,2. BRAUN, F.-M. "Aqua y Espiritu," SelecTeol 4 (13, 19654) 68-76. CREHAN, J. The Theology of St. John (1965) 125-28. FREED, E. D. Old Testament Quotations in the Gospel of John (1965) 21-38. HOOKE, S. H. "The Spirit was not yet," NTS 9 (1962-1963) 372f. CORTES, J. B. "Yet Another Look at Jn 7,37-38," CBQ 29 (2, 1967) 75-86. SMITH, M. Tannaitic Parallels to the Gospels (1968) 8 b n 10. DUNN, J. D. G. Baptism in the Holy Spirit (1970) 179f., 188. NÖTSCHER, F., Altorientalischer und alttestamentlicher Auferstehungsglaube (Darmstadt 1970 = 1926) 322-23. PORSCH, F., Pneuma und Wort (Frankfurt 1974) 57-58, 60-65. REIM, G., Studien zum Alttestamentlichen Hintergrund des Johannesevangeliums (Cambridge 1974) 56-88, 106-108, 193-96, 280.

7:37 GRILL, J. Untersuchungen über die Entstehung des vierten Evangeliums II (1923) 105, 110, 128, 130, 356. GILS, F. Jésus Prophète D'Aprés Les Evangiles Synoptiques (1957) 29-30, 34-35. DANIELOU, J. "Joh 7,37 et Ezéch. 47,1-11," in: Studia Evangelica II (1964) F. L. Cross, ed., 158-63. DAVIES, W. D., The Gospel and the Land (London 1974) 292.

7:38-39 FLEW, R. N. Jesus and His Church (1956) 173. BRAUN, H. Qumran und NT II (1966) 26ff., 77, 131, 133, 253ff., 315. HEER, J. "Ströme Lebendigen Wassers werden aus seinem Leib fliessen," Sein und Sendung 35 (11, 1968) 483-98. SUMMERS, R. The Secret Sayings of the Living Jesus (1968) 20.

7:38 NESTLE, E. "Jn 7:38 im Brief der gallischen Christen," ZNW 10 (1909) 323. PALLIS, A. Notes on St. John and the Apocalypse (London 1928) 17-18. NOACK, B. Zur Johanneischen Tradition (1954) 80-81. MENARD, J.-E. "L'interprétation patristique de Jean VII,38," ROU 25 (1, 1955) 5-25. ELLIS, E.

E. Paul's Use of the Old Testament (1957) 21f., 35. BROWN, R. E., "The Qumran Scrolls and the Johannine Gospel and Epistles" in: K. Stendahl (ed.) The Scrolls and the New Testament (New York 1957) 200; [orig. in CBQ 17 (1955) 403-19, 559-74]; GT: "Die Schriftrollen von Qumran und das Johannesevangelium und die Johannesbriefe" in: K. H. Rengstorf (ed.) Johannes und sein Evangelium (Darmstadt 1973) 515-16. NIEWALDA, P. Sakramentssymbolik im Johannesevangelium² (1958) 68ff. AUDET, J.-P. "La soif, l'eau et la parole," RevBi 66 (3, 1959) 379-86. BOISMARD, M.-E. "Les citations targumiques du quatrième évangile," RevBi 66 (3, 1959) 374-78. GRELOT, P, " 'De son ventre couleront des fleuves d'eau.' La citation scripturaire de Jean VII, 38," RevBi 66 (3, 1959) 369-74. GRELOT, P. "A propos de Jean VII, 38," RevBi 67 (2, 1960) 224-25. BRUCE, F. F., "The Book of Zechariah and the Passion Narrative," BJRL 43 (1960-1961) 348. GRELOT, P. "Jean, VII, 38: Eau du rocher ou source du temple?" RevBi 70 (1, 1963) 43-51. BAUER, J. B. "Drei Cruces," BZ 9 (1, 1965) 84-91. McNAMARA, M. The New Testament and the Palestinian Targum to the Pentateuch (1966) 32n156. BALAGUE, M., "Flumina de ventre credentis (Jn. 7:38)," EstBi 26 (2, 1967) 187-201. NICKELS, P. Targum and New Testament (1967) 55. BAUER, J. B. Scholia Biblica & Patristica (1972) 82-89. BROWNLEE, W. H. "Whence the Gospel According to John?" in: John and Qumran (1972) J. H. Charlesworth ed., 186-87. PORSCH, F., Pneuma und Wort (Frankfurt 1974) 59-60.

7:39 GRILL, J. Untersuchungen über die Entstehung des vierten Evangeliums II (1923) 23, 220, 290, 359, 373. DUPONT, J. Essais sur la Christologie de Saint Jean (1951) 204, 205, 211, 258, 261. BROWNLEE, W. H. "Messianic Motifs of Qumran and the New Testament," NTS 3 (1956-1957) 29f. ROBINSON, J. M. Kerygma und historischer Jesus (1960) 71. WAINWRIGHT, A. W. The Trinity in the New Testament (1962) 261-62. DELLING, G. Die Taufe im Neuen Testament (1963) 58. WOODHOUSE, H. F. "Hard Sayings -IX. John 7.39," Theology 67 (529, 1964) 310-12. KUHL, J. Die Sendung Jesu und der Kirche nach dem Johannes-Evangelium (1967) 135, 167. CADMAN, W. H. The Open Heaven (1969) G. B. Caird ed., 6, 92, 122, 169, 190. OLSSON, B., Structure and Meaning in the Fourth Gospel (Lund 1974) 45, 64, 67, 69-70, 93, 189, 217, 262-65, 271. PORSCH, F., Pneuma und Wort (Frankfurt 1974) 53-81, 332-39. CONZELMANN, H. und LINDEMANN, A., Arbeitsbuch zum Neuen Testament (Tübingen 1975) 27. SCHNACKENBURG, R., "Die johanneische Gemeinde und ihre Geisterfahrung'' in: R. Schnackenburg et al. (eds.) Die Kirche des Anfangs. FS. H. Schürmann (Freiburg 1978) 283-87. SCHWEIZER, E., Heiliger Geist (Berlin 1978) 143. CLARK, K. W., "The Text of the Gospel of John in Third-Century Egypt" in: The Gentile Bias and Other Essays (Leiden 1980) 162. LÉON-DUFOUR, X., "Towards a Symbolic Reading of the Fourth Gospel" NTS 27 (1980-1981) 450.

7:40ff HAHN, F. Christologische Hoheitstitel (1963) 397.

7:40-44 SMITH, C. H. "Tabernacles in the Fourth Gospel and Mark," NTS 9 (1962-1963) 137f. BURGER, C. Jesus als Davidssohn (1970) 153-58.

7:40-44 de JONGE, M., Jesus: Stranger from Heaven and Son of God (Missoula 1977) 54-57, 93-94.

7:40-41 GLASSON, T. F. Moses in the Fourth Gospel (1963) 27ff. REIM, G., Studien zum Alttestamentlichen Hintergrund des Johannesevangeliums (Cambridge 1974) 122-23.

7:40 VOLZ, P. Die Eschatologie der jüdischen Gemeinde (1934) 193. DAVIES, W. D. Torah in the Messianic Age and/or the Age to come (1952) 44. BOUSSET, W. Die Religion des Judentums im Späthellenistischen Zeitalter (1966 = 1926) 233. SCHEL-KLE, K. H. "Jesus - Lehrer und Prophet," in: Orientierung an Jesus (1973) P. Hoffmann ed., 305f. SCHNIDER, F. Jesus der Prophet (1973) 19, 116, 191, 223ff.

7:41-42 HAHN, F. Christologische Hoheitstitel (1963) 224, 245, 253, 269. DELLING, G. Wort und Werk Jesu im Johannes-Evangelium (1966) 91f. "Bethlehem" in: TRE 5 (1980) 760.

7:42-52 SCHILLEBEECKX, E., Christ: the Christian Experience in the Modern World (London 1980) 318-19; GT: Christus und die Christen (Freiburg/Basel/Wien 1977) 305.

7:42 STONEHOUSE, N. B. The Witness of Matthew and Mark to Christ (1944) 223. FREED, E. D. Old Testament Quotations in the Gospel of John (1965) 39-59. BRAUN, H. Qumran und NT II (1966) 305, 312. REIM, G., Studien zum Alttestamentlichen Hintergrund des Johannesevangeliums (Cambridge 1974) 18-21, 89-95.

7:44 METZGER, B. M., The Early Versions of the New Testament (Oxford 1977) 198n.3.

7:45-52 RIVKIN, E., A Hidden Revolution (Nashville 1978) 99-100.

7:45-49 PANCARO, S., The Law in the Fourth Gospel (Leiden 1975) 7, 87, 101-105, 120, 148.

7:46 IBUKI, Y. Die Wahrheit im Johannesevangelium (1972) 47f., 72. REIM, G., Studien zum Alttestamentlichen Hintergrund des

Johannesevangeliums (Cambridge 1974) 123. METZGER, B. M., The Early Versions of the New Testament (Oxford 1977) 436.

7:48ff KAESEMANN, E. Exegetische Versuche und Besinnungen (1964) I 181.

7:48-49 AVANZO, M., "Las Relaciones entre los Rabinos y el Pueblo" RevBi 37 (1975) 9-15.

7:49 MOORE, G. F. Judaism (1946) II 160n. BOUSSET, W. Die Religion des Judentums im Späthellenistischen Zeitalter (1966 = 1926) 165, 187. METZGER, B. M., The Early Versions of the New Testament (Oxford 1977) 162.

7:50ff BROER, I. Die Urgemeinde und das Grab Jesu (1972) 233f.

7:50-52 MAHONEY, R., Two Disciples at the Tomb (Frankfurt 1974) 127-30. de JONGE, M., Jesus: Stranger from Heaven and Son of God (Missoula 1977) 34-37. STASIAK, K., "The Man Who Came By Night" BiTod 20 (1982) 84-89.

7:50 BERGMEIER, R., Glaube als Gabe nach Johannes (Stuttgart 1980) 214.

7:51 BLANK, J. Krisis (1964) 49. PANCARO, S., "The Metamorphosis of a Legal Principle in the Fourth Gospel. A Closer Look at Jn 7,51," Biblica 23 (3, 1972) 340-51. PANCARO, S., The Law sin he Fourth Gospel (Leiden 1975) 114, 129, 130, 138-25b.

7:52 DUPONT, J. Essais sur la Christologie de Saint Jean (1951) 297, 208. SMOTHERS, E. H. "Two Readings in Papyrus Bodmer II," HThR 51 (3, 1958) 109-22. MEHLMANN, J. "O Profeta du Leuteronomic," ACT 11 (3, 1962) 192-298. SMITH, D. M. The Composition and Order of the Fourth Gospel (1965) 132, 156, 158, 160, 162. MEHLMANN, J. "Propheta a Moyse promissus in Jo 7,52 citatus," VerDbom 44 (2, 1966) 79-88. SCHNIDER, F., Jesus der Prophet (1973) 191, 223ff. DAVIES, W. D. The Gospel and the Land (1973) 322, 323, 324, 330. REIM, G., Studien zum Alttestamentlichen Hintergrund des Johannesevangeliums (Cambridge 1974) 123. BERGMEIER, A., Glaube als Gabe nach Johannes (Stuttgart 1980) 214. KRAFT, H., Die Entstehung des Christentums (Darmstadt 1981) 79.

7:53-8:11 BLASS, F. Philosophy of the Gospel (1898) 89f., 155ff. BAUER, W. Das Johannesevangelium (1925) 111-13. TAYLOR, V. The Formation of the Gospel Tradition (1949) 83f. RUCKSTUHL, E. Die literarische Einheit des Johannesevangeliums (1951) 216f. STREETER, B. H. The Four Gospels (1951) 123f. MANSON, T. W. "The Pericope de Adultera (Joh 7,53-8,11)," ZNW 44 (1952-1953) 255f. GUILDING, A. The Fourth Gospel and Jewish Worship (1960) 110-12. MER-LIER, O. "Pericope de la femme adultère," in: Le Quatraième Evangile (1961) 139-49. TAYLOR, V. The Text of the New Testament (1961) 35f. BECKER, U. Jesus und die Ehebrech-erin (1963). DERRETT, J. D. M. "Law in the New Testament: The Story of the Woman Taken in Adultery," NTS 10 (1, 1963) 1-26. HAHN, F. Christologische Hoheitstitel (1963) 76. DER-RETT, J. D. M. "The Woman Taken in Adultery (John 7,53-8,11). Its Legal Aspects," in: Studia Evangelica II (1964) F. L. Cross ed., 170-73. FASCHER, E. ThLZ 89 (12, 1964) 911-917. HENNECKE, E./SCHNEEMELCHER, W. Neutestament-liche Apokryphen (1964) I 78. BRAUN, H. Qumran und NT II (1966) 104. JOHNSON, A. F. "A Stylistic Trait of the Fourth Gospel in the Pericope Adulterae?" BullEvangTheolSoc 9 (2, 1966) 91-96. OSBORNE, R. E., "Pericope Adulterae," CanJournTheol 12 (4, 1966) 281-83. BALTENSWEILER, H. Die Ehe im Neuen Testament (1967) 120-35. COLEMAN, B. W. "The Woman Taken in Adultery. Studies in Texts: John 7:53-8:11," Theology 73 (603, 1970) 409-10. DERRETT, J. D. M. Law in the New Testament (1970) 156-88. RIESEN-FELD, H. The Gospel Tradition (1970) 95-110. BEUTLER, J. Martyria (1972) 265f. TRITES, A. A. "The Woman Taken in Adultery," BiblSa 131 (522, 1974) 137-46. TEMPLE, S., The Core of the Fourth Gospel (London 1975) 158. CAMPEN-HAUSEN, H. F. von., "Zur Perikope von der Ehebrecherin (Joh 7:53 - 8:11)" ZNW 68 (1977) 164-75. METZGER, B. M., The Early Versions of the New Testament (Oxford 1977) 40, 48, 55, 132, 198. "Agrapha" in: TRE 2 (1978) 104. LINDARS, B., "Jesus and the Pharisees" in: E. Bammel et al. (eds.) Donum Gentilicium. FS. D. Daube (Oxford 1978) 56-68. RAYAN, S., The Holy Spirit: Heart of the Gospel and Christian Hope (New York 1978) 57. ROUSSEAU, F., "La femme adultère. Struc-ture de Jn 7,53-8,11" Biblica 59 (1978) 463-80. BECKER, J., Das Evangelium nach Johannes (Gütersloh/Würzburg 1979) 280 (lit!). HODGES, Z. C., "Problem Passages in the Gospel of John. Part 8: The Woman Taken in Adultery (John 7:53-8:11): The Text" BiblSa 136 (1979) 318-32. JAMES, S. A., "The Adulteress and the Death Penalty" JEThS 22 (1979) 45-53. METZGER, B. M., "The Practice of the New Testament Tex-tual Criticism" in: V. L. Tollers/J. R. Maier (eds.) The Bible in Its Literary Milieu (Grand Rapids 1979) 247-49. METZ-GER, B. M., "St. Jerome's Explicit References to Variant Readings in Manuscripts of the New Testament" in: E. Best/R.

McL. Wilson (eds.) Text and Interpretation. FS. M. Black (Cambridge 1979) 183. NEWMAN, B. M., " 'Verses marked with brackets . . . ' " BTr 30 (1979) 233-36. SWIDLER, L., Biblical Affirmations of Woman (Philadelphia 1979) 220, 224, 275. GERSTENBERGER, E. S. und SCHRAGE, W., Frau und Mann (Stuttgart 1980) 165-66. GOLDMAN, E., "Who Raises up the Fallen" Hebrew Studies 20-21 (Madison , WI 1979-1980) 54-59. HAENCHEN, E., Das Johannesevangelium (Tübingen 1980) 363-64 (lit!). HODGES, Z. C., "Problem Passages in the Gospel of John. Part 9: The Woman Taken in Adultery (John 7:53-8:11): Exposition" BiblSa 137 (1980) 41-53. "Cajetan" in: TRE 7 (1981) 544. METZGER, B. M., Manuscripts of the Greek Bible (Oxford 1981) 120. "Einleitungswissenschaft" in: TRE 9 (1982) 470.

7:53-8:1 SCHILLING, F. A. "The story of Jesus and the adulteress (Joh. 7,53-8,1)," AThR XXXVII (2, 1955) 91-106. BLINZLER, J. Der Prozess Jesu (1969⁴) 237, 240f.

8-12 BECKER, H., Die Reden des Johannesevangeliums und der Stil der gnostischen Offenbarungsrede (Göttingen 1956) 114-16.

8 STRATHMANN, H. Das Evangelium ncah Johannes (1956) 152. BECKER, H., Die Reden des Johannesevangeliums und der Stil der gnostischen Offenbarungsrede (Göttingen 1956) 77-78. van den BUSSCHE, H., "La Structure de Jean I-XII" in: M. Boismard et al., L'Evangile de Jean: études et problèmes (Bruges 1958) 100-101. SCHULZ, S., Komposition und Herkunft der Johanneischen Reden (Stuttgart 1960) 74-76, 99-102. SMITH, D. M. The Composition and Order of the Fourth Gospel (1965) 155-63. NICKELS, P. Targum and New Testament (1967) 55. RIEDEL, J. Das Heilswerk Jesu nach Johannes (1973) 379-406.

8:1-20 MATSUNAGA, K. "Is John's Gospel Anti-Sacramental?-A New Solution in the Light of the Evangelist's Milieu" NTS 27 (1980-1981) 522-23.

8:1-11 YATES, K. M. Preaching from John's Gospel (1964) 80-86. KRUSCHE, W. GPM 21 (3, 1966) 256-62. SWIDLER, L., Biblical Affirmations of Woman (Philadelphia 1979) 187, 250, 289. SMIT, D., Speelruimte: Eeen structurele lezing van het evangelie (Hilversum 1981). "Ehe" in: TRE 9 (1982) 360.

8:1-2 SWIDLER, L., Biblical Affirmations of Woman (Philadelphia 1979) 275.

8:2-11 GILL, J. H., "Jesus, Irony, and the 'New Quest' " Encounter (1980) 139-51.

8:4 HAHN, F. Christologische Hoheitstitel (1963) 76.

8:5 BLINZLER, J. "Die Strafe für Ehebruch in Bibel und Halacha. Zur Auslegung von Joh. VIII.5," NTS 4 (1, 1957) 32-47.

8:6 DANIEL, S. "Znaczenie Wyrazenia 'Palec Bozy' w Pismie swietym (Vis Digiti Dei in Scriptura Sacra subiect)," RBL 10 (4-5, 1957) 247-60.

8:7-11 SWIDLER, L. Biblical Affirmations of Woman (Philadelphia 1979) 286.

8:7.9 NICKELS, P. Targum and New Testament (1967) 46, 55.

8:7 SANFORD, J. A., The Kingdom Within (New York 1970) 159-60.

8:11 "Ablass" in: TRE 1 (1977) 349.

8:12ff NORDEN, E. Agnostos Theos (1956 = 1912) 298f.

8:12-59 GUILDING, A. The Fourth Gospel and Jewish Worship (1960) 107-10. TROADEC, H. "Le témoignage de la Lumière. Jean 8,12-59," BVieC 49 (1963) 16-26. YATES, K. M. Preaching from John's Gospel (1964) 87-92. CADMAN, W. H. The Open Heaven (1969) G. B. Caird ed., 107-16. THOMA, C. Kirche aus Juden und Heiden (1970) 88-90. HAENCHEN, E., Das Johannesevangelium (Tübingen 1980) 366-67 (lit!).

8:12-58 KERN, W. "Der symmetrische Gesamtaufbau von Jo 8,12-58," ZKTh 78 (1956) 451-54.

8:12-30 LOCKYER, H. All the Parables of the Bible (1963) 322ff. TEMPLE, S., The Core of the Fourth Gospel (London 1975) 158-61. TSUCHIDO, K., "Tradition and Redaction in John 8:12-30" AJBI 6 (1980) 56-75.

8:12-29 ODEBERG, H. The Fourth Gospel (1968) 286ff.

8:12-20 RUCKSTUHL, E. Die literarische Einheit des Johannes-evangeliums (1951) 236f., 247. WIKENHAUSER, A. Das Evangelium nach Johannes (1957) 170-72. BLANK, J. Krisis (1964) 183. BRAUN, F.-M. Jean le Théologien (1966) 119-21. BEUTLER, J. Martyria (1972) 27f., 30f., 265-71. RIVKIN, E., A Hidden Revolution (Nashville 1978) 99-100. BECKER, J., Das Evangelium nach Johannes (Gütersloh/Würzburg 1979) 286 (lit!). HORST, U., "Jesus als Licht der Welt" Anzeiger für die katholische Geistlichkeit 88 (1979) 306. TSUCHIDO, K.,

"Tradition and Redaction in John 8:12-30" AJBI 6 (1980) 60, 63-64.

8:12-16 FRINDTE, D. GPM 23 (1, 1968) 43-50. MARGENFELD, D. "Offenes Geheimnis" in: Weihnachten heute gesagt (1970) H. Nitschke ed., 88-95. BRANDENBURGER, E./MERKEL, F. GPM 29 (1, 1974) 42-46. HUEBNER, E. GPM 29 (1, 1974) 46-56. MÜLLER, H. M. und LINDNER, I. W.-V., in: P. Krusche et al. (eds.) Predigtstudien für das Kirchenjahr 1974-1975, III/1 (Stuttgart 1974) 56-63. LAUFF, W., in: GPM 35 (1980) 53-58. RIESS, H., und STAMMLER, E., in: P. Krusche et al. (eds.) Predigtstudien für das Kirchenjahr 1980-1981. III/1 (Stuttgart 1980) 54-60.

8:12 BAUER, W. Das Johannesevangelium (1925) 114f. MORGAN, G. C. The Parables and Metaphors of Our Lord (1943) 303ff. DUPONT, J. Essais sur la Christologie de Saint Jean (1961) 27, 51, 72, 92, 97, 189, 205, 206. MUSZNER, F. Z. Ω H. Die Anschauung vom "Leben" im vierten Evangelium (1952) 167f. BARRETT, C. K. The New Testament Background (1956) 159. ANON., "Ich bin das Licht der Welt (Jn 8,12)," GuL 30 (3, 1957) 222-30. WILKENS, W. Die Entstehungsgeschichte des vierten Evangeliums (1958) 108-11. WILES, M. F. The Spiritual Gospel (1960) 73-76, 97, 135. SCHWEIZER, E. Erniedrigung und Erhöhung bei Jesus und seinen Nachfolgern (1962) § 11g. GLASSON, T. F. Moses in the Fourth Gospel (1963) 58, Ch. VIII, 72, 107. HAHN, F. Das Verständnis der Mission im Neuen Testament (²1965) 136. SMITH, D. M. The Composition and Order of the Fourth Gospel (1965) 21, 131, 132, 156, 157, 158, 160, 162. BRAUN, H. Qumran und NT II (1966) 24, 78, 120f., 130, 135, 138, 140, 179, 215, 228. DELLING, G. Wort und Werk Jesu im Johannes-Evangelium (1966) 119-21, 139. ALVAREZ, C. G. " 'Soy luz' (Jn 8,12),; 'sois luz' (Mt 5,14)," CiDi 180 (2, 1967) 257-63. NICKELS, P. Targum and New Testament (1967) 55. CHARLESWORTH, J. H., "A Critical Comparison of the dualism in IQS III. 13-IV 26 and the 'Dualism' contained in the Fourth Gospel," NTS 15 (1968-1969) 413ff. CADMAN, W. H. The Open Heaven (1969) G. B. Caird ed., 21, 100, 117, 125. OTTO, G. Denken - um zu glauben (1970) 18-21. SCHOTTROFF, L. Der Glaubende und die feindliche Welt (1970) 228-29, 231, 283. BEUTLER, J. Martyria (1972) 265-67, 348. DAUER, A., Die Passionsgeschichte im Johannesevangelium (1972) 142, 257, 303. MUELLER, T. Das Heilsgeschehen im Johannesevangelium n.d., 14-18, 90. REIM, G., Studien zum Alttestamentlichen Hintergrund des Johannesevangeliums

(Cambridge 1974) 163-66. PANCARO, S., The Law in the Fourth Gospel (Leiden 1975) 278, 452, 453, 485-87. FISCHER, U., Eschatologie und Jenseitserwartung im hellenistischen Diasporajudentum (Berlin 1978) 68. BERGMEIER, R. Glaube als Gabe nach Johannes (Stuttgart 1980) 192n,30, 204, 215, 235, 272n.592, 598. TSUCHIDO, K., "Tradition and Redaction in John 8:12-30" AJBI 6 (1980) 56, 59-60, 63. PHILONENKO-SAYAR, B. und PHILONENKO, M., "Die Apokalypse Abrahams" in: JüdSchr V/5 (1982) 429n.IX.2.

8:13ff MAURER, C. Ignatius von Aniochien und das Johannesevangelium (1949) 45ff., 51f. HAHN, F., Das Verständnis der Mission im Neuen Testament (^{2}1965) 140.

8:13-20 WILKENS, W. Die Entstehungsgeschichte des vierten Evangeliums (1958) 98-108. SMITH, D. M. The Composition and Order of the Fourth Gospel (1965) 130-34, 140, 155, 156, 159, 160, 161, 212n.

8:13-16 BEUTLER, F. Martyria (1972) 268f.

8:13-14 RUCKSTUHL, E. Die literarische Einheit des Johannesevangeliums (1951) 69, 226f. BROX, N. Zeuge und Märtyrer (1961) 73ff.

8:13 BEUTLER, J. Martyria (1972) 230f. TSUCHIDO, K., "Tradition and Redaction in John 8:12-30" AJBI 6 (1980) 57, 60.

8:14-18 von WAHLDE, U. C., "The Witness to Jesus in John 5:31-40 and Belief in the Fourth Gospel" CBQ 43 (1981) 393, 395.

8:14 MAURER, C. Ignatius von Antiochien und das Johannesevangelium (1949) 25ff., 45ff., 51. SMITH, C. H., "Tabernacles in the Fourth Gospel and Mark," NTS 9 (1962-1963) 134f. DELLING, G. Wort und Werk Jesu im Johannes-Evangelium (1966) 47, 85f. BEUTLER, J. Martyria (1972) 230f., 270f. IBUKI, Y., Die Wahrheit im Johannesevangelium (1972) 164f. BERGMEIER, R., Glaube als Gabe nach Johannes (Stuttgart 1980) 191n.19, 248n.212, 253n.301. TSUCHIDO, K., "Tradition and Redaction in John 8:12-30," AJBI 6 (1980) 57, 60-61. DAHMS, J. V., "Isaiah 55:11 and the Gospel of John" EQ 53 (1981) 78-88.

8:15.17-20 BEUTLER, J. Martyria (1972) 230f., 268f., 269-71.

8:15 KAESEMANN, E. Exegetische Versuche und Besinnungen (1964) II 172. KAESEMANN, E. New Testament Questions of Today (1969) 157. PANCARO, S., The Law in the Fourth Gospel (Leiden 1975) 272-74. BERGMEIER, R., Glaube als Gabe nach Johannes (Stuttgart 1980) 215, 219.

8:16 IBUKI, Y. Die Wahrheit im Johannesevangelium (1972) 166f. TSUCHIDO, K., "Tradition and Redaction in John 8:12-30" AJBI 6 (1980) 58, 60, 63, 70.

8:17-18 REUSS, J., "Presbyter Ammonius' Kommentar zum Jo-Evangelium," Biblica 44 (1963) 166. PANCARO, S., The Law in the Fourth Gospel (Leiden 1975) 265, 266, 275-78.

8:17 CHARLIER, J.-P. "L'exégèse johannique d'un précepte légal: Jean VIII 17," RevBi 67 (4, 1960) 503-15. DAUER, A. Die Passionsgeschichte im Johannesevangelium (1972) 141, 300, 301. REIM, G., Studien zum Alttestamentlichen Hintergrund des Johannesevangeliums (Cambridge 1974) 21-22, 89-91, 93-94. TSUCHIDO, K. "Tradition and Redaction in John 8:12-30" AJBI 6 (1980) 57, 60.

8:18 DELLING, G. Wort und Werk Jesu im Johannesevangelium (1966) 47-49, 65, 101, 114. KUHL, J. Die Sendung Jesu und der Kirche nach dem Johannes-Evangelium (1967) 88-94.

8:19-24 ORIGENES, Das Evangelium nach Johannes (1959) R. Gögler ed., 286-302.

8:19 GRILL, J. Untersuchungen über die Entstehung des vierten Evangeliums II (1923) 125f., 242, 329. WILES, M. F. The Spiritual Gospel (1960) 30, 85, 91-92, 113, 151.

8:20 SMITH, D. M. The Composition and Order of the Fourth Gospel (1965) 119, 131, 140, 160, 241. PETZKE, G. Die Traditionen über Apollonius von Tyana und das Neue Testament (1970) 76, 170. TSUCHIDO, K., "Tradition and Redaction in John 8:12-30" AJBI 6 (1980) 56, 59, 61, 63.

8:21-30 HINZ, GPM 21 (1, 1966) 120-31. BECKER, J., Das Evangelium nach Johannes (Gütersloh/Würzburg 1979) 292 (lit!). TSUCHIDO, K., "Tradition and Redaction in John 8:12-30" AJBI 6 (1980) 56, 64, 66-67. GEBHARDT, R. und BEISHEIM, J., in: P. Krusche et al. (eds.) Predigtstudien für das Kirchenjahr 1982-1983. V/I (Stuttgart 1982) 143-51.

8:21-29 GRAESSER, E. NTS 11 (1964-1965) 84f. SMITH, D. M. The Composition and Order of the Fourth Gospel (1965) 156, 157, 160, 161. RIEDL, J., "Wenn ihr den Menschensohn erhöht habt, werdet ihr erkennen (Joh 8,28)" in: R. Pesch/R. Schnackenburg (eds.) Jesus und der Menschensohn (Freiburg/Basel/Wien 1975) 355-60. COLLINS, R. F., "The Search for Jesus. Reflections on the Fourth Gospel" LThPh 34 (1978) 27-48.

8:21-28 THUESING, W. Die Erhöhung und Verherrlichung Jesu im Johannesevangelium (1970) 15-17.

8:21-22 LEROY, H. Rätsel und Missverständnis (1968) 51-67. DAHMS, J. V., "Isaiah 55:11 and the Gospel of John" EQ 53 (1981) 78-80.

8:21 LAZURE, N., Les Valeurs Morales de la Théologie Johannique (Paris 1965) 295-96. STROBEL, A. Erkenntnis und Bekenntnis der Sünde in neutestamentlicher Zeit (1968) 46. BERGMEIER, R., Glaube als Gabe nach Johannes (Stuttgart 1980) 255n.326. TSUCHIDO, K., "Tradition and Redaction in John 8:12-30" AJBI 6 (1980) 63, 65-66.

8:22 TSUCHIDO, K., "Tradition and Redaction in John 8:12-30" AJBI 6 (1980) 64-67.

8:23ff CHARLESWORTH, J. H., "A Critical Comparison of the dualism in IQS III 13-IV 26 and the 'Dualism' contained in the Fourth Gospel," NTS 15 (1968-1969) 403ff., 412ff.

8:23-34 JEWETT, P. K., Infant Baptism and the Covenant of Grace (Grand Rapids 1978) 228.

8:23 ORIGENES, Das Evangelium nach Johannes (1959) R. Gögler ed., 122-28. WILES, M. F. The Spiritual Gospel (1960) 76-78, 97. DSS: The Hymn of the Intitiants-Manual of Discipline 11, 1-2. BÜHNER, J.-A. Der Gesandte und sein Weg im 4. Evangelium (Tübingen 1977) 381-82. RUDOLPH, K., Die Gnosis (Göttingen 1978) 324. BERGMEIER, R., Glaube als Gabe nach Johannes (Stuttgart 1980) 10, 191n.16, 220-221, 223, 256n.342, 349. TSUCHIDO, K., "Tradition and Redaction in John 8:12-30" AJBI 6 (1980) 67-69.

8:24.28 HARNER, P. B. The "I Am" of the Fourth Gospel (1970) 43-45.

8:24 FLEW, R. N. Jesus and His Church (1956) 176. REUSS, J. "Presbyter Ammonius' Kommentar zum Jo-Evangelium" Biblica 44 (1963) 166-67. LAZURE, N., Les Valeurs Morales de la Théologie Johannique (Paris 1965) 295-97. DELLING, G. Wort und Werk Jesu im Johannes-Evangelium (1966) 38, 40, 44, 50, 54, 141. DAUER, A., Die Passionsgeschichte im Johannesevangelium (1972) 243f., 258. IBUKI, Y. Die Wahrheit im Johannesevangelium (1972) 224f. LINDARS, B. "The Son of Man in the Johannine Christology," in: Christ and the Spirit in the New Testament (1973) B. Lindars/S. S. Smalley eds., 53f. HOWARD, V. P., Das Ego in den Synoptischen Evangelien (Marburg 1975) 253-54. BERGMEIER, R., Glaube als Gabe nach Johannes (Stuttgart 1980) 211.33. TSUCHIDO, K., "Tradition and Redaction in John 8:12-30" AJBI 6 (1980) 63-65. FREED, E. D., "*Ego Eimi* in John VIII:24 in the Light of its Context and Jewish Messianic Belief" JThS 33 (1982) 163-67.

8:25 GRILL, J. Untersuchungen über die Entstehung des vierten Evangeliums II (1923) 329f., 243, 343, 356, 359. CELADA,

B. "El nuevo papiro Bodmer II aclara un pasaje de San Juan (Jn 8:25)," CultBib 15 (163, 1958) 381. FUNK, R. W. "Papyrus Bodmer II (P⁶⁶) and John 8,25," HThR 51 (2, 1958) 95-100. IBUKI, Y. Die Wahrheit im Johannesevangelium (1972) 48f. TSUCHIDO, K. "Tradition and Redaction in John 8:12-30" AJBI 6 (1980) 15, 68-69.

8:26-28 BERGMEIER, R., Glaube als Gabe nach Johannes (Stuttgart 1980) 239n.54.

8:26.28-29 IBUKI, Y. Die Wahrheit im Johannesevangelium (1972) 40ff., 146ff.

8:26.28 DELLING, G. Wort und Werk Jesu im Johannes-Evangelium (1966) 35, 38, 40, 63, 72, 80, 95, 101, 112, 113, 125. NICK-ELS, P. Targum and New Testament (1967) 56.

8:26 DAUER, A. Die Passionsgeschichte im Johannesevangelium (1972) 248, 256, 288. TSUCHIDO, K., "Tradition and Redaction in John 8:12-30" AJBI 6 (1980) 59, 67.

8:28-29 WILKENS, W. Die Entstehungsgeschichte des vierten Evangeliums (1958) 108-11. BÜHNER, J.-A., Der Gesandte und Sein Weg im 4. Evangelium (Tübingen 1977) 408. HANSON, A. T., The New Testament Interpretation of Scripture (London 1980) 172. LINDARS, B., "Discourse and Tradition: The Use of the Sayings of Jesus in the Discourses of the Fourth Gospel" JSNT 13 (1981) 84-85.

8:28 GRILL, J. Untersuchungen über die Entstehung des vierten Evangeliums II (1923) 216f. SCHULZ, S., Untersuchungen zur Menschensohn-Christologie im Johannesevangelium (Göttingen 1957) 118. GIBLET, J., "Jésus et le 'Père' dans le IVe évangile" in: M. Boismard et al., L'Evangile de Jean: études et problèmes (Bruges 1958) 120-23. ROBINSON, J. M. Kerygma und historischer Jesus (1960) 71. HAHN, F. Christologische Hoheitstitel (1963) 53, 130. BRAUN, F.-M. Jean le Théologien (1966) 177f. McNAMARA, M. The New Testament and the Palestinian Targum to the Pentateuch (1966) 146, 149. LEIVESTAD, R. "Der Apokalyptische Menschensohn ein theologisches Phantom," ASThI VI 1967-1968 (1968) H. Kosmala ed., 49-105. SMALLEY, S. S., "The Johannine Son of Man sayings," NTS 15 (1968-1969) 297ff. CADMAN, W. H. The Open Heaven (1969) G. B. Caird ed., 3, 4, 32, 65, 90, 156. THUESING, W. Die Erhöhung und der Verherrlichung Jesu im Johannesevangelium (1970) 15-22. SMALLEY. S. S., "Diversity and Development in John," NTS 17 (1970-1971) 288f. LINDARS, B. "The Son of Man in the Johannine Gospel," in: Christ and the Spirit in the New Testament (1973) B. Lindars/

S. S. Smalley eds., 44, 53f., 56f. CAVALLIN, H. C. C., Life After Death (1974) 7, 2n18. REIM, G., Studien zum Alttestamentlichen Hintergrund des Johannesevangeliums (Cambridge 1974) 171-72, 253-54. HOWARD, V. P., Das Ego in den Synoptischen Evangelien (Marburg 1975) 253-54. RIEDL, J., "Wenn ihr den Menschensohn erhöht habt, werdet ihr erkennen (Joh 8,28)" in: R. Pesch/R. Schnackenburg (eds.) Jesus und der Menschensohn (Freiburg/Basel/Wien 1975) 355-70. RAYAN, S., The Holy Spirit: Heart of the Gospel and Christian Hope (New York 1978) 82. MORGAN-WYNNE, J. E., "The Cross and the Revelation of Jesus in the Fourth Gospel (John 8:28)" in: E. A. Livingstone (ed.) Studia Biblica 1978/II (Sheffield 1980) 219-26. TSUCHIDO, K., "Tradition and Redaction in John 8:12-30" AJBI 6 (1980) 63, 65, 66-68, 70.

8:29 MAURER, C. Ignatius von Antiochien und das Johannes-evangelium (1949) 41. KUHL, J. Die Sendung Jesu und der Kirche nach dem Johannes-Evangelium (1967) 97-99. BÜHNER, J.-A., Der Gesandte und sein Weg im 4. Evangelium (Tübingen 1977) 236-37.

8:30ff HAHN, F. Das Verständnis der Mission im Neuen Testament (²1965) 138.

8:30-59 MAURER, C. Ignatius von Antiochien und das Johannes-evangelium (1949) 58ff. WILKENS, W. Die Entstehungsge-schichte des vierten Evangeliums (1958) 142-45. BLANK, J., Krisis (1964) 226. GRAESSER, E. NTS 11 (1964-1965) 84f. GREINER, A. "Trois études bibliques. La Parole créatrice, La Parole incarnée, La Parole éclairée par le Saint-Esprit,"RevR 19 (3-4, 1968) 1-16. ODEBERG, H. The Fourth Gospel (1968) 296ff.

8:30-47 "Abraham" in: TRE 1 (1977) 377.

8:30-40 SMITH, D. M. The Composition and Order of the Fourth Gospel (1965) 139-41, 150-52, 155, 157, 158, 161, 166-68.

8:30-35 MUSZNER, F. ZΩH. Die Anschauung vom "Leben" im vierten Evangelium (1952) 90f. IWAND, H.-J. Predigt-Meditationen (1964) 576-84. BERGMEIER, R., Glaube als Gabe nach Johannes (Stuttgart 1980) 259n.401.

8:30-32 GRUNDMANN, W. "Verständnis und Bewegung des Glaubens im Johannes-Evangelium," KuD 6 (1960) 139.

8:30 TSUCHIDO, K., "Tradition and Redaction in John 8:12-30" AJBI 6 (1980) 63, 66-69.

8:31ff NORDEN, E. Agnostos Theos (1956 = 1912) 298f.

8:31-59 BARTINA, S. "Maternitas Mariae virginalis in Evangelis ex Judaeorum quoque testimonio confirmata (Jo 8,31-59)," EphM 15 (2-3, 1965) 301-306. TEMPLE, S., The Core of the Fourth Gospel (London 1975) 161-68. MANNS, F., "La verité vous fera libres," Étude exégétique de Jean 8/31-59 (Jerusalem 1976) passim. LONA, H. E., Abraham in Johannes 8. Ein Beitrag zur Methodenfrage (Bern 1976) passim; Recension: OLSSON, B., "Ett bidrag till metodfråagan" SEA 45 (1980) 110-21. BRAUN, F. M., "La Réduction du Pluriel au Singulier dans l'Evangile et la Première lettre de Jean" NTS 24 (1977-1978) 41-45. BECKER, J., Das Evangelium nach Johannes (Gütersloh/ Würzburg 1979) 298-99 (lit!). DOZEMAN, F. B., "*Sperma Abraam* in John 8 and Related Literature" CBQ 42 (1980) 342-58. TSUCHIDO, K., "Tradition and Redaction in John 8:12-30" AJBI 6 (1980) 67-69. SEGOVIA, F., "The Love and Hatred of Jesus and Johannine Sectarianism" CBQ 43 (1981) 267-68, 270. WIESER, F. E. Das Johanneische Abrahambild (Rüschlikon Th.M. Thesis 1981) passim.

8:31-58 DODD, C. H. "Behind a Johannine Dialogue," More New Testament Studies (1968) 41-57. LINDARS, B., "Discourse and Tradition: The Use of the Sayings of Jesus in the Discourses of the Fourth Gospel" JSNT 13 (1981) 89-97.

8:31-47 BRAUN, F.-M. Jean le Théologien (1966) 127-32. IBUKI, Y. Die Wahrheit im Johannesevangelium (1972) 88-116. VEL-LANICKAL, M., The Divine Sonship of Christians in the Johannine Writings (Rome 1977) 252-60.

8:31-45 DAHINTEN, G., in: GPM 33 (1979) 171-77.

8:31-37 MARTYN, J. L., The Gospel of John in Christian History (New York 1978) 109-15, 120.

8:31-36 STECK, K. G. "Ueber Johannes 8,31-36," EvTh 15 (1950) 439-45. OBENDIEK, H. in: Herr, tue meine Lippen auf Bd. 3 (1964) G. Eichholz ed., 378ff. STECK, K. G. in: Hören und Fragen Bd. 5, 3 (1967) G. Eichholz/A. Falkenroth eds., 573ff. WEBER, O. Predigtmeditationen (1967) 57-61. LATEGAN, B. C. "The truth that sets man free. John 8:31-36," Neotestamentica 2 (1968) 70-80. LANGE, E. ed., Predigtstudien für das Kirchenjahr 1970-1971 (1970) 235-40. KRAUSE, G. GPM 25 (3, 1971) 425-35. CASABO SUQUE, J. M. "La Liberacion en San Juan," RevBi 34 (3, 1972) 225-42. MUELLER, T. Das Heilsgeschenen im Johannesevangelium n. d. 65-67. de la POTTERIE, I., La Vérité dans Saint Jean I/II (Rome 1977) 822-25, 825-28. VELLANICKAL, M., The Divine Sonship of Christians in the Johannine Writings (Rome 1977) 286-94. WILL, K., MEIER, C. und ROESSLER, R., in: P. Krusche et al. (eds.) Predigtstudien für das Kirchenjahr 1976-1977. V/2 (Stuttgart 1977) 236-48. RUDOLPH, K., Die Gnosis (Göttingen 1978) 324. WIESER, F. E. Das Johanneische Abrahambild (Rüschlikon, Th.M. Thesis 1981) 14-30. GREMMELS, C. und HERRMANN, W., in: P. Krusche et al. (eds.) Predigtstudien für das Kirchenjahr 1982-1983. V/1 (Stuttgart 1982) 68-75.

8:31-33 LEROY, H. Rätsel and Missverständnis (1968) 67-74.

8:31-32 FLEW, R. N. Jesus and His Church (1956) 175, 178n, 179n. BECKER, M. Die Reden des Johannesevangelium und der Stil der gnostichen Offenbarungsrede (Göttingen 1956) 114-16. LAZURE, N. Les Valeurs Morales de la Théologie Johannique (Paris 1965) 77-78. HEISE, J. Bleiben (1967) 71-77. IBUKI, Y. Die Wahrheit im Johannesevangelium (1972) 89, 107ff, 230, 249. de la POTTERIE, I. La Vérité dans Saint Jean I/II (Rome 1977) 552-62. VELLANICKAL, M. The Divine Sonship of Christians in the Johannine Writings (Rome 1977) 290-93. RAYAN, S. The Holy Spirit: Heart of the Gospel and Christian Hope (New York 1978) 77. SCHWEIZER, E. Heiliger Geist (Berlin 1978) 136. VELLANICKAL, M. " 'Discipleship' according to the Gospel of John" Jeevadhara 10 (1980) 131-47. LINDARS, B. "Discourse and Tradition: The Use of the Sayings of Jesus in the Discourses of the Fourth Gospel" JSNT 13 (1981) 93-95. SEGALLA, G. "Un appello alla perseveranza nella fede in Gv 8:31-32?" Biblica 62 (1981) 387-89.

8:31 WILES, M. F. The Spiritual Gospel (1960) 87-89. DSS: Manual of Discipline 1,10; 5,10. PANCARO, S. The Law in the Fourth Gospel (Leiden 1975) 197, 200, 400, 414, 415-18. SWETNAM, J. "The Meaning of pepisteukotas in John 8:31" Biblica 61 (1980) 106-109. TSUCHIDO, K. "Tradition and Redaction in John 8:12-30" AJBI 6 (1980) 60, 67-69. LINDARS, B. "Discourse and Tradition: The Use of the Sayings of Jesus in the Discourses of the Fourth Gospel" JSNT 13 (1981) 86-87. von WAHLDE, U. C. "The Johannine 'Jews': A Critical Survey" NTS 28 (1982) 50-51.

8:32-36 BARUN, H. Qumran und NT II (1966) 122.

8:32-34 FLEW, R. N. Jesus and His Church (1956) 174.

8:32 BUECHSEL, F. Das Evangelium nach Johannes (1946) 106f. RUDOLPH, K. Die Mandäer I (1960) 174. McNAMARA, M. The New Testament and the Palestinian Targum to the Pentateuch (1966) 170 n.58. SCHILSON, A. " 'Die Wahrheit wird euch frei machen!' (Jo 8:32). Philosophisch-theologische Ueberlegungen zum Verhältnis von Wahrheit und Freiheit," ThG 59 (1, '69) 29-56. DAUER, A. Die Passionsgeschichte im

Johannesevangelium (1972) 247, 257, 259, 260, 289. SABU-
GAL, S. " ' . . . Y la Verdad os hara libres' (Jn 8:32 a la luz
de TPI Gen 15:11)," Augustinianum 14 (1, '74) 177-81.
HOANG DAC-ANH, S. "La liberté par la vérité (Jn 8:32) (I)"
Angelicum 54 (1977) 536-65. de la POTTERIE, I. La Vérité
dans Saint Jean I/II (Rome 1977) 550-75, 816-66. *MARTINS
TERRA, J. E. "Teologia da Libertação em São João. A Ver-
dade vos Libertará (Jo 8:32)" RCB 2 (1978) 3-34. BEIER-
WALTES, W. "Deus est veritas" in: E. Dassmann/K. S. Frank
(eds.) Pietas. FS. B. Kötting (Münster 1980) 24. BERG-
MEIER, R. Glaube als Gabe nach Johannes (Stuttgart 1980) 231.
GEORGI, D. "Weisheit Salomos" in: JüdSchr III/4 (1980) 15
n.3a.

8:33-47　DODD, C. H. "A l'arrière-plan d'un dialogue Johannique,"
RHPhR 37 (1, '57) 5-17.

8:33-44　BRUCE, F. F. The Time is Fulfilled (Exeter 1978) 63.

8:33-36　DELLING, G. Die Taufe im Neuen Testament (1963) 141.
BÖHLIG, A. "Vom 'Knecht' zum 'Sohn' " in: Mysterion und
Wahrheit (Leiden 1968) 64-66. LINDARS, B. "Discourse and
Tradition: The Use of the Sayings of Jesus in the Discourses of
the Fourth Gospel" JSNT 13 (1981) 94-97.

8:33.39　MOORE, G. F. Judaism I (1946) 543n. BOUSSET, W. Die
Religion des Judentums im Späthellenistischen Zeitalter
(1966 = 1926) 199.

8:33　IBUKI, Y. Die Wahrheit im Johannesevangelium (1972) 89f.

8:34　de la POTTERIE, I. La Vérité dans Saint Jean I/II (Rome 1977)
828-33.

8:35-36　HAHN, F. Christologische Hoheitstitel (1963) 329.

8:35　HEISE, J. Bleiben (1967) 77-79. HUNTER, A. M. According
to John (1970²) 81. IBUKI, Y. Die Wahrheit im Johannesevangelium (1972) 90f. de la POTTERIE, I. La Vérité dans Saint
Jean I/II (Rome 1977) 858-66. LINDARS, B. "Discourse and
Tradition: The Use of the Sayings of Jesus in the Discourses of
the Fourth Gospel" JSNT 13 (1981) 91-92.

8:36-38　de JONGE, M. "The Beloved Disciple and the Date of the Gospel of John" in: E. Best/R. McL. Wilson (eds.) Text and Interpretation. FS. M. Black (Cambridge 1979) 100.

8:36　VELLANICKAL, M. The Divine Sonship of Christians in the
Johannine Writings (Rome 1977) 288-90.

8:37-47　GRAESSER, E. "Die Juden als Teufelssöhne in Johannes 8:37-
47," Antijudaismus im Neuen Testament? (1967) W. P. Eck-
ert/N. P. Levinson/M. Stöhr eds., 157-70. HOFRICHTER, P.

Nicht aus Blut sondern monogen aus Gott geboren (Würzburg 1978) 60-67. BERGMEIER, R. Glaube als Gabe nach Johannes (Stuttgart 1980) 224-28. FRICKEL, J. "Die Zöllner, Vorbild der Demut und wahrer Gottesverehrung" in: E. Dassmann/ K. S. Frank (eds.) Pietas, FS. B. Kötting (Münster 1980) 369-70. WIESER, F. E. Das Johanneische Abrahambild (Rüschlikon, Th.M. Thesis 1981) 31-42.

8:37-44 BRAUN, H. Qumran and NT II (1966) 49, 121, 124.

8:37-38 IBUKI, Y. Die Wahrheit im Johannesevangelium (1972) 91-95, 146ff.

8:37 PALLIS, A. Notes on St. John and the Apocalypse (London 1928) 18-19. GREGOR, D. B. "La traduko de *chōrein* ĉe s-ta Johano VIII:37" BiRe 16 (1980) 14-15.

8:38-45 NICKELS, P. Targum and New Testament (1967) 56.

8:38 BÜHNER, J.-A. Der Gesandte und sein Weg im 4. Evangelium (Tübingen 1977) 378-79. METZGER, B. M. The Early Versions of the New Testament (Oxford 1977) 178, 391. BERGMEIER, R. Glaube als Gabe nach Johannes (Stuttgart 1980) 224, 227, 239 n.54, 263 n.469. CLARK, K. W. "The Text of the Gospel of John in Third-Century Egypt" in: The Gentile Bias and other Essays (Leiden 1980) 162.

8:39ff.53ff. KAESEMANN, E. Exegetische Versuche und Besinnungen (1964) I 181.

8:39-41 IBUKI, Y. Die Wahrheit im Johannesevangelium (1972) 95ff., 146-49.

8:39 PANCARO, S. The Law in the Fourth Gospel (Leiden 1975) 181, 182, 389-97, 415. BERGMEIER, R. Glaube als Gabe nach Johannes (Stuttgart 1980) 224, 259 n.400. LINDARS, B. "Discourse and Tradition: The Use of the Sayings of Jesus in the Discourses of the Fourth Gospel" JSNT 13 (1981) 95.

8:40 GRILL, J. Untersuchungen über die Entstehung des vierten Evangeliums II (1923) 329f. WILES, M. F. The Spiritual Gospel (1960) 112-15, 131. DELLING, G. Wort und Werk Jesu im Johannes-Evangelium (1966) 35, 67, 110, 125. de la POTTERIE, I. La Vérité dans Saint Jean I/II (Rome 1977) 64-75. RAYAN, S. The Holy Spirit: Heart of the Gospel and Christian Hope (New York 1978) 82. BERGMEIER, R. Glaube als Gabe nach Johannes (Stuttgart 1980) 224-25, 227-28, 259 n.397. 408-409.

8:41-47 de JONGE, M. Jesus: Stranger from Heaven and Son of God (Missoula 1977) 144-46.

8:41 BERGMEIER, R. Glaube als Gabe nach Johannes (Stuttgart 1980) 223, 225ff., 258 n.385, 259 n.400.413, 261 n.434. KÜGLER, J. "Wir stammen nicht aus einem Ehebruch (Joh 8:41). Eine Kritik an Günther Schwarz" BN 16 (1981) 27-29. SCHWARZ, G. "ημεις εκ πορνειας ου γεγεννημεθα (Johannes 8:41)" BN 14 (1981) 50-53.

8:42ff NORDEN, E. Agnostos Theos (1956 = 1912) 189f.

8:42.55 SUMMERS, R. The Secret Sayings of the Living Jesus (1968) 71.

8:42-47 WALTER, L. L'incroyance des croyants selon saint Jean (Paris 1976) 92-103. de la POTTERIE, I. La Vérité dans Saint Jean I/II (Rome 1977) 918-40.

8:42 GRILL, J. Untersuchungen über die Entstehung des vierten Evangeliums II (1923) 124f. KUHL, J. Die Sendung Jesu und der Kirche nach dem Johannes-Evangelium (1967) 63f., 172. IBUKI, Y. Die Wahrheit im Johannesevangelium (1972) 98f., 112, 260f. DSS: The Manual of Discipline 4, 9. LATTKE, M. Einheit im Wort (München 1975) 107-14. BERGMEIER, R. Glaube als Gabe nach Johannes (Stuttgart 1980) 225ff., 248 n.212. DAHMS, J. V. "Isaiah 55:11 and the Gospel of John" EQ 53 (1981) 78-88.

8:43-44 TILLICH, P. Das Neue Sein (1959) 67-77. BERGMEIER, R. Glaube als Gabe nach Johannes (Stuttgart 1980) 11, 108 n.328, 125, 189, 220-21, 223, 225ff., 228, 231, 258 n.385, 259 n.408, 260 n.421, 261 n.433, 263 n.469, 269 n.530.

8:43 BONSIRVEN, J. "Les aramaismes de S. Jean l'evangéliste?" Biblica 30 ('49) 418-19. PALLIS, A. Notes on St. John and the Apocalypse (London 1928) 19.

8:44-46 LINDARS, B. "Discourse and Tradition: The Use of the Sayings of Jesus in the Discourses of the Fourth Gospel" JSNT 13 (1981) 93.

8:44 DRACHMANN, A. "Zu Johannes 8:44," ZNW 12 (1911) 84. GRILL, J. Untersuchungen über die Entstehung des vierten Evangeliums II (1923) 12, 44, 47, 125, 328, 331, 337, 356. BAUER, W. Das Johannesevangelium (1925) 125. VON LOEWENICH, W. Das Johannes-Verständnis im zweiten Jahrhunderts (1932) 7, 23, 67, 94, 130, 132, 143, 144. RUCKSTUHL, E. Die literarische Einheit des Johannesevangelium (1951) 50, 69, 86, 252, 253. LINDESKOG, G. Studien zum neutestamentlichen Schöpfungsgedanken I (1952) 198, 199, 205. STRATHMANN, H. Das Evangelium nach Johannes (1955) 152. DAHL, N. A. "Manndraperen og hans far (Joh 8:44)"/ The Murderer and His Father/, NTT 64 (3, '63) 129-62. DAHL, N. A. "Der Erstgeborene Satans und der Vater des Teufels

(Polyk. 7:1 und Joh 8:44)," in: Apophoreta (1964) 70-84.
HENNECKE, E./SCHNEEMELCHER, W. Neutestament-
liche Apokryphen (1964) II 74. TURNER, N. Grammatical In-
sights into the New Testament (1965) 148ff. BEYSCHLAG, K.
Clemens Romanus und der Frühkatholizismus (1966) 53ff.
BOUSETT, W. Die Religion des Judentums im Spät-
hellenistischen Zeitalter (1966 = 1926) 335. DELLING, G. Wort
und Werk Jesu im Johannes-Evangelium (1966) 51f., 54f.
NICKELS, P. Targum and the New Testament (1967) 56.
DAUER, A. Die Passionsgeschichte im Johannesevangelium
(1972) 107, 253, 254, 262. IBUKI, Y. Die Wahrheit im
Johannesevangelium (1972) 100-104, 347, 350. LEANEY,
A. R. C. "The Johannine Paraclete and the Qumran Scrolls,"
in: John and Qumran (1972) J. H. Charlesworth ed., 54-55.
FORESTELL, J. T. The Word of the Cross: Salvation as Revelation in the Fourth Gospel (Rome 1974) 151, 152, 153, 176.
de la POTTERIE, I. La Vérité dans Saint Jean I/II (Rome 1977)
920-34. "Antichrist" in: TRE 3 (1978) 22. "Antisemitismus"
in: TRE 3 (1978) 123, 126. RUDOLPH, K. Die Gnosis (Göttingen 1978) 324. GEORGI, D. "Weisheit Salomos" in:
JüdSchr III/4 (1980) 2 n.23a, 24b. THOMAS, J. " 'Menteur et
homicide depuis l'origine.' Lecture de Jean 8:44" Christus 27
(Paris 1980) 225-35.

8:45-59   MOLLAT, D. "Avant qu'Abraham fut je suis," AssS 34 ('63)
          54-63.

8:45-46   de la POTTERIE, I. La Vérité dans Saint Jean I/II (Rome 1977)
          61-64, 980-91. BERGMEIER, R. Glaube als Gabe nach Johan-
          nes (Stuttgart 1980) 227, 233, 259 n.397.

8:45.47.48-59   IBUKI, Y. Die Wahrheit im Johannesevangelium (1972) 62f.,
          104ff.

8:45   WILES, M. F. The Spiritual Gospel (1960) 88-89.

8:46-59   KAESEMANN, E. GPM 4 (1949/50) 106ff. TRAUB, GPM 9
          (1954/55) 92ff. IWAND, H.-J. in: Herr, tue meine Lippen auf
          Bd. 1 (1957) G. Eichholz ed., 111-14. DOERNE, M. Er kommt
          auch noch heute (1961) 63-65. KAESEMANN, E. Exegetische
          Versuche und Besinnungen (1964) I 248-53.

8:46-47   BLANK, J. Schriftauslegung in Theorie und Praxis (1969) 207f.

8:46   LAZURE, N. Les Valeurs Morales de la Théologie Johannique
          (Paris 1965) 297-98. PORSCH, F. Pneuma und Wort (Frank-
          furt 1974) 282-83.

8:47-48.51   REUSS, J. "Presbyter Ammonius' Kommentar zum Jo-Evan-
          gelium," Biblica 44 ('63) 167-68.

8:47 FORESTELL, J. T. The Word of the Cross: Salvation as Revelation in the Fourth Gospel (Rome 1974) 84, 109, 124, 151, 152, 153, 178. PORSCH, F. Pneuma und Wort (Frankfurt 1974) 114. HOFRICHTER, P. Nicht aus Blut sondern monogen aus Gott geboren (Würzburg 1978) 62-65. BERGMEIER, R. Glaube als Gabe nach Johannes (Stuttgart 1980) 27, 220, 223, 233, 259 n.396.

8:48-59 BUECHSEL, F. Das Evangelium nach Johannes (1946) 110-12. BLANK, J. Schriftauslegung in Theorie und Praxis (1969) 207-20. SCHNIDER, F. Jesus der Prophet (1973) 191, 221ff., 239. WIESER, F. E. Das Johanneische Abrahambild (Rüschlikon, Th.M. Thesis 1981) 43-58.

8:48-50 SMITH, D. M. The Composition and Order of the Fourth Gospel (1965) 152-55, 157, 162.

8:48 GRILL, J. Untersuchungen über die Entstehung des vierten Evangeliums II (1923) 12, 17, 52, 241f., 329. MEHLMANN, J. "John 8:48 in Some Patristic Quotations," Biblica 44 (2, '63) 206-209. PALLIS, A. Notes on St. John and the Apocalypse (London 1928) 20.

8:49 HANSON, A. T. The New Testament Interpretation of Scripture (London 1980) 162-66.

8:51-53 LEROY, H. Rätsel und Missverständnis (1968) 74-82. BERGMEIER, R. Glaube als Gabe nach Johannes (Stuttgart 1980) 207.

8:51-52 LINDARS, B. "Discourse and Tradition: The Use of the Sayings of Jesus in the Discourses of the Fourth Gospel" JSNT 13 (1981) 95-98.

8:51 GEORGI, D. "Weisheit Salomos" in: JüdSchr III/4 (1980) 6 n.18b.

8:52 KNOW, W. L. The Sources of the Synoptic Gospels II (1957) 154. LE DEAUT, R. "Gouter le calice de la mort," Biblica 43 ('62) 82-86. SCHRAGE, W. Das Verhältnis der Thomas-Evangeliums zur Synoptischen Tradition und zu den Koptischen Evangelienübersetzungen (1964) 28. CHILTON, B. D. " 'Not to Taste Death': A Jewish, Christian, and Gnostic Usage" in: E. A. Livingstone (ed.) Studia Biblica 1978/II (Sheffield 1980) 29-36.

8:53ff KAESEMANN, E. Exegetische Versuche und Besinnungen (1964) I 181.

8:53-54 BERGMEIER, R. Glaube als Gabe nach Johannes (Stuttgart 1980) 259 n.400.

8:53 NICKELS, P. Targum and New Testament (1967) 56.

8:54-55 SMITH, D. M. The Composition and Order of the Fourth Gospel (1965) 152-55, 157, 162.

8:54 BÜHNER, J.-A. Der Gesandte und sein Weg im 4. Evangelium (Tübingen 1977) 293-95.

8:55 DELLING, G. Wort and Werk Jesu im Johannesevangelium (1966) 39f. BAUMERT, N. Täglich Sterben und Auferstehen (München 1973) 90. GEORGI, D. "Weisheit Salomos" in: JüdSchr III/4 (1980) 2 n.13b.

8:56-59 DAVIES, W. D. The Gospel and the Land (London 1974) 294.

8:56-58 LEROY, H. Rätsel und Missverständnis (1968) 82-88. URBAN, L. and HENRY, P. " 'Before Abraham Was I Am': Does Philo Explain John 8:56-58?" StPh 6 (1979-1980) 157-95.

8:56-57 MAURER, C. Ignatius von Antiochien und das Johannesevangelium (1949) 64f. REGUL, J. Die Antimarcionitischen Evangelienprologe (1969) 135, 156-58.

8:56 VOLZ, P. Die Eschatologie der jüdischen Gemeinde (1934) 219. RIESENFELD, H. Jésus Transfiguré (1947) 93, 95. LERCH, D. Isaaks Opferung christlich gedeutet (1950) 107f. DUPONT, J. Essais sur la Christologie de Saint Jean (1951) 271, 272. FLEW, R. N. Jesus and His Church (1956) 66. McNAMARA, M. The New Testament and the Palestinian Targum to the Pentateuch (1966) 240f., 241 n.6. NICKELS, P. Targum and New Testament (1967) 56. REIM, G. Studien zum Alttestamentlichen Hintergrund des Johannesevangeliums (Cambridge 1974) 100-101. "Abraham" in: TRE 1 (1977) 376. BRUCE, F. F. The Time is Fulfilled (Exeter 1978) 63-64. BERGMEIER, R. Glaube als Gabe nach Johannes (Stuttgart 1980) 16, 259 n.400. THYEN, H. " 'Das Heil kommt von den Juden' " in: D. Lührmann/G. Strecker (eds.) Kirche. FS. G. Bornkamm (Tübingen 1980) 183. BERGER, K. "Das Buch der Jubiläen" in: JüdSchr II/3 (1981) 404 n.21a.

8:57-58 BERGMEIER, R. Glaube als Gabe nach Johannes (Stuttgart 1980) 228.

8:57 SANDMEL, S. We Jews and Jesus (New York 1977) 20, 28. CLARK, K. W. "The Text of the Gospel of John in Third-Century Egypt" in: The Gentile Bias and other Essays (Leiden 1980) 162.

8:58 VON LOEWENICH, W. Das Johannes-Verständnis im zweiten Jahrhundert (1932) 14, 15, 29, 132, 138 n.2. BLAIR, E. P. Jesus in the Gospel of Matthew (1960) 98. CAVALLETTI, S. "La visione messianica di Abramo (Giov. 8:58)," BiOr 3 (5, '61) 179-81. HARNER, P. B. The "I Am" of the Fourth Gospel (1970) 37-43. DAUER, A. Die Passionsgeschichte im Johannesevangelium (1972) 88, 244, 303. LINDARS, B. "The Son of Man in the Johannine Christology," in: Christ and the Spirit in the New Testament (1973) B. Lindars/S. S. Smalley eds., 54f. ROBINSON, J. A. T. "The Use of the Fourth Gospel for Christology," in: Christ and the Spirit in the New Testament (1973) B. Lindars/S. S. Smalley eds., 75f. HOWARD, V. P. Das Ego in den Synoptischen Evangelien (Marburg 1975) 254-55. HANSON, A. T. The New Testament Interpretation of Scripture (London 1980) 162-66.

8:59 GRILL, J. Untersuchungen über die Entstehung des vierten Evangeliums II (1923) 12, 123, 130f. WILLEMSE, J. NTS 11 (1964/65) 358f. KUENZI, M. Das Naherwartungslogion Matthäus 10:23 (1970) 14, 61, 81. DAUER, A. Die Passionsgeschichte im Johannesevangelium (1972) 88, 245, 247, 265. DAVIES, W. D. The Gospel and the Land (1974) 290-95 passim, 313, 319, 322. TSUCHIDO, K. "Tradition and Redaction in John 8:12-30" AJBI 6 (1980) 59, 68.

9-10 WIKENHAUSER, A. Das Evangelium nach Johannes (1957) 193. van den BUSSCHE, H., "La Structure de Jean I-XII" in: M. Boismard et al., L'Evangile de Jean: études et problèmes (Bruges 1958) 101-103.

9:1-10:21 TEMPLE, S., The Core of the Fourth Gospel (London 1975) 169-78. SCHILLEBEECKX, E., Christ: the Christian Experience in the Modern World (London 1980) 391; GT: Christus und die Christen (Freiburg/Basel/Wien 1977) 377.

9 BAUER, W. Das Johannesevangelium (1925) 132f. BECKER, H., Die Reden des Johannesevangeliums und der Stil der gnostischen Offenbarungsrede (Göttingen 1956) 83-84. GRUNDMANN, W., "Verständnis und Bewegung des Glaubens im Johannes-Evangelium," KuD 6 (1960) 141f., 148f. GUILDING, A. The Fourth Gospel and Jewish Worship (1960) 122-25, 216-20. LINDIJER, C. H. De Sacramenten in het Vierde Evangelie (1964) 84f. SMITH, D. M. The Composition and Order of the Fourth Gospel (1965) 155-63. BLIGH, J. "Four Studies in St. John, I: The Man Born Blind," HeyJ 7 (2, 1966) 129-44. DELLING, G. Wort und Werk Jesu im Johannes-

Evangelium (1966) 16, 22f., 147. MEEKS, W. A. The Prophet-King, Moses Traditions and the Johannine Christology (1967) 294-95, 317. MUSSNER, F. Die Wunder Jesu (1967) 55f. NICKELS, P. Targum and New Testament (1967) 56. STROBEL, A. Erkenntnis und Bekenntnis der Sünde in neutestamentlicher Zeit (1968) 60. WILKENS, W., Zeichen und Werke (Zürich 1969) 41-42. OTOMO, Y. Nachfolge Jesu und Anfänge der Kirche im Neuen Testament (1970) 141-44. RIEDL, J. Das Heilswerk Jesu nach Johannes (1973) 283-343. DAVIES, W. D., The Gospel and the Land (London 1974) 313-17. OLSSON, B., Structure and Meaning in the Fourth Gospel (Lund 1974) 18, 29-30, 33, 39, 47, 54, 58-61, 68, 80, 100, 111, 115-16, 187, 203, 220. BARTLETT, D. L., Fact and Faith (Valley Forge 1975) 62-63. CONZELMANN, H. und LINDEMANN, A., Arbeitsbuch zum Neuen Testament (Tübingen 1975) 73. LOHSE, E., "Miracles in the Fourth Gospel" in: M. Hooker/C. Hickling (eds.) What About the New Testament? FS. C. Evans (London 1975) 69-70. PANCARO, S., The Law in the Fourth Gospel (Leiden 1975) 7, 9, 10, 11, 15, 16-30, 45. FITZGERALD, R. R., Jr., "The Blind Man and the Cave" BiTod 93 (1977) 1420-26. GERSTENBERGER, G. und SCHRAGE, W., Leiden (Stuttgart 1977) 198, ET: J. E. Steely (trans.) Suffering (Nashville 1980) 229-31. de JONGE, M., Jesus: Stranger from Heaven and Son of God (Missoula 1977) 61-63. SABUGAL, S., La curación del ciego de nacimiento (Jn 9,1-4). Análisis exegético y teológico (Madrid 1977). SANFORD, J. A., Healing and Wholeness (New York 1977) 22. TRITES, A. A., The New Testament Concept of Witness (Cambridge 1977) 107-108. GRYGLEWICZ, F., "Die Pharisäer und die Johanneskirche" SNTU 3 (1978) 144-58. REIM, G., "Joh 9 — Tradition and zeitgenössische messianische Diskussion" BZ 22 (1978) 245-53. SEYBOLD, K. und MÜLLER, U., Krankheit und Heilung (Stuttgart 1978) 143-44, 147. STAGG, E. and F., Women in the World of Jesus (Philadelphia 1978) 237-38. BECKER, J., Das Evangelium nach Johannes (Gütersloh/Würzburg 1979) 314-15 (lit!). HAENCHEN, E., Das Johannesevangelium (Tübingen 1980) 375-77 (lit!). BRODIE, T. L., "Jesus as the New Elisha: Cracking the Code" ET 93 (1981) 39-42. CARSON, D. A., "Historical Tradition in the Fourth Gospel: After Dodd, What?" in: R. T. France/B. Wenham (eds.) Gospel Perspectives II (Sheffield 1981) 109-11.LEIDIG, E., Jesu Gespräch mit der Samaritanerin (Basel 1981) 218-23. PAINTER, J., "The Farewell Discourses and the History of Johannine Christianity" NTS 27 (1980-1981) 538, 542.

9:1ff WILKENS, W., Die Entstehungsgeschichte des vierten Evangeliums (1958) 51, 52, 53, 54, 55.

9:1-41 ZIENER, G. "Weisheitsbuch und Johannesevangelium," Biblica 38 (1957) 412-13. CORELL, A. Consummatum Est (1958) 67-69. MOLLAT, D. "La guérison de l'avengle-né," BVieC 23 (1958) 22-31. WILES, M. F. The Spiritual Gospel (1960) 55-56. YATES, K. M. Preaching from John's Gospel (1964) 93-99. ROLOFF, J. Das Kerygma und der irdische Jesus (1970) 135-41. BORNKAMM, G. Geschichte und Glaube II (1971) 65-72. SCHNIDER, F. Jesus der Prophet (1973) 200ff., 238.

9:1-39 CULLMANN, O. Urchristentum und Gottesdienst (1950) 88, 99ff. BIEDER, W., Die Verheissung der Taufe im Neuen Testament (Zürich 1966) 271-72.

9:1-38 HOFBECK, G. Semeion (1966) 126-36.

9:1-17 CRIBBS, F. L., "The Agreements that Exist Between John and Acts" in: C. H. Talbert (ed.) Perspectives on Luke-Acts (Danville 1978) 45.

9:1-8 FORTNA, R. T. The Gospel of Signs (1970) 70-74.

9:1-7 WEBER, O. Predigtmeditationen (1967) 50-53. NICOL, W. The Sēmeia in the Fourth Gospel (1972) 16, 35, 59f., 112. MARTYN, J. L., The Gospel of John in Christian History (New York 1978) 24, 28.

9:1-7.13- CZEGLEDY, I. GPM 17 (3, 1963) 303-306. FROER, K. GPM
17.32-39 23 (4, 1968) 328-34. FISCHER, K. M. GPM 29 (3, 1975) 386, 391. GEBHARDT, R./JUNG, H.-G. "Johannes 9,1-7.13-17.32-39: Fortschreitende Aufklärung," in: Predigtstudien für das Kirchenjahr 1975 (1975) P. Krusche/E. Lange/D. Roessler/R. Roessler eds., 191-205.

9:1-3 BOUSSET, W. Die Religion des Judentums im Späthellenistischen Zeitalter (1966 = 1926) 391, 412.

9:1 MOORE, G. F. Judaism II (1946) 322. TEMPLE, S., The Core of the Fourth Gospel (London 1975) 122-23. BÖHLIG, A., Die Gnosis III: Der Manichäismus (Zürich/München 1980) 344n.59.

9:2-5 TEMPLE, S., The Core of the Fourth Gospel (London 1975) 173-75.

9:2-3 HAHN, F. Christologische Hoheitstitel (1963) 43, 75.

9:2 BOUSSET, W. Die Religion des Judentums im Späthellenistischen Zeitalter (1966 = 1926) 210.

9:3-7 KUHL, J. Die Sendung Jesu und der Kirche nach dem Johannes-Evangelium (1967) 69f.

9:3-5 NICOL, W. The Sēmeia in the Fourth Gospel (1972) 118f.

9:3-4 DELLING, G. Wort und Werk Jesu im Johannes-Evangelium (1966) 31, 60, 73, 106.

9:3 CADMAN, W. H. The Open Heaven (1969) G. B. Caird ed., 37, 86, 115, 157.

9:4-5 SMITH, M. Tannaitic Parallels to the Gospel (1968) 2.70.

9:4.5.39-41 ODEBERG, H. The Fourth Gospel (1968) 310ff.

9:4 IBUKI, Y. Die Wahrheit im Johannesevangelium (1972) 352f. BACCHIOCCHI, S., "John 5:17: Negation or Clarification of the Sabbath" AUSS 19 (1981) 10, 13, 16, 19. "Chiliasmus" in: TRE 7 (1981) 727, 728.

9:5 MUSZNER, F. ΖΩΗ. Die Anschauung vom "Leben" im vierten Evangelium (1952) 168f. BROWN, R. E. "The Qumran Scrolls and the Johannine Gospel and Epistles" CBQ 17 (1955) 403-19, 559-74; also in: K. Stendahl (ed.) The Scrolls and the New Testament (New York 1957) 187-88; GT: "Die Schriftrollen von Qumran und das Johannesevangelium und die Johannesbriefe" in: K. H. Rengstorff (ed.) Johannes und sein Evangelium (Darmstadt 1973) 495. HAHN, F. Das Verständnis der Mission im Neuen Testament (²1965) 136. BRAUN, H. Qumran und NT II (1966) 126, 130, 269. REIM, G. Studien zum Alttestamentlichen Hintergrund des Johannesevangeliums (Cambridge 1974) 164-66.

9:6.8.31.37 ORIGENES, Das Evangelium nach Johannes (1959) R. Gögler ed., 333-36.

9:6 PALLIS, A., Notes on St. John and the Apocalypse (London 1928) 20-21. RUCKSTUHL, E. Die literarische Einheit des Johannesevangeliums (1951) 196f., 225. BETZ, H. D. Lukian von Samosata und das Neue Testament (1961) 150. BACCHIOCCHI, S., "John 5:17: Negation or Clarification of the Sabbath" AUSS 19 (1981) 9.

9:7 DELLING, G. Die Zueignung des Heils in der Taufe (1961) 75. HOOKE, S. H., "The Spirit was not yet," NTS 9 (1962-1963) 376f. van der LOOS, H. The Miracles of Jesus (1965) 428-31. WIEAND, D. J. NTS 12 (1965-1966) 396f. MUELLER, K. "Joh 9,7 und das jüdische Verständnis des Siloh-Spruches," BZ 13 (2, 1969) 251-56. DUNN, J. D. G. Baptism in the Holy Spirit (1970) 188. DAVIES, W. D. The Gospel and the Land (1974) 313, 314, 335n.97.

9:8-41 NICOL, W. The Sēmeia in the Fourth Gospel (1972) 36, 102, 108f., 146.

9:8-34 BORNKAMM, G. Geschichte und Glaube II (1971) 69-71.

9:8-12 BLANK, J. Krisis (1964) 254.

9:8 BLACK, M. An Aramaic Approach to the Gospels and Acts (1967) 78f.

9:9 HOWARD, V. P., Das Ego in den Synoptischen Evangelien (Marburg 1975) 253.

9:13-34 BLANK, J. Krisis (1964) 255.

9:13-17 FROER, K. GPM 23 (4, 1968) 328-34.

9:14-17 SWIDLER, L., Biblical Affirmations of Woman (Philadelphia 1979) 181.

9:14 BACCHIOCCHI, S., "John 5:17: Negation or Clarification of the Sabbath?" AUSS 19 (1981) 9, 18.

9:15 METZGER, B. M. The Early Versions of the New Testament (Oxford 1977) 176.

9:16.24 BOUSSET, W. Die Religion des Judentums im Spät-hellenistischen Zeitalter (1966 = 1926) 126.

9:16.22 GRAESSER, E. NTS 11 (1964-1965) 77f., 89f.

9:16 PANCARO, S., The Law in the Fourth Gospel (Leiden 1975) 26, 27, 28, 30-52, 75, 86. MEYER, B. F., The Aims of Jesus (London 1979) 162-68. BERGMEIER, R., Glaube als Gabe nach Johannes (Stuttgart 1980) 248n.213.

9:17 HAHN, F. Christologische Hoheitstitel (1963) 397. SCHNI-DER, P. Jesus der Prophet (1973) 191, 223ff. REIM, G., Studien zum alttestamentlichen Hintergrund des Johannes-Evangeliums (Cambridge 1974) 124. CLARK, K. W. T., "The Text of the Gospel of John in Third Century Egypt" in: The Gentile Bias and other Essays (Leiden 1980) 162.

9:22-23 LANGBRANDTNER, W., Weltferner Gott oder Gott der Liebe (Frankfurt a.M./Bern/Las Vegas 1977) 71-76. BERGMEIER, R., Glaube als Gabe nach Johannes (Stuttgart 1980) 211.

9:22 "Antisemitismus" in: TRE 3 (1979) 127. THYEN, H., " 'Das Heil kommt von den Juden' " in: D. Lührmann/G. Strecker (eds.) Kirche. FS. G. Bornkamm (Tübingen 1980) 180-81. CARSON, D. A. "Historical Tradition in the Fourth Gospel: After Dodd, What?" in: R. T. France/D. Wenham (eds.) Gospel Perspectives II (Sheffield 1981) 123-25.

9:24-41 OBENDIEK, H. in: Herr, tue meine Lippen auf Bd. 3 (1964) 427ff.

9:24-34 PANCARO, S. The Law in the Fourth Gospel (Leiden 1975) 105-11, 120, 330, 468.

9:25 BURCHARD, C. "Ei nach einem Ausdruch des Wissens oder Nichtwissens Joh 9:25, Act 19:2, 1 Cor. 1:16, 7:16," ZNW 52 (1-2, 1961) 73-82. METZGER, B. M., The Early Versions of the New Testament (Oxford 1977) 144, 178.

9:28ff KAESEMANN, E. Exegetische Versuche und Besinnungen (1964) I 181.

9:28 SAITO, T. Die Mosevorstellungen im Neuen Testament (Bern 1977) 117-18.

9:29 HENNECKE, E./SCHNEEMELCHER, W. Neutestamentliche Apokryphen (1964) I 60. REIM, G. Studien zum Alttestamentlichen Hintergrund des Johannesevangeliums (Cambridge 1974) 137-38. METZGER, B. M., The Early Versions of the New Testament (Oxford 1977) 253.

9:30 LJUNVIGK, H. NTS 10 (1963-1964) 291f.

9:31 PETZKE, G. Die Traditionen über Apollonius von Tyana und das Neue Testament (1970) 180, 207, 228. BERGMEIER, R., Glaube als Gabe nach Johannes (Stuttgart 1980) 227, 259n.403.

9:32-39 FROER, K. GPM 23 (4, 1968) 328-34.

9:33 BERGMEIER, R., Glaube als Gabe nach Johannes (Stuttgart 1980) 248n.213.

9:34-35 KAESEMANN, E. Exegetische Versuche und Besinnungen (1964) I 170.

9:34 SCHRAGE, W. Die konkreten Einzelgebote in der paulinischen Paränese (1961) 49. PANCARO, S., The Law in the Fourth Gospel (Leiden 1975) 357, 358-62, 481. MARTYN, J. L. The Gospel of John in Christian History (New York 1978) 73.

9:35-36 SCHNACKENBURG, R. NTS 11 (1964-1965) 125f.

9:35 LEIVESTAD, R. "Der Apokalyptische Menschensohn ein theologisches Phantom," ASThI VI 1967-1968 (1968) 49-105. SMALLEY, S. S. T., "The Johannine Son of Man Sayings," NTS 15 (1968-1969) 295, 297f. BERGMEIER, R., Glaube als Gabe nach Johannes (Stuttgart 1980) 40n.218.

9:36 PANCARO, S., The Law in the Fourth Gospel (Leiden 1975) 328, 330, 332, 339, 344-50.

9:37 IBUKI, Y. Die Wahrheit im Johannesevangelium (1972) 50f., 321.

9:38-39 METZGER, B. M., The Early Versions of the New Testament (Oxford 1977) 139.

9:38-39a PORTER, C. L. "John ix, 38,39a: A Liturgical Addition to the Text," NTS 13 (4, 1967) 387-94.

9:39-41 TILLICH, P. Das Neue Sein (1959) 120-27. BLANK, J. Krisis (1964) 246. MUSSNER, F., Die Wunder Jesu (1967) 71f. SI-MONIS, A. J. Die Hirtenrede im Johannes-Evangelium (1967) 82ff. CADMAN, W. H. The Open Heaven (1969) G. B. Caird ed., 21, 35, 75, 109. BERGMEIER, R., Glaube als Gabe nach Johannes (Stuttgart 1980) 211, 233.

9:39 HESSE, F. Das Verstockungsproblem im Alten Testament (1955) 64, 66. WILES, M. F. The Spiritual Gospel (1960) 24, 80-81, 92. PALLIS, A. Notes on St. John and the Apocalypse (London 1928) 21-22. BÜHNER, J.-A., Der Gesandte und sein Weg im 4. Evangelium (Tübingen 1977) 150-51. BERG-MEIER, R., Glaube als Gabe nach Johannes (Stuttgart 1980) 233. LINDEMANN, A., "Gemeinde und Welt im Johannes-evangelium" in: B. Lührmann/G. Strecker (eds.) Kirche. FS. G. Bornkamm (Tübingen 1980) 145.

9:40-41 BERGMEIER, R., Glaube als Gabe nach Johannes (Stuttgart 1980) 231.

9:41 FLEW, R. N. Jesus and His Church (1956) 176. LAZURE, N., Les Valeurs Morales de la Théologie Johannique (Paris 1965) 298-99. HEISE, J., Bleiben (1967) 55-57. STROBEL, A. Er-kenntnis und Bekenntnis der Sünde in neutestamentlicher Zeit (1968) 46.

10 SCHWEIZER, E. Ego Eimi (Göttingen 1939) 141-51. HAN-SON, S. The Unity of the Church in the New Testament (1946) 162f. SCHNEIDER, J. "Zur Komposition von Joh. 10" in: Coniectanea Neotestamentica (1947) 220-25. BECKER, H., Die Reden des Johannesevangeliums und der Stil der gnostischen Offentbarungsrede (Göttingen 1956) 84-89. SCHULZ, S. Komposition und Herkunft der Johanneischen Reden (Stuttgart 1960) 76-79, 103-107. EMERTON, J. A. "Some New Testa-ment Notes," JThS 11 (2, 1960) 329-36. GUILDING, A. The Fourth Gospel and Jewish Worship (1960) 129-32. MINEAR, P. S. Images of the Church in the New Testament (1960) 84ff. LINDIJER, C. H. De Sacramenten in het vierde Evangelie (1964) 85. SMITH, D. M. The Composition and Order of the Fourth Gospel (1965) 21, 93, 117, 155-63, 165, 176. BRAUN, H. Qumran und NT II (1966) 149, 330. BORIG, R. Der Wahre

Weinstock (1967) 15, 25, 177, 205, 229, 252. MEEKS, W. A. The Prophet-King, Moses Traditions and the Johannine Christology (1967) 66-68. KUENZI, M. Das Naherwartungslogion Matthäus 10,23 (1970) 40, 43, 45, 113. OTOMO, Y. Nachfolge und Anfänge der Kirche im Neuen Testament (1970) 144-46. GOULDER, M. D. Midrash and Lection in Matthew (1974) 392, 399. GRYGLEWICZ, F., "Jezsus jako brama i pasterz," in: F. Gryglewicz (ed.) Egzegeza Ewangelii sw. Jana (Lublin 1976) 33-47. BÜHNER, J.-A., Der Gesandte und sein Weg im 4. Evangelium (Tübingen 1977) 178-80. HOLM-NIELSEN, S., "Die Psalmen Salomos" in: JüdSchr IV/2 (1977) 105n.40b. LANGBRANDTNER, W., Weltferner Gott oder Gott der Liebe (Frankfurt. a.M/Bern/Las Vegas 1977) 46-50. MINEAR, P. S., To Die and to Live (New York 1977) 110-11. TRITES, A. A., The New Testament Concept of Witness (Cambridge 1977) 108-109. BERGER, P. R., "Hirte und Mietling Joh 10" in: Theokratia: Jahrbuch Institutum Judaicum Delitzschlanum III/1973-1975 (Leiden 1979) 60-67. HAHN, F., "Die Hirtenrede in Joh 10" in: C. Andresen et al. (eds.) Theologia crucis-signum crucis. FS. E. Dinkler (Tübingen 1979) 185-200. BERGMEIER, R., Glaube als Gabe nach Johannes (Stuttgart 1980) 23, 155n.135. HAENCHEN, E., Das Johannesevangelium (Tübingen 1980) 386-87 (lit!). LINDEMANN, A., "Gemeinde und Welt im Johannesevangelium" in: D. Lührmann/G. Strecker (eds.) Kirche. FS. G. Bornkamm (Tübingen 1980) 149.

10:1ff MAURER, C. Ignatius von Antiochien und das Johannesevangelium (1949) 30f., 43. KNOX, W. L. The Sources of the Synoptic Gospels II (1957) 157.

10:1-38 CADMAN, W. H. The Open Heaven (1969) G. B. Caird, ed., 117-21.

10:1-30 WIKENHAUSER, A. Der Evangelium nach Johannes (1957) 199f. MUELLER, T. Das Heilsgeschehen im Johannesevangelium n.d., 54-58. BRUCE, F. F., The Time is Fulfilled (Exeter 1978) 49-50.

10:1-21 HAWKIN, D. J., "Orthodoxy and Heresy in John 10:1-21 and 15:1-17" EQ 47 (1975) 208-213. *STACHOWIAK, L., "Dobry Pasterz (J 10, 1-21) (Der gute Hirt)" RTK 22 (1975) 75-84. *CHEVALLIER, M. A., "L'analyse littéraire des textes du Nouveau Testament (Conseils aux édudiants)" RHPR 57 (1977) 367-78.

10:1-18 BAUER, W., Das Johannesevangelium (1925) 138f. PIROT, J. Paraboles et Allégories Evangeliques (1949) 178-84. MEYER, P. W. "A Note on John 10:1-18," JBL 75 (1956) 232-

35. WILKENS, W. Die Entstehungsgeschichte des vierten Evangeliums (1958) 145, 146, 147, 148. BLAIR, E. P., Jesus in the Gospel of Matthew (1960) 74. BRUNS, J. E. "The Discourse on the Good Shepherd and the Rite of Ordination," AER 149 (6, 1963) 386-91. LOCKYER, H. All the Parables of the Bible (1963) 327ff. O'ROURKE, J. J. "Jo 10,1-18: Series Parabolarum?" VerbDom 42 (1, 1964) 22-25. SMITH, D. M. The Composition and Order of the Fourth Gospel (1965) 155, 156, 163. KIEFER, O. Die Hirtenrede (1967). SIMONIS, A. J. Die Hirtenrede im Johannes-Evangelium (1967). ODEBERG, H. The Fourth Gospel (1968) 313ff. DE VILLIERS, J. L. "The Shepherd and his Flock," Neotestamentica 2 (1968) 89-103. WEAD, D. W. The Literary Devices in John's Gospel (1970) 87-92. DERRETT, J. D. M. "The Good Shepherd: St. John's Use of Jewish Halakah and Haggadah," StTh 27 (1, 1973) 25-50. LANGBRANDTNER, W., Weltferner Gott oder Gott der Liebe (Frankfurt 1977) 46-49. O'GRADY, J. F., "The Good Shepherd and the Vine and the Branches" BThB 8 (1978) 86-89. BECKER, J., Das Evangelium nach Johannes (Gütersloh/ Würzburg 1979) 324 (lit!).

10:1-16 FLEW, R. N. Jesus and His Church (1956) 172-73.

10:1-15 LE FORT, P. Les Structures de L'Eglise militante selon saint Jean (1970) 80-87.

10:1-11 IWAND, H.-J. Predigt-Meditationen (1964) 302-306. HAHN, F. Das Verständnis der Mission im Neuen Testament (²1965) 139. WEBER, O. Predigtmeditationen (1967) 35-39.

10:1-10 GEORGE, A. "Je suis la porte des bebris. Jean 10,1-10," BVieC 51 (1963) 18-25. PROVERA, M., "La parabole du Bon Pasteur (Jn 10,1-10)," La Terre Sainte 1 (1975) 16-19.

10:1-9 MORGAN, G. C. The Parables and Metaphors of Our Lord (1943) 309ff.

10:1-6 BUECHSEL, F. Das Evangelium nach Johannes (1946) 119f. SCHILLEBEECKX, E., Christ: The Christian Experience in the Modern World (London 1980) 391-94; GT: Christus und die Christen (Freiburg/Basel/Wien 1977) 377-80.

10:1-5.27-30 FUERST, W. GPM 19 (1, 1965) 181-86. HARDER, G. in: Hören und Fragen Bd. 5, 3 (1967) G. Eichholz/A. Falkenroth eds., 277ff. KOCSIS, E. GPM 25 (1, 1971) 205-11. LANGE, E. ed., Predigtstudien für das Kirchenjahr 1970-1971 (1970) 60-66.

10:1-5 ROBINSON, J. A. T. "The Parable of John 10,1-5," ZNW 46 (3-4, 1955) 233-40. Also in: Twelve New Testament Studies (1962) 67-75. SMITH, D. M. The Composition and Order of the Fourth Gospel (1965) 163, 164, 165, 166. HUNTER, A. M. According to John (1970²) 81f. BRÄNDLE, R. und BUESS, E., in: P. Krusche et al. (eds.) Predigtstudien für das Kirchenjahr 1976/1977. V/2 (Stuttgart 1977) 33-39. SCHUNACK, G., in: GPM 31 (1976-1977) 196-203.

10:1-3.9 LOCKYER, H. All the Parables of the Bible (1963) 324ff.

10:1-2 BIEDER, W. Die Verheissung der Taufe im Neuen Testament (Zürich 1966) 242-48.

10:1 BERGMEIER, R., Glaube als Gabe nach Johannes Stuttgart (1980) 44n.307.

10:2 GRILL, J. Untersuchungen über die Entstehung des vierten Evangeliums II (1923) 148f., 150.

10:3 PALLIS, A. Notes on St. John and the Apocalypse (London 1928) 22. BERGMEIER, R., Glaube als Gabe nach Johannes (Stuttgart 1980) 11.

10:4-5.27-28 SCHWEIZER, E. Erniedrigung und Erhöhung bei Jesus and seinen Nachfolgern (1962) § 11ghk.

10:4 "Autorität" in: TRE 5 (1980) 33.

10:5 METZGER, B. M., The Early Versions of the New Testament (Oxford 1977) 390.

10:6ff FINDLAY, J. A. Jesus and His Parable (1951) 1ff.

10:6 BERGMEIER, R., Glaube als Gabe nach Johannes (Stuttgart 1980) 225.

10:7-14 DEISSMANN, A. Licht vom Osten (1923) 113f.

10:7-11 BERGMEIER, R., Glaube als Gabe nach Johannes (Stuttgart 1980) 44n.307.

10:7-9 BISHOP, E. F. F. " 'The Door of the Sheep' (Egō eimi hē thura tōn probatōn)-John x. 7-9," ET 71 (10, 1960) 307-309. GOETTMAN, J. "La porte de la vie," BVieC 51 (1963) 37-59. CREHAN, J. The Theology of St. John (1965) 72-74.

10:7.9 MAURER, C. Ignatius von Antiochien und das Johannesevangelium (1949) 20, 30ff., 58ff., 77.

10:7 PALLIS, A., Notes on St. John and the Apocalypse (London 1928) 22-23. BIEDER, W., Die Verheissung der Taufe im Neuen Testament (Zürich 1966) 242-48. WEIGANDT, P. "Zum Text von Joh. X 7. Ein Beitrag zum Problem der koptischen Bibelübersetzung," NovTest 9 (1, 1967) 43-51. LADD, G. E. A Theology of the New Testament (1974) 216, 250, 282. METZGER, B. M., The Early Versions of the New Testament (Oxford 1977) 140. "Benediktionen" in: TRE 5 (1980) 170.

10:8-9 VON LOEWENICH, W., Das Johannes-Verständnis im zweiten Jahrhundert (1932) 65, 67, 68, 81n.1, 106, 109, 137.

10:8 BOISMARD, M. E., "Importance de la critique textuelle pour établir l'origine araméenne du quatrième évangile" in: M. Boismard et al., L'Evangile de Jean: études et problèmes (Bruges 1958) 44-45.

10:9 BIEDER, W. Die Verheissung der Taufe im Neuen Testament (Zürich 1966) 242-48. DELLING, G. Wort und Werk Jesu im Johannes-Evangelium (1966) 116f., 121.

10:10 KUHL, J. Die Sendung Jesu und der Kirche nach dem Johannes-Evangelium (1967) 119f., 182. MEEKS, W. A. The Prophet-King, Moses Traditions and the Johannine Christology (1967) 309-310. LADD, G. E. A Theology of the New Testament (1974) 248, 250, 254.

10:11f POPKES, W. Christus Traditus (1967) 190ff., 247, 267, 269, 284, 288. SMITH, M. Tannaitic Parallels to the Gospels (1968) 3 b n 38. KUENZI, M. Das Naherwartungslogion Matthäus 10,23 (1970) 33, 69, 111.

10:11-18 MORGAN, G. C. The Parables and Metaphors of Our Lord (1943) 314ff. MOLLAT, D. "Le bon pasteur (Jean 10:11-18, 26-30)," BVieC 52 (1963) 25-35.

10:11-16 IWAND, H.-J. GPM 4 (1949-1950) 134ff. FUCHS, GPM 9 (1954-1955) 122ff. FISCHER, GPM 15 (1960-1961) 133ff. BONHOEFFER, D. in: Herr, tue meine Lippen auf Bd. 1 (1957) G. Eichholz ed., 149-53. DOERNE, M. Er kommt auch noch neute (1961) 80-82. IWAND, H.-J. Predigt-Meditationen (1964) 212-17. HENKYS, J. in: GPM 33 (1979) 203-208.

10:11 DENNEY, J. The Death of Christ (1956³) 142f. TILLICH, P. Das Ewige Jetzt (1964) 70-78. POPKES, W. Christus Traditus (1967) 283f. JEREMIAS, J., Neutestamentliche Theologie I (1971) 272f., 282. LADD, G. E. A Theology of the New Testament (1974) 108, 187, 216, 249. "Abendmahl" in: TRE 1 (1977) 57.

10:12 BÖHLIG, A., Die Gnosis III: Der Manichäismus (Zürich/Würzburg 1980) 344n.53.

10:14ff SCHWEIZER, E. Gemeinde und Gemeinde-Ordnung im Neuen Testament (1959) § 11d.g. "Baptisterium" in: TRE 5 (1980) 203.

10:14-18 DENNEY, J. The Death of Christ (1956³) 143, 146.

10:14-16 MARZOTTO, D., " 'Un solo unico pastore' (Gv. 10,16)" ScuC 103 (1975) 834-43. BERGMEIER, R., Glaube als Gabe nach

Johannes (Stuttgart 1980) 26-27, 44n.307.312, 45n.316.320, 46n.328, 271n.568, 273n.612.

10:14.15.17.18 HIRSCH, E. Die Auferstehungsgeschichte und der christliche Glaube (1940) 125-37.

10:14-15 CERFAUX, L., "L'Evangile de Jean et 'Le Logion Johannique' des synoptiques" in: M. Boismard et al., L'Evangile de Jean: études et problèmes (Bruges 1958) 155-58. WILES, M. F. The Spiritual Gospel (1960) 85-86. GRUNDMANN, W. "Verständnis und Bewegung des Glaubens im Johannes-Evangelium," KuD 6 (1960) 149. IBUKI, Y. Die Wahrheit im Johannesevangelium (1972) 265f.

10:14 CREHAH, J. The Theology of St. John (1965) 41, 72-73, 75-76.

10:15-18 RUCKSTUHL, E. Die literarische Einheit des Johannesevangeliums (1951) 176f.

10:15-16 TAYLOR, V. Jesus and His Sacrifice (1948) 233, 235, 237, 244, 246-48.

10:15 HAHN, F. Christologische Hoheitstitel (1963) 330. DELLING, G. Wort und Werk Jesu im Johannes-Evangelium (1966) 40, 78, 101, 117. RIEDL, J. BuL 41 (1968) 108-109. JEREMIAS, J. Neutestamentliche Theologie I (1971) 66, 272f., 282. DAUER, A. Die Passionsgeschichte im Johannesevangelium (1972) 39, 294, 313. LADD, G. E. A Theology of the New Testament (1974) 187, 248, 249. "Abendmahl" in : TRE 1 (1977) 57.

10:16 GRILL, J. Untersuchungen über die Entstehung des vierten Evangeliums II (1923) 54, 66, 88, 152, 156, 209, 357. RUCKSTUHL, E. Die literarische Einheit des Johannesevangeliums (1951) 34, 176f., 252. FLEW, R. N. Jesus and His Church (1956) 177n. HAHN, F. Das Verständnis der Mission im Neuen Testament (1965²) 138. SMITH, D. M. The Composition and Order of the Fourth Gospel (1965) 222, 225, 233f. HOFIUS, O. "Die Sammlung der Heiden zur Herde Israels (Joh 10:16, 11:51f)," ZNW 58 (3-4, 1967) 289-91. KUHL, J. Die Sendung Jesu und der Kirche nach dem Johannes-Evangelium (1967) 198, 220-22. LE FORT, P. Les Structures de L'Eglise militante selon Saint Jean (1970) 88-90. BEUTLER, J. Martyria (1972) 346-49. LEISTNER, R., Antijudaismus im Johannesevangelium? (Bern 1974) 148. APPOLD, M. L., The Oneness Motif in the Fourth Gospel (Tübingen 1976) 246-60.

10:17-18 SCHELKLE, K. H. Die Passion Jesu in der Verkündigung des Neuen Testaments (1949) 72f. HAHN, F. Christologische Hoheitstitel (1963) 49. CADMAN, W. H. The Open Heaven (1969)

G. B. Caird ed., 39, 93, 115, 121. THUESING, W. Die Erhöhung und Verherrlichung Jesu im Johannesevangelium (1970) 277-79. JEREMIAS, J. Neutestamentliche Theologie I (1971) 272f., 282. DAUER, A. Die Passionsgeschichte im Johannesevangelium (1972) 279, 293, 294. IBUKI, Y. Die Wahrheit im Johannesevangelium (1972) 263-70. GREER, R. A. The Captain of Our Salvation (1973) 278-79. RIEDL, J. Das Heilswerk Jesu nach Johannes (1973) 106-12, 113-18. LEISTNER, R., Antijudaismus im Johannesevangelium? (Bern 1974) 145-46. LATTKE, M., Einheit im Wort (München 1975) 122-31. DALY, R. J. Christian Sacrifice (Washington, D. C. 1978) 292. BERGMEIER, R., Glaube als Gabe nach Johannes (Stuttgart 1980) 44n.307.

10:17 PALLIS, A., Notes on St. John and the Apocalypse (London 1928) 23. WILES, M. F., The Spiritual Gospel (1960) 127-28. CADMAN, W. H. The Open Heaven (1969) G. B. Caird ed. 16, 40, 50, 180. LATTKE, M., Einheit im Wort (München 1975) 19, 114-31. GEORGI, D., "Weisheit Salomos" in: JüdSchr III/4 (1980) 8n.3b.

10:18 BORIG, R. Der Wahre Weinstock (1967) 30, 65, 233, 235, 243. PANCARO, S., The Law in the Fourth Gospel (Leiden 1975) 322, 338, 438, 439-42. BÜHNER, J.-A., Der Gesandte und sein Weg im 4. Evangelium (Tübingen 1977) 199-201.

10:19-29 KÜMMEL, W. G. Einleitung in das Neue Testament (1973) 170f.

10:19-21 WILKENS, W. Die Entstehungsgeschichte des vierten Evangeliums (1958) 108-11. SIMONIS, A. J. Die Hirtenrede im Johannes-Evangelium (1967) 27, 40f., 44. BECKER, J., Das Evangelium nach Johannes (Gütersloh/Würzburg 1979) 314-15 (lit!).

10:19 CREHAN, J. The Theology of St. John (1965) 75-76. van WAHLDE, U. C., "The Johannine 'Jews': A Critical Survey" NTS 28 (1982) 51.

10:20 GRILL, J. Untersuchungen über die Entstehung des vierten Evangeliums II (1923) 12, 17, 79, 127, 226, 241.

10:21 IBUKI, Y. Die Wahrheit im Johannesevangelium (1972) 63f.

10:22-42 TEMPLE, S., The Core of the Fourth Gospel (London 1975) 178-83. BECKER, J., Das Evangelium nach Johannes (Gütersloh/Würzburg 1979) 335-36 (lit!).

10:22-39 WILKENS, W. Die Entstehungsgeschichte des vierten Evangeliums (1958) 148-50. SIMONIS, A. J. Die Hirtenrede im Johannes-Evangelium (1967) 59ff. VOUGA, F., Le cadre historique et l'intention théologique de Jean (Paris 1977) 50-61. SCHILLEBEECKX, E., Christ: the Christian Experience in the Modern World (London 1980) 391-94; GT: Christus und die Christen (Freiburg/Basel/Wien 1977) 377-80.

10:22-23 BRAUN, H. Qumran und NT I (1966) 101. DAVIES, W. D., The Gospel and the Land (London 1974) 291, 292. VOUGA, F., Le cadre historique et l'intention théologique de Jean (Paris 1977) 53-54.

10:22 BARRETT, C. K. The New Testament Background (1956) 111.

10:23-30 NIESEL, W. in: Herr, tue meine Lippen auf Bd. 3 (1964) G. Eichholz ed., 453ff.

10:24-39 BOISMARD, E. "Jésus, le Prophète par excellence, d'après Jean 10,24-39," in: Neues Testament und Kirche (1974) J. Gnilka ed., 160-71.

10:24-25 DELLING, G. Wort und Werk Jesu im Johannes-Evangelium (1966) 74, 92f. KLEIN, H., "Die lukanisch-johanneische Passionstradition" in: M. Limbeck (ed.) Redaktion und Theologie des Passionsberichtes nach den Synoptikern (Darmstadt 1981) 375-77.

10:24 PALLIS, A., Notes on St. John and the Apocalypse (London 1928) 23-24. KNOX, W. L. The Sources of the Synoptic Gospels II (1957) 143. SCHNEIDER, G. Verleugnung, Verspottung und Verhör Jesu nach Lukas 22,54-71 (1969) 34, 56, 57, 61, 68, 113, 114. VOUGA, F., Le cadre historique et l'intention théologique de Jean (Paris 1977) 54. HANSON, A. T., The New Testament Interpretation of Scripture (London 1980) 167.

10:25-38 ODEBERG, H. The Fourth Gospel (1968) 330ff.

10:25-30 SIMONIS, A. J. Die Hirtenrede im Johannes-Evangelium (1967) 26, 39, 42ff. VOUGA, F., Le cadre historique et l'intention théologique de Jean (Paris 1977) 54-57.

10:25-26 THEYSSEN, G. W. "Unbelief" in the New Testament (Rüschlikon 1965) 46f.

10:25.32-37 RIEDL, J., Das Heilswerk Jesu nach Johannes (1973) 187-282.

10:25.29 SCHUETZ, R. "Jn 10:25,29," ZNW 10 (1909) 324.

10:25 DELLING, G. Die Zueignung des Heils in der Taufe (1961) 43, 45. DELLING, G. Wort und Werk Jesu im Johannes-Evangelium (1966) 34, 48, 60, 73f., 102. BEUTLER, J. Martyria (1972) 23, 175, 223, 259, 272-74, 279, 282, 293, 299, 311, 339, 357. UNTERGASSMAIR, F. G., Im Namen Jesu: Der Namensbegriff im Johannesevangelium (Stuttgart 1973) 56-63.

10:26ff BERGMEIER, R., Glaube als Gabe nach Johannes (Stuttgart 1980) 215.

10:26-30 MOLLAT, D. "Le bon pasteur (Jean 10,11-18.26-30)," BVieC 52 (1963) 25-35.

10:26-29 LE FORT, P. Les Structures de L'Eglise militante selon saint Jean (1970) 80-87.

10:26 FLEW, R. N. Jesus and His Church (1956) 172-73. METZ-GER, B. M., The Early Versions of the New Testament (Oxford 1977) 391.

10:27-30 BRÄNDLE, R. und BUESS, E., in: P. Krusche et al. (eds.) Predigtstudien für des Kirchenjahr 1976-1977. V/2 (Stuttgart 1977) 33-39. SCHUNACK, G., in: GPM 31 (1976-1977) 196-203.

10:27-29 BERGMEIER, R., Glaube als Gabe nach Johannes (Stuttgart 1980) 132, 160n.255-256, 233, 236, 249n.225, 269n.530, 272, 273n.612.

10:27-28 DUPONT, J. Essais sur la Christologie de Saint Jean (1951) 189, 190. SIMONIS, A. J. Die Hirtenrede im Johannes-Evangelium (1967) 26.

10:27 METZGER, B. M., The Early Versions of the New Testament (Oxford 1977) 144.

10:28 DELLING, G. Wort und Werk Jesu im Johannes-Evangelium (1966) 105 143f. "Dordrechter Synode" in: TRE 9 (1982) 141.

10:29-30 SCHUETZ, R. "Ev Jn 10:29-30," ZNW 18 (1917-1918) 223. BÜHNER, J.-A., Der Gesandte und sein Weg im 4. Evangelium (Tübingen 1977) 214-17.

10:29 BIRDSALL, J. N. "John x. 29," JThS 11 (2, 1960) 342-44. REYNOLDS, S. M. "The Supreme Importance of the Doctrine of Election and the Eternal Security of the Elect as Taught in the Gospel of John," WThJ 28 (1, 1965) 38-41. WHITTAKER, J. "A Hellenistic Context for John 10:29," VigChr 24 (4, 1970) 241-60. FISCHER, U., Eschatologie und Jenseitserwartung im hellenistischen Diasporajudentum (Berlin 1978) 94.

10:30 POLLARD, T. E. "The Exegesis of John 10:30 in the Early Trinitarian Controversies," NTS 3 (4, 1957) 334-49. WILES, M. F. The Spiritual Gospel (1960) 112-13, 117, 118-19, 125-26, 131. GAERTNER, B. The Temple and the Community in Qumran and the New Testament (1965) 119. HAHN, F. Das Verständnis der Mission im Neuen Testament (²1965) 140. SUMMERS, R. The Secret Sayings of the Living Jesus (1968) 59. CADMAN, W. H. The Open Heaven (1969) G. B. Caird ed., 1, 16, 28, 75, 124, 146. LE FORT, P. Les Structures de L'Eglise militante selon saint Jean (1970) 106-108. MARAN-

GONI, V. O., "Juan 10,30 en la argumentacion escrituristica de San Atanasio," Stromata 26 (1-2, 1970) 3-57. SMALLEY, S. S., "Diversity and Development in John," NTS 17 (1970-1971) 288f. APPOLD, M. L. The Oneness Motif in the Fourth Gospel (Tübingen 1976) 246-60. BÜHNER, J.-A., Der Gesandte und sein Weg im 4. Evangelium (Tübingen 1977) 214-17. "Baha'ismus" in: TRE 5 (1980) 122. BERGMEIER, R., Glaube als Gabe nach Johannes (Stuttgart 1980) 273n.612.

10:31-38 DUNN, J. D. G., Christology in the Making (London 1980) 58.

10:31-33 SIMONIS, A. J. Die Hirtenrede im Johannes-Evangelium (1967) 27. VOUGA, F., Le cadre historique et l'intention théologique de Jean (Paris 1977) 57-58. von WAHLDE, U. C., "The Johannine 'Jews': A Critical Survey" NTS 28 (1982) 45.

10:31.40 ORIGENES, Das Evangelium nach Johannes (1959) R. Gögler ed., 336-37, 360.

10:31 HENNECKE, E./SCHNEEMELCHER, W. Neutestamentliche Apokryphen (1964) I 60. DAUER, A. Die Passionsgeschichte im Johannesevangelium (1972) 88, 103, 247.

10:33-37 DAVIES, W. D., The Gospel and the Land (London 1974) 293.

10:33-36 HANSON, A. T. "John's Citation of Psalm lxxxii John x 33-6," NTS 11 (2, 1965) 158-62.

10:33-34 TENNANT, R. "Hard Sayings-IV. John 10:33-34," Theology 66 (521, 1963) 457-58.

10:33 NICKELS, P. Targum and New Testament (1967) 56. ROBINSON, J. A. T. "The Use of the Fourth Gospel in Jn 10:33 for Christology Today," in: Christ and the Spirit in the New Testament (1973) B. Lindars/S. S. Smalley eds., 61, 72, 74. KLEIN, H., "Die lukanisch-johanneische Passionstradition" in: M. Limbeck (ed.) Redaktion und Theologie des Passionsberichtes nach den Synoptikern (Darmstadt 1981) 375-77. MATSUNAGA, K., "The 'Theos' Christology as the Ultimate Confession of the Fourth Gospel" AJBI 7 (1981) 129, 130-31, 135.

10:34-38 PANCARO, S., The Law in the Fourth Gospel (Leiden 1975) 129, 175-92, 275, 280. VOUGA, F., Le cadre historique et l'intention théologique de Jean (Paris 1977) 58-60.

10:34-36 JUNGKUNTZ, E., "An Approach to the Exegesis of John 10:34-36," CThM 35 (9, 1964) 556-65. EMERTON, J. A. "Melchizedek and the Gods: Fresh Evidence for the Jewish Background of John X. 34-36," JThS 17 (2, 1966) 399-401. BÜHNER, J.-A., Der Gesandte und sein Weg im 4. Evangelium (Tübingen 1977) 393-96.

10:34 FREED, E. D. Old Testament Quòtations in the Gospel of John
(1965) 60-65. ACKERMAN, J. S. "The Rabbinic Interpretation of Psalm 82 and the Gospel of John: John 10:34," HThR
59 (2, 1966) 186-91. HANSON, A., "John's Citation of Psalm
lxxxii Reconsidered," NTS 13 (4, 1967) 363-67. SANFORD,
J. A., The Kingdom Within (New York 1970) 89. BEUTLER,
J. Martyria (1972) 270, 273, 354. DAUER, A., Die
Passionsgeschichte im Johannesevangelium (1972) 184, 300,
301. REIM, G., Studien zum Alttestamentlichen Hintergrund
des Johannesevangeliums (Cambridge 1974) 23-26, 89-91, 93-
95. BÜHNER, J.-A., Der Gesandte und sein Weg im 4. Evangelium (Tübingen 1977) 408-11. HANSON, A. T., The New
Testament Interpretation of Scripture (London 1980) 159-62.

10:36.39 SMITH, M. Clement of Alexandria and a secret Gospel of Mark
(1973) 225f., 247.

10:36 HAHN, F. Christologische Hoheitstitel (1963) 235, 330.
HAHN, F. Das Verständnis der Mission im Neuen Testament
(^{2}1965) 140. DELLING, G. Wort und Werk Jesu im Johannes-
Evangelium (1966) 57, 65, 67, 79, 100f., 105, 114. KUHL, J.,
Die Sendung Jesu und der Kirche nach dem Johannes-Evangel-
ium (1967) 65-70, 109. CADMAN, W. H., The Open Heaven
(1969) G. B. Caird ed., 14, 22, 52, 55, 75, 78, 209. IBUKI,
Y. Die Wahrheit im Johannesevangelium (1972) 13f., 134-37.
KLEIN, H., "Die lukanisch-johanneische Passionstradition"
in: M. Limbeck (ed.) Redaktion und Theologie des Passionsbe-
richtes nach den Synoptikern (Darmstadt 1981) 375-77. MAT-
SUNAGA, K., "The 'Theos' Christology as the Ultimate
Confession of the Fourth Gospel" AJBI 7 (1981) 132-33.

10:37-38 DELLING, G. Die Zueignung des Heils in der Taufe (1961) 45.
IBUKI, Y. Die Wahrheit im Johannesevangelium (1972) 221f.
235f. BEUTLER, J., Martyria (1972) 259, 273, 299, 357.
BACCHIOCCHI, S., "John 5:17: Negation or Clarification of
the Sabbath?" AUSS 19 (1981) 14.

10:38-39 HENNECKE, E./SCHNEEMELCHER, W. Neutestamentliche Apokryphen (1964) I 60; I 135; II 208.

10:38 HAHN, F. Christologische Hoheitstitel (1963) 330. BORIG, R.
Der Wahre Weinstock (1967) 203, 208, 215f., 218, 228. LADD,
G. E. A Theology of the New Testament (1974) 248, 262, 271.
BÜHNER, J.-A., Der Gesandte und sein Weg im 4. Evangel-
ium (Tübingen 1977) 214-17. BÖHLIG, A., Die Gnosis III: Der
Manichäismus (Zürich/München 1980) 343n.25.

10:39 ORIGENES, Das Evangelium nach Johannes (1959) R. Gögler
ed., 348-49. VOUGA, F., Le cadre historique et l'intention
théologique de Jean (Paris 1977) 60.

10:40-21:24 GYLLENBERG, R., "Intåget ; Jerusalem och Johannesevangeliets uppbyggnad" SEA 41-42 (1976-1977) 81-86.

10:40-12:33 SMITH, D. M. The Composition and Order of the Fourth Gospel 33 (1965) 148-58, 166-68.

10:40-41 RUDOLPH, K. Die Mandäer I (1960) 77, 165. SASS, G. Die Auferweckung des Lazarus (1967) 32. WINK, W. John the Baptist in the Gospel Tradition (1968) 97-98. LENTZEN-DEIS, F. Die Taufe nach den Synoptikern (1970) 81. IBUKI, Y. Die Wahrheit im Johannesevangelium (1972) 235ff., 344. DAVIES W. D. The Gospel and the Land (1974) 319, 321, 324. de JONGE, M., Jesus: Stranger from Heaven and Son of God (Missoula 1977) 120.

10:40 HEISE, J., Bleiben. μένειν in den Johanneischen Schriften (Tübingen 1967) 47-50. CRIBBS, F. L. in: SBL Seminar Papers 2 (1973) MacRae, G. ed. 3.

10:41 BAMMEL, E. " 'John did no miracle'," Miracles, ed. C. F. D. Moule (London 1965) 179-202. CRIBBS, F. L., "The Agreements that Exist Between John and Acts" in: C. H. Talbert (ed.) Perspectives on Luke-Acts (Danville 1978) 48.

11:1-12:50 GRUNDMANN, W. Zeugnis und Gestalt des Johannes-Evangeliums (1961) 58-64.

11-12 van den BUSSCHE, H., "La Structure de Jean I-XII," in: M. Boismard et al., L'Evangile de Jean. Études et problèmes (Bruges 1958) 103-107. de MERODE, M., "L'accueil triomphal de Jésus selon Jean, 11-12" RThL 13 (1982) 49-62.

11 GRILL, J. Untersuchungen über die Entstehung des vierten Evangeliums II (1923) 163, 171f., 175, 185, 191. BECKER, H., Die Reden des Johannesevangeliums und der Stil der gnostischen Offenbarungsrede (Göttingen 1956) 90-91. DUNKERLY, R., "Lazarus," NTS 5 (1959) 321-27. SCHULZ, S., Komposition und Herkunft der Johanneischen Reden (Stuttgart 1960) 79-81, 107-109. BECKER, J. NTS 16 (1969-1970) 146f. PETZKE, G. Die Traditionen über Apollonius von Tyana und das Neue Testament (1970) 109, 136. SCHILLE, G. Das vorsynoptische Judenchristentum (1970) 79f. NÖTSCHER, F., Altorientalischer und alttestamentlicher Auferstehungsglaube

(Darmstadt 1970=1926) 303. HANSON, A. T., "The Old Testament Background to the Raising of Lazarus" StEv 6 (1973) 252-55. POLLARD, T. E., "The Raising of Lazarus (Jn 11)" StEv 6 (1973) 434-43. McNEIL, B., "The Raising of Lazarus" DRev 92 (1974) 269-75. LOHSE, E., "Miracles in the Fourth Gospel" in: M. Hooker/C. Hickling (eds.) What About the New Testament? FS. C. Evans (London 1975) 70-72. MICHIELS, R., "De opwekking van Lazarus" Collationes 21 (1975) 433-47. de JONGE, M., Jesus: Stranger from Heaven and Son of God (Missoula 1977) 124-27. TRITES, A. A., The New Testament Concept of Witness (Cambridge 1977) 109-10. STAGG, E. and F., Women in the World of Jesus (Philadelphia 1978) 238. BROWN, R. E., The Community of the Beloved Disciple (London 1979) 190-92. BÖHLIG, A., Die Gnosis III: Der Manichäismus (Zürich/München 1980) 344n.54. DESCAMPS, A.-L. et al., Genèse et structure d' un texte de Nouveau Testament. Etude interdisciplinaire du chapitre 11 de L'Evangile de Jean (Paris 1981).

11:1ff HAHN, F. Christologische Hoheitstitel (1963) 94.

11:1-54 MUELLER, T. Das Heilsgeschehen im Johannesevangelium n.d., 100-103.

11:1-45 FORTNA, R. T. The Gospel of Signs (1970) 74-87. STENGER, W. "Die Auferweckung des Lazarus (Joh 11,1-45). Vorlage und johanneische Redaktion," TThZ 83 (1, 1974) 17-34. TEMPLE, S., The Core of the Fourth Gospel (London 1975) 183-93. CRIBBS, F., "The Agreements that Exist Between John and Acts" in: C. H. Talbert (ed.) Perspectives on Luke-Acts (Danville 1978) 45. LEIDIG, E., Jesu Gespräch mit der Samaritanerin (Basel 1981) 223-26.

11:1-44 BAUER, W. Das Johannesevangelium (1925) 149f. ZIENER, G. "Weisheitsbuch und Johannesevangelium," Biblica 38 (1957) 409-11. WILKENS, W. "Die Erweckung des Lazarus," ThZ 15 (1959) 22-39. FULLER, R. H. Interpreting the Miracles (1963) 105ff. MARTIN, J. P. "History and Eschatology in the Lazarus Narrative, John 11.1-44" SJTh 17 (3, 1964) 332-43. DELLING, G., Wort und Werk Jesu im Johannes-Evangelium (1966) 16, 23, 76, 97. TRUDINGER, P. "A 'Lazarus Motif' in Primitive Christian Preaching," ANQ 7 (1, 1966) 29-32. CADMAN, W. H. The Open Heaven (1969) G. B. Caird ed., 122-32. WILKENS, W., Zeichen und Werke (Zürich 1969) 42-43. SABOURIN, L. "Resurrectio Lazari (Jo 11,1-44)," VerDom 46 (6, 1969) 339-50. NICOL, W. The Sēmeia in the Fourth Gospel (1972) 37ff., 47, 60, 75, 109f. MOULE, C. F. D., "The Meaning of 'Life' in the Gospels and

Epistles of St. John. A Study in the Story of Lazarus. John 11:1-44," Theology 78 (1975) 114-25. TRUDINGER, L. P., "The Meaning of 'Life' in St. John. Some Further Reflections" BThB 6 (1976) 258-63. TRUDINGER, P., "The Raising of Lazarus — A Brief Response" DRev 94 (1976) 287-90. MARTYN, J. L., The Gospel of John in Christian History (New York 1978) 24-25. SABOURIN, L., "A Resurreição de Lázaro (Jo 11,1-44)" RCB 2 (1978) 293-98. BECKER, J., Das Evangelium nach Johannes (Gütersloh/Würzburg 1979) 343 (lit!). SWIDLER, L., Biblical Affirmations of Woman (Philadelphia 1979) 218, 220, 224. BECKER, J., "Wunder und Christologie. Zum literar-kritischen und christologischen Problem der Wunder im Johannesevangelium" in: A. Suhl (ed.) Der Wunderbegriff im Neuen Testament (Darmstadt 1980) 446-47, 458-61. GIBLIN, C. H., "Suggestion, Negative Response, and Positive Action in St. John's Portrayal of Jesus (John 2.1-11; 4.46-54; 7.2-14; 11:1-44.)" NTS 26 (1980) 197-211. HAENCHEN, E., Das Johannesevangelium (Tübingen 1980) 396-97 (lit!). MENOUD, P.-H. "Die Bedeutung des Wunders nach dem Neuen Testament" in: A. Suhl (ed.) Der Wunderbegriff im Neuen Testament (Darmstadt 1980) 288-89.

11:1-11 BORNKAMM, G. in: Herr, tue meine Lippen auf Bd. 3 (1964) G. Eichholz ed., 402ff. IWAND, H.-J. Predigt-Meditationen (1964) 95-99.

11:1-10 WEBER, O. Predigtmeditationen (1967) 9-12.

11:1-5 SASS, G. Die Auferweckung des Lazarus (1967) 32-37.

11:1.3.17-27 IWAND, H.-J. Predigt-Meditationen (1964) 659-65. HEINTZE, G. in: Hören und Fragen Bd. 5,3 (1967) G. Eichholz/A. Falkenroth eds., 468ff. HERBERT, K. GPM 25 (3, 1971) 389-96. LANGE, E. ed., Predigtstudien für das Kirchenjahr 1970-1971 (1970) 202-208.

11:1-6 FORTNA, R. T. The Gospel of Signs (1970) 75ff.

11:1 BECKER, J. und ROSENBOOM, E., in: P. Krusche et al. (eds.) Predigtstudien für das Kirchenjahr 1976-1977. V/2 (Stuttgart 1977) 196-202. "Aramäisch" in: TRE 3 (1978) 608.

11:2 HAHN, F. Christologische Hoheitstitel (1963) 94. REUSS, J. "Presbyter Ammonius' Kommentar zum Jo-Evangelium," Biblica 44 (1963) 168.

11:3 LATTKE, M., Einheit im Wort (München 1975) 11, 19. BECKER, J. und ROSENBOOM, E., in: P. Krusche et al. (eds.) Predigtstudien für das Kirchenjahr 1976-1977. V/2 (Stuttgart 1977) 196-202.

11:4 DUPONT, J. Essais sur la Christologie de Saint Jean (1951) 248, 279, 281, 286. HAHN, F. Christologische Hoheitstitel (1963) 330. DELLING, G. Wort und Werk Jesu im Johannes-Evangelium (1966) 67, 69, 75f., 100. THUESING, W. Die Erhöhung und Verherrlichung Jesu im Johannesevangelium (1970) 229-31. NICOL, W. The Sēmeia in the Fourth Gospel (1972) 121, 129f. BERGMEIER, R., Glaube als Gabe nach Johannes (Stuttgart 1980) 40n.218.

11:5 PALLIS, A. Notes on St. John and the Apocalypse (London 1928) 24-25. SANDERS, J. N. "Those Whom Jesus Loved" (John XI,6), NTS 1 (1954) 29-41. LATTKE, M., Einheit im Wort (München 1975) 11, 19. "Aramäisch" in: TRE 3 (1978) 608.

11:6-16 SASS, G. Die Auferweckung des Lazarus (1967) 37-42.

11:6 HEISE, J., Bleiben. μένειν in den Johanneischen Schriften (Tübingen 1967) 47-50. METZGER, B. M., The Early Versions of the New Testament (Oxford 1977) 369n.1.

11:7-16 FORTNA, R. T., The Gospel of Signs (1970) 78f.

11:7-8 BAMMEL, E. The Trial of Jesus (1970) 14ff.

11:7 BÖHLIG, A., Die Gnosis III: Der Manichäismus (Zürich/München 1980) 343n.37.

11:8 HAHN, F. Christologische Hoheitstitel (1963) 75.

11:9-10 ODEBERG, H. The Fourth Gospel (1968) 333.

11:9 PALLIS, A., Notes on St. John and the Apocalypse (London 1928) 25. LADD, G. E. A Theology of the New Testament (1974) 223, 224, 225.

11:11ff BERGMEIER, R., Glaube als Gabe nach Johannes (Stuttgart 1980) 250n.241.

11:11-15.23-26 LOCKYER, All the Parables of the Bible (1963) 332f.

11:11-15 MORGAN, G. C. The Parables and Metaphors of Our Lord (1943) 319ff.

11:11-13 HANSON, A. T., The New Testament Interpretation of Scripture (London 1980) 167-68.

11:11 HOFFMANN, P. Die Toten in Christus (1966) 202, 204.

11:12 METZGER, B. M., The Early Versions of the New Testament (Oxford 1977) 144.

11:13 BERGMEIER, R., Glaube als Gabe nach Johannes (Stuttgart 1980) 227.

11:14 BLACK, M. An Aramaic Approach to the Gospels and Acts (1967) 129f.

11:16 KAESEMANN, E. Exegetische Versuche und Besinnungen (1964) I 259. SUMMERS, R. The Secret Sayings of the Living Jesus (1968) 19. BAMMEL, E. The Trial of Jesus (1970) 14ff.

11:17-44 GROSSOUW, W. K. "Ich bin die Auferstehung und das Leben," Schrift 9 (1970) 98-102.

11:17-31 FORTNA, R. T. The Gospel of Signs (1970) 79-81.

11:17-27 SASS, G. Die Auferweckung des Lazarus (1967) 42-50. BECKER, J. und ROSENBOOM, E., in: P. Krusche et al. (eds.) Predigtstudien für das Kirchenjahr 1976-1977 V/2 (Stuttgart 1977) 196-202.

11:17 METZGER, B. M., The Early Versions of the New Testament (Oxford 1977) 144.

11:19-39 "Aramäisch" in: TRE 3 (1978) 608.

11:19 METZGER, B. M., The Early Versions of the New Testament (Oxford 1977) 437.

11:20-27 BORNKAMM, G. in: Herr, tue meine Lippen auf Bd. 3 (1964) G. Eichholz ed., 119ff. SANDERS, J. T., Ethics in the New Testament (Philadelphia 1975) 98.

11:21-28 SCHWEIZER, E., Heiliger Geist (Berlin 1978) 157-59. SCHWEIZER, E., "Auferstehung — Wirklichkeit oder Illusion?" EvTh 41 (1981) 14-15.

11:21-27 ROLOFF, J. Neues Testament (Neukirchen-Vluyn 1979) 148-50.

11:23-26 DUPONT, J., Essais sur la Christologie de Saint Jean (1951) 188, 189.

11:24ff CULLMANN, O. Urchristentum und Gottesdienst (^{2}1950) 54. DAVIES, W. D., The Gospel and the Land (London 1974) 332.

11:24-27 "Auferstehung" in: TRE 4 (1979) 460.

11:24-25 VOLZ, P. Die Eschatologie der jüdischen Gemeinde (1934) 270. NÖTSCHER, F., Altorientalischer und alttestamentlicher Auferstehungsglaube (Darmstadt 1970 = 1926) 305, 308.

11:24 STAUFFER, E., "Agnostos Theos: Joh. xi,24 und die Eschatologie des vierten Evangeliums," in: The Background of the New Testament and Its Eschatology (1956) W. D. Davies/D. Daube eds., 281-99. BERGMEIER, R., Glaube als Gabe nach Johannes (Stuttgart 1980) 13.

11:25-26 ODEBERG, H. The Fourth Gospel (1968) 333f. BÜHNER, J.-A., Der Gesandte und sein Weg im 4. Evangelium (Tübingen 1977) 173-74. RUDOLPH, K., Die Gnosis (Göttingen 1978) 324. BERGMEIER, R., Glaube als Gabe nach Johannes (Stuttgart 1980) 13, 204, 207, 220, 232, 270n.544.

11:25 REUSS, J. "Presbyter Ammonius' Kommentar zum Jo-Evangelium," Biblica 44 (1963) 168. DELLING, G. Wort und Werk Jesu im Johannes-Evangelium (1966) 41, 76, 120, 144. KUHL, J. Die Sendung Jesu und der Kirche nach dem Johannes-Evangelium (1967) 70f., 83, 181-83. BENOIT, P./MURPHY, R. Immortality and Resurrection (1970) 68-77. MARXSEN, W., The Resurrection of Jesus of Nazareth (1970) 136, 185. ROMANIUK, K. " 'I am the Resurrection and the Life' (Jn 11,25)," Concilium 60 (1970) 68-77. BOHREN, R. Predigtlehre (1971) 257f. LADD, G. E. A Theology of the New Testament (1974) 216, 148, 250, 257, 274. REIM, G., Studien zum Alttestamentlichen Hintergrund des Johannesevangeliums (Cambridge 1974) 248-49. SWIDLER, L., Biblical Affirmations of Woman (Philadelphia 1979) 223. "Bestattung" in: TRE 5 (1980) 755. SCHILLEBEECKX, E., Christ: the Christian Experience in the Modern World (London 180) 394; GT: Christus und die Christen (Freiburg/Basel/Wien 1977) 380.

11:26 METZGER, B. M., The Early Versions of the New Testament (Oxford 1977) 252.

11:27-28 HAHN, F. Christologische Hoheitstitel (1963) 77, 80, 219, 224, 330.

11:27 KUHL, J. Die Sendung Jesu und der Kirche nach dem Johannes-Evangelium (1967) 70-74. LADD, G. E. A Theology of the New Testament (1974) 225, 243, 271. DUNN, J. D. G., Unity and Diversity in the New Testament (London 1977) 47. SWIDLER, L., Biblical Affirmations of Woman (Philadelphia 1979) 216, 217, 223. BECKER, J., "Wunder und Christologie. Zum literar-kritischen und christologischen Problem der Wunder im Johannesevangelium" in: A. Suhl (ed.) Der Wunderbegriff im Neuen Testament (Darmstadt 1980) 448-54. BÖHLIG, A., Die Gnosis III: Der Mauichäismus (Zürich/München 1980) 343n.23. KRAFT, H., Die Entstehung des Christentums (Darmstadt 1981) 133.

11:28-44 SASS, G. Die Auferweckung des Lazarus (1967) 50-58.

11:31-37 METZGER, B. M., Manuscripts of the Greek Bible (Oxford 1981) 66.

11:32-46 FORTNA, R. T. The Gospel of Signs (1970) 81-84, 144-55.

11:32 METZGER, B. M., The Early Versions of the New Testament (Oxford 1977) 369n.1.

11:33-38 BEUTLER, J. "Psalm 42/43 im Johannesevangelium" NTS 25 (1978) 33-57.

11:33-36 SWIDLER, L., Biblical Affirmations of Woman (Philadelphia 1979) 283.

11:33 BOISMARD, M. E., "Importance de la critique textuelle pour établir l'origine araméenne du quatrième évangile" in: M. Boismard et al., L'Evangile de Jean. Études et problèmes (Bruges 1958) 49-51. NICKELS, P. Targum and New Testament (1967) 56. WILES, M. F. The Spiritual Gospel (1960) 66, 146-47, 150. PORSCH, F., Pneuma und Wort (Frankfurt 1974) 328-30.

11:34 WILES, M. F. The Spiritual Gospel (1960) 116-17, 142-44. SMITH, M. Tannaitic Parallels to the Gospels (1968) 2, 68*.

11:36 LATTKE, M., Einheit im Wort (München 1975) 11, 19.

11:38 METZGER, B. M., The Early Versions of the New Testament (Oxford 1977) 369n.1.

11:39ff HENNECKE, E./SCHNEEMELCHER, W., Neutestamentliche Apokryphen (1964) I 128.

11:39 STREETER, B. H. The Four Gospels (1951) 87f. BETZ, H. D. Lukian von Samosata und das Neue Testament (1961) 147, 161. METZGER, B. M., The Early Versions of the New Testament (Oxford 1977) 41.

11:40 THEYSSEN, G. W. "Unbelief" in the New Testament (Rüschlikon 1965) 49ff. DELLING, G. Wort und Werk Jesu im Johannes-Evangelium (1966) 16, 37, 44, 69. CADMAN, W. H. The Open Heaven (1969) G. B. Caird ed., 36, 37, 161, 205. THUESING, W. Die Erhöhung und Verherrlichung Jesu im Johannesevangelium (1970) 229-31, 245f.

11:41-54 SMTIH, M. Clement of Alexandria and a secret Gospel of Mark (1973) 153, 155f., 222, 224.

11:43-45.47-48 ORIGENES, Das Evangelium nach Johannes (1959) R. Gögler ed., 340-48.

11:41.43-44 BETZ, H. D. Lukian vom Samosata und das Neue Testament (1961) 71, 155, 157.

11:41-42 ODEBERG, H. The Fourth Gospel (1968) 334. JEREMIAS, J., Neutestamentliche Theologie I (1971) 68, 70, 72, 186. WILCOX, M., "The 'Prayer' of Jesus in John XI.41b-42" NTS 24 (1977) 128-32.

11:41 PALLIS, A., Notes on St. John and the Apocalypse (London 1928) 26-27. HANSON, A. T., The New Testament Interpretation of Scripture (London 1980) 167. BERGER, K., "Das Buch der Jubiläen" in: JüdSchr II/3 (1981) 453n.11a.

11:42 KNOX, W. L. The Sources of the Synoptic Gospels (1957) II 8. WILES, M. F. The Spiritual Gospel (1960) 134, 145, 146.

BAUMERT, N. Täglich Sterben und Auferstehen: Der Literalisnn von 2 Kor 4,12 - 5,10 (München 1973) 101.

11:43 NICKELS, P. Targum and New Testament (1967) 56.

11:44ff WILKENS, W. Die Entstehungsgeschichte des vierten Evangeliums (1958) 55, 56, 57, 58, 59, 60, 61, 62.

11:44 OSBORNE, B. "A Folded Napkin in an Empty Tomb: John 11:44 and 20:7 Again," HeyJ 14 (4, 1973) 437-40. "Bestattung" in: TRE 5 (1980) 736.

11:45ff NICOL, W. The Sēmeia in the Fourth Gospel (1972) 100f.

11:45-57 HAENCHEN, E., Das Johannesevangelium (Tübingen 1980) 421 (lit!).

11:45-54 SASS, G. Die Auferweckung des Lazarus (1967) 58-62. BECKER, J., Das Evangelium nach Johannes (Gütersloh/ Würzburg 1979) 364-65 (lit!).

11:45-53 WILKENS, W. Zeichen und Werke (Zürich 1969) 43-44. RIVKIN, E., A Hidden Revolution (Nashville 1978) 100-11.

11:45.46.47-54 SAASS, G. Die Auferweckung des Lazarus (1967) 58-59, 59-62.

11:45 CRIBBS, F. L., "The Agreements that Exist between John and Acts" in: C. H. Talbert (ed.) Persepectives in Luke-Acts (Danville 1978) 58.

11:46-12:11 TEMPLE, S., The Core of the Fourth Gospel (London 1975) 193-99.

11:47ff WILKENS, W. Die Entstehungsgeschichte des vierten Evangeliums (1958) 63, 64. BAMMEL, E. The Trial of Jesus (1970) 32f.

11:47-57 MOHR, T. A., Markus und Johannespassion (Zürich 1982) 125-28.

11:47-53 DODD, C. H. "The Prophecy of Caiaphas (John xi 47-53)," in: Neutestamentica et Patristica (1962) 134-43. Also in: More New Testament Studies (1968) 58-68. DAUER, A. Die Passionsgeschichte im Johannesevangelium (1972) 88, 247, 339. GRIMM, W., "Die Preisgabe eines Menschen zur Rettung des Volkes. Priesterliche Tradition bei Johannes und Josephus" in: O. Betz et al. (eds.) Josephus-Studien. FS. O. Michel (Göttingen 1974) 133-46. APPOLD, M. L., The Oneness Motif in the Fourth Gospel (Tübingen 1976) 237-45. VELLANICKAL, M., The Divine Sonship of Christians in the Johannine Writings (Rome 1977) 214-24. GRIMM, W., "Das Opfer eines Menschen. Eine Auslegung von John 11, 47-53" in: G. Müller (ed.) Israel hat dennoch Gott zum Trost. FS. S.

Ben-Chorin (Trier 1978) 61-82. BERGMANN, W. und NEHB, H., in: P. Krusche et al. (eds.) Predigtstudien für das Kirchenjahr 1982-1983 V/1 (Stuttgart 1982) 166-72.

11:47-52 BRAUN, F.-M. "Quatre 'Signes' Johanniques de L'Unité Chrétienne," NTS 9 (1962-1963) 148f.

11:47-50 WILKENS, W., Zeichen und Werke (Zürich 1969) 72.

11:47-48 LADD, G. E. A Theology of the New Testament (1974) 139, 140, 182.

11:47 BERGMEIER, R., Glaube als Gabe nach Johannes (Stuttgart 1980) 230, 267n.501.

11:48 PANCARO, S., The Law in the Fourth Gospel (Leiden 1975) 118-22, 124, 318.

11:49-52 FLEW, R. N. Jesus and His Church (1956) 178n. PANCARO, S., The Law in the Fourth Gospel (Leiden 1975) 122-25. SCHWEIZER, E., Heiliger Geist (Berlin 1978) 134. BERGMEIER, R., Glaube als Gabe nach Johannes (Stuttgart 1980) 13.

11:49-51 KUHL, J. Die Sendung Jesu und der Kirche nach dem Johannes-Evangelium (1967) 122f.

11:49-50 GRILL, J. Untersuchungen über die Entstehung des vierten Evangeliums II (1923) 14f. MARZOTTO, D. " 'Un solo unico pastore' (Gv. 10,16)" ScuC 103 (1975) 834-43.

11:49.54-55.57 ORIGENES, Das Evangelium nach Johannes (1959) R. Gögler ed., 349-60.

11:49 LANGBRANDTNER, W., Weltferner Gott oder Gott der Liebe (Frankfurt a.M/Bern/Las Vegas 1977) 44-46.

11:50-52 SCHELKLE, K, H. Die Passion Jesu in der Verkündigung des Neuen Testaments (1949) 30f. MEEKS., W. A. The Prophet-King, Moses Traditions and the Johannine Christology (1967) 96-97. PANCARO, S., " 'People of God' in St. John's Gospel" NTS 16 (2, 1970) 114-29.

11:50 SMIH, M. Tannaitic Parallels to the Gospels (1968) 6 b n 5*. BAMMEL, E. The Trial of Jesus (1970) 41ff. DERRETT, J. D. M. Law in the New Testament (1970) 419-23. MUELLER, T. Das Heilsgeschehen im Johannesevangelium n.d., 59-60. BERGMEIER, R., Glaube als Gabe nach Johannes (Stuttgart 1980) 45n.318.

11:51ff DENNEY, J. The Death of Christ (³1956) 143. HAHN, F. Das Verständnis der Mission im Neuen Testament (²1965) 138. DAUER, A. Die Passionsgeschichte im Johannesevangelium (1972) 112, 198, 292, 340.

11:51-52 LEISTNER, R., Antijudaismus im Johannesevangelium? (Bern 1974) 149. OLSSON, B., Structure and Meaning in the Fourth Gospel (Lund 1974) 244, 246-47, 262-65. "Abendmahl" in: TRE 1 (1977) 57. BERGMEIER, R., Glaube als Gabe nach Johannes (Stuttgart 1980) 22ff,26-27, 42n.264, 44n.312, 45n.316. 318ff, 46n.328, 74, 223, 271n.568, 273n.612.

11:51 FOERSTER, W., "Der Heilige Geist im Spätjudentum," NTS 8 (1961-1962) 120f. HAHN, F. Christologische Hoheitstitel (1963) 355. KRAMER, W. Christos Kyrios Gottessohn (1963) § 4c. FRIEDRICH, G., "Beobachtungen zur messianischen Hohepriestererwartung in den Synoptikern" in: Auf das Wort kommt es an (Göttingen 1978) 83.

11:52 FLEW, R. N. Jesus and His Church (1956) 177n. SCHWEIZER, E. Gemeinde und Gemeinde-Ordnung im Neuen Testament (1959) § 11h. HENNECKE, E./SCHNEEMELCHER, W. Neutestamentliche Apokryphen (1964) I 128, 197. HAHN, F. Das Verständnis der Mission im Neuen Testament (²1965) 139. BRAUN, H. Qumran und NT II (1966) 127, 130. DELLING, G. Wort und Werk Jesu im Johannes-Evangelium (1966) 64, 67, 83, 132f. KUHL, J. Die Sendung Jesu und der Kirche nach dem Johannes-Evangelium (1967) 198, 222-24. BEUTLER, J. Martyria (1972) 346f, 349. APPOLD, M. L., The Oneness Motif in the Fourth Gospel (Tübingen 1976) 246-60. DELLING, G., "Die 'Söhne (Kinder) Gottes' im Neuen Testament" in: R. Schnackenburg et al. (eds.) Die Kirche des Anfangs (Freiburg/ Basel/Wien 1978) 626-28. BERGMEIER, R., Glaube als Gabe nach Johannes (Stuttgart 1980) 23-27.

11:54 DALMAN, G. Orte und Wege Jesu (1967) 231f. HEISE, J., Bleiben. μένειν in den Johanneischen Schriften (Tübingen 1967) 47-50. SCHWANK, B., "Efraim in Joh 11,54" EuA 51 (1975) 346-51. von WAHLDE, U. C. "The Johannine 'Jews': A Critical Survey" NTS 28 (1982) 51-52.

11:55-12:50 STRATHMANN, H. Das Evangelium des Johannes (1955) 193.

11:55-12:11 BECKER, J., Das Evangelium nach Johannes (Gütersloh/ Würzburg 1979) 371 (lit!).

11:55ff WILKENS, W. Die Entstehunsgeschichte des vierten Evangeliums (1958) 64.

11:55-57 SASS, G. Die Auferweckung des Lazarus (1967) 62-63.

12 BECKER, H., Die Reden des Johannesevangeliums und der Stil der gnostischen Offenbarungsrede (Göttingen 1956) 91-94. WIKENHAUSER, A. Das Evangelium nach Johannes (1957) 241f. SMITH, D. M. The Composition and Order of the Fourth Gospel (1965) 106, 141, 158, 166, 167, 168, 170. TRITES, A. A., The New Testament Concept of Witness (Cambridge 1977) 110-12. CLARK, K. W., "Today's Problems with the Critical Text of the New Testament" in: The Gentile Bias and other Essays (Leiden 1980) 122-23.

12:1ff REICKE, B. Diakonie, Festfreude und Zelos (1951) 151f. DEEKS, D., "The Structure of the Fourth Gospel," NTS 15 (1968-1969) 124ff.

12:1-11 PALLIS, A., Notes on St. John and the Apocalypse (London 1928) 27-28. MAURER, G. Ignatius von Antiochien und das Johannesevangelium (1949) 18f. VAWTER, B. "The Johannine Sacramentary," TS 17 (1956) 151-66.

12:1-9 KUEMMEL, W. G. Einleitung in das Neue Testament (1973) 166f.

12:1-8 RUCKSTUHL, E. Die literarische Einheit des Johannesevangeliums (1951) 217f. DOERNE, M. Er kommt auch noch heute (1961) 65-67. KOCH, G. GPM 17 (1962-1963) 152ff. BAILEY, J. A. The Traditions Common to the Gospels of Luke and John (1963) 1-8. BORNKAMM, G. in: Herr, tue meine Lippen auf Bd. 3 (1964) 168ff. HAHN, F. Das Verständnis der Mission im Neuen Testament (²1965) 101. STROBEL, A. Erkenntnis und Bekenntnis der Sünde in neutestamentlicher Zeit (1968) 59. FUERST, W. GPM 23 (2, 1968) 143-48. DERRETT, J. D. M. Law in the New Testament (1970) 266-75. FORTNA, R. T. The Gospel of Signs (1970) 149-52. LOHSE, E. et al., eds., Der Ruf Jesu und die Antwort der Gemeinde (1970) 247-58. ROLOFF, J. Das Kerygma und der irdische Jesus (1970) 220-23. NICOL, W. The Sēmeia in the Fourth Gospel (1972) 11, 15, 72f. LÖWE, H. und ZIPPERT, C., in: P. Krusche et al. (eds.) Predigtstudien für das Kirchenjahr 1974-1975 III/1 (Stuttgart 1974) 173-81. DAHINTEN, G., in: GPM 29 (1975) 179-85. FEUILLET, A., "Les deux onctions faites sur Jésus, et Marie-Magdeleine. Contribution à l'études des rapports entre les Synoptiques et le quatrième évangile" RThom 75 (1975) 357-94. TEMPLE, S., The Core of the Fourth Gospel (London 1975) 196-99. RIST, J. M., On the Independence of Matthew and Mark (Cambridge 1978) 83-84. STAGG, E. and F., Women in the World of Jesus (Philadelphia 1978) 117, 120-21, 238-39. SWIDLER, L. Biblical Affirmations of Woman (Philadelphia 1979) 196, 220, 224, 233, 240. HAENCHEN, E.,

Das Johannesevangelium (Tübingen 1980) 431-32 (lit!). HAN-SON, A. T., The New Testament Interpretation of Scripture (London 1980) 118-21, 168. KRAFT, H., Die Entstehung des Christentums (Darmstadt 1981) 120, 193-95. MOHR, T. A., Markus- und Johannespassion (Zürich 1982) 129-47.

12:1-3 MOHR, T. A., Markus- und Johannespassion (Zürich 1982) 130-35.

12:1-2 SWIDLER, L., Biblical Affirmations of Woman (Philadelphia 1979) 311.

12:1 BRAUN, H. Qumran und NT II (1966) 45, 49f. BÖHLIG, A., Die Gnosis III: Der Manichäismus (Zürich/München 1980) 338n.93.

12:2 SCHLATTER, A. Johannes der Täufer (1956) 29f. "Aramäisch" in: TRE 3 (1978) 608. SWIDLER, L., Biblical Affirmations of Woman (Philadelphia 1979) 311. BERGMEIER, R., Glaube als Gabe nach Johannes (Stuttgart 1980) 214.

12:3-8 SCHNIEWIND, J., Die Parallelperikopen bei Lukas and Johannes (Darmstadt 1958 = 1914) 21-26.

12:3-4 SANDERS, J. N., "Those Whom Jesus Loved," NTS 1 (1954-1955) 39ff.

12:3 KOEBERT, R. "Nardos pistike - Kostnarde," Biblica 29 (1948) 279-81. BRUNS, J. E. "A Note on Jn 12,3," CBQ 28 (2, 1966) 219-22. BLACK, M. An Aramaic Approach to the Gospels and Acts (1967) 223f. PRETE, B.,"Un'aporia giovannea: il testo di Giov. 12,3," RivB 25 (1977) 357-73. SWIDLER, L., Biblical Affirmations of Woman (Philadelphia 1979) 196.

12:4-6 MOHR, T. A., Markus- und Johannespassion (Zürich 1982) 135-36.

12:7 RUDOLPH, K. Die Mandäer II (1961) 416, 5. MOHR, T. A., Markus- und Johannespassion (Zürich 1982) 136-42.

12:8 METZGER, B. M., The Early Versions of the New Testament (Oxford 1977) 134.

12:9 LEE, G. M., "John XII: 9 ὁ ὄχλος πολύς" NovT 22 (1980) 95.

12:10 PALLIS, A., Notes on St. John and the Apocalypse (London 1928) 28.

12:11-16 LEUNG TSUNG-YAT, T., " 'Memory' in John's Gospel" Theology Annual 2 (Hong Kong 1978) 3-17.

12:12ff HAHN, F. Christologische Hoheitstitel (1963) 87.

12:12-50 TEMPLE, S., The Core of the Fourth Gospel (London 1975) 199-212.

12:12-26 SCHMIDT, R., in: GPM 33 (1979) 163-70.

12:12-25 SCHULZ, H./DIENST, K. "Palmarum: Johannes 12:12-25," in: Predigtstudien (1972-1973) E. Lange ed., 177-83.

12:12-20 FREED, E. D. "The Entry into Jerusalem in the Gospel of John," JBL 80 (4, 1961) 329-38.

12:12-19 LEIVESTAD, R. Christ the Conqueror (1954) 34ff. BORN-KAMM, G. GPM 9 (1954-1955) 96ff. SCHNIEWIND, J., Die Parallelperikopen bei Lukas und Johannes (Hildesheim 1958) 26-28. SOUCEK, GPM 15 (1960-1961) 107ff. BAILEY, J. A. The Traditions Common to the Gospels of Luke and John (1963) 22-28. MEEKS, W. A. The Prophet-King, Moses Traditions and the Johannine Christology (1967) 83-87. BARTNICKI, R., "Tekst Za 9,9-10 w perykopach Mt 21,1-11 i J 12,12-19" SThV 14 (1976) 47-66. de JONGE, M., Jesus: Stranger from Heaven and Son of God (Missoula 1977) 59-60. RIVKIN, E., A. Hidden Revolution (Nashville 1978) 101. BECKER, J., Das Evangelium nach Johannes (Gütersloh/Würzburg 1979) 376 (lit!). BARTNICKI, R., "Redakcyjne cele ewangelistow w Lk 19,28-40 i J 12,12-19" SThV 18 (1980) 49-82. HAENCHEN, E., Das Johannesevangelium (Tübingen 1980) 442 (lit!). MAERZ, C.-P., "Siehe, dein König kommt zu dir . . . " Eine traditionsgeschichtliche Untersuchung zur Einzugsperikope (Leipzig 1980). KRAFT, H., Die Entstehung des Christentums (Darmstadt 1981) 183-87.

12:12-16 BRAUN, H. Qumran und NT II (1966) 45.

12:12-15 FORTNA, R. T. The Gospel of Signs (1970) 152-55. OLSSON, B., Structure and Meaning in the Fourth Gospel (Lund 1974) 246, 263-66, 280.

12:12-13 TEMPLE, S., The Core of the Fourth Gospel (London 1975) 201-203.

12:13 DELLING, G. Die Zueignung des Heils in der Taufe (1961) 42. WELLS, G., The Jesus of the Early Christians (1971) 100-101. DAUER, A. Die Passionsgeschichte im Johannesevangelium (1972) 123, 184, 301. CRIBBS, F. L., in: SBL Seminar Papers 2 (1973) G. MacRae ed., 4. UNTERGASSMAIR, F. G., Im Namen Jesu: Der Namensbegriff im Johannesevangelium (Stuttgart 1973) 40-46. REIM, G. Studien zum Alttestamentlichen Hintergrund des Johannesevangeliums (Cambridge 1974) 26-29, 89-90, 92-93. PANCARO, S., The Law in the Fourth Gospel (Leiden 1975) 244, 296, 297ff, 300, 330. HANSON, A. T., The New Testament Interpretation of Scripture (London 1980) 157, 167.

12:14ff STRECKER, G. Der Weg der Gerechtigkeit (1962) 75₃.
ROTHFUCHS, W. Die Erfüllungszitate des Matthäus-Evangeliums (1969) 164-66.

12:14-26 SAUTER, G., "Leben in der Einheit von Tod und Leben" EvTh 41 (1981) 55.

12:14-16 BOHREN, R. Predigtlehre (1971) 186f.

12:14-15 GRILL, J. Untersuchungen über die Entstehung des vierten Evangeliums II (1923) 208f. REIM, G., Studien zum Alttestamentlichen Hintergrund des Johannesevangeliums (Cambridge 1974) 29-32, 90-93. MOHR, T. A., Markus und Johannespassion (Zürich 1982) 60-63.

12:15 LINDARS, B. New Testament Apologetic (1961) 26, 98, 113f. HAHN, F. Christologische Hoheitstitel (1963) 187. BRUCE, F. F., The Time is Fulfilled (Exeter 1978) 51-52. KRAFT, H., Die Entstehung des Christentums (Darmstadt 1981) 121-22.

12:16 ROBINSON, J. M. Kerygma und historischer Jesus (1960) 71. BRUCE, F. F. "The Book of Zechariah and the Passion Narrative," BJRL 43 (1960-1961) 347. DELLING, G. Die Taufe im Neuen Testament (1963) 93. METZGER, B. M., The Early Versions of the New Testament (Oxford 1977) 369n.1, 389.

12:17 BROX, N. Zeuge und Märtyrer (1961) 84f. BEUTLER, J. Martyria (1972) 212ff., 282.

12:18 METZGER, B. M., The Early Versions of the New Testament (Oxford 1977) 390.

12:19 SCHNIEWIND, J., Die Parallelperikopen bei Lukas und Johannes (Darmstadt 1958 = 1914) 26-28. BLACK, M. An Aramaic Approach to the Gospels and Acts (1967) 103f. HANSON, A. T., The New Testament Interpretation of Scripture (London 1980) 168-70.

12:20ff HAHN, F. Das Verständnis der Mission im Neuen Testament (²1965) 138.

12:20-36 BLANK, J. Krisis (1964) 262. BECKER, J., Das Evangelium nach Johannes (Gütersloh/Würzburg 1979) 380-81 (lit!). HAENCHEN, E., Das Johannesevangelium (Tübingen 1980) 444-45 (lit!). LEIDIG, E., Jesu Gespräch mit der Samaritanerin (Basel 1981) 227-30.

12:20-33 ARVEDSON, T. Das Mysterium Christi (1937) 127f. WILKENS, W., Zeichen und Werke (Zürich 1969) 102-204. WREGE, H.-T. "Jesusgeschichte und Jüngergeschick," in: Der Ruf Jesu und die Antwort der Gemeinde (1970) E. Lohse et al., eds., 259-88. BERGMEIER, R., Glaube als Gabe nach Johannes (Stuttgart 1980) 271n.568.

12:20-28 WIKENHAUSER, A. Das Evangelium nach Johannes (1957) 236f.

12:20-26 MORGAN, G. C. The Parables and Metaphors of Our Lord (1943) 324ff. DIEM, H. in: Herr, tue meine Lippen auf Bd. 3 (1964) G. Eichholz ed., 225ff. KAESEMANN, E. Exegetische Versuche und Besinnungen (1964) I 254-57. TEMPLE, S., The Core of the Fourth Gospel (London 1975) 205-208. HERBERT, K., in: GPM 33 (1979) 151-57.

12:20-24.27-32 WILKENS, W. Die Entstehungsgeschichte des vierten Evangeliums (1958) 112-14.

12:20-22 KRAFT, H., Die Entstehung des Christentums (Darmstadt 1981) 228.

12:20 MOORE, W. E. "Sir, We Wish to See Jesus-Was this an Occasion of Temptation?" SJTh 20 (1, 1967) 75-93. BEUTLER, J. Martyria (1972) 241, 346f.

12:21ff GLASSON, T. F. Moses in the Fourth Gospel (1963) 35, 72f.

12:21 HENGEL, M. Judentum und Hellenismus (1969) 347. ET.: Judaism and Hellenism (1974) I 190. "Aramäisch" in: TRE 3 (1978) 604.

12:23-36 ODEBERG, H. The Fourth Gospel (1968) 334f.

12:23-33 MUELLER, T. Das Heilsgeschehen im Johannesevangelium (n.d.) 60-62, 90.

12:23-32 LEON-DUFOUR, X. "Trois Chiasmes Johanniques," NTS 7 (3, 1961) 249-55. LEON-DUFOUR, X., "Jésus à Gethsémani: Essai de lecture synchronique" SciE 31 (1979) 251-68.

12:23-28 SCHILLEBEECKX, E., Christ: the Christian Experience in the Modern World (London 1980) 397-99, GT; Christus und die Christen (Freiburg/Basel/Wien 1977) 383-85.

12:23-26 DAVIES, W. D., The Sermon on the Mount (Cambridge 1966) 120.

12:23 TAYLOR, V., Jesus and His Sacrifice (1948) 235-37, 241f., 256. SCHULZ, S., Untersuchungen zur Menschensohn-Christologie im Johannesevangelium (Göttingen 1957) 119. ROBINSON, J. M. Kerygma und historischer Jesus (1960) 71. WILES, M. F. The Spiritual Gospel (1960) 83-84. KUHL, J. Die Sendung Jesu und der Kirche nach dem Johannes-Evangelium (1967) 110-12. CADMAN, W. H. The Open Heaven (1969) G. B. Caird ed., 36-38, 62, 98. THUESING, W. Die Erhöhung und Verherrlichung Jesu im Johannesevangelium (1970) 75f., 105-107. LADD, G. E. A Theology of the New Testament (1974) 231, 244, 245, 249, 275. REIM, G. Studien zum

Alttestamentlichen Hintergrund des Johannesevangeliums (Cambridge 1974) 253-54. BERGMEIER, R., Glaube als Gabe nach Johannes (Stuttgart 1980) 40n.218.

12:24-33 SCHWEIZER, E., "Discipleship and Belief in Jesus as Lord from Jesus to the Hellenistic Church," NTS 2 (1955-1956) 94f.

12:24-26 SCHWEIZER, E. Erniedrigung und Erhöhung bei Jesus und seinen Nachfolgern (1962) § 11ams. LANGBRANDTNER, W., Weltferner Gott oder Gott der Liebe (Frankfurt a.m./Bern/Las Vegas 1977) 50-56.

12:24-25 DAVIES, W. D., The Sermon on the Mount (Cambridge 1966) 121-22. KUHL, J. Die Sendung Jesu und der Kirche nach dem Johannes-Evangelium (1967) 200-202.

12:24.27 DENNEY, J. The Death of Christ (³1956) 143.

12:24 BONHOEFFER, A. Epiktet und das Neue Testament (1911) 56, 328. RASCO, A. "Christus, granum frumenti (Jo 12,24)," VerDom 37 (1, 1959) 12-25; (2, 1959) 65-77. SCHWEIZER, E. Gemeinde und Gemeinde-Ordnung im Neuen Testament (1959) § 11d,g. HEISE, J. Bleiben (1967) 52-55. HUNTER, A. M. According to John (²1970) 83f. THUESING, W. Die Erhöhung und Verherrlichung Jesu im Johannesevangelium (1970) 101-107. MUELLER, T. Das Heilsgeschehen im Johannes-evangelium n.d., 60-62. NÖTSCHER, F., Altorientalischer und alttestamentlicher Auferstehungsglaube (Darmstadt 1970 = 1926) 301. "Amen" in: TRE 2 (1978) 399. RAYAN, S., The Holy Spirit: Heart of the Gospel and Christian Hope (New York 1978) 115. BERGMEIER, R., Glaube als Gabe nach Johannes (Stuttgart 1980) 43n.272, 44n.306, 273n.612.

12:25-26 LARSSON, E. Christus als Vorbild (1962) 43f, 78f., 105. VELLANICKAL, M., " 'Discipleship' according to the Gospel of John" Jeevadhara 10 (1980) 131-47.

12:25 DODD, C. H., "Some Johannine 'Herrenworte' with Parallels in the Synoptic Gospels," NTS 2 (1955-1956) 78ff. ROBINSON, J. M. Kerygma und historischer Jesus (1960) 165. LA-ZURE, N., Les Valeurs Morales de la Théologie Johannique (Paris 1965) 219. DELLING, G. Wort und Werk Jesu im Johannesevangelium (1966) 11, 58, 142, 144. LADD, G. E. A Theology of the New Testament (1974) 232, 257, 302. HOFF-MANN, P. und EID, V., Jesus von Nazareth und eine christliche Moral (Freiburg/Basel/Wien 1975) 212-14. LATTKE, M., Einheit im Wort (München 1975) 12-13.

12:26 SCHULZ, A. Nachfolge und Nachahmen (1962) 163-67. LA-ZURE, N., Les Valeurs Morales de la Théologie Johannique (Paris 1965) 34-36. OTOMO, Y., Nachfolge Jesu und Anfänge der Kirche im Neuen Testament (1970) 131f. THUESING, W. Die Erhöhung und Verherrlichung Jesu im Johannesevangelium (1970) 129-32. BERGMEIER, R., Glaube als Gabe nach Johannes (Stuttgart 1980) 43n.272, 235.

12:27ff MOHR, T. A., Markus- und Johannespassion (Zürich 1982) 245-47.

12:27-30 BOMAN, T. Die Jesus-Ueberlieferung im Lichte der neueren Volkskunde (1967) 208-21.

12:27-29 TEMPLE, S., The Core of the Fourth Gospel (London 1975) 208-209.

12:27-28 SCHELKLE, K. H. Die Passion Jesu in der Verkündigung des Neuen Testaments (1949) 120f. THUESING, W. Die Erhöhung und Verherrlichung Jesu im Johannesevangelium (1970) 75-77, 78-87, 193-198. KUHL, J. Die Sendung Jesu und der Kirche nach dem Johannes-Evangelium (1967) 110-12. DAUER, A. Die Passionsgeschichte im Johannesevangelium (1972) 283, 294, 321. DELLING, G. Der Kreuzestod Jesu in der urchristlichen Verkündigung (1972) 100f., 107f. KLAPPERT, B., "Arbeit Gottes und Mitarbeit des Menschen (Phil 2:6-11)" in: J. Moltmann (ed.) Recht auf Arbeit - Sinn der Arbeit (München 1979) 106, 108.

10:27.31 ORIGENES, Das Evangelium nach Johannes (1959) R. Gögler ed., 360-62.

12:27 PALLIS, A., Notes on St. John and the Apocalypse (London 1928) 29. WILES, M. F. The Spiritual Gospel (1960) 127-28, 146-47. FORTNA, R. T. The Gospel of Signs (1970) 82, 157, 229n. LEON-DUFOUR, X. " 'Père, fais-moi passer sain et sauf à travers cette heure' (Jean 12,27)," in: Neues Testament und Geschichte (1972) H. Baltensweiler/B. Reicke eds., 157-65. DORMEYER, D., Die Passion Jesu als Verhaltensmodell (Münster 1974) 134. DUNN, J. D. G., Jesus and the Spirit (London 1975) 18-19. BEUTLER, J., "Psalm 42/43 im Johannesevangelium" NTS 25 (1978) 33-57.

12:28 UNTERGASSMAIR, F. G., Im Namen Jesu: Der Namensbegriff im Johannesevangelium (Stuttgart 1973) 94-100. PORSCH, F., Pneuma und Wort (Frankfurt 1974) 77-79. BERGMEIER, R., Glaube als Gabe nach Johannes (Stuttgart 1980) 42n.272, 242n.117. EVANS, C. A., "The Voice from Heaven: A Note on John 12:28" CBQ 43 (1981) 405-408.

12:29 BERGMEIER, R., Glaube als Gabe nach Johannes (Stuttgart 180) 43n.272.

12:31-36 DE LA POTTERIE, I. "L'exaltation du Fils de l'homme (Jn. 12,31-36)," Gregorianum 49 (3, 1968) 460-78.

12:31-33 LEISTNER, R., Antijudaismus im Johannesevangelium? (Bern 1974) 148.

12:31-32 TAYLOR, V. Jesus and His Sacrifice (1948) 236f., 244f., 246-48. KAESEMANN, E. Exegetische Versuche und Besinnungen (1964) I 256. BEUTLER, J. Martyria (1972) 29, 252, 298, 314.

12:31 VOLZ, P. Die Eschatologie der jüdischen Gemeinde (1934) 87. BROWN, R. E., "The Qumran Scrolls and the Johannine Gospel and Epistles" CBQ 17 (1955) 403-19, 559-74; also in: K. Stendahl (ed.) The Scrolls and the New Testament (New York 1957) 189; GT: "Die Schriftrollen von Qumran und das Johannesevangelium und die Johannesbriefe" in: K. H. Rengstorf (ed.) Johannes und sein Evangelium (Darmstadt 1973) 497. HAHN, F. Das Verständnis der Mission im Neuen Testament (²1965) 137. BOUSSET, W. Die Religion des Judentums im Späthellenistischen Zeitalter (1966 = 1926) 253, 335. DELLING, G. Wort und Werk Jesu im Johannes-Evangelium (1966) 52f., 59, 82, 126. DAUER, A. Die Passionsgeschichte im Johannesevangelium (1972) 241f., 275, 294. LADD, G. E. A Theology of the New Testament (1974) 226, 227, 228, 231, 273, 303. MUELLER, T. Das Heilsgeschehen im Johannesevangelium n.d., 70-72. GALITIS, G., " 'Ho archōn tou kosmou toutou' (Io. 12, 31. 14, 30. 16, 11) ('The Prince of this World')" DBM 4 (1976) 59-67. RUDOLPH, K., Die Gnosis (Göttingen 1978) 324. BERGMEIER, R., Glaube als Gabe nach Johannes (Stuttgart 1980) 13, 39n.184, 151n.21, 204, 221, 256n.343. KRAFT, H., Die Entstehung des Christentums (Darmstadt 1981) 152.

12:32-34 SCHELKLE, K. H. Die Passion Jesu in der Verkündigung des Neuen Testaments (1949) 124f. ROBINSON, J. M. Kerygma und historischer Jesus (1960) 71.

12:32-33 HAMERTON-KELLY, R. G. Pre-Existence, Wisdom, and the Son of Man (1973) 198, 218, 220, 224, 231, 232, 233. BERGMEIER, R., Glaube als Gabe nach Johannes (Stuttgart 1980) 44n.306-307, 273n.612.

12:32.34 McNAMARA, M. The New Testament and the Palestinian Targum to the Pentateuch (1966) 145-49.

12:32 GRILL, J. Untersuchungen über die Entstehung des vierten Evangeliums II (1923) 54, 211, 216f. 234. BENOIT, P., "Paulinisme et Johannisme," NTS 9 (1962-1963) 203f. BRAUN, F.-M. Jean le Théologien (1966) 175-77. NICKELS, P. Targum and New Testament (1967) 57. THUESING, W. Die Erhöhung

und Verherrlichung Jesu im Johannesevangelium (1970) 22-29.
CAVALLIN, H. C. C. Life After Death (1974) 7, 2, n.18.
OLSSON, B., Structure and Meaning in the Fourth Gospel
(Lund 1974) 45, 72, 136, 246-48. BÜHNER, J.-A. Der Gesandte und sein Weg im 4. Evangelium (Tübingen 1977) 204-
205. METZGER, B. M., The Early Versions of the New Testament (Oxford 1977) 391. HANSON, A. T., The New Testament Interpretation of Scripture (London 1980) 168-70.

12:33   CASSIAN, B., "John 21," NTS 3 (1956-1957) 135f. SMITH,
D. M. The Composition and Order of the Fourth Gospel (1965)
150, 151, 166, 199n., 224, 236n., 237. McNAMARA, M. The
New Testament and the Palestinian Targum to the Pentateuch
(1966) 146f.

12:34-41   MÜLLER, H. M., und GOLDBACH, G., in: P. Krusche et al.
(eds.) Predigtstudien für das Kirchenjahr 1982-1983. V/1
(Stuttgart 1982) 105-13.

12:34-36.44-50   WILKENS, W. Die Entstehungsgeschichte des vierten Evangeliums (1958) 108-11.

12:34-36   SMITH, D. M. The Composition and Order of the Fourth Gospel (1965) 143, 156, 160, 161, 166, 167, 168, 260.

12:34   KNOX, W. L. The Sources of the Synoptic Gospels II (1957)
143. SCHULZ, S., Untersuchungen zur Menschensohn-Christologie im Johannesevangelium (Göttingen 1957) 119-20. VAN
UNNIK, W. C. "The Quotation from the Old Testament in John
12:34," NovTest 3 (3, 1959) 174-79. BLAIR, E. P. Jesus in
the Gospel of Matthew (1960) 68. HAHN, F. Christologische
Hoheitstitel (1963) 53, 130, 224. BOUSSET, W. Die Religion
des Judentums im Späthellenistischen Zeitalter (1966 = 1926)
268. HEISE, J. Bleiben (1967) 70-71. NICKELS, P. Targum
and New Testament (1967) 57. LEIVESTAD, R. "Der Apo-
kalyptische Menschensohn ein theologisches Phantom," ASThI
VI (1968) H. Kosmala, ed., 49-105. SMALLEY, S. S., "The
Johannine Son of Man Sayings," NTS 15 (1968-1969) 297ff.
CAVALLIN, H. C. C. Life After Death (1974) 7, 2n18. LADD,
G. E. A Theology of the New Testament (1974) 139, 244, 245.
VAN UNNIK, W. C., "The Quotation from the Old Testament
in John XII,34" in: Sparsa Collecta I (Leiden 1973) 64-69.
REIM, G., Studien zum Alttestamentlichen Hintergrund des
Johannesevangeliums (Cambridge 1974) 32-34, 89-95. MED-
ALA, S., "Tradycja o wiecznosci Mesjasza i redakcja J 12,34"
RBL 28 (1975) 199-216. PANCARO, S., The Law in the Fourth
Gospel (Leiden 1975) 332, 336-39, 515, 516. de JONGE, M.,
Jesus: Stranger from Heaven and Son of God (Missoula 1977)

94-96. McNEIL, B., "The Quotation at John XII 34" NovT 19 (1977) 22-33. BERGMEIER, R., Glaube als Gabe nach Johannes (Stuttgart 1980) 13. CHILTON, B., "John xii 34 and Targum Isaiah lii 13" NovT 22 (1980) 176-78.

12:35-41 KRECK, W. in: Herr, tue meine Lippen auf Bd. 3 (1964) G. Eichholz ed., 53ff. WEBER, O. Predigtmeditationen (1967) 20-24.

12:35-36 BRAUN, H. Qumran und NT II (1966) 120f., 126, 131, 135, 138, 140. OTTO, G. Denken - um zu glauben (1970) 44-47. HUNTER, A. M. According to John (²1970) 83. VELLAN-ICKAL, M., The Divine Sonship of Christians in the Johannine Writings (Rome 1977) 157-60. BERGMEIER, R., Glaube als Gabe nach Johannes (Stuttgart 1980) 211, 231, 257n.371.

12:35 KAESEMANN, E. Exegetische Versuche und Besinnungen (1964) I 181. LEROY, H., " 'Wer sein Leben gewinnen will . . .' Erlöste Existenz heute" FZThPh 25 (1978) 171-86.

12:36-43 de JONGE, M., Jesus: Stranger from Heaven and Son of God (Missoula 1977) 120-22. LANGBRANDTNER, W., Weltferner Gott oder Gott der Liebe (Frankfurt a.M./Bern/Las Vegas 1977) 71-76. SEGOVIA, F., "The Love and Hatred of Jesus and Johannine Sectarianism" CBQ 43 (1981) 268-70.

12:36 BROWN, R. E., "The Qumran Scrolls and the Johannine Gospel and Epistles" CBQ 17 (1955) 403-19, 559-74: also in: K. Stendahl (ed.) The Scrolls and the New Testament (New York 1957) 194; GT: "Die Schriftrollen von Qumran and das Johannesevangelium und die Johannesbriefe" in: K. H. Rengstorf (ed.) Johannes und sein Evangelium (Darmstadt 1973) 505.

12:37ff HAHN, F. Das Verständnis der Mission im Neuen Testament (²1965) 136.

12:37-50 BLANK, J. Krisis (1964) 294. HAENCHEN, E., Das Johannesevangelium (Tübingen 1980) 450 (lit!).

12:37-43 BECKER, J., Das Evangelium nach Johannes (Gütersloh/Würzburg 1979) 408 (lit!). BERGMEIER, R., Glaube als Gabe nach Johannes (Stuttgart 1980) 211, 228-31. SCHILLE-BEECKX, E., Christ: the Christian Experience in the Modern World (London 1980) 399-400; GT: Christus und die Christen (Freiburg/Basel/Wien 1977) 385-86.

12:37-41 WILKENS, W., Zeichen und Werke (Zürich 1969) 117-18. WALTER, L., L'incroyance des croyants selon saint Jean (Paris 1976) 107-14.

12:37-38 FORTNA, R. T. The Gospel of Signs (1970) 199.

12:37 KNOX, W. L. The Sources of the Synoptic Gospels II (1957)
8. DELLING, G. Wort und Werk Jesu im Johannes-Evangelium (1966) 16, 43f., 74. SCHOTTROFF, L. Der Glaube und die feindliche Welt (1970) 250-53, 265f. NICOL, W. The Sēmeia in the Fourth Gospel (1972) 3, 39, 101, 115, 132.

12:38-40 HANSON, A. T., The New Testament Interpretation of Scripture (London 1980) 158-59.

12:38 DENNEY, J. The Death of Christ (^{3}1956) 144. HENNECKE, E./SCHNEEMELCHER, W. Neutestamentliche Apokryphen (1964) I 145. ROTHFUCHS, W. Die Erfüllungszitate des Matthäus-Evangeliums (1969) 155. REIM, G., Studien zum Alttestamentlichen Hintergrund des Johannesevangeliums (Cambridge 1974) 34-37, 93-94.

12:39-41 SCHNACKENBURG, R. "John 12, 39-41. Zur christologischen Schriftauslegung des vierten Evangelisten," in: Neues Testament und Geschichte (1972) H. Baltensweiler/B. Reicke eds., 167-77. SCHNACKENBURG, R., Aufsätze und Studien zum Neuen Testament (Leipzig 1973) 364-75.

12:39-40 WILES, M. F. The Spiritual Gospel (1960) 109-11. BERGMEIER, R., Glaube als Gabe nach Johannes (Stuttgart 1980) 211, 226, 228ff, 264n.484, 266n.492.

12:40-41 HESSE, F. Das Verstockungsproblem im Alten Testament (1955) 3, 4, 5, 23, 64f.

12:40 LINDARS, B. New Testament Apologetic (1961) 159-61. WAINWRIGHT, A. W. The Trinity in the New Testament (1962) 89-90. ROTHFUCHS, W. Die Erfüllungszitate des Matthäus-Evangeliums (1969) 155-57. REIM, G., Studien zum Alttestamentlichen Hintergrund des Johannesevangeliums (Cambridge 1974) 90-94. METZGER, B. M., The Early Versions of the New Testament (Oxford 1977) 391. BLOCH, R., "Midrash" in: W. S. Green (ed.) Approaches to Ancient Judaism: Theory and Practice (Missoula 1978) 49.

12:41-50 KUHL, J. Die Sendung Jesu und der Kirche nach dem Johannes-Evangelium (1967) 77f.

12:41 DUPONT, J. Essais sur la Christologie de Saint Jean (1951) 269-73, 278. McNAMARA, M. The New Testament and the Palestinian Targum to the Pentateuch (1966) 41. BLACK, M. An Aramaic Approach to the Gospels and Acts (1967) 78f. "Abendmahlsfeier" in: TRE 1 (1977) 244. BERGMEIER, R., Glaube als Gabe nach Johannes (Stuttgart 1980) 17, 228, 230.

12:42-50 BERGMEIER, R., Glaube als Gabe nach Johannes (Stuttgart 1980) 211-12.

12:42-43 WALTER, L., L'incroyance des croyants selon saint Jean (Paris 1976) 114-17. RIVKIN, E., A Hidden Revolution (Nashville 1978) 101-103.

12:42 GRILL, J. Untersuchungen über die Entstehung des vierten Evangeliums II (1923) 16, 17, 20, 361f. MARTYN, J. L., The Gospel of John in Christian History (New York 1978) 75, 77, 87, 92, 104, 109, 120. BERGMEIER, R., Glaube als Gabe nach Johannes (Stuttgart 1980) 246n.181.

12:43 LATTKE, M., Einheit im Wort (München 1975) 12.

12:44-50 TILLICH, P. Das Neue Sein (1959) 97-99. KRAUSE, G. GPM 19 (4, 1964) 45-52. SMITH, D. M. The Composition and Order of the Fourth Gospel (1965) 21, 117, 156, 157, 161, 166, 167, 168. DIEM, H. in: Hören und Fragen Bd. 5, 3 (1967) G. Eichholz/A. Falkenroth eds., 77ff. ODEBERG, H. The Fourth Gospel (1968) 335f. HENKYS, J. GPM 25 (4, 1970) 66-72. JOHNSTON, G. The Spirit-Paraclete in the Gospel of John (1970) 67, 157, 159, 160, 170. KRECK, W. GPM 29 (1, 1974) 87-92. HELBIG, D. und GERLACH, W., in: P. Krusche et al. (eds.) Predigtstudien für das Kirchenjahr 1974-1975 III/1 (Stuttgart 1974) 86-92. HERTEL, F. und BÜRKLE, M., in: P. Krusche et al. (eds.) Predigtstudien für das Kirchenjahr 1976-1977. V/1 (Stuttgart 1976) 62-67. KLAUS, B. und ÖFFNER, E., in: P. Krusche et al. (eds.) Predigtstudien für das Kirchenjahr 1976-1977. V/1 (Stuttgart 1976) 73-82. BÜHNER, J.-A. Der Gesandte und sein Weg im 4. Evangelium (Tübingen 1977) 172-74. von der OSTEN-SACKEN, P., in: GPM 31 (1976-1977) 48-55. BECKER, J., Das Evangelium nach Johannes (Gütersloh/Würzburg 1979) 413 (lit!). BORGEN, P., "The Use of Tradition in John 12, 44-50" NTS 26 (1979) 18-35. SCHILLEBEECKX, E., Christ: the Christian Experience in the Modern World (London 1980) 399-400; GT: Christus und die Christen (Freiburg/Basel/Wien 1977) 385-86.

12:44-46 ORIGENES, Das Evangelium nach Johannes (1959) R. Gögler ed., 364-66.

12:44-45 HAHN, F. Das Verständnis der Mission im Neuen Testament (^{2}1965) 141.

12:44 DELLING, G. Wort und Werk Jesu im Johannes-Evangelium (1966) 41f.

12:45 WILES, M. F. The Spiritual Gospel (1960) 91-92. BÜHNER, J.-A., Der Gesandte und sein Weg im 4. Evangelium (Tübingen 1977) 383-85.

12:46-50 IWAND, H.-J. Predigt-Meditationen (1964) 54-56.

12:46-48 BRAUN, F.-M. Jean le Théologien (1966) 121f.

12:46-47 BÜHNER, J.-A., Der Gesandte und sein Weg im 4. Evangelium (Tübingen 1977) 150-52.

12:46 BROWN, R. E., "The Qumran Scrolls and the Johannine Gospels and Epistles" CBQ 17 (1955) 403-18, 559-74; also in: K. Stendahl (ed.) The Scrolls and the New Testament (1957) 194; GT: "Die Schriftrollen von Qumran und das Johannesevangelium und die Johannesbriefe" in: K. H. Rengstorf (ed.) Johannes und sein Evangelium (Darmstadt 1973) 505. HAHN, F. Das Verständnis der Mission im Neuen Testament (²1965) 136. HEISE, J. Bleiben (1967) 50-52. LADD, G. E. A Theology of the New Testament (1974) 216, 224, 278. BERGMEIER, R., Glaube als Gabe nach Johannes (Stuttgart 1980) 192n.30, 204, 235.

12:47-48 HAHN, F. Das Verständnis der Mission im Neuen Testament (²1965) 137.

12:47f THYEN, H. Studien zur Sündenvergebung (1970) 248f.

12:47 METZGER, B. M., The Early Versions of the New Testament (Oxford 1977) 390.

12:48-49 NICKELS, P. Targum and New Testament (1967) 57.

12:48-50 LANGBRANDTNER, W., Weltferner Gott oder Gott der Liebe (Frankfurt a.M./Bern/Las Vegas 1977) 50-56.

12:48 METZGER, B. M., The Early Versions of the New Testament (Oxford 1977) 390. "Apokalyptik" in: TRE 3 (1978) 254.

12:49-50 IBUKI, Y., Die Wahrheit im Johannesevangelium (1972) 42-45, 268f.

12:49 DELLING, G. Wort und Werk Jesu im Johannes-Evangelium (1966) 65, 112f. PANCARO, S., The Law in the Fourth Gospel (Leiden 1975) 439-42. BERGER, K., "Das Buch der Jubiläen" in: JüdSchr II/3 (1981) 360n.35a.

13-21 REICKE, B. Diakonie, Festfreude und Zelos (1951) 23f. BRUNS, J. E. ThSt 31 (4, 1970) 754-57. BARRETT, C. K. JBL 90 (3, 1971) 256-58.

13-20 GUILDING, A. The Fourth Gospel and Jewish Worship (1960) 52-53. DEEKS, D., "The Structure of the Fourth Gospel," NTS 15 (1968-1969) 119ff.

13-19 RICHTER, G. "Die Deutung des Kreuzestodes Jesu in der Leidensgeschichte des Johannesevangeliums (Jo 13-19)," BuL 9
(1, 1968) 21-36.

13-17 ARVEDSON, T. Das Mysterium Christi (1937) 132f.
BUECHSEL, F. Das Evangelium nach Johannes (1946) 138-40.
LO GIUDICE, C. "La fede degli Apostoli nel IV Vangelo,"
Biblica 28 (1947) 71-82. VAN DEN BUSSCHE, H. Jezus'
woorden aan het afscheidsmaal (1955). BEHLER, G.-M. Les
paroles d'adieux du Seigneur (1960); GT: Die Abschiedsworte
des Herrn (1962); ET.: The Last Discourse of Jesus (1965).
GRUNDMANN, W. Zeugnis und Gestalt des Johannes-Evan-
geliums (1961) 65-80. BAILEY, J. A. The Traditions Common
to the Gospels of Luke and John (1963) 32-46. GLASSON, T.
F. Moses in the Fourth Gospel (1963) Ch. X. JANOT, J.-Em.
Les Adieux de Jésus (1963). LINDIJER, C. H. De Sacramen-
ten in het Vierde Evangelie (1964) 94f. STAGG, F. "The Fare-
well Discourses. John 13-17," RevEx 62 (4, 1965) 459-72.
GUARDINI, R. Johanneische Botschaft (1966). ZIMMER-
MANN, H. "Struktur und Aussageabsicht der johanneischen
Abschiedsreden (Jo 13-17)," BuL 8 (4, 1967) 279-90. JOHN-
STON, G. "The Spirit-Paraclete in the Gospel of John," Per-
spective 9 (1, 1968) 29-37. BECKER, J. "Die Abschiedsreden
Jesu im Johannesevangelium," ZNW 61 (3-4, 1970) 215-46.
PATRICK, J. G. "The Promise of the Paraclete," BiblSa 127
(508, 1970) 333-45. SELBY, D. J., Introduction to the New
Testament (New York 1971) 230, 237, 252-57. HAMMER-
TON-KELLY, R. G. Pre-Existence, Wisdom, and the Son of
Man (1973) 215-16. PERRIN, N., The New Testament: An In-
troduction (New York 1974) 242-44. CONZELMANN, H. und
LINDEMANN, A., Arbeitsbuch zum Neuen Testament (Tübingen 1975) 285. LATTKE, M., Einheit im Wort (München
1975) 132-38. CORTÈS, E., Les discursos de Adiós de Gn 49
a Jn 13-17. Pistas para la historia de un género literario en la
antigua literatura judía (Barcelona 1976). de la POTTERIE, I.,
"The Paraclete" BB 2 (1976) 120-40. REIM, G. "Probleme
der Abschiedsreden" BZ 20 (1976) 117-22. de JONGE, M.,
Jesus: Stranger from Heaven and Son of God (Missoula 1977)
172-75, 177-80. ONUKI, T., "Die johanneischen Abschiedsreden und die synoptische Tradition — eine traditionskritische
und traditionsgeschichtliche Untersuchung" AJBI 3 (1977) 157-
268. TRITES, A. A., The New Testament Concept of Witness
(Cambridge 1977) 113-22. LUSSIER, E., Christ's Farewell
Discourse (Staten Island, New York 1979). McDonald, J. I. H.,
Kerygma and Didache (Cambridge 1980) 86. SCHILLE-
BEECKX, E., Christ: the Christian Experience in the Modern

World (London 1980) 400-407; GT: Christus und die Christen
(Freiburg/Basel/Wien 1977) 386-93. DAHMS, J. V., "Isaiah
55:11 and the Gospel of John" EQ 53 (1981) 78-79. ES-
BROECK, M. van, "Les textes littéraires sur l'Assomption
avant le Xᵉ siècle" in: F. Bovon et al. (eds.) Les Actes Apo-
cryphes des Apôtres (Geneva 1981) 277. PAINTER, J., "The
Farewell Discourses and the History of Johannine Christianity"
NTS 27 (1981) 525-43. PRIEUR, J.-M., "La figure de l'apôtre
dans les Actes apocryphes d'André" in: F. Bovon et al. (eds.)
Les Actes Apocryphes des Apôtres (Geneva 1981) 130. SIM-
OENS, Y., La gloire d'aimer. Structures stylistiques et inter-
prétatives dans le Discours de la Cène (Jn 13-17) (Rome 1981).
WILSON, T. E., The Farewell Ministry of Christ. John 13-17
(Neptune, NJ 1981).

13-16 WIKENHAUSER, A. Das Evangelium nach Johannes (1957)
259f. LE FORT, P. Les Structures de L'Eglise militante selon
saint Jean (1970) 119-28. CARREZ, M., "Les promesses du
Paraclet" ETh 12 (1981) 323-32.

13 - 14 TEMPLE, S., The Core of the Fourth Gospel (London 1975)
212-25.

13 BECKER,H. Die Reden des Johannesevangeliums und der Stil
der gnostischen Offenbarungsrede (Göttingen 1956) 94. WIL-
KENS, W. Die Entstehungsgeschichte des vierten Evangeliums (1958) 68-77. RUDOLPH, K. Die Mandäer II (1961) 391,
4. HEYRAUD, L. "Judas et la nouvelle Alliance dans la cène
selon saint Jean," BVieC 44 (1962) 39-48. MacGREGOR, G.
H. C., "The Eucharist in the Fourth Gospel," NTS 9 (1962-
1963) 113f. HAHN, F. Christologische Hoheitstitel (1963) 94.
KAESEMANN, E. Exegetische Versuche und Besinnungen
(1964) I 216. LINDIJER, C. H. De Sacramenten in het Vierde
Evangelie (1964) 86ff. SMITH, D. M. The Composition and
Order of the Fourth Gospel (1965) 141, 158, 171n., 216, 217.
BIEDER, W. Die Verheissung der Taufe im Neuen Testament
(Zürich 1966) 272-73. FORTNA, R. T. The Gospel of Signs
(1970) 155-58. THYEN, H. "Johannes 13 und die 'Kirchliche
Redaktion' des vierten Evangeliums," in: Tradition und Glaube
(1971) G. Jeremias ed., 343-56. SMITH, M. Clement of Al-
exandria and a Secret Gospel of Mark (1973) 175f. HUNTER,
A. M., Gospel und Apostle (London 1975) 70-75. LATTKE,
M., Einheit im Wort (München 1975) 139-61. NICCACCI, A.,
"L'unità letteraria di Gv 13,1-38" EuD 29 (1976) 291-323.
ROHDEN, W., "Die Handlungslehre nach Johannes 13"
Theologische Versuche 7 (1976) 81-89. DERRETT, J. D. M.,
"The Footwashing in John XIII and the Alienation of Judas Is-

cariot" RIDA 24 (1977) 3-19. LANGBRANDTNER, W., Weltferner Gott oder Gott der Liebe (Frankfurt a.M./Bern/Las Vegas 1977) 50-56. CANCIAN, D., Nuovo Comandamento, Nuovo Aleanza Eucaristia. Nell'interpretazione del capitolo 13 del Vangelo di Giovanni (Collevalenza, Perugia 1978). FRIEDRICH, G., "Das Problem der Autorität im Neuen Testament" in: Auf das Wort kommt es an (Göttingen 1978) 390. de JONGE, M., "The Beloved Disciple and the Date of the Gospel of John" in: E. Best/R. McL. Wilson (eds.) Text and Interpretation. FS. M. Black (Cambridge 1979) 102-103, 107. KLAPPERT, B., "Arbeit Gottes und Mitabeit des Menschen (Phil 2:6-11)" in: J. Moltmann (ed.) Recht auf Arbeit - Sinn der Arbeit (München 1979) 101-103. du RAND, J. A., Johannes 13: By die maaltyd. 'n Eksperiment in metode en uitleg (Pretoria 1979). du RAND, J. A., "Eksegetiese kanttekeninge by Johannes 13" Scriptura (Stellenbosch, S. Africa 1980) 43-51. MANNS, F., "Le lavement des pieds. Essai sur la structure et la signification de Jean 13" RevSR 55 (1981) 149-69.

13:1ff ROBINSON, J. A. T. "The One Baptism," Twelve New Testament Studies (1962) 158-75. GLASSON, T. F. Moses in the Fourth Gospel(1963) 57, 82ff., 97f.

13:1-38 YATES, K. M. Preaching from John's Gospel (1964) 119-25. CADMAN, W. H. The Open Heaven (1969) G. B. Caird ed., 133-42. SIMOENS, V., La gloire d'aimer. Structures stylistiques et interprétatives dans la Discourse de la Cène (Jn 13-17) (Rome 1981).

13:1-30 STRATHMANN, H. Das Evangelium nach Johannes (1955) 201f. WIKENHAUSER, A. Das Evangelium nach Johannes (1957) 255-58. DERRETT, J. D. M., " 'Domine, tu mihi lavas pedes?' (Studio su Giovanni 13,1-30)" BiOr 21 (1979) 13-42. HAENCHEN, E., Das Johannesevangelium (Tübingen 1980) 452-53 (lit!).

13:1-20 CULLMANN, O. Urchristentum und Gottesdienst (1950) 102ff. RUCKSTUHL, E. Die literarische Einheit des Johannesevangeliums (1951) 122-25, 260. CORELL, A. Consummatum Est (1958) 69-73. RICHTER, G. "Die Fusswaschung Joh 13,1-20," MThZ 16 (1-2, 1965) 13-26. HENSS, W. Das Verhältnis zwischen Diatessaron, Christlicher Gnosis und "Western Text" (1967) 12f. KUHL, J. Die Sendung Jesu und der Kirche nach dem Johannes-Evangelium (1967) 202-204. LOHSE, W. Die Fusswaschung (Joh 13,1-20) I (1967). RICHTER, G. Die Fusswaschung im Johannesevangelium (1967). SWETNAM, J. Biblica 49 (3, 1968) 439-44. BROWN, R. E. ThSt 30 (1, 1969) 120-22. DUNN, J. D. G. "The Washing of the Disciples' Feet in John 13:1-20,'' ZNW 61 (3-4, 1970) 247-52. MARTIN, R. P., New Testament Foundations I (Grand Rapids 1975) 306-14. MALATESTAS, E., "Refléxion sur la lavement des pieds (Jn 13:1-20)" Christus 90 (Paris 1976) 209-23. BECKER,J., Das Evangelium nach Johannes (Gütersloh/ Würzburg 1979) 418-19 (lit!). WEISS, H., "Foot Washing in the Johannine Community" NovT 21 (1979) 298-325. BERG-MEIER, R., Glaube als Gabe nach Johannes (Stuttgart 1980) 208. GILL, J. H., "Jesus, Irony, and the 'New Quest' " Encounter (1980) 139-51. "Diakonie" in: TRE 8 (1981) 650. SCHNEIDERS, S. M., "The Foot Washing (John 13:1-20): An Experiment in Hermeneutics" CBQ 43 (1981) 76-92.

13:1-17 MUSSNER, F. "Fusswaschung (Joh 13,1-17). Versuch einer Deutung," GuL 31 (1, 1958) 25-30. WILES, M. F. The Spiritual Gospel (1960) 58-60, 137. ROBINSON, J. A. T. "The Significance of the Footwashing," in: Neotestamentica et Patristica (1962) 144-47. SCHWANK, B., "Die Fusswaschung: Jo 13,1-17," Sein und Sendung 28 (1, 1963) 4-17. BOISMARD, M.-E. "Le Lavement des pieds (Jn. XIII,1-17)," RevBi 71 (1, 1964) 5-24. LINDIJER, C. H. The Sacramenten in het Vierde Evangelie (1964) 90ff. DESPORTES, "Jeudi Saint. Le lavement des pieds. De l'Evangile à la Liturgie," AmiCler 75 (Mar. 25, 1965) 187-91. JAUBERT, A., "Une lecture de lavement des pieds au mardimercredi saint," Muséon 79 (3-4, 1966) 257-86. THUESING, W. Die Erhöhung und Verherrlichung Jesu im Johannesevangelium (1970) 65f., 69f., 88f., 132ff., 135f., 157f. KYSAR, R., The Fourth Evangelist and His Gospel (Minneapolis 1974) 255. LINDEMANN, A., "Gemeinde und Welt im Johannesevangelium" in: D. Lührmann/G. Strecker (eds.) Kirche. FS. G. Bornkamm (Tübingen 1980) 146-48.

13:1-15 BAUER, W. Das Johannesevangelium (1925) 166f. HAHN, F. GPM 4 (1949-1950) 113ff. SURKAU, H. W. GPM 9 (1954-1955) 100ff. DEHN, G. in: Herr, tue meine Lippen auf Bd. 1 (1957) G. Eichholz ed., 122-27. BORNKAMM, G. GPM 15 (1960-1961) 111ff. DOERNE, M. Er kommt auch noch heute (1961) 67-69. SCHWANK, B. "Vom Werden der Kirche," Am Tisch des Wortes I (1965) 38-48. GEBHARDT, R./JUNG, H. G. "Gründonnerstag: Johannes 13,1-15," in: Predigtstudien 1972-1973 (1972) E. Lange ed., 184-90. LAZURE, N. "Le lavement des pied. Jn 13,1-15," AssS 20 (1973) 53-64. WINTER, D., "Motivation in Christian Behavior" in: B. Kaye/G. Wenham (eds.) Law, Morality and the Bible (Downers Grove, Ill. 1978) 210.

13:1-11 MORGAN, G. C. The Parables and Metaphors of Our Lord (1943) 330ff. GILMORE, A. Christian Baptism (1959) 159ff. LOCKYER, H. All the Parables of the Bible (1963) 335ff.

13:1-8 DELLING, G. Die Taufe im Neuen Testament (1963) 93.

13:1-5 HUNTER, A. M. According to John (1970²) 87f.

13:1-4 LANGBRANDTNER, W., Weltferner Gott oder Gott der Liebe (Frankfurt 1977) 51.

13:1-3 GROSSOUW, W. K. "A Note on John xiii 1-3," NovTest 8 (2-4, 1966) 124-31. RICHTER, G. Die Fusswaschung im Johannesevangelium (1967) 298-300. BÜHNER, J.-A., Der Gesandte und sein Weg im 4. Evangelium (Tübingen 1977) 258-59. BERGMEIER, R., Glaube als Gabe nach Johannes (Stuttgart 1980) 243n.128, 248n.212.

13:1 HAHN, F. Das Verständnis der Mission im Neuen Testament (²1965) 139. SMITH, D. M. The Composition and Order of the Fourth Gospel (1965) 170, 171, 172, 241. LAZURE, N., Les Valeurs Morales de la Théologie Johannique (Paris 1965) 219-20. BRAUN, H. Qumran und NT II (1966) 238. DELLING, G. Wort und Werk Jesu im Johannes-Evangelium (1966) 59, 65, 78, 112, 130. NICKELS, P. Targum and New Testament (1967) 57. CADMAN, W. H. The Open Heaven (1969) G. B. Caird ed., 62, 90, 98, 153, 162, 175, 206. DAUER, A. Die Passionsgeschichte im Johannesevangelium (1972) 141, 209, 240, 278, 294. IBUKI, Y. Die Wahrheit im Johannesevangelium (1972) 250f., 263. LATTKE, M., Einheit im Wort (München 1975) 138-61. RUDOLPH, K., Die Gnosis (Göttingen 1978) 324. DAHMS, J. V., "Isaiah 55:11 and the Gospel of John" EQ 53 (1981) 78-88.

13:2-17 "Abendmahl" in: TRE 1 (1977) 215.

13:2-16 EISLER, R. "Zur Fusswachung am Tage vor dem Passah," ZNW 14 (1913) 268.

13:2.5.6-10 ORIGENES, Das Evangelium nach Johannes (1959) R. Gögler ed., 363-64, 366-71.

13:2.27a BAILEY, J. A. The Traditions Common to the Gospels of Luke and John (1963) 29-31.

13:2 BOUSSET, W. Die Religion des Judentums im Späthellenistischen Zeitalter (1966 = 1926) 335. DELLING, G. Wort und Werk Jesu im Johannes-Evangelium (1966) 52f., 81, 136. HEIN, K., "Judas Iscariot: Key to the Last Supper Narratives?" NTS 17 (1970-1971) 228f. "Antichrist" in: TRE 3 (1978) 22. KLEIN, H., "Die lukanisch-johanneische Passionstradition" in: M. Limbeck (ed.) Redaktion und Theologie des

Passionsberichtes nach den Synoptikern (Darmstadt 1981) 374-75.

13:3-12 NICOL, G. G., "Jesus' Washing the Feet of the Disciples: A Model for Johannine Christology?" ET 91 (1979) 20-21.

13:3 RICHTER, G. Die Fusswaschung im Johannesevangelium (1967) 299f. CADMAN, W. H. The Open Heaven (1969) G. B. Caird ed., 31, 90, 109, 130, 198. DAUER, A. Die Passionsgeschichte im Johannesevangelium (1972) 212, 213, 240. BÜHNER, J.-A., Der Gesandte und sein Weg im 4. Evangelium (Tübingen 1977) 132, 136-37, 148, 198-99, 258-59. DAHMS, J. V., "Isaiah 55:11 and the Gospel of John" EQ 53 (1981) 78-88.

13:4-15 MICHL, J. "Der Sinn der Fusswaschung," Biblica 40 (3, 1959) 697-708.

13:4-11 HOSKINS, E. C. The Fourth Gospel (1956-1957) 443-46.

13:4-10 BERGMEIER, R., Glaube als Gabe nach Johannes (Stuttgart 1980) 209.

13:4-5 KLEIN, H., "Die lukanisch-johanneische Passionstradition" in: M. Limbeck (ed.) Redaktion und Theologie des Passionsberichtes nach den Synoptikern (Darmstadt 1981) 379-81. LEVINE, E., "On the Symbolism of the Pedilavium" ABenR 33 (1982) 21-29.

13:4-5, WILKENS, W. Die Entstehungsgeschichte des vierten Evan-
12-17, 20-35 geliums (1958) 131-32.

13:5-11 DELLING, G. Die Taufe im Neuen Testament (1963) 92-95.

13:5 KUEMMEL, G. ed., Jüdische Schriften aus hellenistisch-römischer Zeit III (1975) 211. METZGER, B. M., The Early Versions of the New Testament (Oxford 1977) 140.

13:6-11 WILKENS, W. Die Entstehungsgeschichte des vierten Evangeliums (1958) 151-52. BROWN, R. E. et al. (eds.) Peter in the New Testament (Minneapolis 1973) 132-33.

13:6-10 VON CAMPHAUSEN, H. "Zur Auslegung von Jo 13:6-10," ZNW 33 (1934) 259. LANGBRANDTNER, W., Weltferner Gott oder Gott der Liebe (Frankfurt 1977) 51-52.

13:6 von WANKE, J., "Kommentarworte" BZ 24 (1980) 213.

13:7ff MUELLER, T. Das Heilsgeschehen im Johannesevangelium n.d., 108.

13:8 DUPONT, J. L'Union Avec Le Christ Suivant Saint Paul (1952) 90-92. WILES, M. F. The Spiritual Gospel (1960) 58-59.

MUELLER, T. Das Heilsgeschehen im Johannesevangelium n.d., 67-70.

13:9-16 BRAUN, H. Qumran und NT II (1966) 35, 40, 42, 129, 133, 288, 295.

13:9-10 DELLING, G. Die Taufe im Neuen Testament (1963) 140.

13:10-11 DELLING, Die Taufe im Neuen Testament (1963) 97, 149.

13:10 BARTH, M., Die Taufe - ein Sakrament? (Zürich 1951) 421ff. WILES, M. F. The Spiritual Gospel (1960) 58-60. SCHRAGE, W. Die konkreten Einzelgebote in der paulinischen Paränese (1961) 49. DUNN, J. D. G. Baptism in the Holy Spirit (1970) 188. LEROY, H., Zur Vergebung der Sünden (Stuttgart 1974) 86-88. LATTKE, M., Einheit im Wort (München 1975) 149-51.

13:12-20 WEISER, A. "Joh 13,12-20 - Zufügung eines späteren Herausgebers?" BZ 12 (2, 1968) 252-57.

13:12-17 LANGBRANDTNER, W., Weltferner Gott oder Gott der Liebe (Frankfurt 1977) 52-53. THÜSING, W., "Die Bitten des Johanneischen Jesus in dem Gebet John 17 und die Intentionen Jesu von Nazaret" in: R. Schnackenburg et al. (eds.) Die Kirche des Anfangs. FS. H. Schürmann (Freiburg/Basel/Wien 1978) 322-28. KLEIN, H., "Die lukanisch-johanneische Passionstradition" in: M. Limbeck (ed.) Redaktion und Theologie des Passionsberichtes nach den Synoptikern (Darmstadt 1981) 379-81.

13:13-14 HAHN, F. Christologische Hoheitstitel (1963) 77, 80, 94, 95, DELLING, G. Wort und Werk Jesu im Johannes-Evangelium (1966) 71, 97f.

13:13 WREGE, H.-T., Die Ueberlieferungsgeschichte der Bergpredigt (1968) 147f.

13:14-16 MUELLER, T. Das Heilsgeschehen im Johannesevangelium n.d., 80-87.

13:14 SANDERS, J. T. Ethics in the New Testament (Philadelphia 1975) 97.

13:15 DE BOER, W. P. The Imitation of Paul (1962) 54ff.

13:16f.20 BERGER, K. Die Amen-Worte Jesu (1970) 95-99.

13:16.20 HAHN, F. Das Verständnis der Mission im Neuen Testament (²1965) 141.

13:16 DODD, C. H., "Some Johannine 'Herrenworte' with parallels in the Synoptic Gospels," NTS 2 (1955-1956) 75ff. FLEW, R. N. Jesus and His Church (1956) 80. KNOX, W. L. The Sources of the Synoptic Gospels II (1957) 10. HAHN, F. Christologische Hoheitstitel (1963) 78. KUHL, J. Die Sendung Jesu und der Kirche nach dem Johannes-Evangelium (1967) 131, 148f. 165. WREGE, H.-T. Die Ueberlieferungsgeschichte der Bergpredigt (1968) 127f. LINTON, O. "Le parallelismus membrorum dans le Nouveau Testament grec," in: Mélanges Bibliques en hommage au R. P. Béda Rigaux (1970) A. Descamps/A. de Halleux eds., 505-506. SNYDER, G. F. "John 13:16 and the Anti-Petrinism of the Johannine Tradition" BR 16 (1971) 5-15. LATTKE, M., Einheit im Wort (München 1975) 19-20, 22, 64-85. "Amt" in: TRE 2 (1978) 517. KRAFT, H., Die Entstehung des Christentums (Darmstadt 1981) 145.

13:17 SMITH, M. F. "The Ascending Christ's Farewell Discourse," Worship 34 (6, 1960) 320-25. JOHNSTON, G. The Spirit-Paraclete in the Gospel of John (1970) 70-75, 155.

13:18-30 SCHWANK, B. " 'Einer von euch wird mich verraten: Jo 13, 18-30," Sein und Sendung 28 (2, 1963) 52-66. MORETON, M. B., "The Beloved Disciple Again" in: E. A. Livingstone (ed.) Studia Biblica 1978/II (Sheffield 1980) 216-18.

13:18-19 WILES, M. F. The Spiritual Gospel (1960) 66-67, 110-11, 146-47. DAUER, A. Die Passionsgeschichte im Johannesevangelium (1972) 41, 245f., 339.

13:18 GRILL, J. Untersuchungen über die Entstehung des vierten Evangeliums II (1923) 46, 204, 225, 357. BISHOP, E. F. F. " 'He that eateth bread with me hath lifted up his heel against me.'-Jn xiii. 18 (ps xli. 9)," ET 70 (11, 1959) 331-33. BLAIR, E. P. Jesus in the Gospel of Matthew (1960) 31. LINDARS, B. New Testament Apologetic (1961) 98, 121, 267. FREED, E. D. Old Testament Quotations in the Gospel of John (1965) 89-93. ELLIS, E. E./WILCOX, M. eds., Neotestamentica et Semitica (1969) 143-47, 153ff. ROTHFUCHS, W. Die Erfüllungszitate des Matthäus-Evangeliums (1969) 157f. RUPPERT, L., Jesus als der leidende Gerechte? (Stuttgart 1972) 50a.28. REIM, G., Studien zum Alttestamentlichen Hintergrund des Johannesevangeliums(Cambridge 1974) 39-42, 89-93. HANSON, A. T., The New Testament Interpretation of Scripture (London 1980) 158-59.

13:19-33 Origenes, Das Evangelium nach Johannes (1959) R. Gögler ed., 371-95, 400-405.

13:19 HARNER, P. B. The "I Am" of the Fourth Gospel (1970) 37-43. IBUKI, Y. Die Wahrheit im Johannesevangelium (1972) 40, 224f. HOWARD, V. P., Das Ego in den Synoptischen Evangelien (Marburg 1975) 253-54. BERGMEIER, R., Glaube als Gabe nach Johannes (Stuttgart 1980) 192n.34.

13:20 BÜHNER, J.-A., Der Gesandte und sein Weg im 4. Evangelium (Tübingen 1977) 251-54. DODD, C. H., "Some Johannine 'Herrenworte' with parallels in the Synoptic Gospels," NTS
2 (1955-1956) 81ff. FLEW, R. N., Jesus and His Church (1956)
174. KUHL, J. Die Sendung Jesu und der Kirche nach dem Johannes-Evangelium (1967) 148f.

13:21-30 RUCKSTUHL, E. Die literarische Einheit des Johannes-
evangeliums (1951) 125f. LORENZEN, T. Die Bedeutung des
Lieblingsjüngers für die Johanneische Theologie (Rüschlikon
1969) 1-19. WILCOX, M. "The Composition of John 13:21-
30," in: Neotestamentica et Semitica (1969) E. E. Ellis/M.
Wilcox eds., 143-56. DAUER, A. Die Passsionsgeschichte im
Johannesevangelium (1972) 318f., 320, 331, 339. MAHO-
NEY, R., Two Disciples at the Tomb (Bern/Frankfurt 1974) 80-
95, 295-300. BECKER, J., Das Evangelium nach Johannes
(Gütersloh/Würzburg 1979) 430-31 (lit!). de JONGE, M., "The
Beloved Disciple and the Date of the Gospel of John" in: E. Best/
R. McL. Wilson (eds.) Text and Interpretation. FS. M. Black
(Cambridge 1979) 100-101. MOHR, T. A., Markus- und Jo-
hannespassion (Zürich 1982) 181-84.

13:21 BEUTLER, J. Martyria (1972) 212ff., 215, 325ff. PORSCH,
F., Pneuma und Wort (Frankfurt 1974) 328-30. BEUTLER, J.,
"Psalm 42/43 im Johannesevangelium" NTS 25 (1978) 33-57.
FERRARO, G., " 'Pneuma' in Giov. 13,21" RivB 28 (1980)
185-211.

13:22-31 BRACHT, H. "O Söffne du die Herzen!" in: Kleine Predigt-
Typologie III (1965) L. Schmidt ed., 358-66.

13:22 PALLIS, A., Notes on St. John and the Apocalypse (London
1928) 29-30. KLEIN, H., "Die lukanisch-johanneische
Passionstradition" in: M. Limbeck (ed.) Redaktion und Theologie des Passionsberichtes nach den Synoptikern (Darmstadt
1981) 377-78.

13:23ff KAESEMANN, E. Exegetische Versuche und Besinnungen
(1963) I 180. HENSS, W. Das Verhältnis zwischen Diatessaron, Christlicher Gnosis und "Western Text" (1967) 46f.

13:23-26 BROWN, R. E. et al. (eds.) Peter in the New Testament (Minneapolis 1973) 134-35.

13:23 BAUER, W. Das Johannesevangelium (1925) 168f. DEL-
LING, G. Die Taufe im Neuen Testament (1963) 94. COL-
SON, J. L'Enigma du Disiciple que Jésus aimait (1969) 16, 89,
110. LATTKE, M., Einheit im Wort (München 1975) 11, 19,
21. WILCKENS, U., "Der Paraklet und die Kirche" in: D.
Lührmann/G. Strecker (eds.) Kirche. FS. G. Bornkamm (Tü-

bingen 1980) 200-201. BERGER, K., "Das Buch der Jubiläen," in: JüdSchr II/3 (1981) 440n.2a.

13:24 BRAUN, H. Qumran und NT II (1966) 35f., 134.

13:26-27 MAHONEY, R., Two Disciples at the Tomb (Bern/Frankfurt 1974) 91-95. BÖHLIG, A., Die Gnosis III: Der Manichäismus (Zürich/München 1980) 344n.52.

13:27 DELLING, G. Wort und Werk Jesu im Johannes-Evangelium (1966) 52f., 81. CRIBBS, F. L. in: SBL Seminar Papers 2 (1973) G. MacRae ed., 4., "Antichrist" in: TRE 3 (1978) 22. KLEIN, H., "Die lukanisch-johanneische Passionstradition" in: M. Limbeck (ed.) Redaktion und Theologie des Passionsberichtes nach den Synoptikern (Darmstadt 1981) 374-75.

13:30ff GLASSON, T. F. Moses in the Fourth Gospel (1963) 72f.

13:30-32 HENSS, W. Das Verhältnis zwischen Diatessaron, Christlicher Gnosis und "Western Text" (1967) 27f.n.18.

13:30 DELLING, G. Die Taufe im Neuen Testament (1963) 95. BRAUN, H. Qumran und NT II (1966) 46, 50. NICKELS, P. Targum and New Testament (1967) 57. DAUER, A. Die Passionsgeschichte im Johannesevangelium (1972) 28, 250f. KLEIN, H., "Die lukanisch-johanneische Passionstradition" in: M. Limbeck (ed.), Redaktion und Theologie des Passionsberichtes nach den Synoptikern (Darmstadt 1981) 383-86.

13:31-17:26 SCHNEIDER, J. "Die Abschiedsreden Jesu. Ein Beitrag zur Frage der Komposition von Joh. 13,31-17,26," in: Gott und die Götter (1958) 103-12. LANGBRANDTNER, W., Weltferner Gott oder Gott der Liebe (Frankfurt a.M./Bern/Las Vegas 1977) 56-59. PAINTER, J., "Glimpses of the Johannine Community in the Farewell Discourses" AusBR 28 (1980) 21-38.

13:31-16:33 LACOMARA, A. "Deuteronomy and the Farewell Discourse (Jn 13:31-16:33)," CBQ 36 (1, 1974) 65-84. BOYLE, J. L., "The Last Discourse (Jn 13:31 - 16:31) and Prayer (Jn. 17): Some Observations on Their Unity and Development" Biblica 56 (1975) 210-22.

13:31-14:31 JOHNSTON, G. The Spirit-Paraclete in the Gospel of John (1970) 165-67. REESE, J. M. "Literary Structure of Jn 13:31-14:31, 16:5-6, 16-33," CBQ 34 (3, 1972) 321-31. de KERGARADEC, Y., " 'Nul ne vient au Père que par moi.' Le premier discours de Jésus après la Cène (Jn 13,31 - 14,31)" Christus 25 (1978) 199-208. MIGLIASSO, S., La presenza dell'Assente. Saggio di analisi letterario-strutturale e di sintesi teologica di Gv. 13, 31 - 14,31 (Rome 1979). WOLL, D. B., "The

Departure of 'The Way': The First Farewell Discourse in the Gospel of John" JBL 99 (1980) 225-39. PAINTER, J., "The Farewell Discourse and the History of Johannine Christianity" NTS 27 (1980-1981) 526, 528, 530-34. SEGOVIA, F., "The Love and Hatred of Jesus and Johannine Sectarianism" CBQ 43 (1981) 258-72. WOLL, D. B., Johannine Christianity in Conflict (Chico, Cal. 1981) passim.

13:31-14:11 SCHWANK, B. "Der Weg zum Vater: Jo. 13,31-14,11," Sein und Sendung 28 (3, 1963) 100-14.

13:31-14:3 WOLL, D. B., Johannine Christianity in Conflict (Chico, Cal. 1981) 37-46.

13:31ff CULLMANN, O. Urchristentum und Gottesdienst (1950) 106ff.

13:31-38 SCHELKLE, K. H. Die Passion Jesu in der Verkündigung des Neuen Testaments (1949) 121f. BECKER, J. Das Evangelium nach Johannes (Gütersloh/Würzburg 1979) 446-47 (lit!). HAENCHEN, E., Das Johannesevangelium (Tübingen 1980) 467-68 (lit!).

13:31-35 KLEIN, G. GPM 17 (1, 1963) 146-52. BORNKAMM, G. in: Herr, tue meine Lippen auf Bd. 3 (1964) G. Eichholz ed., 161ff. WEBER, O. Predigtmeditationen (1967) 181-84. MARXSEN, W. Predigten (1968) 39-45. GROO, G. GPM 23 (2, 1968) 138-42. LAZURE, N. "Louange au Fils de l'homme et commande-ment nouveau. Jn. 13,31-33a, 34-35," AssS 26 (1973) 73-80. GERBER, H. und BUHLER, K.-W., in: P. Krusche et al. (eds.) Predigtstudien für das Kirchenjahr 1974-1975. III/1 (Stuttgart 1974) 156-72. LAUFF, W., in: GPM 29 (1975) 175-79.

13:31-32 SCHULZ, S., Untersuchungen zur Menschensohn-Chri-stologie im Johannesevangelium (Göttingen 1957) 120-24. HIGGINS, A. J. B. Menschensohn-Studien (1965) 46-48. KUHL, J. Die Sendung Jesu und der Kirche nach dem Johan-nes-Evangelium (1967) 217f. CADMAN, W. H. The Open Heaven (1969) G. B. Caird ed., 36-41, 161. WILKENS, W., Zeichen und Werke (Zürich 1969) 100-102. THUESING, W. Die Erhöhung und Verherrlichung Jesu im Johannes-evangelium (1970) 175f., 233-39. DAUER, A. Die Passionsgeschichte im Johannesevangelium (1972) 238f. RIEDL, J. Das Heilswerk Jesu nach Johannes (1973) 123f., 124-28. OLSSON, B., Structure and Meaning in the Fourth Gospel (Lund 1974) 70-72, 247, 263.

13:31 BISHOP, C., "John 21," NTS 3 (1956-1957) 135f. ROBIN-SON, J. M. Kerygma und historischer Jesus (1960) 71. WILES, M. F. The Spiritual Gospel (1960) 39, 81-84, 114. PASTOR, M. M. "Une significacion de doxa y doxazein en la exégesis

origeniana de Jn 13,31," MisC 42 (1964) 173-82. BERG-
MEIER, R., Glaube als Gabe nach Johannes (Stuttgart 1980)
40n.218.

13:33 - 14:6 de la POTTERIE, I., La Vérité dans Saint Jean I/II (Rome 1977)
249-53.

13:32 HAHN, F. Christologische Hoheitstitel (1963) 130. RIEDL, J.
Das Heilswerk Jesu nach Johannes (1973) 121-23, 169-75.

13:33-35 DE BOER, W. P. The Imitation of Paul (1962) 56f.

13:33 KAESEMANN, E. Exegetische Versuche und Besinnungen
(1964) I 181. COLLINS, R. F., "The Search for Jesus. Reflections on the Fourth Gospel" LThPh 34 (1978) 27-48.
WOLL, D. B., "The Departure of 'The Way': The First Farewell Discourse in the Gospel of John" JBL 99 (1980) 229, 237-
38. DAHMS, J. V., "Isaiah 55:11 and the Gospel of John" EQ
53 (1981) 78-88.

13:34ff KRAGERUD, A. "Das Liebesgebot im Johannesevangelium," NTT 57 (3, 1956) 137-49 /In Norwegian/.

13:34-35 TILLICH, P. Das Neue Sein (1959) 33-36. KELLY, J. "What
did Christ Mean by the Sign of Love?" AfrER 13 (2, 1971) 113-
21. GLASSON, T. F. Moses in the Fourth Gospel (1963) 80,
92f. HAACKER, K. Die Stiftung des Heils (1972) 72-74.
BROWN, R. E., "The Qumran Scrolls and the Johannine Gospels and Epistles" CBQ 17 (1955) 403-19, 559-74; also in: K.
Stendahl (ed.) The Scrolls and the New Testament (New York
1957) 119; GT: "Die Schriftrollen von Qumran und das
Johannesevangelium und die Johannesbriefe" in: K. H. Rengstorf (ed.) Johannes und sein Evangelium (Darmstadt 1973) 514.
LATTKE, M., Einheit im Wort (München 1975) 19, 206-18.
VOUGA, F., Le cadre historique et l'intention théologique de
Jean (Paris 1977) 93. THÜSING, W., "Die Bitten des johan-
neischen Jesus in dem Gebet Joh 17 und die Intentionen Jesu
von Nazaret" in: R. Schnackenburg et al. (eds.) Die Kirche des
Anfangs. FS. H. Schürmann (Freiburg/Basel/Wien 1978) 322-
28. LINDEMANN, A., "Gemeinde und Welt im Johannes-
evangelium" in: D. Lührmann/G. Strecker (ed.) Kirche. FS. G.
Bornkamm (Tübingen 1980) 148-49. WILCKENS, U., "Der
Paraklet und die Kirche" in: D.Lührmann/G. Strecker (eds.)
Kirche. FS. G. Bornkamm (Tübingen 1980) 186-87.

13:34 DAVIES, W. D. Torah and the Messianic Age and/or the Age
to come (1952) 92. FARRER, A. St. Matthew and St. Mark
(1954) 184. HARRISVILLE, R. A. The Concept of Newness
in the New Testament (1960) 91ff. SCHRAGE, W. Die konkreten Einzelgebote in der paulinischen Paränese (1961) 99.

HENNECKE, E./SCHNEEMELCHER, W. Neutestamentliche Apokryphen (1964) I 135. LAZURE, N., Les Valeurs
Morales de la Théologie Johannique (Paris 1965) 220. HAHN,
F. Das Verständnis der Mission im Neuen Testament (²1965)
144. BORIG, R. Der Wahre Weinstock (1967) 59f., 233f.
KUHL, J. Die Sendung Jesu und der Kirche nach dem Johan-
nes-Evangelium (1967) 177, 195-97. IBUKI, Y. Die Wahrheit
im Johannesevangelium (1972) 253f. LADD, G. E. A Theol-
ogy of the New Testament (1974) 279, 280, 616. HUNTER, A.
M., Gospel and Apostle (London 1975) 76-80. LATTKE, M.,
Einheit im Wort (München 1975) 19, 21, 25. SANDERS, J. T.,
Ethics in the New Testament (Philadelphia 1975) 91-94.
"Abendmahl" in: TRE 1 (1977) 215. COLLINS, R. F., " 'A
New Commandment I Give to You, That You Love One An-
other . . .' (Jn 13:34)" LThPh 35 (1979) 235-61. "Bibel" in:
TRE 6 (1980) 18.

13:35 FLEW, R. N. Jesus and His Church (1956) 176. WULF, F.
"Wer seinen Bruder liebt, liebt auch Gott," GuL 37 (6, 1964)
405-407. KUHL, J. Die Sendung Jesu und der Kirche nach dem
Johannes-Evangelium (1967) 138f., 195-200.

13:36ff SCHWEIZER, E. Erniedrigung und Erhöhung bei Jesus und
seinen Nachfolgern (1962) § llk.

13:36-38 SCHNIEWIND, J., Die Parallelperikopen bei Lukas und Jo-
hannes (Darmstadt 1958 = 1914) 28-32. BROWN, R. E. et al.
(eds.) Peter in the New Testament (Minneapolis 1973) 133.
OTOMO, Y. Nachfolge Jesu und Anfänge der Kirche im Neuen
Testament (1970) 132f. DAUER, A. Die Passionsgeschichte im
Johannesevangelium (1972) 77, 315, 339. CRIBBS, F. L. in:
SBL Seminar Papers 2 (1973) G. MacRae ed., 4. KLEIN, H.,
"Die lukanisch-johanneische Passionstradition" in: M. Lim-
beck (ed.) Redaktion und Theologie des Passionsberichtes nach
den Synoptikern (Darmstadt 1981) 381-82. MOHR, T. A.,
Markus- und Johannespassion (Zürich 1982) 213-18.

13:36-37 BERGMEIER, R., Glaube als Gabe nach Johannes (Stuttgart
1980) 272n.592.

13:36 IBUKI, Y. Die Wahrheit im Johannesevangelium (1972) 211f.
WOLL, D. B., "The Departure of 'The Way': The First Farewell Discourse in the Gospel of John" JBL 99 (1980) 229.
DAHMS, J. V., "Isaiah 55:11 and the Gospel of John" EQ 53
(1981) 78-88.

13:38 STREETER, B. H. The Four Gospels (1951) 404f.

14-17 MUNCK, J. "Discours d'adieu dans le Nouveau Testament et dans la litterature biblique," in: Aux Sources de la Tradition Chrètienne (1950) M. M. Goguel ed., 155-70. BOYD, W. J. P. "The Ascension according to St. John. Chapters 14-17 not pre-passion but post-resurrection," Theology 70 (563, 1967) 207-11. FORTNA, R. T. The Gospel of Signs (1970) 157f. GRANADO, C. "El Espiritu Santo revelado como Persona en el Sermon de la Cena," EstBi 32 (2, 1973) 157-73. SCHICK, E., Das Vermächtnis des Herrn. Biblische Besinnungen zu den Abschiedsreden Jesu und dem Hohenpriesterlichen Gebet (Joh 14,1 - 17, 26) (Kevelaer 1977). STEINMETZ, F.-J., " '. . . und ich gene nimmer, wann ich geh'-'. Zum Verständnis der johanneischen Abschiedsreden" GuL 51 (1978) 85-99. CARSON, D. A., The Farewell Discourse and Final Prayer of Jesus. An Exposition of John 14 - 17 (Grand Rapids 1980).

14-16 ADLER, N. Das erste christliche Pfingstfest (1938) 70, 148, 157f. BECKER, H., Die Reden des Johannesevangeliums und der Stil der gnostischen Offenbarungsrede (Göttingen 1956) 119-20. STOCKTON, E. "The Paraclete," ACR 39 (3, 1962) 255-63. MIGUENS, M. El Paraclito (1963). SCHWANK, B. "Vom Wirken des dreieinigen Gottes in der Kirche Christi: Jo 14,12-26," Sein und Sendung 28 (4, 1963) 147-49. BEHLER, G.-M., The Last Discourse of Jesus (1965) 75-218. LAZURE, N., Les Valeurs Morales de la Théologie Johannique (Paris 1965) 100-109. JANKOWSKI, A., "Eschatologiczne poslannictwo Ducha Parakleta" AC 7 (1975) 537-62. SANCHEZ MIELGO, G., "Presencia y actuación del Paráklētos en la Iglesia (Jn. 14-16)," Telogía Espiritual 24 (Valencia 1980) 79-117. CARSON, D. A., "Historical Tradition in the Fourth Gospel: After Dodd, What?" in: R. T. France/D. Wenham (eds.) Gospel Perspectives II (Sheffield 1981) 122-23.

14 BECKER, H., Die Reden des Johannesevangeliums und der Stil der gnostischen Offenbarungsrede (Göttingen 1956) 105-109. WILKENS, W. Die Entstehungsgeschichte des vierten Evangeliums (1958) 114-18. GUILDING, A. The Fourth Gospel and Jewish Worship (1960) 86-91.SCHULZ, S., Komposition und Herkunft der Johanneischen Reden (Stuttgart 1960) 81-83, 109-14. KAESEMANN, E. Exegetische Versuche und Besinnungen (1964) II 134, 154. SMITH, D. M. The Composition and Order of the Fourth Gospel (1965) 93, 168, 170, 174. 239.

BORNKAMM, G. Geschichte und Glaube (1968) 117f. LATTKE, M., Einheit im Wort (München 1975) 218-45. MINEAR, P. S., To Die and to Live (New York 1977) 40-51. NICCACCI, A., "Esame letterario di Gv 14" EuD 31 (1978) 209-60. BERGMEIER, R., Glaube als Gabe nach Johannes (Stuttgart 1980) 33n.32, 192n.34. HAENCHEN, E., Das Johannesevangelium (Tübingen 1980) 471-74 (lit!). LÉGASSE, S., "Le retour du Christ d'après l'évangile de Jean, chapitre 14 et 16: une adaptation du motif de la Parousie" BLE 81 (1980) 161-74.

14:1ff CLARKE, W. K. L. New Testament Problems (1929) 96ff.

14:1-31 YATES, K. M. Preaching from John's Gospel (1964) 126-34. CADMAN, W. H. The Open Heaven (1969) G. B. Caird ed., 143-74. SIMEONS, Y., La gloire d'aimer. Structures stylistiques et interprétatives dans le Discours de la Cène (Jn 13-17) (Rome 1981).

14:1-26 BECKER,J., Das Evangelium nach Johannes (Gütersloh/ Würzburg 1979) 458 (lit!).

14:1-22 PEISKER, C. H., in: GPM 31 (1976-1977) 237-44.

14:1-20 KOESTER, H. "John xiv. 1-20: A Meditation," ET 73 (3, 1961) 88.

14:1-14 IWAND, H.-J. Predigt-Meditationen (1964) 639-46. TRAUB, H. GPM 19 (1, 1965) 205-11. SCHNEIDER, G. Der Herr unser Gott (1965) 156-61. VOUGA, F., Le cadre historique et l'intention théologique de Jean (Paris 1977) 77-84.

14:1-12 DIETZFELBINGER, W. in: Hören und Fragen Bd. 5,3 (1967) G. Eichholz/A. Falkenroth eds., 308ff. FISCHER, K. M. GPM 25 (1, 1971) 229-37. LANGE, E. ed., Predigtstudien für das Kirchenjahr 1970-1971 (1970) 85-89. ROSSETTO, G. "La route vers le Père, Jn 14,1-12," AssS 26 (1973) 18-30. HOLZE, H. und ZABEL, H., in: P. Krusche et al. (eds.) Predigtstudien für das Kirchenjahr 1976-1977. V/2 (Stuttgart 1977) 59-65.

14:1-9 BEUTLER, J., "Psalm 42/43 im Johannesevangelium" NTS 25 (1978) 33-57.

14:1-7 SCHAEFER, O. "Der Sinn der Rede Jesu von den vielen Wohnungen in seines Vaters Hause," ZNW 32 (1933) 210.

14:1-6 LOCKYER, H. All the Parables of the Bible (1963) 337ff. BORNKAMM, G. in: Herr, tue meine Lippen auf Bd. 3 (1964) G. Eichholz ed., 217ff. VOUGA, F., Le cadre historique et l'intention théologique de Jean (Paris 1977) 78-81. BAUER, G., in: GPM 35 (1980) 76-83. WIMMER, U. und HERMANN, C., in: P. Krusche et al. (eds.), Predigtstudien für das Kirchenjahr 1980-1981). III/1 (Stuttgart 1980) 76-83.

14:1-5 IBUKI, Y. Die Wahrheit im Johannesevangelium (1972) 208-18.

14:1-4 CLARKE, W. K. L. New Testament Problems (1929) 96-100.

14:1-3 SCHULZ, S., Untersuchungen zur Menschensohn-Christologie im Johannesevangelium (Göttingen 1957) 159-64. BÜHNER, J.-A. Der Gesandte und sein Weg im 4. Evangelium (Tübingen 1977) 218-20. ESTALAYO ALONSO, V., "La Vuelta de Cristo en el Evangelio de Juan. Análisis Literario de Jn 14,1-3" Estudios Teológicos 5 (Guatemala City 1978) 3-70. WOLL, D. B., "The Departure of 'The Way': The First Farewell Discourse in the Gospel of John" JBL 99 (1980) 229.

14:1-2 GLASSON, T. F. Moses in the Fourth Gospel (1963) 83f.

14:2ff GRILL, J. Untersuchungen über die Entstehung des vierten Evangeliums II (1923) 211, 214, 231, 331. PORSCH, F., Pneuma und Wort (Frankfurt 1974) 381-83.

14:2-6 MORGAN, G. C. The Parables and Metaphors of Our Lord (1943) 335ff.

14:2-5 DAHMS, J. V., "Isaiah 55:11 and the Gospel of John" EQ 53 (1981) 78-88.

14:2-3 MUSZNER, F. ZΩH. Die Anschauung vom "Leben" im vierten Evangelium (1952) 179f. BEYSCHLAG, K. Clemens Romanus und der Frühkatholizismus (1966) 326. HUNTER, A. M. According to John (1970²) 86. FISCHER, G., Die himmlischen Wohnungen. Untersuchungen zu Joh 14,2f (Frankfurt 1975). BECKER, J., Auferstehung der Toten im Urchristentum (Stuttgart 1976) 118-23. "Apokalyptik" in: TRE 3 (1978) 254. McNAMARA, M. " 'To Prepare a Resting-Place for You'. A Targumic Expression and John 14:2f.," Milltown Studies 3 (Dublin 1979) 100-108. BERGMEIER, R., Glaube als Gabe nach Johannes (Stuttgart 1980) 34n.93, 240n.63.

14:2 PALLIS, A., Notes on St. John and the Apocaplyse (London 1928) 30-31. VOLZ, P. Die Eschatologie der jüdischen Gemeinde (1934) 406. RIESENFELD, H. Jésus Transfiguré (1947) 199, 275, 302. FOSTER, J. "Go and make ready (Luke XXII,8; John XIV,2)," ET LXIII (1952) 193. BOISMARD, M. E., "Importance de la critique textuelle pour établir l'origine araméenne du quatrième évangile" in: M. Boismard et al., L'Evangile de Jean: études et problèmes (Bruges 1958) 52-53. RUDOLPH, K. Die Mandäer II (1961) 22, 420. GUNDRY, R. H. " 'In my Father's House are Many Monai' (John 14:2)," ZNW 58 (1-2, 1967) 68-72. HEISE, J. Bleiben (1967) 93-101. SMITH, M. Tannaitic Parallels to the Gospels (1968) 8 end. SANDVIK, B. Das Kommen des Herrn beim Abendmahl (1970)

121, 122, 126. WIDENGREN, G. "En la maison de mon Père sont demeures nombreuses," SEA 37-38 (1972-1973) 9-15. CAVALLIN, H. C. C. Life After Death (1974) 4, II, 3, 4, IIn.4. KLIJN, A. F. J., "Die syrische Baruch-Apokalypse" in: JüdSchr V/2 (1976) 151n.6b. FISCHER, U., Eschatologie und Jenseitserwartung im hellenistischen Diasporajudentum (Berlin 1978) 56. "Eschatologie" in: TRE 10 (1982) 288. PHILO-NENKO-SAYAR, B. und PHILONENKO, M., "Die Apokalypse Abrahams" in: JüdSchr V/5 (1982) 439n.16.

14:3 ORIGENES, Das Evangelium nach Johannes (1959) R. Gögler ed., 404-405. CADMAN, W. H. The Open Heaven (1969) G. B. Caird ed., 34, 44, 62, 109, 134, 165, 211. MACK, B. L. Logos und Sophia (1973) 114. METZGER, B. M., The Early Versions of the New Testament (Oxford 1977) 177.

14:4-11 WOLL, D. B., "The Departure of 'The Way': The First Farewell Discourse in the Gospel of John" JBL 99 (1980) 230-31, 233-34, 237. WOLL, D. B., Johannine Christianity in Conflict (Chico, Cal. 1981) 47-68.

14:4-7 BÜHNER, J.-A., Der Gesandte und sein Weg im 4. Evangelium (Tübingen 1977) 219-21.

14:4 WOLL, D. B., "The Departure of 'The Way': The First Farewell Discourse in the Gospel of John" JBL 99 (1980) 230.

14:5 WOLL, D. B., "The Departure of 'The Way': The First Farewell Discourse in the Gospel of John" JBL 99 (1980) 230.

14:6-11 VOUGA, F., Le cadre historique et l'intention théologique de Jean (Paris 1977) 82-83.

14:6-9 IBUKI, Y., Die Wahrheit im Johannesevangelium (1972) 218f.

14:6 VON LOEWENICH, W. Das Johannes-Verständnis im zweiten Jahrhundert (1932) 35, 97, 99, 106, 109, 138 n.2. MAURER, C. Ignatius von Antiochien und des Johannes-evangelium (1949) 30ff., 58ff., 77. DUPONT, J. Essais sur la Christologie de Saint Jean (1951) 213, 214, 215. MUSZNER, F. ΖΩΗ. Die Anschauung vom "Leben" im vierten Evangelium (1952) 89f. LEAL, J. "Ego sum vie et veritas et vita," VD 33 (1955) 336-41. ORIGENES, Das Evangelium nach Johannes (1959) R. Gögler ed., 128-30. WILES, M. F. The Spiritual Gospel (1960) 68-71, 112-13, 137. RUDOLPH, K. Die Mandäer II (1961) 143,9. LAZURE, N., Les Valeurs Morales de la Théologie Johannique (Paris 1965) 146-49. BRAUN, H. Qumran und NT II (1966) 121, 123, 162, 213. DELLING, G. Wort und Werk Jesu im Johannes-Evangelium (1966) 13, 50, 67,72, 117, 120, 125, 139. DE LA POTTERIE, I. " 'Je suis la Voie, la Vérité et la Vie' (Jn 14,6)," NRTh 88 (9, 1966) 907-42.

BORIG, R. Der Wahre Weinstock (1967) 25, 28, 31, 36, 203. GOLLWITZER, H. "Ausser Christus kein Heil? (Johannes 14,6)," Antijudaismus im Neuen Testament (1967) W. P. Eckert ed., 171-94. KUHL, J. Die Sendung Jesu und der Kirche nach dem Johannes-Evangelium (1967) 82-84, 100, 101f., 186. BORNKAMM, G. Geschichte und Glaube (1968) I 87f. FENSHAM, F. C. "I am the Way, the Truth and the Life," Neotestamentica 2 (1968) 81-88. CADMAN, W. H. The Open Heaven (1969) G. B. Caird ed., 51, 111, 155, 198, 209. THUESING, W. Die Erhöhung und Verherrlichung Jesu im Johannesevangelium (1970) 146-49. BEUTLER, J. Martyria (1972) 267, 277, 323. HOFIUS, O. Der Vorhang vor dem Thron Gottes (1972) 83f., 95. IBUKI, Y. Die Wahrheit im Johannesevangelium (1972) 208f., 222-30, 282f. LADD, G. E. A Theology of the New Testament (1974) 216, 250, 257, 264, 266, 294. MUELLER, T. Das Heilsgeschehen im Johannesevangelium n.d., 90-93, 99. de la POTTERIE, I., La Vérité dans Saint Jean I/II (Rome 1977) 241-78, 466-71. "Baha'ismus" in: TRE 5 (1980) 122. BEIERWALTES, W., "Deus est veritas" in: E. Dassmann/K. S. Frank (eds.) Pietas. FS. B. Kötting (Münster 1980) 23-24. BERGMEIER, R., Glaube als Gabe nach Johannes (Stuttgart 1980) 180, 244n.162. BÖHLIG, A., Die Gnosis III: Der Manichäismus (Zürich/München 1980) 342n.4. SCHILLEBEECKX, E., Christ: the Christian Experience in the Modern World (London 1980) 395; GT: Christus und die Christen (Freiburg/Basel/Wien 1977) 380-81. WOLL, D. B., "The Departure of 'The Way': The First Farewell Discourse in the Gospel of John" JBL 99 (1980) 226. "Dogmatik" in: TRE 9 (1982) 112.

14:7-11 IBUKI, Y. Die Wahrheit im Johannesevangelium (1972) 223f., 228f.

14:7-10 DELLING, G. Die Taufe im Neuen Testament (1963) 91.

14:7 HAHN, F. Christologische Hoheitstitel (1963) 330. DELLING, G. Wort und Werk Jesu im Johannes-Evangelium (1966) 37, 39f., 102. SCHNACKENBURG, R., "Johannes 14:7" in: J. K. Elliott (ed.) Studies in New Testament Language and Text. FS. G. D. Kilpatrick (Leiden 1976) 345-56.

14:8ff BULTMANN, R. Theologie des Neuen Testaments (1965) 402f., 424.

14:8-11 SEIDENSTICKER, P. Die Auferstehung Jesu in der Botschaft der Evangelisten (1968) 113f.

14:8 KORTEWEG, T., "The Reality of the Invisible. Some Remarks on St. John XIV 8 and Greek Philosophic Tradition" in:

M. J. Vermaseren (ed.) Studies in Hellenistic Religions (Leidden 1979) 50-102.

14:9-11 KUHL, D., Die Sendung Jesu und der Kirche nach dem Johannes-Evangelium (1967) 100f.

14:9 WILES, M. F. The Spiritual Gospel (1960) 30, 91-92, 118-19, 151. HAENCHEN, E., "Der Vater, der mich gesandt hat," NTS 8 (1962-1963) 211f. HAHN, F. Christologische Hoheitstitel (1963) 330. SUMMERS, R. The Secret Sayings of the Living Jesus (1968) 59. IBUKI, Y. Die Wahrheit im Johannesevangelium (1972) 223ff., 229. BÜHNER, J.-A. Der Gesandte und sein Weg im 4. Evangelium (Tübingen 1977) 218-20, 383-85. METZGER, B. M., The Early Versions of the New Testament (Oxford 1977) 162. "Baha'ismus" in: TRE 5 (1980) 122.

14:10-21 HENNECKE, E./SCHNEEMELCHER, W. Neutestamentliche Apokryphen (1964) I 135, 139; II 99.

14:10-11 IBUKI,Y. Die Wahrheit im Johannesevangelium (1972) 23f, 219-22. RIEDL, J. Das Heilswerk Jesu nach Johannes (1973) 187-282. "Antiochien" in: TRE 3 (1978) 105. BÖHLIG, A., Die Gnosis III: Der Manichäismus (Zürich/München 1980) 343n.25. WOLL, D. B., "The Departure of 'The Way': The First Farewell Discourse in the Gospel of John" JBL 99 (1980) 230-31, 235.

14:10 DELLING, G. Die Zueignung des Heils in der Taufe (1961) 45. BORIG, R. Der Wahre Weinstock (1967) 28, 42, 53, 208ff., 215f., 218. HEISE, J. Bleiben (1967) 79-80. IBUKI, Y. Die Wahrheit im Johannesevangelium (1972) 45ff. BÜHNER, J.-A., Der Gesandte und sein Weg im 4. Evangelium (Tübingen 1977) 215-17, 221-24, 233-34. BERGER, K., "Das Buch der Jubiläen" in: JüdSchr II/3 (1981) 360n.35a.

14:11 TAYLOR, V. The Formation of the Gospel Tradition (1949) 133f. WILES, M. F. The Spiritual Gospel (1960) 118-20. BORIG, R. Der Wahre Weinstock (1967) 208f., 215f., 218. IBUKI, Y., Die Wahrheit im Johannesevangelium (1972) 278f., 280, 282.

14:12ff HAHN, F. Das Verständnis der Mission im Neuen Testament (1965²) 141. IBUKI, Y., Die Wahrheit im Johannesevangelium (1972) 278-83.

14:12-24 WOLL, D. B., Johannine Christianity in Conflict (Chico, Cal. 1981) 69-96.

14:12-17 WOLL, D. B., "The Departure of 'The Way': The First Farewell Discourse in the Gospel of John" JBL 99 (1980) 231-35, 238.

14:12-14 VOUGA, F., Le cadre historique et l'intention théologique de Jean (Paris 1977) 83-84.

14:12-13 THUESING, W. Die Erhöhung und Verherrlichung Jesu im Johannesevangelium (1970) 114-17.

14:12 KAESEMANN, E. Exegetische Versuche und Besinnungen (1964) II 101. LAZURE, N., Les Valeurs Morales de la Théologie Johannique (Paris 1965) 36-37. KUHL, J. Die Sendung Jesu und der Kirche nach dem Johannes-Evangelium (1967) 176-78. KAESEMANN, E. New Testament Questions of Today (1969) 103. IBUKI, Y., Die Wahrheit im Johannesevangelium (1972) 273ff. RIEDL, J. Das Heilswerk Jesu nach Johannes (1973) 283-343. WOLL, D. B., "The Departure of 'The Way': The First Farewell Discourse in the Gospel of John" JBL 99 (1980) 231, 235. DAHMS, J. V., "Isaiah 55:11 and the Gospel of John" EQ 63 (1981) 78-88.

14:13ff IBUKI, Y. Die Wahrheit im Johannesevangelium (1972) 274, 276ff., 281ff., 287, 289.

14:13-14 DELLING, G. Die Zueignung des Heils in der Taufe (1961) 58, 59.

14:13 HAHN, F. Christologische Hoheitstitel (1963) 329f. DELLING, G. Wort und Werk Jesu im Johannes-Evangelium (1966) 100-101. UNTERGASSMAIR, F. G., Im Namen Jesu: Der Namensbegriff im Johannesevangelium (Stuttgart 1973) 108-24. BERGMEIER, R., Glaube als Gabe nach Johannes (Stuttgart 1980) 40n.218. SCHÜRMANN, H., "Christliche Weltverantwortung im Licht des Neuen Testaments" Biblica 34 (1980) 107.

14:14-20 FUERST, W. GPM 21 (3, 1966) 286-91.

14:14 UNTERGASSMAIR, F. G., Im Namen Jesu: Der Namensbegriff im Johannesevangelium (Stuttgart 1973) 125-28.

14:15-26 SEGOVIA, F., "The Love and Hatred of Jesus and Johannine Sectarianism," CBQ 43 (1981) 262-65, 269.

14:15-24 LATTKE, M., Einheit im Wort (München 1975) 222-32. WENHAM, D., "Spirit and Life: Some Reflections on Johannine Theology," Themelios 6 (1980) 4-8. PAINTER, J., "The Farewell Discourses and the History of Johannine Christianity," NTS 27 (1980-1981) 532-33.

14:15-21 LANG, F. in: Herr, tue meine Lippen auf Bd. 3 (1964) G. Eichholz ed., 266ff. KLEIN, G. GPM 21 (1966) 224-28. MUELLER, T. Das Heilsgeschehen im Johannesevangelium n.d., 82-84.

14:15-17 SCHULZ, S., Untersuchungen zur Menschensohn-Christologie im Johannesevangelium (Göttingen 1957) 143-45. KUHL, J. Die Sendung Jesu und der Kirche nach dem Johannes-Evangelium (Tübingen 1967) 157-58. BÜHNER, J.-A., Der Gesandte und sein Weg im 4. Evangelium (Tübingen 1977) 219-21. CARREZ, M., "Les Promesses du Paraclet," ETh 12 (1981) 323-32.

14:15 DAVIES, W. D. Torah in the Messianic Age and/or the Age to come (1951) 92. TOMOI, K. "Is not John xiv, 15 a Dislocation?" ET 72 (1,1960) 31. SESBOUE, B. " 'Si vous m'aimez, vous garderez mes commandements," Christus 8 (30, 1961) 192-206. DAVIES, W. D., The Sermon on the Mount (Cambridge 1966) 124. IBUKI, Y. Die Wahrheit im Johannesevangelium (1972) 258f., 275. LATTKE, M., Einheit im Wort (München 1975) 19, 23. BERGMEIER, R., Glaube als Gabe nach Johannes (Stuttgart 1980) 203. GEORGI, D., "Weisheit Salomos," in: JüdSchr III/4 (1980) 6n.186.

14:16-18 BERGMEIER, R., Glaube als Gabe nach Johannes (Stuttgart 1980) 19.

14:16f.26 BORNKAMM, G., "Die Zeit des Geistes," in: Geschichte und Glaube I (1968) 90-103.

14:16-18 BRAUN, H. Qumran und NT II (1966) 121f., 254f.

14:16-17 BROWN, R. E., "The Qumran Scrolls and the Johannine Gospel and Epistles," CBQ 17 (1955) 403-19, 559-74; also in: K. Stendahl (ed.) The Scrolls and the New Testament (New York 1957) 196; GT: "Die Schriftrollen von Qumran und das Johannesevangelium und die Johannesbriefe," in: K. H. Rengstorf (ed.) Johannes und sein Evangelium (Darmstadt 1973) 508. MUSSNER, F. "Die johanneischen Parakletsprüche und die apostolische Tradition," BZ 5 (1961) 56-70. SCHRAGE, W. Die konkreten Einzelgebote in der paulinischen Paränese (1961) 87. RIEGER, J. "Spiritus Sanctus suum praeparat adventum (Jo 14,16-17)," VerbDom 43 (1, 1965) 19-27. MUSSNER, F. "Die johanneischen Parakletsprüche und die apostolische Tradition," in: Praesentia Salutis (1967) 146. BORNKAMM, G. Geschichte und Glaube I (1968) 68-69. JOHNSTON, G. The Spirit-Paraclete in the Gospel of John (1970) 29-31. LE FORT, P. Les Structures de L'Eglise militante selon saint Jean (1970) 122-28. PORSCH, F., Pneuma und Wort (Frankfurt 1974) 240-53. de la POTTERIE, I., La Vérité dans Saint Jean I/II (Rome 1977) 341-61. SANCHEZ MIELGO, G., "Presencia y Actuación del Páráklētos en la Iglesia (Jn. 14-16)," Theología Espiritual 24 (Valencia 1980) 79-117. WILCKENS, U. "Der Paraklet und die Kirche," in: D. Lührmann/G. Strecker (eds.) Kirche. FS. G. Bornkamm (Tübingen 1980) 189. GRAYSTON, K., "The Meaning of *PARACLE-TOS*," JSNT 13 (1981) 67-82.

14:16.26 BOUSSET, W. Die Religion des Judentums im Spät-hellenistischen Zeitalter (1966 = 1926) 226.

14:16 PALLIS, A., Notes on St. John and the Apocalypse (London 1928) 31. HOSKYNS, E. C. The Fourth Gospel (1947) 465-70. WAINWRIGHT, A. W. The Trinity in the New Testament (1962) 261-62. STRAUSS, L., The Epistles of John (New York 1962) 14. LEE, G. M. "John xiv, 16," ET 76 (8, 1965) 254. KUHL, J. Die Sendung Jesu und der Kirche nach dem Johannes-Evangelium (1967) 131, 135, 136, 137. NICKELS, P. Targum and New Testament (1967) 57. HAACKER, K. Die Stiftung des Heils (1972) 152-54. PORSCH, F., Pneuma und Wort (Frankfurt 1974) 310-11. BÖHLIG, A. Die Gnosis III: Der Manichäismus (Zürich/München 1980) 308n.79, 318n.40. WOLL, D. B., "The Departure of 'The Way': The First Farewell Discourse in the Gospel of John," JBL 99 (1980) 231-34. LOADER, W. R. G., Sohn und Hoherpriester. Eine traditions-geschichtliche Untersuchung zur Christologie des Hebräer-briefes (Neukirchen-Vluyn 1981) 156. PAINTER, J. "The Farewell Discourses and the History of Johannine Christian-ity," NTS 27 (1980-1981) 529, 532.

14:17.26 KAESEMANN, E. Exegetische Versuche und Besinnungen (1964) I 184.

14:17 DELLING, G. Wort und Werk Jesu im Johannes-Evangelium (1966) 36f. HEISE, J. Bleiben (1967) 64-66. DUNN, J. D. G. Baptism in the Holy Spirit (1970) 181f., 196. JOHNSTON, G. The Spirit-Paraclete in the gospel of John (1970) 16, 88, 90, 93, 122. METZGER, B. M., The Early Versions of the New Testament (Oxford 1977) 365. SCHNACKENBURG, R., "Die johanneische Gemeinde und ihre Geisterfahrung," in: R. Schnackenburg et al. (eds.) Die Kirche des Anfangs. FS. H. Schürmann (Freiburg/Basel/Wien 1978) 283-87. MORGAN-WYNNE, J. E., "A Note on John 14. 17b," BZ 23 (1979) 93-96. BERGMEIER, R., Glaube als Gabe nach Johannes (Stutt-gart 1980) 176n.526, 255n.326. WOLL, D. B. "The Depar-ture of 'The Way': The First Farewell Discourse in the Gospel of John," JBL 99 (1980) 233-34.

14:18ff KAESEMANN, E. Exegetische Versuche und Besinnungen (1963) II 146. IBUKI, Y. Die Wahrheit im Johannes-evangelium (1972) 275, 283-86. WILCKENS, U., "Der Par-aklet und die Kirche;" in: D. Lührmann/G. Strecker (eds.) Kirche. FS. G. Bornkamm (Tübingen 1980) 194-95.

14:18-24 MUSZNER, F. ZΩH. Die Anschauung vom "Leben" im vierten Evangelium (1952) 155f. WOLL, D. B., "The Departure of 'The Way': The First Farewell Discourse in the Gospel of John," JBL 99 (1980) 231-35, 237-38.

14:18-23 SCHULZ, S., Untersuchungen zur Menschensohn-Christologie im Johannesevangelium (Göttingen 1957) 164-67. PORSCH, F., Pneuma und Wort (Frankfurt 1974) 383-84.

14:18 KUENZI, M. Das Naherwartungslogion Matthäus 10,23 (1970) 103f., 110.

14:19 DUPONT, J. Essais sur la Christologie de Saint Jean (1951) 208, 209, 210, 211, 212, 229. KAESEMANN, E. Exegetische Versuche und Besinnungen (1964) I 181. RENKEWITZ, H. "Ich lebe und ihr sollt auch leben," in: Kleine Predigt-Typologie III (1965) L. Schmidt ed., 185-91. LINDEMANN, A., "Gemeinde und Welt im Johannesevangelium," in: D. Lührmann/ G. Strecker (eds.) Kirche. FS. G. Bornkamm (Tübingen 1980) 146. WOLL, D. B., "The Departure of 'The Way': The First Farewell Discourse in the Gospel of John," JBL 99 (1980) 232-34.

14:20-22 IBUKI, Y., Die Wahrheit im Johannesevangelium (1972) 158ff., 207, 216f., 274-78, 286f., 288f.

14:20 RUCKSTUHL, E. Die literarische Einheit des Johannesevangeliums (1951) 252. MUSSNER, F. Die Johanneische Sehweise und die Frage nach dem historischen Jesus (1965) 26, 28, 29, 33, 59. CADMAN, W. H. The Open Heaven (1969) G. B. Caird ed., 16, 28, 35, 40, 51, 91, 119, 123, 146. BÜHNER, J.-A., Der Gesandte und sein Weg im 4. Evangelium (Tübingen 1977) 221-24. WOLL, D. B., "The Departure of 'The Way': The First Farewell Discourse in the Gospel of John," JBL 99 (1980) 231, 232, 234-35, 238.

14:21 LATTKE, W., Einheit im Wort (München 1975) 19, 23. BERGMEIER, R., Glaube als Gabe nach Johannes (Stuttgart 1980) 203. GEORGI, D., "Weisheit Salomos," in: JüdSchr III/ 4 (180) 6n.16a, 186.

14:22ff HAHN, F. Das Verständnis der Mission im Neuen Testament (²1965) 139.

14:22 LINDEMANN, A., "Gemeinde und Welt im Johannesvangelium," in: D. Lührmann/G. Strecker (eds.) Kirche. FS. G. Bornkamm (Tübingen 1980) 146.

14:23-32 BLANK, J. "Das Wort, der Geist und die Gemeinde," Am Tisch des Wortes 3 (1965) 28-44.

14:23-31 BONHOEFFER, D., in: Herr, tue meine Lippen auf Bd. 1 (1957) G. Eichholz ed., 184-89. KAESEMANN, E. Exegetische Versuche und Besinnungen (1964) I 257-63. BLANK, J. Schriftauslegung in Theorie und Praxis (1969) 188-206. OTTO, G. Denken- zum zu glauben (1970) 35-39.

14:23-27 KAESEMANN, E. GPM 4 (1949-1950) 166ff. GOLLWITZER, GPM 9 (1954-1955) 146ff. WEBER, O. GPM 15 (1960-1961) 167ff. DOERNE, M. Er kommt auch noch heute (1961) 94-96. WEBER, O. Predigt-Meditationen (1967) 289-93. KLEIN, G. GPM 27 (2, 1973) 278-85. SURKAU, H.-W., in: GPM 33 (1979) 244-52.

14:23-24 BLANK, J. Schriftauslegung in Theorie und Praxis (1969) 192-94.

14:23 VON LOEWENICH, W. Das Johannes-Verständnis im zweiten Jahrhundert (1932) 5, 9, 10, 16, 19, 23, 29, 32, 58. RUDOLPH, K. Die Maudäer II (1961) 420. LUTHER, M. Predigten über die Christus-Botschaft (1966) 208-16. HEISE, J. Bleiben (1967) 102-103. JOHNSTON, G. The Spirit-Paraclete in the gospel of John (1970) 45, 81, 93, 114, 177. SANDVIK, B. Das Kommen des Herrn beim Abendmahl (1970) 121, 122, 125, 139. VOEGTLE, A. Das Neue Testament und die Zukunft des Kosmos (1970) 24f. IBUKI, Y. Die Wahrheit im Johannesevangelium (1972) 257-60, 276f., 286f. PORSCH, F., Pneuma und Wort (Frankfurt 1974) 390-91. LATTKE, M., Einheit im Wort (München 1975) 19, 23. BERGMEIER, R., Glaube als Gabe nach Johannes (Stuttgart 1980) 176n.526. GEORGI, D., "Weisheit Salomos," in: JüdSchr III/4 (1980) 6n.18b.

14:24-27 LUTHER, M. Predigten über die Christus-Botschaft (1966) 217-24.

14:24-26 IBUKI, Y. Die Wahrheit im Johannesevangelium (1972) 32ff., 259f., 277f., 287f.

14:24 DELLING, G., Wort und Werk Jesu im Johannes-Evangelium (1966) 34, 45, 65, 72, 101, 113. BERGMEIER, R., Glaube als Gabe nach Johannes (Stuttgart 1980) 214.

14:25-31 SMIT, D. M. The Composition and Order of the Fourth Gospel (1965) 168, 171, 172, 174, 239. LATTKE, M. Einheit im Wort (München 1975) 233-45.

14:25-26 SCHULZ, S., Untersuchungen zur Menschensohn-Christologie im Johannesevangelium (Göttingen 1957) 145-46. MUSSNER, F., Die Johanneische Sehweise und die Frage nach dem historischen Jesus (1965) 56f. Le FORT, P. Les Structures de L'Eglise militante selon saint Jean (1970) 122-28, 165. BLANK, J., "Bindung und Freiheit. Das Verhältnis der nachapostolischen Kirche zu Jesus von Nazaret,'' BuK 33 (1978) 19-22. CARREZ, M., ''Les Promesses du Paraclet,'' ETh 12 (1981) 323-32. WOLL, D. B., Johannine Christianity in Conflict (Chico, Cal., 1981) 97-105.

14:25 HEISE, J. Bleiben (1967) 63-64.

14:26ff THYEN, H. Studien zur Sündenvergebung (1970) 246f., 251.

14:26 GRILL, J. Untersuchungen über die Entstehung des vierten Evangeliums II (1923) 42, 220f., 331, 336. DELLING, G. Die Zueignung des Heils in der Taufe (1961) 59. SCHRAGE, W. Die konkreten Einzelgebote in der paulinischen Paränese (1961) 87, 89. STRAUSS, L., The Epistles of John (New York 1962) 14. WAINWRIGHT, A. W. The Trinity in the New Testament (1962) 261-62. DELLING, G. Die Taufe im Neuen Testament (1963) 108. KAESEMANN, E. Exegetische Versuche und Besinnungen (1964) I 185. HAHN, F. Das Verständnis der Mission im Neuen Testament (²1965) 141. DELLING, G. Wort und Werk Jesu im Johannes-Evangelium (1966) 64, 84, 126f. KUHL, J. Die Sendung Jesu und der Kirche nach dem Johannes-Evangelium (1967) 130, 153f., 184-86. NICKELS, P. Targum and New Testament (1967) 57. BORNKAMM, G. ''Der Paraklet im Johannes-Evangelium,'' in: Geschichte und Glaube I (1968) 68-89. WREGE, H.-T. Die Ueberlieferungsgeschichte der Bergpredigt (1968) 170f. CADMAN, W. H. The Open Heaven (1969) G. B. Caird ed., 6, 55, 91, 105, 179, 181, 188, 194. JOHNSTON, G. The Spirit-Paraclete in the gospel of John (1970) 16, 31, 32, 39, 69, 81, 84, 86, 89, 93, 128, 164. BEUTLER, J. Martyria (1972) 242, 274f, 303. HAACKER, K. Die Stiftung des Heils (1972) 154-56. IBUKI, Y. Die Wahrheit im Johannesevangelium (1972) 300f., 306f. BAMMEL, E. ''Jesus und der Paraklet in Johannes 16,'' in: Christ and the Spirit in the New Testament (1973) B. Lindars/S. S. Smalley eds., 201f., 204. UNTERGASSMAIR, F. G. Im Namen Jesu: Der Namensbegriff im Johannesevangelium (Stuttgart 1973) 167-71. OLSSON, B., Structure and Meaning in the Fourth Gospel (Lund 1974) 73, 267-70. PORSCH, F., Pneuma und Wort (Frankfurt 1974) 253-67. DUNN, J. D. G., Jesus and the Spirit (London 1975) 350-52. NEILL, S., Jesus Through Many Eyes (Philadephia 1976) 150-52. DUNN, J. D. G., Unity and Diversity in the New Testament (London 1977) 78. de la POTTERIE, I., La Vérité dans Saint Jean I/II (Rome 1977) 361-78, 392-93. ''Apostel,'' in: TRE 3 (1978) 481. MARTIN, A. G., ''Le Saint-Esprit et l'évangile de Jean dans une perspective trinitaire,'' RevR 29 (1978) 141-51. RAYAN, S., The Holy Spirit: Heart of the Gospel and Christian Hope (New York 1978) 84.

BERGMEIER, R., Glaube als Gabe nach Johannes (Stuttgart 1980) 176n.526, 239n.54. BÖHLIG, A., Die Gnosis III: Der Manichäismus (Zürich/München 1980) 308n.79, 318n.40. RUSSELL, E. A., "The Holy Spirit in the Fourth Gospel: Some Observations," IBS 2 (1980) 84-94. SANCHEZ MIELGO, G., "Presencia y Actuación del Paráklētos en la Iglesia (Jn. 14-16)," Theología Espiritual 24 (Valencia 1980) 79-117. WILCKENS, U., "Der Paraklet und die Kirche," in: D. Lührmann/G. Strecker (eds.) Kirche. FS. G. Bornkamm (Tübingen 1980) 189. WOLL, D. B., "The Departure of 'The Way': The First Farewell Discourse in the Gospel of John," JBL 99 (1980) 228, 233, 238. BERGER, K., "Das Buch der Jubiläen" in: JüdSchr II/3 (1981) 485n.25c. GRAYSTON, K., "The Meaning of *PARAKLĒTOS*" JSNT 13 (1981) 80-81. PAINTER, J., "The Farewell Discourses and the History of Johannine Christianity," NTS 27 (1980-1981) 535, 539.

14:27-31 SCHWANK, B. " 'Frieden hinterlasse ich euch': Jo 14,27-31," Sein und Sendung 28 (4, 1963) 196-203. BECKER, J., Das Evangelium nach Johannes (Gütersloh/Würzburg 1979) 458 (lit!). SEGOVIA, F., "The Love and Hatred of Jesus and Johannine Sectarianism," CBQ 43 (1981) 262, 265-66.

14:27-28 SCHULZ, S., Untersuchungen zur Menschensohn-Christologie im Johannesevangelium (Göttingen 1957) 167-68. BLANK, J. Schriftauslegung in Theorie und Praxis (1969) 198-202.

14:27 IBUKI, Y. Die Wahrheit im Johannesevangelium (1972) 373f. BEUTLER, J., "Psalm 42/43 im Johannesevangelium," NTS 25 (1978) 33-57. SWIDLER, L., Biblical Affirmations of Woman (Philadelphia 1979) 285. WOLL, D. B., "The Departure of 'The Way': The First Farewell Discourse of the Gospel of John," JBL 99 (1980) 226-27.

14:28-31 LUTHER, M. Predigten über die Christus-Botschaft (1966) 225-33.

14:28 WILES, M. F. The Spiritual Gospel (1960) 39, 122-25, 131. DELLING, G. Wort und Werk Jesu im Johannes-Evangelium (1966) 63, 85f. KUHL, J. Die Sendung Jesu und der Kirche nach dem Johannes-Evangelium (1967) 56f., 125f. CADMAN, W. H. The Open Heaven (1969) G. B. Caird ed., 16, 44, 90, 148, 181. THUESING, W. Die Erhöhung und Verherrlichung Jesu im Johannesevangelium (1970) 210-12. SMALLEY, S. S., "Diversity and Development in John," NTS 17 (1970-1971) 288f. BARRETT, C. K. "The Father is greater than I (Jn 14,28): Subordinationist Christology in the New Testament," in: Neues

Testament und Kirche (1974) J. Gnilka ed., 144-59. LADD, G.
E. A Theology of the New Testament (1974) 294, 300, 304.
CIGNELLI, L., "Giovanni 14,28 nell'esegesi di Origene"
SBFLA 25 (1975) 136-63. LATTKE, M., Einheit im Wort
(München 1975) 19, 23. CIGNELLI, L., "Giovanni 14,28
nell'esegesi di S. Ireneo," SBFLA 27 (1977) 137-96. SCHIL-
LEBEECKX, E., Die Auferstehung Jesu als Grund der Erlö-
sung (Basel 1979) 147-48. WOLL, D. B., "The Departure of
'The Way': The First Farewell Discourse in the Gospel of John,"
JBL 99 (1980) 227. "Byzanz" in: TRE 7 (1981) 515. DAHMS,
J. V., "Isaiah 55:11 and the Gospel of John," 53 (1981) 78-88.

14:29-31 BLANK, J. Schriftauslegung in Theorie und Praxis (1969) 202-
204.

14:30 FRIES, S. A. "Was bedeutet der Fürst der Welt?" ZNW 6
(1905) 159. BOUSSET, W. Die Religion des Judentums im
Späthellenistischen Zeitalter (1966 = 1926) 253, 335. DEL-
LING, G. Wort und Werk Jesu im Johannes-Evangelium (1966)
52f., 81f., 112. DAUER, A. Die Passionsgeschichte im
Johannesevangelium (1972) 37, 241, 294. BOISMARD, M. E.,
"Importance de la critique textuelle pour établir l'origine ara-
méenne du quatrième évangile" in: M. Boismard et al., L'E-
vangile de Jean: études et problèmes (Bruges 1958) 53-56.
"Antichrist" in: TRE 3 (1978) 22. RUDOLPH, K., Die Gnosis
(Göttingen 1978) 324.

14:31 BORIG, R. Der Wahre Weinstock (1967) 19ff. CADMAN, W.
H. The Open Heaven (1969) G. B. Caird ed., 16, 22, 163, 169,
180. DAUER, A. Die Passionsgeschichte im Johannesevangelium (1972) 279f. IBUKI, Y. Die Wahrheit im
Johannesevangelium (1972) 269-71.

14:31 HAMMER, J., "Eine Klare Stellung zu Joh 14,31b," BuK 14
(2, 1959) 33-40. FORTNA, R. T. The Gospel of Signs (1970)
157. LATTKE, M., Einheit im Wort (München 1975) 19.
PANCARO, S., The Law in the Fourth Gospel (Leiden 1975)
425, 439-42, 449. METZGER, B. M., The Early Versions of
the New Testament (Oxford 1977) 437. BERGMEIER, R.,
Glaube als Gabe nach Johannes (Stuttgart 1980) 211-12. WOLL,
D. B., "The Departure of 'The Way': The First Farewell Discourse in the Gospel of John," JBL 99 (1980) 227. MOHR, T.
A., Markus- und Johannespassion (Zürich 1982) 245-47.

15-17 BAUER, W. Das Johannesevangelium (1925) 182f. STRATH-
MANN, H. Das Evangelium nach Johannes (1955) 213f. TEM-
PLE, S., The Core of the Fourth Gospel (London 1975) 226-27.
WILCKENS, U., "Der Paraklet und die Kirche" in: D. Lühr-
mann/G. Strecker (eds.) Kirche. FS. G. Bornkamm (Tübingen
1980) 185-203. "Eschatologie" in: TRE 10 (1982) 289.

15-16 KAESEMANN, E. Exegetische Versuche und Besinnungen
(1964) II 134, 154. WILKENS, W. Die Entstehungsgeschichte
des vierten Evangeliums (1958) 152-56. THÜSING, W., "Die
Bitten des johanneischen Jesus in dem Gebet Joh 17 und die Intentionen Jesu von Nazaret" in: R. Schnackenburg et al. (eds.)
Die Kirche des Anfangs. FS. H. Schürmann (Freiburg/Basel/
Wien 1978) 322-28. NICCACCI, A. "Esame letterario di Gv
15-16" Antonianum 56 (1981) 43-71.

15:1-16:33 YATES, K. M. Preaching from John's Gospel (1964) 135-41.

15:1-16:24 GUILDING, A. The Fourth Gospel and Jewish Worship (1960)
112-20, 122-23.

15:1-16:4 RINALDI, G., "Amore e odio (Giov. 15,1-16,4a)" BiOr 22
(1980) 97-106. PAINTER, J., "The Farewell Discourses and
the History of Johannine Christianity" NTS 27 (1980-1981) 526,
528, 534-36.

15:1-16:3 SIMOENS, Y., La gloire d'aimer. Structures stylistiques et interprétatives dans le Discours de la Cène (Jn 13-17) (Rome
1981).

15 SCHWEIZER, E. Ego Eimi (Göttingen 1939) 157-61. MOR-
GAN, G. C. The Parables and Metaphors of Our Lord (1943)
341ff. BECKER, H., Die Reden des Johannesevangeliums und
der Stil der gnostischen Offenbarungsrede (Göttingen 1956) 109-
13. NIEWALDA, P. Sakramentsymbolik im Johannes-
evangelium? (1958) 76-79. MINEAR, P. S. Images of the
Church in the New Testament (1960) 47ff., 158f. SCHULZ, S.
Komposition und Herkunft der Johanneischen Reden (Stuttgart
1960) 83-84, 114-17. LOCKYER, H. All the Parables of the
Bible (1963) 339ff. JAUBERT, A. "L'image de la Vigne (Jean
15)," in: Oikonomia (1967) F. Christ ed., 93-99. SANDVIK,
B. "Joh 15 als Abendmahlstext," ThZ 23 (5, 1967) 323-28.
OTOMO, Y. Nachfolge Jesu und Anfänge der Kirche im Neuen
Testament (1970) 147—49. BONHOEFFER, D. Gesammelte
Schriften 5 (1972) E. Bethge ed., 95-106. RIEDL, J. Das

Heilswerk Jesu nach Johannes (1973) 344-78. ROSSCUP, J. E. Abiding in Christ (1973). MUELLER, T. Das Heilsgeschehen im Johannesevangelium n.d., 80-87. SCHNACKENBURG, R., "Aufbau und Sinn von Johannes 15" in: Homenaje a Juan Prado (Madrid 1975) 405-20. BÜHNER, J.-A., Der Gesandte und sein Weg im 4. Evangelium (Tübingen 1977) 178-80. BERG-MEIER, R., Glaube als Gabe nach Johannes (Stuttgart 1980) 212.

15:1ff SCHWEIZER, E. Gemeinde und Gemeinde-Ordnung im Neuen Testament (1959) § 11b,g. SCHWEIZER, E. Erniedrigung und Erhöhung bei Jesus und seinen Nachfolgern (1962) § 5e,f,6g. SANDVIK, B. Das Kommen des Herrn beim Abendmahl (1970) 121ff. FURNISH, V. P. The Love Command in the New Testament (1972) 139-43. "Ethik" in: TRE 10 (1982) 455.

15:1-27 GOLLWITZER, H./HAMEL, J. Ihr sollt mein Volk sein (1959). CADMAN, W. H. The Open Heaven (1969) G. B. Caird ed., 175-88.

15:1-17 PIROT, J. Paraboles et Allégories Evangeliques (1949) 452-64. CORELL, A. Consummatum Est (1958) 73-74. GEORGE, A. "Lettura della Bibbia. Gesù, La Vite Vera (Giov. 15,1-17)," BiOr 3 (4, 1961) 121-25. SCHWANK, B. " 'Ich bin der wahre Weinstock': Joh 15,1-17," Sein und Sendung 28 (6, 1963) 244-58. BEHLER, G.-M. The Last Discourse of Jesus (1965) 135-63. KUHL, J. Die Sendung Jesu und der Kirche nach dem Johannes-Evangelium (1967) 205-209. THUESING, W. Die Erhöhung und Verherrlichung Jesu im Johannesevangelium (1970) 109f., 117-20, 123-26. IBUKI, Y. Die Wahrheit im Johannesevangelium (1972) 290f., 295. BAKER, J. A., "The Myth of the Church. A Case Study in the Use of the Scripture for Christian Doctrine" in: M. Hooker/C. Hickling (eds.) What about the New Testament. FS. C. Evans (London 1975) 173-74. HAWKIN, D. J., "Orthodoxy and Heresy in John 10:1-21 and 15:1-17" EQ 47 (1975) 208-13. RIGOPOULOS, G., "Jēsous Christos 'hē Ampelos hē Alēthinē' (Iō. 15,1-17)" DBM 4 (1976) 161-80. MINEAR, P. S., To Die and to Live. Christ's Resurrection and Christian Vocation (New York 1977) 111-12. BECKER, J., Das Evangelium nach Johannes (Gütersloh/Würzburg 1979) 479 (lit!). HAENCHEN, E., Das Johannesevangelium (Tübingen 1980) 480-81 (lit!). LINDEMANN, A., "Gemeinde und Welt im Johannesevangelium" in: D. Lührmann/G. Strecker (eds.) Kirche. FS. G. Bornkamm (Tübingen 1980) 150. PEDERSEN, S., "Agape—der eschatologische Hauptbegriff bei Paulus" in: S. Pedersen (ed.) Die Paulinische Literatur und Theologie (Arhus/Göttingen 1980) 173-74.

15:1-16 MUELLER, T. Das Heilsgeschehen im Johannesevangelium n.d., 22-24, 67-69.

15:1-11 BARTH, C. "Bible Study IV. The Disciples of the Servant. John 15:1-11," SEAJTh 6 (4, 1965); 7 (1, 1965) 14-16.

15:1-10 BORIG, R. Der Wahre Weinstock (1967). RICHTER, G. MThZ 20 (1, 1969) 72-73. SCHILLEBEECKX, E., Christ: The Christian Experience in the Modern World (London 1980) 395-96; GT: Christus und die Christen (Freiburg/Basel/Wien 1977) 381-82. PAINTER, J., "The Farewell Discourses and the History of Johannine Christianity" NTS 27 (1980-1981) 534, 536.

15:1-8 FLEW, R. N. Jesus and His Church (1956) 172-73. VAN DEN BUSSCHE, H. "La Vigne et ses fruits (Jean 15,1-8)" BVieC 26 (1959) 12-18. KIIVIT, J. GPM 17 (2, 1963) 267-73. NIE-SEL, W. in: Herr, tue meine Lippen auf Bd. 3 (1964) 435ff. BEHLER, G.-M. The Last Discourse of Jesus (1965) 135-48. WEBER, O. Predigtmeditationen (1967) 12-15. BRAUN, H. GPM 23 (3, 1968) 290-93. LE FORT, P. Les Structures de L'Eglise militante selon saint Jean (1970) 90-96, 162, 167-68. WEAD, D. W., The Literary Devices in John's Gospel (1970) 92-94. RADERMAKERS, J. "Je suis la vraie vigne. Jn 15,1-8," AssS 26 (1973) 46-58. KABITZ, U./ROESSLER, I. "Johannes 15,1-8: Anhänglichkeit oder Abhängigkeit," in: Predigtstudien für das Kirchenjahr 1975 (1975) P. Krusche/E. Lange/D. Rössler/R. Roessler eds., 153-61. NIEBERGALL, A. GPM 29 (3, 1975) 347-54. VOUGA, F., Le cadre historique et l'intention théologique de Jean (Paris 1977) 93-94. STEWART, R. A., "Engrafting: A Study in New Testament Symbolism and Baptismal Application" EQ 50 (1978) 8-22. PEISKER, H., in: GPM 33 (1979) 209-16. BERGMEIER, R., Glaube als Gabe nach Johannes (Stuttgart 1980) 236.

15:1-7 THUESING, W. Die Erhöhung und Verherrlichung Jesu im Johannesevangelium (1970) 118-120. HEIN, K., Eucharist and Excommunication (Bern/Frankfurt 1975) 34-37. "Abendmahl" in: TRE 1 (1977) 57.

15:1-6 MUSZNER, F. ZΩH. Die Anschauung vom "Leben" im vierten Evangelium (1952) 148-50.

15:1-4 STECK, K. GPM 21 (2, 1966) 200-208.

15:1-2 HUNTER, A. M. According to John (1970²) 86f.

15:1 CLEMEN, C. Primitive Christianity and Its Non-Jewish Sources (1912) 363f. WULF, F. " 'Ich bin der wahre Weinstock' (Jo 15:1). Anleitung zur Meditation über die Selbstaussagen Jesu," GuL 30 (4, 1957) 301-306. WILES, M. F. The Spiritual Gospel (1960) 69-70, 157. STANLEY, D. M. " 'I Am the Genuine

Vine' John 15:1,'' Bible Today 1 (8, 1963) 484-91. LADD, G.
E. A Theology of the New Testament (1974) 216, 231, 250, 267.
METZGER, B. M., The Early Versions of the New Testament
(Oxford 1977) 34-35. BÖHLIG, A., Die Gnosis III: Der Mani-
chäismus (Zürich/München 1980) 343n.29.

15:2-3 BARTH, M., Die Taufe - ein Sakrament? (Zürich 1951) 420ff.
LEROY, H., Zur Vergebung der Sünden (Stuttgart 1974) 88-
89.

15:3 GRILL, J. Untersuchungen über die Entstehung des vierten
Evangeliums II (1923) 45, 140f. IBUKI, Y. Die Wahrheit im
Johannesevangelium (1972) 31f. MUELLER, T. Das Heilsge-
schehen im Johannesevangelium n.d., 22-24, 132-35.

15:4-7.9f.16 HEISE, J. Bleiben (1967) 80-92.

15:4-5 ROESSLER, R., in: P. Krusche et al (eds.) Predigtstudien für
das Kirchenjahr (1980-1981) III/1 (Stuttgart 1980) 68-75.

15:4 SANDVIK, B. Das Kommen des Herrn beim Abendmahl (1970)
121, 123, 124.

15:5.8 FOSTER, J. "A Note on St. Polycarp," ET 77 (10, 1966) 319.

15:5 van der MINDE, H. J., "Theologia crucis und Pneumaaussa-
gen bei Paulus" Catholica 34 (1980) 108.

15:7ff KAESEMANN, E. Exegetische Versuche und Besinnungen
(1964) I 184.

15:7-17 MIELGO, G. S. "Aspectos eclesiales en San Juan. Estudio ex-
egético-teologico de Jn. 15.7-17." EsVe 1 (1971) 9-58.

15:7-8 PANCARO, S., The Law in the Fourth Gospel (Leiden 1975)
151, 414, 418-20, 426, 427.

15:7 UNTERGASSMAIR, F. G., Im Namen Jesu: Der Namensbe-
griff im Johannesevangelium (Stuttgart 1973) 140-46. KÜM-
MEL, W. G. ed., Jüdische Schriften aus hellenistisch-römischer
Zeit III (1975) 222.

15:8 BOUSSET, W. Die Religion des Judentums im Späthellenistischen Zeitalter (1966 = 1926) 416. KUHL, J. Die
Sendung Jesu und der Kirche nach dem Johannes-Evangelium
(1967) 138f. THUESING, W. Die Erhöhung und Verherrlichung Jesu im Johannesevangelium (1970) 107-10.

15:9-17 LANG, F. in: Herr, tue meine Lippen auf Bd. 3 (1964) G. Eichholz ed., 274ff. BEHLER, G.-M. The Last Discourse of Jesus
(1965) 148-63. STECK, K. G. in: Hören und Fragen Bd. 5,3
(1967) 332ff. STECK, K. G. GPM 25 (1, 1971) 249-57.
LATTKE, M., Einheit im Wort (München 1975) 162-88.
SCHNATH, G. und TILMAN, R., in: P. Krusche et al. (eds.)

Predigtstudien für das Kirchenjahr 1976-1977. V/2 (Stuttgart 1977) 80-86.

15:9-13 DAVIES, W. D., The Sermon on the Mount (Cambridge 1966) 124.

15:9-12 VOUGA, F., " 'Aimez-vous les uns les autres.' Une étude sur l'église de Jean" BCPE 26 (1974) 5-31. VOUGA, F., Le cadre historique et l'intention théologique de Jean (Paris 1977) 92-93.

15:9-11 LAZURE, N., Les Valeurs Morales de la Théologie Johannique (Paris 1965) 217-19. LATTKE, M., Einheit im Wort (München 1975) 165-76.

15:9-10 HEISE, J., Bleiben. μένειν in den Johanneischen Schriften (Tübingen 1967) 80-92. IBUKI, Y. Die Wahrheit im Johannesevangelium (1972) 246ff., 252., 268f. LATTKE, M., Einheit im Wort (München 1975) 12, 19, 25.

15:9 DELLING, G. Wort und Werk Jesu im Johannes-Evangelium (1966) 66, 101, 130, 133. KUHL, J. Die Sendung Jesu und der Kirche nach dem Johannes-Evangelium (1967) 81-88. SCHLIER, H. "Die Bruderliebe nach dem Evangelium und den Briefen des Johannes," in: Mélanges Bibliques en hommage au R. P. Béda Rigaux (1970) A. Descamps/A. deHalleux eds., 237, 239-40. GEORGI, D., "Weisheit Salomos" in: JüdSchr III/4 (1980) 8n.3b.

15:10 HENNECKE, E./SCHNEEMELCHER, W. Neutestamentliche Apokryphen (1964) I 139. GEORGI, D., "Weisheit Salomos" in: JüdSchr III/4 (1980) 6n.18b.

15:11 TILLICH, P. Das Neue Sein (1959) 135-43.

15:12-17 WEBER, O. Predigtmeditationen (1967) 43-46. LATTKE, M., Einheit im Wort (München 1975) 176-88.

15:12-15.17 IBUKI, Y. Die Wahrheit im Johannesevangelium (1972) 244-52, 252ff., 263.

15:12-13 THUESING, W. Die Erhöhung und Verherrlichung Jesu im Johannesevangelium (1970) 124-26.

15:12.17 HAHN, F. Das Verständnis der Mission im Neuen Testament (²1965) 144.

15:12 LAZURE, N., Les Valeurs Morales de la Théologie Johannique (Paris 1965) 220. KUHL, J. Die Sendung Jesu und der Kirche nach dem Johannes-Evangelium (1967) 196f. SCHLIER, H. "Die Bruderliebe nach dem Evangelium und den Briefen des Johannes," in: Mélanges Bibliques en hommage au R. P. Béda Rigaux (1970) A. Descamps/A. deHalleux eds., 241-42. LATTKE, M., Einheit im Wort (München 1975) 19, 25. SAN-

DERS, J. T., Ethics in the New Testament (Philadelphia 1975) 91-94.

15:13ff LATTKE, M. Einheit im Wort (München 1975) 19.

15:13-16 GRUNDMANN, W. "Das Wort von Jesu Freunden (Joh. XV, 13-16) und das Herrenmahl," NovTest 3 (1-2, 1959) 62-69.

15:13-14 HAHN, F. Das Verständnis der Mission im Neuen Testament (²1965) 139.

15:13 DIBELIUS, M. Botschaft und Geschichte I (1953) 204-20. DENNEY, J. The Death of Christ (³1956) 144. JACOBS, L. "Greater Love Hath No Man . . . The Jewish Point of View of Self-Sacrifice," Judaism 6 (1957) 41-47. POPKES, W. Christus Traditus (1967) 284f. DAUER, A. Die Passionsgeschichte im Johannesevangelium (1972) 210, 294, 313. LATTKE, M., Einheit im Wort (München 1975) 178-83. JERVELL, J., Ingen har større kjaerlighet . . . Fra Johannesevangeliets Jesusbilde (Oslo/Bergen/Tromsø 1978). GEORGI, D., "Weisheit Salomos" in: JüdSchr III/4 1980) 6n.18b.

15:14 BARRETT, C. K. The New Testament Background (1956) 221. LEE, G. M. "John XV 14 'Ye are my friends'," NovTest 15 (4, 1973) 260.

15:15 BÖHLIG, A., "Vom 'Knecht' zum 'Sohn' " in: Mysterion und Wahrheit (Leiden 1968) 63.

15:16 DELLING, G. Die Zueignung des Heils in der Taufe (1961) 59. GLASSON, T. F. Moses in the Fourth Gospel (1963) 84f. LAZURE, N., Les Valeurs Morales de la Théologie Johannique (Paris 1965) 33-34. HEISE, J., Bleiben. μένειν in den Johanneischen Schriften (Tübingen 1967) 80-92. KUHL, J. Die Sendung Jesu und der Kirche nach dem Johannes-Evangelium (1967) 142-45, 205-209. CADMAN, W. H. The Open Heaven (1969) G. B. Caird ed., 119, 160, 164, 193, 196. THUESING, W. Die Erhöhung und Verherrlichung Jesu im Johannes-Evangelium (1970) 111-14. UNTERGASSMAIR, F. G., Im Namen Jesu: Der Namensbegriff im Johannesevangelium (Stuttgart 1973) 129-39. "Erwählung" in: TRE 10 (1982) 196.

15:17 LATTKE, M., Einheit im Wort (München 1975) 19. SANDERS, J. T., Ethics in the New Testament (Philadelphia 1975) 91-94.

15:18 - 16:15 SÁNCHEZ MIELGO, G., "La Iglesia en el mundo (Jn 15,18-16,15)" EsVe 11 (1981) 437-62.

15:18 - 16:4 SCHWANK, B. " 'Da sie mich verfolgt haben, werden sie auch euch verfolgen': Jo 15,18-16,4a," Sein und Sendung 28 (7, 1963) 292-301. BEHLER, G.-M. The Last Discourse of Jesus

(1965) 163-79. REIM, G., Studien zum Alttestamentlichen Hintergrund des Johannesevangeliums (Cambridge 1974) 44-45. VOUGA, F., Le cadre historique et l'intention théologique de Jean (Paris 1977) 97-106. BECKER, J. Das Evangelium nach Johannes (Gütersloh/Würzburg 1979) 488 (lit!). PIETRAN-TONIO, R., "El sufrimiento en la persecución por causa de la Palabra. Juan 15,18-16,4a" RevBi 42 (1980) 11-19.

15:18-27 de la POTTERIE, I., La Vérité dans Saint Jean I/II (Rome 1977) 408-409. HAENCHEN, E., Das Johannesevangelium (Tübingen 1980) 484-86 (lit!).

15:18-25 IBUKI, Y. Die Wahrheit im Johannesevangelium (1972) 290f. BERGMEIER, R., Glaube als Gabe nach Johannes (Stuttgart 1980) 16. LINDEMANN, A. "Gemeinde und Welt im Johannesevangelium" in: D. Lührmann/G. Strecker (eds.) Kirche. FS. G. Bornkamm (Tübingen 1980) 151. PAINTER, J., "The Farewell Discourses and the History of Johannine Christianity" NTS 27 (1980-1981) 530, 534, 542.

15:18-21 IWAND, H.-J. Predigt-Meditationen (1964) 557-61. VOUGA, F., Le cadre historique et l'intention théologique de Jean (Paris 1977) 99-100.

15:18 PALLIS, A., Notes on St. John and the Apocalypse (London 1928) 32-33. LATTKE, M., Einheit im Wort (München 1975) 12.

15:19 DELLING, G. Wort und Werk Jesu im Johannes-Evangelium (1966) 55, 132f. HEINZ, D. "Brief Translation Note on John 15:19," CThM 39 (11, 1968) 775. IBUKI, Y. Die Wahrheit im Johannesevangelium (1972) 346ff. BERGMEIER, R., Glaube als Gabe nach Johannes (Stuttgart 1980) 27, 110n.373, 220ff, 256n.348f., 264n.484. "Erwählung" in: TRE 10 (1982) 196.

15:20 KNOX, W. L. The Sources of the Synoptic Gospels II (1957) 10. HAHN, F. Christologische Hoheitstitel (1963) 78. HEN-NECKE, E./SCHNEEMELCHER, W. Neutestamentliche Apokryphen (1964) I 156. DAVIES, W. D., The Sermon on the Mount (Cambridge 1966) 124-25. WREGE, H. "T. Die Ueber-lieferungsgeschichte der Bergpredigt (1968) 127f. von WANKE, J., "Kommentarworte" BZ 24 (1980) 213.

15:21 DELLING, G. Die Zueignung des Heils in der Taufe (1961) 40. UNTERGASSMAIR, F. G., Im Namen Jesu: Der Namensbe-griff im Johannesevangelium (Stuttgart 1973) 177-79.

15:22-25 VOUGA, F., Le cadre historique et l'intention théologique de Jean (Paris 1977) 101-102.

15:22-24 BERGMEIER, R., Glaube als Gabe nach Johannes (Stuttgart 1980) 231, 233, 260n.420.

15:22.24 STROBEL, A. Erkenntnis und Bekenntnis der Sünde in neutestamentlicher Zeit (1968) 46. BEUTLER, J. Martyria (1972) 274f., 299.

15:22 LAZURE, N., Les Valeurs Morales de la Théologie Johannique (Paris 1965) 299.

15:24 LAZURE, N., Les Valeurs Morales de la Théologie Johannique (Paris 1965) 299. METZGER, B. M., The Early Versions of the New Testament (Oxford 1977) 390.

15:25 FREED, E. D. Old Testament Quotations in the Gospel of John (1965) 94-95. ROTHFUCHS, W. Die Erfüllungszitate des Matthäus-Evangeliums (1969) 158f. REIM, G. Studien zum alttestamentlichen Hintergrund des Johannesevangeliums (Cambridge 1974) 42-43, 89-91, 93-94. HANSON, A. T., The New Testament Interpretation of Scripture (London 1980) 158-59.

15:26-16:4 KLAAS, W. in: Herr, tue meine Lippen auf Bd. 1 (1957) G. Eichholz ed., 173-84. IWAND, H.-J. Predigt-Meditationen (1964) 16-19. GEORGE, A. "Les témoins de Jésus devant le monde," AssS 50 (1966) 30-40. STOEVESANDT, H. GPM 27 (2, 1973) 266-78. KÜNKEL, K. in: GPM 33 (1979) 235-44. LINDEMANN, A., "Gemeinde und Welt im Johannesevangelium" in: D. Lührmann/G. Strecker (eds.) Kirche. FS. G. Bornkamm (Tübingen 1980) 151-52.

15:26-27 CREHAN, J., The Theology of St. Luke (1965) 28, 100-101, 146. MUSSNER, F. Die Johanneische Sehweise und die Frage nach dem historischen Jesus (1965) 58f., 62f. LE FORT, P. Les Structures de L'Eglise militante selon saint Jean (1970) 122-28, 162. THUESING, W. Die Erhöhung und Verherrlichung Jesu im Johannesevangelium (1970) 142-44. BEUTLER, J. Martyria (1972) 273ff., 298f., 303f. IBUKI, Y. Die Wahrheit im Johannesevangelium (1972) 290-95, 306-10. de la POTTERIE, I., La Vérité dans Saint Jean I/II (Rome 1977) 378-99. VOUGA, F., Le cadre historique et l'intention théologique de Jean (Paris 1977) 102-103. CRIBBS, F. L., "The Agreements that Exist Between John and Acts" in: C. H. Talbert (ed.) Perspectives on Luke-Acts (Danville 1978) 49-50. SÁNCHEZ MIELGO, G., "Presencia y Actuación del Paráklētos en la Iglesia (Jn. 14-16)" Theología Espiritual 24 (Valencia 1980) 79-117. CARREZ, M., "Les Promesses du Paraclet" ETh 12 (1981) 323-32. GRAYSTON, K., "The Meaning of *PARAKLĒTOS*" JSNT 13 (1981) 80-81. PAINTER, J., "The Farewell Discourses and the History of Johannine Christianity" NTS 27 (1980-1981) 535.

15:26 GRILL, J. Untersuchungen über die Entstehung des vierten Evangeliums II (1923) 220f., 331f., 336. SCHULZ, S., Untersuchungen zur Menschensohn-Christologie im Johannesevangelium (Göttingen 1957) 146-47. STRAUSS, L., The Epistles of John (New York 1962) 14. KAESEMANN, E. Exegetische Versuche und Besinnungen (1964) I 184. HAHN, F. Das Verständnis der Mission im Neuen Testament (²1965) 141. DELLING, G. Wort und Werk Jesu im Johannes-Evangelium (1966) 126f. KUHL, J. Die Sendung Jesu und der Kirche nach dem Johannes-Evangelium (1967) 129-37, 183f. NICKELS, P. Targum and New Testament (1967) 57. BORNKAMM, G. Geschichte und Glaube (1968) I 68ff., 90-103. CADMAN, W. H. The Open Heaven (1969) G. B. Caird ed., 6, 55, 105, 164, 166. JOHNSTON, G. The Spirit-Paraclete in the gospel of John (1970) 32-34. LADD, G. E. A Theology of the New Testament (1974) 268, 275, 295, 296. PORSCH, F., Pneuma und Wort (Frankfurt 1974) 267-75. MARTIN, A. G., ''La Saint-Esprit et l'Evangile de Jean dans une perspective trinitaire'' RevR 29 (1978) 141-51. RAYAN, S., The Holy Spirit: Heart of the Gospel and Christian Hope (New York 1978) 85. BERGMEIER, R., Glaube als Gabe nach Johannes (Stuttgart 1980) 239n.54. BÖHLIG, A., Die Gnosis III: Der Manichäismus (Zürich/München 1980) 308n.79, 318n.40, 322n.54. WILCKENS, U., ''Der Paraklet und die Kirche'' in: D. Lührmann/G. Strecker (eds.), Kirche. FS. G. Bornkamm (Tübingen 1980) 189, 196-97.

15:27 HAHN, F. Das Verständnis der Mission im Neuen Testament (²1965) 142, 143. KUHL, J. Die Sendung Jesu und der Kirche nach dem Johannes-Evangelium (1967) 183f.

---

16 BECKER, H., Die Reden des Johannesevangeliums und der Stil der gnostischen Offenbarungsrede (Göttingen 1956) 96-105. CADMAN, W. H. The Open Heaven (1969) G. B. Gaird ed., 189-98. BAMMEL, E. ''Jesus und der Paraklet in Johannes 16,'' in: Christ and the Spirit in the New Testament (1973) B. Lindars/S. S. Smalley eds., 199-217. MUELLER, T. Das Heilsgeschehen im Johannesevangelium n.d., 80-87. BERGMEIER, R., Glaube als Gabe nach Johannes (Stuttgart 1980) 212. HAENCHEN, E., Das Johannesevangelium (Tübingen 1980)

492 (lit!). LEGASSE, S., "Le rétour du Christ d'après l'évangile de Jean, chapitre 14 et 16: une adaption du motif de la Parousie" BLE 81 (1980) 161-74.

16:1-24 LEANEY, A. R. C. "The Johannine Paraclete and the Qumran Scrolls," in: John and Qumran (1972) J. H. Charlesworth ed., 59-60.

16:1-11 LINDEMANN, A., "Gemeinde und Welt im Johannesevangelium" in: D. Lührmann/G. Strecker (eds.) Kirche. FS. G. Bornkamm (Tübingen 1980) 152-53.

16:1-4 VOUGA, F., Le cadre historique et l'intention théologique de Jean (Paris 1977) 103-104. PAINTER, J., "The Farewell Discourses and the History of Johannine Christianity" NTS 27 (1980-1981) 534-35.

16:2 PALLIS, A., Notes on St. John and the Apocalypse (London 1928) 33-34. STRECKER, G. Der Weg der Gerechtigkeit (1962) 30n.4. IBUKI, Y. Die Wahrheit im Johannesevangelium (1972) 291f. BERGMEIER, R., Glaube als Gabe nach Johannes (Stuttgart 1980) 211. KLEIN, H., "Die lukanisch-johanneische Passionstradition" in: M. Limbeck (ed.) Redaktion and Theologie des Passionsberichtes nach den Synoptikern (Darmstadt 1981) 383-86.

16:3-4 SCHRAGE, W. Die konkreten Einzelgebote in der paulinischen Paränese (1961) 89.

16:3 HAHN, F. Christologische Hoheitstitel (1963) 330.

16:4-33 REHLER, G.-M. The Last Discourse of Jesus (1965) 181-218. PAINTER, J., "The Farewell Discourses and the History of Johannine Christianity" NTS 27 (1980-1981) 526, 536-37. SIMOENS, Y., La gloire d'aimer. Structures stylistiques et interprétatives dans le Discours de la Cène (Jn 13 - 17) (Rome 1981).

16:4-15 SCHWANK, B. " 'Es ist gut für euch, dass ich fortgehe': Jo 16,4b-15," Sein und Sendung 28 (8, 1963) 340-51. BECKER, J., Das Evangelium nach Johannes (Gütersloh/Würzburg 1979) 494 (lit!).

16:4-11 SCHULZ, S., Untersuchungen zur Menschensohn-Christologie im Johannesevangelium (Göttingen 1957) 147-48. BLANK, J., Krisis (1964) 310.

16:4-7 WILCKENS, U., "Der Paraklet und die Kirche" in: D. Lührmann/G. Strecker (eds.), Kirche. FS. G. Bornkamm (Tübingen 1980) 190-92.

16:4 KLEIN, H., "Die lukanisch-johanneische Passionstradition" in: M. Limbeck (ed.) Redaktion und Theologie des Passionsberichtes nach den Synoptikern (Darmstadt 1981) 383-86.

16:5-15 ASMUSSEN, H. in: Herr, tue meine Lippen auf Bd. 1 (1957) G. Eichholz ed., 158-63. IWAND, H.-J. Predigt-Meditationen (1964) 440-46. ZERWICK, M. "Vom Wirken des Heiligen Geistes in uns. Meditationsgedanken zu Jo 16,5-15," GuL 38 (3, 1965) 224-30. BORNKAMM, G., "Die Zeit des Geistes," in: Geschichte und Glaube I (1968) 90-103. BAUER, K.-A., GPM 27 (2, 1973) 243-49. KOEPPEN, W. und WOLF, B., in: P. Krusche et al. (eds.) Predigtstudien für das Kirchenjahr 1980-1981 (Stuttgart 1981) 69-81. STECK, K. G., in: GPM 35 (1981) 280-89.

16:5-11 BORNKAMM, G. "Der Paraklet im Johannes-Evangelium," in: Geschichte und Glaube I (1968) 68-89. BÜHNER, J.-A., Der Gesandte und sein Weg im 4. Evangelium (Tübingen 1977) 259-60.

16:5-10 DAHMS, J. V., "Isaiah 55:11 and the Gospel of John" EQ 53 (1981) 78-88.

16:5-7.12-15 FRICK, GPM 4 (1949-1950) 144ff. IWAND, H.-J. GPM 9 (1954-1955) 128ff. DOERNE, M. Er kommt auch noch heute (1961) 84-87.

16:7-15 LE FORT, P. Les Structures de L'Eglise militante selon saint Jean (1970) 122-28, 131-32, 161, 165. MARTIN, A. G., "Le Saint-Esprit et l'Evangile de Jean dans une perspective trinitaire" RevR 29 (1978) 141-51. WILCKENS, U., "Der Paraklet und die Kirche" in: D. Lührmann/G. Strecker (eds.) Kirche. FS. G. Bornkamm (Tübingen 1980) 189. CARREZ, M., "Les Promesses du Paraclet" ETh 12 (1981) 323-32.

16:7-13 BAMMEL, E. "Jesus und der Paraklet in Johannes 16," in: Christ and the Spirit in the New Testament (1973) B. Lindars/S. S. Smalley eds., 216f.

16:7-11 JOHNSTON, G. The Spirit-Paraclete in the gospel of John (1970) 34-36, 125, 137. LEANEY, A. R. C. "The Johannine Paraclete and the Qumran Scrolls," in: John and Qumran (1972) J. H. Charlesworth ed., 44-45, 58-59. PORSCH, F., Pneuma und Wort (Frankfurt 1974) 275-89. de la POTTERIE, I., La Vérité dans Saint Jean I/II (Rome 1977) 399-421. CARSON, D. A., "The Function of the Paraclete in John 16:7-11" JBL 98 (1979) 547-66. SÁNCHEZ MIELGO, G., "Presencia y Actuación del Paráklētos en la Iglesia (Jn. 14-16)" Theología Espiritual 24 (Valencia 1980) 79-117. GRAYSTON, K., "The Meaning of *PARAKLĒTOS*" JSNT 13 (1981) 80-81.

16:7-10.12-15 HAHN, F. Das Verständnis der Mission im Neuen Testament (²1965) 141.

16:7 STRATHMANN, H. Das Evangelium nach Johannes (1955) 225-27. STRAUSS, L., The Epistles of John (New York 1962) 14. WAINWRIGHT, A. W. The Trinity in the New Testament (1962) 261-62. MUSSNER, F. Die Johanneische Sehweise und die Frage nach dem historischen Jesus (1965) 58f. BOUSSET, W. Die Religion des Judentums im Späthellenistischen Zeitalter (1966 = 1926) 226. JOHNSTON, G., The Spirit-Paraclete in the gospel of John (1970) 31, 39, 81, 84. BEUTLER, J. Martyria (1972) 242, 274f. IBUKI, Y. Die Wahrheit im Johannesevangelium (1972) 306f., 309f. BAMMEL, E. "Jesus und der Paraklet in Johannes 16," in: Christ and the Spirit in the New Testament (1973) B. Lindars/S. S. Smalley eds., 199f., 202, 207, 209f. PORSCH, F., Pneuma und Wort (Frankfurt 1974) 277-79. METZGER, B. M., The Early Versions of the New Testament (Oxford 1977) 252. de la POTTERIE, I., La Vérité dans Saint Jean I/II (Rome 1977) 55-61. "Apostel" in: TRE 3 (1978) 481. RAYAN, S., The Holy Spirit: Heart of the Gospel and Christian Hope (New York 1978) 2. BÖHLIG, A., Die Gnosis III: Der Manichäismus (Zürich/München 1980) 308n.79, 318n.40. BERGER, K., "Das Buch der Jubiläen" in: JüdSchr II/3 (1981) 496n.6b. "Erbauungsliteratur" in: TRE 10 (1982) 50.

16:8-15 BEHLER, G.-M. "La double fonction de l'Esprit. Avocat et guide," VieS 102 (462, 1960) 614-25.

16:8-11 LILLIE, W. Studies in New Testament Ethics (1961) 54f. KUHL, J. Die Sendung Jesu und der Kirche nach dem Johannesevangelium (1967) 157f., 213-16. LINDARS, B. "Δικαιοσύνη in Jn. 16.8 and 10," in: Mélanges Bibliques en hommage au R. P. Béda Rigaux (1970) A. Descamps/A. DeHalleux eds., 278-85. MUELLER, T. Das Heilsgeschehen im Johannesevangelium n.d., 84. PORSCH, F., Pneuma und Wort (Frankfurt 1974) 279-89. SCHNACKENBURG, R., "Die johanneische Gemeinde und ihre Geisterfahrung" in: R. Schnackenburg et al. (eds.) Die Kirche des Anfangs. FS. H. Schürmann (Freiburg/Basel/Wien 1978) 291.

16:8-9 LAZURE, N., Les Valeurs Morales de la Théologie Johannique (Paris 1965) 299. BERGMEIER, R., Glaube als Gabe nach Johannes (Stuttgart 1980) 271n.564.

16:8 PALLIS, A., Notes on St. John and the Apocalypse (London 1928) 34. PORSCH, F., Pneuma und Wort (Frankfurt 1974) 280-81. STENGER, W., "Δικαιοσύνη in Jo. xvi 8.10" NovT 21 (1979) 2-12. GEORGI, D., "Weisheit Salomos" in: JüdSchr III/4 (1980) 1n.3b,6c.

16:8.10 LINDARS, B. "Δικαιοσύνη in Jn. 16.8 and 10," in: Mélanges Bibliques en hommage au R. P. Béda Rigaux (1970) A. Descamps/A. deHalleux eds., 275-85.

16:8 BAMMEL, E. "Jesus und der Paraklet in Johannes 16," in: Christ and the Spirit in the New Testament (1973) B. Lindars/ S. S. Smalley eds., 202f., 207f., 210f., 214, 217.

16:9-11 BAMMEL, E. "Jesus und der Paraklet in Johannes 16," in: Christ and the Spirit in the New Testament (1973) B. Lindars/ S. S. Smalley eds., 201f., 212f., 217.

16:9 STROBEL, A. Erkenntnis und Bekenntnis der Sünde in neutestamentlicher Zeit (1968) 46.

16:10 STENGER, W., "Δικαιοσύνη in Jo. xvi 8.10" NovT 21 (1979) 2-12.

16:11 FRIES, S. A. "Was bedeutet der Fürst der Welt?" ZNW 6 (1905) 159. HAHN, F. Das Verständnis der Mission im Neuen Testament (²1965) 137. DELLING, G. Wort und Werk Jesu im Johannes-Evangelium (1966) 52f., 59, 82. BOUSSET, W. Die Religion des Judentums im Späthellenistischen Zeitalter (1966 = 1926) 253, 335. LADD, G. E. A Theology of the New Testament (1974) 226, 227, 228. GALITIS, G., " 'Ho archōn tou kosmou toutou' (Iō. 12:31; 14:30; 16:10)" DBM 4 (1976) 59-67. "Antichrist" in: TRE 3 (1978) 22. RUDOLPH, K., Die Gnosis (Göttingen 1978) 324. BERGMEIER, R., Glaube als Gabe nach Johannes (Stuttgart 1980) 204, 239n.54. "Edessa" in: TRE 9 (1982) 279.

16:12ff DUNN, J. D. G., Jesus and the Spirit (London 1975) 351-52. BERGMEIER, R., Glaube als Gabe nach Johannes (Stuttgart 1980) 239n.54.

16:12-15 SCHULZ, S., Untersuchungen zur Menschensohn-Christologie im Johannesevangelium (Göttingen 1957) 148-49. MUSSNER, F. Die Johanneische Sehweise und die Frage nach dem historischen Jesus (1965) 59f., 61. BORNKAMM, G. "Der Paraklet im Johannes-Evangelium," in: Geschichte und Glaube I (1968) 68-89. JOHNSTON, G. The Spirit-Paraclete in the gospel of John (1970) 36-39, 66, 67. IBUKI, Y. Die Wahrheit im Johannesevangelium (1972) 295-306. GEORGE, A. "L'Esprit, guide vers la vérité plénière. Jn 16,12-15," AssS 31 (1973) 40-47. ROBINSON, J. A. T. "The Use of the Fourth Gospel for Christology Today," in: Christ and the Spirit in the New Testament (1973) B. Lindars/S. S. Smalley eds., 66f. de la POTTERIE, I. La Vérité dans Saint Jean I/II (Rome 1977) 422-66. SÁNCHEZ MIELGO, G., "Presencia y Actuación del Paráklētos en la Iglesia (Jn. 14-16)" Theología Espiritual 24

(Valencia 1980) 79-117. PAINTER, J. "The Farewell Discourses and the History of Johannine Christianity" NTS 27 (1980-1981) 539-40.

16:12 PALLIS, A., Notes on St. John and the Apocalypse (London 1928) 34-35. PORSCH, F., Pneuma und Wort (Frankfurt 1974) 289-93. de la POTTERIE, I., La Vérité dans Saint Jean I/II (Rome 1977) 423-31.

16:13-15 PORSCH, P., Pneuma und Wort (Frankfurt 1974) 289-303. de la POTTERIE, I., La Vérité dans Saint Jean I/II (Rome 1977) 438-66. SCHNACKENBURG, R., "Die johanneische Gemeinde und ihre Geisterfahrung" in: R. Schnackenburg et al. (eds.) Die Kirche des Anfangs. FS. H. Schürmann (Freiburg/Basel/Wien 1978) 297.

16:13 WILES, M. F. The Spiritual Gospel (1960) 68-70. SCHRAGE, W. Die konkreten Einzelgebote in der paulinischen Paränese (1961) 87. KAESEMANN, E. Exegetische Versuche und Besinnungen (1964) I 184, 223. BRAUN, H. Qumran und NT II (1966) 122. DELLING, G. Wort und Werk Jesu im Johannes-Evangelium (1966) 35, 50, 125f. NICKELS, P. Targum and New Testament (1967) 57. JOHNSTON, G. The Spirit-Paraclete in the gospel of John (1970) 31, 44, 78, 91, 96, 137. THUESING, W. Die Erhöhung und Verherrlichung Jesu im Johannesevangelium (1970) 146-53. RIEDL, J. "Der Heilige Geist wird euch in alle Wahrheit einführen (Joh 16,13): Eine Heilige-Geist-Besinnung anhand der Apostelgeschichte," BuLit 44 (2, 1971) 89-94. BEUTLER, J. Martyria (1972) 273, 278, 303. CHARLESWORTH, J. H. "A Critical Comparison of the Dualism in 1QS 3:13-4:26 and the 'Dualism' in the Gospel of John," in: John and Qumran (1972) J. H. Charlesworth ed., 98-99. HAACKER, K. Die Stiftung des Heils (1972) 154-56. BAMMEL, E. "Jesus und der Paraklet in Johannes 16," in: Christ and the Spirit in the New Testament (1973) B. Lindars/ S. S. Smalley eds. 200-207, 210, 214ff. FERRE, N. F. S. The Extreme Center (1973) 150-55. LADD, G. E. A Theology of the New Testament (1974) 268, 295, 296. METZGER, B. M., The Early Versions of the New Testament (Oxford 1977) 251, 390. de la POTTERIE, I., La Vérité dans Saint Jean I/II (Rome 1977) 431-38. "Amt" in: TRE 2 (1978) 517. KREMER, J., "Jesu Verheissung des Geistes. Zur Verankerung der Aussage von Joh 16:13 im Leben Jesu" in: R. Schnackenburg et al. (eds.) Die Kirche des Anfangs. FS. H. Schürmann (Freiburg/Basel/ Wien 1978) 247-76. RAYAN, S., The Holy Spirit: Heart of the Gospel and Christian Hope (New York 1978) 8, 85. SCHNACKENBURG, R., "Die johanneische Gemeinde und ihre Geisterfahrung" in: R. Schnackenburg et al. (eds.) Die Kirche des Anfangs. FS. H. Schürmann (Freiburg/Basel/Wien 1978) 303. SCHWEIZER, E., Heiliger Geist (Berlin 1978) 145. DUNN, J. D., Christology in the Making (London 1980) 320n.84. WILCKENS, U., "Der Paraklet und die Kirche" in: D. Lührmann/G. Strecker (eds.) Kirche. FS. G. Bornkamm (Tübingen 1980) 193.

16:14-15 THUESING, W. Die Erhöhung und Verherrlichung Jesus im Johannesevangelium (1970) 144-46, 153-59.

16:14 GRILL, J. Untersuchungen über die Entstehung des vierten Evangeliums II (1923) 220f. THUESING, W. Herrlichkeit und Einheit (Düsseldorf 1962) 52-64. PORSCH, F., Pneuma und Wort (Frankfurt 1974) 300-301.

16:15 KUHL, J. Die Sendung Jesu und der Kirche nach dem Johannes-Evangelium (1967) 101f. PORSCH, F. Pneuma und Wort (Frankfurt 1974) 301-302.

16:16ff KAESEMANN, E. Exegetische Versuche und Besinnungen (1964) I 181.

16:16-33 SCHWANK, B. "Sieg und Friede in Christus: Jo 16,16-33," Sein und Sendung 28 (9, 1963) 388-400. BEHLER, G.-M. The Last Discourse of Jesus (1965) 200-18. BECKER, J., Das Evangelium nach Johannes (Gütersloh/Würzburg 1979) 500, 503 (lit!). DIETZFELBINGER, C., "Die eschatologische Freude der Gemeinde in der Angst der Welt. Joh 16,16-33" EvTh 40 (1980) 420-36. LINDEMANN, A., "Gemeinde und Welt im Johannesevangelium" in: D. Lührmann/G. Strecker (eds.) Kirche. FS. G. Bornkamm (Tübingen 1980) 153-54. WILCKENS, U., "Der Paraklet und die Kirche" in: D. Lührmann/G. Strecker (eds.) Kirche. FS. G. Bornkamm (Tübingen 1980) 194-95.

16:16-28 PORSCH, F., Pneuma und Wort (Frankfurt 1974) 384-87.

16:16-24 PAINTER, J., "The Farewell Discourses and the History of Johannine Christianity" NTS 27 (1980-1981) 536-37.

16:16-23 BRUNNER, E. GPM 4 (1949-1950) 139ff. BRAUN, H. GPM 9 (1954-1955) 123ff. ASMUSSEN, H. in: Herr, tue meine Lippen auf Bd 1 (1957) G. Eichholz ed., 153-58. SCHMAUCH, GPM 15 (1960-1961) 142ff. DOERNE, M. Er kommt auch noch heute (1961) 82-84. KRAUSE, O. GPM 27 (2, 1973) 236-43. HINZ, C., in: GPM 35 (1981) 232-39. KATZENSTEIN, E.-U. und TER-NEDDEN-AMSLER, B., in: P. Krusche et al. (eds.) Predigtstudien für das Kirchenjahr 1980-1981. III/3 (Stuttgart 1981) 41-48.

16:16-22 IBUKI, Y. Die Wahrheit im Johannesevangelium (1972) 296f.

16:16f.19 JEREMIAS, J. "Die Drei-Tage-Worte der Evangelien," in: Tradition und Glaube (1971) G. Jeremias ed., 221-29.

16:16.19 GRILL, J. Untersuchungen über die Entstehung des vierten Evangeliums II (1923) 49, 172, 214f.

16:16 SCHULZ, S., Untersuchungen zur Menschensohn-Christologie im Johannesevangelium (Göttingen 1957) 168-71. SCHILDENBERGER, J. "Parallelstellen als Ursache von Textveränderungen," Biblica 40 (1959) 189-90. KUENZI, M. Das Naherwartungslogion Matthäus 10,23 (1970) 99, 109, 113.

16:20-23 SCHULZ, S., Untersuchungen zur Menschensohn-Christologie im Johannesevangelium (Göttingen 1957) 168-71.

16:20-22 TILLICH, P. Das Neue Sein (1959) 135-43.

16:21-22 MORGAN, G. C. The Parables and Metaphors of Our Lord (1943) 347ff. RUCKSTUHL, E. Die literarische Einheit des Johannesevangeliums (1951) 27f. BROWNLEE, W. H. "Messianic Motifs of Qumran and the New Testament," NTS 3 (1956-1957) 29. BRAUN, H. Qumran und NT II (1966) 66, 83, 107.

16:21 VOLZ, P. Die Eschatologie der jüdischen Gemeinde (1934) 147. FEUILLET, A. "L'heure de la femme (Jn 16,21) et l'heure de la Mère de Jésus (Jn 19,25-27)," Biblica 47 (2, 1966) 169-84; (2, 1966) 557-73. HUNTER, A. M. According to John (1970²) 84ff. METZGER, B. M., The Early Versions of the New Testament (Oxford 1977) 390.

16:23-33 FÜRST, W., in: GPM 33 (1979) 222-27.

16:23-30 GEORGE, A. "La nouveauté de Paques," AssS 48 (1965) 39-46.

16:23-24 DELLING, G. Die Zueignung des Heils in der Taufe (1961) 59.

16:23 BORIG, R. Der Wahre Weinstock (1967) 21, 54, 76, 211, 235. IBUKI, Y. Die Wahrheit im Johannesevangelium (1972) 296f. UNTERGASSMAIR, F. G., Im Namen Jesu: Der Namensbegriff im Johannesevangelium (Stuttgart 1973) 163-66. METZGER, B. M., The Early Versions of the New Testament (Oxford 1977) 365.

16:23b-33 ASMUSSEN, H. in: Herr, tue meine Lippen auf Bd 1 (1957) G. Eichholz ed., 163-68. IWAND, H.-J. Predigt-Meditationen (1964) 13-16, 218-22. STOEVESANDT, H. GPM 27 (1, 1973) 56-69.

16:23b-27 IWAND, H.-J. GPM 4 (1949-1950) 150ff. SCHOTT, GPM 9 (1954-1955) 134ff. KIIVIT, GPM 15 (1960-1961) 151ff. DOERNE, M. Er kommt auch noch heute (1961) 87-89. BEHLER, G.-M. The Last Discourse of Jesus (1965) 207-11.

16:24 UNTERGASSMAIR, F. G., Im Namen Jesu: Der Namensbegriff im Johannesevangelium (Stuttgart 1973) 147-52. SCHÜRMANN, H., "Christliche Weltverantwortung im Licht des Neuen Testaments" Catholica 34 (1980) 107.

16:25-17:26 GUILDING, A. The Fourth Gospel and Jewish Worship (1960) 139-42.

16:25ff FINDLAY, J. A. Jesus and His Parables (1951) 1ff.

16:25 IBUKI, Y. Die Wahrheit im Johannesevangelium (1972) 296f., 299f. MORAN, L. R. "Revelacion en enigmas y revelacion en claridad. Analisis exegético de Jn 16,25," Salmanticensis 19 (1, 1972) 107-44. OLSSON, B., Structure and Meaning in the Fourth Gospel (Lund 1974) 73, 192, 196, 270-72. BERGMEIER, R., Glaube als Gabe nach Johannes (Stuttgart 1980) 265n.491.

16:26-27 DELLING, G. Die Zueignung des Heils in der Taufe (1961) 59. UNTERGASSMAIR, F. G., Im Namen Jesu: Der Namensbegriff im Johannesevangelium (Stuttgart 1973) 153-57.

16:27-30 DAHMS, J. V., "Isaiah 55:11 and the Gospel of John" EQ 53 (1981)78-88.

16:27-28 BERGMEIER, R., Glaube als Gabe nach Johannes (Stuttgart 1980) 248n.212.

16:27 DELLING, G. Wort und Werk Jesu im Johannes-Evangelium (1966) 63f. IBUKI, Y. Die Wahrheit im Johannesevangelium (1972) 98f., 257f., 260f., 296f. LATTKE, M., Einheit im Wort (München 1975) 13, 19-20, 23, 188-94.

16:28.31 SCHOTTROFF, L. Der Glaubende und die feindliche Welt (1970) 231, 233, 252, 254, 276, 283, 292.

16:28 HAHN, F. Das Verständnis der Mission im Neuen Testament (^{2}1965) 140. DELLING, G. Wort und Werk Jesu im Johannes-Evangelium (1966) 85f. KUHL, J. Die Sendung Jesu und der Kirche nach dem Johannes-Evangelium (1967) 123f. SMITH, M. Tannaitic Parallels to the Gospels (1968) 8 end. CADMAN, W. H. The Open Heaven (1969) G. B. Caird ed., 198-202. BEUTLER, J. Martyria (1972) 268, 271, 324. BÜHNER, J.-A., Der Gesandte und sein Weg im 4. Evangelium (Tübingen 1977) 132, 148-52. METZGER, B. M., The Early Versions of the New Testament (Oxford 1977) 369n.1.

16:29-30 IBUKI, Y. Die Wahrheit im Johannesevangelium (1972) 98f., 299ff.

16:29 BERGMEIER, R., Glaube als Gabe nach Johannes (Stuttgart 1980) 265n.491.

16:30 MUSSNER, F. Die Johanneische Sehweise und die Frage nach dem historischen Jesus (1965) 33f. MYERS, J. M./REIM-HERR, O./BREAM, H. N. Search the Scriptures (1969) 49-74. PETZKE, G. Die Traditionen über Apollonius von Tyana und das Neue Testament (1970) 175f. BERGMEIER, R., Glaube als Gabe nach Johannes (Stuttgart 1980) 248n.212.

16:31-32 DE LA POTTERIE, I, "Das Wort Jesu, 'Siehe, deine Mutter' und die Annahme der Mutter durch den Jünger (Joh 19,27b)," in: Neues Testament und Kirche (1974) J. Gnilka ed., 192, 208, 210, 211, 213f. MORGAN-WYNNE, J. E., "The Cross and the Revelation of Jesus in the Fourth Gospel (John 8:28)," in: E. A. Livingstone (ed.) Studia Biblica 1978/II (Sheffield 1980) 221-23.

16:32-33 FUERST, GPM 15 (1960-1961) 47ff. LAUTNER, G./KNUD-SEN, C./AHRENDT, R. "Neujahr: Johannes 16,32-33," in: Predigtstudien (1972) E. Lange ed. 72-77. RUHBACH, G. GPM 27 (2, 1973) 249-57.

16:32 FASCHER, E. "Eine Studie zur Geschichte der Schrift-auslegung . . ." ZNW 39 (1940) 171. FEINE, D. P./BEHM, D. J. Einleitung im das Neue Testament (1950) 112f. DAUER, A. Die Passionsgeschichte im Johannesevangelium (1972) 199, 312, 313, 339. NEIRYNCK, F., "ΕΙΣ ΤΑ ΙΔΙΑ Jn 19,27 (et 16,32)" EphT 55 (1979) 357-65. MOHR, T. A. Markus- und Johannespassion (Zürich 1982) 213-18.

16:33 BONHOEFFER, A. Epiktet und das Neue Testament (1911) 177, 319. BROWN, R. E., "The Qumran Scrolls and the Johannine Gospel and Epistles" CBQ 17 (1955) 403-19, 559-74; also in K. Stendahl (ed.) The Scrolls and the New Testament (New York 1957) 189; GT: "Die Schriftrollen von Qumran and das Johannesevangelium und die Johannesbriefe" in: K. H. Rengstorf (ed.) Johannes und sein Evangelium (Darmstadt 1973) 497. DELLING, G. Die Zueignung des Heils in der Taufe (1961) 60. SCHWEIZER, E. Erniedrigung und Erhöhung bei Jesus und seinen Nachfolgern (1962) § 13c. HAHN, F. Das Verständnis der Mission im Neuen Testament (²1965) 137. BRUNS, J. E. "A Note on John 16:33 and I John 2:13-14," JBL 86 (4, 1967) 451-53. LINDEMANN, A., Die Aufhebung der Zeit (Gütersloh 1975) 258-59. THEUNISSEN, M., "ὁ αἰτῶν λαμβάνει. Der Gebetsglaube Jesu und die Zeitlichkeit des Christseins" in: Jesus, Ort der Erfahrung Gottes (Basel 1976) 20. SWIDLER, L., Biblical Affirmations of Woman (Philadelphia 1979) 285.

17 BAUER, W. Das Johannesevangelium (1925) 201f. HAN-
SON, S. The Unity of the Church in the New Testament (1946)
163f. GEORGE, A. "L'heure de Jean XVII," RB 61 (1954)
392-97. GIBLET, J. "Sanctifie-les dans la vérité (Jean 17,1-
26)," BVieC 19 (1957) 58-73. GOES, H./LUTZ, W. Das Letzte
Gebet Jesu (1958). WILKENS, W. Die Entstehungsgeschichte
des vierten Evangeliums (1958) 156-57. HAMMAN, A.
"Lignes maîtresses de la prière johannique," in: The Gospels
Reconsidered (1960) 78-89. WILES, M. F. The Spiritual Gospel (1960) 144-45. THUESING, W. Herrlichkeit und Einheit
(1962). YATES, K. M. Preaching from John's Gospel (1963)
142-51. KAESEMANN, E. Exegetische Versuche und Besinnungen (1964) II 282f. PERRET, J. "Notes Bibliques. La prière
sacerdotale (Jean 17)," VerbCaro 18 (69, 1964) 119-26. MOR-
RISON, C. D. "Mission and Ethic. An Interpretation of John
17," Interpretation 19 (3, 1965) 259-73. POELMAN, R. "The
Sacerdotal Prayer. John XVII," LuVit 20 (1, 1965) 43-66.
SMITH, D. M. The Composition and Order of the Fourth Gospel (1965) 170, 171, 172, 174, 176, 217, 237. BORNKAMM,
G. Geschichte und Glaube (1968) I 104ff. KAESEMANN, E.
The Testament of Jesus (1968). BATTAGLIA, O. "Preghiera
sacerdotale ed innologia ermetica (Giov 17-CH. 1,31-32e XIII,
18-20)," RivB 17 (3, 1969) 209-32. BECKER, J. "Aufbau,
Schichtung und theologiegeschichtliche Stellung des Gebetes
in Johannes 17," ZNW 60 (1-2, 1969) 56-83. KAESEMANN,
E. New Testament Questions of Today (1969) 278. QUINN, J.
"The Prayer of Jesus to his Father," Way 9 (2, 1969) 90-97.
LE FORT, P. Les Structures de L'Eglise militante selon saint
Jean (1970) 97-119. LOHSE, E. et al., eds., Der Ruf Jesu und
die Antwort der Gemeinde (1970) 117-19, 129f. RIGAUX, B.
"Die Jünger Jesu in Johannes 17," ThQ 150 (2, 1970) 202-13.
RIGAUX, B. "Les destinataires du IVe Evangile à la lumière
de Jn 17," RThL 1 (3, 1970) 289-319. MALATESTA, E. "The
Literary Structure of John 17," Biblica 52 (2, 1971) 190-214.
VAN BOXEL, P. "Die präexistente Doxa Jesu im Johannes-
evangelium," Bijdragen 34 (3, 1973) 268-81. PINTARD, J.
"Que nous enseigne l'Ecriture sur le sacerdoce du Christ et de
ses ministres? D'après un ouvrage récent," EsVie 83 (2, 1973)
17-22. HAMERTON-KELLY, R. G. Pre-Existence, Wisdom
and the Son of Man (1973) 215-224. HAY, D. M. Glory at the
Right Hand (1973) 130-31. RADERMAKERS, J. "La prière

de Jésus. Jn 17,'' AssS 29 (1973) 48-86. SCHNACKEN-
BURG, R. "Strukturanalyse von Joh 17," BZ 17 (1, 1973) 67-
78; (2, 1973) 196-202. MUELLER, T. Das Heilsgeschehen im
Johannesevangelium n.d., 24-29, 62-65. BOYD, W. J. P., "The
Ascension according to St. John" StEv 6 (1973) 20-27. UN-
TERGASSMAIR, F. G. Im Namen Jesu: Der Namensbegriff
im Johannesevangelium (Stuttgart 1973) 63-70, 291-302.
BALAGUE, M., "La oracion sacerdotal (Juan 17,1-26)" CuBi
31 (1974) 67-90. HANSON, A. T., "Hodayoth xv and John 17:
A comparison of content and form" Hermathena 118 (Dublin
1974) 48-58. STACHOWIAK, L., "Modlitwa arcykaplanska
(J 17). Refleksje egzegetyczne" RTK 21 (1974) 85-94. BOYLE,
J. L., "The Last Discourse (Jn 13,31-16,33) and Prayer (Jn 17):
Some Observations on Their Unity and Development" Biblica
56 (1975) 210-22. SANDERS, J. T., Ethics in the New Testament (Philadelphia 1975) 94-97. APPOLD, M. L., The Oneness Motif in the Fourth Gospel (Tübingen 1976) 157-236.
BÜHNER, J.-A., Der Gesandte und sein Weg im 4. Evangelium (Tübingen 1977) 224-25, 258-61. MARZOTTO, D.,
"Giovanni 17 e il Targum di Esodo 19-20" RivB 25 (1977) 375-
88. APPOLD, M., "Christ Alive! Church Alive! Reflections
on the Prayer of Jesus in John 17" CuThM 5 (1978) 365-73.
FRIEDRICH, G., "Die Fürbitte im Neuen Testament" in: Auf
das Wort kommt es an (Göttingen 1978) 438-39. NEWMAN,
B. M., "The Case of the Eclectic and the Neglected Ek of John
17" BTr 29 (1978) 339-41. SÁNCHEZ MIELGO, G., "La un-
idad de la Iglesia según Juan 17" EsVe 8 (1978) 9-58. SENFT,
C., "L'évangile de Jean et la théologie de la croix" BCPE 30
(1978) 65-73. THÜSING, W. "Die Bitten des johanneischen
Jesu in dem Gebet Joh 17 und die Intentionen Jesu von Naza-
ret" in: R. Schnackenburg et al. (eds.) Die Kirche des Anfangs.
FS. H. Schürmann (Freiburg/Basel/Wien 1978) 307-37.
BECKER, J., Das Evangelium nach Johannes (Gütersloh/
Würzburg 1979) 508 (lit!). CRESSEY, M. H., "In the World
but not of it—New Testament perspectives on World, Church
and Mission" IBS 1 (1979) 227-41. RITT, H., Das Gebet zum
Vater. Zur Interpretation von Joh 17 (Würzburg 1979). BERG-
MEIER, R., Glaube als Gabe nach Johannes (Stuttgart 1980)
16, 21, 40n.213, 46n.328, 212, 239n.54, 273n.612. CAHILL,
M., "A Structuralist Approach to Prayer in the New Testament" PIBA 4 (1980) 12-20. HAENCHEN, E., Das Johannesevangelium (Tübingen 1980) 499-500 (lit!). LINDEMANN, A.,
"Gemeinde und Welt im Johannesevangelium" in: D. Lühr-
mann/G. Strecker (eds.) Kirche. FS. G. Bornkamm (Tübingen
1980) 155-60. PAINTER, J., "The Farewell Discourses and the

History of Johannine Christianity" NTS 27 (1980-1981) 526, 540. SIMOENS, Y., La gloire d'aimer. Structures stylistiques et interpretatives dans le Discours de la Cène (Jn 13-17) (Rome 1981). MOLONEY, F., "John 17: The Prayer of Jesus' Hour" CIR 67 (1982) 79-83. WALKER, W. O., "The Lord's Prayer in Matthew and in John" NTS 28 (1982) 237-56.

17:1ff BUECHSEL, F. Das Evangelium nach Johannes (1946) 158f. NICOL, W. The Sēmeia in the Fourth Gospel (1972) 127f.

17:1-10 WILKENS, W., Zeichen und Werke (Zürich 1969) 104-106.

17:1-8 IWAND, H.-J. Predigt-Meditationen (1964) 632-38. KOCSIS, E. GPM 19 (1, 1969) 140-46. LANG, F. in: Hören und Fragen Bd. 5, 3 (1967) G. Eichholz/A. Falkenroth eds., 221ff. LANGE, E. ed., Predigtstudien für das Kirchenjahr 1970-1971 (1970) 174-79. DEMKE, C. GPM 25 (1, 1971) 161-67. HOLZE, H. und ZABEL, H., in: P. Krusche et al. (eds.) Predigtstudien für das Kirchenjahr 1976-1977 V/1 (Stuttgart 1976) 169-76. SCHELLONG, D. in: GPM 31 (1976-1977) 157-63. HENNIG, P. und GORSKI, R., in: P. Krusche et al. (eds.) Predigtstudien für das Kirchenjahr 1982-1983 V/1 (Stuttgart 1982) 172-79.

17:1-5 SCHELKLE, K. H. Die Passion Jesu in der Verkündigung des Neuen Testaments (1949) 121f. WIKENHAUSER, A. Das Evangelium nach Johannes (1957) 303f. SCHWANK, B., " 'Vater, verherrliche deinen Sohn': Jo 17,1-5," Sein und Sendung 28 (19, 1963) 436-49. BEHLER, G.-M. The Last Discourse of Jesus (1965) 221-31. RIEDL, J. Das Heilswerk Jesu nach Johannes (1973) 79-80. BÜHNER, J.-A., Der Gesandte und sein Weg im 4. Evangelium (Tübingen 1977) 293-94.

17:1-3 DUPONT, J. Essais sur la Christologie de Saint Jean (1951) 175-79. THUESING, W. Herrlichkeit und Einheit (Düsseldorf 1962) 46-51.

17:1 CASSIAN, B. "John 21" NTS 3 (1956-1957) 135f. ROBINSON, J. M. Kerygma und historischer Jesus (1960) 71. WILES, M. F. The Spiritual Gospel (1960) 82-83. HAHN, F. Christologische Hoheitstitel (1963) 329f. DELLING, G. Wort und Werk Jesu im Johannes-Evangelium (1966) 100f., 112f. KUHL, J. Die Sendung Jesu und der Kirche nach dem Johannes-Evangelium (1967) 218f. CADMAN, W. H. The Open Heaven (1969) G. B. Caird ed., 37-40, 62-98, 122-24, 161. DAUER, A. Die Passionsgeschichte im Johannesevangelium (1972) 239, 251, 278, 294. THUESING, W., Herrlichkeit und Einheit (Düsseldorf 1962) 17-22.

17:2-3 DELLING, G. Wort und Werk Jesu im Johannes-Evangelium (1966) 143f.

17:2.6-7 HAHN, F. Das Verständnis der Mission im Neuen Testament
(² 1965) 138.

17:2 KAESEMANN, E. Exegetische Versuche und Besinnungen
(1964) II 172. KAESEMANN, E. New Testament Questions of
Today (1969) 157. BÜHNER, J.-A. Der Gesandte und sein Weg
im 4. Evangelium (Tübingen 1977) 199-200. METZGER, B.
M., The Early Versions of the New Testament (Oxford 1977)
390. BERGMEIER, R., Glaube als Gabe nach Johannes (Stuttgart 1980) 160n.255, 236, 249n.225, 269n.530.

17:3-5 VOLZ, P. Die Eschatologie der jüdischen Gemeinde (1934) 224,
270.

17:3 WILES, M. F. The Spiritual Gospel (1960) 120-21. HAHN, F.
Das Verständnis der Mission im Neuen Testament (²1965) 140.
BRAUN, H. Qumran und NT II (1966) 129. LADD, G. E. A
Theology of the New Testament (1974) 242, 260, 264, 267.
METZGER, B. M., The Early Versions of the New Testament
(Oxford 1977) 251. GEORGI, D., "Weisheit Salomos" in:
JüdSchr III/4 (1980) 15n.3a. WENHAM, D., "Spirit and Life:
Some Reflections on Johannine Theology" Themelios 6 (1980)
4-8.

17:4-5 THUESING, W. Die Erhöhung und Verherrlichung Jesu im
Johannesevangelium (1970) 47-49, 71-75, 183f., 205-209, 219-
21, 233-39.

17:4 VANHOYE, A. "L'heuvre du Christ, don du Père (Jn. V. 36
et XVII, 4)," RechSR 48 (3, 1960) 377-419. THUESING, W.,
Herrlichkeit und Einheit (Düsseldorf 1962) 23-38. KUHL, J. Die
Sendung Jesu und der Kirche nach dem Johannes-Evangelium
(1967) 112-15, 176f. CADMAN, W. H. The Open Heaven
(1969) G. B. Caird ed., 56, 157, 180, 181. DAUER, A. Die
Passionsgeschichte im Johannesevangelium (1972) 288f.
RIEDL, J. Das Heilswerk Jesu nach Johannes (1973) 69-182,
183-86. BÜHNER, J.-A. Der Gesandte und sein Weg im 4.
Evangelium (Tübingen 1977) 203, 238-39. METZGER, B. M.,
The Early Versions of the New Testament (Oxford 1977) 254.

17:5.9 SCHOTTROFF, L. Der Glaubende und die feindliche Welt
(1970) 231-32, 235-36, 239, 244, 285.

17:5 LAURENTIN, A. "Jean, XVII, 5 et le prédestination du Christ
á la gloire chez S. Augustin et ses prédécesseurs," in: L'Evan-
gile de Jean (1958) Boismard et al., eds., 225-48. BLAIR, E.
P. Jesus in the Gospel of Matthew (1960) 98. ROBINSON, J.
M. Kerygma und historischer Jesus (1960) 71. THUESING, W.,
Herrlichkeit und Einheit (Düsseldorf 1962) 39-45, 65-69.
LAURENTIN, A. "We'attah - Kai nun. Formule caractéris-

tique des textes juridiques et liturgiques (à propos de Jean 17,5)," Biblica 45 (2, 1964) 168-97; (3, 1964) 413-32. DELLING, G. Wort und Werk Jesu im Johannes-Evangelium (1966) 59, 63, 86, 101, 108, 114, 123. CADMAN, W. H. The Open Heaven (1969) G. B. Caird ed., 36-40. THUESING, W. Die Erhöhung und Verherrlichung Jesu im Johannesevangelium (1970) 47-49, 205-209, 219-21. DAUER, A. Die Passionsgeschichte im Johannesevangelium (1972) 239, 251, 294. LAURENTIN, A. Doxa (1972). PORSCH, F., Pneuma und Wort (Frankfurt 1974) 77.

17:6-19 SCHWANK, B. " 'Für sie heilige ich mich, die du mir gegeben hast': Jo 17,6-19," Sein und Sendung 28 (11, 1963) 484-97.

17:6-8 IBUKI, Y. Die Wahrheit im Johannesevangelium (1972) 120-24.

17:6.26 BRAUN, F.-M. Jean le Theologien (1966) 112-16.

17:6 DELLING, G. Wort und Werk Jesu im Johannes-Evangelium (1966) 32f. QUISPEL, G. "Qumran, John and Jewish Christianity," in: John and Qumran (1972) J. H. Charlesworth ed., 149-50. UNTERGASSMAIR, F. G., Im Namen Jesu: Der Namensbegriff im Johannesevangelium (Stuttgart 1973) 70-81. LADD, G. E. A Theology of the New Testament (1974) 226, 227, 245, 268. PANCARO, S., The Law in the Fourth Gospel (Leiden 1975) 407, 411, 414, 423, 424-27. BERGMEIER, R., Glaube als Gabe nach Johannes (Stuttgart 1980) 27, 108n.336, 236, 249n.225, 269n.530.

17:7 BERGMEIER, R., Glaube als Gabe nach Johannes (Stuttgart 1980) 248n.213, 249n.225, 269n.530.

17:8 HAHN, F. Christologische Hoheitstitel (1963) 330. NICKELS, P. Targum and New Testament (1967) 57. BERGMEIER, R., Glaube als Gabe nach Johannes (Stuttgart 1980) 248n.212. DAHMS, J. V., "Isaiah 55:11 and the Gospel of John" EQ 53 (1981) 78-88.

17:9-19 FRICK, GPM 15 (1960-1961) 103ff. RAISER, K./LOTZ, D. "Judica: Johannes 17,9-19," in: Predigtstudien (1972-1973) E. Lange ed., 171-76.

17:9ff.15ff HAHN, F. Das Verständnis der Mission im Neuen Testament (²1965) 139.

17:9-11 THUESING, W., Herrlichkeit und Einheit (Düsseldorf 1962) 70-81.

17:9 BERGMEIER, R., Glaube als Gabe nach Johannes (Stuttgart 1980) 27, 236, 269n.530.

17:10 THUESING, W. Die Erhöhung und Verherrlichung Jesu im Johannesevangelium (1970) 174-76, 178-81, 185f.

17:11-16 THUESING, W. Herrlichkeit und Einheit (Düsseldorf 1962) 82-90.

17:11.21-23 D'ARAGON, J.-L. "La notion johannique de l'unité," Sci-Eccl 11 (1, 1959) 111-19.

17:11-12 DELLING, G. Die Zueignung des Heils in der Taufe (1961) 43, 44.

17:11 GRILL, J. Untersuchungen über die Entstehung des vierten Evangeliums II (1923) 1, 66, 88, 163, 214, 220f., 336. ORIGENES, Das Evangelium nach Johannes (1959) R. Gögler ed., 406-407. BRAUN, H. Qumran und NT II (1966) 127, 130. LE FORT, P. Les Structures de L'Eglise militante selon saint Jean (1970) 105-19. IBUKI, Y. Die Wahrheit im Johannesevangelium (1972) 125f., 127-31. QUISPEL, G. "Qumran, John and Jewish Christianity," in: John and Qumran (1972) J. H. Charlesworth ed., 149-50. UNTERGASSMAIR, F. G., Im Namen Jesu: Der Namensbegriff im Johannesevangelium (Stuttgart 1973) 81-94. BÜHNER, J.-A., Der Gesandte und sein Weg im 4. Evangelium (Tübingen 1977) 224-25, 230-34. de la POTTERIE, I., La Vérité dans Saint Jean I/II (Rome 1977) 721-34. BERGMEIER, R., Glaube als Gabe nach Johannes (Stuttgart 1980) 273n.612. DAHMS, J. V., "Isaiah 55:11 and the Gospel of John" EQ 53 (1981) 78-88.

17:12 PALLIS, A., Notes on St. John and the Apocalypse (London 1928) 35. BLAIR, E. P. Jesus in the Gospel of Matthew (1960) 31. FREED, E. D. Old Testament Quotations in the Gospel of John (1965) 96-98. REIM, G., Studien zum Alttestamentlichen Hintergrund des Johannesevangeliums (Cambridge 1974) 45-47, 89-91, 93. BERGMEIER, R., Glaube als Gabe nach Johannes (Stuttgart 1980) 108n.336. HANSON, A. T., The New Testament Interpretation of Scripture (London 1980) 158-59. SCHRAGE, W., "Die Elia-Apokalypse" in: JüdSchr V/3 (1980) 248n.29f. BERGER, K., "Das Buch der Jubiläen" in: JüdSchr II/3 (1981) 378n.3g.

17:13 DU TOIT, A. B. Der Aspekt der Freude im urchristlichen Abendmahl (1965) 46-48, 151f. IBUKI, Y. Die Wahrheit im Johannesevangelium (1972) 246f. DAHMS, J. V., "Isaiah 55:11 and the Gospel of John" EQ (1981) 78-88.

17:14 BERGMEIER, R., Glaube als Gabe nach Johannes (Stuttgart 1980) 220ff, 256n.349.

17:15.18 KAESEMANN, E. New Testament Questions of Today (1969) 278.

17:15 PALLIS, A., Notes on St. John and the Apocalypse (London 1928) 35-36. ENSLIN, M. S. The Literature of the Christian Movement (1956) 476f. KAESEMANN, E. Exegetische Versuche und Besinnungen (1964) II 284. LINDEMANN, A., Die Aufhebung der Zeit (Gütersloh 1975) 258-59. "Antichrist" in: TRE 3 (1978) 22. GEORGI, D., "Weisheit Salomos" in: JüdSchr III/4 (1980) 4n.10a. ROTTENBERG, I. C., The Promise and the Presence (Grand Rapids 1980) 81.

17:16 BERGMEIER, R., Glaube als Gabe nach Johannes (Stuttgart 1980) 27, 220-21.

17:17ff IBUKI, Y. Die Wahrheit im Johannesevangelium (1972) 130f.

17:17-19 BROWN, R. E., "The Qumran Scrolls and the Johannine Gospel and Epistles" CBQ 17 (1955) 403-19, 559-74; also in: K. Stendahl (ed.) The Scrolls and the New Testament (New York 1957) 197; GT: "Die Schriftrollen von Qumran und das Johannesevangelium und die Johannesbriefe" in: K. H. Rengstorf (ed.) Johannes und sein Evangelium (Darmstadt 1973) 511. BROWNLEE, W. H. "Messianic Motifs of Qumran and the New Testament," NTS 3 (1956-1957) 28f. THUESING, W. Herrlichkeit und Einheit (Düsseldorf 1962) 91-98. CREHAN, J. The Theology of St. John (1965) 92-93. BRAUN, H. Qumran und NT II (1966) 127f., 253ff. THUESING, W. Die Erhöhung und Verherrlichung Jesu im Johannesevangelium (1970) 186-90. de la POTTERIE, I., La Vérité dans Saint Jean I/II (Rome 1977) 706-83.

17:17-18 HAHN, F. Christologische Hoheitstitel (1963) 235.

17:17 LAZURE, N., Les Valeurs Morales de la Théologie Johannique (Paris 1965) 78. IBUKI, Y. Die Wahrheit im Johannesevangelium (1972) 135f. de la POTTERIE, I., La Vérité dans Saint Jean I/II (Rome 1977) 721-58. BEIERWALTES, W., "Deus est veritas" in: E. Dassmann/K. S. Frank (eds.) Pietas. FS. B. Kötting (Münster 1980) 23-24.

17:18-19 MINEAR, P. S. Images of the Church in the New Testament (1960) 137f.

17:18 GRILL, J. Untersuchungen über die Entstehung des vierten Evangeliums II (1923) 153, 155, 233, 388. FLEW, R. N. Jesus and His Church (1956) 175. KAESEMANN, P. Exegetische Versuche und Besinnungen (1964) II 284. HAHN, F. Das Verständnis der Mission im Neuen Testament (²1965) 142. KUHL, J. Die Sendung Jesu und der Kirche nach dem Johannes-Evangelium (1967) 131f., 142-45. RIEDL, J. "Die Funktion der Kirche nach Johannes. 'Vater, wie du mich in die Welt gesandt hast, so habe ich auch sie in die Welt gesandt' (John 17,18),"

BuK 28 (1, 1973) 12-14. de la POTTERIE, I., La Vérité dans saint Jean I/II (Rome 1977) 775-81.

17:19 CYRIL OF ALEXANDRIA, "Pour eux, Je me sanctifie moi-même (Jean 17,19)," BVieC 19 (1957) 55-57. HAHN, F. Christologische Hoheitstitel (1963) 235. CADMAN, W. H. The Open Heaven (1969) G. B. Caird ed., 49-53, 88, 90. IBUKI, Y. Die Wahrheit im Johannesevangelium (1972) 137f. FORESTELL, J. T., The Word of the Cross: Salvation as Revelation in the Fourth Gospel (Rome 1974) 77, 78, 80, 81, 193, 194. de la POTTERIE, I., La Vérité dans Saint Jean I/II (Rome 1977) 758-75. BERGMEIER, R., Glaube als Gabe nach Johannes (Stuttgart 1980) 108n.336.

17:20ff SCHWEIZER, E. Gemeinde und Gemeinde-Ordnung im Neuen Testament (1959) § 11 d,h.

17:20-26 CADIER, J. "The Unity of the Church," Interpretation 11 (1, 1957) 166-76. BENCKERT, H. GPM 17 (1, 1963) 206-210. SCHWANK, B. " 'Damit alle eins seien': Jo 17,20-26," Sein und Sendung 28 (12, 1963) 531-46. SCHMITHALS, W. GPM 23 (2, 1968) 205-11. ADOLPHSEN, H./KNUTH, H.-C. "Johannes 17,20-26: Wir sind schon eins," in: Predigtstudien für das Kirchenjahr 1975 (1975) P. Krusche/E. Lange/D. Rössler/ R. Rössler eds. 59-68. KRUSE, M., in: GPM 29 (1975) 251-57. LATTKE, M., Einheit im Wort (München 1975) 194-206. VOUGA, F., Le cadre historique et l'intention théologique de Jean (Paris 1977) 93.

17:20-24 MINEAR, P. S., To Die and to Live (New York 1977) 107-22.

17:20-23 MAURER, C. Ignatius von Antiochien und das Johannesevangelium (1949) 58ff. FLEW, R. N. Jesus and His Church (1956) 178-80. WILES, M. F. The Spiritual Gospel (1960) 125-26, 153-55, 157. THUESING, W., Herrlichkeit und Einheit (Düsseldorf 1962) 99-112. RANDALL, J. F. "The Theme of Unity in John 17:20-23," EphT 41 (3, 1965) 373-94. WEBER, O. Predigtmeditationen (1967) 39-43. APPOLD, M. L., The Oneness Motif in the Fourth Gospel (Tübingen 1976) 157-93. MINEAR, P. S., "Evangelium, Ecumenism, and John Seventeen" ThT 35 (1978) 5-13. SCHWEIZER, E., Heiliger Geist (Berlin 1978) 319-40.

17:20-22 BERGMEIER, R., Glaube als Gabe nach Johannes (Stuttgart 1980) 44n307, 273n.612.

17:20-21 BOHREN, R. Predigtlehre (1971) 434f.

17:20 HAHN, F. Das Verständnis der Mission im Neuen Testament (²1965) 139. JOHNSTON, G. The Spirit-Paraclete in the gospel of John (1970) 34, 44, 50, 68, 124, 160. LE FORT, P. Les

Structures de L'Eglise militante selon saint Jean (1970) 99-101, 109. IBUKI, Y. Die Wahrheit im Johannesevangelium (1972) 124, 126f., 130. SCHNACKENBURG, R. "Die johanneische Gemeinde und ihre Geisterfahrung" in: R. Schnackenburg et al. (eds.) Die Kirche des Anfangs. FS. H. Schürmann (Freiburg/Basel/Wien 1978) 297-98. SWIDLER, L. Biblical Affirmations of Woman (Philadelphia 1979) 190.

17:21ff BORIG, R. Der Wahre Weinstock (1967) 213, 216, 219f., 236, 246.

17:21-23 HENNECKE, E./SCHNEEMELCHER, W. Neutestamentliche Apokryphen (1964) I 135. KUHL, J. Die Sendung Jesu und der Kirche nach dem Johannes-Evangelium (1967) 103, 161-64. LE FORT, P. Les Structures de L'Eglise militante selon saint Jean (1970) 105-19. IBUKI,Y. Die Wahrheit im Johannesevangelium (1972) 127-30, 256f. APPOLD, M. L., The Oneness Motif in the Fourth Gospel (Tübingen 1976) passim. BÜHNER, J.-A., Der Gesandte und sein Weg im 4. Evangelium (Tübingen 1977) 214-15. MARZOTTO, D. L'unità degli uomini nel vangelo di Giovanni (Paideia 1977). de la POTTERIE, I., La Vérité dans Saint Jean I/II (Rome 1977) 777-81.

17:21 MUZSNER, F. ZΩH. Die Anschauung vom "Leben" im vierten Evangelium (1952) 153f. WIKENHAUSER, A. Das Evangelium nach Johannes (1957) 309f. POLLARD, T. E. " 'That They All May Be One' (John xvii. 21)-and the Unity of the Church," ET 70 (5, 1959) 149-50. WENGER, E. L. " 'That They All May Be One'," ET 70 (11, 1959) 333. EVDOKIMOV, P. "L'Esprit saint et la prière pour l'unité," VerbCaro 14 (55, 1960) 250-64. GALVAN, C. J. "Ut Omnes Unum Sint (Jo 17,21)," RCT 7 (23, 1963) 36-59; (24, 1963) 47-60. EARWAKER, J. C. "John xvii. 21," ET 75 (10, 1964) 316-17. DELLING, G. Wort und Werk Jesu im Johannes-Evangelium (1966) 130f. BORIG, R. Der Wahre Weinstock (1967) 215ff. LADD, G. E. A Theology of the New Testament (1974) 227, 276, 277. RUDOLPH, K., Die Gnosis (Göttingen 1978) 324. BÖHLIG, A. Die Gnosis III: Der Manichäismus (Zürich/München 1980) 343n.25.

17:22ff THUESING, W. Die Erhöhung und Verherrlichung Jesu im Johannesevangelium (1970) 137f., 181-85, 214-18.

17:22-23 HANSON, S. The Unity of the Church in the New Testament (1946) 167ff.

17:22 GLASSON, T. F. Moses in the Fourth Gospel (1963) 81ff. METZGER, B. M., The Early Versions of the New Testament (Oxford 1977) 436.

17:23-26 LATTKE, M., Einheit im Wort (München 1975) 19, 21.

17:23-24 GEORGI, O., "Weisheit Salomos" in: JüdSchr III/4 (1980) 8n.3b.

17:23 HAHN, F. Christologische Hoheitstitel (1963) 330. LATTKE, M., Einheit im Wort (München 1975) 13, 19-20, 25.

17:24 DUPONT, J. L'Union Avec Le Christ Suivant Saint Paul (1952) 96-97. ROBINSON, J. M. Kerygma und historischer Jesus (1960) 71. STRECKER, G. Der Weg der Gerechtigkeit (1962) 71_1. THUESING, W., Herrlichkeit und Einheit (Düsseldorf 1962) 113-16. SHIMADA, K., The Formulary Material in First Peter. A Study According to the Method of Traditionsge-schichte (Th.D. Diss., Ann Arbor, 1966) 288-92. DELLING, G. Wort und Werk Jesu im Johannes-Evangelium (1966) 101f., 108f. KUHL, J. Die Sendung Jesu und der Kirche nach dem Jo-hannes-Evangelium (1967) 97, 103f. METZGER, B. M., The Early Versions of the New Testament (Oxford 1977) 390. BERGMEIER, R., Glaube als Gabe nach Johannes (Stuttgart 1980) 108n.336, 236, 249n.225, 269n.530, 273n.612.

17:25-26 THUESING, W., Herrlichkeit und Einheit (Düsseldorf 1962) 117-22.

17:25 LADD, G. E. A Theology of the New Testament (1974) 226, 248, 262.

17:26 KUHL, J. Die Sendung Jesu und der Kirche nach dem Johan-nes-Evangelium (1967) 78f. BOHREN, R. Predigtlehre (1971) 106. IBUKI, Y. Die Wahrheit im Johannesevangelium (1972) 246ff., 255-58. UNTERGASSMAIR, F. G., Im Namen Jesu: der Namensbegriff im Johannesevangelium (Stuttgart 1973) 70-81. LATTKE, M., Einheit und Wort (München 1975) 24-25. STOEVESANDT, H., in: GPM 29 (1975) 257-66. GEORGI, D., "Weisheit Salomos" in: JüdSchr III/4 (1980) 8n.3b.

———————————

18-21 DIBELIUS, M. Botschaft und Geschichte I (1953) 221-47. BORGEN, P. "John and the Synoptics in the Passion Narra-tive," NTS 5 (4, 1959) 246-59. SUMMERS, R. "The Death and Resurrection of Jesus. John 18-21," RevEx 62 (1965) 473-81. WEISE, M. "Passionswoche und Epiphaniewoche im Johannesevangelium. Ihre Bedeutung für Komposition und

Konzeption des vierten Evangeliums," KuD 12 (1, 1966) 48-62. BENOIT, P. Passione e risurrezione del Signore (1967). EVANS, C. F. Explorations in Theology 2 (London 1977) 50-66.

18-20 SELBY, D. J. Introduction to the New Testament (1971) 230, 257-61. PERRIN, N. The New Testament: An Introduction (New York 1974) 244-46. APPOLD, M. L., The Oneness Motif in the Fourth Gospel (Tübingen 1976) 103-38. TOVAR, S. T., Pasión y Resurrección en el IV Evangelio Interpretación de un cristian de primera hora (Salamanca 1976).

18:1-20:29 GRUNDMANN, W., Zeugnis und Gestalt des Johannes-Evangeliums (1961) 81-94.

18-19 GARDNER-SMITH, P. Saint John and the Synoptic Gospels (1938) 56-72. BUECHSEL, F. Das Evangelium nach Johannes (1946) 162f. BUSE, I. "St. John and the Marcan Passion Narrative," NTS 4 (3, 1958) 215-19. DODD, C. H. The Interpretation of the Fourth Gospel (1958 = 1953) 423-43. WILKENS, W. Die Entstehungsgeschichte des vierten Evangeliums (1958) 77-86. STANLEY, D. M. "The Passion according to St. John," Worship 33 (4, 1959) 210-30. JANSSENS DE VAREBEKE, A. "La structure des scènes de récit de la passion en Joh., XVIII-XIX," EphT 38 (3, 1962) 504-22. BUSE, I. "St. John and the Passion Narratives of St. Matthew and St. Luke," NTS 7 (1, 1960) 65-76. RIAUD, J. "La gloire et la royauté de Jésus dans la Passion selon Saint Jean," BVieC 56 (1964) 28-44. YATES, K. M. Preaching from John's Gospel (1964) 152-59. LEISTNER, R., Antijudaismus im Johannesevangelium? Darstellung des Problems in der neueren Auslegungsgeschichte und Untersuchung der Leidensgeschichte (Bern/Frankfurt 1974). BROWN, R. E., "The Passion According to John: Chapters 18 and 19" Worship 49 (1975) 126-34. PFITZNER, V. C. "The Coronation of the King—Passion Narrative and Passion Theology of the Gospel of St. John" LThJ 10 (1976) 1-12. TOWNSEND, J. T. A Liturgical Interpretation of Our Lord's Passion in Narrative Form (New York 1977). BECKER, J., Das Evangelium nach Johannes (Gütersloh/Würzburg 1979) 529-31 (lit!). McHUGH, J., "The Glory of the Cross: The Passion According to St. John" ClR 67 (1982) 117-27.

18:1-19:30 DAUER, A. Die Passionsgeschichte im Johannesevangelium (1972). REUSS, J. ThR 68 (5, 1972) 376-78. HAENCHEN, E. "History and Interpretation in the Johannine Passion Narrative," Interpretation 24 (2, 1970) 198-219.

18:1-19:16 WILSON, W. R. The Execution of Jesus (1970) 63-73.

18:1-19:7 SCHWANK, B. "Jesus überschreitet den Kidron: Jn 18,1-11," Sein und Sendung 29 (1, 1964) 3-15; "Petrus verleugnet Christus: Jo 18,12-27," (2, 1964) 51-65; "Pilatus begegnet dem Christus: Jo 18,28-38a," (3, 1963) 100-12; "Der Dornengekrönte: Jo 18, 39b-19,7," (4, 1963) 148-60.

18 CHURCH, W. R. "The Dislocutions in the 18th Chapter of John," JBL 49 (1930) 375-83.

18:1-27 KRIEGER, N. "Der Knecht des Hohenpriesters," NovTest 2 (1, 1957) 73-74. TEMPLE, S. The Core of the Fourth Gospel (London 1975) 227-35. HAENCHEN, E., Das Johannesevangelium (Tübingen 1980) 515-16 (lit!).

18:1-12 BAILEY, J. A. The Traditions Common to the Gospels of Luke and John (1963) 47-54. RICHTER, G. "Die Gefangennahme Jesu nach dem Johannesevangelium (18, 1-12)," BuL 10 (1, 1969) 26-39. FORTNA, R. T. The Gospel of Signs (1970) 114-17, 158.

18:1-11 RUCKSTUHL, E. Die literarische Einheit des Johannesevangeliums (1951) 127f. SCHNIEWIND, J. Die Parallelperikopen bei Lukas und Johannes (Darmstadt 1958 = 1914) 32-37. HAENCHEN, E. "Historie und Geschichte in den Johanneischen Passionsberichten," Die Bibel und Wir (1968) 182-207. DAUER, A. Die Passionsgeschichte im Johannesevangelium (1972) 21-61, 280-84. LEISTNER, R. Antijudaismus im Johannesevangelium? (Bern 1974) 80-93. APPOLD, M. L., The Oneness Motif in the Fourth Gospel (Tübingen 1976) 125-26. SABBE, M. "The Arrest of Jesus in Jn 18, 1-11 and its Relation to the Synoptic Gospels: A Critical Evaluation of Dauer's Hypothesis" Bibliotheca Ephemeridum Theologicarum Lovaniensium 44 (Louvain 1977) 203-34.

18:1-2 COLSON, J. L'Enigme du Disciple que Jésus aimait (1969) 91-94. KLEIN, H., "Die lukanisch-johanneische Passionstradition" in: M. Limbeck (ed.) Redaktion und Theologie des Passionsberichtes nach den Synoptikern (Darmstadt 1981) 382-83.

18:1 DALMAN, G. Orte und Wege Jesu (1967) 340f. BERGMEIER, R., Glaube als Gabe nach Johannes (Stuttgart 1980) 212. SCHUNCK, K.-D., "1. Makkabäerbuch" in: JüdSchr I/4 (1980) 352n.37a. MOHR, T. A., Markus- und Johannespassion (Zürich 1982) 245-47.

18:2-12 BRUCE, F. F., "The Trial of Jesus in the Fourth Gospel" in: R. T. France/D. Wenham (eds.) Gospel Perspectives I (Sheffield 1980) 8-10. MOHR, T. A. Markus- und Johannespassion (Zürich 1982) 250-51.

18:2-11 BENOIT, P. Passion et Résurrection du Seigneur (1966) 56-59. BLINZLER, J., Der Prozess Jesu (1969) 73-101.

18:2 REYNEN, H. "Synagesthai Joh 18,2," BZ 5 (1, 1961) 86-90.

18:3 GRILL, J. Untersuchungen über die Entstehung des vierten Evangeliums II (1923) 13f. RIVKIN, E., A Hidden Revolution (Nashville 1978) 102.

18:4-8 BARTINA, S. " 'Yo soy Yahweh.' Nota exegética a Io 18,4-8," EstEc 32 (127, 1958) 403-26.

18:4 COLLINS, R. F., "The Search for Jesus. Reflections on the Fourth Gospel" LThPh 34 (1978) 27-48.

18:5.6.8 HARNER, P. B. The "I Am" in the Fourth Gospel (1970) 45.

18:5-6 RUDOLPH, K. Die Mandäer I (1960) 115.

18:5 PALLIS, A., Notes on St. John and the Apocalypse (London 1928) 36-37. HOWARD, V. P. Das Ego in den Synoptischen Evangelien (Marburg 1975) 253.

18:6 MEIN, P. "A Note on John XVIII," ET 65 (9, 1954) 286-87.

18:7 COLLINS, R. F. "The Search for Jesus: Reflections on the Fourth Gospel" LThPh 34 (1978) 27-48.

18:8 HOWARD, V. P., Das Ego in den Synoptischen Evangelien (Marburg 1976) 253.

18:9 BERGMEIER, R., Glaube als Gabe nach Johannes (Stuttgart 1980) 230.

18:10-11 BROWN, R. E. et al. (eds.) Peter in the New Testament (Minneapolis 1973) 133.

18:10 PALLIS, A., Notes on St. John and the Apocalypse (London 1928) 37-38. BRUCE, F. F. "The Book of Zechariah and the Passion Narrative," BJRL 43 (1960-1961) 351f. CRIBBS, F. L. in: SBL Seminar Papers 2 (1973) G. MacRae ed., 4. KLEIN, H. "Die lukanisch-johanneische Passionstradition" in: M. Limbeck (ed.) Redaktion und Theologie des Passionsberichtes nach den Synoptikern (Darmstadt 1981) 390.

18:11 NICKELS, P. Targum and New Testament (1967) 58. WILLIAMS, J. A., A Conceptual History of Deuteronomism in the Old Testament, Judaism, and the New Testament (Ph.D. Diss, Louisville 1976) 317. MOHR, T. A., Markus- and Johannespassion (Zürich 1982) 245-47.

18:12ff MAHONEY, A. "A New Look on an Old Problem (John 18,12-14, 19-24)," CBQ 27 (3, 1965) 137-44.

18:12-28 LANGBRANDTNER, W., Weltferner Gott oder Gott der Liebe (Frankfurt a.M./Bern/Las Vegas 1977) 44-46.

18:12-27 BAUER, W. Das Johannesevangelium (1925) 207f. RUCK-
STUHL, E. Die literarische Einheit des Johannesevangeliums
(1951) 128-30. SCHNEIDER, J. "Zur Komposition von Joh
18,12-27. Kaiphas und Hannas," ZNW 48 (1-2, 1957) 111-19.
SCHNIEWIND, J., Die Parallelperikopen bei Lukas und Johannes (Darmstadt 1958 = 1914) 37-62. HAENCHEN, E.
"Historie und Geschichte in den johanneischen Passionsbeti-
chten," Die Bibel und Wir (1968) 182-207. BLINZLER, J. Der
Prozess Jesu (1969) 129-36. DAUER, A. Die Passinsges-
chichte im Johannesevangelium (1972) 62-69, 341f. LEIST-
NER, R.,, Antijudaismus im Johannesevangelium? (Bern 1974)
94-108. APPOLD, M. L., The Oneness Motif in the Fourth
Gospel (Tübingen 1976) 126-28.

18:12-19.25-27 BENOIT, P. Passion et Résurrection du Seigneur (1963) 81-83.

18:12-16 BUECHSEL, F. Das Evangelium nach Johannes (1946) 168f.

18:12-14.19-24 CHEVALIER, M. A. "La comparution de Jésus devant Hanne
et devant Caiphe," in: Neues Testament und Geschichte (1972)
H. Baltensweiler/B. Reicke eds., 179-85.

18:12-13 KLEIN, H., "Die lukanisch-johanneische Passionstradition"
in: M. Limbeck (ed.) Redaktion und Theologie des Passionsberichtes nach den Synoptikern (Darmstadt 1981) 372-74.

18:13ff BLASS, F. Philosophy of the Gospels (1898) 56ff.

18:13-28 BAILEY, J. A. The Traditions Common to the Gospels of Luke
and John (1963) 55-63. FORTNA, R. T. The Gospel of Signs
(1970) 117-22.

18:13-27 FORTNA, R. T., "Jesus and Peter at the High Priest's House:
A Test Case for the Question of the Relation Between Mark's
and John's Gospels" NTS 24 (1978) 371-83.

18:13-24 BRUCE, F. F., "The Trial of Jesus in the Fourth Gospel" in:
R. T. France/D. Wenham (eds.) Gospel Perspectives I (Sheffield 1980) 10-11.

18:13-14 MOHR, T. A., Markus- und Johannespassion (Zürich 1982)
271-74.

18:13 DAUER, A. Die Passionsgeschichte im Johannesevangelium
(1972) 71f. METZGER, B. M., The Early Versions of the New
Testament (Oxford 1977) 172.

18:14 BERGMEIER, R., Glaube als Gabe nach Johannes (Stuttgart
1980) 45n.318.

18:15-18 LORENZEN, T. Die Bedeutung des Lieblingsjüngers für die
Johanneische Theologie (Rüschlikon 1969) 44-52. LOREN-
ZEN, T. Der Lieblingsjünger im Johannesevangelium (1971)

46ff. DAUER, A. Die Passionsgeschichte im Johannes-evangelium (1972) 314f. de JONGE, M., "The Beloved Disciple and the Date of the Gospel of John" in: E. Best/R. McL. Wilson (eds.) Text und Interpretation. FS. M. Black (Cambridge 1979) 103-104. STURCH, R. L., "The Alleged Eyewitness Material in the Fourth Gospel" in: E. A. Livingstone (ed.) Studia Biblica 1978/II (Sheffield 1980) 320-23. MOHR, T. A., Markus- und Johannespassion (Zürich 1982) 276-77.

18:15-16 BROWN, R. F. et al. (eds.) Peter in the New Testament (Minneapolis 1973) 135-36. MAHONEY, R., Two Disciples at the Tomb (Bern/Frankfurt 1974) 297-99. NEIRYNCK, F., "The 'Other Disciple' in Jn 18,15-16" EphT 51 (1975) 113-41. WILCKENS, U., "Der Paraklet und die Kirche" in: D. Lührmann/G. Strecker (eds.) Kirche. FS. G. Bornkamm (Tübingen 1980) 201.

18:15 PALLIS, A., Notes on St. John and the Apocalypse (London 1928) 38-39.

18:16-27 PALLIS, A., Notes on St. John and the Apocalypse (London 1928) 40.

18:16-17 BOISMARD, M. E., "Importance de la critique textuelle pour établir l'origine araméenne du quatrième évangile" in: M. Boismard et al., L'Evangile de Jean: Études et problèmes (Bruges 1958) 45-46. NICKELS, P. Targum and New Testament (1967) 58.

18:16 BENOIT, P. Passion et Résurrection du Seigneur (1966) 28-30.

18:17-18 BROWN, R. E., et al. (eds.) Peter in the New Testament (Minneapolis 1973) 135.

18:17 BERGMEIER, R., Glaube als Gabe nach Johannes (Stuttgart 1980) 214, 227. KLEIN, H. "Die lukanisch-johanneische Passionstradition" in: M. Limbeck (ed.) Redaktion und Theologie des Passionsberichtes nach den Synoptikern (Darmstadt 1981) 377.

18:18 PALLIS, A. Notes on St. John and the Apocalypse (London 1928) 37.

18:19-24 BENOIT, P. Passion et Résurrection du Seigneur (1966) 95-98. CRIBBS, F. L. in: SBL Seminar Papers 2 (1973) G. MacRae ed., 62-65. PANCARO, S., The Law in the Fourth Gospel (Leiden 1975) 7, 87, 111-15, 504, 538. LEIDIG, E., Jesu Gespräch mit der Samaritanerin (Basel 1981) 260-63. MOHR, T. A., Markus- und Johannespassion (Zürich 1982) 271-74.

18:19-21 LEISTNER, R., Antijudaismus im Johannesevangelium? (Bern 1974) 101-105.

18:19 BRAUN, F.-M. Jean le Théologien (1966) 165-67.

18:20 MULDER, H. " 'En Hij leerde in hun synagogen'," HomRib 21 (7, 1962) 147-51. BOUSSET, W. Die Religion des Judentums im Späthellenistischen Zeitalter (1966 = 1926) 167. BRAUN, H. Qumran und NT II (1966) 95. SMITH, M. Tannaitic Parallels to the Gospels (1968) 8 b n 7. DAUER, A. Die Passionsgeschichte im Johannesevangelium (1972) 80-82, 343f. von WAHLDE, U. C., "The Johannine 'Jews': A Critical Survey" NTS 28 (1982) 53.

18:22-23 CRIBBS, F. L. in: SBL Seminar Papers 2 (1973) G. MacRae ed., 61-62.

18:22 HOOKER, M. D. Jesus and the Servant (1959) 89-91.

18:23 BEUTLER, J. Martyria (1972) 210, 224, 282, 321.

18:25-27 NICKLE, K. F. The Collection (1966) 66. BROWN, R. E. et al. (eds.) Peter in the New Testament (Minneapolis 1975) 135. STURCH, R. L., "The Alleged Eyewitness Material in the Fourth Gospel" in: E. A. Livingstone (ed.) Studia Biblica 1978/II (Sheffield 1980) 320-23. MOHR, T. A., Markus- und Johannespassion (Zürich 1982) 276-77.

18:25 BERGMEIER, R., Glaube als Gabe nach Johannes (Stuttgart 1980) 214. KLEIN, H., "Die lukanisch-johanneische Passionstradition" in: M. Limbeck (ed.) Redaktion und Theologie des Passionsberichtes nach den Synoptikern (Darmstadt 1981) 377.

18:26 KUHL, J. Die Sendung Jesu und der Kirche nach dem Johannes-Evangelium (1967) 92f.

18:28-19:42 PANCARO, S., The Law in the Fourth Gospel (Leiden 1975) 307-10.

18:28-19:24 ESCANDE, J., "Jésus devant Pilate. Jean 18,28-19,24" FV 73 (1974) 66-81.

18:28-19:22 MEEKS, W. A. The Prophet-King, Moses Traditions and the Johannine Christology (1967) 61-81. DAUER, A. Die Passionsgeschichte im Johannesevangelium (1972) 249-75.

18:28-19:16 BAUER, W. Das Johannesevangelium (1925) 214f. STRATH-MANN, H. Das Evangelium nach Johannes (1955) 241f. SCHLIER, H. Die Zeit der Kirche (1956) 56-74. SCHNIE-WIND, J., Die Parallelperikopen bei Lukas und Johannes (Darmstadt 1958 = 1914) 62-77. BLANK, J. "Die Verhandlung vor Pilatus Joh 18,28-19,16 im Lichte johanneischer Theologie," BZ 3 (1, 1959) 60-81. FORTNA, R. T. The Gospel of Signs (1970) 122-28. HAHN, F., "Der Prozess Jesu nach dem Johannesevangelium. Eine redaktionsgeschichtliche Untersuchung" EKK (Vor) 2 (1970) 23-96. BEUTLER, J. Mar-

tyria (1972) 319f. DAUER, A. Die Passionsgeschichte im
Johannesevangelium (1972) 100f., 119-21. JAUBERT, A., "La
comparution devant Pilate selon Jean. Jean 18,28-19,16" FV
73 (1974) 3-12. LEISTNER, R., Antijudaismus im Johannesevangelium? (Bern 1974) 109-35. TEMPLE, S., The Core of
the Fourth Gospel (London 1975) 235-38. APPOLD, M. L., The
Oneness Motif in the Fourth Gospel (Tübingen 1976) 128-38.
de JONGE, M., Jesus: Stranger from Heaven and Son of God
(Missoula 1977) 66-69. HORST, U., "Jesus als König. Zu Joh
18, 28-19,16" Anzeiger für die katholische Geistlichkeit 88
(1979) 352-54. HAENCHEN, E., Das Johannesevangelium
(Tübingen 1980) 533 (lit!). KLEIN, H., "Die lukanisch-johanneische Passionstradition" in: M. Limbeck (ed.) Redaktion und
Theologie des Passionsberichtes nach dem Synoptikern (Darmstadt 1981) 386-89.

18:28-19:15 HAENCHEN, E. "Jesus vor Pilatus (Joh. 18,28-19,15). (Zur
Methode der Auslegung)," ThLZ 85 (2, 1960) 93-102. Also in:
Gott und Mensch (1965) 144-57.

18:28-19:6 HAENCHEN, E. "Historie und Geschichte in den johanneischen Passionsberichten," Die Bibel und Wir (1968) 182-
207.

18:28-38 MOLLAT, D. "Jésus devant Pilate (Jean 18,28-38)," BVieC
39 (1961) 23-31. BENOIT, P. Passion et Résurrection du Seigneur (1966) 168-73.

18:28 JEREMIAS, J. Die Abendmahlsworte Jesu (1960) 13-15, 76f.
BOUSSET, W. Die Religion des Judentums im Spät-
hellenistischen Zeitalter (1966 = 1926) 93. BRAUN, H. Qum-
ran und NT II (1966) 45. NICKELS, P. Targum and New
Testament (1967) 58. WILKENS, W., Zeichen und Werke
(Zürich 1969) 73-74. BROER, I. Die Urgemeinde und das Grab
Jesu (1972) 190. 215f., 241. DAUER, A. Die Passionsge-
schichte im Johannesevangelium (1972) 121f., 132-43. DOR-
MEYER, D., Die Passion Jesu als Verhaltensmodell (Münster
1974) 119n.340. METZGER, B. M., The Early Versions of the
New Testament (Oxford 1977) 391. MULDER, H., "John
XVIII 28 and the Date of the Crucifixion" in: Baarda, T. et al.
(eds.) Miscellanea Neotestamentica (Leiden 1978) 87-105.
MOHR, T. A., Markus- und Johannespassion (Zürich 1982)
282-84.

18:29-19:16 BAILEY, J. A. The Traditions Common to the Gospels of Luke
and John (1963) 64-77. BRUCE, F. F., "The Trial of Jesus in
the Fourth Gospel" in: R. T. France/D. Wenham (eds.) Gospel
Perspectives I (Sheffield 1980) 12-18.

18:29-38 SCHELKLE, K. H. Die Passion Jesu in der Verkündigung des Neuen Testaments (1949) 25f.

18:29-31 NICKELS, P. Targum and New Testament (1967) 58.

18:30-38 HENNECKE, E./SCHNEEMELCHER, W. Neutestament-liche Apokryphen (1964) I 337f.

18:30 BAUMERT, N., Täglich Sterben und Auferstehen (München 1973) 101.

18:31-34 METZGER, B. M. Manuscripts of the Greek Bible (Oxford 1981) 62.

18:31 BLINZLER, J. Der Prozess Jesu (1969) 229-32. BAMMEL, E. The Trial of Jesus (1970) 78ff. DERRETT, J. D. M. Law in the New Testament (1970) 428-29. CATCHPOLE, D. R. The Trial of Jesus (1971) 247. PANCARO, S., The Law in the Fourth Gospel (Leiden 1975) 7, 115, 308, 309, 310-12. SHERWIN-WHITE, A. N., Roman Society and Roman Law in the New Testament (Grand Rapids 1978) 32. STROBEL, A. Die Stunde der Wahrheit (Tübingen 1980) 43-45.

18:32 CASSIAN, B. "John 21," NTS 3 (1956-1957) 135f. PAN-CARO, S., The Law in the Fourth Gospel (Leiden 1975) 197, 319-63. BERGMEIER, R., Glaube als Gabe nach Johannes (Stuttgart 1980) 230.

18:33-38 HEMPEL, J. GPM 21 (1, 1966) 17-23. MEEKS, W. A. The Prophet-King, Moses Traditions and the Johannine Christology (1967) 63-67. FORTNA, R. T. The Gospel of Signs (1970) 123f. DAUER, A. Die Passionsgeschichte im Johannesevangelium (1972) 112-17, 252-62, 308f. BEUTLER, J. Martyria (1972) 319f. CRIBBS, F. L. in: SBL Seminar Papers 2 (1973) G. MacRae ed., 4.

18:33-37 DELLING, G. Die Taufe im Neuen Testament (1963) 79. BOISMARD, C. "La royauté universelle du Christ. Jn 18,33-37," AssS 65 (1973) 36-46.

18:33 SELBY, D. J. Introduction to the New Testament (New York 1971) 228-29. DAUER, A. Die Passionsgeschichte im Johannesevangelium (1972) 122f. IBUKI, Y. Die Wahrheit im Johannesevangelium (1972) 142f. SANDMEL, S., We Jews and Jesus (New York 1977) 35.

18:33-38 LEIDIG, E., Jesu Gespräch mit der Samaritanerin (Basel 1981) 230-36.

18:33-37 SWIDLER, L., Biblical Affirmations of Woman (Philadelphia 1979) 288.

18:36-37 SCHNACKENBURG, R. Gottes Herrschaft und Reich (1959) 230-32.

18:36 VOLZ, P. Die Eschatologie der jüdischen Gemeinde (1934) 319. RUCKSTUHL, E. Die literarische Einheit des Johannesevangeliums (1951) 69, 230, 245, 252, 253, 255. BLAIR, E. P. Jesus in the Gospel of Matthew (1960) 51. HAHN, F. Christologische Hoheitstitel (1963) 173. DAUER, A. Die Passionsgeschichte im Johannesevangelium (1972) 254-58. LADD, G. E. A Theology of the New Testament (1974) 63, 104, 216, 224, 243. METZGER, B. M., The Early Versions of the New Testament (Oxford 1977) 437. MOTT, S., "Pacifism? Come Now!" The Other Side (Savannah, OH 1977) 64-69. ALEGRE, X., " 'Mi reino no es de este mundo' (Jn 18,36). Conflictividad de la existencia cristiana en el mundo según el cuarto evangelio" EstEc 54 (1979) 499-525. "Autorität" in: TRE 5 (1980) 42. BERGMEIER, R., Glaube als Gabe nach Johannes (Stuttgart 1980) 256n.344.

18:37-38 METZGER, B. M., Manuscripts of the Greek Bible (Oxford 1981) 62.

18:37 HAHN, F. Christologische Hoheitstitel (1963) 187. HAHN, F. Das Verständnis der Mission im Neuen Testament ([2]1965) 140. LAZURE, N., Les Valeurs Morales de la Théologie Johannique (Paris 1965) 75-76. DELLING, G. Wort und Werk Jesu im Johannes-Evangelium (1966) 35, 48f., 57. KUHL, J. Die Sendung Jesu und der Kirche nach dem Johannes-Evangelium (1967) 91f., 182, 205. THUESING, W. Die Erhöhung und Verherrlichung Jesu im Johannesevangelium (1970) 29-31. BEUTLER, J. Martyria (1972) 318-25, 331f. IBUKI, Y. Die Wahrheit im Johannesevangelium (1972) 139f., 142-46, 172-75. LADD, G. E. A Theology of the New Testament (1974) 225, 266, 268, 277, 294. MUELLER, T. Das Heilsgeschehen im Johannesevangelium n.d., 136-37. BÜHNER, J.-A., Der Gesandte und sein Weg im 4. Evangelium (Tübingen 1977) 151-52. de la POTTERIE, I., La Vérité dans Saint Jean I/II (Rome 1977) 100-16, 624-31. BEIERWALTES, W., "Deus est veritas" in: E. Dassmann/K. S. Frank (eds.), Pietas. FS. B. Kötting (Münster 1980) 24. BERGMEIER, R., Glaube als Gabe nach Johannes (Stuttgart 1980) 27, 73, 203, 220, 223, 225, 233.

18:38-40 MEEKS, W. A., The Prophet-King, Moses Traditions and the Johannine Christology (1967) 67-68. FORTNA, R. T. The Gospel of Signs (1970) 124f. MOHR, T. A. Markus- und Johannespassion (Zürich 1982) 297-301.

18:38 PALLIS, A., Notes on St. John and the Apocalypse (London 1928) 41.

18:39-19:16 BENOIT, P. Passion et Résurrection du Seigneur (1966) 168-73.

18:39-40 BLINZLER, J. Der Prozess Jesu (1969) 301-20. STROBEL, A., Die Stunde der Wahrheit (Tübingen 1980) 118-31.

18:39 SELBY, D. J., Introduction to the New Testament (New York 1971) 228-29. METZGER, B. M., The Early Versions of the New Testament (Oxford 1977) 392. SANDMEL, S., We Jews and Jesus (New York 1977) 35.

38:40 BAJSIC, A. "Pilatus, Jesus and Barabbas," Biblica 48 (1967) 11-15. SCHALIT, A. König Herodes (1969) 721. CRIBBS, F. L. in: SBL Seminar Papers 2 (1973) G. MacRae ed., 72.

19-20 NEIRYNCK, F., "Les Femmes au Tombeau: Etude de la rédaction Matthéenne," NTS 15 (1968-1969) 169ff.

19 YATES, K. M. Preaching from John's Gospel (1964) 160-66. BAJSIC, A. "Pilatus, Jesus and Barabbas," Biblica 48 (1967) 11-12.

19:1-16 SCHELKLE, K. H. Die Passion Jesu in der Verkündigung des Neuen Testaments (1949) 25f.

19:1-12 BLINZLER, J. Der Prozess Jesu (1969) 321-33.

19:1-8 DAUER, A. Die Passionsgeschichte im Johannesevangelium (1972) 309f.

19:1-3 MEEKS, W. A. The Prophet-King, Moses Traditions and the Johannine Christology (1967) 68-69. FORTNA, R. T. The Gospel of Signs (1970) 126-27. DAUER, A. Die Passionsgeschichte im Johannesevangelium (1972) 166f., 262f. CRIBBS, F. L. in: SBL Seminar Papers 2 (1973) G. MacRae ed., 4.

19:2-4 MASSAUX, E. Influence de L'Evangile des saint Matthieu sur la littérature chrétienne avant saint Irénée (1950) 71-73.

19:2-3 MOHR, T. A., Markus- und Johannespassion (Zürich 1982) 306-308.

19:2 DAUER, A. Die Passionsgeschichte im Johannesevangelium (1972) 126f., 154.

19:3 SANDMEL, S., We Jews and Jesus (New York 1977) 35.

19:4-16 DAUER, A. Die Passionsgeschichte im Johannesevangelium (1966) 263-69.

19:4-7 MEEKS, W. A. The Prophet-King, Moses Traditions and the Johannine Christology (1967) 69-72.

19:4 BONSERVIN, J. "Hora Talmudica," Biblica 33 (1952) 511-15.

19:5 MARCUS, R. "A Note on Origen in Ev. Joannis XIX,5 (PG XIV, 568b-c)," HThR XLVII (1954) 317-18. BRAUN, H. Qumran und NT II (1966) 83. SCHNACKENBURG, R., "Die Ecce-Homo-Szene und der Menschensohn" in: R. Pesch/R. Schnackenburg (eds.) Jesus und der Menschensohn. FS. A. Vögtle (Freiburg 1975) 371-86. HOULDEN, J. L., "John 19:5: 'And he said to them, Behold the man' " ET 92 (1981) 148-49.

19:6 DERRETT, J. D. M. Law in the New Testament (1970) 428-29. KLEIN, H., "Die lukanisch-johanneische Passionstradition" in: M. Limbeck (eds.) Redaktion und Theologie des Passionsberichtes nach den Synoptikern (Darmstadt 1981) 390.

19:7 HAHN, F. Christologische Hoheitstitel (1963) 330. NICKELS, P.. Targum and New Testament (1967) 58. WEAD, D. W. "We have a Law," NovTest 11 (3, 1969) 185-89. LEISTNER, R. Antijudaismus in Johanesevangelium? (Bern 1974) 125-30. MATSUNAGA, K., "The 'Theos' Christology as the Ultimate Confession of the Fourth Gospel" AJBI 7 (1981) 132-33.

19:8-42 SCHWANK, B. "Der königliche Richter: Jo 19,8-16a," Sein und Sendung 29 (5, 1964) 196-208; "Der erhöhte König: Jo 19,16b-22," (6, 1964) 244-54; "Die ersten Gaben des erhöhten Königs: Jo 19,23-30," (7, 1964) 292-309; " 'Sie werden schauen auf Ihn, den sie durchbohrt haben': Jo 19,31-42," (8, 1964) 340-53.

19:8 MURMELSTEIN, B. "Das Lamm in Test. Jos. 19:8," ZNW 58 (3-4, 1967) 273-79.

19:9-11 DAUER, A. Die Passionsgeschichte im Johannesevangelium (1972) 117-19.

19:9 HOOKER, M. D. Jesus and the Servant (1959) 87-89.

19:10-16 MTEZGER, B. M., Manuscripts of the Greek Bible (Oxford 1981) 114.

19:10 FRIEDRICH, G., "Das Problem der Autorität im Neuen Testament" in: Auf das Wort kommt es an (Göttingen 1978) 405. SWIDLER, L., Biblical Affirmations of Woman (Philadelphia 1979) 288.

19:11-22:15 RISSI, M. The Future of the World (1972).

19:11 VON CAMPENHAUSEN, H. "Zum Verständnis von Joh. 19,11," ThLZ 73 (1948) 387-92. DELLING, G. Die Taufe im Neuen Testament (1963) 90. LAZURE, N., Les Valeurs Morales de la Théologie Johannique (Paris 1965) 299-300. POPKES, W. Christus Traditus (1967) 164, 174, 182, 283. ALEGRE, X., " 'Mi reino no es de este mundo' (Jn. 18,36). Conflictividad de la existencia cristiana en al mundo según el cuarto evangelio" EstEc 54 (1979) 499-525. "Autorität" in: TRE 5 (1980) 42. BERGMEIER, R., Glaube als Gabe nach Johannes (Stuttgart 1980) 231, 249n.223f. GEORGI, D., "Weisheit Salomos" in: JüdSchr III/4 (1980) 6n.3a.

19:12 HAHN, F. Christologische Hoheitstitel (1963) 187. HENNECKE, E./SCHNEEMELCHER, W. Neutestamentliche Apokryphen I (1964) 339. NICKELS, P. Targum and New Testament (1967) 58. CRIBBS, F. L., "The Agreements that Exist Between John and Acts" in: C. H. Talbert (ed.) Perspectives on Luke-Acts (Danville 1978) 45.

19:13 KURFESS, A., " 'Εκάθισεν ἐπὶ βήματος (Jo 19,13)," Biblica 34 (1953) 271. DE LA POTTERIE, I. "Jésus, roi et juge d'après Jn 19,13: ekathisen epi bēmatos," Biblica 41 (3, 1960) 217-24. DE LA POTTERIE, I., "Jesus King and Judge According to John 19:13," Scripture 13 (24, 1961) 97-111. O'-ROURKE, J. J. "Two Notes on St. John's Gospel," CBQ 25 (2, 1963) 124-28. BLINZLER, J. Der Prozess Jesu (1969) 346-56. BALAGUÉ, M., "Y lo sentó en el tribunal (Jn 19,13)" EstBi 33 (1974) 63-67. METZGER, B. M., The Early Versions of the New Testament (Oxford 1977) 392. "Aramäisch" in: TRE 3 (1978) 604. ZABALA, A. M., "The Enigma of John 19:13 Reconsidered (A Survey of the Contemporary Discussion and a Suggestion)" SEAJTh 22 (1981) 16-28.

19:14-15 SANDMEL, S., We Jews and Jesus (New York 1977) 35.

19:14.31 LIGHTFOOT, R. H. History and Interpretation in the Gospels (1934) 135f.

19:14 BARTINA, S. "Ignotum episēmon gabex," VerbDom 36 (1, 1958) 16-37. BRAUN, H. Qumran und NT (1966) 45, 50. WILKENS, W. Zeichen und Werke (Zürich 1969) 73-74. BROER, I., Die Urgemeinde und das Grab Jesu (1972) 215ff., 221ff. DAUER, A. Die Passionsgeschichte im Johannesevangelium (1972) 132-43. SZEWC, L., "Symbolicne znaczenie notatki chronologicznej J 19,14" ZNKUL 21 (1978) 10-18. KLEIN, H., "Die lukanisch-johanneische Passionstradition" in: M. Limbeck (ed.) Redaktion und Theologie des Passionsberichtes nach den Synoptikern (Darmstadt 1981) 391.

19:15 HAHN, F. Christologische Hoheitstitel (1963) 187. METZ-
GER, B. M., The Early Versions of the New Testament (Oxford 1977) 252.

19:16-42 SCHNIEWIND, J. Die Parallelperikopen bei Lukas und Johannes (Darmstadt 1958 = 1914) 77-85. HAENCHEN, E., Das Jo-
hannevangelium (Tübingen 1980) 549-50 (lit!).

19:16-37 TEMPLE, S., The Core of the Fourth Gospel (London 1975)
239-46.

19:16b-37 SCHENK, W. Der Passionsbericht nach Markus (1974) 123ff.

19:16-30 FRIEDRICH, GPM 9 (1954-1955) 103ff. HROMADKA, GPM
15 (1960-1961) 116ff. DAUER, A. Die Passionsgeschichte im
Johannesevangelium (1972) 165-226. HOWALD, M./NEID-
HART, W. "Karfreitag: Johannes 19,16-30," in: Predigtstudien (1972) E. Lange ed., 191-96. KOCH, E., in: GPM 33
(1979) 178-83. MOHR, T. A., Markus- und Johannespassion
(Zürich 1982) 347-50.

19:16-18 BLINZLER, J. Der Prozess Jesu (1969) 229f.

19:16 STROBEL, A., Die Stunde der Wahrheit (Tübingen 1980) 105-
106.

19:17ff LEE, E. K., "St. Mark and the Fourth Gospel," NTS 3 (1956-
1957) 55ff.

19:17-42 STRATHMANN, H. Das Evangelium nach Johannes (1955)
253f. BAILEY, J. A. The Traditions Common to the Gospels
of Luke and John (1963) 78-84. LEISTNER, R., Antijudaismus im Johannesevangelium? (Bern 1974) 136-41.

19:17-37 WINANDY, J. "Le témoignage du sang et de l'eau (Jean 19,
17-37)," BVieC 31 (1960) 19-27. RAMOS, F. F., "El Espiritu
Santo y Maria en los escritos joanicos" EphM 28 (1978) 169-
90.

19:17-30 BLINZLER, J. Der Prozess Jesu (1969) 357-74.

19:17-18 CRIBBS, F. L. in: SBL Seminar Papers 2 (1973) G. MacRae
ed., 76-77. DAUER, A. Die Passionsgeschichte im Johannesevangelium (1972) 167-74.

19:17 GLASSON, T. F. Moses in the Fourth Gospel (1963) 98f.
SMITH, M. Clement of Alexandria and a secret Gospel of Mark
(1973) 259f.

19:18 METZGER, B. M., "Names for the Nameless in the New Testament: a Study in the Growth of Christian Tradition" in: New
Testament Studies: Philological, Versional, and Patristic (Leiden 1980) 33-38

19:19ff DAUER, A. Die Passionsgeschichte im Johannesevangelium
(1972) 174-77, 177-82, 221, 345.

19:19-21 SANDMEL, S. We Jews and Jesus (New York 1977) 35.

19:19 RUDOLPH, K. Die Mandäer I (1960) 115.

19:20 "Bibel" in: TRE 6 (1980) 60. von WAHLDE, U. C. "The Johannine 'Jews': A Critical Survey," NTS 28 (1982) 53.

19:21 von WAHLDE, U. C., "The Johannine 'Jews': A Critical Survey" NTS 28 (1982) 53-54.

19:23-24 STRECKER, G. Der Weg der Gerechtigkeit (1962) 18. BRAUN, F.-M., "Quatre 'Signes' Johanniques de L'Unité Chrétienne," NTS 9 (1962-1963) 150f. DAUER, A. Die Passionsgeschichte im Johannesevangelium (1972) 275-77. de la POTTERIE, I. "La tunique sans couture, symbole du Christ grand prêtre?" Biblica 60 (1979) 255-69.

19:23 HAHN, F. Christologische Hoheitstitel (1963) 235.

19:24-28 DE GOEDT, M., "Un Scheme Revelation dans le Quatrième Evangile," NTS 8 (1961-1962) 145-50.

19:24.36 BLAIR, E. P. Jesus in the Gospel of Matthew (1960) 31.

19:24 NEPPER-CHRISTENSEN, P. Das Matthäusevangelium (1958) 141-42, 148. STRECKER, G. Der Weg der Gerechtigkeit (1962) 71₃. FREED, E. D. Old Testament Quotations in the Gospel of John (1965) 99-103. ROTHFUCHS, W. Die Erfüllungszitate des Matthäus-Evangeliums (1969) 159f. LINTON, O. "Le parallelismus membrorum dans le Nouveau Testament," in: Mélanges Bibliques en hommage au R. P. Béda Rigaux (1970) A. Descamps/A. deHalleux, eds., 493-94. DAUER, A. Die Passionsgeschichte im Johannesevangelium (1972) 297f. RUPPERT, L., Jesus als der leidende Gerechte? (Stuttgart 1972) 50n.31. REIM, G., Studien zum Alttestamentlichen Hintergrund des Johannesevangeliums (Cambridge 1974) 47-48, 89-90, 92-94. PANCARO, S., The Law in the Fourth Gospel (Leiden 1975) 328, 330, 332, 339-44. HANSON, A. T., The New Testament Interpretation of Scripture (London 1980) 158-59.

19:25-27 THYES, A. "Jean 19, 25-27 et la Maternité spirituelle de Marie," Marianum 18 (1956) 80-117. "Marie et les écrits johanniques," AmiCl 66 (1956) 687-689. CEROKE, C.P. "Mary's Maternal Role in John 19, 25-27" MarStud 11 (1960) 123-151. KERRIGAN, A. "Jn. 19, 25-27 in the Light of Johannine Theology and the Old Testament," Antonianum 35 (3-4, 1960) 369-416. *LANGKAMMER, T. "Znaczenie mariologiczne tekstu ewangelii sw. Jana 19, 25-27," RTK 9 (3, 1962) 99-113. GALLUS, T. Die Mutter Jesu im Johannesevangelium (1963). FEUILLET, A. "Les adieux du Christ à sa mère (Jn 19,

25-27) et la maternité spirituelle de Marie,'' NRTh 86 (5, 1964) 469-489. ZERWICK, M. ''The Hour of the Mother-John 19:25-27,'' BibToday 1 (18, 1965) 1187-94. FEUILLET, A. ''L'heure de la femme (Jn 16, 21) et l'heure de la Mère de Jésus (Jn 19, 25-27),'' Biblica 47 (3, 1966) 361-80. DAUER, A. ''Das Wort des Gekreuzigten an seine Mutter und den 'Jünger, den er liebte.' Eine traditionsgeschichtliche und theologische Untersuchung zu Joh 19, 25-27,'' BZ 11 (2, 1967) 222-39. SPEDALIERI, F. ''Il Testamento del Signore,'' EphT 17 (1, 1967) 55-87. DAUER, A. ''Das Wort des Gekreuzigten an seine Mutter und den 'Jünger, den er liebte.' Eine traditionsgeschichtliche und theologische Untersuchung zu Joh 19, 25-27,'' BZ 12 (1, 1968) 80-93. ZERWICK, M. ''La hora de la Madre (J 19, 25-27),'' RevBi 30 (4, 1968) 197-205. COLSON, J. L'Enigme du Disciple que Jesus aimait (1969) 10, 16, 27, 97, 110. LORENZEN, T. Die Bedeutung des Lieblingsjüngers für die Johanneische Theologie (1969) 11-18. LE FORT, P. Les Structures de L'Eglise militante selon saint Jean (1970) 152-156. SCHUERMANN, H. Ursprung und Gestalt (1970) 13-15,18,19,23-26. LORENZEN, T. Der Lieblingsjünger im Johannesevangelium (1971) 18ff. MAHONEY, R., Two Disciples at the Tomb (Bern/Frankfurt 1974) 95-103, 295-300. OLSSON, B., Structure and Meaning in the Fourth Gospel (Lund 1974) 30,41-43. OBERLINNER, L., Historische Ueberlieferung und christologische Aussage (Stuttgart 1975) 120-135. CZAJKOWSKI, M., ''Maria u progu i kresu dziela des Wirkens des Messias; Joh 2,1-11; 19,25-27)'' in: F.Gryglewicz (ed.) Egzegeza Ewangelii św.Jana (Lublin 1976) 101-112. DIP, G., ''Maria en el Nuovo Testamento'' CuBi 34 (1977) 83-98. LANGBRANDTNER,W., Weltferner Gott oder Gott der Liebe (Frankfurt a.M./Bern/Las Vegas 1977) 33-35. WULF,F., ''Das marianische Geheimnis der Kirche im Licht des Johannesevangeliums'' GuL 50 (1977) 326-334. STAGG,E. and F., Woman in the World of Jesus (Philadelphia 1978) 239. VANNI,U., ''La decodificazione 'del grande segno' in Apocalisse 12,1-6'' Marianum 40 (1978) 121-152. ALFARO,J.I., ''La mariologia del Cuarto Evangelio. Ensayo de teologia biblica'' RevBi 41 (1979) 193-209. RUETHER,R.R., Mary - The Feminine Face of the Church (London 1979) 31-35. SWIDLER, L., Biblical Affirmations of Woman (Philadelphia 1979) 185, 199, 209, 221. FEUILLET, A., ''La doctrine mariale du Nouveau Testament et la Médaille Miraculeuse. Une révélation privée au service de la Grande Révélation'' EsVie 90 (1980) 657-75.

19:25   BISHOP,E. ''Mary Clopas-Joh 19,25,'' ET 65 (9, 1954) 286-287. BISHOP, E. F. F., ''Mary (of) Clopas and Her Father,''

ET 73 (11, 1962) 339. MEHLMANN,J. "Salomé. A Mãe Dos
Filhos De Zebedeu, 'Irmã' De Nossa Senhora (Jo 19,25)," RCB
3 (2,'63) 56-84. NICKELS,P. Targum and New Testament
(1967) 58. BLINZLER,J., Die Brüder und Schwestern Jesu
(Stuttgart 1967) 111-118. WANKE,J., Die Emmauserzählung
(Leipzig 1973) 124. SWIDLER,L., Biblical Affirmations of
Woman (Philadelphia 1979) 208,234.

19:26ff KAESEMANN,E. Exegetische Versuche und Besinnungen
(1964) I 180. SCHUERMANN,H. Ursprung und Gestalt (1970)
151-166,170-187.

19:26-27 GRILL,J. Untersuchungen über die Entstehung des vierten
Evangeliums II (1923) 25f.,29,196f.,386. RUCKSTUHL,E.
Die literarische Einheit des Johannesevangeliums (1951) 139f.
SQUILLACI, D. "La Maternità spirituale della Madonna,"
PaCl 37 (13, 1958) 685-91. UNGER,D. "The Meaning of John
19,26-27 in the Light of Papal Documents," Marianum 21 (3-
4, 1959) 186-221. LANGKAMMER,H. "Christ's 'Last Will
and Testament' (Jn 19,26.27) in the Interpretation of the Fa-
thers of the Church and the Scholastics," Antonianum 43 (1,
1968) 99-109. SCHUERMANN,H. Ursprung und Gestalt
(1970) 13-28. DAUER, A. Die Passionsgeschichte im
Johannesevangelium (1972) 196-200, 318-33. KEAR-
NEY,P.J., "Gen. 3:15 and Johannine Theology" MSt 27 (1976)
99-109. SABOURIN,L., "As Sete Palavras de Jesus na Cruz"
RcB 2 (1978) 299-303. TOUS,L., "María y la Iglesia. La madre
de Jesús en el IV evangelio" ByF 6 (1980) 226-234. WILCK-
ENS,U., "Der Paraklet und die Kirche" in: D.Lührmann/
G.Strecker (eds.) Kirche. FS. G.Bornkamm (Tübingen 1980)
201.

19:26 PALLIS, A., Notes on St. John and the Apocalypse (London
1928) 43. MICHL, J. "Der Weibessame (Gen 3,15) in Spätjü-
discher und frühchristlicher Auffassung," Biblica 33 (1952)
390-93. SMEREKA, L. "Ecce Mater Tua," RBL 9 (1956) 244-
261. HAENCHEN, E., "Der Vater, der Mich Gesandt Hat,"
NTS 9 (1962/63) 214f. NICKELS,P. Targum and New Testament (1967) 58. SMITH,M. Tannaitic Parallels to the Gospels
(1968) 2.25*. LATTKE,M., Einheit im Wort (München 1975)
12,19.

19:27 DE LA POTTERIE, I. "Das Wort Jesu "Siehe deine Mutter'
und die Annahme der Mutter durch den Jünger (Joh 19,27b),"
in: Neues Testament und Kirche (1974) J.Gnilka ed., 191-219,
esp. 203-216. DE LA POTTERIE,I. "La parole de Jésus 'Voici
ta Mère' et l'accueil du Disciple (Jn 19,27b)," Marianum 36
(1, 1974) 1-39. VOIGT,S., "O Discípulo Amado Recebe a Mae

de Jesus 'Eis Ta Idia': Velada Apologia de João em Jo 19,27?''
REB 35 (1975) 771-823. NEIRYNCK,F., *"EIS TA IDIA*: Jn
19,27 (et 16,32)'' EphT 55 (1979) 357-365. de la POT-
TERIE,I., "Et à partir de cette heure, le Disciple l'accueillit dans
son intimité' (Jn 19,27b). Réflexions méthodologiques sur l'interprétation d'un verset johannique'' Marianum 42 (1980) 84-
125. NEIRYNCK,F., "La traduction d'un verset johannique:
Jn 19, 27b'' EphT 57 (1981) 83-106.

19:28-30 PANCARO,S., The Law in the Fourth Gospel (Leiden 1975)
346, 352-357, 362, 363. SCHNEIDER,G., "Die theologische
Sicht des Todes Jesu in den Kreuzigungsberichten der Evangelien'' TPQ 126 (1978) 14-22. FARICY,R., Praying for Inner
Healing (London 1979) 37-38. MOHR,T.A., Markus- und Johannespassion (Zürich 1982) 322-325.

19:28-29 ROTHFUCHS,W. Die Erfüllungszitate des Matthäus-Evangeliums (1969) 160f. WILKENS,W., Zeichen und Werke (Zürich
1969) 74-76. THUESING,W. Die Erhöhung und Verherrlichung Jesu im Johannesevangelium (1970) 64-69. DAUER,A.
Die Passionsgeschichte im Johannesevangelium (1972) 298f.
HANSON,A.T., The New Testament Interpretation of Scripture (London 1980) 158-159.

19:28.30 KUHL,J. Die Sendung Jesu und der Kirche nach dem Johannes-Evangelium (1967) 110,113-116. DAUER,A. Die
Passionsgeschichte im Johannesevangelium (1972) 201f., 202-
207,286-294,305f.

19:28 GRILL,J. Untersuchungen über die Entstehung des vierten
Evangeliums II (1923) 201,357f. FREED,E.D. Old Testament
Quotations in the Gospel of John (1965) 104-107. BRAUN,H.
Qumran und NT II (1966) 312. MORETTO,G. "Giov. 19,28:
La sete di Cristo in croce," RivB 15 (3, 1967) 249-274. SPUR-
RELL,J.M. "An Interpretation of 'I Thirst'," Church-
QuartRev 167 (362, 1966) 12-18. BAMPFYLDE,G. "John XIX
28, a case for a different translation," NovTest 11 (4, 1969) 247-
260. REIM,G., Studien zum Alttestamentlichen Hintergrund des
Johannesevangeliums (Cambridge 1974) 48-50,89-97. BEUT-
LER,J., "Psalm 42/43 im Johannesevangelium" NTS 25 (1978)
33-57. SABOURIN, L., "As Sete Palavras de Jesus na Cruz"
RCB 2 (1978) 299-303.'' ''Erbauungsliteratur'' in: TRE 10
(1982) 66.

19:29-30 MÜLLER,U.B., "Die griechische Esra-Apokalypse" in:
JüdSchr V/2 (1976) 93n.25a.

19:30-37 LEFEVRE,A. "Die Seitenwunde Jesu," GuL 33 (2, 1960) 86-
96.

19:30 GRILL,J. Untersuchungen über die Entstehung des vierten Evangeliums II (1923) 203f.,210,386. NIEWALDA,P. Sakramentssymbolik im Johannesevangelium? (1958) 12-14. ROBINSON,J.A.T. "The One Baptism," Twelve New Testament Studies (1962) 158-175. BRAUN,F.-M. Jean le Théologien (1966) 150-152. STROBEL,A. Erkenntnis und Bekenntnis der Sünde in neutestamentlicher Zeit (1968) 57. DUNN, J.D.G. Baptism in the Holy Spirit (1970) 177. THYEN,H. Studien zur Sündenvergebung (1970) 246f. DAUER,A. Die Passionsgeschichte im Johannesevangelium (1972) 209-216,305f. PORSCH,F., Pneuma und Wort (Frankfurt 1974) 327-340,377-378. SABOURIN,L., "As Sete Palavras de Jesus na Cruz" RCB 2 (1978) 299-303. HENGEL,M., The Atonement (London 1981) 74,76n.6.

19:31ff GRASS,H. Ostergeschehen und Osterberichte (1970) 174ff.

19:31-42 BROER,I. Die Urgemeinde und das Grab Jesu (1972) 201-249. MAHONEY,R., Two Disciples at the Tomb (Bern/Frankfurt 1974) 121-140. MOHR,T.A., Markus- und Johannespassion (Zürich 1982) 359-364.

19:31-37 GRILL,J. Untersuchungen über die Entstehung des vierten Evangeliums II (1923) 203f,365. GILMORE,A. Christian Baptism (1959) 163ff. WILKENS,W. Die Entstehungsgeschichte des vierten Evangeliums (1958) 25,26. WILKENS,W., Zeichen und Werke (Zürich 1969) 73-74. BRAUN,F.-M. "Avoir soif et boire (Jn 4,10-14; 7,37-38)," in: Mélanges Bibliques en hommage au R.P.Béda Rigaux (1970) A.Descamps/A.DeHalleux eds., 255-257. FORTNA,R.T. The Gospel of Signs (1970) 131. MAHONEY,R., Two Disciples at the Tomb (Bern/Frankfurt 1974) 121-126. DUNLOP,L., "The Pierced Side. Focal Point of Johannine Theology" BiTod 86 (1976) 960-965. VENETZ,H.-J., "Zeuge des Erhöhten. Ein exegetischer Beitrag zu Joh 19,31-37" FZPhTh 23 (1976) 81-111. MOHR,T.A., Markus-und Johannespassion (Zürich 1982) 359-362.

19:31 BRAUN,H. Qumran und NT (1966) II 45. HEISE,J., Bleiben. μένειν in den Johanneischen Schriften (Tübingen 1967) 47-50. WOOD,J.E. "Isaac Typology in the New Testament," NTS 14 (1968) 583-589.

19:32-34 BLINZLER,J. Der Prozess Jesu (1969) 383f.

19:33ff MAURER,C. Ignatius von Antiochien und das Johannesevangelium (1949) 83.

19:33-37 RUCKSTUHL,E. Die literarische Einheit des Johannesevangeliums (1951) 172f.,250. BRUCE,F.F. "The Book of

Zechariah and the Passion Narrative,'' BJRL 43 (1960/61) 341f.
PONCELET,M. Le mystère du sang et de l'eau dans l'Evangile
de Saint Jean (1961).

19:33-34 WILLEMSE,J. ''Christus' doorstoken zijde, oorsprung van de
Kerk. De achtergrond van Joh. 19,33-34'' TvTh 5 (2, 1965) 113-
135.

19:33 BORCHERT,G.L. ''They Brake Not His Legs,'' ChrTo 6 (16,
1962) 572. HAHN,F. Christologische Hoheitstitel (1963) 55.

19:34-35 BARTH,M., Die Taufe - ein Sakrament? (Zürich 1951) 407ff.
ROBINSON,J.M. Kerygma und historischer Jesus (1960) 66.
CULLMANN,O. Urchristentum und Gottesdienst (1950) 110ff.
ROBINSON,J.A.T. ''The One Baptism.'' Twelve New Tes-
tament Studies (1962) 158-175. LE FORT,P. Les Structures de
L'Eglise militante selon saint Jean (1970) 67-69,162.
DAUER,A. Die Passionsgeschichte im Johannesevangelium
(1972) 331f. KEMPTHORNE,R., '''As God is my Witness.'
John 19,34-35'' StEv 6 (1973) 287-290. DUNN,J.D.G., Unity
and Diversity in the New Testament (London 1977) 301-302.
LANGBRANDTNER,W., Weltferner Gott oder Gott der Liebe
(Frankfurt a.m./Bern/Las Vegas 1977) 33-35.

19:34b-35 LORENZEN,T. Die Bedeutung des Lieblingsjüngers für die
Johanneische Theologie (1969) 53-62. LORENZEN,T. Der
Lieblingsjünger im Johannesevangelium (1971) 53ff.

19:34 GRILL,J. Untersuchungen über die Entstehung des vierten
Evangeliums II (1923) 202f.,360,398. PALLIS,A., Notes on
St. John and the Apocalypse (London 1928) 43-44. RUCK-
STUHL,E. Die literarische Einheit des Johannesevangeliums
(1951) 34,172-174,178. CORELL,A. Consummatum Est
(1958) 74-75. NIEWALDA,P. Sakramentssymbolik im
Johannesevangelium? (1958) 68ff. SAVA,A.F. ''The Blood and
Water from the Side of Christ,'' AER 138 (5, 1958) 341-345.
RUDOLPH,K. Die Mandäer II (1961) 127,2. DELLING,G. Die
Taufe im Neuen Testament (1963) 95. GLASSON,T.F. Moses
in the Fourth Gospel (1963) 51ff. SCHWEIZER,E. Neotesta-
mentica (1963) 379-384. MIGUENS,M. '''Salio sangre y agua'
(Jn. 19,34),'' SBFLA 14 (1963-1964) 5-31. LINDIJER,C.H.
De Sacramenten in het Vierde Evangelie (1964) 96f.
BRAUN,F.-M. Jean le Théologien (1966) 167-169.
BIEDER,W., Die Verheissung der Taufe im Neuen Testament
(Zürich 1966) 274-275. FORD,J.M., '''Mingled Blood' from
the Side of Christ (John xix.34),'' NTS 15 (3, 1969) 337-338.
DUNN,J.D.G. Baptism in the Holy Spirit (1970) 187f. RICH-
TER, G. ''Blut und Wasser aus der durchbohrten Seite Jesu (Joh

19,34b)," MThZ 21 (1, 1970) 1-21. THUESING,W. Die Er-
hühung und verherrlichung Jesu im Johannesevangelium (1970)
21f., 161f.,171-173,281f. BEUTLER,J. Martyria (1972) 360f.
KUEMMEL,W.G. Einleitung in das Neue Testament (1973)
175f. KYSAR,R., The Fourth Evangelist and His Gospel (Minneapolis 1974) 256. PORSCH,F., Pneuma und Wort (Frankfurt
1974) 327-340,377-378. REIM,G., Studien zum Alttestamentlichen Hintergrund des Johannesevangeliums (Cambridge 1974)
58-61. PANCARO,S., The Law in the Fourth Gospel (Leiden
1975) 357-362. WILKINSON,J., "The Incident of the Blood
and Water in John 19.34" SJTH 28 (1975) 149-172. "Abendmahl" in: TRE 1 (1977) 57-58. CHMIEL,J., "Krew i woda.
Proba interpretacji J 19,34,"RBL 30 (1977) 291-296. VEL-
LANICKAL,M., "Blood and Water" Jeevadhara 8 (1978) 218-
230. BÖHLIG,A., Die Gnosis III: Der Manichäismus (Zürich/
München 1980) 344n.74. METZGER,B.M., "Names for the
Nameless in the New Testament: a Study in the Growth of
Christian Tradition" in: New Testament Studies: Philological,
Versional, and Patristic (Leiden 1980) 38-39.

19:35-36 BLASS,F. Philosophy of the Gospels (1898) 225ff. de
JONGE,M., "The Beloved Disciple and the Date of the Gospel
of John" in: E.Best/R.McL.Wilson (eds.) Text and Interpretation. FS.M. Black (Cambridge 1979) 104.

19:35 PALLIS,A., Notes on St. John and the Apocalypse (London
1928) 44-45. RUCKSTUHL,E. Die literarische Einheit des
Johannesevangeliums (1951) 5f., 225-228. SCHWEIZER, E.
Gemeinde und Gemeinde-Ordnung im Neuen Testament (1959)
§§11c,24b. BROX,N. Zeuge und Märtyrer (1961) 80ff.,83f.
KAESEMANN,E. Exegetische Versuche und Besinnungen
(1964) I 180. SMITH,D.M. The Composition and Order of the
Fourth Gospel (1965) 214,216,221,222,227,233. KUHL,J. Die
Sendung Jesu und der Kirche nach dem Johannes-Evangelium
(1967) 179f. BEUTLER,J. Martyria (1972) 36f. BERG-
MEIER,R., Glaube als Gabe nach Johannes (Stuttgart 1980)
202.

19:36-37 FREED, E., D. Old Testament Quotations in the Gospel of John
(1965) 108-16. NELLESSEN,E. Das Kind und seine Mutter
(1969) 37f. ROTHFUCHS, W. Die Erfüllungszitate des Matthäus-Evangeliums (1969) 161ff. DAUER,A. Die Passionsgeschichte im Johannesevangelium (1972) 139-141,299.
SEYNAEVE,J., "Les citations scripturaires en Jn., 19,36-37:
une preuve en faveur de la typologie de l'Agneau pascal?" RATh
1 (1977) 67-76. HANSON,A.T., The New Testament Interpretation of Scripture (London 1980) 158-159.

19:36 BARTON,G.A. "A bone of him shall not be broken," JBL 49 (1930) 13-19. HAHN,F. Christologische Hoheitstitel (1963) 55. NICKELS,P. Targum and New Testament (1967) 58. SCHUERMANN,H. Ursprung und Gestalt (1970) 199,200,201,202. RUPPERT,L., Jesus als der leidende Gerechte? (Stuttgart 1972) 66. REIM,G., Studien zum Alttestamentlichen Hintergrund des Johannesevangeliums (Cambridge 1974) 51-57,89-90,93. BRUCE,F.F., The Time is Fulfilled (Exeter 1978) 48. BERGER,K., "Das Buch der Jubiläen" in: JüdSchr II/3 (1981) 549n.13a.

19:37 SQUILLACI,D. "Il Cuore di Gesù trafitto (Giov. 19,37; Zacc. 12,10)," PaCl 37 (12, 1958) 628-631. BRUCE,F.F. "The Book of Zechariah and the Passion Narratives," BJRL 43 (1960/61) 350f. GLASSON,T.F. Moses in the Fourth Gospel (1963) 34f. BRAUN,F.-M. Jean le Théologien (1966) 178-180. THUESING,W. Die Erhöhung und Verherrlichung Jesu im Johannesevangelium (1970) 19-22. SCHUESSLER-FIORENZA,E. Priester für Gott (1972) 191f. REIM,G., Studien zum Alttestamentlichen Hintergrund des Johannesevangeliums (Cambridge 1974) 54-56,89-90,92-93. PANCARO,S., The Law in the Fourth Gospel (Leiden 1975) 344,350-352,357,358. LANGBRANDTNER,W., Weltferner Gott oder Gott der Liebe (Frankfurt a.M./Bern/Las Vegas 1977) 33-35. BERGMEIER,R., Glaube als Gabe nach Johannes (Stuttgart 1980) 267n.504.

19:38ff GRILL,J. Untersuchungen über die Entstehung des vierten Evangeliums II (1923) 176f.

19:38-20:10 TEMPLE, S., The Core of the Fourth Gospel (London 1975) 246-50.

19:38-42 BENOIT,P. Passion et Résurrection du Seigneur (1966) 248-251. FORTNA,R.T. The Gospel of Signs (1970) 131f. CRIBBS,F.L. in: SBL Seminar Papers 2 (1973) G.MacRae ed., 79-81. MAHONEY,R., Two Disciples at the Tomb (Bern/Frankfurt 1974) 122-124. SCHREIBER,J., "Die Bestattung Jesu. Redaktionsgeschichtliche Beobachtungen zu Mk 15:42-47" ZNW 72 (1981) 166-172. MOHR,T.A., Markus- und Johannespassion (Zürich 1982) 362.

19:38 FLEW,R.N. Jesus and His Church (1956) 175. METZGER,B.M., The Early Versions of the New Testament (Oxford 1977) 11,435.

19:39-42 STASIAK,K., "The Man Who Came by Night" BiTod 20 (1982) 84-89.

19:39 PALLIS,A., Notes on St. John and the Apocalypse (London 1928) 45. MAHONEY,R., Two Disciples at the Tomb (Bern/ Frankfurt 1974) 126-128.

19:40 RUDOLPH,K. Die Mandäer II (1961) 416,5. CHARBEL,A., "A Sepultura de Jesus como Resulta dos Evangelhos" RCB 2 (1978) 351-362.

19:41-20:18 KRETSCHMAR,G., "Kreuz und Auferstehung Jesu Christi. Das Zeugnis der Heiligen Stätten" EuA 54 (1978) 423-431; 55 (1979) 12-26.

19:41-42 KLEIN,H., "Die lukanisch-johanneische Passionstradition" in: M.Limbeck (ed.) Redaktion und Theologie des Passionsberichtes nach den Synoptikern (Darmstadt 1981) 389.

19:41 HENNECKE,E./SCHNEEMELCHER,W. Neutestamentliche Apokryphen (1964) I 122. CRIBBS,F.L. in: SBL Seminar Papers 2 (1973) G. MacRae ed., 4. MAHONEY,R., Two Disciples at the Tomb (Bern/Frankfurt 1974) 133-138. METZGER,B.M., The Early Versions of the New Testament (Oxford 1977) 365.

20-21 GARDNER-SMITH, P. Saint John and the Synoptic Gospels (1938) 73-87. LO GIUDICE, C. "La fede degli Apostoli nel IV Vangelo," Biblica 28 (1947) 264-274. BAILEY, J. A. The Traditions Common to the Gospels of Luke and John (1963) 85-102. HAHN, F. Christologische Hoheitstitel (1963) 94,123f. SCHWANK, B. "Das leere Grab: Jo 20,1-18," Sein und Sendung 29 (9, 1964) 388-400; "'Selig, die nicht sehen und doch glauben': Jo 20, 19-31," (10, 1964) 435-50; "Der geheimnisvolle Fischfang: Jo 21, 1-14," (11, 1964) 484-98; "Christi Stellvertreter: Jo 21, 15-25," (12, 1964) 531-42. SCHWANK, B. "Die Ostererscheinungen des Johannesevangeliums und die Postmortem-Erscheinungen der Parapsychologie," EuA 44 (1, 1968) 36-53. BODE, E.L. The First Easter Morning (1970) 72-73. FEUILLET, A., "Les christophanies pascales du quatrième évangile sont-elles des signes?" NRTh 97 (1975) 577-592. MINEAR, P. S., To Die and to Live (New York 1977) 109-110. VELLANICKAL, M., "Resurrection of Jesus in St. John" BB 3 (1977) 131-54.

20:1-21:23 KREMER, J., Die Osterevangelien—Geschichten um Geschichte (Stuttgart/Klosterneuburg).

20 LIGHTFOOT, R. H. Locality and Doctrine in the Gospels (1938) 101ff. LEANEY, R., "The Resurrection Narratives in Luke (XXIV, 12-53)," NTS 2 (1955/56) 111ff. SCHNIE-WIND, J., Die Parallelperikopen bei Lukas und Johannes (Darmstadt 1958 = 1914) 85-95. WILKENS, W. Die Entstehungsgeschichte des vierten Evangeliums (1958) 87-93. LINDARS, B. "The Composition of John XX," NTS 7 (2, 1961) 142-147. HARTMANN, G. "Die Vorlage der Osterberichte in Joh 20," ZNW 55 (3-4, 1964) 197-220. YATES, K. M. Preaching from John's Gospel (1964) 167-173. KAMP-HAUS, F. Von der Exegese zur Predigt (1968) 57-62. NEI-RYNCK, F., "Les Femmes au Tombeau: Etude de la Rédaction Matthéenne (Matt. XXVIII. 1-10)," NTS 15 (1968/69) 168ff. DUPONT, L. et al., "Récherche sur la structure de Jean 20," Biblica 54 (4, 1973) 482-98. GHIBERTI, G. "Gv 20 nell'esegesi contemporanea," StPa 20 (2, 1973) 293-337. MA-HONEY, R., Two Disciples at the Tomb (Bern/Frankfurt 1974) 34-39. BARTLETT, D. L., Fact and Faith (Valley Forge 1975) 118-120. SCHEP, J. A., The Nature of the Resurrection Body (Grand Rapids 1976) 134ff. de SOLAGES, M., Jean et les Synoptiques (Leiden 1979) 187-267. BERGMEIER, R., Glaube als Gabe nach Johannes (Stuttgart 1980) 206. HAENCHEN, E., Das Johannesevangelium (Tübingen 1980) 566-567 (lit!).

20:1ff RENGSTORF, K. H. Die Auferstehung Jesu (1960) passim. GRASS, H. Ostergeschehen und Osterberichte (1970) 51ff.

20:1-31 RUCKSTUHL, E. Die literarische Einheit des Johannesevangeliums (1951) 130, 135, 137f., 177. STANLEY, D. M. "St. John and the Paschal Mystery," Worship 33 (5, 1959) 293-301. CRIBBS, F. L. in: SBL Seminar Papers 2 (1973) G.MacRae ed., 81-82.

20:1-29 NICCACCI, A., "La fede nel Gesù storico et la fede nel Cristo risorto" Antonianum 53 (1978) 423-42.

20:1-20 FORTNA, R. T. The Gospel of Signs (1970) 134-144.

20:1-18 RUCKSTUHL, E. Die literarische Einheit des Johannesevangeliums (1951) 130-134, 137. WIKENHAUSER, A. Das Evangelium nach Johannes (1957) 341. BENOIT, P. "Marie-Madeleine et les Disciples au Tombeau selon Joh 20:1-18," Judentum, Urchristentum und Kirche (1960) 141-152. KAMP-HAUS, F. Von der Exegese zur Predigt (1968) 36-38. KREMER, J. Die Osterbotschaft der vier Evangelien (1968) 87-102. SEIDENSTICKER, P. Die Auferstehung Jesu in der Botschaft der Evangelisten (1968) 119f. GUTBROD, K. Die Auferstehung Jesu im Neuen Testament (1969) 62-64. PEREIRA,

F. "Maria Magdalena aput sepulcrum," VD 47 (1, 1969) 4-21. LEON-DUFOUR, X., The Resurrection and the Message of Easter (London 1974) 169-181. MAHONEY, R., Two Disciples at the Tomb (Bern/Frankfurt 1974) 137-140, 171-228. VELLANICKAL, M., "Feast of the Resurrection (Jn 20:1-18). Identity of the Risen Lord" BB 2 (1976) 91-94. LÖWE, M. und ZIPPERT, C., in: P. Krusche et al. (eds.) Predigtstudien für das Kirchenjahr 1976/1977. V/2 (Stuttgart 1977) 17-24. STAGG, E. and F., Woman in the World of Jesus (Philadelphia 1978) 144-160, 239. "Auferstehung" in: TRE 4 (1979) 506. BECKER, J., Das Evangelium nach Johannes (Gütersloh/ Würzburg 1979) 605 (lit!). BROWN, R. E., The Community of the Beloved Disciple (London 1979) 189-190. MOHR, T.A., Markus- und Johannespassion (Zürich 1982) 388-403.

20:1-13 BODE, E. L. The First Easter Morning (1970) 7-10, 72-86, 184-185. ALSUP, J. E., The Post-Resurrection Appearance Stories of the Gospel-Tradition (Stuttgart 1975) 95ff.

20:1-10 RUCKSTUHL, E. Die literarische Einheit des Johannesevangeliums (1951) 139f. DESCAMPS, A. "La Structure des Récits Evangeliques de la Résurrection," Biblica 40 (1959) 731-733. MAHONEY, R., Two Disciples at the Tomb. The Background and Message of John 20, 1-10 (Bern/Frankfurt 1974) passim. SWIDLER, L., Biblical Affirmations of Woman (Philadelphia 1979) 202, 221, 234.

20:1-2 MARXSEN, W. The Resurrection of Jesus of Nazareth (1970) 56-59. JEREMIAS, J. New Testament Theology I (1971) 304f. MAHONEY, R., Two Disciples at the Tomb (Bern/Frankfurt 1974) 180-182, 189-191. SCHILLEBEECKX, E. Die Auferstehung Jesu als Grund der Erlösung (Basel 1979) 104-105.

20:1.11-13 SCHNIDER, F./STENGER, W. Die Ostergeschichten der Evangelien (1969) 92-107.

20:1 HAHN, F. Christologische Hoheitstitel (1963) 205. FORTNA, R.T. The Gospel of Signs (1970) 135. MAHONEY, R., Two Disciples at the Tomb (Bern/Frankfurt 1974) 184-186, 194-197, 201-214, 237-240. "Auferstehung" in: TRE 4 (1979) 498.

20:2ff KASEMANN, E. Exegetische Versuche und Besinnungen (1964) I 180.

20:2-18 MAHONEY, R., Two Disciples at the Tomb (Bern/Frankfurt 1974) 212-224.

20:2-11 MOHR, T.A., Markus- und Johannespassion (Zürich 1982) 394-396.

20:2-10 LORENZEN, T. Die Bedeutung des Lieblingsjüngers für die Johanneische Theologie (Rüschlikon 1969) 19-32. SCHNIDER, F./STENGER, W. Die Ostergeschichten der Evangelisten (1969) 107-111. GRASS, H. Ostergeschehen und Osterberichte (1970) 54ff. LORENZEN, T. Der Lieblingsjünger im Johannesevangelium (1971) 24ff. DAUER, A. Die Passionsgeschichte im Johannesevangelium (1972) 319f., 331, 347. BROWN, R.E. et al. (eds.) Peter and the New Testament (Minneapolis 1973) 137-138. MAHONEY, R., Two Disciples at the Tomb (Bern/Frankfurt 1974) 72-73, 173-174. LANGBRANDTNER, W., Weltferner Gott oder Gott der Liebe (Frankfurt a.M./Bern/Las Vegas 1977) 30-32. de JONGE, M., ''The Beloved Disciple and the Date of the Gospel of John'' in: E.Best/R.McL.Wilson (eds.) Text and Interpretation. FS. M. Black (Cambridge 1979) 102. MORETON, M. B., ''The Beloved Disciple Again'' in: E. A. Livingstone (ed.) Studia Biblica 1978/II (Sheffield 1980) 215-216. WILCKENS, U., ''Der Paraklet und die Kirche'' in: D.Lührmann/ G. Strecker (eds.) Kirche. FS. G.Bornkamm (Tübingen 1980) 202.

20:2-8. BERGER, K., ''Das Buch der Jubiläen'' in: JüdSchr II/3 (1981) 440n.4a.

20:2 PALLIS, A., Notes on St. John and the Apocalypse (London 1928) 45-46. DELLING, G. Die Taufe im Neuen Testament (1963) 94. HAHN, F. Christologische Hoheitstitel (1963) 123, 124. SMITH, M. Tannaitic Parallels to the Gospels (1968) 2.70*. FORTNA, R. T. The Gospel of Signs (1970) 135f. MAHONEY, R., Two Disciples at the Tomb (Bern/Frankfurt 1974) 173-175. 184-187, 213-217, 239-245. LATTKE, M., Einheit im Wort (München 1975) 19. MINEAR, P.S., '''We don't know where . . . ' John 20:2'' Interp 30 (1976) 125-139.

20:3ff HAHN, F. Christologische Hoheitstitel (1963) 388.

20:3-10 BODE, E.L. The First Easter Morning (1970) 171-172. JEREMIAS, J. Neutestamentliche Theologie I (1971) 289f. MARXSEN, W. The Resurrection of Jesus of Nazareth (1970) 57-60. WANKE, J., Die Emmauserzählung (Leipzig 1973) 73, 76-79, 81-82. MAHONEY, R., Two Disciples at the Tomb (Bern/Frankfurt 1974) 181-185. ALSUP, J. E., The Post-Resurrection Appearance Stories of the Gospel-Tradition (Stuttgart 1975) 98ff. FEUILLET, A., ''La découverte du tombeau vide en Jean 20,3-10 et la Foi au Christ ressuscité'' EsVie 87 (1977) 257-266, 273-284. FEUILLET, A., ''La découverte du tombeau en Jean 20.3-10'' Hokhma 7 (1978) 1-45. ''Auferstehung'' in: TRE 4 (1979) 506. SCHILLEBEECKX, E., Die Auferstehung Jesu als Grund der Erlösung (Basel 1979) 104-105.

20:3-9 MICHEL, O. "Ein johanneischer Osterbericht," in: Studien zum Neuen Testament und zur Patristik (1961) Kommission für spätantike Religionsgeschichte eds., 35-43.

20:3 MAHONEY, R., Two Disciples at the Tomb (Bern/Frankfurt 1974) 244-246.

20:4 BODE, E.L. The First Easter Morning (1970) 76-77. MAHONEY, R., Two Disciples at the Tomb (Bern/Frankfurt 1974) 245-250.

20:5-7 AUER, E.G. Die Urkunde der Auferstehung Jesu (1959). MERCIER, R., "Lo que 'el otro discipulo' vio en la tumba vacia. Juan 20, 5-7" RevBi 43 (1981) 3-32.

20:5 MAHONEY, R., Two Disciples at the Tomb (Bern/Frankfurt 1974) 217-219, 246-253.

20:6-7 BALAGUE, M. "La prueba de la Resurrection (Jn 20, 6-7)," EstBi 25 (2, 1966) 169-192. MAHONEY, R., Two Disciples at the Tomb (Bern/Frankfurt 1974) 251-258. CHARBEL, A., "A Sepultura de Jesus como Resulta dos Evangelhos" RCB 2 (1978) 351-362.

20:7 OSBORNE, B. "A Folded Napkin in an Empty Tomb: John 11:44 and 20:7 Again," HeyJ 14 (4, 1973) 437-440. REISER, W.E. "The Case of the Tidy Tomb: The Place of the Napkins of John 11:44 and 20:7," HeyJ 14 (1, 1973) 47-57. SALVONI, F., "The So-Called Jesus Resurrection Proof (John 20:7)" RestQ 22 (1979) 72-76.

20:8ff GRUNDMANN, W. "Verständnis und Bewegung des Glaubens im Johannes-Evangelium," KuD 6 (1960) 143ff.

20:8-9 BODE, E.L. The First Easter Morning (1970) 78-80, 80-82.

20:8 MAHONEY, R., Two Disciples at the Tomb (Bern/Frankfurt 1974) 257-270.

20:9 MAHONEY, R., Two Disciples at the Tomb (Bern/Frankfurt 1974) 270-274. ZELZER, K., *"Oudepo gar edeisan-* 'denn bisher hatten sie nicht verstanden.' Zu Übersetzung und Kontextbezug von Joh 20,9" BuL 53 (1980) 104-106. ZELZER, K., *OUDEPŌ GAR ĒIDEISAN-* 'denn bisher hatten sie nicht verstanden.' Philologisches zu Übersetzung und Kontextbezug von Jo. 20,9" Wiener Studien 14 (1980) 56-74.

20:10 NEIRYNCK, F., *"Apēlthen pros heauton.* Lc 24, 12 et Jn 20,10" EphT 54 (1978) 104-118.

20:11-30 TEMPLE, S., The Core of the Fourth Gospel (London 1975) 250.

20:11-18 IWAND, H.-J. in: Herr, tue meine Lippen auf Bd 3 (1964) G. Eichholz, ed., 200ff. KUENKEL, K. GPM (1, 1965) 168-174. LUTHER, M. Predigten über die Christus-Botschaft (1966) 182-187. FUERST, W. in: Hören und Fragen Bd 5, 3 (1967) G. Eichholz/A.Falkenroth eds., 259ff. HOOKE, S.H. The Resurrection of Christ as History and Experience (1967) 80-82. BODE, E.L. The First Easter Morning (1970) 82-84, 85-86. MARXSEN, W. The Resurrection of Jesus of Nazareth (1970) 57f., 59ff. FUCHS, E. GPM 25 (1, 1971) 197-200. VON RAD, G. Predigten (1972) 17-22. WANKE, J., Die Emmauserzählung (Leipzig 1973) 5, 13, 36, 124, A.42, 55, 119. MAHONEY, R., Two Disciples at the Tomb (Bern/Frankfurt 1974) 274-277. HAAR, J., GPM 31 (1976/1977) 186-189. COLLINS, R.F., "The Search for Jesus. Reflections on the Fourth Gospel," LThPh 34 (1978) 27-48. FEUILLET, A., "L'apparition du Christ à Marie-Madeleine *Jean 20, 11-18*. Comparaison avec l'apparition aux disciples d'Emmaüs *Luc 24, 13-35*" EsVie 88 (1978) 193-204, 209-223. ROLOFF, J., Neues Testament (Neukirchen-Vluyn 1979) 208-210. SWIDLER, L., Biblical Affirmations of Woman (Philadelphia 1979) 204, 209, 223, 234, 279. LEIDIG, E., Jesu Gespräch mit der Samaritanerin (Basel 1981) 236-239. MOHR, T.A., Markus- und Johannespassion (Zürich 1982) 396-401.

20:11-14 MAHONEY, R., Two Disciples at the Tomb (Bern/Frankfurt 1974) 178-180.

20:11-13 "Auferstehung" in: TRE 4 (1979) 498. SCHILLEBEECKX, E., Die Auferstehung Jesu als Grund der Erlösung (Basel 1979) 104-105.

20:11-12 FORTNA, R.T. The Gospel of Signs (1970) 138f.

20:11 MAHONEY, R., Two Disciples at the Tomb (Bern/Frankfurt 1974) 176-179, 184-186. METZGER, B.M., The Early Versions of the New Testament (Oxford 1977) 369n.1.

20:12 BODE, E.L. The First Easter Morning (1970) 165-171. WANKE, J., Die Emmauserzählung (Leipzig 1973) 74. METZGER, B.M., The Early Versions of the New Testament (Oxford 1977) 437. SCHRAGE, W., "Die Elia-Apokalypse" in: JüdSchr V/3 (1980) 265n.39m.

20:13 HAHN, F. Christologische Hoheitstitel (1963) 123, 124. MAHONEY, R., Two Disciples at the Tomb (Bern/Frankfurt 1974) 215-217, 240-242.

20:14-18 SEIDENSTICKER, P. Die Auferstehung Jesu in der Botschaft des Evangelisten (1968) 120ff. SCHNIDER, F./STENGER, W. Die Ostergeschichten der Evangelien (1969) 111-118. ALSUP, J.E., The Post-Resurrection Appearance Stories of the Gospel-

Tradition (Stuttgart 1975) 206ff., 267-268. DUNN, J.D.G., Jesus and the Spirit (London 1975) 126ff. KELBER, W.H. (ed.) The Passion in Mark (Philadelphia 1976) 142, 143, 144. PAGELS, E.H., "Visions, Appearances, and Apostolic Authority: Gnostic and Orthodox Traditions" in: B.Aland et al. (eds.) Gnosis. FS. H.Jonas (Göttingen 1978) 415.

20:14 BROER, I. Die Urgemeinde und das Grab Jesu (1972) 241f. FORESTELL, J.T., The Word of the Cross (Rome 1974) 22-23. SWIDLER, L., Biblical Affirmations of Woman (Philadelphia 1979) 344.

20:15 MAHONEY, R., Two Disciples at the Tomb (Bern/Frankfurt 1974) 215-217, 240-244. "Auferstehung" in: TRE 4 (1979) 522.

20:16 KNOX, W.L. The Sources of the Synoptic Gospels II (1957) 87. BOISMARD, M.E., "Importance de la critique textuelle pour établir l'origine araméenne du quatrième évangile" in: M.Boismard et al., L'Evangile de Jean: études et problèmes (Bruges 1958) 47-48. HAHN, F. Christologische Hoheitstitel (1963) 75, 76. NICKELS, P. Targum and New Testament (1967) 58. ALSUP, J.E., The Post-Resurrection Appearance Stories of the Gospel-Tradition (Stuttgart 1975) 150ff. "Aramäisch" in: TRE 3 (1978) 608.

20:17-29 THUESING, W. Die Erhöhung und Verherrlichung Jesu im Johannesevangelium (1970) 213f., 263-269, 270f., 275f. de JONGE, M., Jesus: Stranger from Heaven and Son of God (Missoula 1977) 3-7.

20:17-21 HENNECKE, E./SCHNEEMELCHER, W. Neutestamentliche Apokryphen (1964) I 130, II 99, 319.

20:17-19 TALBERT, C.H. Literary Patterns. Theological Themes, and the Genre of Luke-Acts (1974) 113.

20:17 GRILL, J. Untersuchungen über die Entstehung des vierten Evangeliums II (1923) 25, 71, 94, 290, 374, 390. VIOLET, B. "Ein Versuch zu Jn 20:17," ZNW 24 (1925) 78. GRUNDMANN, W. "Zur Rede Jesu vom Vater im Johannesevangelium. Eine redaktions- und bekenntnisgeschichtliche Untersuchung zu Joh 20,17 und seiner Vorbereitung," ZNW 52 (3-4, 1961) 213-230. STRECKER, G. Der Weg der Gerechtigkeit (1962) 211$_2$. DALTON, W.J., Christ's Proclamation to the Spirits (Rome 1965) 185. DELLING, G. Wort und Werk Jesu im Johannes-Evangelium (1966) 61, 64f., 85. DUNN, J.D.G. Baptism in the Holy Spirit (1970) 174, 176f., 182. GRASS, H. Ostergeschehen und Osterberichte (1970) 59ff. LOHFINK, G. Die Himmelfahrt Jesu (1971) 115-118. RICH-

TER, G. "Der Vater und Gott Jesu und seiner Brüder in Joh 20, 17. Ein Beitrag zur Christologie des Johannesevangeliums," MThZ 24 (2, 1973) 95-114. FORESTELL, J.T., The Word of the Cross (Rome 1974) 60, 97, 98, 99, 100. MAHONEY, R., Two Disciples at the Tomb (Bern/Frankfurt 1974) 185-187, 275-277. PORSCH, F., Pneuma und Wort (Frankfurt 1974) 344-349. ALSUP, J.E., The Post-Resurrection Appearance Stories of the Gospel-Tradition (Stuttgart 1975) 150ff. FOWLER, D.C., "The meaning of 'Touch Me Not' in John 20:17" EQ 47 (1975) 16-25. CHARBEL, A., "Giov. 20,17a: 'Nondum enim ascendi ad Patrem'?" BiOr 21 (1979) 79-83. SCHILDENBERGER, J., "Die Vertauschung der Aussagen über Zeichen und Bezeichnetes. Eine hermeneutisch bedeutsame Redeweise" in: Kirche und Bibel. FS. E.Schick (Paderborn 1979) 407. SWIDLER, L., Biblical Affirmations of Woman (Philadelphia 1979) 209. "Erbauungsliteratur" in: TRE 10 (1982) 67.

20:18   HAHN, F. Christologische Hoheitstitel (1963) 123. SWIDLER, L., Biblical Affirmations of Woman (Philadelphia 1979) 213.

20:19-31   DINKLER, E., GPM 4 (1949/50) 130ff. GLOEGE, G., GPM 9 (1954/55) 114ff. BONHOEFFER, D. in: Herr, tue meine Lippen auf Bd 1 (1957) G. Eichholz ed., 145-149. STECK, K. G., GPM 15 (1960/61) 128ff. DOERNE, M. Er kommt auch noch heute (1961) 77-80. SCHMIDT, L. "Nicht sehen-und doch glauben," in: Kleine Predigt-Typologie III (1965) L. Schmidt ed., 303-308. KAMPHAUS, F. Von der Exegese zur Predigt (1968) 93-103. ALSUP, J.E., The Post-Resurrection Appearance Stories of the Gospel-Tradition (Stuttgart 1975) 148ff. LANGBRANDTNER, W., Weltferner Gott oder Gott der Liebe (Frankfurt a.M./Bern/Las Vegas 1977) 35-38.

20:19-29   KREMER, J. Die Osterbotschaft der vier Evangelien (1968) 102-114. THUESING, W. Die Erhöhung und Verherrlichung Jesu im Johannesevangelium (1970) 263-269. WILCKENS, U. Auferstehung (1970) 71-75. SCHMIDT, H. GPM 27 (2, 1973) 221-229. LEON-DUFOUR, X. The Resurrection and the Message of Easter (London 1974) 82-94. SUGGIT, J., "The Eucharistic Significance of John 20.19-29" JThSA 16 (1976) 52-59. LINK, H.-G., in: GPM 33 (1979) 196-203.

20:19-24   LEON-DUFOUR, X., The Resurrection and the Message of Easter (London 1974) 181-189.

20:19-23   BEARE, F.W. "The Risen Jesus Bestows the Spirit: A Study of John 20:19-23," CanJournTheol 4 (2, 1958) 95-100. HAHN, F. Christologische Hoheitstitel (1963) 123. HOOKE, S.H. The

Resurrection of Christ as History and Experience (1967) 82-84.
SEIDENSTICKER, P. Die Auferstehung Jesu in der Botschaft
der Evangelisten (1968) 130ff. KASTING, H. Die Anfänge der
Urchristlichen Mission (1969) 44f., 46. SCHNIDER, F./
STENGER, W. Die Ostergeschichten der Evangelien (1969)
118-127. BURCHARD, C. Der dreizehnte Zeuge (1970) 130f.,
132. GRASS, H. Ostergeschehen und Osterberichte (1970) 64ff.
THYEN, H. Studien zur Sündenvergebung (1970) 243-251.
FEUILLET, A. "La Communication de l'Esprit Saint aux
Apôtres (Jn, XX 19-23) et le ministère sacerdotal de la récon-
ciliation des hommes avec Dieu," EsVie 82 (1, 1972) 2-7.
MICHL, J., "Sündenbekenntnis und Sündenvergebung in der
Kirche des Neuen Testaments" MThZ 24 (1973) 189-207.
WANKE, J., Die Emmauserzählung (Leipzig 1973) 12, 116.
HUBBARD, B.J., "The Matthean Redaction of a Primitive
Apostolic Commissioning: An Exegesis of Matthew 28:16-20
(Missoula 1974) 101-128. PORSCH, F., Pneuma und Wort
(Frankfurt 1974) 344-349, 353-359. SZYMANEK, E., "Zes-
lanie Ducha Świetego wedlug św. Jana spelnieniem obietnicy
(J 20, 19-23) (The Descent of the Holy Spirit according to St.
John: Fulfillment of the Promise; John 20, 19-23)" Stud-
Warmińskie 12 (1975) 463-66. THEOHARIS, A., "Hē em-
phanisis tou anastantos Kyriou kata to Iō. 20, 19-23 en schesei
pros to Prax. keph. II" [The Appearance of the Risen Lord according to Jn 20:19-23 as Compared with Acts cha. 2] DBM 4
(1976) 68-85. "Apostel" in: TRE 3 (1978) 434. "Auferstehung" in: TRE 4 (1979) 491, 507. BECKER, J., Das
Evangelium nach Johannes (Gütersloh/Würzburg 1979) 620
(lit!). "Beichte" in: TRE 5 (1980) 429. KESICH, V., "Resurrection, Ascension, and the Giving of the Spirit" GOThR 25
(1980) 249-260. WOLFF, H.W. "Wie erweist sich Jesus
Christus als der Lebendige?" in: . . . Wie eine Fackel (Neukirchen-Vluyn 1980) 193-201.

20:19-21 DODD, C.H. "The Appearances of the Risen Christ: a study in
form-criticism of the Gospels," in: More New Testament Studies (1968) 102-133.

20:19-20.27 CRIBBS, F.L. in: SBL Seminar Papers 2 (1973) G.MacRae ed.,
85-86.

20:19-20 FLEW, R.N. Jesus and His Church (1956) 175. WANKE, J.,
Die Emmauserzählung (Leipzig 1973) 9,n.409.

20:19 BETZ, H.D. Lukian von Samosata und das Neue Testament
(1961) 162, 170.

20:20 KAESEMANN, E. Exegetische Versuche und Besinnungen (1964) I 216.

20:21-23 GALTIER, P. Aux Origines du Sacrement de Pénitence (1951) 50-55. DENNEY, J. The Death of Christ (³1956) 45f. FLEW, R.N. Jesus and His Church (1956) 174-176. HAHN, F. Das Verständnis der Mission im Neuen Testament (²1965) 142. BRAUN, H. Qumran und NT II (1966) 252-255. LE FORT, P. Les Structures de L'Eglise militante selon saint Jean (1970) 129-137. THUESING, W. Die Erhöhung und Verherrlichung Jesu im Johannesevangelium (1970) 266-268. LEROY, H., Zur Vergebung der Sünden (Stuttgart 1974) 90-93. PORSCH, F., Pneuma und Wort (Frankfurt 1974) 341-378. "Amt" in: TRE 2 (1978) 576. TREVIJANO ETCHEVERRÍA, R., "La misión de la Iglesia Primitiva y los mandatos del Señor en los Evangelios" Salmanticensis 25 (1978) 5-36.

20:21-22 PORSCH, F., Pneuma und Wort (Frankfurt 1974) 363-378.

20:21.23 WAINWRIGHT, A.W. The Trinity in the New Testament (1962) 261-62.

20:21 ETIENNE, P., " 'Comme le Père m'a envoyé, moi aussi je vous envoie' (Saint Jean 20:21)," VerbCaro 15 (58, 1961) 129-31. CREHAN, J. The Theology of St. John (1965) 145-146. KUHL, J. Die Sendung Jesu und der Kirche nach dem Johannes-Evangelium (1967) 145-147. KASTING, H. Die Anfänge der Urchristlichen Mission (1969) 44-45. PORSCH, F., Pneuma und Wort (Frankfurt 1974) 369-370. BÜHNER, J.-A., Der Gesandte und sein Weg im 4. Evangelium (Tübingen 1977) 183-184. "Autorität" in: TRE 5 (1980) 47.

20:22-23 NIEWALDA, P. Sakramentssymbolik im Johannesevangelium? (1958) 6-7. FORTNA, R.T. The Gospel of Signs (1970) 141f. JOHNSTON, G. The Spirit-Paraclete in the gospel of John (1970) 49-51. KREMER, J., Pfingstbericht und Pfingstgeschehen (Stuttgart 1973) 224-228, 237-238. RIGAUX, B. "'Lier et déliér'. Les ministères de Réconciliation dans l'Eglise des Temps apostoliques," MaisDieu 117 (1, 1974) 86-135. PORSCH, F., Pneuma und Wort (Frankfurt 1974) 341-342, 359-363. "Amt" in: TRE 2 (1978) 554.

20:22 BUECHSEL, D.F. Der Geist Gottes im Neuen Testament (1926) 234-240. ADLER, N. Das erste christliche Pfingstfest (1938) 156-158. ADLER, N., Taufe und Handauflegung (Münster 1951) 17, 63, 70, 76-78, 86-87, 103. BETZ, H.D. Lukian von Samosata und das Neue Testament (1961) 107, 174. DELLING, G. Die Taufe im Neuen Testament (1963) 58. GLASSON, T.F. Moses in the Fourth Gospel (1963) 84f. KUHL, J. Die Sendung Jesu und der Kirche nach dem Johannes-Evangelium (1967) 131, 135f., 146. NICKELS, P. Targum and New Testament (1967) 59. DUNN, J.D.G. Baptism in the Holy Spirit (1970) 173ff. KREMER, J., Pfingstbericht und Pfingstgeschehen (Stuttgart 1973) 9, 58, 228, 234, 236, 260. CAVALLIN, H.C.C. Life After Death (1974) 4, I nn30, 31. PORSCH, F., Pneuma und Wort (Frankfurt 1974) 341-353, 374-378. MOULE, C.F.D., The Holy Spirit (London 1978) 48, 85, 91. SCHNACKENBURG, R., "Die johanneische Gemeinde und ihre Geisterfahrung" in: R. Schnackenburg et al. (eds.) Die Kirche des Anfangs, FS. H.Schürmann (Freiburg/Basel/Wien 1978) 283-287, 300-301. RUSSEL, E.A., "The Holy Spirit in the Fourth Gospel. Some Observations" IBS (1980) 84-94.

20:23 STRECKER, G. Der Weg der Gerechtigkeit (1962) 224$_4$, 225$_3$. TURNER, N. Grammatical Insights into the New Testament (1965) 80ff. LAZURE, N., Les Valeurs Morales de la Théologie Johannique (Paris 1965) 300. KUHL, J. Die Sendung Jesu und der Kirche nach dem Johannes-Evangelium (1967) 194f. NICKELS, P. Targum and New Testament (1967) 59. STROBEL, A. Erkenntnis und Bekenntnis der Sünde in neutestamentlicher Zeit (1968) 47, 57. LEE, G.M. "Presbyters and Apostles," ZNW 62 (1-2, 1971) 122. BARRETT, C.K. "Conversion and Conformity: the Freedom of the Spirit in the Institutional Church," in: Christ and the Spirit in the New Testament (1973) B.Lindars/S.S.Smalley eds., 375f. MANTEY, J.R. "Evidence That The Perfect Tense in John 20:23 and Matthew 16:19 is Mistranslated," JEThS 16 (3, 1973) 129-138. PORSCH, F., Pneuma und Wort (Frankfurt 1974) 357-359. METZGER, B.M., The Early Versions of the New Testament (Oxford 1977) 437. MANTEY, J.R. "Distorted Translations in John 20:23; Matthew 16:18-19 and 18:18" RevEx 78 (1981) 409-416.

20:24ff ALSUP, J.E., The Post-Resurrection Appearance Stories of the Gospel-Tradition (Stuttgart 1975) 148ff.

20:24-31 WENZ, H. "Sehen und Glauben bei Johannes," ThZ 17 (1, 1961) 17-25. SCHNIDER,F./STENGER, W. Die Ostergeschichten der Evangelien (1969) 127-133.

20:24-29 HIRSCH, E. Die Auferstehungsgeschichten und der christliche Glaube (1940) 138-144. ERDOZAIN, L. La función del signo en la fe según al cuarto evangelio (Rome 1968). SEIDENSTICKER, P., Die Auferstehung Jesu in der Botschaft der Evangelisten (1968) 134ff. FORTNA, R.T. The Gospel of Signs (1970) 142f. GRASS, H. Ostergeschehen und Osterberichte (1970) 69ff. "Auferstehung" in: TRE 4 (1979) 508. BECKER, J., Das Evangelium nach Johannes (Gütersloh/Würzburg 1979)

625-626 (lit!). LEIDIG, E., Jesu Gespräch mit der Samaritanerin (Basel 1981) 239-241.

20:24.30 FLEW, R.N. Jesus and His Church (1956) 175.

20:24 SUMMERS, R. The Secret Sayings of the Living Jesus (1968) 19. DORMEYER, D., Die Passion Jesu als Verhaltensmodell (Münster 1974) 83n.136. ALSUP, J.E., The Post-Resurrection Appearance Stories of the Gospel-Tradition (Stuttgart 1975) 151ff.

20:25-28 HENNECKE, E./SCHNEEMELCHER, W. Neutestamentliche Apokryphen (1964) I 122, 128, 288; II 152, 364.

20:25.27 THEYSSEN, G.W. "Unbelief" in the New Testament (Rüschlikon 1965) 49ff.

20:25 GIUDICE, C. "La fede degli Apostoli Nel IV Vangelo," Biblica 28 (1947) 267-274. ORIGENES, Das Evangelium nach Johannes (1959) R. Gögler ed., 405-406. HAHN, F. Christologische Hoheitstitel (1963) 123. MAHONEY, R., Two Disciples at the Tomb (Bern/Frankfurt 1974) 267-269.

20:26-29 TALBERT, C.H. Literary Patterns, Theological Themes, and the Genre of Luke-Acts (1974) 60. ALSUP, J.E., The Post-Resurrection Appearance Stories of the Gospel-Tradition (Stuttgart 1975) 148ff. DUNN, J.D.G., Jesus and the Spirit (London 1975) 122, 130.

20:27 DUNN, J.D.G. Baptism in the Holy Spirit (1970) 176. BROER, I. Die Urgemeinde und das Grab Jesu (1972) 205f. CRIBBS, F.L. in: SBL Seminar Papers 2 (1973) G.MacRae ed., 4. ALSUP, J.E., The Post-Resurrection Appearance Stories of the Gospel-Tradition (Stuttgart 1975) 165-166.

20:28-29 GRILL, J. Untersuchungen über die Entstehung des vierten Evangeliums II (1923) 71f., 372f.

20:28 BUECHSEL, F. Das Evangelium nach Johannes (1946) 179f. HAHN, F. Christologische Hoheitstitel (1963) 123, 124. MASTIN, B.A., "The Imperial Cult and the Ascription of the Title Θεός to Jesus (John 20,28)," StEv 6 (1973) 352-365. PORSCH, F., Pneuma und Wort (Frankfurt 1974) 349-351. REIM, G., Studien zum Alttestamentlichen Hintergrund des Johannesevangeliums (Cambridge 1974) 258-259. DUNN, J.D.G., Unity and Diversity in the New Testament (London 1977) 55. MATSUNAGA, K., "The 'Theos' Christology as the Ultimate Confession of the Fourth Gospel" AJBI 7 (1981) 125, 127-128.

20:29 BORNKAMM-BARTH-HELD, Ueberlieferung und Auslegung im Matthäus-Evangelium (²1961) 124. PRETE, B. "Beati coloro che non vendone e credono (Giov. 20, 29)," BiOr 9 (3,

1967) 97-114. WANKE, J., Die Emmauserzählung (Leipzig 1973) 126. METZGER, B.M., The Early Versions of the New Testament (Oxford 1977) 254. BERGMEIER, R., Glaube als Gabe nach Johannes (Stuttgart 1980) 207. LEON-DUFOUR, X., "Towards a Symbolic Reading of the Fourth Gospel" NTS 27 (1980-1981) 450. "Edessa" in: TRE 9 (1982) 278.

20:30-21:24 GRUNDMANN, W. Zeugnis und Gestalt des Johannes-Evangeliums 24 (1961) 81-94.

20:30-31 RUCKSTUHL, E. Die literarische Einheit des Johannes-evangeliums (1951) 5f., 107-109, 134f. YATES, K.M. Preaching from John's Gospel (1964) 1-5. HAHN, F. Das Verständnis der Mission im Neuen Testament (²1965) 140. SMITH, D.M. The Composition and Order of the Fourth Gospel (1965) 35, 38, 66, 176, 214, 222. DELLING, G. Wort und Werk Jesu im Johannes-Evangelium (1966) 20, 23. FORTNA, R.T. The Gospel of Signs (1970) 197-199. SCHOTTROFF, L. Der Glaubende und die feindliche Welt (1970) 246, 250-252. NICOL, W. The Sēmeia in the Fourth Gospel (1972) 9ff. KUEMMEL, W.G. Einleitung in das Neue Testament (1973) 173f. MAHONEY, R., Two Disciples at the Tomb (Bern/Frankfurt 1974) 267-269. OLSSON, B., Structure and Meaning in the Fourth Gospel (Lund 1974) 31, 64-66, 100, 122, 250, 262, 272. REIM, G., Studien zum Alttestamentlichen Hintergrund des Johannesevangeliums (Cambridge 1974) 208-209. CONZELMANN, H. und LINDEMANN, A., Arbeitsbuch zum Neuen Testament (Tübingen 1975) 27, 31, 59, 285. DRURY, C., "'Who's In, Who's Out'" in: M.Hooker/C.Hickling (eds.) What about the New Testament? FS. C. Evans (London 1975) 231-232. DUNN, J.D.G., Unity and Diversity in the New Testament (London 1977) 304. de JONGE, M., Jesus: Stranger from Heaven and Son of God (Missoula 1977) 1-3, 118-120. "Auferstehung" in: TRE 4 (1979) 508. BECKER, J., Das Evangelium nach Johannes (Gütersloh/Würzburg 1979) 632 (lit!). BECKER, J., "Wunder und Christologie. Zum literar-kritischen und christologischen Problem der Wunder im Johannesevangelium" in: A. Suhl (ed.) Der Wunderbegriff im Neuen Testament (Darmstadt 1980) 439-440. BERGMEIER, R., Glaube als Gabe nach Johannes (Stuttgart 1980) 206-207, 241n.97.

20:30 FEINE, D. P./BEHM, D. J., Einleitung in das Neue Testament (1950) 115f. FLEW, R. N., Jesus and His Church (1956) 175. ZIENER, G., "Weisheitsbuch und Johannesevangelium," Biblica 38 (1954) 401-406.

20:31-21:3 TRUDINGER, L.P., "A propos de pêche (Jean 20:31-21:3)" FV 74 (1975) 55-57.

20:31 DELLING, G. Die Zueignung des Heils in der Taufe (1961) 60. DELLING, G. Die Taufe im Neuen Testament (1963) 91. HAHN, F. Christologische Hoheitstitel (1963) 219, 224, 330. BRAUN, H. Qumran und NT II (1966) 29, 39, 70ff. DELLING, G. Wort und Werk Jesu im Johannes-Evangelium (1966) 13, 43, 44, 45, 46, 93, 100, 110, 121. GROENEWALD, E.P. "The Christological meaning of John 20:31," Neotestamentica 2 (1968) 131-140. NEUGEBAUER, F. Die Entstehung des Johannesevangelium (1968) 10ff. BEUTLER, J. Martyria (1972) 23, 30, 32, 245, 318. LADD, G.E. A Theology of the New Testament (1974) 140, 227, 243, 254, 271, 274, 275. UN-TERGASSMAIR, F.G. Im Namen Jesu: Der Namensbegriff im Johannesevangelium (Stuttgart 1973) 175-176. WILCKENS, U. "Der eucharistische Abschnitt der johanneischen Rede vom Lebensbrot (Joh 6, 51c-58)," in: Neues Testament und Kirche (1974) J. Gnilka ed., 233, 234, 235. de KRUIJF, T.C., "'Hold the Faith' or 'Come to Believe'? A Note on John 20,31" Bijdragen 36 (1975) 439-449. DUNN, J.D.G., Unity and Diversity in the New Testament (London, 1977) 47. METZGER, B.M., The Early Versions of the New Testament (Oxford 1977) 437. CRIBBS, F.L., "The Agreements that Exist between John and Acts" in: C.H. Talbert (ed.) Perspectives on Luke-Acts (Danville 1978) 60. HENGEL, M., Zur urchristlichen Geschichtsschreibung (Stuttgart 1979) 34; ET: J. Bowden (trans.) Acts and the History of Earliest Christianity (London 1979) 32.

---

21 GRILL, J. Untersuchungen über die Entstehung des vierten Evangeliums II (1923) 9, 35, 307, 321, 396. BAUER, W. Das Johannesevangelium (1925) 228f. LIGHTFOOT, R. H. Locality and Doctrine in the Gospels (1938) 101ff. STONEHOUSE, N. B. The Witness of Matthew and Mark to Christ (1944) 223. FEINE, D. P./ BEHM, D. J. Einleitung in das Neue Testament (1950) 118f. STREETER, B. H. The Four Gospels (1951) 353ff. BISHOP, C. "John xxi," NTS 3 (2, 1957) 132-136. WIL-KENS, W. Die Entstehungsgeschichte des vierten Evangeliums (1958) 158, 159, 160, 161, 162, 163, 164. CULLMANN, O. Petrus (1960). GUILDING, A. The Fourth Gospel and Jewish Worship (1960) 220-228. MINEAR, P. S. Images of the Church in the New Testament (1960) 32f., 271f. GLASSON,

T. F. Moses in the Fourth Gospel (1963) 84f. KAESEMANN, E. Exegetische Versuche und Besinnungen (1964) II 133, 142, 144, 154. SMITH, D. M. The Composition and Order of the Fourth Gospel (1965) 234-237. AGOURIDES, S., "The Purpose of John 21" in: B. L. Daniels/M. J. Suggs (eds.) Studies in the History and Text of the New Testament. FS. K. W. Clark (Salt Lake City 1967) 127-132. GHIBERTI, G. "Missione e primato di Pietro secondo," Atti Della XIX settimana Biblica Italiana (1967) 167-214. MARROW, S. "Jo 21: Indagatio in Ecclesiologiam Joanneam," VerbDom 45 (1, 1967) 47-51. KAMPHAUS, F. Von der Exegese zur Predigt (1968) 62-64. KASTING, H. Die Anfänge der Urchristlichen Mission (1969) 47-52. REGUL, J. Die Antimarcionitischen Evangelienprologe (1969) 104-106. GRASS, H. Ostergeschehen und Osterberichte (1970) 74ff. TRUDINGER, P. "Subtle Word-Plays in the Gospel of John, and the Problem of Chapter 21," JRTho 28 (1, 1971) 27-31. BROWN, R. E. et al. (eds.) Peter in the New Testament (Minneapolis 1973) 139-147. KUEMMEL, W. G. Einleitung in das Neue Testament (1973) 172-174. MAHONEY, R., Two Disciples at the Tomb (Bern/Frankfurt 1974) 12-40, 286-297. DAVIES, W. D. The Gospel and the Land (1974) 264, 410, 429, 430, 431. SMALLEY, S. S. "The Sign in John xxi," NTS 20 (3, 1974) 275-288. ALSUP, J. E., The Post-Resurrection Appearance Stories of the Gospel-Tradition (Stuttgart 1975) 200ff. BARTLETT, D. L., Fact and Faith (Valley Forge 1975) 120-122. CONZELMANN, H. und LINDEMANN, A., Arbeitsbuch zum Neuen Testament (Tübingen 1975) 59. CULLMANN, O., Der johanneische Kreis (Tübingen 1975) 2, 3, 5, 10, 69, 74, 76, 78, 79, 99. SHAW, A., "Image and Symbol in John 21" ET 86 (1975) 311. TEMPLE, S., The Core of the Fourth Gospel (London 1975) 251. MUSSNER, F., Petrus und Paulus-Pole der Einheit (Freiburg/Basel/Wien 1976) 42-49. REIM, G., "Johannes 21 - Ein Anhang?" in: J. K. Elliott (ed.) Studies in New Testament Language and Text. FS. G. D. Kilpatrick (Leiden 1976) 330-337. LANGBRANDTNER, W., Weltferner Gott oder Gott der Liebe (Frankfurt a. M./Bern/Las Vegas 1977) 25-30. THYEN, H., "Entwicklungen innerhalb der johanneischen Theologie und Kirche im Spiegel von Joh 21 und der Lieblingsjüngertexte des Evangeliums" Bibliotheca ephemeridum theologicarum Lovaniensium 44 (Louvain 1977) 259-299. RUCKSTUHL, E., "Zur Aussage und Botschaft von Johannes 21" in: R. Schnackenburg et al. (eds.) Die Kirche des Anfangs. FS. H. Schürmann (Freiburg/Basel/Wien/1978) 339-362. "Auferstehung" in: TRE 4 (1979) 508. BECKER, J., Das Evangelium nach Johannes (Gütersloh/Würzburg 1979) 635 (lit!). de SOLAGES, B. and VACHEROT, J. -M., "Le Chapitre XXI de Jean est-il de la même plume que le reste de l'Évangile?" BLE 80 (1979) 96-101. de SOLAGES, B., Jean et les Synoptiques (Leiden 1979) 187-267. BERGMEIER, R., Glaube als Gabe nach Johannes (Stuttgart 1980) 205ff., 212. DERRETT, J. D. M., "*Esan gar halieis* (Mkl. 16). Jesus's Fishermen and the Parable of the Net" NovT 22 (1980) 108-137. HAENCHEN, E., Das Johannesevangelium (Tübingen 1980) 582-583 (lit!). OSBORNE, G. R., "John 21: Test Case for History and Redaction in the Resurrection Narratives" in: R. T. France/D. Wenham (eds.) Gospel Perspectives II (Sheffield 1981) 293-328.

21:1ff HAHN, F. Das Verständnis der Mission im Neuen Testament (²1965) 37. DALMAN, G. Orte und Wege Jesu (1967) 147f.

21:1-25 RUCKSTUHL, E. Die literarische Einheit des Johannesevangeliums (1951) 5f., 134-139, 140-149. YATES, K. M. Preaching from John's Gospel (1964) 174-181.

21:1-23 STRECKER, G. Der Weg der Gerechtigkeit (1962) 94₂. KREMER, J. Die Osterbotschaft der vier Evangelien (1968) 115-133.

21:1-19 SCHNIEWIND, J., Die Parallelperikopen bei Lukas und Johannes (Darmstadt 1958 = 1914) 11-16.

21:1-14 BAUER, W. Das Johannesevangelium (1925) 231. MUNCK, J. Paul and the Salvation of Mankind (1959) 274f. BAILEY, J. A. The Traditions Common to the Gospels of Luke and John (1963) 12-17. HAAR, J. GPM 17 (1, 1963) 179-185. LINDIJER, C. H. De Sacramenten in het Vierde Evangelie (1964) 98f. VOOBUS, A. The Gospels in Study and Preaching (1966) 155ff. HOOKE, S. H. The Resurrection of Christ as History and Experience (1967) 85-87. WUELLNER, W. N. The Meaning of "Fishers of Men" (1967) 58f. JETTER, W. GPM 23 (2, 1968) 173-182. KLEIN, G. "Die Berufung des Petrus," in: Rekonstruktion und Interpretation (1969) 11-48. PESCH, R. Der Reiche Fischfang (1969). SCHNIDER, F./ STENGER, W. Die Ostergeschichten der Evangelien (1969) 133-143. FORTNA, R. T. The Gospel of Signs (1979) 87-98. GRASS, H. Ostergeschehen und Osterberichte (1970) 74ff. ITTEL, G. W. Jesus und die Jünger (1970) 23-25. ROLOFF, J. Das Kerygma und der irdische Jesus (1970) 258-260. WILCKENS, U. Auferstehung (1970) 76-85. BROWN, R. E. et al. (eds.) Peter in the New Testament (Minneapolis 1973) 116-117, 140-141. WANKE, J., Die Emmauserzählung (Leipzig 1973) 9, 36, 96, 102-105, 107, 124-125, n. 42, 319. SHAW, A. "The Breakfast by the Shore and the Mary Magdalene Encounter as Eucharistic Narratives,"

JThS 25 (1, 1974) 12-26. MAHONEY, R., Two Disciples at the Tomb (Bern/Frankfurt 1974) 287-289. GRÄSSER, E., in: GPM 29 (1975) 210-220. STOLT, P./ BARUTZKY, M. "Johannes 21, 1-14: Die Schöpfung ausschöpfen," in: Predigtstudien (1975) P. Krusche/E. Lange/D. Rössler/R. Roessler eds., 26-32. de JONGE, M., "The Beloved Disciple and the Date of the Gospel of John" in: E. Best/R. McL. Wilson (eds.) Text and Interpretation. FS. M. Black (Cambridge 1979) 102. HINZ, C., in: GPM 35 (1981) 219-225. LEIDIG, E., Jesu Gespräch mit der Samaritanerin (Basel 1981) 265. OSBORNE, G. R., "John 21: Test Case for History and Redaction in the Resurrection Narratives" in: R. T. France/D. Wenham (eds.) Gospel Perspectives II (Sheffield 1981) 296-306. SCHEIDEWIND, K. und WIESE, W., in: P. Krusche et al. (eds.) Predigtstudien für das Kirchenjahr 1980/1981 III/2 (Stuttgart 1981) 27-34.

21:1-11 BRAUN, F.-M., "Quatre 'Signes' Johanniques de L'Unité Chrétienne," NTS 9 (1962/63) 153f. HAENCHEN, E. "Historie und Verkündigung bei Markus und Lukas," Die Bibel und Wir (1968) 156-181.

21:1-10 TALBERT, C. H. Literary Patterns, Theological Themes, and the Genre of Lukes-Acts (1974) 41.

21:1-7 LORENZEN, T. Der Lieblingsjünger im Johannesevangelium (1971) 59ff.

21:2-13 SCHILLE, G. Die urchristliche Kollegialmission (1967).

21:2 OLSSON, B., Structure and Meaning in the Fourth Gospel (Lund 1974) 26-28, 110, 190, 262-263.

21:4-7 BEYSCHLAG, K. Clemens Romanus und der Frühkatholizismus (1966) 255ff. OSBORNE, G. R., "John 21: Test Case for History and Redaction in the Resurrection Narratives" in: R. T. France/D. Wenham (eds.) Gospel Perspectives II (Sheffield 1981) 299-300.

21:4 METZGER, B. M., The Early Versions of the New Testament (Oxford 1977) 369n.1.

21:5 PALLIS, A., Notes on St. John and the Apocalypse (London 1928) 46-47. BERGMEIER, R., Glaube als Gabe nach Johannes (Stuttgart 1980) 240n.65.

21:7-8 BLASS, F. Philosophy of the Gospels (1898) 239ff. STRECKER, G. Der Weg der Gerechtigkeit (1962) 199. WILCKENS, U., "Der Paraklet und die Kirche" in: D. Lührmann/G. Strecker (eds.) Kirche. FS. G. Bornkamm (Tübingen 1980) 202.

21:7 PALLIS, A., Notes on St. John and the Apocalypse (London 1928) 47. FEINE, D. P./BEHM, D. J. Einleitung in das Neue Testament (1950) 102f. HAHN, F. Christologische Hoheitstitel (1963) 123, 124. HENSS, W. Das Verhältnis zwischen Diatessaron, Christlicher Gnosis und "Western Text" (1967) 46f. KUEMMEL, W. G. Einleitung in das Neue Testament (1973) 201f. MAHONEY, R., Two Disciples at the Tomb (Bern/ Frankfurt 1974) 288-290. LATTKE, M., Einheit im Wort (München 1975) 12, 19.

21:8 BERGER, K. Die Amen-Worte Jesus (1970) 99-101.

21:9 PALLIS, A., Notes on St. John and the Apocalypse (London 1928) 48.

21:11 EMERTON, J. A. "The Hundred and Fifty-Three Fishes in John xxi.11," JThS 9 (1, 1958) 86-89. ACKROYD, P. R. "The 153 Fishes in John XXI. 11-A Further Note," JThS 10 (1, 1959) 94. KRUSE, H. "Magni Pisces Centum Quinquaginta Tres (Jo 21,11)," VerbDom 38 (3, 1960) 129-148. FORTNA, R. T. The Gospel of Signs (1970) 92f., 93f. McELENEY, N. J., "153 Great Fishes (John 21,11)—Gematriacal Atbash" Biblica 58 (1977) 411-417. ROMEO, J. A., "Gematria and John 21:11— The Children of God" JBL 97 (1978) 263-264.

21:12ff ROLOFF, J. Das Kerygma und der irdische Jesus (1970) 254ff.

21:12-13 OSBORNE, G. R., "John 21: Test Case for History and Redaction in the Resurrection Narratives" in: R. T. France/ D. Wenham (eds.) Gospel Perspectives II (Sheffield 1981) 304-305.

21:12.14 HAHN, F. Christologische Hoheitstitel (1963) 123, 124, 204.

21:12 PALLIS, A., Notes on St. John and the Apocalypse (London 1928) 48. WANKE, J., Die Emmauserzählung (Leipzig 1973) 9. METZGER, B. M., The Early Versions of the New Testament (Oxford 1977) 370.

21:13 "Abendmahlsfeier" in: TRE 1 (1977) 230.

21:14 WANKE, J., Die Emmauserzählung (Leipzig 1973) 9.

21:15ff STRECKER, G. Der Weg der Gerechtigkeit (1962) 202$_4$. GLOMBITZA, O. "Petrus, der Freund Jesu. Ueberlegungen zu Joh xxi 15ff.," NovTest 6 (4, 1963) 277-285. HAHN, F. Das Verständnis der Mission im Neuen Testament (^{2}1965) 38. BEYSCHLAG, K. Clemens Romanus und der Frühkatholizismus (1966) 252ff.

21:15-25 SCHNIDER, F./STENGER, W. Die Ostergeschichten der Evangelien (1969) 143-150. de JONGE, M., "The Beloved Disciple and the Date of the Gospel of John" in: E. Best/R. McL. Wilson (eds.) Text and Interpretation. FS. M. Black (Cambridge 1979) 100-102.

21:15-24 LE FORT, P. Les Structures de L'Eglise militante selon saint Jean (1970) 138-146, 162.

21:15-23 MARXSEN, W. The Resurrection of Jesus of Nazareth (1970) 64-65, 86-96.

21:15-22 KARRER, O. "Simon Petrus, Jünger, Apostel, Felsenfundament," BuK 23 (1968) 37-43.

21:15-19 CASALIS, G. GPM 17 (1, 1963) 185-189. BORNKAMM, G. in: Herr, tue meine Lippen auf Bd 3 (1964) G. Eichholz ed., 211ff. BARUTZKY, M./STOLT, P. "Johannes 21, 15-19: Hirtenamt," in: Predigtstudien (1975) P. Krusche/E. Lange/D. Rössler/R. Roessler eds., 33-37. SCHWEIZER, E., in: GPM 29 (1975) 220-226. "Amt" in: TRE 2 (1978) 511.

21:15-18 "Apostel" in: TRE 3 (1978) 434.

21:15-17 CLARKE, W. K. L. New Testament Problems (1929) 100-101. RUCKSTUHL, E. Die literarische Einheit des Johannesevangeliums (1951) 146. SALAS, A. "'Apacienta mis corderos' (Jn 21, 15-17)," CiDi 179 (4, 1966) 672-680. KUHL, J., Die Sendung Jesu und der Kirche nach dem Johannes-Evangelium (1967) 131, 147f., 167. KASTING, H. Die Anfänge der Urchristlichen Mission (1969) 47f. KLEIN, G. "Die Verleugnung des Petrus," in: Rekonstruktion und Interpretation (1969) 49-98. GRASS, H. Ostergeschehen und Osterberichte (1970) 82f. HAHN, F. Christologische Hoheitstitel (1963) 123, 124. BROWN, R.E. et al. (eds.) Peter in the New Testament (Minneapolis 1973) 141-144. KRAFT, H., Die Entstehung des Christentums (Darmstadt 1981) 209. OSBORNE, G.R., "John 21: Test Case for History and Redaction in the Resurrection Narratives" in: R. T. France/D. Wenham (eds.) Gospel Perspectives II (Sheffield 1981) 306-310.

21:15 SHEEHAN, J. F. X. "Feed my Lambs," Scripture 16 (33, 1964) 21-27. LATTKE, M., Einheit im Wort (Müchen 1975) 19.

21:17 PALLIS, A., Notes on St. John and the Apocalypse (London 1928) 56.

21:18-25 LORENZEN, T. Der Lieblingsjünger im Johannesevangelium (1971) 69ff.

21:18-23 BROWN, R. E. et al. (eds.) Peter in the New Testament (Minneapolis 1973) 145-146.

21:18-22 SCHWEIZER, E. Erniedrigung und Erhöhung bei Jesus und seinen Nachfolgern (1962) § 11i.

21:18-21 JART, U. "The Precious Stones in the Revelation of St. John xxi. 18-21," StTh 24 (2, 1970) 150-181.

21:18-19 MAHONEY, R., Two Disciples at the Tomb (Bern/ Frankfurt 1974) 290-294. OSBORNE, G. R., "John 21: Test Case for History and Redaction in the Resurrection Narratives" in: R. T. France/D. Wenham (eds.) Gospel Perspectives II (Sheffield 1981) 310-312.

21:18 GERSTENBERGER, G. und SCHRAGE, W., Leiden (Stuttgart 1977) 207; ET: Steeley, J. E. (trans.) Suffering (Nashville 1980) 239.

21:19-24 LOHSE, E. GPM 19 (4, 1964) 40-44.

21:19.22 DE BOER, W. P. The Imitation of Paul (1962) 53f.

21:20-25 MAHONEY, R., Two Disciples at the Tomb (Bern/ Frankfurt 1974) 288-296. "Apokalypse des Johannes" in: TRE 3 (1978) 187. WILCKENS, U., "Der Paraklet und die Kirche" in: D. Lührmann/G. Strecker (eds.) Kirche. FS. G. Bornkamm (Tübingen 1980) 202.

21:20-23 OSBORNE, G. R. , "John 21: Test Case for History and Redaction in the Resurrection Narratives" in: R. T. France/ D. Wenham (eds.) Gospel Perspectives II (Sheffield 1981) 312-314.

21:20-21 HAHN, F. Christologische Hoheitstitel (1963) 123, 124.

21:20 PALLIS, A., Notes on St. John and the Apocalypse (London 1928) 49. MUSSNER, F. Die Johanneische Sehweise und die Frage nach dem historischen Jesus (1965) 53f. LATTKE, M., Einheit im Wort (München 1975) 12, 19.

21:21-23 RUCKSTUHL, E. Die literarische Einheit des Johannesevangeliums (1951) 137f., 141-143.

21:22-23 HEISE, J., Bleiben. μένειν in den Johanneischen Schriften (Tübingen 1967) 47-50. BERGMEIER, R., Glaube als Gabe nach Johannes (Stuttgart 1980) 204, 206, 240n.65.

21:22 SMITH, D. M. The Composition and Order of the Fourth Gospel (1965) 106, 235, 236, 237.

21:23 STREETER, B. H. The Four Gospels (1951) 477f.

21:24-25 KAESEMANN, E. Exegetische Versuche und Besinnungen (1964) II 133. CREHAN, J. The Theology of St. John (1965) 29-30. DAUER, A. Die Passionsgeschichte im Johannesevangelium (1972) 332f. CONZELMANN, H. und LINDEMANN, A., Arbeitsbuch zum Neuen Testament (Tübingen 1975) 27, 59, 285. BERGMEIER, R., Glaube als Gabe nach Johannes (Stuttgart 1980) 202, 206-207. OSBORNE, G. R., "John 21: Test Case for History and Redaction in the Resurrection Narratives" in: R. T. France/D. Wenham (eds.) Gospel Perspectives II (Sheffield 1981) 314-317.

21:24 RUCKSTUHL, E. Die literarische Einheit des Johannesevangeliums (1951) 141f., 220-242. ROBINSON, J. M. Kerygma und historischer Jesus (1960) 66. BROX, N. Zeuge und
Märtyrer (1961) 82f. KAESEMANN, E. Exegetische Versuche
und Besinnungen (1964) I 180. BEUTLER, J. Martyria (1972)
230ff., 282f. LOHSE, E. Die Einheit des Neuen Testaments
(1973) 197f., 203. CULLMANN, O., Der johanneische Kreis
(Tübingen 1975) 2, 69, 75, 80, 82, 88, 99.

21:25 SCHWARZ, G., "τὸν κόσμον χωρῆσαι (Johannes 21,25)"
BN 15 (1981) 46.

1 John

ΙΩΑΝΝΟΥ Α

1-5 HERRMANN, T., "Miłość braterska wedlug św. Jana świetle ewangelii synoptycznych i św.Pawla"SThV 17 (1979) 43-64. CULPEPPER, R.A., "The Pivot of John's Prologue" NTS 27 (1980-1981) 25-26. LIEU, J. M., "Authority to Become Children of God" NovT 23 (1981) 210-28. PAINTER, J., "The Farewell Discourses and the History of Johannine Christianity" NTS 27 (1980-1981) 541.

1:1-2:22 THOMPSON, P. J. "Psalm 119: a possible Clue to the Structure of the First Epistle of John" in: F. L. Cross (ed.) Studia Evangelica II (1964) 489, 491.

1:1-2:2 DUPREY, P. "On I John 1:1-2:2" in: Mid-Stream. Conference on Church Union Negotiations (Limuru/Kenya 1970) 270-72.

1 PRIERO, G. "La grazia in 1 Jo 1" PaCl 34 (1955) 1081-86.

1:1-10 IBUKI, Y., "Offene Fragen zur Aufnahme des Logoshymnus in das Vierte Evangelium" AJBI 5 (1979) 111.

1:1-5 WENDT, H. H. "Zum zweiten und dritten Johannesbrief" ZNW 23 (1924) 27. LANGBRANDTNER, W. Weltferner Gott oder Gott der Liebe. Der Ketzerstreit in der johanneischen Kirche (1977) 389.

1:1-4 DE KEULENAER, J. "De interpretatione Prologi I Ioannis (1,1-4)" Collectanea Mechliniensia 6 (1932) 167-73. SOUCEK, J. B. GPM 12 (1957/58) 30-33. SCHWEIZER, E. Gemeinde und Gemeindeordnung im Neuen Testament (1959) §24b. SURKAU, H. W. GPM 18 (1963/64) 39-47. IWAND, H.-J. Predigt-Meditationen (1964) 328-33. STECK, K. G. in: G. Eichholz (ed.) Herr, tue meine Lippen auf, Bd. 4 (1965) 33ff. BULTMANN, R. "Die kirchliche Redaktion des ersten Johannesbriefes" in: Exegetica (1967) 381-82. VOIGT, G. Der zerrissene Vorhang I (1969) 44-52. KUENKEL, K. GPM 24 (1969/70) 41-47. BRIGGS, R. C. "Contemporary Study of the Johannine Epistles" RevEx 67 (1970) 415. COOK, D. E. "Interpretation of I John 1-5" RevEx 67 (1970) 445-447. DRUMWRIGHT, H. "Problem Passages in the Johannine Epistles: A Hermeneutical Approach" SouJTh 13 (1970) 53-56. LE FORT, P. Les Structures de l'Eglise militante selon Saint Jean (1970) 58-62. JONES, P. R. "A Structural Analysis of I John" RevEx 67 (1970) 443. FEUILLET, A. "Etude structurale de la première épître de saint Jean" in: H. Baltensweiler and B. Reicke (eds.) Neues Testament und Geschichte. Oscar Cullmann zum 70. Geburtstag (1972) 309-12. FEUILLET, A. "The Structure of First John. Comparison with the 4th Gospel. The Pattern of Christian Life" BThB 3 (1973) 194-216. GIURIS-

ATO, G. "Struttura della prima lettera di Giovanni" RivB 21 (1973) 361-81. SANCHEZ MIELGO, G. "Perspectivas eclesiologicas en la primera carta de Juan" EsVe 4 (1974) 9-64. GEHRKE, H. und SCHIERSE, F. J., in: P. Krusche et al. (eds.) Predigtstudien für das Kirchenjahr 1975/1976. IV/1 (Stuttgart 1975) 57-64. SCHUNACK, G. GPM 30 (1975/76) 38-44. DE JONGE, M. "An Analysis of I John 1,1-4" BTr (1978) 322-30. PANIKULAM, G., Koinōnia in the New Testament: A Dynamic Expression of Christian Life (Rome 1979) 134. GOLD-BACH, G. und HASSELMANN, N., in: P. Krusche et al. (eds.) Predigtstudien für das Kirchenjahr 1979/1980. II/1 (Stuttgart 1979) 70-76. TRAUB, H., in: GPM 34 (1979) 44-49.

1:1-3 DUPONT, J. Essais sur la Christologie de Saint Jean (1951) 27-29, 43-44, 215-16, 278. STRAUSS, L. The Epistles of John (1962) 15. KAESEMANN, E. "Ketzer und Zeuge" in: Exegetische Versuche und Besinnungen I (1964) 181. MUSSNER, F. Die johanneische Sehweise und die Frage nach dem historischen Jesus (1965) 21-22, 68-69. SCHILLE, G. Frühchristliche Hymnen (1965) 109-10. STAGG, F. "Orthodoxy and Orthopraxy in the Johannine Epistles" RevEx 67 (1970) 428. DUNN, J. D., Christology in the Making (London 1980) 245-46, 249.

1:1-2 SALOM, A. P. "Some aspects of the grammatical style of 1 John" JBL 74 (1955) 97, 102. WEISS, K. "Orthodoxie und Heterodoxie im 1.Johannesbrief" ZNW 58 (1967/68) 248-50. WEIR, J. E. "The Identity of the Logos in the First Epistle of John" ET 86 (1975) 118-20.

1:1 WENDT, H. H. "Der Anfang im Beginn des 1.Johannesbriefes" ZNW 21 (1922) 38-42. CONZELMANN, H. " 'Was von Anfang an war' " in: Neutestamentliche Studien für Rudolf Bultmann (1954) 194-201; = in: Theologie als Schriftauslegung (1974) 207-14. NAUCK, W. Die Tradition und der Charakter des ersten Johannesbriefes—Zugleich ein Beitrag zur Taufe im Urchristentum und in der alten Kirche (1957) 84-86. HENNECKE, E. and SCHNEEMELCHER, W. Neutestamentliche Apokryphen I (1959) 128, II (1964) 364; ET: New Testament Apocrypha I (1975) 192, II 518. DIEZ MACHO, A. "El logos y el Espíritu Santo" Atlántida 1 (1963) 381. FILSON, F. V. "First John: Purpose and Message" Interp 23 (1969) 266. STAGG, F. "Orthodoxy and Orthopraxy in the Johannine Epistles" RevEx 67 (1970) 424, 432. GRAYSTON, K. " 'Logos' " in 1 Jn 1:1" ET 86 (1974/75) 279. LOUW, J. P. "Verbal aspects in the first Letter of John" Neotestamentica 9 (1975) 98-104. TRITES, A. A., The New Testament Concept of Witness (Cambridge 1977) 124. "Clemens von Alexandrien" in: TRE 8 (1981) 107.

1:2-11 SONGER, H. S. "The Life Situation of the Johannine Epistles" RevEx 67 (1970) 400-401.

1:2-3 MICHL, J. "Gemeinschaft mit Gott und ewiges Leben" in: Der erste Johannesbrief (1953) 267-68. STRAUSS, L. The Epistles of John (1962) 20-22. FILSON, F. V. "First John: Purpose and Message" Interp 23 (1969) 265-66.

1:2 MUSSNER, F. ZΩH. Die Anschauung vom "Leben" im vierten Evangelium (1952) 83-84. BEUTLER, J. Martyria (1972) 283-84.

1:3-7 BOSMARD, M.-E. "The First Epistle of John and the Writings of Qumran" in: J. H. Charlesworth (ed.) John and Qumran (1972) 160-61.

1:3-4 SONGER, H. S. "The Life Situation of the Johannine Epistles" RevEx 67 (1970) 400.

1:3 STRAUSS, L. The Epistles of John (1962) 30-33, 38-42. MOODY, D. "The Theology of the Johannine Letters" SouJTh 13 (1970) 10. BRAUN, F. M. "La Réduction du Pluriel au Singulier dans l'Evangile et la Première Lettre de Jean" NTS 24 (1977/78) 64. PANIKULAM, G., Koinōnia in the New Testament: A Dynamic Expression of Christian Life (Rome 1979) 130-42.

1:4 HORNER, J. "Introduction to the Johannine Epistles" SouJTh 13 (1970) 47.

1:5-2:29 FEUILLET, A. "The Structure of First John. Comparison with the 4th Gospel. The Pattern of Christian Life" BThB 3 (1973) 194-216.

1:5-2:28 FEUILLET, A. "Etude structurale de la première épître de saint Jean" in: H. Baltensweiler and B. Reicke (eds.) Neues Testament und Geschichte. Oscar Cullmann zum 70. Geburtstag (1972) 312-16. MALATESTA, E. "Covenant and Indwelling" Way 17 (1977) 23-32.

1:5-2:27 COOK, D. E. "Interpretation of I John 1-5" RevEx 67 (1970) 447-52. JONES, P. R. "A Structural Analysis of I John" RevEx 67 (1970) 434-35, 443-44.

1:5-2:11 WINDISCH, H. "Die Polemik in 1,5-2,11" in: Die Katholischen Briefe (1930) 115.

1:5-2:6 GIURISATO, G. "Struttura della prima lettera di Giovanni" RivB 21 (1973) 361-81. HOULDEN, J. L., "Salvation Proclaimed: II. 1 John 1:5-2:6: Belief and Growth" ET 93 (1982)

132-36. PIETRON, J. und BARTELS, C., in: P. Krusche et al. (eds.) Predigtstudien für das Kirchenjahr 1981/1982. IV/2 (Stuttgart 1982) 114-21. SCHUNACK, G., in: GPM 36 (1981-1982) 285-90.

1:5-2:2 KAESEMANN, E. "Ketzer und Zeuge" in: Exegetische Versuche und Besinnungen I (1964) 182-84. DRUMWRIGHT, H. "Problem Passages in the Johannine Epistles: A Hermeneutical Approach" SouJTh 13 (1970) 56-58. MOODY, D. "The Theology of the Johannine Letters" SouJTh 13 (1970) 13-14.

1:5-10 BULTMANN, R. "Analyse des ersten Johannesbriefes" in: Festgabe für Adolf Jülicher (1927) 138-42, 157-58; = in: Exegetica (1967) 106-108, 121-23. DE KEULENAER, J. "De interpretatione I Ioannis I,5-10" Collectanea Mechliniensia 28 (1939) 279-82. RUCKSTUHL, E. Die literarische Einheit des Johannesevangeliums (1951) 40-41. MUSSNER, F. ΖΩΗ. Die Anschauung vom "Leben" im vierten Evangelium (1952) 169-70. BRAUN, H. "Literar-Analyse und theologische Schichtung im ersten Johannesbrief" in: Gesammelte Studien zum Neuen Testament und seiner Umwelt (1962) 212-14. STRAUSS, L. The Epistles of John (1962) 34-37, 38-56. IWAND, H.-J. Predigt-Meditationen (1964) 334-37, 668-74. O'NEILL, J. C. The Puzzle of 1 John. A New Examination of Origins (1966) 8-12. GABRIS, K. GPM 22(1967/68) 49-56. STAGG, F. "Orthodoxy and Orthopraxy in the Johannine Epistles" RevEx (1970) 428, 429, 430. LANGBRANDTNER, W. Weltferner Gott oder Gott der Liebe. Der Ketzerstreit in der johanneischen Kirche (1977) 384-86. McDONALD, J. I. H., Kerygma and Didache (Cambridge 1980) 64.

1:5-7 SUITBERTUS, P. "Die Vollkommenheitslehre des ersten Johannesbriefes" Biblica 39 (1958) 330. BRAUN, H. Qumran und das Neue Testament I (1966) 290-91.

1:5 SCHAEFER, D. "Gott ist Licht, 1.Joh. 1,5" ThSK 105 (1933) 467-76. BROWN, R. E. "The Qumran Scrolls and the Johannine Gospel and Epistles" CBQ 17 (1955) 403-19, 559-74; = in: K. Stendahl (ed.) The Scrolls and the New Testament (1957) 187-88; GT: "Die Schriftrollen von Qumran und das Johannesevangelium und die Johannesbriefe" in: K. H. Rengstorf (ed.) Johannes und sein Evangelium (1973) 495. NAUCK, W. Die Tradition und der Charakter des ersten Johannesbriefes—Zugleich ein Beitrag zur Taufe im Urchristentum und in der alten Kirche (1957) 89. MOODY, D. "The Theology of the Johannine Letters" SouJTh 13 (1970) 11. CHMIEL, J. Lumière et charité d'après la première épître de saint Jean (Diss Rome 1971). IBUKI, Y. Die Wahrheit im Johannesevangelium (1972)

311-12. PHILONENKO-SAYAR, B. und PHILONENKO, M., "Die Apokalypse Abrahams" in: JüdSchr V/5 (1982) 439n. 15.

1:6-2:2 BERGMEIER, R., Glaube als Gabe nach Johannes (Stuttgart 1980) 109n. 345.

1:6-10 NAUCK, W. Die Tradition und der Charakter des ersten Johannesbriefes—Zugleich ein Beitrag zur Taufe im Urchristentum und in der alten Kirche (1957) 19-23. SCHENKE, H. M. "Determination und Ethik im ersten Johannesbrief" ZThK 60 (1963) 206-12. HAHN, F. GPM 21 (1966/67) 76-84. LE FORT, P. Les Structures de L'Eglise militante selon Saint Jean (1970) 19-24. SONGER, H. S. "The Life Situation of the Johannine Epistles" RevEx 67 (1970) 401. SANCHEZ MIELGO, G. "Perspectivas eclesiologicas en la primera carta de Juan" EsVe 4 (1974) 9-64. de la POTTERIE, I., La Vérité dans Saint Jean I/II (Rome 1977) 521-22, 949-52. BRAUN, F. M. "La Réduction du Pluriel au Singulier dans l'Evangile et la Première Lettre de Jean" NTS 24 (1977/78) 48.

1:6-9 WEISS, K. "Orthodoxie und Heterodoxie im 1. Johannes-Brief" ZNW 58 (1967/68) 248-50.

1:6-7 NAUCK, W. Die Tradition und der Charakter des ersten Johannesbriefes—Zugleich ein Beitrag zur Taufe im Urchristentum und in der alten Kirche (1957) 37, 59-62.

1:6 MICHL, J. "Licht und Finsternis" in: Der erste Johannesbrief (1953) 271-72. BROWN, R. E. "The Qumran Scrolls and the Johannine Gospel and Epistles" CBQ 17 (1955) 403-19, 559-74; = in: K. Stendahl (ed.) The Scrolls and the New Testament (1957) 191-92, 196; GT: "Die Schriftrollen von Qumran und das Johannesevangelium und die Johannesbriefe" in: K. H. Rengstorf (ed.) Johannes und sein Evangelium (1973) 502. NAUCK, W. Die Tradition und der Charakter des ersten Johannesbriefes—Zugleich ein Beitrag zur Taufe im Urchristentum und in der alten Kirche (1957) 38-39. LAZURE, N., Les Valeurs Morales de la Théologie Johannique (Paris 1965) 87. de la POTTERIE, I., La Vérité dans Saint Jean I/II (Rome 1977) 520-30, 530-35, 943-49, 954-80.

1:7-2:5 HANSON, A. T. "Elements of a Baptismal Liturgy in Titus" in: Studies in the Pastoral Epistles (1968) 78-96.

1:7-2:2 WENNEMER, K. "Der Christ und die Sünde nach der Lehre des ersten Johannesbriefes" GuL 33 (1960) 370-76.

1:7-9 CARLTON, J. W. "Preaching from the Johannine Epistles" RevEx 67 (1970) 480-83.

1:7.9 KNOX, W. L. The Sources of the Synoptic Gospels, vol. 2 (1957) 26.

1:7 BROWN, R. E. "The Qumran Scrolls and the Johannine Gospel and Epistles" CBQ 17 (1955) 403-19, 559-74; = in: K. Stendahl (ed.) The Scrolls and the New Testament (1957) 194; GT: "Die Schriftrollen von Qumran und das Johannesevangelium und die Johannesbriefe" in: K. H. Rengstorf (ed.) Johannes und sein Evangelium (1973) 506. NAUCK, W. Die Tradition und der Charakter des ersten Johannesbriefes—Zugleich ein Beitrag zur Taufe im Urchristentum und in der alten Kirche (1957) 40-41, 47, 49-59, 129. BULTMANN, R. "Die kirchliche Redaktion des ersten Johannesbriefes" in: Exegetica (1967) 391-92. WARD, R. A. "The Theological Pattern of the Johannine Epistles" SouJTh 13 (1970) 29.

1:8-10 RUCKSTUHL, E. Die literarische Einheit des Johannesevangeliums (1951) 40-41, 56-57, 60-61. BRAUN, H. Qumran und das Neue Testament I (1966) 291-292. MICHL, J. "Sündenbekenntnis und Sündenvergebung in der Kirche des Neuen Testaments" MThZ 24 (1973) 189-207. BUEHNER, J.-A. Der Gesandte und sein Weg im 4. Evangelium (1977) 219-20.

1:8-9 BRAUN, F. M. "La Réduction du Pluriel au Singulier dans l'Evangile et la Première Lettre de Jean" NTS 24 (1977/78) 56.

1:8 LA BONNARDIERE, A. M. "Les commentaires simultanés de Mat. 6:12 et de I Jean 1:8 dans l'oeuvre de saint Augustin" REA 1 (1955) 129-47. STRAUSS, L. The Epistles of John (1962) 14. LAZURE, N., Les Valeurs Morales de la Théologie Johannique (Paris 1965) 86-87. BOGART, J. Orthodox and Heretical Perfectionism in the Johannine Community as Evident in the First Epistle of John (Diss Berkeley 1977). de la POTTERIE, I., La Vérité dans Saint Jean I/II (Rome 1977) 954-80, 991-93.

1:9 ROGERS, L. M. "1 John i.9" ET 45 (1933/34) 527. THORNTON-DUESBERG, J. P. "1 John i.9" ET 45 (1933/34) 183-84. DESCAMPS, A. Les justes et la justice dans les évangiles et le christianisme primitif hormis la doctrine proprement paulinienne (1950) 138-42. NAUCK, W. Die Tradition und der Charakter des ersten Johannesbriefes—Zugleich ein Beitrag zur Taufe im Urchristentum und in der alten Kirche (1957) 47-48. STRAUSS, L. The Epistles of John (1962) 63-64. LAZURE, N., Les Valeurs Morales de la Théologie Johannique (Paris 1965) 309-10. BRAUN, F.. M. "La Réduction du Pluriel au Singulier dans l'Evangile et la Première Lettre de Jean" NTS 24 (1977/78) 55. MARTINO, C., "La riconciliazione in 1 Gv 1, 9" Antonianum 54 (1979) 163-224. "Beichte" in: TRE 5 (1980) 438.

1:10 BRAUN, H. "Literar-Analyse und theologische Schichtung im ersten Johannesbrief" in: Gesammelte Studien zum Neuen Testament und seiner Umwelt (1962) 220-26. BOGART, J. Orthodox and Heretical Perfectionism in the Johannine Community as Evident in the First Epistle of John (Diss Berkeley 1977).

1:16 SALOM, A. P. "Some aspects of the grammatical style of I John" JBL 74 (1955) 99.

1:17 DALTON, W. J. Christ's Proclamation to the Spirits (1965) 118.

1:18 WINDISCH, H. "Der Antichrist" in: Die Katholischen Briefe (1930) 117.

2:1-17 McDONALD, J. I. H., Kerygma and Didache (Cambridge 1980) 64-65.

2:1-6 O'NEILL, J. C. The Puzzle of 1 John. A New Examination of Origins (1966) 13-15.

2:1-5 LAZURE, N. "Les voies de la connaissance de Dieu (1 Jn 2:1-5a)" AssS 24 (1970) 21-28.

2:1-2 BULTMANN, R. "Analyse des ersten Johannesbriefs" in: Festgabe für Adolf Jülicher (1927) 140-43; = in: Exegetica (1967) 107-109. JAMES, A. G. "Jesus Our Advocate. A Free Exposition of 1 John 2,1-2" ET 39 (1927/28) 473-75. DESCAMPS, A. Les justes et la justice dans les évangiles et le christianisme primitif hormis la doctrine proprement paulinienne (1950) 142-45. SCHWEIZER, E. Gemeinde und Gemeindeordnung im Neuen Testament (1959) §12ab. BRAUN, H. "Literar-Analyse und theologische Schichtung im ersten Johannesbrief" in: Gesammelte Studien zum Neuen Testament und seiner Umwelt (1962) 214-15. STRAUSS, L. The Epistles of John (1962) 43-47, 50-53. BRAUN, H. Qumran und das Neue Testament I (1966) 292. CARLTON, J. W. "Preaching from the Johannine Epistles" RevEx 67 (1970) 480-83. MOODY, D. "The Theology of the Johannine Letters" SouJTh 13 (1970) 9. REGOPOULOS, G. Ch. "Iēsous Christos ho 'Paraklētos.' Symbolē eis tēn hermēneian tou horou kata tēn A'Epistolēn tou Hagiou Iōannou" DBM 1 (1971) 52-58. VELLANICKAL, M., The Divine Sonship of Christians in the Johannine Writings (Rome 1977) 249. DALY, R. J., Christian Sacrifice (Washing-

ton D. C. 1978) 293. "Agende" in: TRE 2 (1978) 3. FRIED-
RICH, G. "Die Fürbitte im Neuen Testament" in: Auf das Wort
kommt es an (1978) 439-40.

2:1 RUCKSTUHL, E. Die literarische Einheit des Johannesevangeliums (1951) 40-41, 56-57, 60-61. NAUCK, W. Die
Tradition und der Charakter des ersten Johannesbriefes—Zugleich ein Beitrag zur Taufe im Urchristentum und in der alten
Kirche (1957) 68-70. STRAUSS, L. The Epistles of John (1962)
14, 20-22, 47. HAHN, F. Christologische Hoheitstitel (1963)
233-34. SONGER, H. S. "The Life Situation of the Johannine
Epistles" RevEx 67 (1970) 400. RUPPERT, L., Jesus als der
leidende Gerechte? (Stuttgart 1972) 13. PORSCH, F., Pneuma
und Wort (Frankfurt 1974) 310-11. TRITES, A. A., The New
Testament Concept of Witness (Cambridge 1977) 125-26.
SCHÜRMANN, H., "Christliche Weltverantwortung im Lichte
des Neuen Testaments" Catholica 34 (1980) 105, 107.
GRAYSTON, K., "The Meaning of PARAKLĒTOS" JSNT
13 (1981) 67-82. LOADER, W. R. G., Sohn und Hoherpriester
(Neukirchen-Vluyn 1981) 155.

2:2 WARFIELD, B. B. "Jesus Christ the propitiation of the whole
world" Exp 47, 8th series 21 (1921) 241-53. NAUCK, W. Die
Tradition und der Charakter des ersten Johannesbriefes—Zugleich ein Beitrag zur Taufe im Urchristentum und in der alten
Kirche (1957) 129. STRAUSS, L. The Epistles of John (1962)
82-83. DALTON, W. J. Christ's Proclamation to the Spirits
(1965) 118. SHIMADA, K. The Formulary Material in First
Peter: A Study According to the Method of Traditionsge-
schichte (Th.D. Diss, Union Theological Seminary New York
1966) 324-30, 341. BULTMANN, R. "Die kirchliche Redaktion des ersten Johannesbriefes" in: Exegetica (1967) 392-93.
THORNTON, T. C. G. "Propitiation or Expiation?— = ηΙλαστήριον and Ἱλασμός in Romans and I John" ET 80 (1968/
69) 53-55. LYONNET, S. "The Terminology of Redemption"
in: S. Lyonnet (ed.) Sin, Redemption, and Sacrifice. A Biblical
and Patristic Study (1970) 149-53. SABOURIN, L. "Christ
Made 'Sin' (2 Cor 5:21): Sacrifice and Redemption in the History of a Formula" in: S. Lyonnet (ed.) Sin, Redemption, and
Sacrifice (1970) 256-58. WENGST, K. Christologische Formeln und Lieder des Urchristentums (1972) 90-91. "Dordrechter Synode" in: TRE 9 (1982) 141.

2:3-11 VICENT CERNUDA, A., "Enganan la oscuridad y el mondo:
La luz era y manifesta lo verdadero" EstBi 27 (1968) 153-75,
215-32. MOODY, D. "The Theology of the Johannine Letters" SouJTh 13 (1970) 17. MUÑOZ LÉON, D., "La novedad

del mandamiento del amor en los escritos de S. Juan: Intentos modernos de solución" in: XXIX Semana Biblica Espanola, 1969 (Madrid 1971) 193-231.

2:3-7 DUNN, J. D. G. "Prophetic 'I'-Sayings and the Jesus tradition: The importance of testing prophetic utterances within early Christianity" NTS 24 (1977/78) 190.

2:3-6 SUITBERTUS, P. "Die Vollkommenheitslehre des ersten Johannesbriefes" Biblica 39 (1958) 452, 457-62. SCHENKE, H. M. "Determination und Ethik im ersten Johannesbrief" ZThK 60 (1963) 206-15. de la POTTERIE, I., La Vēritē dans Saint Jean I/II (Rome 1977) 994-96.

2:3-5 STRAUSS, L. The Epistles of John (1962) 78.

2:3-4 DUPONT, J. Essais sur la Christologie de Saint Jean (1951) 74-77. BRAUN, H. "Literar-Analyse und theologische Schichtung im ersten Johannesbrief" in: Gesammelte Studien zum Neuen Testament und seiner Umwelt (1962) 220-26.

2:3 SALOM, A. P. "Some aspects of the grammatical style of I John" JBL 74 (1955) 101. WEISS, K. "Orthodoxie und Heterodoxie im 1. Johannesbrief" ZNW 58 (1967/68) 251-53.

2:4-11 NAUCK, W. Die Tradition und der Charakter des ersten Johannesbriefes (1957) 23-66. LE FORT, P. Les Structures de l'Eglise militante selon Saint Jean (1970) 20-24.

2:4f.9-11 SANCHEZ MIELGO, G. "Perspectivas eclesiologicas en la primera carta de Juan" EsVe 4 (1974) 9-64.

2:4-9 SONGER, H. S. "The Life Situation of the Johannine Epistles" RevEx 67 (1970) 401, 402.

2:4-5 BULTMANN, R. "Analyse des ersten Johannesbriefes" in: Festgabe für Adolf Jülicher (1927) 143-44, 157-58; = in: Exegetica (1967) 109-10, 121-23. NAUCK, W. Die Tradition und der Charakter des ersten Johannesbriefes (1957) 37-38. BRAUN, H. Qumran und das Neue Testament I (1966) 292-93.

2:4 NAUCK, W. Die Tradition und der Charakter des ersten Johannesbriefes (1957) 38-39. BUEHNER, J.-A. Der Gesandte und sein Weg im 4. Evangelium (1977) 220. de la POTTERIE, I., La Vérité dans Saint Jean I/II (Rome 1977) 940-49.

2:5-17 DE KEULENAER, J. "De I Ioannis 2,5-17" Collectanea Mechliniensia 6 (1932) 189-90.

2:5-7 BRAUN, H. "Literar-Analyse und theologische Schichtung im ersten Johannesbrief" in: Gesammelte Studien zum Neuen Testament und seiner Umwelt (1962) 220-26.

2:5-6 SUITBERTUS, P. "Die Vollkommenheitslehre des ersten Johannesbriefes" Biblica 39 (1958) 330-31, 466. BRAUN, H. "Literar-Analyse und theologische Schichtung im ersten Johannesbrief" in: Gesammelte Studien zum Neuen Testament und seiner Umwelt (1962) 215-16. PHILIBERT, P., "Two New Testament Tests of Discipleship" Spiritual Life 24 (Washington, D. C. 1978) 107-13.

2:5 STRAUSS, L. The Epistles of John (1962) 123. LAZURE, N., Les Valeurs Morales de la Théologie Johannique (Paris 1965) 236-37. WEISS, K. "Orthodoxie und Heterodoxie im 1. Johannesbrief" ZNW 58 (1967/68) 251-53. COPPENS, J. "Miscellanées bibliques. LII. 'Agápe et Ágapân dans les Lettres johanniques" EphT 45 (1969) 125-27.

2:6-9 GALTIER, P. Aux origines du sacrement de pénitence (1951) 69-76.

2:6 SALOM, A. P. "Some aspects of the grammatical style of I John" JBL 74 (1955) 101. STRAUSS, L. The Epistles of John (1962) 34-36. HEISE, J. Bleiben (1967) 120-26.

2:7-24 SALOM, A. P. "Some aspects of the grammatical style of I John" JBL 74 (1955) 102.

2:7-17 GIURISATO, G. "Struttura della prima lettera di Giovanni" RivB 21 (1973) 361-81.

2:7-11 O'NEILL, J. C. The Puzzle of 1 John. A New Examination of Origins (1966) 16-19. STAGG, F. "Orthodoxy and Orthopraxy in the Johannine Epistles" RevEx 67 (1970) 430. STEIGER, L., in: GPM 34 (1980) 332-38.

2:7-8 BULTMANN, R. "Analyse des ersten Johannesbriefes" in: Festgabe für Adolf Jülicher (1927) 144, 157-58; = in: Exegetica (1967) 110, 121-23. BRAUN, H. "Literar-Analyse und theologische Schichtung im ersten Johannesbrief" in: Gesammelte Studien zum Neuen Testament und seiner Umwelt (1962) 220-26. STRAUSS, L. The Epistles of John (1962) 108-11. SANCHEZ MIELGO, G. "Perspectivas eclesiologicas en la primera carta de Juan" EsVe 4 (1974) 9-64. SANDERS, J. T., Ethics in the New Testament (Philadelphia 1975) 93.

2:7 RUCKSTUHL, E. Die literarische Einheit des Johannesevangeliums (1951) 232-33. NAUCK, W. Die Tradition und der Charakter des ersten Johannesbriefes (1957) 68, 70, 84-86. CONZELMANN, H. " 'Was von Anfang war' " in: Neutestamentliche Studien für Rudolf Bultmann (1954) 194-201; = in: Theologie als Schriftauslegung (1974) 207-14. ROBINSON, J. A. T. "The Destination and Purpose of the Johannine Epistles," NTS 7 (1960) 57. LOHSE, E., "Kirche im Alltag. Erwägungen zur theologischen Begründung der Ethik im Neuen

Testament'' in: D. Lührmann/G. Strecker (eds.) Kirche. FS. G. Bornkamm (Tübingen 1980) 406.

2:8-3:10 O'NEILL, J. C. The Puzzle of 1 John. A New Examination of Origins (1966) 31-37.

2:8.17 CERNUDA, V. A. ''Engañan la oscuridad y el mundo; la luz era y manifiesta lo verdadero (Esclarecimiento mutuo de Jn 1,9; 1 Cor 7,31; 1 Jn 2,8 y 17)'' EstBi 27 (1968) 153-75, 215-32.

2:8-12 BERGMEIER, R., Glaube als Gabe nach Johannes (Stuttgart 1980) 204, 213, 230, 240n. 59.

2:8-11 DUPONT, J. Essais sur la Christologie de Saint Jean (1951) 74-77. MUSSNER, F. ZΩH. Die Anschauung vom ''Leben'' im vierten Evangelium (1952) 170. BRAUN, H. Qumran und das Neue Testament I (1966) 293-94.

2:8 BROWN, R. E. ''The Qumran Scrolls and the Johannine Gospel and Epistles'' CBQ 17 (1955) 403-19, 559-74; = in: K. Stendahl (ed.) The Scrolls and the New Testament (1957) 189; GT: ''Die Schriftrollen von Qumran und das Johannes-evangelium und die Johannesbriefe'' in: K. H. Rengstorf (ed.) Johannes und sein Evangelium (1973) 497. NAUCK, W. Die Tradition und der Charakter des ersten Johannesbriefes (1957) 68, 70. KILPATRICK, G. D. ''Two Johannine Idioms in the Johannine Epistles'' JThS 12 (1961) 272. LANGBRANDT-NER, W. Weltferner Gott oder Gott der Liebe (1977) 387-89.

2:9-11 BULTMANN, R. ''Analyse des ersten Johannesbriefes'' in: Festgabe für Adolf Jülicher (1927) 144-55, 157-58; = in: Exegetica (1967) 111, 121-23. NAUCK, W. Die Tradition und der Charakter des ersten Johannesbriefes (1957) 38. BRAUN, H. ''Literar-Analyse und theologische Schichtung im ersten Johannesbriefe'' in: Gesammelte Studien zum Neuen Testament und seiner Umwelt (1962) 216. SCHENKE, H. M. ''Determination und Ethik im ersten Johannesbrief'' ZThK 60 (1963) 206-12. BOISMARD, M.-E. ''The First Epistle of John and the Writings of Qumran'' in: J. H. Charlesworth (ed.) John and Qumran (1972) 159-60. LANDBRANDTNER, W. Weltferner Gott oder Gott der Liebe (1977) 384-86. de la POTTERIE, I., La Vérité dans Saint Jean I/II (Rome 1977) 996-98.

2:9.11 STAGG, F. ''Orthodoxy and Orthopraxy in the Johannine Epistles'' RevEx 67 (1970) 427.

2:9-10 BROWN, R. E. ''The Qumran Scrolls and the Johannine Gospel and Epistles'' CBQ 17 (1955) 403-19, 559-74; = in: K. Stendahl (ed.) The Scrolls and the New Testament (1957) 194, 199; GT: ''Die Schriftrollen von Qumran und das Johannes-

evangelium und die Johannesbriefe" in: K. H. Rengstorf (ed.)
Johannes und sein Evangelium (1973) 506, 514.

2:9 NAUCK, W. Die Tradition und der Charakter des ersten Johannesbriefes (1957) 38-39. HEISE, J. Bleiben (1967) 164-70.
de la POTTERIE, I., La Vérité dans Saint Jean I/II (Rome 1977)
998-1001.

2:10-11 CARLTON, J. W. "Preaching from the Johannine Epistles"
RevEx 67 (1970) 444-47.

2:10 LEFEVRE, G. "Le précepte du Seigneur" VieS 96 (1957) 40-
55. NAUCK, W. Die Tradition und der Charakter des ersten Johannesbriefes (1957) 39-40. HEISE, J. Bleiben (1967) 126-30.
de la POTTERIE, I., La Vérité dans Saint Jean I/II (Rome 1977)
993-97.

2:11 STRAUSS, L. The Epistles of John (1962) 34-36.

2:12-27 WENDT, H. H. "Zum zweiten und dritten Johannesbrief"
ZNW 23 (1924) 26-27.

2:12-18 STRAUSS, L. The Epistles of John (1962) 20-22.

2:12-17 WENDT, H. H., "Die Beziehung unseres ersten Johannesbriefes auf den zweiten" ZNW 21 (1922) 140-46. BULTMANN, R. "Analyse des ersten Johannesbriefes" in: Festgabe
für Adolf Jülicher (1927) 145-46; = in: Exegetica (1967) 111.
HUPPENBAUER, H., "*Bsr*, 'Fleisch' in den Texten von
Qumran (Höhle I)" TZ 13 (1957) 298-300. KUHN, K. G.,
"New Light on Temptation, Sin and Flesh in the New Testament" in: K. Stendahl (ed.) The Scrolls and the New Testament
(1957) 94-113. SCHWEIZER, E., "Die hellenistische Komponente im neutestamentlichen *Sarx*-Begriff" ZNW 48 (1957)
237-53. GRUNDMANN, W., "Die *Nēpioi* in der urchristlichen Paränese" NTS 5 (1958-1959) 188-205. MURPHY, R.
E., "*Bsr* in the Qumrân literature and *Sarks* in the Epistle to the
Romans" in: Sacra Pagina 2 (Louvain 1959) 60-76. KLEIN, G.
GPM 18 (1963/64) 349-57. PRYKE, J., " 'Spirit' and 'Flesh'
in the Qumran Documents and some New Testament Texts"
RevQ 5 (1964-1966) 345-60. OBENDIEK, H. in: G. Eichholz
(ed.) Herr, tue meine Lippen auf, Bd.4 (1965) 180ff. O'-
NEILL, J. C. The Puzzle of I John. A New Examination of Origin (1966) 20-22. DUPONT, J., "Les 'simples' *(petâyim)* dans
la Bible et à Qumrân: a propos des *nepioi* de Mt 11, 25; Lc 10,
21" in: G. Buccellati (ed.) Studi sul' Oriente et la Bibbia. FS.
G. Rinaldi (Genova 1967) 329-36. SPICQ, C., "La place ou le
rôle des jeunes dans certaines communautēs nēotestamentaires" RB 76 (1969) 508-27. HEMPEL, J. GPM 24 (1969/70)
406-10. ELLIOT, J. H., "Ministry and Church Order in the New

Testament: A Tradition-Historical Analysis (1 Pt. 5, 1-5 and parrallels)'' CBQ 32 (1970) 367-91. MOODY, D. ''The Theology of the Johannine Letters'' SouJTh 13 (1970) 16.

2:12-14 WENDT, H. H. ''Zum zweiten und dritten Johannesbrief'' ZNW 23 (1924) 18-19. NAUCK, W. Die Tradition und der Charakter des ersten Johannesbriefes (1957) 68-71. SUITBER-TUS, P. ''Die Vollkommenheitslehre des ersten Johannesbriefes'' Biblica 39 (1958) 453-54. NOACK, B. ''On I John ii.12-14'' NTS 6 (1959/60) 236-41. THOMPSON, P. J. ''Psalm 119: a possible Clue to the Structure of the First Epistle of John'' in: F. L. Cross (ed.) Studia Evangelica II (1964) 489. de la POTTERIE, I., ''La connaissance de Dieu dans le dualisme eschatologique d'après 1 Jn, 2:12-14'' in: Au Service de la Parole de Dieu (1969) 77-99. SONGER, H. S. ''The Life Situation of the Johannine Epistles'' RevEx 67 (1970) 400. SANCHEZ MIELGO, G. ''Perspectivas eclesiologicas en la primera carta de Juan'' EsVe 4 (1974) 9-64. VELLANICKAL, M., The Divine Sonship of Christians in the Johannine Writings (Rome 1977) 271-72. STAGG, E. and F. Woman in the World of Jesus (1978) 240-41.

2:12 STRAUSS, L. The Epistles of John (1962) 43-47, 57-64. THOMPSON, P. J. ''Psalm 119: a possible Clue to the Structure of the First Epistle of John'' in: F. L. Cross (ed.) Studia Evangelica II (1964) 487-89. JEWETT, P. K., Infant Baptism and the Covenant of Grace (Grand Rapids 1978) 34.

2:13-14 NAUCK, W. Die Tradition und der Charakter des ersten Johannesbriefes (1957) 84-86. STRAUSS, L. The Epistles of John (1962) 104. BRUNS, J. E., ''A Note on John 16:33 and 1 John 2:13-14'' JBL 86 (1967) 451-53. de la POTTERIE, I., La Vérité dans Saint Jean I/II (Rome 1977) 835-37. ''Antichrist'' in: TRE 3 (1978) 22.

2:13 BERGMEIER, R., Glaube als Gabe nach Johannes (Stuttgart 1980) 258n. 394.

2:14 GIACINTO, S. de, '' ' . . .a voi, giovani, che siete forti' (1 Giov. 2,14)'' BiOr 2 (1960) 81-85. BRAUN, H. ''Literar-Analyse und theologische Schichtung im ersten Johannesbrief'' in: Gesammelte Studien zum Neuen Testament und seiner Umwelt (1962) 220-26. KAESEMANN, E. ''Ketzer und Zeuge'' in: Exegetische Versuche und Besinnungen I (1964) 184. HEISE, J. Bleiben (1967) 130-32.

2:15-17 BRAUN, H. Qumran und das Neue Testament I (1966) 294-95. CARLTON, J. W. ''Preaching from the Johannine Epistles'' RevEx 67 (1970) 477-80. LANGBRANDTNER, W. Weltferner Gott oder Gott der Liebe (1977) 384-86. BRAUN, F. M. "La Réduction du Pluriel au Singulier dans l'Evangile et la Première Lettre de Jean" NTS 24 (1977/78) 51. SANDERS, J. T., Ethics in the New Testament (Philadelphia 1975) 94-95. CLARK, S. B., Man and Woman in Christ (Ann Arbor, Mich. 1980) 276.

2:15-16 SANCHEZ MIELGO, G. "Perspectivas eclesiologicas en la primera carta de Juan" EsVe 4 (1974) 9-64.

2:15 NAUCK, W. Die Tradition und der Charakter der ersten Johannesbriefes (1957) 68, 70. STRAUSS, L. The Epistles of John (1962) 84-85, 88-89. SCHENKE, H. M. "Determination und Ethik im ersten Johannesbrief" ZThK 60 (1963) 206-15. COPPENS, J. "Miscellanées bibliques. LII. 'Agápe et 'Agapân dans les lettres johanniques" EphT 45 (1969) 125-27. SCHRAGE, W., "Die Elia-Apokalypse" in: JüdSchr V/3 (1980) 204, 213n. 96, 231n. 19d.

2:16-17 CARLTON, J. W. "Preaching from the Johannine Epistles," RevEx 67 (1970) 477-80.

2:16 JOUON, P. "1 John 2:16: la présomption des richesses" RechSR 28 (1938) 479-81. STRAUSS, L. The Epistles of John (1962) 92-97. LAZURE, N. "La convoitise de la chair en I Jean ii,16" RB 76 (1969) 161-205. KOUTLEMANIS, P., "The Interpretation of I John 2,16 according to the ascetic theology and the contemporary research" DBM 4 (1976) 117-32. "Anfechtung" in: TRE 2 (1978) 692.

2:17 HARNACK, A. von, Studien zur Geschichte des Neuen Testaments und der Alten Kirche (1931) 138-40. JOHNSTON, G. "The will of God in 1 Peter and 1 John" ET 72 (1960/61) 237, 238-39. STRAUSS, L. The Epistles of John (1962) 89-90. LE DEAUT, R. La Nuit Pascale (1963) 253. HEISE, J. Bleiben (1967) 132-35. DUPLACY, J. " 'Le Texte Occidentale' des Epîtres Catholiques" NTS 16 (1969/70) 398. VOEGTLE, A. Das Neue Testament und die Zukunft des Kosmos (1970) 92-94. BONHOEFFER, D. Gesammelte Schriften, Bd.5 (1972) 452-57. LANGBRANDTNER, W. Weltferner Gott oder Gott der Liebe (1977) 387-89.

2:18ff "Apokalyptik" in: TRE 3 (1978) 253.

2:18-28 BULTMANN, R. "Analyse des ersten Johannesbriefes" in: Festgabe für Adolf Jülicher (1927) 155; = in: Exegetica (1967) 120. GIURISATO, G. "Struttura della prima lettura di Giovanni" RivB 21 (1973) 361-81.

2:18-27 BOUSSET, W., Der Antichrist in der Überlieferung des Judentums, des Neuen Testaments und der alten Kirche (1895). RI-

GAUX, B., L'Antéchrist et l'opposition au royaume messianique dans l'Ancien et le Nouveau Testament (1932). HANSE, H., "Gott Haben" in der Antike und im frühen Christentum (1939) 104-108. MICHL, J., "Der Geist als Garant des rechten Glaubens" in: N. Adler (ed.) Vom Wort des Lebens. FS. M. Meinertz (Münster 1951) 142-51. SCHLIER, H., "Vom Antichrist-Zum 13. Kapitel der Offenbarung Johannes" in: Die Zeit der Kirche (Freiburg 1956) 16-29. BRAUN, H. "Literar-Analyse und theologische Schichtung im ersten Johannesbrief" in: Gesammelte Studien zum Neuen Testament und seiner Umwelt (1962) 237-42. O'NEILL, J. C. The Puzzle of 1 John. A New Examination of Origins (1966) 23-30. LE FORT, P. Les Structures de l'Eglise militante selon Saint Jean (1970) 25-39. de la POTTERIE. I., "Anointing of the Christian by Faith" in: I. de la Potterie/ S. Lyonnet, The Christian Lives by the Spirit (Staten Island 1971) 79-143. SANCHEZ MIELGO, G. "Perspectivas eclesiologicas en la primera carta de Juan" EsVe 4 (1974) 9-64. YATES, R., "The Antichrist" EQ 46 (1974) 42-50. LANGBRANDTNER, W. Weltferner Gott oder Gott der Liebe (1977) 374-77, 382. RUDOLPH, K. Die Gnosis (1978) 324-27.

2:18-26 RUCKSTUHL, E. Die literarische Einheit des Johannesevangeliums (1951) 233-35.

2:18-25 SCHNACKENBURG, R. "Zum Begriff der 'Wahrheit' in den beiden kleinen Johannesbriefen" BZ 11 (1967) 253-54. DRUMWRIGHT, H. "Problem Passages in the Johannine Epistles: A Hermeneutical Approach" SouJTh 13 (1970) 58-60. BERGMEIER, R., Glaube als Gabe nach Johannes (Stuttgart 1980) 202.

2:18-22 BRAUN, H. Qumran und das Neue Testament 1 (1966) 295-96.

2:18.22 BOUSSET, W. Die Religion des Judentums im Späthellenistischen Zeitalter (1926 = 1966) 254-56. RIDDERBOS, H. Paul. An Outline of His Theology (1975) 513-26. "Antichrist" in: TRE 3 (1978) 22.

2:18-19 ROBINSON, J. A. T. "The Destination and Purpose of the Johannine Epistle," NTS 7 (1960) 58-59. FILSON, F. V. "First John: Purpose and Message" Interp 23 (1969) 267, 271.

2:18 MICHL, J. "Der Antichrist" in: Der erste Johannesbrief (1953) 279-81. NAUCK, W. Die Tradition und der Charakter des ersten Johannesbriefes (1957) 71-72. ROELS, E. D. God's Mission (1962) 268-69. MOODY, D. "The Theology of the Johannine Letters" SouJTh 13 (1970) 19. BRAUN, F. M. "La

Réduction du Pluriel au Singulier dans l'Evangile et la Première Lettre de Jean'' NTS 24 (1977/78) 51, 54, 58, 59. ''Antichrist'' in: TRE 3 (1978) 22. BERGMEIER, R., Glaube als Gabe nach Johannes (Stuttgart 1980) 204, 239n. 58, 240n. 65. ''Eschatologie'' in: TRE 10 (1982) 290.

2:19 SALOM, A. P. ''Some aspects of the grammatical style of 1 John'' JBL 74 (1955) 102. NAUCK, W. Die Tradition und der Charakter des ersten Johannesbriefes (1957) 72-73. SCHWEIZER, E. Gemeinde und Gemeindeordnung im Neuen Testament (1959) §12be. STRAUSS, L. The Epistles of John (1962) 68-69. HEISE, J. Bleiben (1967) 135-36. WEISS, K. ''Orthodoxie und Heterodoxie im 1. Johannesbrief'' ZNW 58 (1967/68) 253. SONGER, H. S. ''The Life Situation of the Johannine Epistles'' RevEx 67 (1970) 401. BERGMEIER, R., Glaube als Gabe nach Johannes (Stuttgart 1980) 213-14, 240n. 68, 264n. 484.

2:20-27 LE FORT, P. Les Structures de l'Eglise militante selon Saint Jean (1970) 29-39, 71-73.

2:20f.27 SCHWEIZER, E. Heiliger Geist (1978) 139.

2:20-21 SUITBERTUS, P. ''Die Vollkommenheitslehre des ersten Johannesbriefes'' Biblica 39 (1958) 456. de la POTTERIE, I., La Vérité dans Saint Jean I/II (Rome 1977) 583-87.

2:20 HARNACK, A. von, Studien zur Geschichte des Neuen Testaments und der Alten Kirche (1931) 140-41. NAUCK, W. Die Tradition und der Charakter des ersten Johannesbriefes (1957) 94-96. SCHWEIZER, E. Gemeinde und Gemeindeordnung im Neuen Testament (1959) §12. DELLING, G. Die Taufe im Neuen Testament (1963) 107-108. LAZURE, N., Les Valeurs Morales de la Théologie Johannique (Paris 1965) 113-16. DUNN, J. D. G. Baptism in the Holy Spirit (1970) 195-200. MOODY, D. ''The Theology of the Johannine Letters'' SouJTh 13 (1970) 12. BERGMEIER, R., Glaube als Gabe nach Johannes (Stuttgart 1980) 176n. 526. SCHILLEBEECKX, E., Christ: the Christian Experience in the Modern World (London 1980) 421-23; GT: Christus und die Christen (Freiburg/Basel/Wien 1977) 407-408.

2:21-25 BERGMANN, W., und NEHB, H., in: P. Krusche et al. (eds.) Predigtstudien für das Kirchenjahr 1981/1982. IV/1 (Stuttgart 1981) 60-65. STECK, K. G., in: GPM 36 (1981) 48-55.

2:21 WENDT, H. H. ''Zum zweiten und dritten Johannesbrief'' ZNW 23 (1924) 18-19. LAZURE, N., Les Valeurs Morales de la Théologie Johannique (Paris 1965) 84-86. WEISS, K. ''Orthodoxie und Heterodoxie im 1. Johannesbrief'' ZNW 58 (1967/

68) 253. SONGER H. S. "The Life Situation of the Johannine Epistles" RevEx 67 (1970) 400. de la POTTERIE, I., La Vérité dans Saint Jean I/II (Rome 1977) 583-92, 619-22, 943-49. BERGMEIER, R., Glaube als Gabe nach Johannes (Stuttgart 1980) 202, 214, 222.

2:22-3:18 THOMPSON, P. J. "Psalm 119: a possible Clue to the Structure of the First Epistle of John" in: F. L. Cross (ed.) Studia Evangelica 2 (1964) 489, 491.

2:22-28 STRAUSS, L. The Epistles of John (1962) 20-22.

2:22-24 SALOM, A. P. "Some aspects of the grammatical style of 1 John" JBL 74 (1955) 97. STRAUSS, L. The Epistles of John (1962) 32-33, 69-72. BERGMEIER, R., Glaube als Gabe nach Johannes (Stuttgart 1980) 202, 207.

2:22-23 SKRINJAR, A. "Errores in epistola I Jo impugnati" VD 41 (1963) 60-72. SONGER, H. S. "The Life Situation of the Johannine Epistles" RevEx 67 (1970) 401, 402. STAGG, F. "Orthodoxy and Orthopraxy in the Johannine Epistles" RevEx 67 (1970) 427. WARD, R. A. "The Theological Pattern of the Johannine Epistles" SouJTh 13 (1970) 31. MUELLER, U. B. Die Geschichte der Christologie in der johanneischen Gemeinde (1975) 53-57. DUNN, J. D. G. "Prophetic 'I'-Sayings and the Jesus tradition: The importance of testing prophetic utterances within early Christianity" NTS 24 (1977/78) 190, 192.

2:22 NAUCK, W. Die Tradition und der Charakter des ersten Johannesbriefes (1957) 72. ROBINSON, J. A. T. "The Destination and Purpose of the Johannine Epistles" NTS 7 (1960) 60. KILPATRICK, G. D. "Two Johannine Idioms in the Johannine Epistles" JThS 12 (1961) 272. DUNN, J. D. G. Unity and Diversity in the New Testament (1977) 44-45.

2:23 BULTMANN, R. "Analyse des ersten Johannesbriefes" in: Festgabe für Adolf Jülicher (1927) 157-58; = in: Exegetica (1967) 121-23. NAUCK, W. Die Tradition und der Charakter des ersten Johannesbriefes (1957) 76-77, 86-88. THOMPSON, P. J. "Psalm 119: a possible Clue to the Structure of the First Epistle of John" in: F. L. Cross (ed.) Studia Evangelica II (1964) 487-89. McDONALD, J. I. H., Kerygma and Didache (Cambridge 1980) 65-66.

2:24-29 IWAND, H.-J. Predigt-Meditationen (1964) 129-33.

2:24.27 DUNN, J. D. G. Jesus and the Spirit (1975) 352.

2:24 CONZELMANN, H. " 'Was von Anfang war' ' in: Neutestamentliche Studien für Rudolf Bultmann (1954) 194-201; = in: Theologie als Schriftauslegung (1974) 207-14. NAUCK, W.

Die Tradition und der Charakter des ersten Johannesbriefes (1957) 68, 70, 84-86. SUITBERTUS, P. "Die Vollkommenheitslehre des ersten Johannesbriefes" Biblica 39 (1958) 456. HEISE, J. Bleiben (1967) 136-38. FILSON, F. V. "First John: Purpose and Message" Interp 23 (1969) 266. DUNN, J. D. G. "Prophetic 'I'-Sayings and the Jesus tradition: The importance of testing prophetic utterances within early Christianity" NTS 24 (1977/78) 190.

2:26-27 SUITBERTUS, P. "Die Vollkommenheitslehre des ersten Johannesbriefes" Biblica 39 (1958) 456.

2:26 STRAUSS, L. The Epistles of John (1962) 65. SONGER, H. S. "The Life Situation of the Johannine Epistles" RevEx 67 (1970) 400, 401.

2:27 NAUCK, W. Die Tradition und der Charakter des ersten Johannesbriefes (1957) 73, 94-96. GRIFFITHS, D. R. "Baptism in the Fourth Gospel and the First Epistle of John" in: A. Gilmore (ed.) Christian Baptism (1959) 166-67. SCHWEIZER, E. Gemeinde und Gemeindeordnung im Neuen Testament (1959) §12c. DELLING, G. Die Taufe im Neuen Testament (1963) 107-108. KAESEMANN, E. "Ketzer und Zeuge" in: Exegetische Versuche und Besinnungen I (1964) 184-85. LAZURE, N., Les Valeurs Morales de la Théologie Johannique (Paris 1965) 113-16. BRAUN, H. Qumran und das Neue Testament I (1966) 296. HEISE, J. Bleiben (1967) 138-42. WEISS, K. "Orthodoxie und Heterodoxie im 1. Johannesbrief" ZNW 58 (1967/68) 253. CARDER, M. M. "A Caesarean Text in the Catholic Epistles?" NTS 16 (1969/70) 256. DUNN, J. D. G. Baptism in the Holy Spirit (1970) 195-200. MOODY, D. "The Theology of the Johannine Letters" SouJTh 13 (1970) 12. PORSCH, F., Pneuma und Wort (Frankfurt 1974) 116-17, 260. de la POTTERIE, I., La Vérité dans Saint Jean I/II (Rome 1977) 583-87. SCHNACKENBURG, R. "Die johanneische Gemeinde und ihre Geisterfahrung" in: R. Schnackenburg et al. (eds.) Die Kirche des Anfangs. FS. Heinz Schürmann (1978) 294-96. BERGMEIER, R., Glaube als Gabe nach Johannes (Stuttgart 1980) 176n. 526. SCHILLEBEECKX, E., Christ: the Christian Experience in the Modern World (London 1980) 421-23; GT: Christus und die Christen (Freiburg/Basel/Wien 1977) 407-408.

2:28-4:6 COOK, D. E. "Interpretation of 1 John 1-5" RevEx 67 (1970) 452-56. JONES, P. R. "A Structural Analysis of 1 John" RevEx 67 (1970) 434-35, 444.

2:28-3:12 BRAUN, H. "Literar-Analyse und theologische Schichtung im ersten Johannesbrief" in: Gesammelte Studien zum Neuen Testament und seiner Umwelt (1962) 210-12. McDONALD, J. I. H., Kerygma and Didache (Cambridge 1980) 65.

2:28-3:10 BOISMARD, M.-E., "Une liturgie baptismale dans la Prima Petri" RB 63 (1956) 182-208; RB 64 (1957) 161-83. van UNNIK, W. C., "The Christian's Freedom of Speech in the New Testament" BJRL 44 (1961-1962) 466-88. MOODY, D. "The Theology of the Johannine Letters" SouJTh 13 (1970) 14-15. la RONDELLE, H. K., Perfection and Perfectionism (Berrien Springs, MI 1975) 227-36.

2:28-3:6 SCHRAGE, W. GPM 20 (1965/66) 33-41.

2:28-29 MOODY, D. "The Theology of the Johannine Letters" SouJTh 13 (1970) 19.

2:28 PETERSON, E., "Zur Bedeutungsgeschichte von *Parresia*" in: W. Koepp (ed.) FS. R. Seeburg. I (Leipzig 1929) 283-97. NAUCK, W. Die Tradition und der Charakter des ersten Johannesbriefes (1957) 129-33. STRAUSS, L. The Epistles of John (1962) 128-32. LAZURE, N., Les Valeurs Morales de la Théologie Johannique (Paris 1965) 277. BULTMANN, R. "Die kirchliche Redaktion des ersten Johannesbriefes" in: Exegetica (1967) 388-89. HEISE, J. Bleiben (1967) 142-45. BERGMEIER, R., Glaube als Gabe nach Johannes (Stuttgart 1980) 204.

2:29-4:6 MALATESTA, E. "Covenant and Indwelling" Way 17 (1977) 23-32.

2:29-3:24 BULTMANN, R. "Analyse des ersten Johannesbriefes" in: Festgabe für Adolf Jülicher (1927) 146-51; = in: Exegetica (1967) 112-17.

2:29-3:10 NAUCK, W. Die Tradition und der Charakter des ersten Johannesbriefes (1957) 15-19, 26-66. SUITBERTUS, P. "Die Vollkommenheitslehre des ersten Johannesbriefes" Biblica 39 (1958) 331-32, 466-67. BRAUN, H. Qumran und das Neue Testament I (1966) 296. LE FORT, P. Les Structures de l'Eglise militante selon Saint Jean (1970) 19-24. GIURISATO, G. "Struttura della prima lettera di Giovanni" RivB 21 (1973) 361-81. SANCHEZ MIELGO, G. "Perspectivas eclesiologicas en la primera carta de Juan" EsVe 4 (1974) 9-64. VELLANICKAL, M., The Divine Sonship of Christians in the Johannine Writings (Rome 1977) 232-62. SEGALLA, G., "L'impeccabilità del credente in *I Giov*. 2, 29-3, 10 alla luce dell'analisi strutturale" RivB 29 (1981) 331-41.

2:29-3:3 LANGBRANDTNER, W. Weltferner Gott oder Gott der Liebe (1977) 390, 391.

2:29-3:2 DELLING, G. "Die 'Söhne (Kinder) Gottes' im Neuen Testament" in: R. Schnackenburg et al. (eds.) Die Kirche des Anfangs. FS. Heinz Schürmann (1978) 628-29.

2:29 BULTMANN, R. "Analyse des ersten Johannesbriefes" in: Festgabe für Adolf Jülicher (1927) 157-58; = in: Exegetica (1967) 121-23. BRAUN, H. "Literar-Analyse und theologische Schichtung im ersten Johannesbrief" in: Gesammelte Studien zum Neuen Testament und seiner Umwelt (1962) 227-31. STRAUSS, L. The Epistles of John (1962) 22-24. SCHENKE, H. M. "Determination und Ethik im ersten Johannesbrief" ZThK 60 60 (1963) 206-12. SHIMADA, K. The Formulary Material in First Peter: A Study According to the Method of Traditionsgeschichte (Th.D. Diss, Union Theological Seminary New York 1966) 186-91, 196-98. VICENT CERNUDA, A., "La filiación divina según *kai* en 1 Jn 2, 29 y 3, 1" EstBi 36 (1977) 85-90. HOFRICHTER, P., Nicht aus Blut sondern monogen aus Gott geboren (Würzburg 1978) 60-67.

3:1-5:12 FEUILLET, A. "Etude structurale de la première épître de saint Jean" in: H. Baltensweiler and B. Reicke (eds.) Neues Testament und Geschichte. Oscar Cullmann zum 70. Geburtstag (1972) 316-22. FEUILLET, A. "The Structure of First John. Comparison with the 4th Gospel. The Pattern of Christian Life" BThB 3 (1973) 194-216.

3:1-10 BOISMARD, M. E. Quatre Hymnes Baptismales dans la Première Epître de Pierre (1961) 129-32.

3:1-8 BORNKAMM, G. GPM 7 (1952/53) 18-21.

3:1-6 KIIVIT, J. GPM 14 (1959/60) 24-30. STECK, K. G. GPM 26 (1971/72) 34-43. TONKS, H. and HOLLENWEGER, W. J. in: Predigtstudien für das Kirchenjahr 1977/78, Perikopenreihe VI/1 (1977) 46-51. FISCHER, K. M., in: GPM 36 (1981) 39-44. WREGE, H.-T, und KLEINERT, U., in: P. Krusche et al. (eds.) Predigtstudien für das Kirchenjahr 1981/1982. IV/1 (Stuttgart 1981) 45-52.

3:1-5 IWAND, H.-J. in: G. Eichholz (ed.) Herr, tue meine Lippen auf, Bd. 4 (1965) 43ff.

3:1-3 BULTMANN, R. "Analyse des ersten Johannesbriefes" in: Festgabe für Adolf Jülicher (1927) 146; = in: Exegetica (1967) 112-13. FUERST, W. GPM 32 (1977/78) 32-37. BERGMEIER, R., Glaube als Gabe nach Johannes (Stuttgart 1980) 255n 329.

3:1-2 GROSHEIDE, F. W. "Kol 3,1-4; I Petr 1,3-5; 1Jo 3,1-2" GThT 54 (1954) 139-57. NAUCK, W. Die Tradition und der Charakter des ersten Johannesbriefes (1957) 72. SMYTH-FLORENTIN, F. "Voyez quel grand amour le Père nous a donné (1 John 3:1-2)" AssS 25 (1969) 32-38. VELLANICKAL, M., The Divine Sonship of Christians in the Johannine Writings (Rome 1977) 331-47.

3:1 STRAUSS, L. The Epistles of John (1962) 20-22, 86, 115-16. VELLANICKAL, M., The Divine Sonship of Christians in the Johannine Writings (Rome 1977) 313-15. VICENT CERNUDA, A., "La filiacion divina segun *kai* en 1 Jn. 2, 29 y 3, 1" EstBi 36 (1977) 85-90. BERGMEIER, R., Glaube als Gabe nach Johannes (Stuttgart 1980) 213.

3:2-3 STRAUSS, L. The Epistles of John (1962) 128-32, 135-37. LAZURE, N., Les Valeurs Morales de la Théologie Johannique (Paris 1965) 278-80.

3:2 SYNGE, F. C. "1 John 3,2" JThS 3 (1952) 79. NAUCK, W. Die Tradition und der Charakter des ersten Johannesbriefes (1957) 129-33. STRAUSS, L. The Epistles of John (1962) 138-41. BULTMANN, R. "Die kirchliche Redaktion des ersten Johannesbriefes" in: Exegetica (1967) 389-90. BUEHNER, J.-A. Der Gesandte und sein Weg im 4. Evangelium (1977) 220. BRAUN, F. M. "La Réduction du Pluriel au Singlier dans l'Evangile et la Première Lettre de Jean" NTS 24 (1977/78) 52. BERGMEIER, R., Glaube als Gabe nach Johannes (Stuttgart 1980) 204, 213. "Bild Gottes" in: TRE 6 (1980) 500-501. "Bloch" in: TRE 6 (1980) 719. SCHWEIZER, E., "Auferstehung—Wirklichkeit oder Illusion?" EvTh 41 (1981) 2-3.

3:3-16 SALOM, A. P. "Some aspects of the grammatical style of 1 John" JBL 74 (1955) 101.

3:3 NAUCK, W. Die Tradition und der Charakter des ersten Johannesbriefes (1957) 75. VELLANICKAL, M., The Divine Sonship of Christians in the Johannine Writings (Rome 1977) 349-50.

3:4-10 WINDISCH, H. "Die Unsündlichkeit des Christen" in: Die Katholischen Briefe (1930) 121-22. SCHWEIZER, E. Gemeinde und Gemeindeordnung im Neuen Testament (1959) §12b. WENNEMER, K. "Der Christ und die Sünde nach der Lehre des ersten Johannesbriefes" GuL 33 (1960) 370-76.

DRUMWRIGHT, H. "Problem Passages in the Johannine Epistles: A Hermeneutical Approach" SouJTh 13 (1970) 56-58. BRAUN, F. M. "La Réduction du Pluriel au Singulier dans l'Evangile et la Première Lettre de Jean" NTS 24 (1977/78) 53, 55, 56. DUNN, J. D. G. "Prophetic 'I'-Sayings and the Jesus tradition: The importance of testing prophetic utterances within early Christianity" NTS 24 (1977/78) 190. BERGMEIER, R., Glaube als Gabe nach Johannes (Stuttgart 1980) 109n. 345.

3:4-9 STRAUSS, L. The Epistles of John (1962) 43-53. LYONNET, S., "The Notion of Sin in the Johannine Writings" in: S. Lyonnet/L. Sabourin, Sin, Redemption and Sacrifice (Rome 1970) 38-45.

3:4-5 BULTMANN, R. "Analyse des ersten Johannesbriefes" in: Festgabe für Adolf Jülicher (1927) 147; = in: Exegetica (1967) 113. ARGYLE, A. W. "1 John III,4f" ET 65 (1953/54) 62-63.

3:4 BULTMANN, R. "Analyse des ersten Johannesbriefes" in: Festgabe für Adolf Jülicher (1927) 157-58; = in: Exegetica (1967) 121-23. CLAPPERTON, J. A. "Τὴν = ἡ Ἀμαρτίαν (1 John iii,4)" ET 47 (1935-36) 92-93. de la POTTERIE, I. "Le péché, c'est l'iniquité (1 Joh., III,4)" NRTh 78 (1956) 785-97; = Lumen 5 (1956) 364ff. ROBINSON, J. A. T. "The Destination and Purpose of the Johannine Epistles" NTS 7 (1960) 60. LAZURE, N., Les Valeurs Morales de la Théologie Johannique (Paris 1965) 307-309. LYONNET, S. "The Notion of Sin" in: S. Lyonnet (ed.) Sin, Redemption, and Sacrifice. A Biblical and Patristic Study (1970) 42-43. COOPER, E. J. "The Consciousness of Sin in 1 John" LThPh 28 (1972) 237-48. SEGALLA, G., "Il Dio inaccessibile de Giovanni" in: Dio nella Bibbia e nelle culture ad essa contemporaneo (Turin 1980) 84-123. "Böse" in: TRE 7 (1981) 10.

3:5 de la POTTERIE, I., La Vérité dans Saint Jean I/II (Rome 1977) 987-88. BRAUN, F. M. "La Réduction du Pluriel au Singulier dans l'Evangile et la Première Lettre de Jean" NTS 24 (1977/78) 52-53, 55.

3:6-11 SCHENKE, H. M. "Determination und Ethik im ersten Johannesbrief" ZThK 60 (1963) 206-12.

3:6-9 BULTMANN, R. "Analyse des ersten Johannesbriefes" in: Festgabe für Adolf Jülicher (1927) 147-48, 157-58; = in: Exegetica (1967) 113-14, 121-23. de la POTTERIE, I., "L'impeccabilité du chrétien d'après I Joh. 3,6-9" in: Boismard et al. (eds.) L'Evangile de Jean (1958) 161-77.

3:6.9 GALTIER, P. "Le Chrétien impeccable (1 Jean 3,6.9)" MSR 4 (1947) 137-54.

3:6 SUITBERTUS, P. "Die Vollkommenheitslehre des ersten Johannesbriefes" Biblica 39 (1958) 453, 458-62. HEISE, J. Bleiben (1967) 145-47. SONGER, H. S. "The Life Situation of the Johannine Epistles" RevEx 67 (1970) 402. BOGART, J. Orthodox and Heretical Perfectionism in the Johannine Community as Evident in the First Epistle of John (Diss Berkeley 1977). VELLANICKAL, M., The Divine Sonship of Christians in the Johannine Writings (Rome 1977) 272-74. GEORGI, D., "Weisheit Salomos" in: JüdSchr III/4 (1980) 15n. 3a.

3:7-12 BOISMARD, M.-E. "The First Epistle of John and the Writings of Qumran" in: J. H. Charlesworth (ed.) John and Qumran (1972) 156-65.

3:7-10 BRAUN, H. "Literar-Analyse und theologische Schichtung im ersten Johannesbrief" in: Gesammelte Studien zum Neuen Testament und seiner Umwelt (1962) 216. BRAUN, H. Qumran und das Neue Testament I (1966) 296-97. LANGBRANDTNER, W. Weltferner Gott oder Gott der Liebe 1977) 386-87.

3:7 STRAUSS, L. The Epistles of John (1962) 20-22. SANCHEZ MIELGO, G. "Perspectivas eclesiologicas en la primera carta de Juan" EsVe 4 (1973) 9-64.

3:8-15 ROBINSON, J. A. T. "The Destination and Purpose of the Johannine Epistles" NTS 7 (1960) 57.

3:8-12 LE DEAUT, R. Liturgie juive et Nouveau Testament (1965) 60-61.

3:8.11 SALOM, A. P. "Some aspects of the grammatical style of 1 John" JBL 74 (1955) 102.

3:8 WINDISCH, H. "Gotteszeugung" in: Die Katholischen Briefe (1930) 122-23. NAUCK, W. Die Tradition und der Charakter des ersten Johannesbriefes (1957) 84-86. STRAUSS, L. The Epistles of John (1962) 98-100, 102-105. CARLTON, J. W. "Preaching from the Johannine Epistles" RevEx 67 (1970) 480-83. BERGMEIER, R., Glaube als Gabe nach Johannes (Stuttgart 1980) 179, 213, 258n. 385, 394. "Böse" in: TRE 7 (1981) 15.

3:9-10 BULTMANN, R. "Analyse des ersten Johannesbriefes" in: Festgabe für Adolf Jülicher (1927) 149, 157-58; = in: Exegetica (1967) 114, 121-23. HARNACK, A. von, Studien zur Geschichte des Neuen Testaments und der Alten Kirche (1931) 112, 141-43. DELLING, G. "Die 'Söhne (Kinder) Gottes' im Neuen Testament" in: R. Schnackenburg et al. (eds.) Die Kirche des Anfangs. Für Heinz Schürmann (1978) 629.

3:9 BARRETT, C. K. The New Testament Background: Selected Documents (1956) 89. NAUCK, W. Die Tradition und der

Charakter des ersten Johannesbriefes (1957) 64. BRAUN, H. "Literar-Analyse und theologische Schichtung im ersten Johannesbrief" in: Gesammelte Studien zum Neuen Testament und seiner Umwelt (1962) 227-31. BRAUN, F. M. Jean le Théologien (1966) 116-18. HEISE, J. Bleiben (1967) 147-50. KUBO, S. "I John 3:9: Absolute or Habitual?" AUSS 7 (1969) 47-56. DUNN, J. D. G. Baptism in the Holy Spirit (1970) 195-200. STAGG, F. "Orthodoxy and Orthopraxy in the Johannine Epistles" RevEx 67 (1970) 428. PORSCH, F., Pneuma und Wort (Frankfurt 1974) 114-16. Du PREEZ, J. " 'Sperma autou' in 1 John 3:9" Neotestamentica 8 (1975) 105-12; = NGTT 17 (1976) 35-43. BOGART, J. Orthodox and Heretical Perfectionism in the Johannine Community as Evident in the First Epistle of John (Diss Berkeley 1977). INKMAN, V. K. "Distinctive Johannine Vocabulary and the Interpretation of 1 John 3:9" WThJ 40 (1977) 136-44. de la POTTERIE, I., La Vérité dans Saint Jean I/II (Rome 1977) 987-88. VELLANICKAL, M., The Divine Sonship of Christians in the Johannine Writings (Rome 1977) 265-70, 272-74. HOFRICHTER, P., Nicht aus Blut sondern monogen aus Gott geboren (Würzburg 1978) 60-67. RUDOLPH, K. Die Gnosis (1978) 324-27. BERGMEIER, R., Glaube als Gabe nach Johannes (Stuttgart 1980) 213, 255n. 329.

3:10-24 SALOM, A. P. "Some aspects of the grammatical style of 1 John" JBL 74 (1955) 101.

3:10-20 CARDER, M. M. "A Caesarean Text in the Catholic Epistles?" NTS 16 (1969/70) 267-68.

3:10-19 O'NEILL, J. C. The Puzzle of 1 John. A New Examination of Origins (1966) 38-41.

3:10-18 SISTI, P.A., "La caritá dei figli di Dio (1 Giov. 3, 10-18)" BiOr 9 (1967) 77-87. MOODY, D. "The Theology of the Johannine Letters" SouJTh 13 (1970) 17-18.

3:10-17 MICHL, J. "Die Bruderliebe" in: Der erste Johannesbrief (1953) 287-90.

3:10-12 BULTMANN, R. "Analyse des ersten Johannesbriefes" in: Festgabe für Adolf Jülicher (1927) 149; = in: Exegetica (1967) 114-15. VELLANICKAL, M., The Divine Sonship of Christians in the Johannine Writings (Rome 1977) 295-302.

3:10-11 CARDER, M. M. "A Caesarean Text in the Catholic Epistles?" NTS 16 (1969/70) 260. VISSCHERS, L., "Een nieuwe weg voor de mens! Uit de eerste brief van Johannes" Schrift 57 (1978) 100-106.

3:10 STRAUSS, L. The Epistles of John (1962) 34-36, 102-103. SONGER, H. S. "The Life Situation of the Johannine Epistles" RevEx 67 (1970) 402. STAGG, F. "Orthodoxy and Orthopraxy in the Johannine Epistles" RevEx 67 (1970) 427. BERGMEIER, R., Glaube als Gabe nach Johannes (Stuttgart 1980) 189, 213, 223.

3:11-24 WENDT, H. H., "Zum ersten Johannesbrief" ZNW 22 (1923) 57-79. BAUER, J. B., "Il misfatto di Caino nel guidizio di S. Giovanni" RivB 2 (1954) 325-28. MUSSNER, F., "Eine neutestamentliche Kurzformel für das Christentum" TThZ 79 (1970) 49-52.

3:11-22 GIURISATO, G. "Struttura della prima lettera di Giovani" RivB 21 (1973) 361-81.

3:11-18 SCHOENHERR, A. GPM 16 (1961/62) 230-34.

3:11 NAUCK, W. Die Tradition und der Charakter des ersten Johannesbriefes (1957) 84-86. STRAUSS, L. The Epistles of John (1962) 116. CONZELMANN, H. " 'Was von Anfang war' " in: Neutestamentliche Studien für Rudolf Bultmann (1954) 194-201; = in: Theologie als Schriftauslegung (1974) 207-14. SANDERS, J. T., Ethics in the New Testament (Philadelphia 1975) 91-94. BRAUN, F. M. "La Réduction du Pluriel au Singulier dans l'Evangile et la Première Lettre de Jean" NTS 24 (1977/78) 49, 50. DUNN, J. D. G. "Prophetic 'I'-Sayings and the Jesus tradition: The importance of testing prophetic utterances within early Christianity" NTS 24 (1977/78) 190.

3:12-15 BERGMEIER, R., Glaube als Gabe nach Johannes (Stuttgart 1980) 204, 213, 223, 226, 240n. 58, 261n. 433, 264n. 484, 270n. 544.

3:12 BAUER, G. B. "Il misfatto di Caino nel giudizio di S. Giovanni" Salesianum 2 (1954) 325-28. NAUCK, W. Die Tradition und der Charakter des ersten Johannesbriefes (1957) 88-89. GRELOT, P. "Les Targums du Pentateuque" Semitica 9 (1959) 59-88. RAMON DIAZ, J. "Dos notas sobre el Targum palestinense" Sefarad 19 (1959) 134-36. LE DEAUT, R. "Traditions targumiques dans le corpus paulinien?" Biblica 42 (1961) 30-36. VERMES, G. "The Targumic Versions of Genesis 4, 3-16" ALUOS 3 (1961/62) 81-114. STRAUSS, L. The Epistles of John (1962) 87, 100-101. DIEZ MACHO, A. "Targum y Nuevo Testamento" in: Mélanges E. Tisserant (1964) 164. McNAMARA, M. The New Testament and the Palestinian Targum to the Pentateuch (1966) 156-60. KUEMMEL, W. G., Einleitung in das neue Testament (1973¹⁷) 386. BRAUN, F. M. "La Réduction du Pluriel au Singulier dans l'Evangile et la Première Lettre de Jean" NTS 24 (1977/78) 50. de KRUIJF, T. C.,

" 'Nicht wie Kain (der) vom Bösen war . . . ' (1 Joh. 3, 12)"
Bijdragen 41 (1980) 47-63.

3:13-24 CARDER, M. M. "A Caesarean Text in the Catholic epistles?" NTS 16 (1969/70) 261-62.

3:13-18 BULTMANN, R. "Analyse des ersten Johannesbriefes" in: Festgabe für Adolf Jülicher (1927) 149-50; = in: Exegetica (1967) 115. OGARA, F. "Scimus quoniam translati sumus de morte ad vitam! (1 John 3:13-18)" VD 18 (1938) 161-67. EHRENBERG, H. GPM 5 (1950/51) 144-47. FRIEDRICH, G. GPM 10 (1955/56) 164-67. DUPONT, J. "Comment aimer ses frères (1 Jean 3:13-18)" AssS 55 (1962) 24-31. MAURER, C. in: G. Eichholz (ed.) Herr, tue meine Lippen auf, Bd. II (1966⁵) 352-57. DOERNE, M. Die alten Episteln (1967) 157-61. HAAR, J. GPM 22 (1967/68) 289-96.

3:13-17 LANGBRANDTNER, W. Weltferner Gott oder Gott der Liebe (1977) 390-91.

3:13 STRAUSS, L. The Epistles of John (1962) 86-87. BRAUN, H. Qumran und das Neue Testament 1 (1966) 297. CARDER, M. M. "A Caesarean Text in the Catholic Epistles?" NTS 16 (1969/70) 256.

3:14-19 SCHENKE, H. M. "Determination und Ethik im ersten Johannesbrief" ZThK 60 (1963) 206-15.

3:14-15 BULTMANN, R. "Analyse des ersten Johannesbriefes" in: Festgabe für Adolf Jülicher (1927) 157-58; = in: Exegetica (1967) 121-23. DUPONT, J. Essais sur la Christologie de Saint Jean (1951) 182-84.

3:14 ROBINSON, J. A. T. "The Destination and Purpose of the Johannine Epistles" NTS 7 (1960) 57. STRAUSS, L. The Epistles of John (1962) 78-79. HEISE, J. Bleiben (1967) 150-53. SONGER, H. S. "The Life Situation of the Johannine Epistles" RevEx 67 (1970) 402. SANDERS, J. T., Ethics in the New Testament (Philadelphia 1975) 93. THYEN, H., " ' . . . denn wir lieben die Brüder' (1 John 3, 14)" in: J. Friedrich et al. (eds.) Rechtfertigung. FS. E. Käsemann (Tübingen/Göttingen 1976) 527-42.

3:15 BEYSCHLAG, K. Clemens Romanus und der Frühkatholizismus (1966) 68. HEISE, J. Bleiben (1967) 153-54.

3:16-18 BULTMANN, R. "Analyse des ersten Johannesbriefes" in: Festgabe für Adolf Jülicher (1927) 150; = in: Exegetica (1967) 115. STAGG, F. "Orthodoxy and Orthopraxy in the Johannine Epistles" RevEx 67 (1970) 430-31. SANDERS, J. T., Ethics in the New Testament (Philadelphia 1975) 99-100.

3:16-17 COPENS, J. "Miscellanées bibliques. LII. 'Agápe et 'Agapân dans les Lettres johanniques" EphT 45 (1969) 125-27.

3:16 DENNEY, J. The Death of Christ (1956³) 151-52. NAUCK, W. Die Tradition und der Charakter des ersten Johannesbriefes (1957) 68-70. STRAUSS, L. The Epistles of John (1962) 112. KUHL, J. Die Sendung Jesu und der Kirche nach dem Johannesevangelium (1967) 197-98. POPKES, W. Christus Traditus (1967) 248-49, 283-84. WARD, R. A. "The Theological Pattern of the Johannine Epistles" SouJTh 13 (1970) 28.

3:17-18 STRAUSS, L. The Epistles of John (1962) 119-21. BRAUN, F. M. "La Réduction du Pluriel au Singulier dans l'Evangile et la Première Lettre de Jean" NTS 24 (1977/78) 50.

3:17 STRAUSS, L. The Epistles of John (1962) 88-89. GERSTENBERGER, G. und SCHRAGE, W., Leiden (Stuttgart 1977) 225; ET: J. E. Steely (trans.) Suffering (Nashville 1980) 259-60. "Armenfürsorge" in: TRE 4 (1979) 17. "Barmherzigkeit" in: TRE 5 (1980) 226, 227.

3:18-4:21 THOMPSON, P. J. "Psalm 119: a possible Clue to the Structure of the First Epistle of John" in: F. L. Cross (ed.) Studia Evangelica 2 (1964) 489, 491.

3:18-24 STECK, K. G. GPM 26 (1971/72) 419-27. de la POTTERIE, I. "Aimer ses frères et croire en Jésus Christ. 1 Jn 3,18-24" AssS 26 (1973) 39-45. ENGELHARDT, K. GPM 32 (1977/78) 401-406.

3:18-19 de la POTTERIE, I., La Vérité dans Saint Jean I/II (Rome 1977) 622-24.

3:18 STRAUSS, L. The Epistles of John (1962) 20-22. WEISS, K. "Orthodoxie und Heterodoxie im 1. Johannesbrief" ZNW 58 (1967/68) 251-53. LAZURE, N., Les Valeurs Morales de la Théologie Johannique (Paris 1965) 87-88. de la POTTERIE, I., La Vérité dans Saint Jean I/II (Rome 1977) 663-73, 891-92.

3:19-24 BULTMANN, R. "Analyse des ersten Johannesbriefes" in: Festgabe für Adolf Jülicher (1927) 150-51; = in: Exegetica (1967) 115-16. FRIEDERICH, G. GPM 7 (1952/53) 243-48. O'NEILL, J. C. The Puzzle of 1 John (1966) 42-45. MOODY, D. "The Theology of the Johannine Letters" SouJTh 13 (1970) 12-13. SCHROEER, H. in: Predigtstudien für das Kirchenjahr 1971/72, Perikopenreihe VI/2 (1972) 226-29.

3:19-22 NAUCK, E. Die Tradition und der Charakter des ersten Johannesbriefes (1957) 78-83.

3:19-21 SPICQ, C. "La justification du charitable (1 Jo 3,19-21)" Biblica 40 (1959) 915-27.

3:19-20 PRATSCHER, W. "Gott ist grösser als unser Herz. Zur Interpretation von 1.Joh, 3,19f" ThZ 32 (1976) 272-81. RICHARDSON, C. C., "The Exegesis of 1 John 3. 19-20—An Ecumenical Misinterpretation?" in: D. F. Winslow (ed.) Disciplina Nostra. FS. R. F. Evans (Cambridge, MA 1979) 31-52.

3:19 LAZURE, N., Les Valeurs Morales de la Théologie Johannique (Paris 1965) 86.

3:20 REBSTOCK, B. "Gott ist grösser als unser Herz" Benediktinische Monatsschrift 18 (1936) 321-33. SKRINJAR, A. "Major est Deus corde nostro (1 Jo 3:20)" VD 20 (1940) 340-50.

3:21 BULTMANN, R. "Analyse des ersten Johannesbriefes" in: Festgabe für Adolf Jülicher (1927) 150-51; = in: Exegetica (1967) 116.

3:22-24 BRAUN, H. "Literar-Analyse und theologische Schichtung im ersten Johannesbrief" in: Gesammelte Studien zum Neuen Testament und seiner Umwelt (1962) 220-26.

3:23-5:4 GIURISATO, G. "Struttura della prima lettera di Giovanni" RivB 21 (1973) 361-81.

3:23-24 BRAUN, F. M. "La Réduction du Pluriel au Singulier dans l'Evangile et la Première Lettre de Jean" NTS 24 (1977/78) 49, 51.

3:23 STRAUSS, L. The Epistles of John (1962) 116-17. MUSSNER, F. "Eine neutestamentliche Kurzformel für das Christentum" TThZ 79 (1970) 49-52. SANDERS, J. T., Ethics in the New Testament (Philadelphia 1975) 91-94.

3:24 BULTMANN, R. "Analyse des ersten Johannesbriefes" in: Festgabe für Adolf Jülicher (1927) 157-58; = in: Exegetica (1967) 121-23. NAUCK, W. Die Tradition und der Charakter des ersten Johannesbriefes (1957) 75. SUITBERTUS, P. "Die Vollkommenheitslehre des ersten Johannesbriefes" Biblica 39 (1958) 456. STRAUSS, L. The Epistles of John (1962) 79. SCHENKE, H. M. "Determination und Ethik im ersten Johannesbrief" ZThK 60 (1963) 206-12. HEISE, J. Bleiben (1967) 157-60. WEISS, K. "Orthodoxie und Heterodoxie im 1. Johannesbrief" ZNW 58 (1967/68) 251-53. de la POTTERIE, I., La Vérité dans Saint Jean I/II (Rome 1977) 290-97. DUNN, J. D. G. "Prophetic 'I'-Sayings and the Jesus tradition: The importance of testing prophetic utterances within early Christianity" NTS 24 (1977/78) 190. SCHNACKENBURG, R. "Die johanneische Gemeinde und ihre Geisterfahrung" in: R. Schnackenburg et al. (eds.) Die Kirche des Anfangs. Für Heinz Schürmann (1978) 283-87.

4:1ff DUNN, J. D. G. "Prophetic 'I'-Sayings and the Jesus tradition: The importance of testing prophetic utterances within early Christianity" NTS 24 (1977/78) 187, 190.

4:1-12 DRUMWRIGHT, H. "Problem Passages in the Johannine Epistles: A Hermeneutical Approach" SouJTh 13 (1970) 58-60.

4:1-8 BRAUN, H. GPM 7 (1952/53) 192-94. BORNKAMM, G. GPM 14 (1959/60) 300-305. IWAND, H.-J. Predigt-Meditationen (1964) 137-41. FUERST, GPM 20 (1965/66) 394ff. KUENKEL, K. GPM 26 (1971/72) 401-407.

4:1-6 WINDISCH, H. "Die Irrlehrer" in: Die Katholischen Briefe (1930) 127-28. RUCKSTUHL, E. Die literarische Einheit des Johannesevangeliums (1951) 233-35. BROWN, R. E. "The Qumran Scrolls and the Johannine Gospel and Epistles" CBQ 17 (1955) 403-19, 559-74; = in: K. Stendahl (ed.) The Scrolls and the New Testament (1957) 196; GT: "Die Schriftrollen von Qumran und das Johannesevangelium und die Johannesbriefe" in: K. H. Rengstorf (ed.) Johannes und sein Evangelium (1973) 509. SERAFIN de AUSEJO, "El concepto de 'carne' aplicado a Cristo en el IV Evangelio" EstBi 17 (1958) 411-27. ROBINSON, J. A. T. "The Destination and Purpose of the Johannine Epistles" NTS 7 (1960) 61. BRAUN, H. "Literar-Analyse und theologische Schichtung im ersten Johannesbrief" in: Gesammelte Studien zum Neuen Testament und seiner Umwelt (1962) 237-42. BRAUN, H. Qumran und das Neue Testament 1 (1966) 297-300. O'NEILL, J. C. The Puzzle of 1 John (1966) 46-48. FILSON, F. V. "First John: Purpose and Message" Interp 23 (1969) 267-71, 274. LE FORT, P. Les Structures de l'Eglise militante selon Saint Jean (1970) 40-47. MOODY, D. "The Theology of the Johannine Letters" SouJTh 13 (1970) 12-13, 16-17, 19. SONGER, H. S. "The Life Situation of the Johannine Epistles" RevEx 67 (1970) 401-402. SCHROEER, H. and BOEHMIG, W. in: Predigtstudien für das Kirchenjahr 1971/72, Perikopenreihe VI/2 (1972) 213-18. BOISMARD, M.-E. "The First Epistle of John and the Writings of Qumran" in: J. H. Charlesworth (ed.) John and Qumran (1972) 156-65. de la CIGOÑA, J. R. F. "El discernimiento de espíritus en la primera carta de San Juan" Manresa 46 (1974) 123-30. SANCHEZ MIELGO, G. "Perspectivas eclesiologicas en la primera carta de Juan" EsVe 4 (1974) 9-64. DUNN, J. D. G. Jesus and the Spirit (1975) 352-53, 356. de la POTTERIE, I., La Vérité dans Saint Jean I/II (Rome 1977) 282-310. "Antichrist" in: TRE 3 (1978) 22. RUDOLPH, K. Die Gnosis (1978) 324-27. SCHWEIZER, E., Heiliger Geist (1978) 141. McDONALD, J. I. H., Kerygma and Didache (Cambridge 1980) 66. PAINTER, J., "The Farewell Discourses and the History of Johannine Christianity" NTS 27 (1980-1981) 532, 539.

4:1-3 HORNER, J. "Introduction to the Johannine Epistles" SouJTh 13 (1970) 44-45. STAGG, F. "Orthodoxy and Orthopraxy in the Johannine Epistles" RevEx 67 (1970) 427. DUNN, J. D. G. Unity and Diversity in the New Testament (1977) 55, 303. LANGBRANDTNER, W. Weltferner Gott oder Gott der Liebe (1977) 282, 377-80. "Antichrist" in: TRE 3 (1978) 34.

4:1 STRAUSS, L. The Epistles of John (1962) 72. DUNN, J. D. G. "Prophetic 'I'-Sayings and the Jesus tradition: The importance of testing prophetic utterances within early Christianity" NTS 24 (1977/78) 186. "Antichrist" in: TRE 3 (1978) 22. SCHNACKENBURG, R. "Die johanneische Gemeinde und ihre Geisterfahrung" in: R. Schnackenburg et al. (eds.) Die Kirche des Anfangs. Für Heinz Schürmann (1978) 302-303. ALAND, K., "Noch einmal: Das Problem der Anonymität und Pseudonymität in der christlichen Literatur der ersten beiden Jahrhunderte" in: E. Dassmann/K. S. Frank (eds.) Pietas. FS. B. Kötting (Münster 1980) 136. BERGMEIER, R., Glaube als Gabe nach Johannes (Stuttgart 1980) 204.

4:2-17 SALOM, A. P. "Some aspects of the grammatical style of 1 John" JBL 74 (1955) 101.

4:2-3 HARNACK, A. von, Studien zur Geschichte des Neuen Testaments und der Alten Kirche (1931) 132-37. NAUCK, W. Die Tradition und der Charakter des ersten Johannesbriefes (1957) 76-77. BRAUN, H. "Literar-Analyse und theologische Schichtung im ersten Johannesbrief" in: Gesammelte Studien zum Neuen Testament und seiner Umwelt (1962) 217-18. STRAUSS, L. The Epistles of John (1962) 32-33, 73. "Bekenntnisschriften" in: TRE 5 (1980) 490.

4:2 NAUCK, W. Die Tradition und der Charakter des ersten Johannesbriefes (1957) 86-88. SERAFIN de AUSEJO, "El concepto de 'carne' aplicado a Cristo en el IV Evangelio" EstBi 17 (1958) 416-20. WAINWRIGHT, A. W. The Trinity in the New Testament (1962) 261-63. KRAMER, W. Christos Kyrios Gottessohn (1963) §16d. COPPENS, J. "Miscellanées bibliques. LII. 'Agápe et 'Agapân dans les Lettres johanniques" EphT 45 (1969) 125-27. BRIGGS, R. C. "Contemporary Study of the Johannine Epistles" RevEx 67 (1970) 416. CARLTON, J. W.

"Preaching from the Johannine Epistles" RevEx 67 (1970) 477-80. MINEAR, P. S. "The Idea of Incarnation in First John" Interp 24 (1970) 291-302. de la POTTERIE, I., La Vérité dans Saint Jean I/II (Rome 1977) 290.

4:3 von der GOLTZ, E. F., "Eine textkritische Arbeit des zehnten bzw. sechsten Jahrhunderts" TU 17 (1899) 48-50. BOUSSET, W. Die Religion des Judentums in späthellenistischen Zeitalter (1926 = 1966) 254-56. NAUCK, W. Die Tradition und der Charakter des ersten Johannesbriefes (1957) 77. BRAUN, F. M. "La Réduction du Pluriel au Singulier dans l'Evangile et la Première Lettre de Jean" NTS 24 (1977/78) 58. "Antichrist" in: TRE 3 (1978) 22. BERGMEIER, R., Glaube als Gabe nach Johannes (Stuttgart 1980) 204, 239n. 58.

4:4-13 SALOM, A. P. "Some aspects of the grammatical style of 1 John" JBL 74 (1955) 97.

4:4-6 BULTMANN, R. "Analyse des ersten Johannesbriefes" in: Festgabe für Adolf Jülicher (1927) 155; = in: Exegetica (1967) 199-20. NAUCK, W. Die Tradition und der Charakter des ersten Johannesbriefes (1957) 74-75. LANGBRANDTNER, W. Weltferner Gott oder Gott der Liebe (1977) 383-84.

4:4 STRAUSS, L. The Epistles of John (1962) 20-22. HOFRICHTER, P., Nicht aus Blut sondern monogen aus Gott geboren (Würzburg 1978) 60-67.

4:5-6 BERGMEIER, R., Glaube als Gabe nach Johannes (Stuttgart 1980) 202, 213.

4:5 BULTMANN, R. "Analyse des ersten Johannesbriefes" in: Festgabe für Adolf Jülicher (1927) 157-58; = in: Exegetica (1967) 121-23. STRAUSS, L. The Epistles of John (1962) 87.

4:6-8 SCHENKE, H. M. "Determination und Ethik im ersten Johannesbriefe" ZThK 60 (1963) 206-12. WARD, R. A. "The Theological Pattern of the Johannine Epistles" SouJTh 13 (1970) 33.

4:6 MUSSNER, F. ZΩH. Die Anschauung vom "Leben" im vierten Evanglium (1952) 175. SUITBERTUS, P. "Die Vollkommenheitslehre des ersten Johannesbriefes" Biblica 39 (1958) 451-52. STRAUSS, L. The Epistles of John (1962) 73. LAZURE, N., Les Valeurs Morales de la Théologie Johannique (Paris 1965) 110-11. PORSCH, F., Pneuma und Wort (Frankfurt 1974) 231-33. de la POTTERIE, I., La Vérité dans Saint Jean I/II (Rome 1977) 286-310. HOFRICHTER, P., Nicht aus Blut sondern monogen aus Gott geboren (Würzburg 1978) 60-67.

4:7-5:13 COOK, D. D "Interpretation of 1 John 1-5" RevEx 67 (1970) 456-58. MALATESTA, E. "Covenant and Indwelling" Way 17 (1977) 23-32.

4:7-5:12 JONES, P. R. "A Structural Analysis of 1 John" RevEx 67 (1970) 434-35, 444. McDONALD, J. I. H., Kerygma and Didache (Cambridge 1980) 66-67.

4:7-5:4 SCHÜTZ, R., Die Vorgeschichte der johanneischen Formel *Ho Theos Agape Estin* (Göttingen 1917). SPICQ, C., "Notes d'exégèse johannique: La charité est amour manifeste" RB 65 (1958) 358-70. BULTMANN, R. "Analyse des ersten Johannesbriefes" in: Festgabe für Adolf Jülicher (1927) 152; = in: Exegetica (1967) 117. MENESTRINA, G. "Agapé nelle Lettere di Giovanni" BiOr 19 (1977) 77-80.

4:7-21 DE KEULENAER, J. "De interpretatione I Ioannis 4,7-21" Collectanea Mechliniensia 5 (1931) 639-43. DAVIES, W. D. The Sermon on the Mount (1966) 117-18. MOODY, D. "The Theology of the Johannine Letters" SouJTH 13 (1970) 18. VELLANICKAL, M., The Divine Sonship of Christians in the Johannine Writings (Rome 1977) 303-304.

4:7-18 O'NEILL, J. C. The Puzzle of 1 John (1966) 49-53.

4:7-16 MICHALKO, J. GPM 16 (1961/62) 279-81. SCHNEIDER, G. Der Herr unser Gott (1965) 185-88.

4:7-13 CHARLIER, C. "L'Amour en Esprit" BVieC 10 (1955) 57-72.

4:7-12 DINKLER, E. GPM 8 (1953/54) 216-18. LANGBRANDT-NER, W. Weltferner Gott oder Gott der Liebe (1977) 390, 391-92. KRUSCHE, G., in: GPM 34 (1980) 346-53. ORTH, G. und RENNER, U., in: P. Krusche et al. (eds.) Predigtstudien für das Kirchenjahr 1979/1980. II/2 (Stuttgart 1980) 191-97.

4:7-10 BOURGIN, C. "L'Eglise fraternité dans l'amour divin" AssS 27 (1970) 24-29.

4:7-8 BULTMANN, R. "Analyse des ersten Johannesbriefes" in: Festgabe für Adolf Jülicher (1927) 157-58; = in: Exegetica (1967) 121-23. PERRIN, J.-M. "Voir vos frères, c'est voir Dieu" VieS 72 (1945) 372-89. BROWN, R. E. "The Qumran Scrolls and the Johannine Gospel and the Epistles" CBQ 17 (1955) 403-19, 559-74; = in: K. Stendahl (ed.) The Scrolls and the New Testament (1957) 199; GT: "Die Schriftrollen von Qumran und das Johannesevangelium und die Johannesbriefe" in: K. H. Rengstorf (ed.) Johannes und sein Evangelium (1973) 514. SUITBERTUS, P. "Die Vollkommenheitslehre des ersten Johannesbriefes" Biblica 39 (1958) 453, 457-62.

STRAUSS, L. The Epistles of John (1962) 20, 22-27, 117-18. MIRANDA, J. P. Marx and the Bible (1977) 61-64. VELLAN-ICKAL, M., The Divine Sonship of Christians in the Johannine Writings (Rome 1977) 302-12.

4:7 WINDISCH, H. ''Gegenseitige Liebe'' in: Die Katholischen Briefe (1930) 129. NAUCK, W. Die Tradition und der Charakter des ersten Johannesbriefes (1957) 75-76. BRAUN, H. ''Literar-Analyse und theologische Schichtung im ersten Johannesbrief'' in: Gesammelte Studien zum Neuen Testament und seiner Umwelt (1962) 227-31. SHIMADA, K. The Formulary Material in First Peter (Th.D. Diss, Union Theological Seminary New York 1966) 186-91, 196-98. BOUTRY, A. ''Quiconque aime, est né de Dieu (1 Jn 4:7)'' BVieC 82 (1968) 66-70. De JONGE, M. '' 'Geliefden, laten wij elkander liefhebben, want de liefde is uit God' (1 Joh. 4:7)'' NedThT 22 (1968) 352-67. COPPENS, J. ''Miscellanées bibliques. LII. 'Agápe et 'Agapân dans les Lettres johanniques'' EphT 45 (1969) 125-27. de JONGE, M., ''To Love as God Loves (1 John 4:7)'' in: Jesus: Inspiring and Disturbing Presence (Nashville 1974) 110-27. LANGBRANDTNER, W. Weltferner Gott oder Gott der Liebe (1977) 386-87. BRAUN, F. M. ''La Réduction de Pluriel au Singulier dans l'Evangile et la Première Lettre de Jean'' NTS 24 (1977/78) 49. HOFRICHTER, P., Nicht aus Blut sondern monogen aus Gott geboren (Würzburg 1978) 60-67.

4:8 NAUCK, W. Die Tradition und der Charakter des ersten Johannesbriefes (1957) 75-76. LAZURE, N., Les Valeurs Morales de la Théologie Johannique (Paris 1965) 237-39. CHMIEL, J. Lumière et charité d'après la première épître de saint Jean (Diss Rome 1971). DIDEBERG, D., ''Esprit Saint et charité: L'exégèse augustinienne de 1 Jn 4, 8 et 16'' NRTh 97 (1975) 97-109, 229-50.

4:9-16 EHRENBERG, H. GPM 7 (1952/53) 42-45.

4:9-14 DIEM, H. in: G. Eichholz (ed.) Herr, tue meine Lippen auf, Bd. 4 (1965) 282ff. WARD, R. A. ''The Theological Pattern of the Johannine Epistles'' SouJTh 13 (1970) 30.

4:9-12 BULTMANN, R. ''Analyse des ersten Johannesbriefes'' in: Festgabe für Adolf Jülicher (1927) 152; = in: Exegetica (1967) 117. WEBER, O. Predigtmeditationen (1967) 70-73.

4:9-10 BUEHNER, J.-A. Der Gesandte und seine Weg im 4. Evangelium (1977) 94, 409-12. IBUKI, Y. Die Wahrheit im Johannesevangelium (1972) 157-58, 256, 311.

4:9 NAUCK, W. Die Tradition und der Charakter des ersten Johannesbriefes (1957) 68-70. KILPATRICK, G. D. ''Two Johannine Idioms in the Johannine Epistles'' JThS 12 (1961) 272-73. KRAMER, W. Christos Kyrios Gottessohn (1963) §25b. MOODY, D. ''The Theology of the Johannine Letters'' SouJTh 13 (1970) 10. SCHWEIZER, E. ''Zum religionsgeschichtlichen Hintergrund der 'Sendungsformel' Gal 4, 4f, Röm 8,3f, Joh 3,16f, 1 Joh 4,9'' in: Beiträge zur Theologie des Neuen Testaments (1970) 83-95. BUEHNER, J.-A. Der Gesandte und sein Weg im 4. Evangelium (1977) 128-29 n 21, 264-65. SCHRAGE, W., ''Die Elia-Apokalypse'' in: JüdSchr V/3 (1980) 232n. 20d.

4:10ff FUCHS, J. ''El amor de Dios en 1 Jn 4,10ss'' Revista Biblica con sección Litúrgica 18 (1956) 142ff.

4:10 MORRIS, L. The Apostolic Preaching of the Cross (1955) 178-79. NAUCK, W. Die Tradition und der Charakter des ersten Johannesbriefes (1957) 68-70, 129. KILPATRICK, G. D. ''Two Johannine Idioms in the Johannine Epistles'' JThS 12 (1961) 272-73. STRAUSS, L. The Epistles of John (1962) 43-47, 50-53, 113-14. DALTON, W. J. Christ's Proclamation to the Spirits (1965) 118. SHIMADA, K. The Formulary Material in First Peter (Th.D. Diss, Union Theological Seminary New York 1966) 324-30, 341. BULTMANN, R. ''Die kirchliche Redaktion des ersten Johannesbriefes'' in: Exegetica (1967) 393. THORNTON, T. C. G. ''Propitiation or Expiation? = ηΙλαστήριον and = ηΙλασμός in Romans and 1 John'' ET 80 (1968/69) 53-55. LYONNET, S. ''The Terminology of Redemption'' in: S. Lyonnet (ed.) Sin, Redemption, and Sacrifice (1970) 154-55. MOODY, D. The Theology of the Johannine Letters'' SouJTh 13 (1970) 9. SABOURIN, L. ''Christ Made 'Sin' (2 Cor 5:21): Sacrifice and Redemption in the History of a Formula'' in: S. Lyonnet (ed.) Sin, Redemption and Sacrifice (1970) 256-58. WENGST, K. Christologische Formeln und Lieder des Urchristentums (1972) 91. BRAUN, F. M. ''La Réduction du Pluriel au Singulier dans l'Evangile et la Première Lettre de Jean'' NTS 24 (1977/78) 52. DALY, R., Christian Sacrifice (Washington D. C. 1978) 293. LOHSE, E., ''Kirche im Alltag. Erwägungen zur theologischen Begründung der Ethik im Neuen Testament'' in: D. Lührmann/G. Strecker (eds.) Kirche. FS. G. Bornkamm (Tübingen 1980) 406.

4:11-16 BOURGIN, C. ''L'amour fraternel chrétien, expérience de Dieu. 1 Jn 4,11-16'' AssS 29 (1973) 31-37.

4:11-13 SCHWEIZER, E. Heiliger Geist (1978) 140.

4:11-12 SCHENKE, H. M. ''Determination und Ethik im ersten Johannesbrief'' ZThK 60 (1963) 206-15. BRAUN, F. M. ''La Réduction du Pluriel au Singulier dans l'Evangile et la Première Lettre de Jean'' NTS 24 (1977/78) 49.

4:11 SCHULZ, A. Nachfolgen und Nachahmen (1962) 248-51. CARLTON, J. W. ''Preaching from the Johannine Epistles'' RevEx 67 (1970) 444-47.

4:12f.15f HEISE, J. Bleiben (1967) 160-64.

4:12-13 MIRANDA, J. P. Marx and the Bible (1977) 223-24. VEL-LANICKAL, M., The Divine Sonship of Christians in the Johannine Writings (Rome 1977) 312-13.

4:12 BULTMANN, R. ''Analyse des ersten Johannesbriefes'' in: Festgabe für Adolf Jülicher (1927) 157-58; = in: Exegetica (1967) 121-23. MOORE. W. E. ''L John IV, 12a'' ET 65 (1953/ 54) 29-30. NAUCK, W. Die Tradition und der Charakter des ersten Johannesbriefes (1957) 75. STRAUSS, L. The Epistles of John (1962) 123-24. LAZURE, N., Les Valeurs Morales de la Théologie Johannique (Paris 1965) 236-37. WEISS, K. ''Orthodoxie und Heterodoxie im 1. Johannesbrief'' ZNW 58 (1967/ 68) 250-51. COPPENS, J. ''Miscellanées bibliques. LII. 'A-gape et 'Agapân dans les Lettres johanniques'' EphT 45 (1969) 125-27. STAGG, F. ''Orthodoxy and Orthopraxy in the Johannine Epistles'' RevEx 67 (1970) 430-31. VAN DER HORST, P. W. ''A Wordplay in Joh 4:12?'' ZNW 63 (1972) 280-82. BUEHNER, J.-A. Der Gesandte und sein Weg im 4. Evangelium (1977) 65, 220. BRAUN, F. M. ''La Réduction du Pluriel au Singulier dans l'Evangile et la Première Lettre de Jean'' NTS 24 (1977/78) 51.

4:13-16 BULTMANN, R. ''Analyse des ersten Johannesbriefes'' in: Festgabe für Adolf Jülicher (1927) 153; = in: Exegetica (1967) 118. MOODY, D. ''The Theology of the Johannine Letters'' SouJTh 13 (1970) 12-13.

4:13-14 NAUCK, W. Die Tradition und der Charakter des ersten Johannesbriefes (1957) 68-70.

4:13 SUITBERTUS, P. ''Die Vollkommenheitslehre des ersten Johannesbriefes'' Biblica 39 (1958) 456. STRAUSS, L. The Epistles of John (1962) 79. BRAUN, H. Qumran und das Neue Testament I (1966) 300-301. de la POTTERIE, I., La Vérité dans Saint Jean I/II (Rome 1977) 297-306. SCHNACKEN-BURG, R. ''Die johanneische Gemeinde und ihre Geisterfahrung'' in: R. Schnackenburg et al. (eds.) Die Kirche des Anfangs. Für Heinz Schürmann (1978) 283-87.

4:14 KILPATRICK, G. D. ''Two Johannine Idioms in the Johannine Epistles'' JThS 12 (1961) 272-73. STRAUSS, L. The Epistles of John (1962) 20-22, 83-84, 105. CARLTON, J. W.

"Preaching from the Johannine Epistles" RevEx 67 (1970) 480-83. BEUTLER, J. Martyria (1972) 283-84. BUEHNER, J.-A. Der Gesandte und sein Weg im 4. Evanglium (1977) 409, 410 n. 16, 412. TRITES, A. A., The New Testament Concept of Witness (Cambridge 1977) 124. BRAUN, F. M. "La Réduction de Pluriel as Singulier dans l'Evangile et la Première Lettre de Jean" NTS 24 (1977/78) 52.

4:15-16 SCHENKE, H. M. "Determination und Ethik im ersten Johannesbrief" ZThK 60 (1963) 206-12.

4:15 NAUCK, W. Die Tradition und der Charakter des ersten Johannesbriefes (1957) 68-70. ROBINSON, J. A. T. "The Destination and Purpose of the Johannine Epistles" NTS 7 (1960) 60. STRAUSS, L. The Epistles of John (1962) 32-33. SONGER, H. S. "The Life Situation of the Johannine Epistles" RevEx 67 (1970) 401, 402. MUELLER, U. B. Die Geschichte der Christologie in der johanneischen Gemeinde (1975) 53-57. LANGBRANDTNER, W. Weltferner Gott oder Gott der Liebe (1977) 380-82. DUNN, J. D. G. "Prophetic 'I'-Sayings and the Jesus tradition: The importance of testing prophetic utterances within early Christianity" NTS 24 (1977/78) 190.

4:16-21 FRICK, R. GPM 5 (1950/51) 139-43. STECK, K. G. GPM 10 (1955/56) 159-63. TRILLHAAS, W. "Gott ist Liebe" in: L. Schmidt (ed.) Kleine Predigt-Typologie III (1965) 52-56. TRAUB, H. in: G. Eichholz (ed.) Herr, tue meine Lippen, auf, Bd. 2 (1966⁵) 347-52. DOERNE, M. Die alten Episteln (1967) 153-57. HARBSMEIER, C. GPM 22 (1967/68) 284-89. KNUTH, H. C. und ADOLPHSEN, H., in: P. Krusche et al. (eds.) Predigtstudien für das Kirchenjahr 1979/1980. II/2 (Stuttgart 1980) 107-14. TRÖGER, K. W., in: GPM 34 (1980) 263-68.

4:16 BULTMANN, R. "Analyse des ersten Johannesbriefes" in: Festgabe für Adolf Jülicher (1927) 157-58; = in: Exegetica (1967) 121-23. NAUCK, W. Die Tradition und der Charakter des ersten Johannesbriefes (1957) 75. GREENLEE, J. H. "A Misinterpreted Nomen Sacrum in P⁹" HThR 51 (1958) 187. SUITBERTUS, P. "Die Vollkommenheitslehre des ersten Johannesbriefes" Biblica 39 (1958) 455. LAZURE, N., Les Valeurs Morales de la Théologie Johannique (Paris 1965) 237-39. BRAUN, H. Qumran und das Neue Testament 1 (1966) 301. BEHLER, G.-M. "Nous avons cru en l'amour (1 Jn 4:16)" VieS 119 (1968) 296-318. CHMIEL, J. Lumière et charité d'après la première épître de saint Jean (Diss Rome 1971). IBUKI, Y. Die Wahrheit im Johannesevangelium (1972) 311-12. DIDEBERG, D., "Esprit Saint et charité: L'exégèse augustinienne de 1 Jn 4, 8 et 16'' NRTh 97 (1975) 97-109, 229-50. LOUW, J. P. "Verbal aspects in the first Letter of John" Neotestamentica 9 (1975) 98-104. LOHSE, E., "Kirche im Alltag. Erwägungen zur theologischen Begründung der Ethik im Neuen Testament" in: D. Lührmann/G. Strecker (eds.) Kirche. FS. G. Bornkamm (Tübingen 1980) 406.

4:17-21 BULTMANN, R. "Analyse des ersten Johannesbriefes" in: Festgabe für Adolf Jülicher (1927) 153-55; = in: Exegetica (1967) 118-19.

4:17-18 STANGE, C. "Die Ueberwindung der Furcht (1 Joh. 4,17.18)" Allgemein-evangelisch-lutherische Kirchenzeitung 64 (1931) 217-19. STRAUSS, L. The Epistles of John (1962) 124-25. ROMANIUK, K. " 'Perfecta caritas foras mittit timorem' (1 Jn 4,17-18)" RBL 16 (1963) 80-87. ROMANIUK, K. " 'Die vollkommene Liebe treibt die Furcht aus.' Eine Auslegung von 1 Jo 4,17-18" BiLe 5 (1964) 80-84. LAZURE, N., Les Valeurs Morales de la Théologie Johannique (Paris 1965) 248-49, 277-78.

4:17 HARRISON, E. F., "A Key to the Understanding of First John" BiblSa 111 (1954) 39-46. NAUCK, W. Die Tradition und der Charakter des ersten Johannesbriefes (1957) 68, 71, 129-33. BULTMANN, R. "Die kirchliche Redaktion des ersten Johannesbriefes" in: Exegetica (1967) 390-91. DUPLACY, J. " 'Le Texte Occidentale' des Epîtres Catholiques" NTS 16 (1969/70) 398. MOODY, D. "The Theology of the Johannine Letters" SouJTh 13 (1970) 19-20. WARD, R. A. "The Theological Pattern of the Johannine Epistles" SouJTh 13 (1970) 33-34. HAGE, W., "Die griechische Baruch-Apokalypse" in: JüdSchr V/1 (1974) 23n. 7b. BERGMEIER, R., Glaube als Gabe nach Johannes (Stuttgart 1980) 204.

4:18 NAUCK, W. Die Tradition und der Charakter des ersten Johannesbriefes (1957) 68, 71. MOELLER, C. Von der Predigt zum Text (1970) 177-89.

4:19-5:13 O'NEILL, J. C. The Puzzle of 1 John. A New Examination of Origins (1966) 54-60.

4:19-21 STRAUSS, L. The Epistles of John (1962) 121-22.

4:19 SCHULZ, A. Nachfolgen und Nachahmen (1962) 248-51. CLARK, K. W., "The Making of the Twentieth Century New Testament" in: The Gentile Bias and other Essays (Leiden 1980) 155.

4:20-21 NAUCK, W. Die Tradition und der Charakter des ersten Johannesbriefes (1957) 73. COPPENS, J. "Miscellanées bibliques. LII. 'Agape et 'Agapân dans les Lettres johanniques" EphT 45 (1969) 125-27.

4:20 BRAUN, H. Qumran und das Neue Testament 1 (1966) 301. SONGER, H. S. "The Life Situation of the Johannine Epistles" RevEx 67 (1970) 401. STAGG, F. "Orthodoxy and Orthopraxy in the Johannine Epistles" RevEx 67 (1970) 427, 430. de la POTTERIE, I., La Vérité dans Saint Jean I/II (Rome 1977) 943-49.

4:21 BRAUN, H. "Literar-Analyse und theologische Schichtung im ersten Johannesbrief" in: Gesammelte Studien zum Neuen Testament und seiner Umwelt (1962) 220-26. DAVIES, W. D. The Sermon on the Mount (1966) 117-18. SANDERS, J. T., Ethics in the New Testament (Philadelphia 1975) 93ff.

_____

5 THOMPSON, P. J. "Psalm 119: a possible Clue to the Structure of the First Epistle of John" in: F. L. Cross (ed.) Studia Evangelica 2 (1964) 489, 491.

5:1-6 de la POTTERIE, I. "Le croyant qui vaincu le monde" AssS 23 (1971) 34-43.

5:1-5 BORNKAMM, G. GPM 5 (1950/51) 105-108. BINDER, H. GPM 16 (1961/62) 171-75. MAURER, C. in: G. Eichholz (ed.) Herr, tue meine Lippen auf, Bd. 2 (1966⁵) 269-76. DOERNE, M. Die alten Episteln (1967) 115-18. KLEIN, G. GPM 22 (1967/68) 205-12. KITTLER, R. "Erweis der Bruderliebe an der Bruderliebe?! Versuch der Auslegung eines 'fast unverständlichen' Satzes im 1. Johannesbrief" KuD 16 (1970) 223-28.

5:1-4 VELLANICKAL, M., The Divine Sonship of Christians in the Johannine Writings (Rome 1977) 317-30. SCHRÖER, H., in: GPM 34 (1980) 206-12. THEURICH, H., und SCHRÖER, H., in: P. Krusche et al. (eds.) Predigtstudien für das Kirchenjahr 1979/1980. II/2 (Stuttgart 1980) 51-58.

5:1-3 COPPENS, J. "Miscellanées bibliques. LII. 'Agape et 'Agapân dans les Lettres johanniques" EphT 45 (1969) 125-27.

5:1-2 SONGER, H. S. "The Life Situation of the Johannine Epistles" RevEx 67 (1970) 402. DELLING, G. "Die 'Söhne (Kinder) Gottes' im Neuen Testament" in: R. Schnackenburg et al. (eds.) Die Kirche des Anfangs. Für Heinz Schürmann (1978) 628.

5:1 BULTMANN, R. "Analyse des ersten Johannesbriefes" in: Festgabe für Adolf Jülicher (1927) 157-58; = in: Exegetica (1967) 121-23. NAUCK, W. Die Tradition und der Charakter des ersten Johannesbriefes (1957) 75. SUITBERTUS, P. "Die Vollkommenheitslehre des ersten Johannesbriefes" Biblica 39 (1958) 457-62. ROBINSON, J. A. T. "The Destination and Purpose of the Johannine Epistles" NTS 7 (1960) 60. BRAUN, H. "Literar-Analyse und theologische Schichtung im ersten Johannesbrief" in: Gesammelte Studien zum Neuen Testament und seiner Umwelt (1962) 227-31. STRAUSS, L. The Epistles of John (1962) 20, 22-27, 32-33, 118. SHIMADA, K. The Formulary Material in First Peter (Th.D. Diss, Union Theological Seminary New York 1966) 186-91, 196-98. MUELLER, U. B. Die Geschichte der Christologie in der johanneischen Gemeinde (1975) 53-57. DUNN, J. D. G. Unity and Diversity in the New Testament (1977) 44-45. LANGBRANDTNER, W. Weltferner Gott oder Gott der Liebe (1977) 380-82. BRAUN, F. M. "La Réduction du Pluriel au Singulier dans l'Evangile et la Première Lettre de Jean" NTS 24 (1977/78) 58. DUNN, J. D. G. "Prophetic 'I'-Sayings and the Jesus tradition: The importance of testing prophetic utterances within early Christianity" NTS 24 (1977/78) 190. HOFRICHTER, P., Nicht aus Blut sondern monogen aus Gott geboren (Würzburg 1978) 60-67. RUDOLPH, K. Die Gnosis (1978) 324-27. BERGMEIER, R., Glaube als Gabe nach Johannes (Stuttgart 1980) 213.

5:2-3 BRAUN, H. "Literar-Analyse und theologische Schichtung im ersten Johannesbrief" in: Gesammelte Studien zum Neuen Testament und seiner Umwelt (1962) 220-26. BRAUN, F. M. "La Réduction du Pluriel au Singulier dans l'Evangile et la Première Lettre de Jean" NTS 24 (1977/78) 49, 51. DUNN, J. D. G. "Prophetic 'I'-Sayings and the Jesus tradition: The importance of testing prophetic utterances within early Christianity" NTS 24 (1977/78) 190.

5:2 SALOM, A. P. "Some aspects of the grammatical style of 1 John" JBL 74 (1955) 101. NAUCK, W. Die Tradition und der Charakter des ersten Johannesbriefes (1957) 68-70. WEISS, K. "Orthodoxie und Heterodoxie im 1. Johannesbriefe" ZNW 58 (1967/68) 251-53. KITTLER, R., "Erweis der Bruderliebe an der Bruderliebe? Versuch der Auslegung eines 'fast unverständlichen' Satzes im 1. Johannesbrief" KuD 16 (1970) 223-28. HERRMANN, T., "Proby nowej interpretacji 1 J 5, 2" RBL 28 (1975) 229-30.

5:3 NAUCK, W. Die Tradition und der Charakter des ersten Johannesbriefes (1957) 68-70. LAZURE, N., Les Valeurs Morales de la Théologie Johannique (Paris 1965) 134-37. GEORGI, D., "Weisheit Salomos" in: JüdSchr III/4 (1980) 6n. 18a.

5:4-12 DENNEY, J., "He That Came by Water and Blood" The Expositor VII/5 (1908) 416-428. WINTERBOTHAM, R., "The Spirit and the Water and the Blood" The Expositor VIII/2 (1911) 62-71. de la POTTERIE, I., "La notion de témoignage dans Saint Jean" Sacra Pagina 2 (Louvain 1959) 193-208. RICHTER, G., "Blut und Wasser aus der durchbohrten Seite Jesu (1 Joh. 19, 34b)" MThZ 21 (1970) 1-21.

5:4-10 OGARA, F. "Quis est qui vincit mundum, nisi qui credit quoniam Jesus est Filius Dei?" VD 18 (1938) 97-103. TRAUB, H. GPM 10 (1955/56) 111-15.

5:4-5 STRAUSS, L. The Epistles of John (1962) 20, 22-27, 91. CLARK, S. B., Man and Woman in Christ (Ann Arbor, Mich. 1980) 276.

5:4 BULTMANN, R. "Analyse des ersten Johannesbriefes" in: Festgabe für Adolf Jülicher (1927) 157-58; = in: Exegetica (1967) 121-23. NAUCK, W. Die Tradition und der Charakter des ersten Johannesbriefes (1957) 75. BRAUN, H. "Literar-Analyse und theologische Schichtung im ersten Johannesbriefe" in: Gesammelte Studien zum Neuen Testament und seiner Umwelt (1962) 227-31. FILSON, F. V. "First John: Purpose and Message" Interp 23 (1969) 274-75. VELLANICKAL, M., The Divine Sonship of Christians in the Johannine Writings (Rome 1977) 272. HOFRICHTER, P., Nicht aus Blut sondern monogen aus Gott geboren (Würzburg 1978) 60-67.

5:5-21 BULTMANN, R. "Analyse des ersten Johannesbriefes" in: Festgabe für Adolf Jülicher (1927) 155-57; = in: Exegetica (1967) 120.

5:5-17 GIURISATO, G. "Struttura della prima lettera di Giovanni" RivB 21 (1973) 361-81.

5:5-12 BRONX, N. Zeuge und Märtyrer (1961) 86-90.

5:5-8 GRIFFITHS, D. R. "Baptism in the Fourth Gospel and the First Epistle of John" in: A. Gilmore (ed.) Christian Baptism (1959) 167-69. LANGBRANDTNER, W. Weltferner Gott oder Gott der Liebe (1977) 380-82. RUDOLPH, K. Die Gnosis (1978) 324-27.

5:5-6 MUELLER, U. B. Die Geschichte der Christologie in der johanneischen Gemeinde (1975) 58-59.

5:5 ROBINSON, J. A. T. "The Destination and Purpose of the Johannine Epistles" NTS 7 (1960) 60.

5:6ff CLEMEN, C. Primitive Christianity and Its Non-Jewish Sources
(1912) 227-28. DUNN, J. D. G. "Prophetic 'I'-Sayings and the
Jesus tradition: The importance of testing prophetic utterances
within early Christianity" NTS 24 (1977/78) 190.

5:6-13 KEPPLER, P. W., "Geist, Wasser und Blut. Zur Erklärung von
1 Joh. 5, 6-13 (ev. Joh. 19, 34)" ThQ 68 (1886) 3-25.

5:6-12 DUNN, J. D. G. Baptism in the Holy Spirit (1970) 200-204.
DRUMWRIGHT, H. "Problem Passages in the Johannine
Epistles: A Hermeneutical Approach" SouJTh 13 (1970) 60-62.
MOODY, D. "The Theology of the Johannine Letters" SouJTh
13 (1970) 12-13. BEUTLER, J. Martyria (1972) 276-81.
TRITES, A. A., The New Testament Concept of Witness
(Cambridge 1977) 126-27.

5:6-10 DUNN, J. D. G. Jesus and the Spirit (1975) 353.

5:6-8 MANSON, T. W., "Entry into Membership of the Early
Church" JThS 48 (1947) 25-32. BRAUN, F. M. "L'eau et
l'Esprit" RThom 49 (1949) 5-30. BARTH, M. Die Taufe—ein
Sakrament? (1951) 395ff. BROOKS, O. S., "The Johannine
Eucharist. Another Interpretation" JBL 82 (1963) 293-300.
DELLING, G. Die Taufe im Neuen Testament (1963) 95-96.
SCHWEIZER, E. "Das johanneische Zeugnis vom Herrenmahl" in: Neotestamentica (1963) 375-79. LAZURE, N., Les
Valeurs Morales de la Théologie Johannique (Paris 1965) 111-
13. BIEDER, W. Die Verheissung der Taufe im Neuen Testament (1966) 274-75. BRAUN, F. M. Jean le Théologien (1966)
169-70. BRAUN, H. Qumran und das Neue Testament 1 (1966)
301-302. LE FORT, P. Les Structures de l'Eglise militante selon Saint Jean (1970) 65-71. STAGG, F. "Orthodoxy and Orthopraxy in the Johannine Epistles" RevEx 67 (1970) 427.
THUESING, W. Die Erhöhung und Verherrlichung Jesu im
Johannesevangelium (1970) 165-74. MIGUENS, M. "Tres
testigos: Espíritu, agua, sangre" Studii biblici Franciscani liber
Annuus 22 (1972) 74-94. PORSCH, F., Pneuma und Wort
(Frankfurt 1974) 334-37. HEIN, K. Eucharist and Excommunication (1975) 165-71. MOULE, C. F. D., The Holy Spirit
(London 1978) 80-81. "Blut" in: TRE 6 (1980) 736.

5:6.8 CALMET, A. "Le témoignage de l'eau, du sang, de l'Esprit.
1 Jean 5,6.8" BVieC 53 (1963) 35-36.

5:6-7 SCHELKLE, K. H. Die Passion Jesu in der Verkündigung des
Neuen Testaments (1949) 184-85. DENNEY, J. The Death of
Christ (1956³) 151ff. "Abendmahl" in: TRE 1 (1977) 74.

5:6 ROBINSON, J. A. T. "The Destination and Purpose of the Johannine Epistles" NTS 7 (1960) 62; = in: Twelve New Testament Studies (1962) 134-36. SKRINJAR, A. "Errores in

epistola I Jo impugnati" VD 41 (1963) 60-72. LAZURE, N., Les Valeurs Morales de la Théologie Johannique (Paris 1965) 81-84. HORNER, J. "Introduction to the Johannine Epistles" SouJTh 13 (1970) 45-46. PORSCH, F., Pneuma und Wort (Frankfurt 1974) 233-36. de la POTTERIE, I., La Vérité dans Saint Jean I/II (Rome 1977) 310-28, 466-71.

5:7-8 WINDISCH, H. "Comma Johanneum" in: Die Katholischen Briefe (1930) 133. GREIFF, A. "Die drei Zeugen in 1 Joh. 5:7f" ThQ 114 (1933) 465-80. JENKINS, C. "A newly discovered reference to the 'heavenly witnesses' in a manuscript of Bede" JThS 43 (1942) 42-45. DEL ALAMO, M. "El Comma Joaneo" EstBi 2 (1943) 75-105. AYUSOMARAZUELA, T. "Neuvo estudio sobre el Comma Johanneum" Biblica 28 (1947) 83-112, 216-35; 29 (1948) 52-76. NAUCK, W. Die Tradition und der Charakter des ersten Johannesbriefes (1957) 147-82. THIELE, W. "Beobachtungen zum Comma Iohanneum (1 Joh 5:7f)" ZNW 50 (1959) 61-73. HIEBERT, D. E. An Introduction to the Non-Pauline Epistles (1962) 217-18. KUEMMEL, W. G. Einleitung in das Neue Testament (1973[17]) 388. "Abendmahl" in: TRE 1 (1977) 58. JAUBERT, A., "O Espirito, e Agua, e o Sangue (1 Jo 5,7-8)" in: S.Voigt/F.Vier (eds.) Actualidades Biblicas. FS. J. Padreira de Castro (Petropolis, Brazil 1971) 616-20. "Bibel" in: TRE 6 (1980) 75. de JONGE, H. J. "Erasmus and the Comma Johanneum" EphT 56 (1980) 381-89. ALAND, K., et al., Der Text des Neuen Testaments (Stuttgart 1982) 313-14. "Einleitungswissenschaft" in: TRE 9 (1982) 470.

5:7 DE JONGE, M. "Declaratio circa decretum 1 Jo. 5,7" Collationes Brugenses 27 (1927) 452-55. HARNACK, A. von, Studien zur Geschichte des Neuen Testaments und der Alten Kirche (1931) 151-52. KRETZMANN, P. E. "Das Comma Johanneum, 1 Joh. 5,7" CThM 4 (1933) 349-54. DEL ALAMO, M. "Los 'Tres testificantes' de la primera Epistola de S. Juan, V,7" Cultura Biblica 4 (1947) 11-14. STRAUSS, L. The Epistles of John (1962) 20-22, 32-33. JANSSEN, E. "Testament Abrahams" in: W. G. Kümmel (ed.) Jüdische Schriften aus hellenistisch-römischer Zeit, Bd.III: Unterweisung in lehrhafter Form (1975) 235.

5:8-9 DUPLACY, J. " 'Le Texte Occidentale' des Epîtres Catholiques" NTS 16 (1969/70) 398.

5:9-13 RONGY, H. "La notion de témoignage chez S. Jean" Revue Ecclesiastique Liége 29 (1937) 34-39. DUPONT, J. Essais sur la Christologie de Saint Jean (1951) 218-21. HARBSMEIER, G. GPM 24 (1969/70) 75-82. HOWALD, M. und NEID-

HART, W., in: P.Krusche et al. (eds.) Predigtstudien für das Kirchenjahr 1975/1976. IV/1 (Stuttgart 1975) 91-97.

5:9 NAUCK, W. Die Tradition und der Charakter des ersten Johannesbriefes (1957) 72.

5:10-12 BULTMANN, R. ''Analyse des ersten Johannesbriefes'' in: Festgabe für Adolf Jülicher (1927) 157-58; = in: Exegetica (1967) 121-23. STRAUSS, L. The Epistles of John (1962) 32-33.

5:10 BULTMANN, R. ''Analyse des ersten Johannesbriefes'' in: Festgabe für Adolf Jülicher (1927) 156, 157-58; = in: Exegetica (1967) 120, 121-23. NAUCK, W. Die Tradition und der Charakter des ersten Johannesbriefes (1957) 76-77, 86-88. STRAUSS, L. The Epistles of John (1962) 79.

5:11-13 STECK, K. G. GPM 12 (1957/58) 47-52. HAAR, J. GPM 18 (1963/64) 75-79. VOIGT, G. Der zerrissene Vorhang I (1969) 76-82. STECK, K. G. GPM 30 (1975/76) 74-81.

5:11-12 MOODY, D. ''The Theology of the Johannine Letters'' SouJTh 13 (1970) 9. de la POTTERIE, I., La Vérité dans Saint Jean I/II (Rome 1977) 311-15.

5:11 NAUCK, W. Die Tradition und der Charakter des ersten Johannesbriefes (1957) 68-70.

5:12 BULTMANN, R. ''Analyse des ersten Johannesbriefes'' in: Festgabe für Adolf Jülicher (1927) 156, 157-58; = in: Exegetica (1967) 121-23. NAUCK, W. Die Tradition und der Charakter des ersten Johannesbriefes (1957) 76-77.

5:13-21 BAUERFEIND, O., ''Die Fürbitte angesichts der 'Sünde zum Tode' '' in: Von der Antike zum Christentum. FS. V. Schultze (Stettin 1931) 43-54. O'NEILL, J. C. The Puzzle of 1 John (1966) 61-64. BRIGGS, R. C. ''Contemporary Study of the Johannine Epistles'' RevEx 67 (1970) 415. FRANCIS, F. O., ''The Form and Function of the Opening and Closing Paragraphs of James and 1 John'' ZNW 61 (1970) 110-26. JONES, P. R. ''A Structural Analysis of 1 John'' RevEx 67 (1970) 444. FEUILLET, A. ''Etude structurale de la première épître de saint Jean'' in: H. Baltensweiler and B. Reicke (eds.) Neues Testament und Geschichte. Oscar Cullmann zum 70. Geburtstag (1972) 322-25. REYNOLDS, S. M., ''The Sin unto Death and Prayers for the Dead'' Reformation Review 20 (1973) 130-39.

5:13 ROBINSON, J. A. T. ''The Destination and Purpose of the Johannine Epistles'' NTS 7 (1960) 56. STRAUSS, L. The Epistles of John (1962) 74-78. THOMPSON, P. J. ''Psalm 119: a possible Clue to the Structure of the First Epistle of John'' in:

F. L. Cross (ed.) Studia Evangelica 2 (1964) 487-89. BULT-
MANN, R. "Die kirchliche Redaktion des ersten Johannes-
briefes" in: Exegetica (1967) 382-83. HORNER, J.
"Introduction to the Johannine Epistles" SouJTh 13 (1970) 47.
SONGER, H. S. "The Life Situation of the Johannine Epis-
tles" RevEx 67 (1970) 400. FEUILLET, A. "The Structure of
First John. Comparison with the 4th Gospel. The Pattern of
Christian Life" BThB 3 (1973) 194-216.

5:14-21 NAUCK, W. Die Tradition und der Charakter des ersten Johannesbriefes (1957) 133-46. BULTMANN, R. "Die kirchliche Redaktion des ersten Johannesbriefes" in: Exegetica (1967)
382-88. JONES, P. R. "A Structural Analysis of 1 John" RevEx
67 (1970) 458-59. FEUILLET, A. "The Structure of First John.
Comparison with the 4th Gospel. The Pattern of Christian Life"
BThB 3 (1973) 194-216. KUEMMEL, W. G. Einleitung in das
Neue Testament (1973[17]) 388.

5:14-17 MOODY, D. "The Theology of the Johannine Letters" SouJTh
13 (1970) 15.

5:16ff DAMMERS, A. H. "Hard Sayings—II. I John 5,16ff" Theology 66 (1963) 370-72.

5:16-18 STRAUSS, L. The Epistles of John (1962) 43-50, 53-56.
DRUMWRIGHT, H. "Problem Passages in the Johannine
Epistles: A Hermeneutical Approach" SouJTh 13 (1970) 56-58.
BERGMEIER, R., Glaube als Gabe nach Johannes (Stuttgart
1980) 109n.

5:16-17 HARNACK, A. von, Studien zur Geschichte des Neuen Tes-
taments und der Alten Kirche (1931) 143-49. NAUCK, W. Die
Tradition und der Charakter des ersten Johannesbriefes (1957)
141-46. TOWNSEND, J. "The Sin unto Death" RestQ 6 (1962)
147-50. LAZURE, N., Les Valeurs Morales de la Théologie
Johannique (Paris 1965) 310-14. FILSON, F. V. "First John:
Purpose and Meaning" Interp 23 (1969) 273. SONGER, H. S.
"The Life Situation of the Johannine Epistles" RevEx 67 (1970)
406-407. TRUDINGER, P. "Concerning Sins, Mortal and
Otherwise. A Note on 1 John 5,16-17" Biblica 52 (1972) 541-
42. SCHOLER, D. M. "Sin within and sins without: An Interpretation of 1 John 5:16-17" in: G. F. Hawthorne (ed.) Current
Issues in Biblical and Patristic Interpretation. Studies in Honor
of Merrill C. Tenney (1975) 230-46.

5:16 BUJANDA, J. "El 'peccatum ad mortem' interpretado por el
Card. Toledo" Archivo Teológico Granadino 3 (1940) 69-84.
HERKENRATH, J. "Sünde zum Tode (1 Jo 5,16)" in: Fest-
schrift F. Tillmann (1950) 119-38. BROWN, R. E. "The Qum-

ran Scrolls and the Johannine Gospel and Epistles CBQ 17 (1955) 403-19, 559-74; = in: K. Stendahl (ed.) The Scrolls and the New Testament (1957) 201; GT: "Die Schriftrollen von Qumran und das Johannesevangelium und die Johannesbriefe" in: K. H. Rengstorf (ed.) Johannes und sein Evangelium (1973) 517. WENNEMER, K. "Der Christ und die Sünde nach der Lehre des ersten Johannesbriefes" GuL 33 (1960) 370-76. BRAUN, H. Qumran und das Neue Testament 1 (1966) 302-304. LYONNET, S., "The Notion of Sin in the Johannine Writings" in: S. Lyonnet/L. Sabourin, Sin, Redemption and Sacrifice (Rome 1970) 38-45. COOPER, E. J. "The Consciousness of Sin in 1 John" LThPh 28 (1972) 237-48. MIG-UENS, M., "Sin, Prayer, Life in 1 Jn 5,16" in: Studie Hierosolymitana. FS. B. Bagatti II (Jerusalem 1976) 64-82. FRIEDRICH, G. "Die Fürbitte im Neuen Testament" in: Auf das Wort kommt es an (1978) 450. HERRMANN, T., "Grzech, ktory sprowadza smierc; 1 J 5,16 (Le péché qui porte la morte; 1 Jean 5,16)" RBL 32 (1979) 115-24. "Busse" in: TRE 7 (1981) 457.

5:17 LAZURE, N., Les Valeurs Morales de la Théologie Johannique (Paris 1965) 309-10.

5:18-21 HARNACK, A. von, Studien zur Geschichte des Neuen Testaments und der Alten Kirche (1931) 109-111. GIURISATO, G. "Struttura della prima lettera di Giovanni" RivB 21 (1973) 361-81. MALATESTA, E. "Covenant and Indwelling" Way 17 (1977) 23-32.

5:18-20 SEGOND, A. "1re Epître de Jean, chap. 5:18-20" RHPR 45 (1965) 349-51. VELLANICKAL, M., The Divine Sonship of Christians in the Johannine Writings (Rome 1977) 276-86.

5:18-19 BERGMEIER, R., Glaube als Gabe nach Johannes (Stuttgart 1980) 213-14.

5:18 HARNACK, A. von, Studien zur Geschichte des Neuen Testaments und der Alten Kirche (1931) 105-15. WENNEMER, K. "Der Christ und die Sünde nach der Lehre des ersten Johannesbriefes" GuL 33 (1960) 370-76. BRAUN, H. "Literar-Analyse und theologische Schichtung im ersten Johannesbrief" in: Gesammelte Studien zum Neuen Testament und seiner Umwelt (1962) 227-31. LANGBRANDTNER, W. Weltferner Gott oder gott der Liebe (1977) 386-87. VELLANICKAL, M., The Divine Sonship of Christians in the Johannine Writings (Rome 1977) 276-78. BRAUN, F. M. "La Réduction du Pluriel au Singulier dans l'Evangile et la Première Lettre de Jean" NTS 24 (1977/78) 55. DUNN, J. D. G. "Prophetic 'I'-Sayings and the Jesus tradition: The importance of testing prophetic utterances within early Christianity" NTS 24 (1977/78) 190. HOFRICHTER, P., Nicht aus Blut sondern monogen aus Gott geboren (Würzburg 1978) 60-67. JEWETT, P. K., Infant Baptism and the Covenant of Grace (Grand Rapids 1978) 34.

5:19 MUSSNER, F. ZΩH. Die Anschauung vom "Leben" im vierten Evangelium (1952) 66. SALOM, A. P. "Some aspects of the grammatical style of 1 John" JBL 74 (1955) 97. JOHNSTON, G. "The will of God in 1 Peter and 1 John" ET 72 (1960/61) 237, 238-39. STRAUSS, L. The Epistles of John (1962) 85. BRAUN, H. Qumran und das Neue Testament 1 (1966) 304. CARLTON, J. W. "Preaching from the Johannine Epistles" RevEx 67 (1970) 477-83. BOISMARD, M.-E. "The First Epistle of John and the Writings of Qumran" in: J. H. Charlesworth (ed.) John and Qumran (1972) 158-59. "Böse" in: TRE 7 (1981) 9.

5:20 HARNACK, A. von, Studien zur Geschichte des Neuen Testaments und der Alten Kirche (1931) 149-51. DUPONT, J. Essais sur la Christologie de Saint Jean (1951) 222-25. KILPATRICK, G. D. "Two Johannine Idioms in the Johannine Epistles" JThS 12 (1961) 272. STRAUSS, L. The Epistles of John (1962) 32-33. CARDER, M. M. "A Caesarean Text in the Catholic Epistles?" NTS 16 (1969/70) 257. DUPLACY, J. " 'Le Texte Occidentale' des Epîtres Catholiques" NTS 16 (1969/70) 398.

5:21 STRAUSS, L. The Epistles of John (1962) 20-22. LAZURE, N., Les Valeurs Morales de la Théologie Johannique (Paris 1965) 314-17. BRAUN, H., Qumran und das Neue Testament I (1966) 304. BOISMARD, M.-E., "The First Epistle of John and the Writings of Qumran" in: J. H. Charlesworth (ed.) John and Qumran (1972) 161. SKA, J.-L., " 'Petits enfants, prenez garde aux idoles' 1 Jn 5, 21" NRTh 101 (1979) 860-74.

2 John

ΙΩΑΝΝΟΥ Β

1-13 RAMSAY, W. M., "Note on the Date of Second John" The Expositor VI/3 (1901) 354-56. GIBBINS, H. J., "The Second Epistle of St. John" The Expositor VI/6 (1902) 228-36. CHAPMAN, J., "The Historical Setting of the Second and Third Epistles of St. John" JThS 5 (1904) 357-68, 517-34. BARTLET, V., "The Historical Setting of the Second and Third Epistles of St. John" JThS 6 (1905) 204-16. GIBBINS, H. J., "The Problem of the Second Epistle of St. John" The Expositor VI/12 (1905) 412-24. BRESKY, B., Das Verhältnis des zweiten Johannesbriefes zum Dritten (Münster 1906) passim. BAUER, W. Die Katholischen Briefe (1910) 60-64. SCHEPENS, P., " 'Johannes in epistula sua' (Saint Cyprien, passim)" RechSR 11 (1921) 87-89. MARTY, J., "Contribution à l'ètude des problémes johannique: Les petites êpitres 'II et III Jean' " RHR 91 (1925) 200-11. KÄSEMANN, E., "Ketzer und Zeuge: Zum johanneischen Verfasserproblem" ZThK 48 (1951) 292-311. HIEBERT, D. E. An Introduction to the Non-Pauline Epistles (1962) 222-40. FUNK, R. W., "The Form and Structure of II and III John" JBL 86 (1967) 424-30. LE FORT, P. Les Structures de L'Eglise militante selon Saint Jean (1970). SELBY, D. J. Introduction to the New Testament (1971) 449-50. GRAU, J. El amor y la veridad. El mensaje de la segunda carta de Juan (1973). VIELHAUER, P. Geschichte der urchristlichen Literatur (1975) 475-81. LANGBRANDTNER, W., Weltferner Gott oder Gott der Liebe (Frankfurt a.M./Bern/ Las Vegas 1977) 382, 400-404. van UNNIK, W. C., "The Authority of the Presbyters in Iranaeus' Works" in: J. Jervell/W. A. Meeks (eds.) God's Christ and His People. FS. N. A. Dahl (Oslo 1977) 248-60.

1-3 POLHILL, J. B. "An Analysis of 2 and 3 John" RevEx 67 (1970) 462-64. HANSON, A. T., The New Testament Interpretation of Scripture (London 1980) 101-102.

1-2 STRAUSS, L. The Epistles of John (1962) 147-48. BERGMEIER, R. "Zum Verfasserproblem des II und III Johannesbriefes" ZNW 57 (1966/67) 98, 99. LANDBRANDTNER, W. Weltferner Gott oder Gott der Liebe. Der Ketzerstreit in der johanneischen Kirche (1977) 401.

1 BACON, B. W., "Marcion, Papias and 'The Elders' " JThS 23 (1922) 134-60. WENDT, H. H. "Zum zweiten und dritten Johannesbrief" ZNW 23 (1924) 19. DOELGER, F. J. "Domina Mater Ecclesia und die 'Herrin' im 2. Johannesbrief" Antike und Christentum 5 (1936) 211-17. MUNCK, J., "Presbyters and Disciples of the Lord in Papias" HThR 52 (1959) 223-43. HIEBERT, D. E. An Introduction to the Non-Pauline Epistles

(1962) 231-34. STRAUSS, L. The Epistles of John (1962) 146-47. BERGMEIER, R. "Zum Verfasserproblem des II und III Johannesbriefes" ZNW 57 (1966/67) 97-98. SCHNACKEN-BURG, R. "Zum Begriff der 'Wahrheit' in den beiden kleinen Johannesbriefen" BZ 11 (1967) 255. BRIGGS, R. C. "Contemporary Study of the Johannine Epistles" RevEx 67 (1970) 416-18. DRUMWRIGHT, H. "Problem Passages in the Johannine Epistles: A Hermeneutical Approach" SouJTh 13 (1970) 62-63. LE FORT, P. Les Structures de L'Eglise militante selon Saint Jean (1970) 54-58. de la POTTERIE, I., La Vérité dans Saint Jean I/II (Rome 1977) 539-52, 657-63. SCHNACKEN-BURG, R. "Die johanneische Gemeinde und ihre Geisterfahrung" in: R. Schnackenburg et al. (eds.) Die Kirche des Anfangs. Für Heinz Schürmann (1978) 281. STAGG, E. and F. Woman in the World of Jesus (1978) 242. PRAST, F., Presbyter und Evangelium in nachapostolischer Zeit (Stuttgart 1979) 417n. 175. BERGMEIER, R., Glaube als Gabe nach Johannes (Stuttgart 1980) 201-202.

2-3 BERGMEIER, R., Glaube als Gabe nach Johannes (Stuttgart 1980) 200-201, 238n. 24.

2 BERGMEIER, R. "Zum Verfasserproblem des II und III Johannesbriefes" ZNW 57 (1966/67) 97. HEISE, J. Bleiben (1967) 164-70. SCHNACKENBURG, R. "Zum Begriff der 'Wahrheit' in den beiden kleinen Johannesbriefen" BZ 11 (1967) 258.

3 STRAUSS, L. The Epistles of John (1962) 148-49. BERG-MEIER, R. "Zum Verfasserproblem des II und III Johannesbriefes" ZNW 57 (1966/67) 98. SCHNACKENBURG, R. "Zum Begriff der 'Wahrheit' in den beiden kleinen Johannesbriefen" BZ 11 (1967) 258. "Amt" in: TRE 2 (1978) 517. "Barmherzigkeit" in: TRE 5 (1980) 226. "Benediktionen" in: TRE 5 (1980) 563. BERGMEIER, R., Glaube als Gabe nach Johannes (Stuttgart 1980) 200.

4-7 BERGMEIER, R. "Zum Verfasserproblem des II und III Johannesbriefes," ZNW 57 (1966/67) 96.

4-6 MOODY, D. "The Theology of the Johannine Letters" SouJTh 13 (1970) 18. POLHILL, J. B. "An Analysis of 2 and 3 John" RevEx 67 (1970) 464. LANGBRANDTNER, W. Weltferner Gott oder Gott der Liebe. Der Ketzerstreit in der johanneischen Kirche (1977) 400-401.

4 WENDT, H. H. "Zum zweiten und dritten Johannesbrief" ZNW 23 (1924) 20. BROWN, R. E. "The Qumran Scrolls and the Johannine Gospel and Epistles" CBQ 17 (1955) 403-19, 559-

74; = in: K. Stendahl (ed.) The Scrolls and the New Testament (1957) 196; GT: "Die Schriftrollen von Qumran und das Johannesevangelium und die Johannesbriefe" in: K. H. Rengstorf (ed.) Johannes und sein Evangelium (1973) 510. STRAUSS, L. The Epistles of John (1962) 149-50. BRAUN, H. Qumran und das Neue Testament 1 (1966) 306. BERGMEIER, R. "Zum Verfasserproblem des II und III Johannesbriefes" ZNW 57 (1966/67) 96. SCHNACKENBURG, R. "Zum Begriff der 'Wahrheit' in den beiden kleinen Johannesbriefen" BZ 11 (1967) 254-55, 258. DRUMWRIGHT, H. "Problem Passages in the Johannine Epistles: A Hermeneutical Approach" SouJTh 13 (1970) 62-63. HORNER, J. "Introduction to the Johannine Epistles" SouJTh 13 (1970) 50. de la POTTERIE, I., La Vérité dans Saint Jean I/II (Rome 1977) 646-57.

5-6 WENDT, H. H. "Zum zweiten und dritten Johannesbrief" ZNW 23 (1924) 20-21. DUNN, J. D. G. "Prophetic 'I'-Sayings and the Jesus Tradition: The importance of testing prophetic utterances within early Christianity" NTS 24 (1977/78) 190.

5 STRAUSS, L. The Epistles of John (1962) 150-51. CARDER, M. M. "A Caesarean Text in the Catholic Epistles?" NTS 16 (1969/70) 257. SANDERS, J. T., Ethics in the New Testament (Philadelphia 1975) 91-94. BRAUN, F. M. "La Réduction du Pluriel au Singulier dans l'Evangile et la Première lettre de Jean" NTS 24 (1977/78) 49. STAGG, E. and F. Woman in the World of Jesus (1978) 242.

6 STRAUSS, L. The Epistles of John (1962) 151-52.

7-11 FILSON, F. V. "First John: Purpose and Message" Interp 23 (1969) 266. de la POTTERIE, I., La Vérité dans Saint Jean I/II (Rome 1977) 511-12. LANDBRANDTNER, W. Weltferner Gott oder Gott der Liebe. Der Ketzerstreit in der johanneischen Kirche (1977) 282.

7-9 POLHILL, J. B. "An Analysis of 2 and 3 John" RevEx 67 (1970) 464-65.

7-8 DRUMWRIGHT, H. "Problem Pasages in the Johannine Epistles: A Hermeneutical Approach," SouJTh 13 (1970) 58-60. BERGMEIER, R., Glaube als Gabe nach Johannes (Stuttgart 1980) 202-203.

7 WENDT, H. H. "Zum zweiten und dritten Johannesbrief" ZNW 23 (1924) 20, 21. BOUSSET, W. Die Religion des Judentums im späthellenistische Zeitalter (1926 = 1966) 254-56. RUCKSTUHL, E. Die litterarische Einheit des Johannesevangeliums (1951) 227-35. SERAFIN de AUSEJO, "El con-

cepto de 'carne' aplicado a Cristo en el IV Evangelio" EstBi 17 (1958) 416-20. STRAUSS, L. The Epistles of John (1962) 152. HENNECKE, E. and SCHNEEMELCHER, W. Neutestamentliche Apokryphen 2 (1964) 473; ET: New Testament Apocrypha 2 (1975) 669. BRIGGS, R. C. "Contemporary Study of the Johannine Epistles" RevEx 67 (1970) 418, 419. HORNER, J. "Introduction to the Johannine Epistles" SouJTh 13 (1970) 44-45, 51. MOODY, D. "The Theology of the Johannine Letters" SouJTh 13 (1970) 19. STAGG, F. "Orthodoxy and Orthopraxy in the Johannine Epistles" RevEx 67 (1970) 427. BRAUN, F. M. "La Réduction du Pluriel au Singulier dans l'Evangile et la Première lettre de Jean" NTS 24 (1977/78) 58-59. "Antichrist" in: TRE 3 (1978) 22. "Apokalyptik" in: TRE 3 (1978) 253.

8-9 SCHENKE, H. M. "Determination und Ethik im ersten Johannesbrief" ZThK 60 (1963) 206-15.

8 WENDT, H. H. "Zum zweiten und dritten Johannesbrief" ZNW 23 (1924) 24. STRAUSS, L. The Epistles of John (1962) 152-53. ROBINSON, J. A. T. "The Destination and Purpose of the Johannine Epistles" NTS 7 (1960) 58.

9-10 WENDT, H. H. "Zum zweiten und dritten Johannesbrief" ZNW 23 (1924) 22-23. SCHNACKENBURG, R. "Zum Begriff der 'Wahrheit' in den beiden kleinen Johannesbriefen" BZ 11 (1967) 253-54. DUNN, J. D. G. "Prophetic 'I'-Sayings and the Jesus Tradition: The importance of testing prophetic utterances within early Christianity" NTS 24 (1977/78) 190. BERGMEIER, R., Glaube als Gabe nach Johannes (Stuttgart 1980) 201-202, 239n. 54.

9 BULTMANN, R. "Analyse des ersten Johannesbriefes" in: Festgabe für Adolf Jülicher (1927) 157-58; = in: Exegetica (1967) 121-23. STRAUSS, L. The Epistles of John (1962) 153-54. ROBINSON, J. A. T. "The Destination and Purpose of the Johannine Epistles," NTS 7 (1960) 60. BERGMEIER, R. "Zum Verfasserproblem des 2 und 3 Johannesbriefes" ZNW 57 (1966/67) 96. HEISE, J. Bleiben (1967) 164-70. BERGMEIER, R., Glaube als Gabe nach Johannes (Stuttgart 1980) 201.

10-11 WENDT, H. H. "Zum zweiten und dritten Johannesbrief" ZNW 23 (1924) 23. STRAUSS, L. The Epistles of John (1962) 154-55. BRIGGS, R. C. "Contemporary Study of the Johannine Epistles" RevEx 67 (1970) 418, 419. POLHILL, J. B. "An Analysis of 2 and 3 John" RevEx 67 (1970) 465-66. LANGBRANDTNER, W. Weltferner Gott oder Gott der Liebe. Der Ketzerstreit in der johanneischen Kirche (1977) 400.

10 KAESEMANN, E. "Ketzer und Zeuge" in: Exegetische Versuche und Besinnungen 1 (1964) 172-73.

11 DUPLACY, J. " 'Le Texte Occidentale' des Epîtres Catholiques" NTS 16 (1969/70) 398.

12-13 POLHILL, J. B. "An Analysis of 2 and 3 John" RevEx 67 (1970) 466.

12 WENDT, H. H. "Zum zweiten und dritten Johannesbrief" ZNW 23 (1924) 19. STRAUSS, L. The Epistles of John (1962) 155.

13 WENDT, H. H. "Zum zweiten und dritten Johannesbrief" ZNW 23 (1924) 19. HIEBERT, D. E. An Introduction to the Non-Pauline Epistles (1962) 231-34. STRAUSS, L. The Epistles of John (1962) 155. SCHNACKENBURG, R. "Zum Begriff der 'Wahrheit' in den beiden kleinen Johannesbriefen" BZ 11 (1967) 254-55. DRUMWRIGHT, H. "Problem Passages in the Johannine Epistles: A Hermeneutical Approach" SouJTh 13 (1970) 62-63. HORNER, J. "Introduction to the Johannine Epistles" SouJTh 13 (1970) 50.

3 JOHN

ΙΩΑΝΝΟΥ Γ

1-15 von HARNACK, A., "Über den dritten Johannesbrief" TU 15 (1897) 3-27. BAUER, W. Die Katholischen Briefe des Neuen Testaments (1910) 60-64. SCHNACKENBURG, R., "Der Streit zwischen dem Verfasser von 3 Joh. und Diotrephes und seine verfassungs-geschichtliche Bedeutung" MThZ 4 (1953) 18-26. ROBINSON, J. A. T. "The Destination and Purpose of the Johannine Epistles" NTS 7 (1960/61) 58-59. HIEBERT, D. E. An Introduction to the Non-Pauline Epistles (1962) 222-40. HAHN, F. Das Verständnis der Mission im Neuen Testament (1965²) 144-45. LE FORT, P. Les Structures de L'Eglise militante selon Saint Jean (1970). RELING, J. Hermas and Christian Prophecy (1973) 11-12. VIELHAUER, P. Geschichte der urchristlichen Literatur (1975) 475-81. HALL, D. R., "Fellow-workers with the Gospel" ET 85 (1973-1974) 119-20. LANGBRANDTNER, W., Weltferner Gott oder Gott der Liebe (Frankfurt 1977) 395-400. MALHERBE, A. J., "The Inhospitality of Diotrephes" in: J. Jervell/W. A. Meeks (eds.) God's Christ and His People. FS. N. A. Dahl (Oslo 1977) 222-32.

1-8 STRAUSS, L. The Epistles of John (1962) 160-65.

1-4 POLHILL, J. B. "An Analysis of 2 and 3 John" RevEx 67 (1970) 466-67.

1-2 BARTINA, S., "Un papiro copto de 3 Jn 1-2 (PPallau Rib. inv. 20)" StPap 6 (1967) 95-97.

1 WENDT, H. H. "Zum zweiten und dritten Johannesbrief" ZNW 23 (1924) 19. WINDISCH, H. "Der Presbyter" in: Die Katholischen Briefe (1930) 143-44. BERGMEIER, R. "Zum Verfasserproblem des 2 und 3 Johannesbriefes" ZNW 57 (1966/67) 97-98. SCHNACKENBURG, R. "Zum Begriff der 'Wahrheit' in den beiden kleinen Johannesbriefen" BZ 11 (1967) 255-56. BRIGGS, R. C. "Contemporary Study of the Johannine Epistles" RevEx 67 (1970) 416-18. LE FORT, P. Les Structures de L'Eglise militante selon Saint Jean (1970) 54-58. HORNER, J. "Introduction to the Johannine Epistles" SouJTh 13 (1970) 51. de la POTTERIE, I., La Vérité dans Saint Jean I/II (Rome 1977) 657-63. SCHNACKENBURG, R. "Die johanneische Gemeinde und ihre Geisterfahrung" in: R. Schnackenburg et al. (eds.) Die Kirche des Anfangs. Für Heinz Schürmann (1978) 281. PRAST, F., Presbyter und Evangelium in nachapostolischer Zeit (Stuttgart 1979) 417n. 175.

2-8 LANGBRANDTNER, W. Weltferner Gott oder Gott der Liebe. Der Ketzerstreit in der johanneischen Kirche (1977) 396-98.

3-8 LE FORT, P. Les Structures de L'Eglise militante selon Saint Jean (1970) 64-65. de la POTTERIE, I., La Vérité dans Saint Jean I/II (Rome 1977) 876-80, 895-98.

3-4 BRAUN, H. Qumran und das Neue Testament I (1966) 306. de
la POTTERIE, I., La Vérité dans Saint Jean I/II (Rome 1977)
646-657. BERGMEIER, R., Glaube als Gabe nach Johannes
(Stuttgart 1980) 201-203, 238n. 39.

3 WENDT, H. H. "Zum zweiten und dritten Johannesbrief"
ZNW 23 (1924) 25. BROWN, R. E. "The Qumran Scrolls and
the Johannine Gospel and Epistles" CBQ 17 (1955) 403-19, 559-
74; = in: K. Stendahl (ed.) The Scrolls and the New Testament
(1957) 196; GT: "Die Schriftrollen von Qumran und das
Johannesevangelium und die Johannesbriefe" in: K. H. Rengstorf (ed.) Johannes und sein Evangelium (1973) 510. BERG-
MEIER, R. "Zum Verfasserproblem des 2 und 3
Johannesbriefes" ZNW 57 (1966/67) 96. SCHNACKEN-
BURG, R. "Zum Begriff der 'Wahrheit' in den beiden kleinen
Johannesbriefen" BZ 11 (1967) 255-56. BEUTLER, J. Martyria (1972) 325. TRITES, A. A., The New Testament Concept
of Witness (Cambridge 1977) 125.

4 WENDT, H. H. "Zum zweiten und dritten Johannesbrief"
ZNW 23 (1924) 19. BERGMEIER, R. "Zum Verfasserprob-
lem des 2 und 3 Johannesbriefes" ZNW 57 (1966/67) 96.
SCHNACKENBURG, R. "Zum Begriff der 'Wahrheit' in den
beiden kleinen Johannesbriefen" BZ 11 (1967) 254-55.
DRUMWRIGHT, H. "Problem Passages in the Johannine
Epistles: A Hermeneutical Approach" SouJTh 13 (1970) 62-63.

5-8 WENDT, H. H. "Zum zweiten und dritten Johannesbrief"
ZNW 23 (1924) 25. POLHILL, J. B. "An Analysis of 2 and 3
John" RevEx 67 (1970) 467-68. SCHNACKENBURG, R.
"Die johanneische Gemeinde und ihre Geisterfahrung" in: R.
Schnackenburg et al. eds.) Die Kirche des Anfangs. Für Heinz
Schürmann (1978) 303.

6 ROBINSON, J. A. T. "The Destination and Purpose of the Johannine Epistles" NTS 7 (1960) 58. BEUTLER, J. Martyria
(1972) 221, 325. BERGMEIER, R., Glaube als Gabe nach Johannes (Stuttgart 1980) 203, 238n. 39.

7 KNOX, W. L. The Sources of the Synoptic Gospels 2 (1957)
33. ROBINSON, J. A. T. "The Destination and Purpose of the
Johannine Epistles" NTS 7 (1960) 58. THOMPSON, P. J.
"Psalm 119: a possible Clue to the Structure of the First Epistle
of John" in: F. L. Cross (ed.) Studia Evangelica 2 (1964) 488.
HORNER, J. "Introduction to the Johannine Epistles" SouJTh
13 (1970) 51. de la POTTERIE, I., La Vérité dans Saint Jean
I/II (Rome 1977) 880-82.

8 WENDT, H. H. "Zum zweiten und dritten Johannesbrief" ZNW 23 (1924) 25. BERGMEIER, R. "Zum Verfasserproblem des 2 und 3 Johannesbriefes" ZNW 57 (1966/67) 98-99. SCHNACKENBURG, R. "Zum Begriff der 'Wahrheit' in den beiden kleinen Johannesbriefen" BZ 11 (1967) 255-56, 258. de la POTTERIE, I., La Vérité dans Saint Jean I/II (Rome 1977) 867-904.

9-12 de la POTTERIE, I., La Vérité dans Saint Jean I/II (Rome 1977) 895-98.

9-11 STRAUSS, L. The Epistles of John (1962) 165-69. BRAUN, R. M. "La Réduction du Pluriel au Singulier dans l'Evangile et la Première lettre de Jean" NTS 24 (1977/78) 51.

9-10 SCHNACKENBURG, R. "Zum Begriff der 'Wahrheit' in den beiden kleinen Johannesbriefen" BZ 11 (1967) 255-56. FILSON, F. V. "First John: Purpose and Message" Interp 23 (1969) 266. BRIGGS, R. C. "Contemporary Study of the Johannine Epistles" RevEx 67 (1970) 418. DRUMWRIGHT, H. "Problem Passages in the Johannine Epistles: A Hermeneutical Approach" SouJTh 13 (1970) 63-64. LE FORT, P. Les Structures de L'Eglise militante selon Saint Jean (1970) 50-54. POLHILL, J. B. "An Analysis of 2 and 3 John" RevEx 67 (1970) 468-70. KUEMMEL, W. G. Einleitung in das Neue Testament (1973[17]) 394-96. DUNN, J. D. G. Unity and Diversity in the New Testament (1977) 238. LANGBRANDTNER, W. Weltferner Gott oder Gott der Liebe. Der Ketzerstreit in der johanneischen Kirche (1977) 396-98. MALHERBE, A. J. "The Inhospitality of Diotrephes" in: J. Jervell and W. A. Meeks (eds.) God's Christ and His People. Studies in Honour of Nils Alstrup Dahl (1977) 222-32.

9 WENDT, H. H. "Zum zweiten und dritten Johannesbrief" ZNW (1924) 19, 24-25. WINDISCH, H. "Diotrephes" in: Die Katholischen Briefe (1930) 141-42. SCHWEIZER, E. Gemeinde und Gemeindeordnung im Neuen Testament (1959) §§ 11i, 12c, 14ab. CARDER, M. M. "A Caesarean Test in the Catholic Epistles?" NTS 16 (1969/70) 257. "Amt" in TRE 2 (1978) 517.

10 WENDT, H. H. "Zum zweiten und dritten Johannesbrief" ZNW 23 (1924) 25. "Amt" in: TRE 2 (1978) 517. "Bann" in: TRE 5 (1980) 166.

11-12 WENDT, H. H. "Zum zweiten und dritten Johannesbrief" ZNW 23 (1924) 26. POLHILL, J. B. "An Analysis of 2 and 3 John" RevEx 67 (1970) 470. LANGBRANDTNER, W. Weltferner Gott oder Gott der Liebe. Der Ketzerstreit in der Johanneischen Kirche (1977) 398-400.

11 DE BOER, W. P. The Imitation of Paul (1962) 85. SCHENKE, H. M. "Determination und Ethik im ersten Johannesbrief" ZThK 60 (1963) 206-15. HORVATH, T. "3 Jn 11ᵇ: An Early Ecumenical Creed?" ET 85 (1973/74) 339-40. TRITES, A. A., The New Testament Concept of Witness (Cambridge 1977) 125.

12-14 STRAUSS, L. The Epistles of John (1962) 169-71.

12 GRILL, J. Untersuchungen über die Entstehung des vierten Evangeliums, Bd. II: Das Mysterienevangelium des hellenisierten kleinasiatischen Christentums (1923) 405-406. RUCK-STUHL, E. Die literarische Einheit des Johannesevangeliums (1951) 227-35. KILPATRICK, G. D. "Two Johannine Idioms in the Johannine Epistles" JThS 12 (1961) 272. KAESE-MANN, E. "Ketzer und Zeuge" in: Exegetische Versuche und Besinnungen 1 (1964) 180. BERGMEIER, R. "Zum Verfasserproblem des 2 und 3 Johannesbriefes" ZNW 57 (1966/67) 99. SCHNACKENBURG, R. "Zum Begriff der 'Wahrheit' in den beiden kleinen Johannesbriefen" BZ 11 (1967) 255-56. BERGMEIER, R., Glaube als Gabe nach Johannes (Stuttgart 1980) 201ff., 238n. 39.

13-15 POLHILL, J. B. "An Analysis of 2 and 3 John" RevEx 67 (1970) 471.

15 BARRETT, C. K. The New Testament Background: Selected Documents (1956) 29.